Risk Management Planning Handbook

A Comprehensive Guide to Hazard Assessment, Accidental Release Prevention and Consequence Analysis

A. Roger Greenway, QEP, CCM
RTP Environmental Associates, Inc.

Government Institutes
Rockville, MD

Government Institutes, Inc., 4 Research Place, Rockville, Maryland
20850, USA.

Library of Congress Cataloging-in-Publication Data

Greenway, A. Roger.
Risk management planning : a comprehensive guide to hazard
assessment, accidental release prevention, and consequence analysis
/ by A. Roger Greenway.
                p.   cm.
        Includes index.
        ISBN: 0-86587-615-0
        1. Risk management. 2. Risk assessment. 3. Decision-making.
I. Title.
    HD61.G733   1998
    658.15'5--dc21

                                                98-10411
                                                CIP

Printed in the United States of America

Table of Contents

List of Tables and Figures

Preface

It was a windy and chilly December night in the city of Bhopal, India. None of the residents of the city were aware that the events that would transpire over the next several hours that night in an otherwise unheard of city in India would change the managerial policies of industrial facilities across the world, cause Fortune 500 companies to re-evaluate their potential financial liabilities, and ignite the United States legislature to develop legislation for Risk Management Plans.

On December 3, 1984, workers on the night shift at the Union Carbide plant in Bhopal complained that their eyes were aching intensely. What they soon realized was that there was a methyl isocyanate (MIC) leak in their facility. A few of the workers investigated the MIC storage tank and discovered a drip of liquid about 50 feet off the ground that was accompanied by an off-gassing of yellow-ish-white vapors. The pressure in the tank had reached 40 PSI, the operational capacity. As the pressure in the tank began to increase rapidly, that small drip turned into a heavy stream. Workers ran for safety as the concrete slab on top of the storage tank began to shake. Sounds of a boiling cauldron began to reverberate from the tank as a white cloud drifted over the nearby neighborhoods. When a number of workers scrambled back to the control room, they realized that the pressure indicator had reached 55 PSI and the safety valve had opened, releasing dangerous levels of MIC.

The plant supervisor ordered the leak to be sprayed with water, but the water jet failed to reach the top of the 120 foot stack, which was spewing the MIC. The supervisor then turned on the vent gas scrubber, but it was out of order.

At 1 A.M., the factory turned on the public siren, but the streets were already filled with people fleeing from their homes. During the following two hours, the safety valve remained open and released more than 50,000 lbs of MIC. The danger of MIC is that it forms Phosgene—the deadly World War I poison—spontaneously in the presence of water. It is likely that a large, lethal amount of Phosgene was formed in the cloud of gas that entombed the Bhopal neighborhoods that night. A survey conducted three months after the accident revealed that more than 250,000 people had been exposed to the gas emitted from the Union Carbide facility, that 65,000 had been subjected to severe medical disability, and that more than 3,500 people had died.

A lot has changed since the Bhopal disaster of 1984. Risk management planning has evolved in response to that disaster as several states and the federal government have developed voluntary and, later, mandatory programs to assess the potential risks and consequences of chemical releases. Some of these programs involve the identification of onsite materials and are aimed at providing first responders—such as fire departments, first aid squads, and National Guard units—the information they need to know, before they enter a site, about the hazardous or toxic materials that may exist there. Other programs relate to providing information on discharges of hazardous or toxic substances to the environment. Still others relate to examining processes to ascertain whether they are safe and to identify ways in which process safety can be improved. In February 1992, similar regulations were promulgated by the Occupational Safety and Health Administration (OSHA), namely the Process Safety Management Regulations. The Process Hazard Assessment portion of these OSHA regulations are incorporated into the EPA Risk Management Plan (RMP) regulations of 40 CFR Part 68.

This handbook will examine the background of risk management planning and will address in detail the regulations developed by U.S. EPA under the Clean Air Act Amendments of 1990 (Section 112(r)). Additionally, it will offer specific recommendations on how to set up and implement risk management programs, how to identify worst-case emissions from potential accidental releases, how to plan for minimizing the potential for an accidental release, and how to minimize the consequences if a release does occur.

This handbook is recommended for use by anyone who needs to understand the requirements of the RMP regulations, needs advice on cost-effective compliance, or works with outside experts in preparing RMPs.

This handbook has been prepared by RTP Environmental Associates, Inc., and is published by Government Institutes. It relies heavily on the Clean Air Act Amendments of 1990, on U.S. EPA background material, as well as on regulations published pursuant to the Clean Air Act Amendments of 1990. In addition, OSHA PSM regulations are heavily referenced since the hazard assessment provisions of RMP, in turn, reference the OSHA regulations. This handbook incorporates the experiences of several RTP principals, each with over twenty-five years of practice in environmental consulting, primarily in air quality issues.

Acknowledgments

This book would not be possible without significant material developed by the U.S. EPA and NASA and its work groups. References to printed material, as well as Internet references, are provided for further reading and for participation in this important program as it develops.

Finally, I would like to acknowledge the co-authors of this book, including Paul E. Neil, Principal of the RTP Environmental Associates, Inc., office in San Diego, California; John A. Green, Director of Environmental Assurance at Domino Sugar Corporation; and Brian L. Lubbert, Project Manager at RTP Environmental Associates, Inc.

Biographies of the Author and Contributors

A. Roger Greenway

A. Roger Greenway is a principal of RTP Environmental Associates, Inc., Green Brook, New Jersey. He is a Qualified Environmental Professional (QEP) and a Certified Consulting Meteorologist (CCM), and he has more than twenty-five years of experience in environmental consulting. Mr. Greenway has conducted risk management studies, including air quality dispersion modeling, for a wide range of facilities. He has also assisted clients in obtaining air quality and environmental permits for a diverse range of facilities, including electric power plants, manufacturing facilities, petrochemical facilities, and other types of facilities. He has conducted environmental impact analyses for new construction, as well as environmental assessments for industrial petrochemical and transportation projects. In addition, he has conducted many indoor air quality and asbestos projects and is an Accredited Asbestos Inspector, Management Planner, and Abatement Project Designer.

Mr. Greenway is a frequent lecturer at Government Institutes' Professional Education courses and seminars and is an organizer of the Clean Air Compliance Institute and the New Jersey Environmental Laws and Compliance courses. He is also a lecturer at Government Institutes' Risk Management Planning Under the Clean Air Act course.

Mr. Greenway is active in volunteer activities, serving as an Environmental Commissioner on the Harding Township Environmental Commission, Harding Township, New Jersey, and he also serves on other local committees. He is a member of a number of professional societies and organizations, including the American Meteorological Society, the Air and Waste Management Association, the New York Academy of Sciences, the National Association of the Advancement of Science, as well as a number of environmental organizations.

Mr. Greenway holds a Bachelor of Science in Meteorology, with a minor in Physics, and a Master of Science in Meteorological/Environmental Science from Rutgers University. He also holds a Master of Business Administration from Fairleigh Dickinson University, New Jersey.

John A. Green

A graduate of the Polytechnic Institute of Brooklyn with a Bachelor of Science in Chemical Engineering, John Green has been in the regulatory affairs field for more than 20 years and has been the Director of Environmental Assurance at Domino Sugar Corporation since 1992.

Mr. Green's experience includes being the Chairman of the 24-member Technical Defense Committee in the $100 million Charles George Landfill Superfund Case brought by the EPA (Region I) and the Commonwealth of Massachusetts.

Mr. Green is also experienced in clean air compliance, ground water remediation, waste minimization, and regulatory auditing. He has participated as an instructor in professional development seminars dealing with asbestos compliance, environmental auditing, and occupational safety and health compliance issues.

Paul E. Neil

Mr. Neil is a principal of RTP Environmental Associates, Inc., San Diego, California. He has been the permitting manager for numerous facilities throughout the United States, including obtaining environmental permits for industrial landfills, municipal solid waste-to-energy facilities, biomass facilities, fossil fuel power plants and industrial/manufacturing facilities. He has extensive consulting experience in California, especially with regard to the Toxic Hot Spot Act, the Toxic Pit Act, Proposition 65, and environmental business plans.

Mr. Neil has also conducted industrial environmental compliance audits, prepared hazardous material and emergency contigency plans, and managed the environmental compliance programs at five facilities.

Mr. Neil is a diplomat of the American Academy of Environmental Engineers, a Professional Engineer in the States of California, Florida, and South Carolina, a Registered Environmental Assessor in the State of California, and a Certified Hazardous Material Manager, Master Level. He holds a Bachelor of Science in Chemistry from the University of South Carolina and a Master of Science in Environmental Engineering from Washington State University.

Brian L. Lubbert

Mr. Lubbert is a Project Manager with RTP Environmental Associates, Inc., Green Brook, New Jersey. He has conducted numerous air quality projects, including Title V Operating Permit applications, amounting to more than eighty air permit applications, including air permit audits at numerous facilities. Mr. Lubbert is experienced in conducting air monitoring of volatile organic compounds (VOCs), as well as volatile organic acids (VOAs) and particulate matter. He has additional monitoring experience in sulfur dioxide, ozone, and particulate SO_4 pollutants. Mr. Lubbert recovered and chemically analyzed daily precipitation samples at a central Pennsylvania acidic precipitation collection site, co-located with the National Deposition Program and the Canadian Air Pollution Monitoring Network.

Mr. Lubbert holds a Bachelor of Science from the University of Wisconsin-Madison, and a Master of Science in Meteorology from Pennsylvania State University. He is a member of the Air and Waste Management Association, the American Meteorological Society, and the Meteorological Honor Society (Chi Epsilon Pi).

Chapter 1

Overview

The Risk Management Plan: What It Is and Why You Need One

Background on the Chemical Accidental Release Prevention Regulations

The chemical accidental release prevention regulations of 40 CFR Part 68 require the owner or operator of stationary sources at which a regulated substance is present in more than a threshold quantity to prepare and implement a risk management plan to detect and prevent or minimize accidental releases of such substances from the stationary source, and to provide a prompt emergency response to any such releases in order to protect human health and the environment.

These risk management plans must include a hazard assessment that specifically evaluates the potential effects of an accidental release of any regulated substance. The hazard assessment must include an estimate of potential release quantities and downwind effects, including potential exposure to populations. The assessment also must include a five-year release history, including the size, concentration, and duration of releases, and must consider worst-case release scenarios. The risk management plan must also document a complete prevention program, including safety precautions, maintenance, monitoring, and employee training measures. The final element that must be documented in the risk management plan is an emergency response program that provides specific actions to be taken in response to a release to protect human health and the environment, including informing the public and local agencies, emergency health care, and employee training.

The risk management program addresses the general requirements of CAA Section 112(r)(7)(B)(i) for regulations to provide for accidental release detection and prevention. The risk management plan, referred to as the RMP in this book, addresses the specific requirements of CAA section 112(r)(7)(B)(ii) for a plan that provides governmental entities and the public with information on the hazards found at facilities and the facilities' plans for addressing the hazards. These hazards are to be identified and addressed through implementation of the risk management program elements. Therefore, the RMP summarizes the results of hazard assessments and analyses and the implementation of the risk management program requirements. The submission requirements (registration and the RMP) address the requirements of the Clean Air Act Section 112(r)(7)(B)(iii), as does the requirement for a system to audit RMPs.

These risk management plan requirements are only the most recent in a long series of attempts to mitigate the effects of hazardous or toxic releases from chemical and other facilities and, as these attempts to mitigate efforts have evolved, to look at ways of preventing such releases in the first place.

Accident Rate Comparisons

Ever since man has been using hazardous, toxic, and explosive substances, accidents have occurred. However, there is a growing awareness that the frequency of accidents can be reduced, and many that can be prevented. Not all accidents can be prevented, but when

1

one looks at the record of safety of various industries, it is apparent that some industries and some activities are safer than others. The air transportation industry is an example of what can be done to provide a highly safe transportation system. Given the myriad components of modern aircraft and the number of flight operations on a daily basis, it is a testament to the efforts of the men and women of the air transportation sector that there are not more air transportation accidents. Air travel is, in fact, one of the safest means of travel.

The chemical industry has, over the last decade, worked to significantly improve its own safety record. Table 1.3 shows the frequency of occupational injury and illness rates in the U.S. Table 1.4 lists notable explosions in the U.S. since 1910.

Table 1.1: U.S. Airline Safety, Scheduled Commercial Carriers[1]

Year	Departures	Fatal Accidents	Fatalities	Fatal Accidents Per One Million Departures
1980	5,400,000	0	0	0.0
1985	5,800,000	4	187	0.7
1990	6,900,000	6	39	0.9
1995	8,100,000	2	166	0.3

Source: National Transportation Safety Board

Table 1.2: Rates of Transportation Deaths in the United States in 1995

	Automobile	Airplane
Miles Traveled	2.4 trillion	540 billion
Deaths	43,600	166
Deaths Per One Billion Miles Traveled	18.2	0.3
Miles Traveled Per Death	60 million	3.25 billion

Calculations above based on information found in the *World Almanac*.

Lessons of Tragedy

When looking at the relative accident frequencies by industry, it is apparent that the chemical industry has done much over the last decade to improve its safety record. The fact that the accident record has dramatically improved in the last decade is probably a function of several factors. First, after the Bhopal accident in India where more than 3,500 people died, it became more apparent that the risks of chemical accidents and the consequences of current chemical accidents could be significant in terms of human and environmental health. A subsequent chemical release in Institute, West Virginia, sent more than 100 people to the hospital and made Americans aware that such incidents can—and do—happen in the United States. Over the last several decades, we have seen an expanding chemical industry and an expanded use of hazardous and toxic substances, often in areas of high population densities. This makes the consequences of an accidental release more significant, since more people can be affected by a chemical release or sub-

sequent explosion. April 16-18, 1997 was the 50th anniversary of the worst chemical accident in American history. In 1947, the French freighter *Grandcamp* was docked at Texas City, Texas, when the 2,300 tons of ammonium nitrate aboard the ship caught fire and subsequently exploded. At least 576 people were killed, and more than 3,000 others were injured. Most of the city, including 1,000 buildings, was destroyed.

The risks of litigation resulting from an accidental release and subsequent potential offsite exposure, the costs of insurance, and other liability-related issues have also contributed to a rising interest in reducing the frequency of such accidents. The chemical industry itself has taken several steps to improve plant safety. One of the most significant of these is the Chemical Manufacturers Association (CMA) Responsible Care Program. CMA's Responsible Care Program is designed to improve performance in health and safety, and in environmental quality. The program is based on codes of management practices that outline safe work procedures for every aspect of chemical transporting and handling. Responsible Care is also designed as a public outreach program, designed to open dialogues with key audiences.

Table 1.3: Incidents of Injury and Illness in Manufacturing Industries Per 100 Employees[2]					
Rank	Industry	SIC	Injury and Illness Incidents	Injury and Illness Lost Work Days Incidents	Injury Incidents	Injury Lost Work Days Incidents
1	Primary metal industries...............	3300	16.5	7.2	14.9	6.7
2	Food and kindred products..............	2000	16.3	8.7	13.0	6.9
3	Fabricated metal products..............	3400	15.8	6.9	14.5	6.3
4	Lumber and wood products...............	2400	14.9	7.0	14.2	6.7
5	Furniture and fixtures..................	2500	13.9	6.4	12.5	5.7
6	Rubber and misc. plastics products......	3000	12.9	6.5	11.7	5.8
7	Stone, clay, and glass products.........	3200	12.3	5.7	11.3	5.3
8	Leather and leather products............	3100	11.4	4.8	9.0	3.7
9	Industrial machinery and equipment......	3500	11.2	4.4	10.1	4.0
10	Paper and allied products...............	2600	8.5	4.2	7.8	3.9
11	Textile mill products...................	2200	8.2	4.1	7.0	3.6
12	Apparel and other textile products......	2300	8.2	3.6	6.3	2.7
13	Electronic and other electric equipment.	3600	7.6	3.3	6.0	2.6
14	Printing and publishing.................	2700	6.4	3.0	5.8	2.7
15	Tobacco products........................	2100	5.6	2.6	5.2	2.5
16	Chemicals and allied products...........	2800	5.5	2.7	4.8	2.4
17	Petroleum and coal products.............	2900	4.8	2.4	4.6	2.3

a. The incidence rates represent the number of injuries and illnesses per 100 full-time workers and were calculated as: (N/EH) X 200,000 where N = number of injuries and illnesses; EH = total hours worked by all employees during the calendar year; 200,000 = base for 100 equivalent full-time workers; (working 40 hours per week, 50 weeks per year).
b. SIC is the Standard Industrial Classification Manual, 1987 Edition.
c. Lost work day totals include cases involving restricted work activity only, in addition to days-away from work cases with or without restricted work activity.

Source: Department of Labor, 1995.

History of Occupational Safety and Health

Mining Disasters

The history of occupational safety in the U.S. began with the founding of the Bureau of Mines in 1910. Mine disasters, typically defined as accidents occurring in mines and resulting in 5 or more deaths, were once appallingly common. For instance, the single year of 1907 saw 18 coal mine disasters, plus two more disasters in the metal and nonmetal mining industries. Among the disasters in 1907 was the worst in United States history—the Monongah coal mine explosion. The incident, which claimed 362 lives, stimulated Congress to create the Bureau of Mines in 1910 by Public Law 61-179.

The first federal safety standards for occupation hazards were adopted in 1947 by Public Law 80-328. The standards covered bituminous coal and lignite mines. Since then, more strengthened mine safety regulations have been adopted and implemented by the Department of Labor's Mine Safety and Health Administration .

After decades of research, technology, and preventive programs, mine accidents have declined dramatically in number and severity. Today, mine accidents resulting in five or more deaths are very uncommon. However, the dangers should not be forgotten, and preventing a recurrence of disasters like those of the past should remain a top priority, requiring constant vigilance by management, labor, and government. Table 1.5 shows a list of mine disasters.

OSHA

The federal Occupational Safety and Health Administration (OSHA) has developed regulations aimed specifically at reducing the possibility of chemical accidents. While OSHA is primarily responsible for health and safety in the workplace, U.S. EPA regulations primarily relate to the exposure of the general public to hazardous or toxic chemicals, and this exposure is limited to ambient air quality. Ambient air quality is defined as the air in the outdoor environment to which people off-site may be generally exposed. OSHA, by contrast, regulates the concentrations of chemicals to which workers in chemical or other facilities that use, generate or store hazardous or toxic substances may be exposed. This leads to an important distinction. First, the general public that may live at the fence line of a chemical facility has no choice as to what air they breathe and what that air may contain. Additionally, the general public does not have protective devices available to them, nor do they receive training in emergency situations—until this program, that is. The general public has been, for all intents and purposes, at the mercy of their industrial neighbor. They also have lacked the ability to enter the facility to learn about the company's operations, safety measures, and housekeeping practices.

Industrial employees, on the other hand, covered by OSHA, are given training in handling the materials that may be hazardous or toxic, are given protective equipment to use in case of emergencies, and are paid to work with these potentially hazardous materials. The industrial employees are also typically on site only eight hours per day, while residents outside the property line may live with atmospheric pollution twenty-four hours per day.

OSHA has developed a number of regulations over the last decade also developed permissible expo-

sure levels (PELs), which define the maximum exposure of a hazardous or toxic substance which a worker may be exposed to for eight hours per day.

In comparison, it is difficult to extrapolate OSHA regulations to the general public. First, as noted, the general public may be present twenty-four hours per day, seven days a week to a given exposure, has no training in emergency situations, and does not have access to protective equipment. Therefore, the OSHA PEL levels are not readily adaptable in setting appropriate ambient levels to which the general public may be exposed. Additionally, the PELs specify what levels may be ac-

Table 1.4: Notable Explosions in the United States Since 1910[3]

Date	Plant	City	Deaths
1917, Apr 10	Munitions Plant	Eddystone, PA	133
1918, May 18	Chemical Plant	Oakdale, PA	193
1918, Oct 4	Shell Plant	Morgan Station, NJ	64
1919, May 22	Food Plant	Cedar Rapids, IA	44
1924, Jan 3	Food Plant	Perkin, IL	42
1940, Sept 12	Hercules Power	Kenvil, NJ	55
1942, June 5	Ordinance Plant	Elwood, IL	49
1944, Oct 21	Liquid Gas Plant	Cleveland, OH	135
1947, Apr 16	Pier	Texas City, TX	576
1950, May 19	Munitions	South Amboy, NJ	30
1958, May 22	Nike Missiles	Leonardo, NJ	10
1963, Jan 2	Packing Plant	Terre Haute, IN	16
1967, Feb 17	Chemical Plant	Hawthorne, NJ	11
1973, Feb 10	Liquid Gas Tank	Staten Island, NY	40
1977, Dec 22	Grain Elevator	Westwago, LA	35
1988, May 5	Shell Oil Company	Norco, LA	7
1995, April 21	Napp Technologies	Lodi, NJ	5

Table 1.5: Historical Number of Documented Mine Disasters (5 or more deaths)

Historical Period	Coal Mines	Metal and Nonmetal Mines	Total
Through 1875	19	4	23
1876-1900	101	17	118
1901-1925	305	51	356
1926-1950	147	23	170
1951-1975	35	9	44
1976 to Present	13	1	14

Source: United States Department of Labor: Mine Safety and Health Administration

ceptable for an average eight-hour workday, day-in day-out. This does not necessarily translate to appropriate levels of general public exposure—either for routine releases, or for releases due to accidents, explosions, or fires.

OSHA regulations have included the development of specific training for workers dealing with hazardous and toxic substances as well as hazard communication (HAZCOM) requirements. OSHA HAZCOM regulations require that workers who may be exposed to hazardous or toxic substances receive training and be informed of the hazards associated with materials they work with and the protective equipment and handling techniques needed to minimize risks from exposure to those materials.

Until recently, the bulk of federal and state regulations have dealt with routine exposures to workers and routine releases to the air and other environmental media. Examples include OSHA HAZCOM, EPA Emergency Planning and Community Right-to-Know (EPCRA, 1986), and various related regulations including the Form "R" reporting requirements under EPCRA. It is only very recently that proactive regulations dealing with minimizing potential releases and reducing their potential for even occurrence have been developed.

Regulating Hazardous Chemicals

One of the first of these regulations was the OSHA Process Safety Management of Highly Hazardous Chemicals. These regulations, promulgated in February 1992, require many of the same types of investigations as the current RMP regulations under Title III of the Clean Air Act Amendments of 1990 which are the subject of this book. These require specific actions to identify potential hazards in processes, to train operators in measures to reduce potential catastrophic releases, and to undertake other measures all designed to reduce the likelihood of emergency process releases. These OSHA PSM regulations represent the first OSHA regulations developed pursuant to the Clean Air Act.

On the EPA side, the Clean Air Act Amendments of 1990 required EPA to develop regulations to require risk management programs for chemical accidental release prevention. These are required under Clean Air Act Amendments of 1990, Section 112(r)(7). These regulations, and subsequent guidance, require facilities that store, manufacture, or otherwise handle hazardous and toxic substances to develop risk management programs that include hazard assessments of all processes utilizing or generating the material along with appropriate prevention and emergency response. U.S. EPA,

Table 1.6: Regulated Categories and Entities[4]	
Category	**Examples of Regulated Entities**
Chemical Manufacturers	Industrial organics and inorganics, paints, pharmaceuticals, adhesives, sealants, fibers
Petrochemical	Refineries, industrial gases, plastics and resins, synthetic rubber
Other Manufacturing	Electronics, semiconductors, paper, fabricated metals, industrial machinery, furniture, textiles
Agriculture	Fertilizers, pesticides
Public Sources	Drinking and waste water treatment works
Utilities	Electric and gas utilities
Others	Food and cold storage, propane retail, warehousing and wholesalers
Federal Sources	Military and energy installations

in its final regulations published on June 20, 1996, made the program consistent with the OSHA Process Safety Management Regulations, where possible, for facilities with processes in certain industrial categories and with a history of accidental releases.[5] The final RMP regulations specify threshold quantities below which facilities that utilize the regulated substances need not comply with the rule. The types of processes covered by the RMP regulations include those listed in Table 1.6.

The final rule for accidental release prevention requires industries to first determine their applicability by comparing their onsite quantities of hazardous or toxic substances to the threshold quantities (TQs) defined in the regulations (Sections 68.130) and in the proposed modifications (40 1 FR 16598) of April 15, 1996, along with the applicability requirements defined in Section 68.10 of the final rule. These aspects of the rule will be discussed in detail in subsequent chapters.

State Regulatory Programs

A number of similar programs also have been developed by individual states. In particular, California, New Jersey, Nevada, and Louisiana have developed state programs regarding risk management analysis and planning for regulated entities. For a number of years after the 1990 Clean Air Act Amendments, states with programs continued to regulate toxic and hazardous chemicals used and processed in their states under their own regulations. As the federal regulations became more codified, and in particular with the publication in June of 1996 of the final RMP regulations, these states have indicated that they will revise their programs to be consistent with the federal requirements. This is a good development since, without such modifications of the state program, operating facilities in states with their own RMP program (e.g., The Toxic Catastrophe Prevention Act in New Jersey) would be required to have two plans, which would need to be tailored to reflect the specific requirements of the state program as well as the federal program. For facilities also covered by OSHA PSM requirements, the facility could have potentially been required to have three separate plans with much duplicated material. The problem with this is that, although there may be significant overlap in the plans, the plans themselves and the form of the plans could be different. It is also possible for facilities to be fined for not following a plan, raising interesting compliance challenges where required plan elements conflict. Recently, we have seen that the U.S. EPA, OSHA and the states have cooperated to minimize duplicative work.

Regulation of Risk Planning

The rapidly evolving series of regulations governing the assessment and management of risk and risk planning and response planning for accidental releases can be traced back to the early 1980s when the Union Carbide's plant in Bhopal, India had a major accidental release in December 1984. This release exposed a large community to concentrations of methyl isocyanate at levels that caused significant health impacts. While it is likely that smaller releases had been occurring previous to this incident, more than any other event, this disaster focused worldwide attention on the potentially devastating consequences of large industrial accidents involving hazardous or toxic substances. It also focused worldwide attention on the fact that communities living in close proximity to chemical and other facilities that use, manufacture, or transport hazardous or toxic substances often have no information about what materials are on site, what the conditions of storage and use are, and what precautions are being taken by the facility to minimize the potential for an accidental release. Furthermore, communities often have no advance information that would be helpful in planning for the event of an accidental release.

Once worldwide attention was focused on the problem because of the Bhopal incident, the media pounced on every other minor release, no matter where it might have occurred. As a result, there was widespread press coverage about other releases in the United States and in particular in the New Jersey area, where there was a series of releases from petrochemical facilities along the Arthur Kill near Newark.

Chemical Emergency Preparedness Program

In 1985, U.S. EPA developed a voluntary program called the Chemical Emergency Preparedness Program (CEPP). The program's mission was to provide leadership, advocacy, and assistance in order to prevent and prepare for chemical emergencies; to respond to environmental crises; to inform the public about chemical hazards in the community; and to protect human health and the environment. The CEPP develops, implements, and coordinates regulatory and nonregulatory safety programs.

The CEPP program was developed to encourage state and local authorities to identify hazards in their areas and to plan for potential chemical emergencies. This local planning complemented emergency response planning already being carried out at the national and regional levels.

Community Right-to-Know

In 1986, Congress enacted many of the elements of CEPP in the Emergency Planning and Community Right-to-Know Act of 1986, also known as Title III of the Superfund Amendments and Reauthorization Act of 1986 (SARA). SARA Title III requires states to establish State Emergency Response Commissions (SERCs) and Local Emergency Planning Committees (LEPCs), and to develop emergency response plans for each community. SARA Title III also requires facilities to make information available to the public on the hazardous chemicals in storage (Tier I/Tier II forms of 40 CFR 370) and in use onsite (Form R of 40 CFR 372). Title III's reporting requirements foster a valuable dialogue between industry and local communities on hazards to help citizens become more informed about the presence of hazardous chemicals that might affect public health and the environment.

Chemical Accident Prevention Program

EPA recognized that accident prevention, preparedness, and response are not discrete processes, but form a safety continuum. Therefore, in 1986, EPA established its Chemical Accident Prevention Program, integrating it with the Chemical Emergency Preparedness Program.

Under the Chemical Accident Prevention Program, EPA developed the Accidental Release Information Program (ARIP) to collect data on the causes of accidents and to establish the steps facilities need to take in order to prevent recurrences. EPA also developed its Chemical Safety Audit Program to gather and disseminate information on practices at facilities that mitigate and prevent chemical accidents. Another significant component of EPA's Chemical Accident Prevention Program involves outreach to small and medium-sized enterprises, which are generally less aware of risks than larger facilities.

The first prevention initiative began collecting information on chemical accidents. Then EPA began working with other stakeholder groups to increase knowledge of prevention practices and encourage industry to improve safety at facilities.

SARA Requirements

In 1986, the Superfund legislation was reauthorized as the Superfund Amendment and Reauthorization Act (SARA). Title III of this Act was entitled Emergency Planning and Community Right-to-Know (EPCRA). This legislation (EPCRA 311) required, for the first time, detailed identification and reporting of hazardous and toxic substances present at facilities that handled, stored (40 CFR Part 370), manufactured, or otherwise used haz-

ardous and toxic substances. The regulations developed under SARA (312) require companies to identify the onsite inventories of hazardous and toxic substances that exceed threshold levels. This is the annual Tier I/Tier II reporting required by March 1 of each year. EPCRA 302 requires industry to report on 360 extremely hazardous substances that are "otherwise being used." This "use" includes routine releases to the air, water, to solid waste, to the land, and to off-site facilities for possible disposal or recycling. The list of 360 extremely hazardous substances can be found in Appendix A.

SARA (313) also requires the reporting of other releases—including accidental releases of hazardous toxic substances—as part of an annual report quantifying all releases to the environment. This SARA 313 reporting is commonly known as the Form R submission and is required by July 1 of every calendar year for all covered facilities by the regulations found in 40 CFR 372.

SARA Title III Emergency Planning and Community Right-to-Know also requires the formation of emergency planning commissions and local emergency planning committees (LEPCs). The latter were envisioned to be committees formed by potential first responders (i.e., fire department, first aid squad, National Guard, State police) and representatives of the companies in a particular community or county. The LEPC was charged with developing emergency response plans for the industries within its planning area. Coordination with the state emergency planning commission was also required under SARA Title III.

Obligations of Companies

The most important benefit of SARA 313 (also known as Emergency Planning and Community Right-to-Know, EPCRA, 42 U.S.C. 11003) is that for the first time, companies had to tabulate the quantities of materials of listed extremely hazardous substances onsite, and had to participate in local emergency planning committees to plan for an appropriate response in case of accidental releases. It also required industries to plan for response to accidental releases and carried a requirement for industries to conduct dispersion modeling and scenario assessment to identify the worst-case accident and to predict the maximum off-site concentrations. It is required in the regulations that companies plan for appropriate response to accidental releases. There is, however, no requirement for industries to study the processes at their facilities and to look for ways to minimize the possibility of an accident occurring in the first place. This is a key distinction between the RMP program and EPCRA.

Nonetheless, EPCRA was very helpful in focusing community attention on the industrial use of hazardous and toxic substances. One reason this happened is that EPA made the results of the annual filings publicly available. They are now available on-line. As a result, environmental action groups and community groups have been able to identify the largest emitters of toxic substances in their community, county, and state. The resultant public pressure to reduce emissions to the environment has been a key factor in reducing the amount of hazardous and toxic substances used and generated on site as well as discharges to the environment.

The response of industries to the filing under EPCRA has also been a key factor in embracing pollution prevention planning (P3) as a desirable goal in their manufacturing processes.

OSHA PSM Program

The Clean Air Act Amendments of 1990 also required the Occupational Safety and Health Administration (OSHA) to develop regulations to improve process safety management (Section 304 CAA 1990). OSHA promulgated its PSM standard in February of 1992. The OSHA program required industries in certain Standard Industrial Classification (SIC) codes to develop standard operating procedures for operating processes and to respond to abnormal conditions that could lead to accidental releases, including explosions and fires. The goal of the OSHA PSM program was the "proactive identification, evaluation, and mitigation or prevention of chemical releases that could occur as a result of failures and processes, procedures or equipment."[6] The OSHA PSM regulations are discussed in detail in Chapter 12 of this book. Most importantly, the OSHA regulations focus on hazard assessments of industrial facilities based on their Standard Industrial Classification (SIC) code and the presence of a threshold planning quantity of one of 137 listed chemicals or a flammable liquid or gas in quantities of 10,000 pounds or more. In many ways, OSHA PSM parallels 112 (r) risk management planning requirements. A key difference, however, is that OSHA PSM, while it focuses on evaluating processes and minimizing the possibility of an accident resulting in a release, does *not* include requirements for

addressing the offsite impacts nor for participating with local emergency planning officials. It is understood, however, that many of these facilities will be covered by Emergency Planning and Community Right-to-Know or by the RMP regulations that do require such participation.

Risk Management Programs

The Clean Air Act Amendments of 1990 amend Section 112 of the Clean Air Act and add paragraph (r). The intent of the 1990 amendments, as codified in Section 112(r), is to prevent the accidental releases to the air and to mitigate the consequences of such releases by focusing on prevention measures and focusing particularly on chemicals that pose the greatest risk to the public and the environment.

U.S. EPA, in its final rule making, indicated that it coordinated with OSHA and that the final regulations are also consistent with EPCRA and with the Department of Transportation regulations which govern the transport of hazardous and toxic substances. To the extent possible, "covered sources will not face inconsistent requirements under these agency's rules" (U.S. EPA 40 CFR Part 68, 6/20/96). U.S. EPA has defined a list of regulated substances and thresholds. Appendix B provides a list of the U.S. EPA defined substances and thresholds. It also contains the threshold planning quantities for related chemical reporting and risk management programs, including Sections 302, Section 304, and Section 313. The Resource Conservation Recovery Act (RCRA) code is also reported.

This consolidated list, provided by EPA, is available through the National Technical Information Service and

Table 1.7: Reporting Requirements

Regulatory Requirement	Description
Section 302 - Clean Air Act	Definitions
Section 304 - Clean Air Act	Citizen Suits
Section 313 -SARA-Title III	EPCRA: Emergency Planning and Community Right-to-Know

on-line at www.epa.gov/swercepp/. The other reporting requirements include those shown in Table 1.7.

Following the consolidated list can be found an alphabetical listing of chemical name and Chemical Asbstract Service (CAS) number for each of the listed chemicals or compounds.

The U.S. EPA final list includes 77 acutely toxic substances with threshold quantities ranging from 500 to 20,000 pounds, as shown in Table 1.8 (See pages 10-11.), 63 flammable substances with a 10,000 pound threshold, as shown in Table 1.9 (See pages 12-13.).

Clean Air Act Amendments of 1990

Section 112(r)

The Clean Air Act Amendments of 1990 are the regulatory basis for the RMP program currently being implemented by U.S. EPA. The goal is to prevent the accidental release into the atmosphere of regulated substances and other extremely hazardous substances. Of particular note, the Clean Air Act establishes a "general duty" requirement for facilities to identify hazards that may result from releases, to design and maintain a safe facility, and to minimize the consequences of any releases that occur. This general duty provision was effective upon promulgation of the Act in 1990. Therefore, any facility with quantities of material covered under the Act (or any facilities that handle such substances) has a "general duty to identify hazards, to design and maintain a safe facility, and to minimize a consequences of any releases that occur." Therefore, all facilities that fall into this category have been covered since 1990 by this general duty provision. If an accidental release occurred any time after 1990, whether or not final regulations and RMP plans have been developed, there exists this general duty provision that requires facilities to have identified their hazards, to have designed and maintained a safe facility, and to have minimized the consequences of any releases that may occur. Therefore, it is important—especially for facilities that handle, use, or generate hazardous substances in threshold quantities—to begin immediately with the above-mentioned tasks under the general duty provision. Since many such facilities are also covered by OSHA PSM or by one of the several state programs that have existed for several years, much of this work may already have been undertaken. Additionally, some components of the RMP program may have been undertaken as part of the Environmental Planning Community Right-to-Know requirements of SARA, Title III (1986).

The issue under the general duty clause is one of potential liability. Should an accident occur, the general duty provisions may be used by U.S. EPA to undertake enforcement action for lack of compliance with these provisions.

Section 112(r)(7)

Section 112(r)(7) covers certain specific stationary activities at facilities that use, store, or generate listed substances. The covered activities under these regulations include the use of these listed substances, the operation of equipment that uses the substances, the repair, replacement, and maintenance of that equipment, the use of the equipment and the repair, replacement, and maintenance of equipment used to monitor or detect releases to the environment. In addition, equipment used in inspecting other, related equipment is covered, as is equipment used to control accidental releases.

> *Stationary source* means any buildings, structures, equipment, installations, or substance-emitting stationary activities which belong to the same industrial group, which are located on one or more contiguous properties, which are under the control of the same person (or persons under common control), and from which an accidental release may occur. The term *stationary source* does not apply to transportation, including storage incident to transportation, of any regulated substance or any other extremely hazardous substance under the provisions of this part. A stationary source includes transportation containers used for storage not incident to transportation and transportation containers connected to equipment at a stationary source for loading and unloading. Transportation includes, but is not limited to, transportation subject to oversight or regulation under 49 CFR Parts 192, 193, or 195, or a state natural gas or hazardous liquid program for which the state has in effect a certification to DOT under 49 U.S.C. Section 60105. A stationary source does not include naturally occurring hydrocarbon reservoirs. Properties shall not be considered contiguous solely because of a railroad or pipeline right-of-way. (FR January 6, 1998, Vol. 63, #3.)

Training

Training is another important component of the 112(r) regulations. Training is required of operators in the use and maintenance of equipment and in conducting periin Chapter 5.

Table 1.8: Threshold Quantities of Regulated Toxic Substances for Accidental Release Prevention

CAS No.	Toxic Chemical	Threshold (lbs)
107–02–8	Acrolein [2-Propenal]	5,000
107–13–1	Acrylonitrile [2-Propenenitrile]	20,000
814–68–6	Acrylyl chloride [2-Propenoyl chloride]	5,000
107–18–6	Allyl alcohol [2-Propen-1-ol]	15,000
107–11–9	Allylamine [2-Propen-1-amine]	10,000
7664–41–7	Ammonia (anhydrous)	10,000
7664–41–7	Ammonia (conc 20% or greater)	20,000
7784–34–1	Arsenous trichloride	15,000
7784–42–1	Arsine	1,000
10294–34–5	Boron trichloride [Borane, trichloro-]	5,000
7637–07–2	Boron trifluoride [Borane, trifluoro-]	5,000
353–42–4	Boron trifluoride compound with methyl ether (1:1) [Boron, trifluoro[oxybis[methane]]-, T-4	15,000
7726–95–6	Bromine	10,000
75–15–0	Carbon disulfide	20,000
7782–50–5	Chlorine	2,500
10049–04–4	Chlorine dioxide [Chlorine oxide (ClO2)]	1,000
67–66–3	Chloroform [Methane, trichloro-]	20,000
542–88–1	Chloromethyl ether [Methane, oxybis[chloro-]	1,000
107–30–2	Chloromethyl methyl ether [Methane, chloromethoxy-]	5,000
4170–30–3	Crotonaldehyde [2-Butenal]	20,000
123–73–9	Crotonaldehyde, (E)-, [2-Butenal, (E)-]	20,000
506–77–4	Cyanogen chloride	10,000
108–91–8	Cyclohexylamine [Cyclohexanamine]	15,000
19287–45–7	Diborane	2,500
75–78–5	Dimethyldichlorosilane [Silane, dichlorodimethyl-]	5,000
57–14–7	1,1-Dimethylhydrazine [Hydrazine, 1,1-dimethyl-]	15,000
106–89–8	Epichlorohydrin [Oxirane, (chloromethyl)-]	20,000
107–15–3	Ethylenediamine [1,2-Ethanediamine]	20,000
151–56–4	Ethyleneimine [Aziridine]	10,000
75–21–8	Ethylene oxide [Oxirane]	10,000
7782–41–4	Fluorine	1,000
50–00–0	Formaldehyde (solution)	15,000
110–00–9	Furan	5,000
302–01–2	Hydrazine	15,000
7664–39–3	Hydrochloric acid (conc 50% or greater)	1,000
7647–01–0	Hydrochloric acid (conc 30% or greater)	15,000
74–90–8	Hydrocyanic acid	2,500
7647–01–0	Hydrogen chloride (anhydrous) [Hydrochloric acid]	5,000
7664–39–3	Hydrogen fluoride/Hydrofluoric acid (conc 50% or greater) [Hydrofluoric acid]	1,000
7783–07–5	Hydrogen selenide	500
7783–06–4	Hydrogen sulfide	10,000

Table 1.8 *(cont'd.)*: Threshold Quantities of Regulated Toxic Substances for Accidental Release Prevention

CAS No.	Toxic Chemical	Threshold (lbs)
13463–40–6	Iron, pentacarbonyl- [Iron carbonyl (Fe(CO)5), (TB–5–11)-]	2,500
78–82–0	Isobutyronitrile [Propanenitrile, 2-methyl-]	20,000
108–23–6	Isopropyl chloroformate [Carbonochloride acid, 1-methylethyl ester]	15,000
126–98–7	Methacrylonitrile [2-Propenenitrile, 2-methyl-]	10,000
74–87–3	Methyl chloride [Methane, chloro-]	10,000
79–22–1	Methyl chloroformate [Carbonochloridic acid, methylester]	5,000
60–34–4	Methyl hydrazine [Hydrazine, methyl-]	15,000
624–83–9	Methyl isocyanate [Methane, isocyanato-]	10,000
74–93–1	Methyl mercaptan [Methanethiol]	10,000
556–64–9	Methyl thiocyanate [Thiocyanic acid, methyl ester]	20,000
75–79–6	Methyltrichlorosilane [Silane, trichloromethyl-]	5,000
13463–39–3	Nickel carbonyl	1,000
7697–37–2	Nitric acid (conc 80% or greater)	15,000
10102–43–9	Nitric oxide [Nitrogen oxide (NO)]	10,000
8014–95–7	Oleum (Fuming Sulfuric acid) [Sulfuric acid, mixture with sulfur trioxide]	10,000
79–21–0	Peracetic acid [Ethaneperoxoic acid]	10,000
594–42–3	Perchloromethylmercaptan [Methanesulfenyl chloride, trichloro-]	10,000
75–44–5	Phosgene [Carbonic dichloride]	500
7803–51–2	Phosphine	5,000
10025–87–3	Phosphorus oxychloride [Phosphoryl chloride]	5,000
7719–12–2	Phosphorus trichloride [Phosphorous trichloride]	15,000
110–89–4	Piperidine	15,000
107–12–0	Propionitrile [Propanenitrile]	10,000
109–61–5	Propyl chloroformate [Carbonochloridic acid, propylester]	15,000
75–55–8	Propyleneimine [Aziridine, 2-methyl-]	10,000
75–56–9	Propylene oxide [Oxirane, methyl-]	10,000
7446–09–5	Sulfur dioxide (anhydrous)	5,000
7783–60–0	Sulfur tetrafluoride [Sulfur fluoride (SF4), (T-4)-]	2,500
7446–11–9	Sulfur trioxide	10,000
75–74–1	Tetramethyllead [Plumbane, tetramethyl-]	10,000
509–14–8	Tetranitromethane [Methane, tetranitro-]	10,000
7750–45–0	Titanium tetrachloride [Titanium chloride (TiCl4) (T-4)-]	2,500
584–84–9	Toluene 2,4-diisocyanate [Benzene, 2,4-diisocyanato-1-methyl-]	10,000
91–08–7	Toluene 2,6-diisocyanate [Benzene, 1,3-diisocyanato-2-methyl-]	10,000
26471–62–5	Toluene diisocyanate (unspecified isomer) [Benzene, 1,3-diisocyanatomethyl-]	10,000
75–77–4	Trimethylchlorosilane [Silane, chlorotrimethyl-]	10,000
108–05–4	Vinyl acetate monomer [Acetic acid ethenyl ester]	15,000

Table 1.9: Threshold Quantities of Regulated Flammable Substances for Accidental Release Prevention

CAS No.	Flammable Substance	Threshold (lbs)
75-07-0	Acetaldehyde	10,000
74-86-2	Acetylene	10,000
598-73-2	Bromotrifluroethylene	10,000
106-99-0	1,3-Butadiene	10,000
106-97-8	Butane	10,000
25167-67-3	Butene	10,000
590-18-1	2-Butene-cis	10,000
624-64-6	2-Butene-trans	10,000
106-98-9	1-Butene	10,000
107-01-7	2-Butene	10,000
463-58-1	Carbon oxysulfide	10,000
7791-21-1	Chlorine Monoxide	10,000
590-21-6	1-Chloropropylene	10,000
557-98-2	2-Chloropylene	10,000
460-19-5	Cyanogen	10,000
75-19-4	Cyclopropane	10,000
4109-96-0	Dichlorosilane	10,000
75-37-6	Difluroethane	10,000
124-40-3	Dimethylamine	10,000
463-82-1	2,2-Dimethylpropane	10,000
74-84-0	Ethane	10,000
107-00-6	Ethyl acetylene	10,000
75-04-7	Ethylamine	10,000
75-00-3	Ethyl chloride	10,000
74-85-1	Ethylene	10,000
60-29-7	Ethyl ether	10,000
109-95-5	Ethyl nitrite	10,000
75-08-1	Ethyl mercaptan	10,000
1333-74-0	Hydrogen	10,000
75-28-5	Isobutane	10,000
78-78-4	Isopentane	10,000
78-79-5	Isoprene	10,000
75-31-0	Isopropylamine	10,000
75-29-6	Isopropyl chloride	10,000
74-82-8	Methane	10,000
74-89-5	Methylamine	10,000
563-46-2	2-Methyl-1-butene	10,000
563-45-1	3-Methyl-1-butene	10,000
115-10-6	Methyl ether	10,000
107-31-3	Methyl formate	10,000
115-11-7	2-Methylpropene	10,000
504-60-9	1,3-Pentadiene	10,000
109-66-0	Pentane	10,000

Table 1.9 (*cont'd.*): Threshold Quantities of Regulated Flammable Substances for Accidental Release Prevention

CAS No.	Flammable Substance	Threshold (lbs)
109-67-1	1-Pentene	10,000
646-04-8	2-Pentene, (E)-	10,000
627-20-3	2-Pentene, (Z)-	10,000
463-49-0	Propadiene	10,000
74-98-6	Propane	10,000
115-07-1	Propylene	10,000
74-99-7	Propyne	10,000
7803-62-5	Silane	10,000
116-14-3	Tetrafluroethylene	10,000
75-76-3	Tetramethylsilane	10,000
10025-78-2	Trichlorosilane	10,000
79-38-9	Triflurochloroethylene	10,000
75-50-3	Trimethylamine	10,000
689-97-4	Vinyl acetylene	10,000
75-01-4	Vinyl chloride	10,000
109-92-2	Vinyl ethyl ether	10,000
75-02-5	Vinyl fluoride	10,000
75-35-4	Vinylidene chloride	10,000
75-38-7	Vinylidene fluoride	10,000
107-25-5	Vinyl methyl ether	10,000

The overall approach of the 112(r) regulations for RMPs is really very straightforward.

1. Risk management plans are required.
2. Risk management plans are to be submitted to the U.S. EPA or the designated state agency.
3. Classified information may be protected from public disclosure.

Subsequent chapters will discuss these topics in more detail. Chapter 2 provides guidance on setting up a prevention program.

[1] *The World Almanac* (1997): Farmighetti, R., ed., Funk and Wagnalls, Mahwah, NJ.
[2] U.S. Department of Labor.
[3] *The World Almanac* (1997): Farmighetti, R., ed., Funk and Wagnalls, Mahwah, NJ.
[4] 40 CFR Part 68, 6/20/96.
[5] 40 CFR Part 68, 6/20/96.
[6] OSHA PSM regulations 47 FR 6356, 2/92.

Setting Up a Prevention Program

The final RMP regulations require many facilities throughout the United States to prepare Process Hazard Assessments and Risk Management Plans. The Clean Air Act Amendments of 1990 list 77 toxic substances and 63 flammable substances—as noted in Chapter 1 and as tabulated in the Tables 1.8 and 1.9—that are covered by the act. All facilities with more than threshold quantities of each listed hazardous or toxic substance are required to comply with the regulations.

Applicability

U.S. EPA has estimated that more than 66,000 facilities nationwide will be required to comply with the RMP regulations. This compares to more than 87,800 facilities that are covered by the OSHA Process Safety Management standards. The largest populations of facilities include the following:

❏ Cold storage facilities (ammonia refrigerants)

❏ Public drinking water systems (chlorine)

❏ Publicly-owned treatment works, or POTWs (chlorine)

❏ Manufacturers (for a list of substances)

❏ Propane retailers

❏ Wholesalers and service industries

❏ Farm contractors (ammonia fertilizer)

The RMP is designed to be a multi-purpose document. The Clean Air Act requires the RMP to specifically certify compliance with the regulations and to include the hazard assessment, prevention program, and emergency response programs. EPA is mandated to develop a program for auditing RMPs and to require revisions where appropriate.[7] The RMP must have enough information in it so that U.S. EPA or a designated state agency can assess the extent to which the facility complies with the regulations. The RMP must have sufficient information to provide the public with enough information to understand issues related to accident prevention and preparedness for each facility covered by the regulations.

Although U.S. EPA did not originally exempt gasoline and naturally occurring hydrocarbons (e.g., crude oil), it did not, however, intend to cover regulated flammables in those mixtures. U.S. EPA has proposed to revise the criteria for flammable mixtures and to exclude naturally occurring hydrocarbons prior to processing at the gas processing plant or refinery.[8] Flammable mixtures are covered only if they meet all of National Fire Protection Association-4 (NFPA-4) criteria. Gasoline and crude oil are listed with NFPA-3 flammability rates in NFPA-325M, *Fire Hazard Properties-Flammable Liquids Gases and Solids* (1991).[9] U.S. EPA stayed implementation of the risk management program for substances and processes that would be affected by these proposed changes. (In January 1998, the EPA finalized its exemption for all grades of gasoline with respect to its possible inclusion as a listed flammable substance.) In addition, U.S. EPA did not adopt OSHA's exemption for atmospheric storage of flammables. According to the U.S. EPA regulations, this is because U.S. EPA lists only flammable gases and highly volatile flammable liquids. U.S. EPA considers these substances to be "intrinsically hazardous," regardless of storage conditions and therefore does not believe it appropriate to provide an exemption for such substances.[10]

Affected Facility Areas

What area of an industrial facility is covered by the RMP regulations? The area covered includes any area on the property where a regulated substance is present in quantities exceeding the TQ.

Multiple Substances

What about multiple substances in a single process? The regulations provide that where processes involve multiple listed substances that a single hazard analysis may be undertaken for the process, thereby covering multiple listed substances. This can become complicated if, at the facility, different processes contain different regulated substances and other processes may involve multiple regulated substances. Figure 2.1 illustrates the possible combinations.

ever, Process 1, in which two regulated substances (MEK and formaldehyde) can be found, may also be covered by a single hazard analysis.

Preparing a Prevention Program

What tasks must be undertaken in preparing your prevention program? The final regulation requires that all covered facilities register with the U.S. EPA within three years of June 20, 1996 or by June 20, 1999. These registrations must include, among other things, identification of all regulated substances and quantities for comparison to EPA's List of Lists found in Appendix B.

For all processes at facilities with more than the threshold quantity (TQ) of a regulated substance, the Clean Air Act mandates that the risk management plan document three elements: a hazard assessment, a prevention program, and an emergency response program. This section discusses these elements in order to assist the reader in better understanding the concept of a risk management program and to better develop each of the plan requirements.

Hazard Assessment

The Clean Air Act requires a hazard assessment that includes an evaluation of a range of releases, including worst-case accidental releases; analyses of potential offsite consequences; and a five-year accident history. The language of the act also suggests a more extensive assessment that would require a formal process hazard analysis (e.g., basic data on the source, identification of potential points of release, review of the efficacy of release, and control measures). To allow EPA's prevention program requirements to parallel OSHA's process safety management standard, EPA separated the offsite consequence analysis and five-year accident history from the formal process hazard analysis requirement and requires a hazard assessment that examines a range of accidental release scenarios, selects a worst-case accidental release scenario, analyzes offsite consequences for selected release scenarios, including worst case, and documents a five-year history of significant accidental releases.

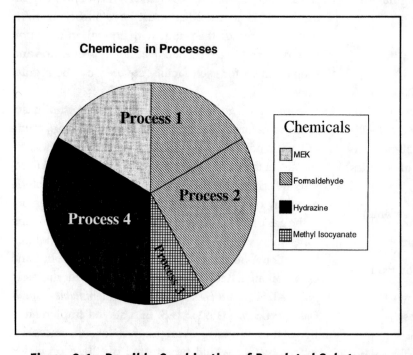

Figure 2.1: Possible Combination of Regulated Substances

Looking at Figure 2.1, we can see Processes 2, 3, and 4 where only single regulated substances are found that must be the subject of individual hazard analyses. How-

In its proposed rule, EPA would require facilities to complete a hazard assessment for each regulated substance present above the threshold quantity. Facilities that use the regulated substance above its threshold in several locations or processes would need to evaluate a range of accidental releases and determine a worst-case release scenario for each location. The range of releases would include only those events that could lead to significant releases (i.e., accidental releases that have the potential to cause offsite death, injury, or serious adverse effects to human health or the environment). However, in its final rule, EPA stated that one worst-case release scenario will be defined to represent all toxics, and one worst-case release scenario would be defined to represent all flammables held above the threshold at the source. Additional worst-case release scenario(s) must be analyzed and reported if such a release from another covered process at the source potentially affects public receptors that would not be potentially affected by the first scenario. EPA recognized that this approach may be problematic for some sources such as batch processors and warehouses where the use of listed substances or inventory may vary considerably within an RMP reporting period. EPA suggests that owners or operators of such processes develop a worst-case scenario for future chemical use and inventory based on past practices to minimize the need for frequent revision of their worst-case scenario. For alternative release scenarios, one scenario is required for each toxic substance and one to represent all flammable substances held in covered processes at the source.

Prevention Program

The Clean Air Act Amendments of 1990 require that the risk management plan include a prevention program that covers safety precautions and maintenance, monitoring, and employee training measures. Although the Act's requirements for the prevention program are general, a consensus exists among industry, professional organizations, labor, public interest groups, and government on what constitutes a good risk management program. In its Review of Emergency Systems, EPA listed elements of good management programs. The American Institute of Chemical Engineers (AIChE) has published Guidelines for Technical Management of Chemical Process Safety, which basically includes the

same elements. Delaware, New Jersey, California, and Nevada have each adopted state risk management program regulations that, again, cover a similar set of elements. The OSHA chemical process safety management standard also covers this same set of elements. The prevention program that EPA adopted consists of elements that the Federal government and several state agencies—as well as trade associations, professional organizations, labor, and public interest groups—believe are necessary in order to have an integrated approach to understanding and managing risks associated with regulated substances at a facility. The elements of this integrated approach are consistent with and fulfill the requirements of the statute.

Nine Procedural Areas

EPA has adopted a prevention program that adopts and builds on OSHA's process safety management standard and covers nine procedural areas: process hazard analysis, process safety information, standard operating procedures (SOPs), training, maintenance, pre-startup review, management of change, safety audits, and accident investigation. The degree of complexity required for compliance with each element will depend on the complexity of the facility. For example, development of process safety information for chlorine storage would take far more time and would require greater expertise at a large petrochemical facility than it would at a small drinking water system. As facility owners or operators develop plans for implementing these elements, they would have to consider the complexity of their chemical use, the hazards potentially posed by the chemicals, and potential consequences of an accidental release.

Need for Integration of Program Elements

The prevention program elements must be integrated with each other on an ongoing basis. For example, each time a new substance is introduced to a process or new equipment is installed, the process hazard analysis must be reviewed, SOPs updated, training and maintenance programs revised, and new training provided. An investigation of a near miss or a safety audit may reveal the need for revised operating and maintenance procedures, which will lead to revisions to SOPs, training, and maintenance. The investigation or audit may also indicate a need to review the process hazard analysis. The management system should ensure that a change in any single element leads to a review of all other elements in order to identify any impacts caused by that change.

Emergency Response Program

The Clean Air Act specifies that the emergency response program include actions to be taken to protect human health and the environment in response to a release, including informing the public and local agencies, emergency health care, and employee training. Emergency response procedures are a necessary part of a risk management program because accidents can occur even with the best safety systems in place. Emergency response procedures can reduce the severity of a release and protect employees, emergency responders, and the public from harmful exposure to the regulated substances. As discussed above, the damage from accidents and risks to responders can be increased if releases have the potential to damage or destroy utilities and equipment needed to respond to the incident. The emergency response plan helps define these worst cases and develop an approach to prevent potential problems.

EPA has adopted the emergency response requirements found in the statute, without additional specific planning requirements beyond those necessary to implement the statute. This action is consistent with the EPA's effort to develop a single federal approach for emergency response planning. The Presidential review of federal release prevention, mitigation, and response authorities (required under Section 112(r)(10) of the Clean Air Act) found that there is seldom harmony in the required formats or elements of response plans prepared to meet various federal regulations. Accordingly, EPA has committed not to specify new plan elements and/or a specific plan format in the final RMP rule beyond those that are statutory required. EPA believes that plans developed to comply with other EPA contingency planning requirements and with the OSHA Hazardous Waste and Emergency Operations (HAZWOPER) rule will meet most of the requirements for the emergency response program.[11] In addition, EPA and other National Response Team (NRT) agencies have prepared the Integrated Contingency Plan Guidance ("One Plan").[12] The NRT and the agencies responsible for reviewing and approving federal response plans to which the one plan option applies agree that integrated response plans pre-

pared in the format provided in this guidance will be acceptable and will be the federally preferred method of response planning. An emergency response plan that includes the elements specified in the EPA guidance can be used to meet the requirements of the final rule. The final rule also provides relief for sources that are too small to respond to releases with their own employees. These sources will not be required to develop emergency response plans provided that procedures for notifying non-employee emergency responders have been adopted and that appropriate responses to their hazards have been addressed in the community emergency response plan developed under EPCRA (42 U.S.C. 11003) for toxics or coordinated with the local fire department for flammables.

Providing for Maintenance of Onsite Documentation

In addition to the RMP, an affected facility is required to maintain onsite documentation of its process hazard analysis, offsite consequence analysis, process information (e.g., P&IDs, MSDSs), training and maintenance programs, SOPs, pre-startup review list, management of change procedures and records, compliance audits, accident investigation procedures and reports, and emergency response plans. This documentation would include schedules for starting and completing actions based on the recommendations of the process hazard analysis, safety audit, and accident investigation. These documentation requirements are similar to those imposed under OSHA's standard.

The certification required by Section 68.58 Compliance Audits includes a requirement that an owner or operator certify that they have evaluated compliance with the revisions of the RMP regulations at least every three years and must include a verification that the procedures and practices developed under the rule are adequate and are being followed. *In effect, this is certification that the facility is operating safely.* If an accident occurs and the RMP developed under the regulations is being followed, then, by definition, the RMP could not have been adequate. Certification may, more than many other requirements under the program, force companies to closely examine all aspects of the RMP development and implementation process.

The RMP must include a certification as to the accuracy and completeness of the information. In addition, the owner or operator of the covered facilities in program levels II and III (to be discussed in a later chapter) are required to develop a management system to oversee the implementation of the risk management program element.[13] The owner/operator is required to assign a qualified person to have overall responsibility for the development, implementation, and integration of the risk management program elements. The regulations allow that the facility may assign a position (as opposed to a person) to this function; however, the lines of responsibility must be assigned throughout the organization and must be documented on an organizational chart or similar document where all names and positions are adequately defined. Finally, all RMPs must be updated either every five years or whenever a new regulated substance or process (including significant changes) is added.

Definitions

The final RMP regulations define several key terms. Among the most important of these is *catastrophic release*. Catastrophic release is defined as a major uncontrolled emission, fire, or explosion, involving one or more regulated substances that presents immediate and substantial endangerment to public health and the environment.[14]

The final regulations define a *worst-case release* as the release of the largest quantity of a regulated substance for a vessel or process line failure that results in the *greatest distance to an endpoint*.[15]

Note that these two definitions are not mutually exclusive. It is entirely possible to have a worst-case release that is not a catastrophic release. It is also possible to have a worst case release from one portion of a site that results from the release of a smaller quantity of material than another release at a different location on the site. Figure 2.2, for example, shows a hypothetical facility. Area A is the main production area of the facility. Area B

is the truck depot for loading and unloading raw materials and final products. While the production Area A has large storage tanks holding several hundreds of thousands of gallons of a regulated substance and terminal Area B has smaller tanks, note that Area B is also closer to the property line. Therefore, it is possible that a release at the truck terminal loading area could result in a greater distance to an offsite impact than a release in production Area A. This concept will be discussed in more detail in Chapter 14.

Any time an analysis of offsite impacts from accidental releases becomes necessary, the question of what constitutes a predicted concentration of concern becomes important. In the past, there have been several approaches to identifying concentrations of concern from accidental releases. Some have been based on levels set by the American Conference of Government Industrial Hygienists, which identified levels that are deemed to be acceptable for an eight-hour exposure (permissible exposure levels or PELs), as well as levels associated with short-term consequences, including Immediate Danger of Life and Health (IDLH) and other similar measures.

Endpoints

U.S. EPA in its final regulations (06/20/96 as amended 08/25/97) provides a table of toxic endpoints, which can be found at the end of this chapter in Table 2.1. The toxic endpoints for the toxic substances on this

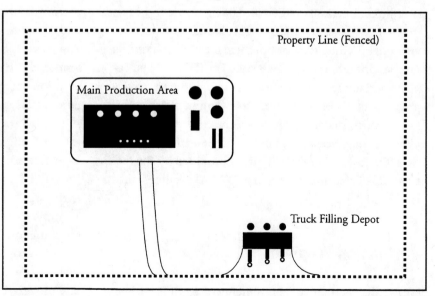

Figure 2.2: Hypothetical Facility

list provide milligrams per liter concentration values for each toxic chemical. In addition, endpoints are defined for flammables included because of the hazards of an explosion, as an overpressure of 1 psi, and for heat, which is 5 kilowatts per square meter for 40 seconds. Additionally, the lower flammability limit is defined as an endpoint.

The concept of endpoints is quite simple. The endpoint is the distance offsite at which the predicted value (i.e., toxic pollutant concentration, explosion over-pressure, or heat load) drops below the stated value. The distance at which the predicted concentration drops below this value is the endpoint distance. Therefore, the worst-case release is one that results in the greatest distance to an offsite endpoint. This is why a release of a moderate quantity near the property line could result in a greater distance to an endpoint than a release in a production area that is located farther from the property line.

Note that the endpoints published by EPA on June 20, 1997 represent only interim guidance on what endpoints should be. EPA has adopted the emergency response planning guideline level 2 (ERPG-2), which references the American Industrial Hygiene Association (AIHA). For substances that had no ERPG-2 value, the endpoint was set at the level of concern (LOC) from the Technical Guidance for Hazard Analysis, updated where necessary to reflect new toxicity data. EPA recognized the limitations of these data and endpoints and is working with other agencies to develop acute exposure guideline limits (AEGLs). The final rule indicates that when these have been developed and peer reviewed, EPA intends to adopt them into rule making as toxic endpoints for the RMP rule. For flammables, vapor cloud explosion distances are to based on an overpressure of 1 PSI. For alternative flammable releases, radiant heat distances are based on an exposure of 5 kW/M2 for 40 seconds. For vapor cloud fires and jet fires, the lower flammability limit provided by the National Fire Protection Association (NFPA) or other source is to used.[16]

Prevention Programs

Under the regulatory requirements of 40 CFR Part 68, processes subject to the RMP standard are divided into three levels of compliance, labeled Programs 1, 2, and

3. Eligibility for any given program is based on process criteria so that classification of one process in a program does not influence the classification of other processes at the source. For example, if a process meets Program 1 criteria, the source need only satisfy Program 1 requirements for that process, even if other processes at the source are subject to Program 2 or Program 3. A source, therefore, could have processes in one or more of the three programs. See Chapter 12, Table 12.1 for more detail. The following is a general discussion of each programs requirements.

Program 1 Requirements

EPA did not to make the presence of environmental receptors a part of the eligibility criteria for Program 1 and has deleted the certification requirement. Instead, owners or operators of all covered processes will have to identify in the RMP any environmental receptors that are within the distance potentially affected by the worst case. Since Program 1 eligibility is now determined on a by-process basis rather than by source-wide criteria, EPA is requiring the owner or operator of a Program 1 process to ensure that any necessary response actions have been coordinated with local response agencies. EPA believes that local responders may become involved in an incident even if the public is not threatened. No additional CAA-related planning activities are required, however.

The CAA requires that all sources with more than a threshold quantity of a listed substance register an RMP, perform a hazard assessment, and develop accidental release prevention and emergency response programs. Therefore, total exemption of processes that meet Program 1 criteria is not possible. Moreover, even if an exemption for processes that exceed a threshold were permissible, the owner or operator would need to take steps that are equivalent to the hazard assessment to establish eligibility for the exemption. The offsite consequence analysis is the most significant burden for a Program 1 process under the standard. The minimal additional actions required in the final rule for Program 1 simply establish a record of eligibility and a response coordination mechanism.

EPA recognizes that emergency responders and site visitors could also be hurt by an accidental release from any process, but notes that responder safety is covered by OSHA and EPA under the HAZWOPER regulations. It is the owners' or operators' responsibility to inform visitors about the hazards and the appropriate steps to take in the event of an accidental release from any process subject to the RMP rule.

Finally, EPA based the registration information requirements in the final rule on the EPCRA section 312 Tier II form. The CAA requires that the RMP be registered with EPA. Because the EPCRA form is not submitted to EPA, it would not substitute for registration with EPA, either in its present or amended form. EPA recognizes the information overlap between the Tier II form and the RMP registration and is planning to take under consideration the possible use of the RMP registration to satisfy the Tier II reporting requirement.

Program 2 Requirements

In promulgating the final standard, EPA retained the prevention program management system requirements proposed in the NPRM, but only for Program 2 and 3 processes.[17] EPA moved the management system requirement from the prevention program section to the general requirements section because it should be designed to oversee the implementation of all elements of the risk management program. The owner or operator must designate a qualified person or position with overall responsibility for the program and specify the lines of authority if the responsibility for implementing individual requirements is assigned to other persons or positions.

EPA developed the following seven specific elements for the Program 2 prevention program which can be referenced in the attached 40 CFR Part 68 regulations found in Appendix C:

- ❏ Safety information (Sec. 68.48)
- ❏ Hazard review (Sec. 68.50)
- ❏ Operating procedures (Sec. 68.52)
- ❏ Training (Sec. 68.54)
- ❏ Maintenance (Sec. 68.56)
- ❏ Compliance audits (Sec. 68.58)
- ❏ Incident investigation (Sec. 68.60)

Most Program 2 processes are likely to be relatively simple and are located at smaller businesses. EPA believed that owners or operators of Program 2 processes can successfully prevent accidents without a program as detailed as the OSHA PSM, which was primarily designed for the chemical industry. EPA combined and tailored elements common to OSHA's PSM and EPA's RMP to generate Program 2 requirements and applied them to non-petrochemical industry processes. EPA is also developing model risk management programs for several industry sectors that will have Program 2 processes. These model guidances will help sources comply by providing standard elements that can be adopted to a specific source. EPA expects that many Program 2 processes will already be in compliance with most of the requirements through compliance with other federal regulations, state laws, industry standards and codes, and good engineering practices.

Program 3 Requirements

The Program 3 prevention program includes the requirements of the OSHA PSM standard, 29 CFR 1910.119 (c) through (m) and (o), with minor wording changes to address statutory differences (refer to Chapter 12). This makes it clear that one accident prevention program to protect workers, the general public, and the environment will satisfy both OSHA and EPA. Keep in mind, however, that the Accident Prevention Program is only part of the RMP.

For elements that are in both the EPA and OSHA rules, EPA has used OSHA's language verbatim, with the following changes:

- ❏ Replacement of terms (See Table 2.1.)
- ❏ Deletion of specific references to workplace impacts or to "safety and health"
- ❏ Changes to specific schedule dates
- ❏ Changes to references within the standard.

Table 2.1: OSHA vs. EPA Terminology	
OSHA	**EPA**
highly hazardous substance	regulated substance
employer	owner or operator
standard	part or rule
acility	stationary source

The "safety and health" and "workplace impacts" references occur in OSHA's PSM standard in process safety information (29 CFR 1910.119 (d)(2)(E)), process hazards analysis (29 CFR 1910.119(e)(3)(vii)), and incident investigation (29 CFR 1910.119(m)(1)). These changes were made to ensure that OSHA retains its oversight of actions designed to protect workers while EPA retains its oversight of actions to protect public health and the environment and to remove possible interpretations that certain elements of process safety management fail to account for offsite impacts.

Under the final rule, process hazard analyses (PHAs) conducted for OSHA are considered adequate to meet EPA's requirements. They will be updated on the OSHA schedule by the fifth anniversary of their initial completion. Documentation for the PHA developed for OSHA will be sufficient to meet EPA's purposes. This approach will eliminate any duplicative analyses.

EPA anticipates that sources whose processes are already in compliance with OSHA PSM will not need to take any additional steps or create any new documentation to comply with EPA's Program 3 prevention program. Any PSM modifications necessary to account for protection of public health and the environment along with protection of workers can be made when PSM elements are updated under the OSHA requirements. EPA has modified the OSHA definition of catastrophic release—which serves as the trigger for an incident investigation—to include events "that present imminent and substantial endangerment to public health and the environment." As a result, the RMP rule requires investigation of accidental releases that pose a risk to the public or the environment, whereas the OSHA rule does not. EPA recognizes that catastrophic accidental releases primarily affect the workplace and that this change will have little effect on incident investigation programs already established. However, EPA needs to ensure under the Clean Air Act requirements for RMP that accidental releases having an exclusively offsite impact are also addressed.

RMP Required Elements

Although subsequent chapters of this book will review in detail the specific requirements for each level of a risk management prevention program, following is a brief topical discussion of 10 of the more important required program elements.

Hazard Review

The Clean Air Act requires a hazard assessment that includes evaluation of a range of releases, including worst-case accidental releases, analyses of potential offsite consequences, and a five-year accident history. The language in the *Conference Report* suggests a more extensive assessment that would require a formal process hazard analysis (e.g., basic data on the source, identification of potential points of release, review of the efficacy of release, and control measures). To allow EPA's prevention program requirements to parallel OSHA's process safety management standard, the offsite consequence analysis and five-year accident history have been separated from the formal process hazard analysis requirement and requires a hazard assessment that examines a range of accidental release scenarios, selects a worst-case accidental release scenario, analyzes offsite consequences for selected release scenarios including worst case, and documents a five-year history of significant accidental releases and accidental releases with the potential for offsite consequences.

Process Safety Information

The process hazard analysis must be based on up-to-date chemical and process information, including information on physical and chemical hazards, process technology (e.g., process chemistry, process parameters), and equipment (e.g., equipment specifications and design, piping and instrumentation drawings). As per OSHA, after the effective date of the rule, facilities would also need to document material and energy balances for new equipment in a process that involves a regulated substance above the threshold quantity to ensure that the equipment is appropriately designed for the process. The material balance is intended only for ensuring the proper design basis for the equipment and is not useful for process inventory accounting or for measurement of chemical loss. For example, it is necessary to know the flow rate in units of mass per unit-time to properly design a heat exchanger; however, this flow rate does not give the mass of the substance consumed or lost in a reaction system. All required process safety information would apply only to affected equipment, not to the facility as a whole. Chemical information is available from Material Safety Data Sheets (MSDSs) mandated under OSHA's hazard communication standard (29 CFR 1910.1200). The level of process technology and equipment information would vary with the type of facility. For warehouses, wholesalers, and service industries, little equipment information would be needed unless special equipment is used with the regulated substances. For manufacturers, more extensive information would be required, including flow charts, piping and instrumentation diagrams (P&IDs) of the facility as it currently exists, and electrical, ventilation, and safety system specifications.

Standard Operating Procedures (SOPs)

The results of the process hazard analysis, information developed during the design of a process, and industry and facility experience combine to define the proper way to conduct operations and maintain equipment. SOPs describe the tasks to be performed by the operator, the operating parameters (e.g., temperature, pressure) that must be maintained, and safety precautions needed for both operations and maintenance activities. SOPs must specify the consequences of deviations from safe operating limits (e.g., if the safe operating temperatures are between 100 and 150 degrees Celsius, the SOP should indicate what happens if the temperature is above or below those limits). Written SOPs provide a guide to safe operations in a form that can be used by employees. Lack of SOPs and inadequate SOPs have been implicated in a number of catastrophic accidents. For example, improper maintenance procedures have been blamed for a release and explosion at a facility in New Castle, Delaware, in 1980, which killed six people, injured twenty-seven others, and caused more than $63 million in property damage to the facility.

SOPs, which define the proper steps to take in these emergency situations, provide a quick source of information that can prevent or mitigate the effects of accidents. SOPs also provide workers and management a standard against which to assess performance, since the procedures clarify for both operators and supervisors how operations should be carried out at the facility. Application of SOPs can result in more cost-effective operations by ensuring that operators adhere to procedures that maximize both the safety and efficiency of a process.

Training

Training provides employees with the information needed to understand what they must do to operate safely and why safe operations are necessary. The required training program is the key to ensuring the effectiveness of other program elements such as SOPs, maintenance programs, pre-startup reviews, and emer-gency response. Refresher training ensures that employees are reminded of appropriate procedures periodically. Training programs often provide immediate benefits to facilities because trained employees have fewer accidents, damage less equipment through mishandling, and conduct more efficient operations. Inadequately trained maintenance workers have been implicated in the 1989 disaster in Pasadena, Texas, which killed twenty-three people, injured 130 others, and destroyed $750 million of property at the facility. In 1988, at a plating facility in Auburn, Indiana, untrained workers used hydrochloric acid to clean a tank that was used to hold zinc cyanide. The resulting hydrogen cyanide killed five workers and sent more than ten others to the hospital.

Maintenance

The Clean Air Act specifies that the prevention program must include requirements for equipment maintenance. Preventive maintenance, inspection, and testing of equipment are critical to safe operations at a facility. Waiting for equipment to fail often means waiting until an accidental release occurs before addressing a problem. This approach is not acceptable, especially considering the extremely hazardous characteristics of the regulated substances. Preventive maintenance, inspection, and testing are needed because many of the potential failures are not obvious from visual inspections. For example, failed alarm systems or detectors may need to be tested to determine if they are functioning properly; detectors and monitors, which can provide early warnings of releases, must be calibrated periodically; corrosion of vessels and piping, a hazard with many chemicals, can be detected through testing well before the vessels or pipes fail; and scheduled cleaning, oiling, or replacement of parts can prevent equipment failure. A large number of the accidents reported in the Marsh and McLennan review of the 100 largest losses in the petrochemical industry were the result of equipment failure that might have been avoided through preventive maintenance.[18] A 1978 fire and explosion at a Texas City, Texas, facility that led to almost $100 million in property damage was attributed to instrument failure and a faulty relief valve. A 1989 accident in Richmond, California, that injured workers and responders was caused by a failed weld.

Besides preventing accidental releases, maintenance programs also provide direct benefits to facilities by decreasing the amount of costly down time that can result from failed equipment. Even in incidents where there is serious property damage, the lost business costs can be significantly greater than the property damage resulting directly from an accident.

Accident Investigation

Accidents can provide valuable information about hazards and the steps needed to prevent accidental releases. Many times, the immediate cause of an accident is the result of a series of other problems that need to be addressed to prevent recurrences. For example, an operator's mistake may be the result of poor training, inappropriate SOPs, or poor design of control systems; equipment failure may result from improper maintenance, misuse of equipment (operating at too high a temperature), or use of incompatible materials. Without a thorough investigation, facilities may miss the opportunity to identify and solve the root problems. Investigations must be initiated within 48 hours of any accident.

The accident investigation should determine, to the extent possible, the initiating event that led to the release, and the root cause(s). EPA emphasizes that identification of the root causes (e.g., a misdesigned piping run) may be more important than identification of the initiating event (e.g., a failed flange). The investigation should be summarized in a report to management; the report should include recommendations for steps that need to be taken to prevent recurrences (e.g., review piping design) and improve emergency response and mitigation measures. Management is required to document its decisions based on the recommendations. As with the management of change procedures, the degree of the accident investigation and documentation will vary with the potential seriousness of the accident. For example, a minor release that was prevented from becoming a major release only by prompt action of operators may require more investigation than a large release that can be quickly attributed to a single failure (e.g., a faulty high-level alarm).

Process Hazard Analysis

The AIChE's Guidelines for Hazard Evaluation Procedures defines a hazard evaluation (also known as a process hazard analysis) as a procedure intended "to identify the hazards that exist, the consequences that may occur as a result of the hazards, the likelihood that events may take place that would cause an accident with

such a consequence, and the likelihood that safety systems, mitigating systems, and emergency alarms and evacuation plans would function properly and eliminate or reduce the consequences."[19]

A process hazard analysis involves the application of a formal technique, such as a "What If" analysis or a hazards and operability study (HAZOP). Formal techniques provide a method for a rigorous, step-by-step examination of processes, process equipment and controls, and procedures to identify each point at which a mishap may occur (e.g., a valve failing, a gauge malfunctioning, human error) and examine the possible consequences of that mishap—by itself and in combination with other possible mishaps. The result of a properly conducted process hazard analysis is a list of possible hazards of the process at the facility that could lead to a loss of containment and release of a regulated substance. Process hazard analyses must be conducted by professionals trained in the techniques and knowledgeable about the process and facility being examined. Such evaluations usually require at least two experts, with other experts contributing to the process when necessary. A HAZOP may require a core team of five to seven people to thoroughly complete the analysis. For a simple process, the process hazard analysis may take a day or two; for complex processes, the evaluation may take six weeks to three months.

Pre-Startup Review

Startup of a new or modified system can be a particularly hazardous time for facilities, especially for complex processes and those that require high temperatures, high pressures, or potentially exothermic reactions. However, even simple facilities need to conduct such reviews. For example, before a chemical distributor accepts a new regulated substance, the distributor should check that the fire suppression system is appropriate for the substance, that workers know how to handle and store the substance, and that emergency response procedures are in place to handle an accidental release.

Management of Change

Chemical processes are integrated systems; changes in one part of the process can have unintended effects in other parts of the system. For example, installation of better seals may increase the pressure in vessels. It is, therefore, important that all changes in processes, chemicals, and procedures be reviewed prior to their implementation to identify any potential hazards that may be created by the modification. Although most changes at facilities are intended to improve safety and efficiency, any modification can have unintended effects and requires a specific review of the safety implications of the change. Other process modifications are instituted in response to a specific problem that arises unexpectedly. It was such an unexamined change in the installation of a temporary bypass at Flixborough, England, that led to a 1974 release and explosion that killed twenty-eight employees, injured eighty-nine people, and damaged almost 2,000 properties offsite.

Compliance Audits

An important tool in ensuring that the process safety management elements are being implemented is the periodic safety audit. The safety audit provides management with a mechanism for oversight of the implementation of the safety elements and of the overall safety of the facility. Safety audits may take several forms—some facilities use audits to check on compliance with specific regulations, some do spot-checks of safety practices, while others review all key aspects of safety management. See Chapter 6 for a more detailed discussion of safety audits.

[7] 40 CFR Part 68, 6/20/96.
[8] 40 CFR Part 68, 6/20/96.
[9] NFPA-325M, *Fire Hazard Properties: Flammable Liquids, Gases and Solids* (1991).
[10] 40 CFR Part 68, 6/20/96.
[11] 29CFR 1910.120.
[12] (NRT, May 1996).
[13] 40 CFR Part 68, 6/20/96.
[14] 40CFR Part 68, 6/20/96.
[15] (68.22(a)).
[16] 40 CFR Part 68, 6/20/96.
[17] 58FR 54190, 7/20/93.
[18] March and McLennan's *Large Property Damage Losses in the Hydrocarbon-Chemical Industries: A Thirty-Year Review,* 1990.
[19] *Guidelines for Hazard Evaluation Procedures: Second Edition with Worked Examples,* New York: Center for Chemical Process Safety of the American Institutes of Chemical Engineers, 1992.

Table 2.2: Table of Toxic Endpoints

CAS No.	Toxic Substances	Endpoint (mg/L)
107–02–8	Acrolein [2-Propenal]	0.0011
107–13–1	Acrylonitrile [2-Propenenitrile]	0.076
814–68–6	Acrylyl chloride [2-Propenoyl chloride]	0.00090
107–18–6	Allyl alcohol [2-Propen-1-ol]	0.036
107–11–9	Allylamine [2-Propen-1-amine]	0.0032
7664–41–7	Ammonia (anhydrous)	0.14
7664–41–7	Ammonia (conc 20% or greater)	0.14
7784–34–1	Arsenous trichloride	0.010
7784–42–1	Arsine	0.0019
10294–34–5	Boron trichloride [Borane, trichloro-]	0.010
7637–07–2	Boron trifluoride [Borane, trifluoro-]	0.028
353–42–4	Boron trifluoride compound with methyl ether (1:1) [Boron, trifluoro[oxybis[methane]]-, T-4	0.023
7726–95–6	Bromine	0.0065
75–15–0	Carbon disulfide	0.16
7782–50–5	Chlorine	0.0087
10049–04–4	Chlorine dioxide [Chlorine oxide (ClO2)]	0.0028
67–66–3	Chloroform [Methane, trichloro-]	0.49
542–88–1	Chloromethyl ether [Methane, oxybis[chloro-]	0.00025
107–30–2	Chloromethyl methyl ether [Methane, chloromethoxy-]	0.0018
4170–30–3	Crotonaldehyde [2-Butenal]	0.029
123–73–9	Crotonaldehyde, (E)-, [2-Butenal, (E)-]	0.029
506–77–4	Cyanogen chloride	0.030
108–91–8	Cyclohexylamine [Cyclohexanamine]	0.16
19287–45–7	Diborane	0.0011
75–78–5	Dimethyldichlorosilane [Silane, dichlorodimethyl-]	0.026
57–14–7	1,1-Dimethylhydrazine [Hydrazine, 1,1-dimethyl-]	0.012
106–89–8	Epichlorohydrin [Oxirane, (chloromethyl)-]	0.076
107–15–3	Ethylenediamine [1,2-Ethanediamine]	0.49
151–56–4	Ethyleneimine [Aziridine]	0.018
75–21–8	Ethylene oxide [Oxirane]	0.090
7782–41–4	Fluorine	0.0039
50–00–0	Formaldehyde (solution)	0.012
110–00–9	Furan	0.0012
302–01–2	Hydrazine	0.011
7647–01–0	Hydrochloric acid (conc 30% or greater)	0.030
74–90–8	Hydrocyanic acid	0.011
7647–01–0	Hydrogen chloride (anhydrous) [Hydrochloric acid]	0.030
7664–39–3	Hydrogen fluoride/Hydrofluoric acid (conc 50% or greater) [Hydrofluoric acid]	0.016
7783–07–5	Hydrogen selenide	0.00066
7783–06–4	Hydrogen sulfide	0.042
13463–40–6	Iron, pentacarbonyl- [Iron carbonyl (Fe(CO)5), (TB–5–11)-]	0.00044

Table 2.2 (*cont'd.*): Table of Toxic Endpoints

CAS No.	Toxic Substances	Endpoint (mg/L)
78–82–0	Isobutyronitrile [Propanenitrile, 2-methyl-]	0.14
108–23–6	Isopropyl chloroformate [Carbonochloride acid, 1-methylethyl ester]	0.10
126–98–7	Methacrylonitrile [2-Propenenitrile, 2-methyl-]	0.0027
74–87–3	Methyl chloride [Methane, chloro-]	0.82
79–22–1	Methyl chloroformate [Carbonochloridic acid, methylester]	0.0019
60–34–4	Methyl hydrazine [Hydrazine, methyl-]	0.0094
624–83–9	Methyl isocyanate [Methane, isocyanato-]	0.0012
74–93–1	Methyl mercaptan [Methanethiol]	0.049
556–64–9	Methyl thiocyanate [Thiocyanic acid, methyl ester]	0.085
75–79–6	Methyltrichlorosilane [Silane, trichloromethyl-]	0.018
13463–39–3	Nickel carbonyl	0.00067
7697–37–2	Nitric acid (conc 80% or greater)	0.026
10102–43–9	Nitric oxide [Nitrogen oxide (NO)]	0.031
8014–95–7	Oleum (Fuming Sulfuric acid) [Sulfuric acid, mixture with sulfur trioxide]	0.010
79–21–0	Peracetic acid [Ethaneperoxoic acid]	0.0045
594–42–3	Perchloromethylmercaptan [Methanesulfenyl chloride, trichloro-]	0.0076
75–44–5	Phosgene [Carbonic dichloride]	0.00081
7803–51–2	Phosphine	0.0035
10025–87–3	Phosphorus oxychloride [Phosphoryl chloride]	0.0030
7719–12–2	Phosphorus trichloride [Phosphorous trichloride]	0.028
110–89–4	Piperidine	0.022
107–12–0	Propionitrile [Propanenitrile]	0.0037
109–61–5	Propyl chloroformate [Carbonochloridic acid, propylester]	0.010
75–55–8	Propyleneimine [Aziridine, 2-methyl-]	0.12
75–56–9	Propylene oxide [Oxirane, methyl-]	0.59
7446–09–5	Sulfur dioxide (anhydrous)	0.0078
7783–60–0	Sulfur tetrafluoride [Sulfur fluoride (SF4), (T-4)-]	0.0092
7446–11–9	Sulfur trioxide	0.010
75–74–1	Tetramethyllead [Plumbane, tetramethyl-]	0.0040
509–14–8	Tetranitromethane [Methane, tetranitro-]	0.0040
7750–45–0	Titanium tetrachloride [Titanium chloride (TiCl4) (T-4)-]	0.020
584–84–9	Toluene 2,4-diisocyanate [Benzene, 2,4-diisocyanato-1-methyl-]	0.0070
91–08–7	Toluene 2,6-diisocyanate [Benzene, 1,3-diisocyanato-2-methyl-]	0.0070
26471–62–5	Toluene diisocyanate (unspecified isomer) [Benzene, 1,3-diisocyanatomethyl-]	0.0070
75–77–4	Trimethylchlorosilane [Silane, chlorotrimethyl-]	0.050
108–05–4	Vinyl acetate monomer [Acetic acid ethenyl ester]	0.26

APPENDIX A TO PART 68: TABLE OF TOXIC ENDPOINTS[As defined in § 68.22 of this part]

Chapter 3

Organizing Process Safety Information

The first step in conducting an assessment of the potential for accidental releases of hazardous or toxic substances from processes requires that the proper safety information be obtained and organized. This is not always an easy task.

The compilation of information concerning process chemicals, technology, and equipment provides the foundation for identifying and understanding the hazards involved in a process and is necessary in the development of a complete and thorough process hazard analysis, as well as the management of change, operating procedures, and incident investigations, etc.

Historically, facilities that manufacture or use hazardous or toxic materials—including explosives and flammables—focus on proper utilization of these materials or production of these materials and their processes. Safety is always a concern, primarily with respect to workers at the facility.

What Must Be Included

Even though safety has always been a concern, scientific and engineering information concerning process safety parameters has, until recently, not been widely available, nor, if available, maintained and updated. Process safety information comprises data of several types. First, it is important to recognize that the regulations (Section 68.65 - 68.87) require the owner/operator to compile written process safety information *before* conducting any process hazard analysis as required under the regulations. The compilation of written process

safety information is necessary, not only to assist the owner or operator in performing the hazard analysis, but also to document to the U.S. EPA, to state emergency planning commissions, and to the public that all appropriate information was available and was used as the starting point in conducting the hazard analysis.

Process safety information must include information relating to the hazards posed by regulated substances used or produced in processes at the facility in quantities exceeding the threshold quantity (TQ). This required process safety information should include toxicity information, permissible exposure limits, physical data, reactivity data, corrosivity data, thermal and chemical stability data, hazardous effects of inadvertent mixing of different materials that could forseeably occur. Most of the information may already be available from the Material Safety Data Sheet (MSDS). MSDSs are acceptable in meeting this requirement to the extent that the required information is available on the MSDS. The regulations list the minimum components of process information, which must be made available as part of the plan in written form.

In accordance with the schedule set forth in Section 68.67, the owner or operator must complete a compilation of written process safety information before conducting any process hazard analysis required by the rule. The compilation of written process safety information is used to enable to owner or operator and the employees involved in operating the process to identify and understand the hazards posed by those processes involving regulated substances. This process safety information must include information pertaining to the hazards of the regulated substances used or produced by the process, information pertaining to the technology of the process, and information pertaining to the equipment in the process.

Regulated Substances Information

Information pertaining to the hazards of the regulated substances in the process must also include at least the following:

1. Toxicity information
2. Permissible exposure limits
3. Physical data
4. Reactivity data
5. Corrosively data
6. Thermal and chemical stability data
7. Hazardous effects of inadvertent mixing of different materials that could foreseeably occur

Technology Information

Information pertaining to the technology of the process must include the following:

1. A block flow diagram or simplified process flow diagram
2. Process chemistry
3. Maximum intended inventory
4. Safe upper and lower limits for such items as temperatures, pressures, flows, or compositions
5. An evaluation of the consequences of deviations

Information about Equipment

Where the original technical information no longer exists, such information may be developed in conjunction with the process hazard analysis in sufficient detail to support the analysis. Required information pertaining to the equipment in the process includes the following:

1. Materials of construction
2. Piping and instrumentation diagrams (P&IDs)
3. Electrical classification
4. Relief system design and design basis
5. Ventilation system design
6. Design codes and standards employed
7. Material and energy balances for processes built after June 21, 1999
8. Safety systems (e.g., interlocks, detection or suppression systems)

The owner or operator must document that equipment complies with recognized and generally accepted good engineering practices.

For existing equipment designed and constructed in accordance with codes, standards, or practices that are no longer in general use, the owner or operator must determine and document that the equipment is designed, maintained, inspected, tested, and operated in a safe manner.

Material Safety Data Sheets

The Material Safety Data Sheet (MSDS) is an important resource in obtaining information about the physical and chemical hazards posed by materials and their processes. MSDSs are available for inputs to the process from the companies providing these materials. For materials generated or manufactured at the facility, these forms must be available onsite under OSHA regulations. Additionally, under the OSHA Hazard Communications Standard[20] it is a requirement of all facilities handling, manufacturing, or otherwise using hazardous toxic substances to have a complete file of current MSDS sheets.

The MSDS has information on toxicity and permissible exposure limits and may also have data on warnings related to hazardous effects of mixing with other materials, which could cause unforeseen reactions. There is much more data listed in this table, however, than can possibly be obtained from an MSDS. For example, this table lists data on the technology of the process; process chemistry (safe limits for temperature, pressure, flows or composition); evaluations of the consequences of deviations; information pertaining to equipment in the process, including the materials of construction, piping instrumentation diagrams, electrical classifications, and design codes and standards; as well as other aspects of the process.

Hazard Evaluation

Hazard evaluations can be performed using available information that can be assembled for this purpose. The adequacy and accuracy of a hazard evaluation, however, depends on the completeness and accuracy of the data assembled in written form on which it is based. Additionally, if available data are not relatively complete, this lack of data can preclude certain levels of analysis related to hazard assessment. For example, HAZOP Analysis and Fault Tree Analysis will not be possible without complete information.

New processes pose specific challenges to determining the potential for accidental release. Information available to perform the hazard analysis will vary over the lifetime of a process. New processes—before operating experience can be developed—will have available very little of the process information that will be needed to conduct a hazard assessment. In the early stages of process development, only limited information on the chemical hazards may be available. In addition, limited information on projected temperatures and pressures throughout the process will not be available. Once the process has reached commercial production, more complete information will be available. Table 3.1 shows examples of information used to perform hazard assessments. This table comes from *Guidelines for Hazard Evaluation Procedures* published by AIChE in 1992.

Table 3.1: Examples of Information Used to Perform an Hazard Evaluation Study[21]

- Chemical reaction equations and stoichiometry for primary and important secondary or side reactions
- Area electrical classification drawings
- Type and nature of catalysts used
- Building and equipment layouts
- Reactive chemical data on all streams, including in-process chemicals
- Electrical classifications of equipment
- Kinetic data for important process reactions, including the order, rate constants, approach to equilibrium, etc.
- Piping and instrumentation drawings
- Kinetic data for undesirable reactions, such as decompositions and autopolymerizations
- Mechanical equipment data sheets
- Process limits stated in terms of pressure, temperature, concentration, feed-to-catalyst ratio, etc., along with a description of the consequences of operating beyond these limits
- Equipment catalogs
- Process flow diagrams and a description of the process steps or unit operations involved, starting with raw material storage and feed prepara-

tion and ending with product recovery and storage
- Vendor drawings and operation and maintenance manuals
- Design energy and mass balance
- Valve and instrumentation data sheets
- Major material inventories
- Fire protection system(s) design basis
- Piping specifications
- Description of general control philosophy (i.e., identifying the primary control variables and the reasons for their selection)
- Utility specifications
- Discussion of special design considerations that are required because of the unique hazards or properties of the chemicals involved
- Test and inspection reports
- Safety, health, and environmental data for raw materials, intermediates, products, by-products, and wastes
- Electrical one-line drawings
- Regulatory limits and/or permit limits
- Instrument loop drawings and logic diagrams
- Applicable codes and standards
- Control system and alarm description
- Variances
- Computer control system hardware and software design
- Plot plans
- Operating procedures (with critical operating parameters)
- Population distribution data
- Maintenance procedures
- Site hydrology data
- Relief system design basis
- Previous safety studies
- Ventilation system design basis
- Internal standards and checklists
- Safety system(s) design basis
- Corporate safety policies
- Relevant industry experience
- Incident reports

Table 3.2: Common Material Property Data for Hazard Identification[22]

Acute toxicity
- inhalation (e.g., LCLO)
- oral (e.g., LD50)
- dermal

Physical properties
- vapor pressure
- density or specific volume
- corrosivity/erosivity
- heat capacity
- specific heats
- freezing point
- coefficient of expansion
- boiling point
- solubility

Chronic toxicity
- inhalation
- oral
- dermal

Persistence in the environment

Odor threshold

Mutagenicity

Flammability/Explosivity
- LEL/LFL
- UEL/UFL
- dust explosion parameters
- minimum ignition energy
- flash point
- autoignition temperature
- energy production[23]

Reactivity
- process materials
- desired reaction(s)
- side reaction(s)
- decomposition reaction(s)
- kinetics
- materials of construction
- raw material impurities
- contaminants (air, water, rust, lubricants, etc.)
- decomposition products
- incompatible chemicals
- pyrophoric materials

Carcinogenicity

Stability
- shock
- temperature
- light polymerization

Exposure limits
- TLV
- PEL
- STEL®
- IDLH
- ERPG

Biodegradability

Aquatic toxicity

Persistence in the environment

Odor threshold

Table 3.2 shows common material property data needed for hazard identification. These material property data relate to both the environmental and health consequences of exposure to released chemicals and also relate to the physical properties of the material, which are needed to assess the potential for accidents to occur in the first place.

Section 68.67 of the final RMP regulations requires that the owner/operator perform an initial process hazard analysis (hazard evaluation) on "covered" processes. These are processes that contain more than the TQ of a regulated substance. The process hazard analysis should be appropriate for the complexity of the process and identify, evaluate, and control the hazards potentially involved in the process. The owner/operator is required to determine and document a priority order for conducting process hazard assessments based on a rational that includes such considerations as the extent of process hazards, number of potentially effected employees, age of the process, and operating history of the process. The process hazard analysis must be conducted *as soon as possible*, but no later than June 21, 1999. The regulated community takes this to generally mean the process hazard analysis should be completed by June 21, 1999. Reflect for a moment, however, on the general duty clause (Chapter 1), which requires all owners and operators who process, utilize, manufacture, or generate hazardous or toxic substances in quantities exceeding the TQ to plan for and mitigate the consequences of hazardous releases.

In the unlikely event of a release that injures offsite parties, a company could find itself in a difficult position having not begun the process hazard analysis. Assuming it had until June 20, 1999, when the final RMP regulations states that it must be "completed as soon as possible."[24] It is incumbent upon owners and operators to begin this process as soon as possible to be in full compliance with these regulations.

Other Important Analyses

There are a number of techniques that are identified in the regulations as being potentially valuable in hazard assessment. These include the following:

1. What-If Analysis
2. Checklist Analysis
3. What-If/Checklist Analysis
4. Hazard and Operability Study (HAZOP)
5. Failure Mode and Effects Analysis (FMEA)
6. Fault Tree Analysis
7. An appropriate equivalent methodology

There are a number of additional hazard evaluation techniques that are described in general terms in *Guidelines for Hazard Evaluation Procedures*, published by the Center for Chemical Process Safety of the American Institute of Chemical Engineers, referenced previously. These other techniques include Safety Reviews. Safety Reviews are intended to identify conditions in plants that could lead to major accidents. Such reviews are fairly simple, including a walk through of the facility and interviews with plant personnel. Safety Reviews can be used to help keep standard operating procedures current and to identify equipment or process changes which may be desirable to improve the safety of the facility. They are inherently non-quantitative in nature.

Checklist Analysis

A Checklist Analysis involves comparing requirements, codes, and standards with constructed processes. The adequacy of a checklist analysis depends on the experience and diligence of the participants. Checklists are useful where relatively inexperienced auditors are sent into a facility because they can check items on the checklist to verify compliance with codes and regulations. A completed checklist will have "Yes," "No," "Needs More Information" answers as responses to each question to be assessed.

Relative Ranking Analysis

Relative Ranking Analysis can be used to compare different processes at a facility to processes at separate facilities to determine the relative risks posed by each.

There are several standardized, well developed, relative ranking approaches available. These include the Dow Fire Explosion Index (FEI). This method is described in publications of the AIChE and evaluates the existence and significance of fire and explosion hazards by dividing a process or activity into separate process units and assigning indices based on the material, physical and chemical characteristics, process conditions, plant arrangement and equipment layout considerations and other factors.[25]

Preliminary Hazard Analysis

A Preliminary Hazard Analysis (PHA) is an analysis that is sometimes conducted early in a process life cycle, before commercial operation, or early into commercial operation. It is an outgrowth of the United States Military Standard System Safety Program requirements.[26] PHA formulates a list of hazards and potentially hazardous situations by considering certain key aspects of processes:

1. Raw materials, intermediate and final product and reactivity
2. Plant equipment
3. Facility layout
4. Operating environment
5. Operational activities (testing, maintenance, etc.)
6. Interfaces among system components

The result of a Preliminary Process Hazard Analysis is a quantitative assessment of the relative risks posed by different processes, materials, locations, and operating conditions. Therefore, it is apparent that this analysis is very helpful at the early stages of development, when decisions about what process to employ, where to locate it, and how to interrelate it to other processes must be undertaken.

What-If Analysis

The What-If Analysis involves hypothesizing various potential catastrophes or failures in the process. Its effectiveness depends on the availability of a very experienced team with extensive knowledge of the process under assessment or of very similar processes. Examples of What-If questions include these:

❏ What if electric power to the condenser cooling the process is interrupted for more than 5 hours which is the amount of time the back-up generators can run before running out of fuel? or

❏ What if the reactor safety vent does not release pressure at its designed rupture pressure in the event of over-pressure?

What-If/Checklist Analysis

The What-If/Checklist Analysis combines the hypothesizing of the What-If scenario analysis with the detail of the Checklist approach. The purpose of the What-If/Checklist Analysis is to identify hazards, consider the general types of accidents that can occur in a process or activity, evaluate in a qualitative fashion the effects of those accidents, and determine appropriate safeguards.[27]

Hazard and Operability Analysis

The Hazard and Operability Analysis (HAZOP) combines an operability analysis with the inclusion of hazards. The operability analysis basically takes certain key parameters—such as flow temperature, pressure, as well as the physical operating parameters of pumps, valves, vessels, heaters, and other process equipment. The Operability Analysis poses questions similar to a What-If Analysis such as "What if there is no flow from a pump?" The HAZOP analysis doesn't actually use the "what-if" phrase, but it does is combine words such as "flow" with other guide words such as "no," "high," "low." As an example, a high flow condition could represent an operability problem for a process. If this operability problem could result in an accident, which could, in turn, lead to an explosion or release of a hazardous or toxic chemical, then possible causes of such high or low deviations are investigated. The HAZOP analysis may identify a range of deviant operational conditions that could lead to hazardous releases. Appropriate corrective measures may be recommended as a result of the analysis. This technique is particularly helpful in developing standard operating procedures since it is likely to result in a tabulation of operation conditions and their normal range of values. Operating parameters

exceeding normal values are those that could lead to accidents and releases.

HAZOP analyses require very detailed process information. Ideally, piping and instrumentation diagrams (P&ID) for the complete process are needed. Additionally, detailed information on the process construction, maintenance, and other aspects are also required.

Failure Modes and Effects Analysis

Failure Modes and Effects Analyses are used to identify potential failures that could occur in a plant and specifically in a process containing more than a TQ of a regulated substance. Failure modes can also include broken vessels and pipe ruptures, and failure modes and effect analysis usually includes assessments of the worst-case consequences of each failure mode identified.

Fault Tree Analysis

The Fault Tree Analysis is a graphical approach to analyzing one particular type of accident or system failure. It provides a means for determining likely causes of an accident. The Fault Tree is a graphical model that displays the various combinations of equipment failures and human errors that could result in an overall system failure. The strength of the Fault Tree Analysis as a qualitative tool is its ability to identify the combinations of basic equipment failures and human errors that could lead to an accident. This allows the hazard assessment to focus on preventive or mitigative measures and to improve the adequacy of standard operating procedures.[28]

The approach taken to hazard assessment will vary depending on the level of information available, as well as the stage the process is in from conceptual design to commercial operation, through decommissioning. Additionally, the level of effort may be adjusted depending on the size of the facility and the potential magnitude of any release that could occur. If the worst-case release from a process will not lead to a concentration beyond the property line that could cause death or other extreme impact, it may not be appropriate to conduct a HAZOP or Fault Tree Analysis.

The data in Table 3.3 shows typical level of effort estimates for hazard evaluation techniques. Note that the overall commitment of time for a HAZOP ranges from

58 to 264 hours for a simple, small process to 264 for complex, large processes, respectively. By contrast, a safety review ranges from 15 for a simple, small to 84 for a complex, large process.

Table 3.3: Cost Estimates for Hazard Evaluation

Task	Prep	Modeling	Evaluation	Documentation	Total Hours	Cost*
Simple/Small						
Safety Review	3	0	6	6	15	$600
Checklist Analysis	3	0	6	6	15	$600
HAZOP Analysis	10	0	16	32	58	$2,300
Cause/Consequence Analysis	16	16	16	32	80	$3,200
Complex/Large						
Safety Review	16	0	32	36	84	$3,360
Checklist Analysis	16	0	32	24	72	$2,880
HAZOP Analysis	24	0	80	160	264	$10,560
Cause/Consequence Analysis	30	60	60	160	310	$12,400

*Assumes cost rate of $40/hour.

[20]OSHA Communication Standard

[22]*Guidelines for Hazard Evaluation Procedures Second Edition with Worked Examples*, New York: Center for Chemical Process Safety of the American Institutes of Chemical Engineers, 1992.

[23]*Guidelines for Hazard Evaluation Procedures Second Edition with Worked Examples*, New York: Center for Chemical Process Safety of the American Institutes of Chemical Engineers, 1992, p.37.

[24]40 CFR Part 68, 6/20/96.

[25]*Guidelines for Hazard Evaluation Procedures Second Edition with Worked Examples*, New York: Center for Chemical Process Safety of the American Institutes of Chemical Engineers, 1992.

[26]*Guidelines for Hazard Evaluation Procedures Second Edition with Worked Examples*, New York: Center for Chemical Process Safety of the American Institutes of Chemical Engineers, 1992.

[27]29 CFR 1910.1200.

[28]*Guidelines for Hazard Evaluation Procedures Second Edition with Worked Examples*, New York: Center for Chemical Process Safety of the American Institutes of Chemical Engineers, 1992.

Chapter 4

Determining Operating Procedures

Several types of activities are required in the RMP regulations, but are not thoroughly prescribed in the final RMP regulations. Determining operating procedures is one of those areas. A variety of tasks may be necessary during a process, such as initial startup, handling special hazards, normal operation, temporary operations, and emergency shutdowns. The appropriate and consistent manner in which the employer expects these tasks and procedures to be performed is often referred to as a *standard operating procedure* (SOP).

General Guidelines

Standard operating procedures are used in many industrial facilities that use both hazardous or nonhazardous chemicals in their manufacturing. These operating procedures should provide clear instructions for safely conducting activities involved in these processes and should also provide for the control of hazards during operations—such as opening process equipment or piping and for the control over entrance into a facility by support personnel such as maintenance, contractor, laboratory, or others. Standard operating procedures inform plant workers of the proper way to perform their jobs. A standard operating procedure can be compared to an instruction booklet for assembling a model airplane or for flying an airplane. A standard operating procedure provides a chronological set of instructions of what to do in a facility when it involves the manufacture, mixture, or transportation of various hazardous or toxic substances.

SOPs Must Be Written

It is important to have written operating procedures so that employees working on a single process can perform a given task in the exact manner. There is less likelihood that incidents will occur if written operating procedures are developed so that even a new employee or one who is relatively inexperienced will respond to a given event in a preconsidered and prescribed manner. It is also important that these procedures be written so that they can be communicated to employees in the most effective manner possible. Such written procedures can comprise an employer's policy with respect to what is to be accomplished, and how it is to be accomplished safely. This ensures that employees will perform the same tasks and procedures in a consistently safe manner and that employees will know what is expected of them. These operating procedures must also be available for ready reference and review during production to make sure the process is operated properly.

Checklist Format

A standard operating procedure is often in checklist form, where operators can check off each step of the procedures as it is undertaken. Standard operating procedures can also incorporate acceptable ranges of parameters for each step of the procedure. For example, to mix two chemicals in an exothermic reaction, certain temperature increases are expected. In this case, the standard operating procedure can have a branch structure whereby as long as the resultant temperatures fall within the acceptable range, the process can continue. If temperatures exceed or fall below the normal range, however, then the standard operating procedure should have instructions about which additional steps must be undertaken. These additional steps will also be described in detail in the standard operating procedures so there is no room for error.

Simple SOP

An example of the contents of a standard operating procedure for a simple mixing and blending operation might look like the one below.

Table 4.1: Standard Operating Procedure: Mixing and Blending Process

Standard Procedures:

Step 1   Inspect mixing tank and mixer.

Step 2   Start loading raw materials.

Step 3   Start mixer motor, adjust to 100 rpm.

Step 4   Run mixer for 30 minutes, checking operating speed every 5 minutes.

Step 5   Draw off 100 gallons and transfer to two 55 gallon drums.

Step 6   Mix additive A. Mix for additional 90 minutes monitoring mixing speed and temperature every 5 minutes.

Step 7   Transfer mixture to reactor.

Step 8   Add new input chemical.

Step 9   Heat to 350° Fahrenheit.

Step 10   Cook for 24 hours.

Step 11   Cool off for 12 hours or until temperature reaches ambient temperature.

Step 12   Open drain valve, turn on pump, transfer completed batch to packaging area.

Acceptable Limits:	Emergency Procedures:
Terpentine	Initial actions to correct problem
Mixer speed	Notifications
Tank/reactor liquid level	Evacuation procedures

This is a very simple example of a standard operating procedure. Please note that at each of these stages—particularly those where exothermic reactions occur and where heat is applied—ranges of acceptable temperatures could be supplied and appropriate corrective

measures added to the standard operating procedure to direct the operators as what to do when certain ranges of temperatures or pressures are encountered.

Until very recently, standard operating procedures were directed at maintaining processes in such a state that they could be effective in manufacturing the intended product at an acceptable quality level. If higher temperatures or pressures were encountered, operators were instructed to take corrective action primarily to maintain product quality.

Unlike the OSHA PSM standard, under the final y regulations, SOPs must be certified to be appropriate to prevent (to the extent possible) explosions, fires, or other catastrophic failures that could lead to releases of hazardous or toxic pollutants to the environment. What is needed then, is that the SOP must be expanded to include appropriate responses to out-of-normal or unusual circumstances for the explicit purpose of preventing (where possible) the occurrence of an explosion, fire, or other event that could cause a catastrophic release.

Incorporating RMP Requirements

SOPs must be amended to incorporate the RMP requirements. This can be done by obtaining information from suppliers of the chemicals used in a process, by chemical engineering calculations, by discussions with companies from which process licenses are obtained, and by other resources. It is not only important that out of range temperatures, pressures, or other conditions be noted so they can be corrected to maintain product quality, but that several ranges of out-of-balance conditions should be included in the SOP with a range of response actions. For example, a slight out-of-bounds temperature or pressure can indicate a simple response of increasing cooling rate or cooling water flow, or slowing down a mixer speed rate, while an out-of-temperature or out-of-pressure condition that exceeds the upper end of the normal range by a certain percentage—say 25 to 50 percent—might indicate a more drastic response. In this case, the recommended procedure for a condition out of the normal range might be to stop the flow of a chemical that is part of an exothermic reaction, or to turn off the heat to a heated process.

For out-of-balance conditions that exceed those which could lead to imminent failure (e.g., temperatures or pressures exceeding normal ranges by as much as 100 percent or even more), drastic response actions might be required to prevent an accidental release. In addition, such a condition might trigger notification of offsite first responders, emergency response personnel, and may also indicate a possible evacuation of the production area.

Remember that the certification under the RMP regulations requires management to certify that the SOPs are adequate to maintaining a safe process. This raises a very troubling question because if an accident, explosion, or other condition does occur, almost by definition, the SOPs were not adequate.

Complete emergency response and notification procedures must be part of the standard operating procedures for each process handling hazard or toxic substances in quantities exceeding the TQ. They must cover each operating phase of the process, including start-up, routine operation, and shutdown. The level of detail for the SOP must be appropriate for the process for which it is written. This level will vary with the complexity of the process, the equipment involved, and other factors. Additional operating procedures might include the required steps for safety permits and other approvals that must be administered before any change, modification, or replacement of parts is allowed in processes that use hazardous or toxic substances.

NASA SOP Example

The NASA Lewis Safety Program includes an example of the operational information that is part of a standard operating procedure. This safety program includes requirements for the following:

❑ Initial checkout plan

❑ Operating procedures/checklist, including normal start-up, shutdown and operations when approved by a knowledgeable supervisor or project authority prior to safety review

❑ Emergency plans and shutdown procedures—an emergency reaction plan that includes all procedures for shutdown, sequence of notifications, and so on must be provided

❑ Equipment or system limits

❑ List of alarms, shutdowns, and permissives

❑ Access control requirements

Maintenance information is also required and includes these components:

❑ Maintenance procedures and schedules (for items that have safety implications)

❑ Log books or maintenance data sheets, for items that have safety implications

❑ Lockout/tagout procedures

❑ Rectification requirements[29]

The NASA Lewis program also includes requirements for submittal of specialized forms including the following:

❑ Safety permit request form—this must be submitted to the safety committee, approximately 60 days prior to initial operations

❑ Safety permit—this indicates that a facility rig, system, experiment, or operation has been reviewed by the safety committee and constitutes a license to operate with the constraints indicated thereon

❑ Safety permit renewal modification requests

❑ Qualified operators list—qualified operators described experience and training requirements for each operator—can only be used in conjunction with a valid safety permit

❑ Users radiological training and experience record for processes involving use of radioactive materials[30]

The NASA program also includes a color-coded sticker program, which affixes a color-coded sticker to the safety permit and provides identification of the potential hazard level and instructions for emergency action to be taken.

Appendix D includes Chapter One of The Lewis Safety Manual and shows the safety permit process that NASA has developed. Note that key decision points are indicated, and sign-offs and records retention requirements are also included.

[29]NASA Lewis Safety Program, www.osma.larc.nasa.gov, Oct. 1997.
[30]NASA Lewis Safety Program, www.osma.larc.nasa.gov, Oct. 1997.

Chapter 5

Organizing an Employee Information and Training Program

Accidents involving the releases of highly hazardous substances are often the result of unplanned occurrences (e.g., a valve that sticks in an open position; a regular employee calls in sick and is replaced by a less trained worker; a "temporary" modification was made that somehow became permanent). Although a list of such occurrences could fill several pages, they are not the root causes of accidents involving the unplanned releases of these materials. All too often the actual cause of such an accident can be traced back to an employee simply not understanding or not being aware of the consequences of his/her actions. An employer's primary line of defense in preventing the accidental releases of toxic and/or highly hazardous substances is often an effective employee information and training program.

EPA Training Requirements

EPA has taken the position that when offsite impacts are possible, it is reasonable to implement additional measures to reduce accidental releases, especially when the burden of measures such as additional training or safety precautions is low. Facilities in Programs 2 and 3 Prevention Programs are given, in the final RMP regulations, flexibility to the appropriate level of effort, of employee information and training. Since the potential of offsite consequences from an accidental release of regulated substances from a facility in Program 1 is considered to be minimal, employee training is not required.

The final RMP regulations require all facilities covered by the regulations of a Program 2 Prevention Program or a Program 3 Prevention Program to develop a training program for all processes that have more than threshold quantity (TQ) levels of regulated substances. In organizing such a program, it should be realized that truly effective training goes beyond the scope of basic classroom teaching. The overall success of any RMP training program requires the active participation of all concerned parties and depends upon the effective two-way communication between the employees who operate and/or maintain the processes that use regulated hazardous substances and the supervisors who oversee such operations. Consequently, when the management of an affected facility considers what their "information and training" goals and objectives should be in establishing an effective RMP, the information and training methods that are covered by both OSHA's Hazard Communication Standard (29 CFR 1910.1200) and Process Safety Management Standard (29 CFR 1910.119) should be reviewed.

Training Objective

The overall objective of an effective RMP training and information program is to help employees understand the nature and causes of problems arising from process operations and to increase employee awareness with the hazards particular to a process. Since an effective training and information program significantly reduces the number and severity of incidents resulting from process operations and can be instrumental in preventing small problems from leading to catastrophic releases, it is imperative that each affected employee involved in operating and/or maintaining a covered process receive the necessary training that allows him/her to better understand and adhere to current operating procedures and safe work practices associated with the process.

Scope of Training Required

This training and information program must cover the initial training of all employees involved in operating and maintaining processes that include more than TQ levels of regulated substances. The training must emphasize safety and health hazards and emergency operation procedures, including shutdowns, start-ups, and safe work practices. Although refresher training is required at least every three years, the frequency of training is left to the owner to determine, based on an assessment of the risks involved in less frequent training.

In addition to the above requirements for conducting such training, the Chemical Accident Prevention Provisions of 40 CFR, Part 68 require owners of covered processes to document the following information as part of their certification:

- ❏ Date of their most recent review or training or revision of training programs
- ❏ Nature of training provided, including indication of where the training was held: in a classroom, a combination classroom/on-the-job, or other
- ❏ Type of competency testing used, including a record of how employees were tested to determine and evaluate comprehension of training materials

The owner and/or operator, in consultation with employees operating the process, must determine the appropriate frequency of refresher training.[31] The regulations also allow that the owner or operator may use training conducted under other programs (for example, the OSHA PSM to comply with this training requirement). In addition, owners and/or operators may use training provided by equipment vendors to satisfy these requirements as long as such training meets the requirements of the final RMP regulations. Finally, the owner and/or operator must ensure that operators are trained in any updated or new procedures prior to start-up of a process after any major changes.

All employees involved with highly hazardous chemicals—including process operators, maintenance workers, and contractor employees—need to fully understand the safety and health hazards of the chemicals and processes they work with for the protection of themselves, their fellow employees, and the citizens of nearby communities. Training conducted in compliance with Section 1910.1200, the OSHA Hazard Communication Standard, will help employees to be more knowledgeable about the chemicals they work with as well as familiarize them with reading and understanding MSDSs. However, additional training in subjects such as standard operating procedures and safety work practices, emergency evacuation and response, incident investigation, safety procedures, routine and non-routine work authorization activities, and other areas pertinent to process safety and health will need to be covered by an employer's information and training program.

Specific Training Required

The RMP information and training requirements are based on the OSHA PSM training requirements and are described in detail in Chapter 12 of this book. The OSHA PSM training requirements focus on the following three areas:

1. **Initial training:** Each employee presently involved in operating a process, and each employee before being involved in operating a newly assigned process, must be trained in both an overview and the operating procedures of the process. The training must include emphasis on the specific safety and health hazards, emergency operations including shutdown, and safe work practices applicable to the employee's job tasks.

   In lieu of initial training for those employees already involved in operating a process on May 26, 1992 (Note: do not confuse this OSHA PSM-specified date with the EPA-specified RMP date of June 21, 1999, contained in the RMP training provisions), an employer may certify in writing that the employee already has the required knowledge, skills, and abilities to safely carry out the duties and responsibilities as specified in the operating procedures.

2. **Refresher training:** Refresher training must be provided at least every three years—and more often if necessary—to each employee involved in operating a process to ensure that the employee understands and adheres to the current operating procedures of the process. The owner/operator, in consultation with the employees involved in operating the process, must determine the appropriate frequency of refresher training.

3. **Training documentation:** The owner/operator must ascertain that each employee involved in operating a process has received and understood the training required by this paragraph. The owner/operator has to prepare a record that identifies the employee, the date of training, and the means used to verify that the employee understood the training.

Organizing the Employee Information and Training Program

In order to effectively organize a RMP information and training program that complies with the requirements of the Chemical Accident Prevention Provisions of 40 CFR, Part 68, it is helpful to remember the three basic management principles of any training program—development, implementation, and evaluation. In developing an information and training program, it is important to recognize that the scope of these requirements varies not only according to the prevention program required (Program 2 Prevention Program vs. Program 3 Prevention Program) but also by the personnel, including outside contractors, who operate and/or maintain the covered process(es). Not only are the basic requirements of these two prevention programs different, but the more complex provisions of the Program 3 Prevention Program actually incorporate by reference the training provisions of other OSHA standards, such as the hot work requirements found in the welding, cutting, and brazing standard (29 CFR 1910.252); confined space entry (29 CFR 1910.146); and the control of hazardous energy sources (lockout/tagout) (29 CFR 1910.147).

Employee-Centered Training

In implementing their training programs, owners/operators should remember that people are vital to the success of risk management. All affected personnel need to be both part of the program and knowledgeable of how their responsibilities are a part of the much bigger picture. Owners/operators must clearly define the employees to be trained and what subjects are to be covered in their training, and, in doing so, must tailor the training to the educational level of their employees. In setting up their training program, owners/operators will need to clearly establish the goals and objectives they wish to achieve with the training. The learning goals or objectives should be written in clear, measurable terms before the training begins. These goals and objectives need to be tailored to each of the specific training modules or segments. Owners/operators should describe the important actions and conditions under which the employee will demonstrate competence or knowledge, as well as what is acceptable performance.

Realistic Training

Hands-on-training—where employees are able to use their senses beyond listening—will enhance learning. For example, operating personnel working in a control room or at control panels would benefit by being trained at a simulated control panel. Upset conditions of various types can be displayed on the simulator, and then the employee can follow the proper operating procedures to bring the simulator panel back to normal operating parameters. A training environment can be created to help the trainee feel the full reality of the situation but, of course, under controlled conditions. This realistic type of training can be very effective in training employees in the correct procedures while allowing them to also see the consequences of not following those established operating procedures. Other training techniques, such as those using videos or on-the-job training, can also be very effective for teaching other job tasks, duties, or important information. An effective training program will allow the employee to fully participate in the training process and to practice their skills or knowledge.

Owners/operators need to periodically evaluate their information and training programs to see if the necessary skills, knowledge, and routines are being properly understood and implemented by their trained employees. The means or methods for evaluating the training should be developed along with the training program goals and objectives. Information and training program evaluation will help employers to determine the amount of training their employees have understood, and whether the desired results were obtained. If, after the evaluation, it appears that the trained employees have not reached the expected level of knowledge and skill, the employer will need to revise the training program, provide retraining, or provide more frequent refresher training sessions until the deficiency is resolved. Those who conducted the training and those who received the training should also be consulted as to how best improve the training process. If there is a language barrier, the language known to the trainees should be used to reinforce the training messages and information.

Since the training requirements of the RMP Standard closely parallel those of the OSHA PSM Standard, it is suggested that the guidelines found in the 1910.119 (g) Training section of OSHA's PSM Compliance Directive be used to help evaluate the effectiveness of the employee RMP information and training program.

Owner/operators will also need to establish methods in which the information-sharing requirements of the RMP Standard (e.g., incident investigation reports) can be effectively achieved. Again, such forums (e.g. classroom, field sessions) will depend on the mutual candid exchange of information.

Strategies for Developing an Information and Training Program

Careful consideration must be given to how the training and information is developed and how the training will be given. Since even a basic Program 2 Prevention Program requires a comprehensive knowledge of potentially facility-specific, complex operating processes and maintenance procedures, only qualified personnel should be selected to actually give the training. Unless a facility has such personnel on staff, it will probably have to go outside its immediate organization to assemble a training team. Usually the composition of a well-balanced training team will consist of both technically oriented, in-house personnel with the required facility-specific, process/maintenance knowledge and qualified outside personnel with the required technical/regulatory/industry experience. This approach helps ensure that the talents of all parties compliment each other in a synergistic manner. For example, if your facility has a process that uses chlorine (CAS# 7782-50-5) at levels above the established TQ of 2,500 lbs., you

may want to consider bringing together qualified in-house process and maintenance personnel, technical representatives of the chlorine industry, and an outside consultant knowledgeable in the regulatory requirements of the RMP Program to ensure that your training program has a solid technical basis. Some facilities will also want to consider bringing in a training professional to better structure the mechanics of delivering the contents of information and training program to the affected employees.

Keeping Training Current

In determining who must be trained, owners/operators must be certain that all affected employees—including maintenance and contract employees—receive current and updated training. For example, if changes are made to a process, impacted employees must be trained in the changes and understand the effects of the changes on their job tasks (e.g., any new operating procedures pertinent to their tasks). Additionally, as already discussed, the evaluation of the employee's absorption of training will influence the need for training.

Incorporating Industry Codes and Standards

Applicable industry codes and standards provide criteria for external inspections for such items as foundations and supports, anchor bolts, concrete or steel supports, guy wires, nozzles and sprinklers, pipe hangers, grounding connections, protective coatings and insulation, and external metal surfaces of piping and vessels, etc. These codes and standards also provide information on methodologies for internal inspection, and frequency formulas based on the corrosion rate of the materials of construction. These codes and/or standards should be incorporated into the content of the facility's training and information program when developing the appropriate training to be provided to maintenance personnel that ensures their understanding of the preventive maintenance program procedures, safe practices, and proper use and application of special equipment or unique tools that may be required.

In the following sections, we will take a look at both the key elements of a RMP information and training program and the requirements of both the Program 2 Prevention Program and the Program 3 Prevention Program to see what is required for effectively complying with the applicable information and training requirements of each. While both programs are considerably focused on SOP training and both share common elements (e.g., use of outside contractors, emergency response) for which training is required, the specific requirements of a Program 3 Prevention Program have been designed towards the more complex processes that use the highly hazardous substances covered by this standard. Consequently, a Program 3 Prevention Program includes more stringent elements, such as the management of change and pre-startup review.

Key Elements of a RMP Information and Training Program

Standard Operating Procedures

A key element of the OSHA PSM training requirements on which the RMP training requirements have been based is the concept of standard operating procedures (SOPs). Standard operating procedures describe tasks to be performed, data to be recorded, operating conditions to be maintained, samples to be collected, and safety and health precautions to be taken. The procedures need to be technically accurate, understandable to employees, and revised periodically to ensure that they reflect current operations. Operating procedures should be reviewed by engineering staff and operating personnel to ensure that they are accurate and provide practical instructions on how to actually carry out job duties safely.

Standard operating procedures and instructions are important in the training of operating personnel. Control room personnel and operating staff, in general, need to have a complete understanding of operating procedures. If workers are not fluent in English, then training instructions need to be prepared in a second language understood by the workers. In addition, operating procedures need to be changed when there is a change in the process as a result of the management of change procedures. Information relating to the consequences of operating procedure changes need to be fully evaluated and conveyed to all affected personnel prior to enacting the change. For example, mechanical changes to the process made by the maintenance department (like changing a valve from steel to brass or other subtle changes) need to be evaluated to determine if operating procedures and practices also need to be changed. All management of change actions must be coordinated and integrated with current operating procedures and operating personnel must be trained in the changes in procedures before the change is made.

Process Interruptions

Training in how to handle upset conditions must be accomplished as well as what operating personnel are to do in emergencies, such as when a pump seal fails or a pipeline ruptures. Communication between operating personnel and workers performing work within the process area, such as non-routine tasks, also must be maintained. The hazards of the tasks are to be conveyed to operating personnel in accordance with established procedures and to those performing the actual tasks. When the work is completed, operating personnel should be informed to provide closure on the job.

Maintenance/Ongoing Mechanical Integrity

The first line of defense an employer has available is to operate and maintain the process as designed, and to keep the chemicals contained within the equipment. This basic requirement is a primary justification for incorporating the maintenance (Program 2) and mechanical integrity (Program 3) elements into a facility's RMP.

Employers will need to review their maintenance programs and schedules to see if there are areas where "breakdown" maintenance is used rather than an ongoing mechanical integrity program. Equipment used to process, store, or handle highly hazardous chemicals needs to be designed, constructed, installed, and maintained to minimize the risk of releases of such chemicals. This requires that a mechanical integrity program be in place to ensure the continued integrity of process equipment. Elements of a mechanical integrity program include the identification and categorization of equipment and instrumentation, inspections and tests, testing and inspection frequencies, development of maintenance procedures, training of maintenance personnel, the establishment of criteria for acceptable test results, documentation of test and inspection results, and documentation of manufacturer recommendations regarding typical operating life.

Management of Change

To properly manage changes to process chemicals, technology, equipment, and facilities, one must define what is meant by change. Under the RMP standard, change includes all modifications to equipment, procedures, raw materials, and processing conditions other than "replacement in kind." These changes need to be properly managed by identifying and reviewing them prior to implementation of the change. For example, the operating procedures contain the operating parameters (pressure limits, temperature ranges, flow rates, etc.) and the importance of operating within these limits. While the operator must have the flexibility to maintain safe operation within the established parameters, any operation outside of these parameters requires review, approval by a written management of change procedure and process operator training.

Management of change covers such topics as changes in process technology and changes to equipment and instrumentation. Changes in process technology can result from changes in production rates, raw materials, experimentation, equipment unavailability, new equipment, new product development, change in catalyst, and changes in operating conditions to improve yield or quality. Equipment changes include, among others, change in materials of construction, equipment specifications, piping pre-arrangements, experimental equipment, computer program revisions, and changes in alarms and interlocks. By establishing means and methods to detect both technical changes and mechanical changes, employers can effectively inform their employees of—and train them in—these changes.

Contractors

Employers who use contractors to perform work in and around processes that involve highly hazardous chemicals will need to establish an effective information sharing program with contract employers (who are responsible for the training of their own employees) to be certain that only contractors who can accomplish the desired job tasks without compromising the safety and health of employees at a facility will be hired. All contractors who are involved with the maintenance of a covered process must be trained in performing the procedures required to maintain the continued mechanical integrity of the process.

Program 2 Prevention Program Training Requirements

The Program 2 requirements contained in Section 68.54 cover training and are a streamlined version of the OSHA PSM requirements. The primary difference with

OSHA PSM training is that the documentation requirements have been dropped. EPA believed that, for Program 2 sources, which generally will have simple processes and few employees involved in the process, the level of documentation required by OSHA PSM is not needed. The pertinent RMP requirement specifically states that training conducted to comply with other federal, state, or industry codes may be used to demonstrate compliance with the section if the training covers the standard operating procedures (SOPs) for the process. Workers must be retrained when SOPs change as a result of a major change.

The Program 2 process operator training provisions of Section 68.54 contain these requirements:

- ❑ The owner or operator must ensure that each employee presently operating a process and each employee newly assigned to a covered process has been trained or tested competent in the operating procedures provided in Section 68.52 that pertain to their duties. For those employees already operating a process on June 21, 1999, the owner or operator may certify in writing that the employee has the required knowledge, skills, and abilities to safely carry out the duties and responsibilities as provided in the operating procedures.

- ❑ Refresher training must be provided at least every three years, and more often if necessary, to each employee operating a process to ensure that the employee understands and adheres to the current operating procedures of the process. The owner or operator, in consultation with the employees operating the process, must determine the appropriate frequency of refresher training.

- ❑ The owner or operator may use training conducted under federal or state regulations or under industry-specific standards or codes or training conducted by covered process equipment vendors to demonstrate compliance with this section to the extent that the training meets the requirements of the regulations.

- ❑ The owner or operator must ensure that operators are trained in any updated or new procedures prior to startup of a process after a major change.

For a Program 2 Prevention Program, these SOPs must include procedures for the following:

❏ Initial startup
❏ Normal operations
❏ Temporary operations
❏ Emergency shutdown and operations
❏ Normal shutdown
❏ Startup following a normal or emergency shutdown or a major change that requires a hazard review
❏ Consequences of deviations and steps required to correct or avoid deviations
❏ Equipment inspections

In determining the scope of information and training requirements of a Program 2 Prevention Program, it is necessary to look beyond the operator training provisions listed immediately above as the following maintenance, incident reporting, and emergency response provisions of Section 68.56, Section 68.60, and Section 68.95, respectively, also apply.

40 CFR 68.56 Maintenance

The owner or operator must train or cause to be trained each employee involved in maintaining the ongoing mechanical integrity of the process. To ensure that the employee can perform the job tasks in a safe manner, each such employee must be trained in the hazards of the process, in how to avoid or correct unsafe conditions, and in the procedures applicable to the employee's job tasks. Any maintenance contractor must ensure that each contract maintenance employee is trained to perform the procedures developed under this section.

40 CFR 68.60 Incident Investigation

The owner or operator must investigate each incident that resulted in, or could reasonably have resulted in, a catastrophic release. An incident investigation must be initiated as promptly as possible, but not later than 48 hours following the incident. A summary must be prepared at the conclusion of the investigation, the findings of which must be reviewed with all affected personnel whose job tasks are affected by the findings. *Training changes may be indicated.*

40 CFR 68.95 Emergency Response Program

The owner or operator must develop and implement an emergency response program for the purpose of protecting public health and the environment. Such a pro-

gram must include training for all employees in relevant procedures including these:

❏ Procedures for informing the public and local emergency response agencies about accidental releases
❏ Procedures and measures for emergency response after an accidental release of a regulated substance
❏ Procedures for the use of emergency response equipment and for its inspection, testing, and maintenance
❏ Procedures to review and update, as appropriate, the emergency response plan to reflect changes at the stationary source and ensure that employees are informed of changes

Therefore, if your facility has a process covered by a Program 2 Prevention Program, your employee information and training program must not only address in-house process operator training, but also ongoing mechanical integrity training associated with both in-house maintenance workers and contracted maintenance personnel; reviewing incident investigation report findings with affected personnel; and emergency response procedural training for all employees.

Program 3 Prevention Program Training Requirements

In general, the training provisions associated with a Program 3 Prevention Program are more complex and comprehensive than those of a Program 2 Prevention Program. The operator training requirements of Section 68.71 have been adopted from OSHA process management training requirements except for changing "employer" to "owner/operator" and other minor changes in referenced sections.

Specifically the Program 3 process operator training provisions of Section 68.71 contain these requirements:

❏ **Initial training:** Each employee presently involved in operating a process, and each employee before being involved in operating a newly assigned process, must be trained in an overview of the process and in the operating procedures as specified in Section 68.69. The training must include emphasis on the specific safety and health hazards, emergency operations including shutdown, and safe work practices applicable to the employee's job tasks. In lieu of initial training for those employees already involved in operating a process on June 21, 1999, an owner or operator may certify in writing that the employee has the required knowledge, skills, and abilities to safely carry out the duties and responsibilities as specified in the operating procedures.

❑ **Refresher training:** Refresher training must be provided at least every three years, and more often if necessary, to each employee involved in operating a process to assure that the employee understands and adheres to the current operating procedures of the process. The owner or operator, in consultation with the employees involved in operating the process, must determine the appropriate frequency of refresher training.

❑ **Training documentation:** The owner or operator must ascertain that each employee involved in operating a process has received and understood the *training* required. The owner or operator must prepare a record which contains the identity of the employee, the date of training, and the means used to verify that the employee understood the training.

These Program 3 process operator training requirements are more comprehensive than those of a Program 2 Prevention Program and must ensure that the following specific operating procedures contained in Section 68.69 are adequately addressed:

1. The owner or operator must develop and implement written operating procedures that provide clear instructions for safely conducting activities involved in each covered process consistent with the process safety information and must address at least the following elements.

Steps for each operating phase
- Initial startup
- Normal operations
- Temporary operations
- Emergency shutdown including the conditions under which emergency shutdown is required and the assignment of shutdown responsibility to qualified operators to ensure that emergency shutdown is executed in a safe and timely manner

- Emergency operations
- Normal shutdown
- Startup following a turnaround, or after an emergency shutdown

Operating limits
- Consequences of deviation
- Steps required to correct or avoid deviation

Safety and health considerations
- properties of, and hazards presented by, the chemicals used in the process
- Precautions necessary to prevent exposure, including engineering controls, administrative controls, and personal protective equipment
- Control measures to be taken if physical contact or airborne exposure occurs
- Quality control for raw materials and control of hazardous chemical inventory levels
- Any special or unique hazards

Safety systems and their functions

2. Operating procedures must be readily accessible to employees who work in or maintain a process.

3. The operating procedures must be reviewed as often as necessary to ensure that they reflect current operating practice, including changes that result from changes in process chemicals, technology, and equipment, and changes to stationary sources. The owner or operator must certify annually that the information contained in these operating procedures is current and accurate.

4. The owner or operator must develop and implement safe work practices to provide for the control of hazards during operations, such as lockout/tagout; confined space entry; opening process equipment or piping; and control over entrance into a stationary source by maintenance, contractor, laboratory, or other support personnel. These safe work practices must apply to employees and contractor employees.

However, as in determining the total scope of a Program 2 Prevention Program's information and training requirements, a similar determination for a Program 3 Prevention Program's requirements must also be predicated on looking past the process operator training requirements listed above, to the following applicable regulations:

40 CFR 68.73 Mechanical Integrity

The owner or operator must train each employee involved in maintaining the ongoing integrity of process equipment in an overview of that process and its hazards and in the procedures applicable to the employee's job tasks to ensure that the employee can perform the job tasks in a safe manner.

40 CFR 68.75 Management of Change

Employees involved in operating a process and maintenance and contract employees whose job tasks will be affected by a change in the process must be informed of, and trained in, the change prior to start-up of the process or affected part of the process.

40 CFR 68.77 Pre-Startup Review

Any pre-startup safety review must confirm that prior to the introduction of regulated substances to a process training of each employee involved in operating a process has been completed.

40 CFR 68.81 Incident Investigation

The owner or operator must investigate each incident that resulted in, or could reasonably have resulted in, a catastrophic release of a regulated substance. An incident investigation must be initiated as promptly as possible, but not later than 48 hours following the incident. A report must be prepared at the conclusion of the investigation with resolutions and corrective actions documented. The information contained in this report must be reviewed with all affected personnel.

40 CFR 68.87 Contractors

When it comes to employing outside contractors, both facility owners and/or operators and contractor employers have information and training obligations under a Program 3 Prevention Program.

The facility owner or operator shall
- ❏ Inform contract owner or operator of the known potential fire, explosion, or toxic release hazards related to the contractor's work; and
- ❏ Inform the contract owner or operator the applicable provisions of the facility's emergency response program.

The contract owner or operator shall
- ❏ Ensure that each contract employee is trained in the work practices necessary to safely perform his/her job;
- ❏ Ensure that each contract employee is trained in the known potential fire, explosion, or toxic release hazards related to his/her job and the process, and the applicable provisions of the emergency action plan;
- ❏ Document that each contract employee has received and understood both the information and the training required by this section. The contract owner or operator shall prepare a record that contains the identity of the contract employee, the date of training, and the means used to verify that the employee understood the training; and
- ❏ Inform the owner or operator of any unique hazards presented by the contract owner or operator's work, or of any hazards found by the contract owner or operator's work.

These requirements apply to contractors performing maintenance or repair, turnaround, major renovation, or specialty work on or adjacent to a covered process. They do not apply to contractors providing incidental services that do not influence process safety, such as janitorial work, food and drink services, laundry, delivery, or other such services. Also, although it is the responsibility of the contractor owners and/or operators to inform and train their employees, it is recommended that the management of facilities in which contractor employees perform tasks on covered processes ensure that this required training is effectively completed.

40 CFR 68.95 Emergency Response Program

The owner or operator must develop and implement an emergency response program for the purpose of protecting public health and the environment. Such a program must include training for all employees in relevant procedures, including the following:
- ❏ Procedures for informing the public and local emergency response agencies about accidental releases
- ❏ Procedures and measures for emergency response after an accidental release of a regulated substance

❏ Procedures for the use of emergency response equipment and for its inspection, testing, and maintenance

❏ Procedures to review and update, as appropriate, the emergency response plan to reflect changes at the stationary source and to ensure that employees are informed of changes

Since both the above Program 3 Prevention Program SOPs and the Hot Work Permit requirements specify the development and implementation of safe work practices associated with other OSHA standards—such as confined space entry (29 CFR 1910.141), lockout/tagout,(29 CFR 1910.146), and welding, cutting, and brazing (29 CFR 1910.252)—the training requirements of these programs have been essentially incorporated into the overall training requirements of a Program 3 Prevention Program and are listed below.

29 CFR 1910.146 Permit-Required Confined Space Entry

The employer shall provide training so that all employees whose work is regulated by this section acquire the understanding, knowledge, and skills necessary for the safe performance of the duties assigned under this section. Training shall be provided to each affected employee in a timely manner:

❏ Before the employee is first assigned duties under this section

❏ Before there is a change in assigned duties

❏ Whenever there is a change in permit space operations that presents a hazard about which an employee has not previously been trained

❏ Whenever the employer has reason to believe either that there are deviations from the required permit space entry procedures or that there are inadequacies in the employee's knowledge or use of these procedures

The training shall establish employee proficiency in the duties required by this section and shall introduce new or revised procedures, as necessary, for compliance with this section.

The employer shall certify that the required training has been accomplished. The certification shall contain each employee's name, the signatures or initials of the trainers, and the dates of training. The certification shall be available for inspection by employees and their authorized representatives.

29 CFR 1910.147 Control of Hazardous Energy (Lockout/Tagout)

The employer shall provide training to ensure that the purpose and function of the energy control program are understood by employees and that the knowledge and skills required for the safe application, usage, and removal of the energy controls are acquired by employees. This training shall include the following:

❏ Each authorized employee shall receive training in the recognition of applicable hazardous energy sources, the type and magnitude of the energy available in the workplace, and the methods and means necessary for energy isolation and control.

❏ Each affected employee shall be informed and instructed in the purpose and use of the energy control procedure.

❏ All other employees whose work operations are or may be in an area where energy control procedures may be utilized, shall be informed and instructed about the procedure, and about the prohibition relating to attempts to restart or re-energize machines or equipment that are locked out or tagged out.

When tagout systems are used, employees shall also be trained in the following limitations of tags:

❏ Tags are essentially warning devices affixed to energy isolating devices, and do not provide the physical restraint on those devices that is provided by a lock.

❏ When a tag is attached to an energy isolating means, it is not to be removed without authorization of the authorized person responsible for it, and it is never to be bypassed, ignored, or otherwise defeated.

❏ Tags must be legible and understandable by all authorized employees, affected employees, and all other employees whose work operations are or may be in the area, in order to be effective.

❏ Tags and their means of attachment must be made of materials that will withstand the environmental conditions encountered in the workplace.

❑ Tags may evoke a false sense of security and their meaning needs to be understood as part of the overall energy control program.

❑ Tags must be securely attached to energy-isolating devices so that they cannot be inadvertently or accidentally detached during use.

Employee Retraining

Retraining shall be provided for all authorized and affected employees whenever there is a change in their job assignments, a change in machines, equipment, or processes that present a new hazard, or when there is a change in the energy control procedures.

Additional retraining shall also be conducted whenever a required periodic inspection reveals, or whenever the employer has reason to believe that there are deviations from or inadequacies in the employee's knowledge or use of the energy control procedures.

The retraining shall reestablish employee proficiency and introduce new or revised control methods and procedures, as necessary.

The employer shall certify that employee training has been accomplished and is being kept up to date. The certification shall contain each employee's name and dates of training.

29 CFR 1910.252 Welding, Cutting, and Brazing

Fire watchers shall have fire extinguishing equipment readily available and be trained in its use. They shall be familiar with facilities for sounding an alarm in the event of a fire. In addition, facility management shall recognize its responsibility for the safe usage of cutting and welding equipment on its property and insist that cutters or welders and their supervisors are suitably trained in the safe operation of their equipment and the safe use of the process.

Management Training

Since effective compliance with the RMP regulations can be a complex process and requires more than operator training and maintaining safe processes, it is recommended that "qualified" personnel provide training to middle and upper management in their responsibilities under the RMP program. For example, owners and/or operators are required to submit RMPs that include an analysis of worse case accidental releases and worse-case off-site impacts along with distances to end points. Since these are not required under OSHA PSM, such training is not specifically required under the regulations. However, these are very important components of the RMP program, and it would be appropriate to include training on how to prepare such plans, and possibly more importantly, on how to interpret off-site consequence impact analysis calculations in such training. This will provide operators with a better feeling for what the potential consequences of out-of-balance conditions and potential accidental releases would be and, in addition, will provide management with a better understanding of why process maintenance training and other aspects of the RMP program are so important. This training for management should include an overview of the RMP regulations, a review of all processes operated at the facility, an overview of the training provided to operators, and a review of the potential offsite consequences of accidental releases that have been developed as part of the hazard assessment and RMP development effort.

A real value of training managers is that they will be better able to see what the possible offsite consequences of various releases are. This could make it easier to affect changes in the facility, resulting in a lessening of the potential for off-site consequences. By involving management in the training, refreshers that are undertaken would more likely facilitate decision making regarding process modifications or changes to the facility that could have resulted in significant offsite impacts. The certification requirements and potential civil and criminal penalties that are possible for noncompliance with these Clean Air Act regulations make it important for management to be involved in the training. Additionally, management approval of the training should be obtained before undertaking the initial training and any refresher training.

OSHA Training Courses

The U.S. Department of Labor, Occupational Safety and Health Administration, provides a large range of courses, including the following:

- ❑ Initial Compliance Course
- ❑ Basic Accident Investigation
- ❑ Advanced Accident Investigation
- ❑ Principles of Industrial Ventilation
- ❑ Respiratory Protection
- ❑ Industrial Toxicology
- ❑ Laboratory Safety and Health
- ❑ Indoor Air Quality
- ❑ Biohazards
- ❑ Evaluation of Safety and Health Standards
- ❑ Safety and Health for Oil and Gas Well Operations

- ❑ Safety and Health for Grain Operations
- ❑ Safety and Health in Saw Mills and Logging Operations
- ❑ Hazardous Waste Site Inspection
- ❑ Emergency Response for the Construction Industry
- ❑ Safety and Health in the Chemical Processing Industries for Construction

The current listing, as of October 1997, lists no specific process safety management training in the training institute schedule of courses.

---

[31]EPA Provisions for Chemical Accident Prevention, Section 68.54, Training: 7/19/96.

Chapter 6

Monitoring Compliance Audits

Purpose of an Audit

The successful implementation of a risk management program, such as that required and envisioned by the new Part 68 Rules as well as existing regulations, such as the OSHA requirements under 29 CFR 1910.119, can only be achieved through a systematic, comprehensive, and committed effort on the part of all facility staff. The use of compliance evaluations or compliance audits is one of the most cost effective ways to ensure that the benefits of the risk management program are maximized for the benefit of all facility staff and the potentially affected public. A compliance audit is also a regulatory requirement, a well-planned, properly conducted audit can result in improvements in environmental compliance, enhanced competitiveness, decreased long-term environmental liability, and increased awareness of environmental management responsibilities.

A comprehensive compliance audit program represents a proactive alternative in assessing environmental compliance, identifying potential environmental impacts, and planning for the future mitigation of such impacts. A remaining alternative is, of course, to naively avoid seriously examining the potential problems, pitfalls, and liabilities of environmental compliance, which would likely result in a crisis management approach each and every time a compliance problem presents itself.

An audit program should be the primary element in an environmental management system designed to identify a facility's responsibilities, policies, practices, procedures, processes, and resources for protecting the environment and managing environmental issues. Industry environmental experts agree that the failure to develop a comprehensive system will result in costs far in excess of those potentially spent in implementing and maintaining such a system.

Planning the Audit

Planning is essential to the success of the auditing process. Each employer needs to establish the format, staffing, scheduling, and verification methods of an audit prior to conducting it. The format should be designed to provide the lead auditor with a procedure or checklist that details the requirements of each section of the standard. The names of the audit team members should be listed as part of the format as well. The checklist, if properly designed, could serve as the verification sheet, which provides the auditor with the necessary information to expedite the review and assures that no requirements of the standard are omitted. This verification sheet format could also identify those elements that will require evaluation or a response to correct deficiencies. This sheet could also be used for developing the follow-up and documentation requirements.

If your facility already has an established audit program or procedure, the audit required under the Risk Management Planning (RMP) regulations can easily be integrated into the process with minimal impact on resources and budgets. If your facility has no such auditing program, the implementation of the RMP audit should be used as a springboard to developing a comprehensive program suited to your facility's needs. It is important to remember that the compliance monitoring audit, required by the RMP regulations and program, must achieve the following goal:

❑ Certification by the owner or operator that they have evaluated compliance with the provisions of 40 CFR 68 at least every three years to verify that the procedures and practices developed under the RMP rule are adequate and are being followed.

The Audit Team

The composition, background, and experience of the members of the facility's audit team will directly affect the scope, breadth, and depth of any audit conducted. The selection of effective audit team members is critical to the success of the program. Team members should be chosen for their experience, knowledge, and training and should be familiar with the facility's processes and with auditing techniques, practices, and procedures. The size of the team will vary depending on the size and complexity of the process under consideration. For a large, complex, highly instrumented plant, it may be desirable to have team members with expertise in process engineering and design, process chemistry, instrumentation and computer controls, electrical hazards and classifications, safety and health disciplines, maintenance, emergency preparedness, warehousing or shipping, and process safety auditing. The team may use part-time members to provide for the depth of expertise required as well as for what is actually done, compared to what is simply written.

Therefore, careful thought should be given to the composition of the audit team. Pursuant to 40 CFR 68.58(b), the audit team must, at a minimum, be composed of at least one person knowledgeable in the process, although an audit team composed of a single person is not recommended.

The audit team should be composed of a mix of individuals having the following expertise and knowledge:

❑ Thorough knowledge of the facility operations, processes, materials used, products produced, and wastestreams generated
❑ Strong regulatory background in the following areas:

1. Risk management process
2. Process health and safety
3. Air and water compliance issues and standards
4. Solid and hazardous waste handling, storage, and disposal issues and regulations

In addition to team members with the types of expertise delineated above, it is important that the team be comprised of facility staff from the various management levels such as:

❑ Production level
❑ Supervisory level
❑ Mid- and/or upper-facility management level

The choice of audit team members across these staff levels will ensure a balanced approach in conducting the audit, identification of problem areas, and resolution of resultant issues. It will also indicate to facility staff and the affected public that the facility has a high degree of confidence and expertise at every staff level and that the chosen team members have displayed the proven ability to independently and systematically conduct the required audit.

Mixed Audit Teams

Of course, it must be acknowledged that not every facility will have this level of experience, background, or expertise present in its internal staff. Therefore, it may be necessary to assemble an audit team that is composed of a mix of internal facility staff, and outside consultant staff experienced with the prevailing regulatory practice. In many instances, audit teams are composed of impartial outside consultants who work with appropriate facility staff (or corporate staff) to produce an independent compliance audit. This arrangement is gaining in popularity because it can result in an unbiased audit-findings report, free from the potential influences and pressures of the various facility management levels. The composition and size of each audit team will, of course, be dictated by the type of facility, complexity of the processes, applicable environmental regulations, and available facility resources.

For instance, based on the author's experience, the audit team for a small non-complex facility that may or may not have an environmental staff person is typically composed of an outside consultant who works with various facility staff at management and production levels to produce the audit. Conversely, the audit team used by one of the nation's prominent pulp and paper companies is composed solely of internal personnel, environmental, and legal staff. The primary core of this audit team remains consistent while the interplay with various facility personnel may change from year to year. As a result, the team maintains a consistent balance and level of expertise and knowledge, while constantly being infused with new perspectives from individual facility staff. Another example is that derived from an independent power company with a national profile. This company utilizes an audit team composed solely of outside consultant staff chosen specifically for their expertise in the respective areas of concern to the company's facilities. The chosen consultant team works with individual facility staff and corporate management to produce a final audit.

Scope of an Audit

An effective audit includes a review of the relevant documentation and process safety information, inspection of the physical facilities, and interviews with all levels of plant personnel. Utilizing the audit procedure and checklist developed in the preplanning stage, the audit team can systematically analyze compliance with the provisions of the standard and any other corporate policies that are relevant. For example, the audit team will review all aspects of the training program as part of the overall audit. The team will review the written training program for adequacy of content, frequency of training, effectiveness of training in terms of its goals and objectives, as well as to how it fits into meeting the standard's requirements, documentation, etc. Through interviews, the team can determine the employee's knowledge and awareness of the safety procedures, duties, rules, emergency response assignments, etc. During the inspection, the team can observe actual practices such as safety and health policies, procedures, and work authorization practices. This approach enables the team to identify deficiencies and determine where corrective actions or improvements are necessary.

Selecting the Audit Sample

An audit is a technique used to gather sufficient facts and information, including statistical information, to verify compliance with standards. Auditors should select, as part of their planning, a sample size sufficient to give a degree of confidence that the audit reflects the level of compliance with the standard. The audit team, through this systematic analysis, should document areas that require corrective action as well as those areas where the process safety management system is effective and working in an effective manner. This provides a record of the audit procedures and findings, and serves as a baseline of operation data for future audits. It will assist future auditors in determining changes or trends from previous audits

Determining Corrective Actions

Corrective action is one of the most important elements of the audit. It includes not only addressing the identified deficiencies, but also planning follow-up and documentation. The corrective action process normally begins with a management review of the audit findings. The purpose of this review is to determine what actions are appropriate, and to establish priorities, timetables, resource allocations, and requirements and responsibilities. In some cases, corrective action may involve a simple change in procedure or minor maintenance effort to remedy the concern. Management of change procedures need to be used, as appropriate, even for what may seem to be a minor change. Many of the deficiencies can be acted on promptly, while others may require engineering studies or an in-depth review of actual procedures and practices. There may be instances where no action is necessary and this is a valid response to an audit finding. All actions taken, including an explanation where no action is taken on a finding, need to be documented as to what was done and why.

It is important to ensure that each identified deficiency is addressed, the corrective action to be taken is noted, and the audit person or team responsible is properly documented by the employer. To control the corrective action process, the employer should consider the use of a tracking system. This tracking system might include periodic status reports shared with affected levels of management, specific reports such as completion of an engineering study, and a final implementation report to provide closure for audit findings that have been through management of change, if appropriate, and then shared with affected employees and management. This type of tracking system provides the employer with the status of the corrective action. It also provides the documentation required to verify that appropriate corrective actions were taken on deficiencies identified in the audit.

The final audit, per 40 CFR 68.58, must incorporate the following items:

❑ The final audit should be in the form of a written report detailing the audit findings.

❑ The facility owner or operator must properly determine and document an appropriate response to each of the audit findings and document that these deficiencies have been corrected. (Some deficiencies necessitate a long-term plan to achieve compliance. These should be carefully delineated in the owner/operator responses and should be included as an integral portion of the audit report.)

❑ The owner/operator must retain the two (2) most recent compliance audit reports, not including any report that is over five (5) years old.

Frequency of Audits

Audits required under the RMP regulations are to be accomplished "at least every three (3) years." Based on the author's experience, it is strongly recommended that the audit of the RMP be incorporated into the existing audit program (if one exists) and that the frequency of the audit be at least annual. At a maximum, audits should be conducted certainly no more than eighteen (18) months apart. The U. S. EPA, in setting the required three-year period, did its best to address the concerns of the business community as well as the intent of the RMP program with respect to the anticipated outcome (i.e., protection of facility staff and the surrounding population from accidental releases of hazardous materials). The three-year period represents a compromise as well as being the required statutory timeframe for the compliance audits. It should not be construed as the appropriate audit timeframe for all processes or facilities. Each facility covered by the RMP regulations presents its own unique set of resources and potential problems. Many existing audit programs are already based on an annual review cycle that corresponds to the renewal of various annual environmental and regulatory permits or operational authorizations. It is this author's belief that the RMP audit—which deals with environmental, health, and safety issues—should be considered at least as important as other regulatory permits and

authorizations, and therefore should be conducted on at least an annual basis. The General Duty Provisions will also dictate more frequent audits for many facilities. Remember, the RMP audit is assessing the safety and reliability of systems, which if neglected, could potentially cause harm to the surrounding population. Additionally, the RMP audit assesses the established response procedures and policies that the facility will use to minimize the potential for accidental releases and impacts on facility staff and the general population.

In addition to the recommended annual audit cycle, the author also recommends that a "mini," or focused, audit be conducted at each initiation of the management of change procedures as outlined in 40 CFR 68.75. The "mini" audit can provide verification of the management of change process, and the results can be incorporated into the next regularly scheduled comprehensive audit.

Confirmation of SOP Implementation and Appropriateness

One of primary purposes of the compliance audit is the review and determination as to whether an update of the Standard Operating Procedures (SOPs) for the various devices and/or processes that could be potential release points for, or cause of a release from, another related system, or a hazardous substance under the RMP program is necessary. SOPs are simply a detailed accounting of all of the important procedures surrounding the operation of a given device or system. SOPs should, at a minimum, contain the following types of procedures and information:

❑ Pre-startup procedure and checklist
❑ Startup procedure
❑ Normal operation guidelines and procedures
❑ Abnormal operating diagnosis procedures and guidelines
❑ Shutdown procedures
❑ Operational interplay with other systems
❑ Information on the minimum and maximum operational tolerances and process parameters for safe operation
❑ Procedures for coordinating system operations with other inter-related systems

Many equipment and/or process manufacturers will typically supply a basic SOP for their equipment as supplied or constructed. This SOP can be used as the foundation for the RMP SOP. Such a SOP should be reviewed for completeness and additional procedures incorporated as required to establish the SOP as an integral part of the RMP.

SOPs may also be established for other areas of the RMP that are not solely confined to process areas, process equipment, or process systems. SOPs may, and should, be established for areas such as these:

- ❑ Adequate process safety information
- ❑ Adequate process operating procedures and mechanical integrity
- ❑ Adequate training
- ❑ Adequate response and incident investigation
- ❑ Adequate development of emergency response plans
- ❑ Adequate protection of facility staff and contractors

In these cases, the SOPs should be used to define the scope and breadth of the information required to develop and implement that portion of the RMP as well as specifying at what juncture revisions or updates are required.

The review of the SOPs, as part of the scheduled audit, should focus on answering the following questions:

- ❑ Is the SOP clear and understandable?
- ❑ Are the resources needed to implement the SOP available?
- ❑ What problems, if any, have been noticed in the SOP since the last comprehensive audit and how were they resolved?
- ❑ Is the SOP effective from a health and safety standpoint?
- ❑ Does the SOP help to minimize potential accidental releases?
- ❑ Are the SOPs adhered to by production and management staff?

These basic questions may be used to evaluate the appropriateness of each SOP and used for determining if revisions are necessary.

Management Participation in a Safely Operated Facility

This section addresses the question, "What is management's role in the safe operation of the facility?" It is certainly no secret that the level of commitment by a company's management will be reflected in all other areas of the company culture, including, but not limited to, quality of product, health and safety, employee concerns, and environmental compliance. We are all aware of both positive and negative examples of corporate management's commitment, or lack thereof, and the outcome. Unfortunately, negative examples are exposed in the daily news, on a frequent basis.

Pursuant to 40 CFR 68.15, management staff is required to be directly involved in the following RMP areas:

- ❑ Development of a management and oversight system to ensure implementation of the RMP elements
- ❑ Appointment of a person and/or staff position to have overall responsibility for the development, implementation, and integration of the RMP elements
- ❑ Responsibility to clearly define, through the use of an organizational chart or similar document, the individual person or persons responsible for individual RMP element implementation, if different from the individual named for overall responsibility

Additionally, within the context of the RMP regulations, the role of management staff is implied in numerous areas through the use of language such as, "the owner or operator shall…." In numerous instances, the required action on the part of the "owner or operator" can only be accomplished either by management staff or as a result of management staff input and/or concurrence. This is certainly the case in the following general areas:

- ❑ Choice of method for the process hazard analysis
- ❑ Participation on the audit team
- ❑ Establishment of SOPs
- ❑ Establishment of training programs and procedures

- ❏ Establishment of emergency response program
- ❏ Investigation of any accidental releases
- ❏ Response to audit findings
- ❏ Certification of compliance

Management staff must participate in these areas in order to ensure a balanced and effective RMP document and process.

Management staff is required (40 CFR 68.79(d)) to prepare responses to each and every finding made in the required compliance audit. Not only must a response be prepared, but management staff must clearly indicate an appropriate response to the findings, (i.e. that the deficiencies have been corrected). These responsibilities must be accomplished prior to owner/operator certification of compliance.

And finally, the commitment to a balanced RMP by management staff should be approached from a "common sense" viewpoint due to the fact that the RMP is designed to protect management equally as well as the facility labor force, supervisory staff, and families that may reside in close proximity to the facility. Therefore, the commitment to the RMP plan development and implementation may have direct health and safety impacts on management staff as well as all other levels of the facility workforce and general public. Self auditing is the best way for owner/operators to assure an effective compliance status!

REFERENCES

Air and Waste Management Association (AWMA). 1997. Accident Prevention and Risk Management - The Challenge, June 1997. Air Course AIR-380.

California Environmental Compliance Monitor. 1996. *A Monitor Special Report: Environmental Auditing*. May 1996.

Greenfield, S.M. 1995. Corporate Planning for the Avoidance of Environmental Liability. April 1995. *National Environmental Journal*.

Grognale, G.G. 1991. *Auditing Answers*. August 1991. G.G. Grognale. Environmental Protection.

Kass and McCarroll. 1995. The Corporate Environmental Audit, *Environmental Protection Magazine*. June 1995. S.L. Kass and J.M. McCarroll.

Latham & Watkins. 1996. Latham & Watkins, et.al. *EPA Environmental Self-Auditing Policy*, Latham & Watkins, Bulletin 35. January 1996. Latham & Watkins, San Diego, California.

Levin, et al. 1994. *Discovery and Disclosure: How to Protect Your Environmental Audit*. January 1994. M.H. Levin, A.D. Hymes, and S. Mullaney. BNA - Analysis and Perspective.

Thomson and LeGrand. 1993. *The Importance of Environmental Auditing*. September 1993. R.P. Thomson and C.H. LeGrand. Industrial Wastewater.

United States Code of Federal Regulations (CFR). 1997. 29 *Code of Federal Regulations 1910*, 1997. (Also known as *Title 29, Part 1910*.)

United States Code of Federal Regulations (CFR). 1997. 40 *Code of Federal Regulations 68*, 1997. (Also known as *Title 40, Part 68*.)

United States Department of Justice. 1991. *Factors in Decisions on Criminal Prosecution for Environmental Violations in the Context of Significant Voluntary Compliance or Disclosure Effort By the Violator*. July 1991. U.S. Department of Justice.

United States Environmental Protection Agency (EPA). 1996. *RMP Off-site Consequence Analysis Guidance*, May 24, 1996. United States Environmental Protection Agency, Office of Air Quality Planning and Standards (OAQPS).

Chapter 7

Incident Investigations

In promulgating the RMP standard, EPA included requirements for incident investigation because a crucial part of any risk management program is the thorough investigation of any incident that resulted in, or could reasonably have resulted in, a catastrophic release of a highly hazardous chemical in the workplace. Such investigations are extremely important for identifying the chain of events leading to the incident and for determining causal factors. Information resulting from the investigation will be invaluable to the development and implementation of corrective measures and for use in subsequent process hazard analyses.

It is important that an incident investigation be initiated promptly so that events can be recounted as clearly as possible, to preserve crucial evidence, and so that there is less likelihood that the scene will have been disturbed. EPA also realizes that circumstances may not facilitate an immediate investigation because of the potential emergency nature of some incidents. This is the reason that the required investigations are to be initiated as promptly as possible, but not later than 48 hours following the incident.

In this chapter, we will take a look at the two major types of accident investigation: those initiated by the facility incurring the accident and those conducted by federal authorities (e.g., the Chemical Safety Board).

Facility Owner/Operator

Accident investigations are a required part of an affected facility's overall prevention program. EPA retained the management system requirement proposed in the Notice of Proposed Rule Making, but only for Program 2 and 3 processes. EPA anticipates that sources whose processes are already in compliance with OSHA PSM will not need to take any additional steps or create any new documentation to comply with EPA's Program 2 and Program 3 Prevention Program. Any PSM modifications necessary to account for protection of public health and the environment, along with protection of workers, can be made when PSM elements are updated under the OSHA requirements. EPA has modified the OSHA definition of catastrophic release, which serves as the trigger for an incident investigation, to include events that "present imminent and substantial endangerment to public health and the environment." As a result, the RMP rule requires investigation of accidental releases that pose a risk to the public or the environment, whereas the OSHA rule does not. EPA recognizes that catastrophic accidental releases primarily affect the workplace and that this change will have little effect on incident investigation programs already established. However, EPA needs to ensure that deviations that could have had only an offsite impact are also addressed.

The incident investigation requirements of a Program 3 are slightly more encompassing than those required by a Program 2. As such, both are listed below to facilitate the reader's review.

Program 2 Incident Investigation Requirements
1. The owner or operator must investigate each incident that resulted in, or could reasonably have resulted in, a catastrophic release.

2. An incident investigation needs to be initiated as promptly as possible, but not later than 48 hours following the incident.
3. A summary is to be prepared at the conclusion of the investigation, which includes, at a minimum:
   a) Date of incident
   b) Date investigation began
   c) A description of the incident
   d) The factors that contributed to the incident
   e) Any recommendations resulting from the in vestigation
4. The owner or operator shall promptly address and resolve the investigation findings and recommendations. Resolutions and corrective actions shall be documented.
5. The findings must be reviewed with all affected personnel whose job tasks are affected by the findings.
6. Investigation summaries shall be retained for five (5) years.

Program 3 Incident Investigation Requirements

1. The owner or operator must investigate each incident that resulted in, or could reasonably have resulted in, a catastrophic release of a regulated substance.
2. An incident investigation must be initiated as promptly as possible, but not later than 48 hours following the incident.
3. An incident investigation team is to be established and consist of at least one person knowledgeable in the process involved, including a contract employee if the incident involved work of the contractor and other persons with appropriate knowledge and experience to thoroughly investigate and analyze the incident.
4. A report must be prepared at the conclusion of the investigation which includes at a minimum:
   a) Date of incident
   b) Date investigation began
   c) A description of the incident
   d) The factors that contributed to the incident
   e) Any recommendations resulting from the in vestigation
5. The owner or operator must establish a system to promptly address and resolve the incident re port findings and recommendations. Resolutions and corrective actions shall be documented.
6. The report needs to be reviewed with all affected personnel whose job tasks are relevant to the incident findings including contract employees where applicable.
7. Incident investigation reports must be retained for five (5) years.

Chemical Safety Board

Clean Air Act Amendments of 1990 required U.S. EPA to establish a Chemical Safety Board (Section 112(r)(5) Chemical Safety Board). The Board is required to be comprised of five members, "including a chairperson who shall be appointed by the president, by and with the advice and consent of the Senate." Members of the Board are be appointed on the basis of technical qualifications, professional standing, and demonstrated knowledge in the fields of accident reconstruction, safety engineering, human factors, toxicology, or air pollution regulations. Members of the Board are appointed for five-year terms. The Board chairman serves as Chief Executive Officer and exercises the executive and administrative functions of the Board. The two functions of the board are these:

1. Investigate (or cause to be investigated), determine and report to the public in writing, the facts, conditions, and circumstances, and the cause or probable cause of any accidental release resulting in a fatality, serious injury, or substantial property damage.
2. Issue periodic reports to the Congress, federal, state, and local agencies, including the Environmental Protection Agency and the Occupational Safety and Health Administration, concerned with safety of the chemical production, processing, handling, and storage and other interested persons recommending measures to reduce the likelihood of the consequences of accidental releases and proposing corrective steps to make chemical production, processing, handling, and storage that is safe and free from risk of injury as much as is possible.

Reporting releases to the National Response Center, in lieu of the Board directly, would satisfy the regulations. The National Response Center was required to notify the Board of any releases that it felt were within the Board's jurisdiction. The Board is also permitted to utilize the experience and expertise of other agencies, for example, OSHA. The Board is also required to coordinate its activities with investigations and studies conducted by other agencies of the U.S. having the responsibility to protect public health and safety. Examples of this could include, besides the Occupational Safety and Health Administration, local emergency planning commissions, local fire departments, National Guard, and other first-responders.

The Board was also required to enter into a Memorandum of Understanding with the National Transportation Safety Board to assure coordination of investigations and to limit duplication of effort. For accidental releases that are deemed to be transportation related, the National Transportation Safety Board was to be designated as the lead investigative agency. The Board was not allowed to investigate marine-related oil spills, which are normally investigated by the National Transportation Safety Board. It was also required to enter into a Memorandum of Understanding with the Occupational Safety and Health Administration to limit duplication of activities under OSHA PSM or other OSHA requirements. The Act did indicate, however, that "in no event shall the Board forgo an investigation when accidental release causes a fatality or serious injury among the general public, or had the potential to cause substantial property damage or a number of deaths or injuries among the general public."[32]

Chemical Accident Investigation Board

The Accident Investigation Board was also authorized by the Act to conduct research studies with respect to potential for accidental releases, whether or not similar releases had occurred in the past. This was permitted where available evidence indicated that a potential hazard existed.

Interestingly, Paragraph G of the Act states "no part of the conclusions, findings, or recommendation of the Board relating to any accidental release or investigation thereof shall be admitted as evidence or used in any action or suit for damages arising out of any matter mentioned in such report."[33]

This limitation may have been designed to free the Board from worry of involvement in litigation; however, it is likely that information developed by the board in its investigation of an accident would be very relevant to such litigation. This may be an area of the Act that the courts may further interpret.

The Board was also charged with several non-investigatory responsibilities, including developing recommendations on hazard assessment and other tools for studying and predicting the impact of accidental releases.

The Board has broad powers to enter facilities that had experienced accidental releases for purposes of inspecting. Inspectors, while they have broad rights to enter facilities for purposes of inspecting, the Act also provided that facility employees and their representatives have the same rights to participate in such inspections as provided under the Occupational Safety and Health Act.

Funding

The Chemical Safety Board was required to submit budget requests and other budget information and legislative recommendations or prepare testimony for Congressional hearings. Recommendations on funding are sent to the President, Secretary of Labor, and Administrator or Director of the Office of Management and Budget. It was also required that the board currently submit a copy of these recommendations to the Congress.

No report to the Board was to be subject to review by the Administrator or enter any federal agency or judicial view in any court. No officer or agency of the United States was to have the authority to require the Board to submit its budget request or estimates, legislative recommendations, prepared testimony, comments, recommendations, or reports to any officer or agency of the United States for approval or review prior to submission of such recommendations or other reference material to the Congress.

This is a very unusual structure for an environmental authority. In other words, Congress controlled the funding of the committee while reports, testimony, and budget requests were to be submitted directly to Congress, not to the EPA administrator or to other agencies. Herein lies a problem with the Board. Congress has previously withheld funding of the Accident Investigation Board. In September 1997, House and Senate Budget negotiators finally agreed to fund the Chemical Safety and Hazard Investigation Board. A budget of four million dollars to fund the Board under fiscal year 1998 spending bill HR2158 for the Departments of Veterans Affairs, Housing and Urban Development, and independent agencies was proposed.[34]

We may now see the Chemical Accident Investigation Board finally constituted and begin its legislatively required functions. In the absence of such a Board, however, U.S. EPA has developed regulations requiring self-investigation by companies suffering accidental releases. In its final rule, published June 20, 1996, the U.S. EPA suggested that the existing reports be used to document causes and resolution of accidental releases. U.S. EPA decided to rely on the five-year accident history for the immediate future and, based on that information, determine whether additional information and requirements were needed. U.S. EPA noted that it had authority under the Clean Air Act Section 114 to investigate releases and to seek additional information as needed under the RMP provisions for Chemical Accident Prevention.[35]

As noted earlier, the House and Senate budget negotiators on September 30, 1997 agreed to fund the Chemical Safety and Hazard Investigation Board originally mandated by the Clean Air Act Amendments of 1990.

The House and Senate committees voted the Board's funding, which had originally been held up by the Congress since it concluded that the administration's approach was not working. According to BNA's *Environment Reporter* of 10/10/97, Congress concluded that U.S. EPA and OSHA could not do the job without the Board and that the Board should be given a chance to work. The Board, originally required by the Clean Air Act Amendments to consist of five members, had been frozen at three members under President Clinton's reinvention strategy to streamline government and never received start-up funding. According to BNA, "To date (U.S. EPA and OSHA) have done an abominable job in investigating chemical accidents" —a quote from a letter sent by 79 groups, including environmental, social justice, religious, health, and labor organizations that was sent to the White House Office of Management and Budget. This letter stated that "recent chemical disasters clearly illustrate the need for this independent Board" (BNA 10/10/97). The group cited a major accident at Napp Technologies in Lodi, New Jersey, that re-

sulted in five worker fatalities. It took EPA more than two years to publish a report on this event. The letter from the groups also called the legal jurisdiction of U.S. EPA and OSHA into question. The letter stated, "For example, following an accident at a Tosco Oil Refinery at Martinez, California, U.S. EPA was barred from entering the facility to investigate the accident because the agency could not provide proof of their authority to enter." Note that this last problem could have been prevented had the U.S. EPA had the proper credentials. The Clean Air Act 112(r) paragraph authorizing creation of the Board does require EPA to provide proof of proper credentials before entering a facility. It does not, however, indicate what sort of proof that must be.[36]

Accidents Investigated

Several accidental releases have been investigated by the Chemical Emergency Preparedness and Prevention Office (CEPPO) of the U.S. EPA since 1994.

The first accident investigation was of Terra Industries of Port Neil, Iowa. This accident involved an explosion of ammonium nitrate. About 5,700 tons of anhydrous ammonia and 25,000 gallons of nitric acid were released. Four workers were killed and 18 others were hospitalized. The investigation was completed on this accident approximately 14 months after it occurred. A regulatory alert for ammonium nitrate is pending.

The second accident investigated was at Powel Duffryn Terminals in Savannah, Georgia. This accident involved a crude sulfate turpentine that was involved in a fire. Hydrogen sulfide was released and 2,000 residents were evacuated. A major investigation report is pending. As a result, an alert for carbon absorption systems was issued in 1997.

Next, the Napp Technologies incident of April 21, 1995, in Lodi, New Jersey, resulted in a release of sodium hydrosulfite aluminum powder, potassium carbonate, and densel dehyde as a result of an explosion. Four employees were killed and numerous others were injured. One of the injured later died as a result of injuries. A major joint investigation report was released in November 1997.

Napp was conducting a blending operation for another company, Technique, involving water-reactive chemicals (aluminum powder and sodium hydrosulfite). The employees conducting the blending operation had noticed an unexpected reaction taking place in the blender, producing increasing heat and a release of foul-smelling gas (sulfur dioxide). The Joint Chemical Accident Investigation Team (JCAIT) formed by OSHA and EPA determined that the most likely cause of the accident was the inadvertent introduction of water and heat into water-reactive materials during the mixing operation. The water caused sodium hydrosulfite in the blender to decompose. The decomposition process became self-sustaining as it generated heat, sulfur dioxide, and additional water. The reaction generated sufficient heat to allow the aluminum powder to rapidly react with the other ingredients and generate more heat. In an effort to mitigate the situation, an emergency operation was conducted to off-load the blender of its reacting contents. During the off-loading operation, the material ignited and a deflagration occurred, which resulted in the deaths of the Napp employees and destruction of the facility.

JCAIT concluded that an inadequate process hazards analysis was conducted and appropriate preventive actions were not taken. Napp's process hazard analysis had identified the water reactivity of the substances involved, but did not identify other potential factors, including sources of water/heat, mitigation measures, recognition of deviations, consequences of failures of controls, and steps necessary to stop a reaction inside the blender. In addition, JCAIT found the decision to re-enter the facility and off-load the blender was based on inadequate information. Napp was aware of, and concerned for, the strong possibility of a fire, but did not understand whether or not off-loading the blender would make the situation worse.[37]

Next, in October 1995, Pennzoil Products Company, Russell, Pennsylvania, experienced a fire and explosion of flammable hydrocarbons. Three workers were killed in the fire and three others were injured. A major investigation report of that incident is still pending.

In January 1997, at a Tosco Refinery in Martinez, California, there was an explosion and fire involving hydrocarbons in which one worker was killed and 44 others were injured. Residents were sheltered in place. Major investigation with CAL/OSHA and local authorities is on-going.

On March 26, 1997, in Haskell, Oklahoma, Chief Supply Corporation experienced a fire and explosion of flammable waste, including paints, oils, thinners, inks, and cleaning solvents. Three workers were injured and one of the injured later died as a result of his injuries. Residents within 1.5 miles of the facility were evacuated from their homes and businesses. An investigation is ongoing.

On April 8, 1997, in Albany, New York, Surpass Chemical Corporation experienced a hydrochloric acid spill. The hydrochloric acid cloud drifted off site, a liquid spill entered city storm drains, and a total of 43 persons including some employees were treated at hospitals, and of these, four were hospitalized. One square block around the facility was evacuated and nearby elementary schools sheltered students and facility in place.

On May 8, 1997, in West Helena, Arkansas, BPS Inc. experienced a fire and explosion. Early reports indicated pesticides involved may have included azine azio-methyl. This apparently has not been confirmed. Three firefighters were killed by a collapsing roof and twenty persons were injured while a three-mile radius area was initially evacuated. A major investigation is ongoing.

On June 22, 1997, in Deer Park, Texas, Shell Chemical Company experienced a fire and explosion involving hydrocarbons in an olefins unit. Major damage to the olefins unit occurred, one employee was hospitalized, and minor injuries occurred to 20 to 30 employees. The nearby community was sheltered in place. Highways west and south of the plant were closed for several hours. Broken window damage was reported in the surrounding areas. A major joint accident investigation is underway.

On June 24, 1997, in Elkhart, Indiana, Accra Pack experienced a fire and explosion that may have involved ethylene oxide. One employee was killed and three others were hospitalized. Fifty-nine people were treated at a hospital and approximately 2,500 people were evacuated for a one mile radius around the plant. A preliminary cause investigation is being coordinated in conjunction with Indiana OSHA.

Observations

Several observations are apparent from this summary. First, there was not a large number of incidents to be investigated. If the Board had been in existence since

1994, it would have investigated only eleven incidents. Secondly, there was a larger number of incidents in 1997 than in any other year. This could be the result of more incidents occurring; however, it is more likely the result of better reporting. Additionally, only one of the investigations of the incidents that occurred in 1995 or later has been completed. Furthermore, only one investigation of incidents that occurred in 1994 has been completed to report stage. This pointed to a need for a fully funded Chemical Safety Board, as noted earlier.

[32]Clean Air Act 112(r)(e).

[33]112(r)(e).

[34]The Bureau of National Affairs, Inc.: *Environment Reporter*, "Chemical Safety: House, Senate Would Fund Safety Board; Lawmakers, Group Seek Clinton Support," October 10, 1997, Vol. 28, No. 23, P. 1160. ©Copyright 1997 by The Bureau of National Affairs, Inc. (800-372-1033) <http://www.bna.com> (Reprinted with permission)

[35]62 FR 45130, 08/25/97.

[36]The Bureau of National Affairs, Inc.: *Environmental Reporter*, "Chemical Safety: House, Senate Would Fund Safety Board; Lawmakers, Group Seek Clinton Support," October 10, 1997, Vol. 28, No. 23, P. 1160. ©Copyright 1997 by The Bureau of National Affairs, Inc. (800-372-1033) <http://www.bna.com> (Reprinted with permission)

[37]United States Environmental Protection Agency, United States Occupational Safety and Health Administration, EPA 550-R-002, October 1997.

Chapter 8

Establishing an Emergency Response Plan

The Clean Air Act Amendments of 1990 require owners or operators of facilities to establish emergency response plans. Section 112r (7), Accident Prevention, requires the owner or operator of a stationary source at which a regulated substance is present in more than a threshold quantity (TQ) to prepare and implement a Risk Management Plan to detect and prevent or minimize accidental releases of such substances from the stationary source, and to provide a prompt emergency response to any such release in order to protect human health in the environment. Ref Section 112r Clean Air Act 1990 paragraph (III) requires "a response program striving for a specific action to be taken in response to an accidental release of a regulated substance so as to protect human health and the environment, including procedures for informing the public and local agencies responsible for responding to accidental releases, emergency health care, and employee training measures."[38]

The final regulations promulgated pursuant to these requirements (Emergency Response Program) require sources to "develop an emergency response plan that defines the steps each employee should take during an accidental release of a regulated substance."[39]

Related Regulations

Certain elements that should be a part of a response program are already required, and sources should already have implemented portions of these under other regulatory programs. For example, the Resource Conservation and Recovery Act (RCRA) requires Spill Pre-vention Control and Countermeasure Plans (SPCC Plans). These plans cover actions that facilities must take to minimize the consequences of releases of hazardous or toxic substances. They include, for example, proper storage of tanks, drums, and other storage containers, including dikes to capture and contain the contents of a spill. They also include procedures employees are to follow to prevent or stop a release, and then to recover releases that occur. These plans stop short, however, of including estimates of the offsite consequences of evaporation from a release of a liquid. Traditionally, OSHA regulations (emergency actions plans, HAZWOPER regulations) provide guidance on actions employees must take in the event of emergency operations.

Finally, SARA (The Superfund Amendment and Reauthorization Act of 1986) contains Title III, Emergency Planning and Community Right-to-Know. (42 U.S.C. 11003). This requires facilities to develop offsite emergency response plans and to file these and coordinate with the local emergency planning committees. In addition, it does not require assessing offsite impacts.

Content of Plans

Given several other regulatory programs that require emergency planning and response, U.S. EPA adopted the statutory language of the Clean Air Act and did not require additional planning elements. U.S. EPA has "committed not to specify new plan elements or a specific planned format in...."[40] U.S. EPA believed that "plans developed to comply with other U.S. EPA contingency planning requirements and the OSHA Hazardous Waste and Emergency Operations (HAZWOPER Rule) (29 CFR 1910.120) will meet the requirements for the emergency response program provided they address the elements in Section 68.95 of the final regulations. Section 68.95 requires the following in the development and implementation of an emergency response program for purposes of protecting public health and the environment. These plans must include the following:

1. An emergency response plan must be maintained at the facility (stationary source) and must contain the following elements:
   * procedures for informing the public and local emergency response agencies about accidental releases
   * documentation of proper first aid and emergency medical treatment necessary to treat accidental human exposures
   * procedures and measures for emergency response to accidental releases of the regulated substance
2. Procedures for the use of emergency response equipment and for its inspection, testing, and maintenance
3. Training for all employees in relevant procedures
4. Procedures to review and update, as appropriate, the emergency response plan to reflect changes in the stationary source and ensure that employees are informed of changes.

The final regulations also indicate that written plans meeting the requirements of the federal government's National Response Team's integrated contingency plan guidance ("One Plan") and including the elements provided in the final RMP regulations will satisfy the requirements of those regulations if the owner or operator also complies with final regulations with respect to the required elements and content of the emergency response plan.

Facilities categorized as Program 1 facilities need not prepare detailed emergency response plans. For facilities and Programs 2 and 3, however, full compliance with the requirements of Section 68.95 of the final regulations (emergency response program) is required. Owners or operators of facilities whose employees will not respond to accidental releases of regulated substances need not comply with Section 68.95 provided they meet the following critieria:

❑ For stationary sources with any regulated toxic substance held in the process above the threshold quantity, the stationary source is required to be included in the community emergency response plan developed under 42 U.S.C. 11003.

❑ For stationary sources of regulated flammable substances only held in a process above the threshold quantity, the owner/operator is required to demonstrate that he or she has coordinated response actions with the local fire department.

❑ Appropriate mechanisms are in place to notify emergency responders when there is a need for a response.

All other facilities designated as Program 2 or 3 are required to have emergency response programs in place.

The emergency response program required by Section 68.95 requires the owner/operator to develop and implement an emergency response program for the "purpose of protection of public health and the environment."[41] An emergency response plan to be maintained at the facility must contain at least the following elements:

❑ Procedures for informing the public and local emergency response agencies about accidental releases

❑ Documentation of proper first aid and emergency medical treatment necessary to treat accidental human exposures

❑ Procedures and measures for emergency response after an accidental release of a highly regulated substance

❑ Procedures for use of emergency response equipment and for its inspection, testing, and maintenance

❑ Training for all employees in relevant procedures and

❑ Procedures to review and update, as appropriate, the emergency response plan to reflect changes at the stationary source and ensure that employees are informed of changes[42]

The RMP regulations require that the emergency response plan developed be coordinated with the community emergency response plan developed under 42 U.S.C. 11003. If requested by the local emergency planning committee or emergency response officials, the owner or operator must provide these officials with information necessary for developing and implementing the community emergency response plan.

Endpoints

An important issue in developing an emergency response plan is determining what offsite concentrations require various levels of response. For example, just because a hypothetical release of a hazardous or toxic substance will produce a concentration exceeding an endpoint off the property line, it does not necessarily mean that an emergency response is necessary. The endpoint constitutes a planning value and if it occurs in an unpopulated area, no response may be needed. Even if it occurs off site and in a populated area, the appropriate emergency response will vary depending on what the chemical at issue is. Some endpoints, for example, can be values at which advisories for staying indoors may be issued, while others may require a more aggressive response.

Certain accidental releases can result in concentrations that greatly exceed the endpoints. In these situations, values may approach those that could require evacuation if there is time. In many instances, by the time the emergency happens, especially depending upon the wind speed, concentrations may already exceed levels of concern off site. Therefore, it is important in the standard operating procedures that if an emergency response is likely to be required, given the progression of events at a process, an early warning must be provided as a component of the emergency response plan so that political bodies, local emergency planning committees, or other entities responsible for informing and possibly evacuating the public will have time to take appropriate action.

Avoiding Unnecessary Evacuation Risks

While most people think of the danger to the public from an accidental release and the potential need for evacuation, there is danger in the evacuation process itself. In a hasty evacuation, it is entirely possible that offsite residents or plant personnel will be involved in traffic accidents, some may have other accidents involving falling due to running or other factors, and members of the public may suffer heart attacks or other medical consequences of the evacuation itself. Therefore, evacuations should be ordered only when they are really necessary.

Scenario Modeling

How does one determine whether sheltering or evacuation is an appropriate emergency response? First, scenario modeling is necessary. This is required under the regulations for Programs 2 and 3 for purposes of determining whether there is an offsite concentration possible that exceeds the published endpoint. Beyond this, however, modeling also may be appropriate, if offsite concentrations may exceed an endpoint, to determine whether concentrations off site could be severe

Table 8.1: Examples of Toxic Endpoints vs. IDLH					
Exposure Limits (mg/L)	NIOSH (TWA)	OSHA (TWA)	IDLH	Toxic Endpoint	Enpoint Basis
Phosgene	0.0004	0.0004	0.0082	0.00081	EHS-LOC(IDLH)
Hydrogen Selenide	0.2000	0.2000	0.0034	0.00066	EHS-LOC(IDLH)
Iron, Pentacarbonyl	0.8000	none	not determined	0.00044	EHS-LOC(Toxic)
Formaldehyde	0.00002	0.0009	0.025 (Carcinogen)	0.01200	ERPG-2
Chlorine	1.4500	3.000	0.295	0.00870	ERPG-2

EHS-LOC(IDLH): Extremely Hazardous Substance: Level of Concern (Immediately Dangerous to Life and Health).

EHS-LOC(Tox): Extremely Hazardous Substance: Level of Concern (Toxic).

ERPG-2: Emergency Response Planning Guideline, Level 2

enough to require sheltering or evacuation. Such modeling can be undertaken in a variety of ways. Emergency response computer systems have been developed by several companies. These systems integrate real-time meteorological monitoring along with plant monitoring to provide a real-time prediction of where a plume from an emergency release is and what direction it is traveling in.

In order for these systems to work, however, the emergency release must be one that can be monitored. Only some types of emergency releases can be monitored. Those that occur through cracked discs and vent lines can be monitored (although usually they are not); however, those that occur from ruptured pipes or broken tanks or truck accidents can clearly not be monitored. In these instances, the operator of the system must be prepared to provide an input value for the quantity released. These emergency response systems are very elegant and provide either a printout or a display on a computer monitor of where the plume is at any moment. From the history of the plume, it is possible to infer where the plume will be in certain forward-moving increments of time (although with increasing uncertainty as the time period is extended).

One problem with use of such systems is that the facility must have trained operators on duty with access to the system at the exact time that the incident occurs. Since (almost by definition) chemical accidents most often occur at 3:00 A.M. on a Sunday morning, this is not always possible.

Hypothetical Modeling

There are alternatives to offsite response planning. Another approach is to conduct hypothetical modeling of all accidental releases and potential accidental releases and to prepare overlays of center-line downwind concentrations. This approach is similar to that taken in the nuclear utility industry before real-time emergency response systems were available. A series of overlays corresponding to different combinations of atmospheric stability and wind speed can be plotted, and using simple meteorological instruments to measure wind speed, wind direction, and some indications of atmospheric stability. An individual at the plant or at the emergency planning committee can take the appropriate overlay; for example, take stable atmosphere with 10 mile-per-hour wind and align it with the wind direction as provided by the meteorological sensors.

Using this approach and aligning the overlay with the wind direction on a base map of the facility and surrounding area, an output similar to that produced by a real time emergency response modeling system can be obtained. Using such an approach, an owner/operator or emergency response official can determine that concentrations could exceed levels that could be life threatening to a distance of 1/2 mile from the site of the accident. Under stable conditions, however, such concentrations might be predicted to extend out to 1-1/2 miles. Therefore, use of such an approach would enable the facility or the emergency response committee to limit an evacuation to 1/2 mile radius rather than a 1 or 1-1/2 mile radius which might be the value predicted using the offsite consequence analysis guidelines and atmospheric stability. Use of either the overlay approach or a refined real-time predictive model will help a facility and an emergency response committee limit potential evacuation to those areas that really need it. This should reduce injuries or deaths that could be attributed to an overly broad evacuation order.

Integrated Contingency Plan

The National Response Team (NRT) published the integrated contingency plan ("One Plan") on June 5, 1996 (61 FR 28642). This One Plan contains the mechanism by which facilities may consolidate multiple emergency response plans into one functional plan. It is an Integrated Facility Response plan (ICP) in a format favored by the federal government. This is not formally required under the final RMP regulations; however a similarly functioning plan is preferable for facilities rather than multiple disparate plans. The ICP is "intended to streamline the emergency planning process of those facilities that may be subject to one or more federal emergency regulations...." While not affecting the substantive requirements of these federal regulations, the NRT developed a mechanism by which the components of the emergency plan may be incorporated into a single document.[43]

This guidance provided in the ICP requires that a plan consist of three parts: the introductory section, the core plan, and a series of supporting annexes or appendixes. The steps necessary to initiate, conduct, and terminate an emergency response action are found in the core plan. The annexes provide detail support information based on procedures detailed in the core plan.[44] The core plan provides only the most essential response steps and will make frequent references to the annexes or appendixes. These may further reference other plans—for example, area contingency plans, local emergency planning committee plans, or other state or local plans. If facilities submit integrated contingency plans under Section 112(r), they should cross reference the interrelated requirements of the other regulatory programs. Note that the integrated facility plan guidance does not address all of the requirements of Section 112(r). The intent, however, is that the ICP could cover the emergency response plan requirements of Program 2 and Program 3 facilities under 112(r).

Training Exercises

Training exercises are not specifically required under the final RMP regulations. These are, however, an excellent way for facilities and local emergency responders to prepare for an incident.

Modeling is a useful tool for determining potential evacuation areas. Such information is valuable for planning real-world training exercises. Details on how to conduct modeling will be discussed in Chapter 14.

---

[38]The Clean Air Act 112r(7)III.

[39]40 CFR Part 68, 6/20/96.

[40]40 CFR Part 68, 6/20/96.

[41]40 CFR Part 68, 6/20/96.

[42]40 CFR Part 68, 6/20/96.

[43]Chemical Emergency Preparedness and Prevention Office (CEPPO), July 1997, CAA Section 112r - Frequently Asked Questions.

[44]Chemical Emergency Preparedness and Prevention Office (CEPPO), July 1997, CAA Section 112r - Frequently Asked Questions.

Chapter 9

Handling Registration Procedures

The Clean Air Act Amendments of 1990 Title III, Section 112r (7) - Accident Prevention (III) require the owner or operator to register a risk management plan prepared under the final RMP regulations with the EPA Administrator (or delegated state agency) within three years of the effective date of regulations developed pursuant to the legislation (by June 21, 1999) in such form as may be required by the administrator. The form of the submittal is looking more and more like it will be an electronic format. Additionally, plans must be submitted to the Chemical Safety Board (now funded) and also to any states in which stationary sources are located, and as well as, to any local agency or entity having responsibility for planning or for responding to an accidental release that may occur at regulated facilities. These plans, furthermore, are to be made available to the public under Section 114(c). The EPA Administrator, under the Clean Air Act, is required to establish an auditing system for regular review and, if necessary, to require revisions in risk management plans to ensure that the plans comply with the legislation. Finally, each plan is required to be updated periodically, or as may be required by the administrator or regulations.

Registration Requirements

Under the final RMP regulations, RMPs need not be formally submitted until June 21, 1999, or the date on which a regulated substance first becomes present above a threshold quantity in a process—whichever is later (40 CFR 68.10)(a)). For substances that may be added to the list of TQs (new chemicals or compounds), the due date for RMP submissions will be three years after the date in which the regulated substance was first listed by EPA. Update filings are required every five years if there are no significant changes in the facility. Update filings are required within six months of a change that requires a revised process hazard analysis or hazard review (40 CFR 68.190)(b)(5)). Also, a revised offsite consequence analysis, or any change that alters a program level as it applies to any covered process, requires an update filing.[45]

Unlike some other environmental programs requiring registration, there is no preregistration required before the due date for the RMP itself. Note, however, that owners and operators are encouraged by the regulations to begin collecting hazard assessments and risk management program assessments immediately. In addition, recall the General Duty provision (Chapter 1) that holds owners and operators responsible for having done such planning in the event of accidental releases affecting offsite receptors.

Determining which of the three program levels a facility falls under requires facility-specific information. First, a facility is required to comply with Section 112(r)(5) of the Clean Air Act as amended if the threshhold (TQ) quantity of regulated substances in a process is determined to be present at the facility.

The RMP regulations, Section 68.115, Threshold Determination, specifies the procedures for determining whether regulated substances listed in Section 68.130 are present at the facility, and in what quantities. It is important to differentiate between substances in mixtures, substances in regulated flammables, and substances in explosives.

Exemptions

There are exemptions for regulated substances in mixtures. If a regulated substance in a mixture is below one percent by weight of the mixture, the amount of the substance in the mixture need not be considered in the TQ calculation. This could be important for facilities that use very large quantities of mixtures containing regulated substances in low concentrations. There is an additional exemption that applies to all regulated substances, except for oleum, toluene, 2,4-diisocyanate, toluene 2,6-diisocyanate, and toluene diisocyanate. If the concentration of the regulated substance in the mixture is 1% or greater by weight, but the partial pressure of the regulated substance in the mixture, or the solution, under handling or storage conditions in any portion of the process is less than 10 millimeters of mercury, the amount of the substance in the mixture in that portion of the process need not be considered in calculating a threshold quantity. The owner or operator is required to document this partial pressure measurement or estimate.[46]

Flammables

Concentrations of regulated flammable substances in a mixture also follow the 1% by weight exemption. If the concentration of the regulated substance in the mixture is 1% or greater by weight, then the *entire weight of the mixture* is treated as the regulated substance unless the owner or operator can demonstrate that the mixture itself would not be rated with an NFPA flammability rating of 4 [i.e., flashpoint (below 73° F) (22.8° C) and boiling point below 100° F (37.8° C)]. The owner/operator is responsible for documenting these flashpoint and boiling point measurements or estimates.[47]

Other Exemptions and Exclusions

There are other exemptions and exclusions from regulated substance threshold quantity calculations. These include the following:

❑ **Articles:** Regulated substances contained in articles need not be considered when determining TQ for a facility.

❑ **Uses:** Regulated substances when in use for certain purposes need not be included in determining the TQ. These include:
  - use of a structural component as the stationary source
  - use of product for routine janitorial maintenance
  - use of employee's foods, drugs, cosmetics, or other personal items containing the regulated substance
  - use of regulated substances present in process water and non-contact cooling water as drawn from the environment or municipal sources,
  - use of regulated substances present in air used as either compressed air or as products of combustion

Laboratories

There is also an exemption for laboratory use of regulated substances. For example, regulated substances that are manufactured, processed, or used in a laboratory at a facility under the supervision of a technically qualified individual (Section 720.3) (ee) are exempted from RMP. Note that the laboratory exemption does not apply in the following circumstances:

❑ Specialty chemical production
❑ Manufacture, processing, or use of substances and pilot scale operations
❑ Activities conducted outside the laboratory

Electronic Submission

U.S. EPA has several workgroups working on electronic submission capability for filing RMPs. There are several guidance documents that have been prepared by these workgroups. One such useful guidance material is *Risk Management Plan Data Elements*. This document, available from U.S. EPA, provides a detailed list of the requirements for RMP data elements, including registration.[48] Information required for registration is shown in Table 9.1.

Following the overall facility information, for each coverage process, the RMP data elements require the following information for each chemical in each covered process (that is, those with quantities exceeding TQ levels): chemical name, CAS number, quantity, SIC

Table 9.1: Information Required for Electronic Registration

Source Identification

Name: _____

Address: _____

Street: _____

City, County, State Zip: _____

Location (Latitude/Longitude): _____

Credit Information of Source

Source Dunn & Bradstreet Number: _____

Name of Corporate Parent: _____

Dunn & Bradstreet Number of Corporate Parent: _____

Owner/Operator Information

Name: _____

Phone: _____

Mailing Address: _____

_____

_____

Person Responsible for Part 68 Implementation

Name: _____

Title: _____

Emergency Contact

Name: _____

Title: _____

Phone: _____

24 hr. Phone: _____

Chemical Information

Chemical Name	CAS#	Quantity	SIC Code	Program Level

code for the process and program level (either Program 1, 2, or 3, as appropriate).

Additional Data Elements

The additional data elements required in the RMP can be found in Appendix E, which is a complete list, as of this writing, of the RMP data elements.

U.S. EPA established an electronic workgroup in September 1996, under the Accident Prevention Subcommittee of the Clean Air Act federal advisory committee to recommend ways to report risk management plans and to develop the best methods for EPA, state and local governments, and the public to obtain access to this information. The workgroup issued its final report on June 18, 1997. This report supported electronic submission and access to risk management plans and provided some general recommendations for the RMP submission and access systems.[49]

U.S. EPA is contracting the development of RMP*Submit and RMP*Info through EPA's Net*Program, a part of EPA's Mission Oriented Software Engineering Support (MOSES) contract. EPA will publish a final announcement of the method and format for RMP submissions in the *Federal Register* in August of 1998. The timetable for development allows for one year for software development followed by a five-month pilot test. EPA proposes a plan to have RMP*Submit and RMP*Info fully operational by June 4, 1999 to allow sufficient time for industry to submit prior to the initial RMP deadline of June 21, 1999. This is clearly cutting it close. Extensions for filing may be needed.

The RMP management plan elements found in Appendix E represent a work product of the workgroup developing RMP*Info and RMP*Submit capabilities. EPA is seriously considering posting RMPs on the Internet. This represents a unique opportunity to broadly distribute RMP data to the regulated community, to first responders, and to the public. EPA has commissioned a study to ascertain whether this broad dissemination of the information in RMPs would potentially lead to an increase in terrorism.

---

[45]40 CFR Part 68, 6/20/96.
[46]40 CFR Part 68, 6/20/96.
[47]40 CFR Part 68, 6/20/96.
[48](REF EPA 1997).
[49](REF EPA 1997).

Chapter 10

Totaling the Costs

Many facilities will comply with the RMP regulations with little additional cost beyond their compliance with OSHA PSM or other programs, such as state programs of a similar nature. The cost of compliance with RMP, if you are not already covered by OSHA PSM or a similar state program, will vary significantly depending on the nature of your facility. EPA notes that in developing the final rule it has taken actions to streamline requirements wherever possible and has tailored requirements through the use of the program levels. U.S. EPA notes in the proposed rulemaking that to apply the same level of analysis to all sources would not be cost-effective. Use of varied programs enables smaller and remotely located facilities to comply at significantly reduced costs. EPA has also changed its requirements for two elements of the rule—the offsite consequence analyses and the risk management plan. U.S. EPA elected to recommend and allow methods for offsite consequence analyses and include look-up tables so that many facilities would not need to spend resources to obtain and apply air quality dispersion models. EPA also reduced the requirements to define offsite populations by allowing facilities to use census track data rather than to identify only those institutions or developments that appear on local maps. For the RMP, EPA limited the requirements for information to those that can be reported as data elements. The rule, as first proposed, would have required sources to document all major hazards for each process, the major consequences of each of these hazards, and the risk reduction steps taken to address each hazard, as well as the consequences of each risk reduction step. The result, according to EPA estimates, would have been documents of a thousand pages or more for large, complex sources.

Facilities Affected

Based on the final rule, EPA estimates 66,000 sources will be affected by the regulations. Of these, only 360 sources and approximately 410 processes will be eligible for Program 1, the least complex and least expensive program. These sources are primarily gas processes that are remote and generally unstaffed. They are also not covered by OSHA PSM. EPA estimates that Program 2 will include 40,000 plus sources and 47,000 processes. These sources will include retailers, propane users, public drinking water, wastewater systems, and public utilities not subject to OSHA PSM. Wholesalers, processors at federal facilities and non-chemical manufacturers may also qualify for Program 2. Program 3 is expected to cover 25,000 sources and 43,800 processes.

The Program 3 sources include other manufacturers, electric utilities, POTWs, and drinking water systems covered by OSHA PSM, wholesalers, ammonia refrigeration systems, gas utilities, gas producers, and federal facilities. All of these sources are already covered by OSHA PSM for at least one regulated substance. EPA estimates that only about 370 non-OSHA PSM processes require Program 3 submissions.

Facilities that already have a "high-quality" PSM Program would not need to take any additional actions to satisfy the prevention program required under Program 3 of the final RMP regulations. However, the EPA analyses assumed that many sources may still be in the process of improving their PSM programs after achieving initial compliance. The public scrutiny expected to follow submission of an RMP is likely to encourage sources to ensure that their prevention efforts are fully implemented and effective.[50] Therefore, in its cost estimates, EPA assumed that these sources, even though they are covered by OSHA, would improve training, maintenance, and management oversight and, in some cases, institute additional capital improvements.

The RMP regulations have a three-year compliance schedule. The rule also imposes continuing costs on facilities to implement their management programs and to provide ongoing training and modifications of the plans. EPA calculated unit costs of compliance for each element of the program and multiplied this by the number of sources assumed to be affected by the requirements. EPA then adjusted these cost estimates to account for the fact that some sources have already implemented some risk management requirements, for example, training.

Costs of Compliance

EPA estimated that costs for a uniform program for all facilities with comprehensive offsite impact analyses would cost $1.22 billion in initial cost and would have an annual benefit of $174 million, but with an annual cost of $246 million after the initial year, or a net cost of $72 million a year. In Option 2, EPA analyzed that it would cost $642 million to have one program for all types of facilities with a simplified offsite consequence analysis. This carries with it a $142 million annual cost and an annual benefit of $174 million, or a net benefit of $32 million a year. The chosen option, where we have different levels of RMP for different types of facilities and simplified offsite consequence analysis, would cost $494 million initially and $97 million annually with an annual benefit of $174 million, or a net benefit of $77 million a year.

Benefits of Compliance

EPA calculated the annual benefit to accrue from a reduction in damage from accidental releases of regulated substances not already regulated under the OSHA PSM standard. EPA estimates $174 million in savings under each of these three approaches. Types of damages and costs considered in the analyses includes threats to human health (death or injury), response to these threats (evacuations, sheltering), threats to environment, and economic damages such as property damages and litigation. Although EPA assumed that additional benefits might be provided by making information available to the public in the RMP, these cannot be quantified.

It is unlikely that the annual benefits of these three options are exactly the same. For example, doing a detailed offsite consequence analysis will provide more accurate information. Because it is more accurate (i.e., less conservative), less evacuation will be required in response to accidental releases. This will result in a cost savings. Additionally, since the predictions from a comprehensive consequence analysis will be more accurate, it is to be expected that the consequences will be better known and more informed decisions can be made on when evacuations are needed, reducing costs.

It would be in a facility's best interest to conduct a detailed assessment of offsite consequences, EPA's final regulations and guidance notwithstanding. This is because doing so will enable a facility to more accu-

Table 10.1: Estimated Costs of Compliance	
Process	**Amount**
Process hazard analysis	$6,600 - $35,000
Training	$2,400 - $61,000
Process Information (per process)	$25,000 - $36,000
SOPs	$2,500 - $14,000
Overall costs for mfg. plants	$15,000 - $150,000
Non-manufacturers	$8,200 - $9,400
Service/Sales	$1,860 - $2,200
Facilities previously regulated under OSHA or TCPA will cost considerably less	

rately predict its offsite consequences from hypothetical releases and therefore more effectively plan either for sheltering, evacuation, or other contingencies. This will reduce the overall liability to the facility and will be expected to reduce cost resulting from any accidental release.

Estimate of Overall Costs of Compliance

Table 10.1 details the range of costs EPA has estimated for various sizes of facility. The EPA's total cost estimate of $494 million, when spread over 66,000 sources, works out to $7,500 per facility.

Table 10.2 is an analysis based on data contained in "Guidelines for Hazard Evaluation Procedures." It shows the cost just for the hazard assessment portion of an RMP. Note that the costs range for a simple-small facilities of $600 for a safety review to complex-large facilities of $12,400 for a cause/consequence analysis. Checklist analyses and HAZOP analyses fall in-between, ranging from $600 to $2,800 for a checklist analyses for a simple-small to a complex- large facilities and the HAZOP analyses from $2,300 to $10,500 for a complex large facility. These are based on an average labor cost including benefits of $40.00/hr. These numbers are also based on a range of labor hours provided for in the estimates in the guidelines for hazard evaluation procedures. Since filing the RMP with EPA or the state or delegated committee will also require looking at offsite consequences and documenting other aspects of the facility, it would appear that EPA cost estimates may be on the low side. The hazard assessment is only one portion of the costs to prepare and file the RMP.

Table 10.2: Hazard Assessment Techniques						
Task	Prep	Modeling	Evaluation	Documentation	Total Hours	Cost*
Simple/Small						
Safety Review	3	0	6	6	15	$600
Checklist Analysis	3	0	6	6	15	$600
HAZOP Analysis	10	0	16	32	58	$2,300
Cause/ConsequenceAnalysis	16	16	16	32	80	$3,200
Complex/Large						
Safety Review	16	0	32	36	84	$3,360
Checklist Analysis	16	0	32	24	72	$2,880
HAZOP Analysis	24	0	80	160	264	$10,560
Cause/ConsequenceAnalysis	30	60	60	160	310	$12,400

*Assumes cost rate of $40/hour.

Chapter 11

Avoiding Penalties

Like other areas of the Clean Air Act Amendments of 1990 with specific compliance requirements, there are significant penalties possible for noncompliance. Title VII of the Clean Air Act Amendments of 1990 prescribe penalties possible for various types of noncompliance. The penalties for noncompliance with the RMP regulations include up to $25,000 per day of violation and, additionally, can involve criminal penalties for responsible individuals.

The only sure way to avoid potential penalties under the RMP program is to develop a sound plan, follow the plan completely, and have no accidents. In order to follow the plan you have in place, you will need to complete the following actions for all processes with regulated substances in greater than TQ quantities:

❑ Conduct a hazard assessment
❑ Identify offsite consequences of accidental releases
❑ Conduct required training
❑ File the plan

You will also have to notify appropriate regulatory agencies, including the U.S. EPA, the local emergency planning commission, other designated agencies at the state level, and first responders.

Ensuring Compliance

Reporting an accident is the first line of defense in avoiding penalties. If no accidental releases occur, particularly if none occur for more than a five-year period, this will provide strong evidence that the hazard assessment and measures taken to reduce the risks of accidental release have been effective. Likewise, if accidents involving releases of hazardous or toxic substances do occur and no one is killed seriously injured as a result, it could also be argued that the plan worked and was appropriate as well as effective.

If, however, accidental releases occur and employees or offsite residents are injured or killed as a result, it could be argued that, EPA or state agency approval not withstanding, the hazard assessment or plan was not adequate to prevent the accident from occurring or that the response to the accident was inadequate. In this instance, the general duty provisions may also prove troubling for the owner or operator.

There is another potential compliance issue under the RMP regulations. This is the audit program required under Section 68.220. Under this section, the designated agency is required to periodically audit the risk management plan submitted under the final RMP regulations, to review the adequacy of the RMPs, and to require the revision of RMPs, when necessary, to ensure compliance with the regulations.

Compliance Audit Criteria

Implementing agencies are required to select facilities for audits based on the following criteria:

❑ Accident history of the stationary source
❑ Accident history of other stationary sources in the same industry

- ❑ Quantity of regulated substances present at the stationary source
- ❑ Location of the regulated substances present at the stationary source
- ❑ Location of the stationary source and its proximity to the public and environmental receptors
- ❑ Presence of specific regulated substances
- ❑ Hazards identified in the RMP
- ❑ Plan providing for neutral random oversight

There is an automatic exemption for facilities with a "star of merit" ranking under OSHA's Voluntary Protection Program. These facilities are exempt from audits based on the accident history of other sources in the same industry and under the requirement that the audits be based on a plan providing for neutral random oversight.

Inspections and Notices of Deficiency

The implementing agency is required, under the regulations, to have access to the facility, all supporting documentation for the RMP, and access to locations that are part of the facility where an accidental release could occur. As a result of an audit, the agency may issue the owner/operator a written preliminary determination of necessary revisions to the RMP to ensure the RMP meets the requirements of the regulations. Notices of deficiency must include references to appropriate guidance material, including those published by industry groups such as the AIChE, CCPS, ASME, and API. The audit results should include a timetable for implementation. Facilities are required to respond to the audit results in writing, within ninety (90) days of the issuance of a preliminary determination, or within a shorter period of time if an implementing agency specifies in a preliminary determination that this is necessary to protect public health and the environment. Facilities are afforded the opportunity to respond to the audit findings before a final determination is provided by the agency. The implementation schedule will be part of the final determination issued by the implementing agency. A facility will be considered in violation of the RMP requirements if it has not completed all required action within thirty (30) days of the schedule contained in the final determination.

EPA also considered having the public petition process to be one of the factors for setting audits for operating facilities. EPA rejected this approach to date so that public petitions are not a way for a facility to be subject to an audit under the program. Under various Clean Air Act provisions, however, the public does have the right to citizen suit and whistleblower protection. Under these provisions, employees may report their employer for violations of the regulations and, under citizen supervision, members of the public or environmental groups may sue to require a facility to fully comply with the requirements of the Clean Air Act and the RMP regulations.

Accident Investigation

In addition to the other requirements for the RMP, if an accident does occur, a facility must comply with the self investigation requirement of Section 68.81 (Program 3) or Section 68.60 (Program 2), which is required to be completed within 48 hours of the accident. Failure to initiate an investigation, to complete it, and to file a report in a timely manner are possible grounds for penalties.

Chapter 12

Coordinating with OSHA's Process Safety Management Standard

The requirements of both the OSHA Process Safety Management (PSM) (29 CFR 1910.119) Program and EPA's Risk Management Program (RMP) standard are intended to eliminate or mitigate the consequences of releases of extremely hazardous substances. These standards emphasize the application of management controls when addressing the risks associated with handling or working near such hazardous chemicals.

Comparing RMP and PSM

The main differences between the EPA RMP standard and the OSHA PSM standard are those mandated by the CAA, such as the hazard assessment (offsite consequence analysis, the five-year accident history), the emergency response requirements, registration, and the RMP submission to the Chemical Safety Board, implementing agency, SERC, and LEPC. In addition, for some elements of the two programs, OSHA's focus is on workplace impacts while EPA's focus is on offsite consequences, reflecting the differing statutory mandates of the two programs. The OSHA standard includes elements specific to worker issues that EPA has not included in its proposed rule. EPA anticipates that facilities in compliance with the requirements in the OSHA rule also will be in compliance with EPA's prevention program elements. That is, for most prevention program elements, facilities that are in compliance with OSHA's process safety management standard will not need to do anything different or create different onsite documentation to comply with EPA's prevention program requirements.

Because EPA's list of chemicals and thresholds and OSHA's list and thresholds are not identical (EPA covers more substances with acute toxic effects, fewer flammables and explosives, and no reactives) and because OSHA does not cover state and local government employees, the universes of facilities covered by the two rules are not identical, although they substantially overlap.

Since both the PSM standard and the RMP standards have been developed pursuant to requirements of the Clean Air Act Amendments (CAAA) of 1990, section 304(a), there are many common elements between the two standards. While both these standards deal with the prevention of releases of extremely/highly hazardous substances, the OSHA PSM standard is designed to protect workers within a covered facility, while the focus of the EPA RMP Program is to protect the general public outside a covered facility. Although the requirements of both these programs overlap, it is the stated goals of both agencies, OSHA and EPA, that duplicative compliance burdens and requirements should be simplified and minimized. EPA has coordinated with OSHA and the Department of Transportation (DOT) in developing the RMP Standard. To the extent possible, covered sources will not face inconsistent requirements under these agencies' rules.

In this chapter, we will examine the relationships between the OSHA PSM standard and the RMP regulations, review in detail the requirements of the OSHA

PSM program, and determine how their respective compliance requirements can be mutually dependent.

OSHA's PSM Standard for Highly Hazardous Chemicals

OSHA's final rule on the Process Safety Management of Highly Hazardous Chemicals, Explosives and Blasting Agents, published in the *Federal Register* on February 24, 1992 (57 FR 6356), promulgated a standard for the management of hazards associated with processes using highly hazardous chemicals (HHCs). The process safety management standard targets HHCs that have the potential to cause a catastrophic incident. This standard as a whole is aimed at helping employers in their efforts to prevent or mitigate chemical releases that could lead to a catastrophe in the workplace and possibly to the surrounding community. To control these types of hazards, employers are required to develop the necessary expertise, experience, judgment and proactive initiative within their workforce to properly implement and maintain an effective process safety management program. The final PSM rule became effective on May 26, 1992.

Background of the OSHA PSM Standard

Regardless of what industry is using highly hazardous chemicals, there exists a potential for an accidental release if a highly hazardous chemical is not properly controlled. This, in turn, presents the potential for a devastating incident. Recent major incidents included the 1984 Bhopal incident, resulting in more than 2,000 deaths; the October 1989 Phillips 66 Chemical Plant incident, resulting in 24 deaths and 132 injuries; the July 1990 ARCO Chemical incident, resulting in 17 deaths; the July 1990 BASF incident, resulting in 2 deaths and 41 injuries; and the May 1991 IMC incident resulting in 8 deaths and 128 injuries.

After the 1984 Bhopal, India incident, OSHA determined that it was necessary to immediately investigate U.S. producers and users of methyl isocyanate. This investigation indicated that while the chemical industry was subject to OSHA's general industry standards, these standards did not presently contain specific coverage for chemical industry process hazards, nor did they specifically address employee protection from large releases of hazardous chemicals.

The promulgation of the PSM final rule reflected OSHA's conclusions that a standard was necessary to promote safe and healthful places of employment for employees in industries that had processes involving highly hazardous chemicals. Additionally, OSHA was convinced that compliance with the final standard provisions would mitigate many of the hazards present in processes involving highly hazardous chemicals. As a result, OSHA believed the risk of death or injury to employees exposed would be significantly reduced by promulgating the PSM standard.

Finally, the Clean Air Act Amendments of 1990 required OSHA to develop a chemical process safety standard containing certain minimum requirements to prevent accidental releases of chemicals that could pose a threat to employees [Section 304(a)]. In addition to being convinced that a process safety management standard was necessary and appropriate, OSHA fulfilled its obligation under the Clean Air Act Amendments in developing the PSM standard.

Primary Objectives of the PSM Standard

The major objective of process safety management of highly hazardous chemicals is the prevention of releases of hazardous chemicals. In order to accomplish this objective, a systematic approach to evaluating the whole process is needed. Consequently, process design, process technology, operational and maintenance activities and procedures, non-routine activities and procedures, emergency preparedness plans and procedures, training programs, and other elements that impact the process, are all considered in the evaluation. Incorporated design and operational considerations of the process must be evaluated and strengthened to ensure their effectiveness at each level. Process safety management is the proactive identification, evaluation, and mitigation or prevention of chemical releases that could occur as a result of failures in process, procedures, or equipment.

The standard emphasizes the application of management controls, rather than specific engineering guidelines, when addressing the risks associated with handling or working near hazardous chemicals. The

PSM standard focuses on the quantities and types of HHCs, rather than the size of a facility, as the determining factors in ascertaining the degree of risk.

Relationship between OSHA'S PSM Standard and the Clean Air Act Amendments

Approximately four months after the publication of OSHA's proposed standard for process safety management of highly hazardous chemicals, the Clean Air Act Amendments were enacted into law (November 15, 1990). The CAAA required, in Section 304, that the Secretary of Labor, in coordination with the Administrator of the Environmental Protection Agency, promulgate, pursuant to the Occupational Safety and Health Act of 1970, a chemical process safety standard to prevent accidental releases of chemicals that could pose a threat to employees.

The CAAA required that the standard include the development of a list of highly hazardous chemicals to include toxic, flammable, highly reactive, and explosive substances. The CAAA specified the minimum elements that must be covered by the such a standard. Consequently, the OSHA PSM standard requires employers to do the following:

1. Develop and maintain written safety information identifying workplace chemical and process hazards, equipment used in the processes, and technology used in the processes.

2. Perform a workplace hazard assessment, including, as appropriate, identification of potential sources of accidental releases, an identification of any previous release within the facility that had a likely potential for catastrophic consequences in the workplace, estimation of workplace effects of a range of releases, estimation of the health and safety effects of such range on employees.

3. Consult with employees and their representatives on developing and conducting hazard assessments and developing chemical accident prevention plans and providing access to these and other records required under the standard.

4. Establish a system to respond to the workplace hazard assessment findings, which addresses prevention, mitigation, and emergency responses.

5. Periodically review the workplace hazard assessment and response system.

6. Develop and implement written operating procedures for the chemical process, including procedures for each operating phase, operating limitations, and safety and health considerations.

7. Provide written safety and operating information to employees and train employees in operating procedures, emphasizing hazards and safe practices.

8. Ensure contractors and contract employees are provided appropriate information and training.

9. Train and educate employees and contractors in emergency response in a manner as comprehensive and effective as that required by the regulation promulgated pursuant to section 126(d) of the Superfund Amendments and Reauthorization Act.

10. Establish a quality assurance program to ensure that initial process-related equipment, maintenance materials, and spare parts are fabricated and installed consistent with design specifications.

11. Establish maintenance systems for critical process-related equipment including written procedures, employee training, appropriate inspections, and testing of such equipment to ensure ongoing mechanical integrity.

12. Conduct pre-startup safety reviews of all newly installed or modified equipment.

13. Establish and implement written procedures to manage change to process chemicals, technology, equipment, and facilities.

14. Investigate every incident that results in, or could have resulted in, a major accident in the workplace, with any findings to be reviewed by operating personnel and modifications made, if appropriate.

Catastrophic Releases

Catastrophic releases are major uncontrolled emissions, fires, or explosions, involving one or more highly hazardous chemicals that present serious danger to employees in the workplace.

Processes Subject to the Requirements of OSHA'S PSM Standard

The provisions of OSHA's PSM Standard apply to the following processes:

❑ A process that involves a chemical at or above the specified threshold quantities

❑ A process that involves a flammable liquid or gas [as defined in 1910.1200(c) of the regulations] on site in one location, in a quantity of 10,000 pounds (4535.9 kg) or more except for the following:

   • Hydrocarbon fuels used solely for workplace consumption as a fuel (e.g., propane used for comfort heating, gasoline for vehicle refueling), if such fuels are not a part of a process containing another highly hazardous chemical covered by the PSM standard

   • Flammable liquids stored in atmospheric tanks or transferred which are kept below their normal boiling point without benefit of chilling or refrigeration

The requirements of OSHA's PSM Standard do not apply to these facilities:

❑ Retail facilities
❑ Oil or gas well drilling or servicing operations
❑ Normally unoccupied remote facilities

Elements of Process Safety Management Programs

There are fourteen basic elements that are required in the OSHA PSM Program. Since there can be many common elements between an OSHA PSM Program and an EPA RMP Program (especially a Program 2 and/or a Program 3), compliance with the elements of the PSM Standard often is the basis for effective compliance with the RMP standard. Therefore, it is essential to understand what compliance with each of the 14 required PSM elements entails. The following is a brief summary and listing of each of these requirements.

Employee Participation

Employers are required by the PSM Standard to:

❑ Develop a written plan of action regarding the implementation of the employee participation required by the PSM regulation.

❑ Consult with employees and their representatives on the conduct and development of process hazards analyses and on the development of the other elements of process safety management in the PSM standard.

❑ Provide to employees and their representatives access to process hazard analyses and to all other information required to be developed under the PSM standard.

Process Safety Information

Employers are required to complete a compilation of written process safety information before conducting any process hazard analysis required by the standard. The compilation of written process safety information is to enable the employer and the employees involved in operating the process to identify and understand the hazards posed by those processes involving highly hazardous chemicals. This process safety information includes information pertaining to the hazards of the highly hazardous chemicals used or produced by the process, information pertaining to the technology of the process, and information pertaining to the equipment in the process.

Specific information requirements include the following:

❑ **Information pertaining to the hazards of the highly hazardous chemicals in the process**: This information should at least include toxicity information; permissible exposure limits; physical data; reactivity data; corrosivity data; thermal and chemical stability data; hazardous effects of inadvertent mixing of different materials that could foreseeably occur.

❑ **Information pertaining to the technology of the process**: This information should include at least a block flow diagram or simplified process flow diagram, the process chemistry; the maximum intended inventory, the safe upper and lower limits for such items as temperatures, pressures, flows or compositions; and, an evaluation of the consequences of deviations, including those affecting the safety and health of employees.

❑ **Information pertaining to the equipment in the process**: This information should include all known materials of construction, piping and instrument diagrams (PI&D's), electrical classifications, relief system design and design basis, ventilation system design, design codes and standards employed, material and energy balances for processes built after May 26, 1992, and safety systems (e.g. interlocks, detection or suppression systems).

The employer must document that equipment complies with recognized and generally accepted good engineering practices.

For existing equipment designed and constructed in accordance with codes, standards, or practices that are no longer in general use, the employer must determine and document that the equipment is designed, maintained, inspected, tested, and operating in a safe manner.

Process Hazard Analysis

The employer is required to perform an initial process hazard analysis (hazard evaluation) on processes covered by the OSHA PSM standard. This process hazard analysis must be appropriate to the complexity of the process and must identify, evaluate, and control the hazards involved in the process. Employers must determine and document the priority order for conducting process hazard analyses based on a rationale that includes such considerations as extent of the process hazards, number of potentially affected employees, age of the process, and operating history of the process. All initial process hazards analyses are required to have been completed by May 26, 1997.

Process hazard analyses are required to be performed by a team with expertise in engineering and process operations, and the team must include at least one employee who has experience and knowledge specific to the process being evaluated. Also, one member of the team must be knowledgeable in the specific process hazard analysis methodology being used.

Employers must establish a system to promptly address the team's findings and recommendations; ensure that the recommendations are resolved in a timely manner and that the resolution is documented; document what actions are to be taken; complete actions as soon as possible; develop a written schedule of when these actions are to be completed; communicate the actions to operating, maintenance, and other employees whose work assignments are in the process and who may be affected by the recommendations or actions.

At least every five (5) years after the completion of the initial process hazard analysis, the process hazard analysis must be updated and revalidated by a team meeting the necessary requirements, to ensure that the process hazard analysis is consistent with the current process.

Operating Procedures

Employers must develop and implement written operating procedures that provide clear instructions for safely conducting activities involved in each covered process consistent with the process safety information and must address at least the following elements:

❑ Steps for each operating phase
❑ Operating limits
❑ Safety and health considerations
❑ Safety systems and their functions

Operating procedures must always be readily accessible to employees who work in or maintain a process and are required to be reviewed as often as necessary to ensure that they reflect current operating practice, including changes that result from changes in process chemicals, technology, and equipment, and changes to facilities. Employers must certify annually that these operating procedures are current and accurate.

Employers must develop and implement safe work practices to provide for the control of hazards during operations such as lockout/tagout; confined space entry; opening process equipment or piping; and control over entrance into a facility by maintenance, contractor, laboratory, or other support personnel. These safe work practices must apply to both employees and contractor employees.

Training

All employees, including maintenance and contractor employees, involved with highly hazardous chemicals need to fully understand the safety and health hazards of the chemicals and processes they work with for the protection of themselves, their fellow employees, and the citizens of nearby communities. Training conducted in compliance with Section 1910.1200, the Hazard Communication Standard, will help employees to be more knowledgeable about the chemicals they work with, as well as familiarize them with reading and understanding MSDSs. However, additional training in subjects such as operating procedures and safety work practices, emergency evacuation and response, safety procedures, routine and nonroutine work authorization activities, and other areas pertinent to process safety and health need to be covered by an employer's training program.

In establishing their training programs, employers must clearly define the employees to be trained and what subjects are to be covered in their training. Employers in setting up their training program will need to clearly establish the goals and objectives they wish to achieve with the training that they provide to their employees. The learning goals or objectives should be written in clear, measurable terms before the training begins. These goals and objectives need to be tailored to each of the specific training modules or segments. Employers should describe the important actions and conditions under which the employee will demonstrate competence or knowledge as well as what is acceptable performance.

Initial Training

Each employee presently involved in operating a process, and each employee before being involved in operating a newly assigned process, must be trained in an overview of the process and in the operating procedures. The training is required to include emphasis on the specific safety and health hazards, emergency operations including shutdown, and safe work practices applicable to the employee's job tasks. In lieu of initial training for those employees already involved in operating a process on May 26, 1992, an employer may certify in writing that the employee has the required knowledge, skills, and abilities to safely carry out the duties and responsibilities as specified in the operating procedures.

Refresher Training

Employers must provide refresher training at least every three years, and more often if necessary, to each employee involved in operating a process to ensure that the employee understands and adheres to the current operating procedures of the process. The employer, in consultation with the employees involved in operating the process, must determine the appropriate frequency of refresher training.

Training Documentation

The employer must ascertain that each employee involved in operating a process has received and understood the training required by this paragraph. The employer must prepare a record that contains the identity of the employee, the date of training, and the means used to verify that the employee understood the training.

Working with Contractors

The PSM standard applies to contractors performing maintenance or repair, turnaround, major renovation, or specialty work on or adjacent to a covered process. It does not apply to contractors providing incidental services that do not influence process safety, such as janitorial work, food and drink services, laundry, delivery, or other such services.

"Host" Employer Responsibilities

Employers, when selecting a contractor, must obtain and evaluate information regarding the contract employer's safety performance and programs and must inform contract employers of the known potential fire, explosion, or toxic release hazards related to the contractor's work and the process. Employers must explain to contract employers the applicable provisions of the Emergency Action Plan required by the PSM standard.

Employers must also develop and implement safe work practices to control the entrance, presence, and exit of contract employers and contract employees in covered processes, periodically evaluate the performance of contract employers in fulfilling their obligations, and maintain a contract employee injury and illness log related to the contractor's work in process areas.

Contract Employer Responsibilities

Contract employers must ensure that each contract employee is trained in the work practices necessary to safely perform his or her job, must ensure that each contract employee is instructed in potential fire, explosion, or toxic release hazards related to his or her job and the process, and the applicable provisions of the emergency action plan.

In addition, contract employers must document that each contract employee has received and understood the required training and must prepare a record that contains the identity of the contract employee, the date of training, and the means used to verify that the employee understood the training. They must also ensure that each contract employee follows the safety rules of the facility including the safe work practices, and must advise the "host" employer of any unique hazards presented by the contract employer's work, or of any hazards found by the contract employer's work.

Pre-Startup Safety Review

The employer must perform a pre-startup safety review for new facilities and for modified facilities when the modification is significant enough to require a change in the process safety information. The pre-startup safety review must confirm that, prior to the introduction of highly hazardous chemicals to a process, construction and equipment are in accordance with design specifications and that safety, operating, maintenance, and emergency procedures are in place and are *adequate*. For new facilities, pre-startup reviews must confirm that a process hazard analysis has been performed, that recommendations have been resolved or implemented before startup, that modified facilities meet the "management of change" requirements, and that training of each employee involved in operating a process has been completed.

Mechanical Integrity

Employers will need to review their maintenance programs and schedules to see if there are areas where "breakdown" maintenance is used rather than an ongoing mechanical integrity program. Equipment used to process, store, or handle highly hazardous chemicals needs to be designed, constructed, installed, and maintained to minimize the risk of releases of such chemicals. This requires that a mechanical integrity program be in place to ensure the continued integrity of process equipment. Elements of a mechanical integrity program include the identification and categorization of equipment and instrumentation, inspections and tests, test-ing and inspection frequencies, development of maintenance procedures, training of maintenance personnel, the establishment of criteria for acceptable test results, documentation of test and inspection results, and documentation of manufacturer recommendations.

The first line of defense an employer has available is to operate and maintain the process as designed, and to keep the chemicals contained. This line of defense is backed up by the next line of defense, which is the controlled release of chemicals through venting to scrubbers or flares, or to surge or overflow tanks that are designed to receive such chemicals, etc. These lines of defense are the primary lines of defense or means to prevent unwanted releases. The secondary lines of defense include fixed fire protection systems, like sprinklers, water spray, or deluge systems; monitor guns; dikes; designed drainage systems; and other systems that would control or mitigate hazardous chemicals once an unwanted release occurs. These primary and secondary lines of defense are what the mechanical integrity program needs to protect and strengthen.

Application

Mechanical integrity requirements of the PSM standard apply to the following:
- Process equipment
- Pressure vessels and storage tanks
- Piping systems (including piping components such as valves)
- Relief and vent systems and devices
- Emergency shutdown systems
- Controls (including monitoring devices and sensors, alarms, and interlocks)
- Pumps

Written Procedures

The employer must establish and implement written procedures to maintain the ongoing integrity of process equipment.

Training for Process Maintenance Activities

The employer must train each employee involved in maintaining the ongoing integrity of process equipment in an overview of that process and its hazards and in the procedures applicable to the employee's job tasks to ensure that the employee can perform the job tasks in a safe manner.

Inspection and Testing

The employer must ensure that the following procedures are performed:

❑ Inspections and tests are to be performed on process equipment.

❑ Inspection and testing procedures must follow recognized and generally accepted good engineering practices.

❑ The frequency of inspections and tests of process equipment must be consistent with applicable manufacturers' recommendations and good engineering practices, and the frequency should be increased if determined to be necessary by prior operating experience.

❑ Each inspection and test that has been performed on process equipment must be adequately documented. The documentation must identify the date of the inspection or test, the name of the person who performed the inspection or test, the serial number or other identifier of the equipment on which the inspection or test was performed, a description of the inspection or test performed, and the results of the inspection or test.

Equipment Deficiencies

It is the employer's responsibility to correct deficiencies in equipment that are outside acceptable limits before further use or in a safe and timely manner when necessary means are taken to ensure safe operation.

Quality Assurance

The employer must ensure that equipment is properly designed, constructed, and maintained.

❑ In the construction of new plants and equipment, equipment must be suitably fabricated for the process application for which it will be used.

❑ Appropriate checks and inspections must be performed to ensure that equipment is installed properly and is consistent with design specifications and the manufacturer's instructions.

❑ Maintenance materials, spare parts, and equipment must be suitable for the process application for which they will be used.

Hot Work Permit

The employer must issue a hot work permit for hot work operations conducted on or near a covered process, and the permit must document that the fire pre-vention and protection requirements in 29 CFR 1910.252(a) have been implemented prior to beginning the hot work operations. It must indicate the date(s) authorized for hot work, identify the object on which hot work is to be performed, and be kept on file until completion of the hot work operations.

Management of Change

To properly manage changes to process chemicals, technology, equipment, and facilities, one must define what is meant by change. According to the OSHA process safety management standard, change includes all modifications to equipment, procedures, raw materials, and processing conditions other than "replacement in kind." These changes need to be properly managed by identifying and reviewing them prior to implementation of change. For example, the operating procedures contain the operating parameters (pressure limits, temperature ranges, flow rates, etc.) and the importance of operating within these limits. While the operator must have the flexibility to maintain safe operation within the established parameters, any operation outside of these parameters requires review and approval by a written management of change procedure.

Management of change covers changes in process technology and changes to equipment and instrumentation. Changes in process technology can result from changes in production rates, raw materials, experimentation, equipment unavailability, new equipment, new product development, change in catalyst, and changes in operating conditions to improve yield or quality. Equipment changes include, among others, change in materials of construction, equipment specifications, piping pre-arrangements, experimental equipment, computer program revisions, and changes in alarms and interlocks. Employers need to establish means and methods to detect both technical changes and mechanical changes.

Temporary changes have caused a number of catastrophes over the years, and employers need to establish ways to detect temporary changes as well as those that are permanent. It is important that a time limit for temporary changes be established and monitored since, without control, these changes may tend to become permanent.

Temporary changes are subject to the management of change provisions. In addition, the management of change procedures are used to ensure that the equipment and procedures are returned to their original or designed conditions at the end of the temporary change. Proper documentation and review of these changes is invaluable in ensuring that safety and health considerations are being incorporated into the operating procedures and the process.

The employer must establish and implement written procedures to manage changes (except for "replacements in kind") in process chemicals, technology, equipment, and procedures, and changes in facilities that affect a covered process. These procedures must ensure that the following considerations are addressed prior to any change:

- ❑ The technical basis for the proposed change
- ❑ Impact of change on safety and health
- ❑ Modifications to operating procedure
- ❑ Necessary time period for the change
- ❑ Authorization requirements for the proposed change

Employees involved in operating a process and maintenance and contract employees whose job tasks will be affected by a change in the process are required to be informed of, and trained in, the change prior to start-up of the process or affected part of the process. If a change covered by this paragraph results in a change in the process safety information required by the PSM regulations, such information must be updated accordingly. And, if a change covered by this paragraph results in a change in the operating procedures or practices required by the PSM standard, such procedures or practices must be updated accordingly.

Incident Investigation

Incident investigation is the process of identifying the underlying causes of incidents and implementing steps to prevent similar events from occurring. The intent of an incident investigation is for employers to learn from past experiences and thus avoid repeating past mistakes. The incidents for which OSHA expects employers to become aware and to investigate are the types of events that result in or could reasonably have resulted in a catastrophic release. Some of the events are sometimes referred to as "near misses"—meaning that a serious consequence did not occur, but could have.

Employers need to develop in-house capability to investigate incidents that occur in their facilities. A team needs to be assembled by the employer and trained in the techniques of investigation, including how to conduct interviews of witnesses, needed documentation, and report writing. A multidisciplinary team is better able to gather the facts of the event and to analyze them and develop plausible scenarios as to what happened, and why. Team members should be selected on the basis of their training, knowledge, and ability to contribute to a team effort to fully investigate the incident.

Employees in the process area where the incident occurred should be consulted, interviewed, or made members of the team. Their knowledge of the events form a significant set of facts about the incident that occurred. The report, its findings and recommendations, are to be shared with those who can benefit from the information. The cooperation of employees is essential to an effective incident investigation. The focus of the investigation should be to obtain facts and not to place blame. The team and the investigation process should clearly deal with all involved individuals in a fair, open, and consistent manner.

Specific requirements of an incident investigation include the following actions:

- ❑ The employer must investigate each incident that resulted in, or could reasonably have resulted in, a catastrophic release of highly a hazardous chemical in the workplace.
- ❑ An incident investigation must be initiated as promptly as possible, but not later than 48 hours following the incident.
- ❑ An incident investigation team must be established and must consist of at least one person knowledgeable in the process involved, including a contract employee if the incident involved work of the contractor, and other persons with appropriate knowledge and experience to thoroughly investigate and analyze the incident.
- ❑ A report must be prepared at the conclusion of the investigation that includes at a minimum:
  - Date of incident
  - Date investigation began
  - Description of the incident
  - Factors that contributed to the incident
  - Recommendations resulting from the investigation

The employer must establish a system to promptly address and resolve the incident report findings and recommendations. Resolutions and corrective actions must be documented. The report must be reviewed with all affected personnel whose job tasks are relevant to the incident findings, including contract employees, where applicable. Incident investigation reports must be retained for five (5) years.

Emergency Planning and Response

Each employer must address what actions employees are to take when there is an unwanted release of highly hazardous chemicals. Emergency preparedness will be intiated into action when an unwanted release occurs. Employers will need to decide the following: if they want employees to handle and stop small or minor incidental releases; whether they wish to mobilize the available resources at the plant and have them brought to bear on a more significant release; or whether they want their employees to evacuate the danger area and promptly escape to a planned safe zone, allowing the local community emergency response organizations to handle the release; or whether the they want to use some combination of these actions. Employers will need to select the number of emergency preparedness or tertiary lines of defense they plan to have and then develop the necessary plans and procedures for each. They must appropriately train employees in emergency duties and responsibilities before implementing these lines of defense.

At a minimum, employers must have an emergency action plan that will facilitate the prompt evacuation of employees after an unwanted release of a highly hazardous chemical. This means that the employer will have a plan that will be activated by an alarm system to alert employees when to evacuate and that will have the necessary support and assistance to get employees who are physically impaired to the safe zone as well. The intent of these requirements is to alert and move employees to a safe zone quickly. Delaying alarms or confusing alarms are to be avoided. The use of process control centers or similar process buildings in the process area as safe areas is discouraged by OSHA. Recent catastrophes have shown that a large life loss has occurred in these structures because of where they have been sited and because they are not necessarily designed to withstand over-pressures from shockwaves resulting from explosions in the process area.

The employer must establish and implement an emergency action plan for the entire plant in accordance with the provisions of 29 CFR 1910.38(a). In addition, the emergency action plan must include procedures for handling small releases. Employers covered under this standard may also be subject to the hazardous waste and emergency response provisions contained in 29 CFR 1910.120(a), (p) and (q).

Compliance Audits

Employers need to select a trained individual or assemble a trained team of people to audit the process safety management system and program. A small process or plant may need only one knowledgeable person to conduct an audit. The audit is to include an evaluation of the design and effectiveness of the process safety management system and a field inspection of the safety and health conditions and practices to verify that the employer's systems are effectively implemented. The audit should be conducted or led by a person knowledgeable in audit techniques who is impartial towards the facility or area being audited. The essential elements of an audit program include planning, staffing, conducting the audit, evaluation and corrective action, follow-up, and documentation.

*Planning for the Audit**

Planning is essential to the success of the auditing process. Each employer needs to establish the format, staffing, scheduling, and verification methods prior to conducting the audit. The format should be designed to provide the lead auditor with a procedure or checklist that details the requirements of each section of the standard. The names of the audit team members should be listed as well. The checklist, if properly designed, serves as the verification sheet, which provides the auditor with the necessary information to expedite the review and ensures that no requirements of the standard are omitted. This verification sheet format also identifies those elements that will require evaluations or responses to correct deficiencies. This sheet can also be used for developing the follow-up and documentation requirements.

*Selecting Audit Team Members**

The selection of effective audit team members is critical to the success of the program. Team members should be chosen for their experience, knowledge, and training and should be familiar with the processes and with auditing techniques, practices, and procedures. The size of the team will vary, depending on the size and complexity of the process under consideration. For a large, complex, highly instrumented plant, it may be desirable to have team members with expertise in process engineering and design, process chemistry, instrumentation and computer controls, electrical hazards and classifications, safety and health disciplines, maintenance, emergency preparedness, warehousing or shipping, and process safety auditing. The team may use part-time members to provide for the depth of expertise required, as well as for what is actually done or followed, compared to what is written.

Conducting an Effective Audit

An effective audit includes a review of the relevant documentation and process safety information, inspection of the physical facilities, and interviews with all levels of plant personnel. Utilizing the audit procedure and checklist developed in the planning stage, the audit team can systematically analyze compliance with the provisions of the standard and any other corporate policies that are relevant. For example, the audit team will review all aspects of the training program as part of the overall audit. The team will review the written training program for adequacy of content, frequency of training, effectiveness of training in terms of its goals and objectives, as well as to how it fits into meeting the standard's requirements, documentation, etc. Through interviews, the team can determine the employee's knowledge and awareness of the safety procedures, duties, rules, emergency response assignments, etc. During the inspection, the team can observe actual practices, such as safety and health policies, procedures, and work authorization practices. This approach enables the team to identify deficiencies and determine where corrective actions or improvements are necessary.

An audit is a technique used to gather sufficient facts and information, including statistical information, to verify compliance with standards. Auditors should select, as part of their planning, a sample size sufficient to give a degree of confidence that the audit reflects the level of compliance with the standard. The audit team, through this systematic analysis, should document areas that require corrective action, as well as those areas where the process safety management system is effective and working in an effective manner. This provides

a record of the audit procedures and findings, and serves as a baseline of operation data for future audits. It will assist future auditors in determining changes or trends from previous audits.

Employers must certify that they have evaluated compliance with the provisions of the OSHA PSM requirements at least every three years to verify that the procedures and practices developed under the standard are adequate and are being followed. The compliance audit must be conducted by at least one person knowledgeable in the process. A report of the findings of the audit must be developed, and the employer must promptly determine and document an appropriate response to each of the findings of the compliance audit, and further document that deficiencies have been corrected.

Employers must retain the two (2) most recent compliance audit reports.

Trade Secrets

Employers must make all information necessary to comply with the PSM requirements available to those persons responsible for compiling the process safety information, those assisting in the development of the process hazard analysis, those responsible for developing the operating, and those involved in incident, emergency planning and response, and compliance audits without regard to possible trade secret status of such information.

Nothing in the PSM requirements preclude the employer from requiring the persons to whom the information is made available to enter into confidentiality agreements not to disclose the information (as set forth in 29 CFR 1910.1200).

Subject to the rules and procedures set forth in 29 CFR 1910.1200(i)(1) through 1910.1200(i)(12), employees and their designated representatives must have access to trade secret information contained within the process hazard analysis and other documents required to be developed by the PSM standard.

Overlapping Requirements of EPA'S RMP and OSHA'S PSM Program

The Clean Air Act requires EPA to promulgate regulations to prevent accidental releases of regulated sub-

Table 12.1: Program Eligibility Criteria		
Program 1	**Program 2**	**Program 3**
No offsite accident history	The process is not eligible for Program 1 or 3	Process is subject to OSHA PSM
No public receptors in worst-case circle		Process is in SIC code 2611, 2812, 2819, 2821, 2865, 2869, 2873, 2879, or 2911
Emergency response co-ordinated with local responders		

stances and reduce the severity of those releases that do occur. EPA has promulgated rules that apply to all stationary sources with processes that contain more than a threshold quantity of a regulated substance. Processes will be divided into three categories based on the potential for offsite consequences associated with a worst-case accidental release; accident history; or compliance with the prevention requirements under OSHA's Process Safety Management Standard. Processes that have no potential impact on the public in the case of an accidental release will have minimal requirements. For other processes, sources will implement a risk management program that includes more detailed requirements for hazard assessment, prevention, and emergency response. Processes in industry categories with a history of accidental releases and processes already complying with OSHA's Process Safety Management Standard will be subject to a prevention program that is identical to parallel elements of the OSHA Standard. For more specifics, please refer to "Common Elements in OSHA's PSM Standard and EPA's RMP Program," which appears later in this chapter.

Program Applicability

Under the EPA Risk Management Program, processes subject to these requirements are divided into Programs 1, 2, and 3. EPA uses the term "Program" to avoid confusion with Tier I and Tier II forms submitted under EPCRA, also known as Title III of the Superfund Amendments and Reauthorization Act of 1986 (SARA Title III). Eligibility for any given program is based on process criteria so that classification of one process in a program does not influence the classification of other processes

at the source. For example, if a process meets Program 1 criteria, the source need only satisfy Program 1 requirements for that process, even if other processes at the source are subject to Program 2 or Program 3. A source, therefore, could have processes in one or more of the three programs.

Program 1 is applicable to any process that has not had an accidental release with offsite consequences in the five years prior to the submission date of the RMP and has no public receptors within the distance to a specified toxic or flammable endpoint associated with a worst-case release scenario.

Program 3 applies to processes in Standard Industrial Classification (SIC) codes 2611 (pulp mills), 2812 (chlor-alkali), 2819 (industrial inorganics), 2821 (plastics and resins), 2865 (cyclic crudes), 2869 (industrial organics), 2873 (nitrogen fertilizers), 2879 (agricultural chemicals), and 2911 (petroleum refineries). Program 3 also applies to all processes subject to the OSHA Process Safety Management (PSM) standard (29 CFR 1910.119), unless the process is eligible for Program 1. Owners or operators will need to determine individual SIC codes for each covered process to determine whether Program 3 applies.

Common Elements in OSHA'S PSM Standard and EPA's RMP Program

EPA has developed seven specific elements for the Program 2 Prevention Program: safety information (Section 68.48), hazard review (Section 68.50), operating procedures (Section 68.52), training (Section 68.54), maintenance (Section 68.56), compliance audits (Section 68.58), and incident investigation (Section 68.60). Most

Table 12.2: Comparison of Program Requirements		
Program 1	**Program 2**	**Program 3**
Hazard Assessment		
Worst-case analysis 5-year accident history	Worst-case analysis Alternative releases 5-year accident history	Worst-case analysis Alternative releases 5-year accident history
Management Program		
	Document management system	Document management system
Prevention Program		
Certify no additional steps needed	Safety Information Hazard Review Operating Procedures Training Maintenance Incident Investigation Compliance Audit	Process Safety Information Process Hazard Analysis Operating Procedures Training Mechanical Integrity Incident Investigation Compliance Audit Management of Change Pre-startup Review Contractors Employee Participation Hot Work Permits
Emergency Response Program		
Coordinate with local responders	Develop plan and program	Develop plan and program
Risk Management Plan Contents		
Executive Summary Registration Worst-case data 5-year accident history Certification	Executive Summary Registration Worst-case data Alternative release data 5-year accident history Prevention program data Emergency response data Certification	Executive Summary Registration Worst-case data Alternative release data 5-year accident history Prevention program data Emergency response data Certification

Program 2 processes are likely to be relatively simple and located at smaller businesses. EPA believed owners or operators of Program 2 processes could successfully prevent accidents without a program as detailed as the OSHA PSM, which was primarily designed for the chemical industry. EPA combined and tailored elements common to OSHA's PSM and EPA's notice of proposed rulemaking (NPRM) to generate Program 2 requirements and applied them to non-petrochemical industry processes. EPA is also developing model risk management programs (and RMPs) for several industry sectors that will have Program 2 processes. These model guidances will help sources comply by providing standard elements that can be adopted to a specific source. EPA expects that many Program 2 processes will already be in compliance with most of the requirements through compliance with other federal regulations, state laws, industry standards and codes, and good engineering practices. The model RMP EPA has developed is for the propane industry and can be found in Appendix F.

The Program 3 Prevention Program includes the requirements of the OSHA PSM standard, 29 CFR 1910.119(c) through (m) and (o), with minor wording changes to address statutory differences. This makes it clear that one accident prevention program to protect workers, the general public, and the environment will satisfy both OSHA and EPA. For elements that are in both the EPA and OSHA rules, EPA has used OSHA's language verbatim, with the following changes: the replacement of the terms as shown in Table 12.3; the dele-

Table 12.3: OSHA vs. EPA Terminology	
OSHA	**EPA**
highly hazardous substance	regulated substance
employer	owner or operator
standard	part or rule
facility	stationary source

tion of specific references to workplace impacts or to "safety and health"; changes to specific schedule dates; and changes to references within the standard. The "safety and health" and "workplace impacts" references occur in OSHA's PSM standard in process safety information [29 CFR 1910.119 (d)(2)(E)], process hazards analysis [29 CFR 1910.119(e)(3)(vii)], and incident investigation [29 CFR 1910.119(m)(1)].

Under the final rule, PHAs conducted for OSHA are considered adequate to meet EPA's requirements. They will be updated on the OSHA schedule (i.e., by the fifth anniversary of their initial completion). This approach will eliminate any need for duplicative analyses. Documentation for the PHA developed for OSHA will be sufficient to meet EPA's purposes.

EPA anticipates that sources whose processes are already in compliance with OSHA PSM will not need to take any additional steps or create any new documentation to comply with EPA's Program 3 Prevention Program. Any PSM modifications necessary to account for protection of public health and the environment along

with protection of workers can be made when PSM elements are updated under the OSHA requirements.

EPA and OSHA Enforcement Authority

Under the EPA RMP Program, changes are included and designed to ensure that OSHA retains its oversight of actions designed to protect workers while EPA retains its oversight of actions to protect public health and the environment.

EPA has modified the OSHA definition of catastrophic release, which serves as the trigger for an incident investigation, to include events "that present imminent and substantial endangerment to public health and the environment." As a result, the RMP rule requires investigation of accidental releases that pose a risk to the public or the environment, whereas the OSHA rule does not. EPA recognizes that catastrophic accidental releases primarily affect the workplace and that this change will have little effect on incident investigation programs already established. However, EPA needs to ensure that problems that could have had only an offsite impact are also addressed.

In the CAAA of 1990, Congress adopted a number of provisions aimed at reducing the number and severity of chemical accidents. The accident prevention requirements for which EPA is responsible are included primarily in the new subsection (r) of Section 112 of the Clean Air Act (42 U.S.C. 7412), which also establishes a chemical safety and hazard investigation board to investigate chemical accidents. Under subsection (r) and other CAAA provisions, EPA will conduct research on topics related to chemical accident prevention.

EPA and OSHA are working closely to coordinate interpretation and enforcement of PSM and RMP accident prevention programs. Under a recently signed Memorandum of Understanding, OSHA and EPA have jointly assumed the responsibilities for conducting investigations of major facility chemical accidents. The fundamental objectives of the EPA/OSHA chemical accident investigation program is to determine and report to the public the facts, conditions, circumstances and cause or probable root cause of any chemical accident that results in a fatality, serious injury, substantial property damage, or serious offsite impact, including a large scale evacuation of the general public. The ultimate goal of this joint accident investigation is to determine the root cause in order to reduce the likelihood of recurrence, minimize the consequences associated with accidental releases, and to make chemical production, processing, handling, and storage safer. Since both the PSM and RMP final rules are consistent with the mandate of the CAAA, it is anticipated that joint inspection activities related to the PSM standard will now arise between OSHA, the EPA, and the Chemical Safety and Hazard Investigation Board.

EPA activities include developing new and refining existing criteria with OSHA for selection of accidents for joint investigation or independent investigation by the lead agencies, enhancing investigation techniques of significant chemical accidents, and improving training to EPA, OSHA, and other parties on accident investigations techniques. To assist these operations, EPA and OSHA are now conducting activities to support an external expert panel to review accident investigation reports and make recommendations for further prevention and safety. Although this panel, the Chemical Safety and Hazard Investigation Board, was originally mandated by the 1990 Clean Air Act Amendments, there have never been any serious concerted efforts to fully implement it until recently because of White House political opposition and budget cuts. It now appears to be funded, for at least a year.[51]

---

[51]EPA/OSHA Joint Chemical Accident Investigation Report: EPA 550-R-97-002.

Chapter 13

Determining Program Levels of RMP

The final RMP regulations identify three program levels of RMP applicability. In earlier drafts of the regulations, EPA had called these program levels "tiers" of coverage. EPA, in the final regulations, changed the description to "program" levels to avoid confusion with the Emergency Planning and Community Right-to-Know regulations, which have tiers of reporting requirements for quantities of hazardous substances on site. Since these programs are very similar in certain aspects, EPA felt changing the nomenclature of the RMP Program to "programs" would help to avoid confusion.

There are three program levels specified in the final regulations—Program 1, Program 2, and Program 3.

Program 1 Eligibility

In promulgating the RMP standard, EPA revised the Program 1 eligibility requirements to clarify that the criteria are applied to a process, not the source as a whole. EPA has amended the list rule to delete the category of high explosives from the List of Regulated Substances. The types of accidents that will disqualify a process from Program 1 are now specified in the rule as those accidental releases of a regulated substance that lead to offsite exposure to the substance; its reaction products; over-pressure generated by an explosion involving the substance; or radiant heat generated by a fire involving the substance which resulted in offsite death or injury (as defined by the rule), or response or restoration activities at an environmental receptor. These accidental release criteria have eliminated the need for a definition of significant accidental release, which was deleted. Offsite environmental response or restoration includes such activities as collection, treatment, and disposal of soil, shutoff of drinking water, replacement of damaged vegetation, or isolation of a natural areas due to contamination associated with an accidental release. The distance calculation equation for flammables has been dropped, and the worst-case release endpoint for flammables is specified, which allows the source to use the reference tables or their own methodology to determine the distance to the endpoint. The requirement that the community have an EPCRA emergency response plan has been replaced by a requirement that the source coordinate emergency response procedures with local community responders.

Eligibility requirements include the following:

❏ For 5 years prior to the submission of an RMP, the process has not had an accidental release of a regulated substance where exposure to the substance, its reaction products, over-pressure generated by an explosion involving a substance, or radiant heat generated by a fire involving a substance lead to any of the following off site:

- death
- injury
- response or restoration activities for an exposure for an environmental receptor

❏ Additionally, the distance from a toxic or flammable endpoint for a worst-case release assessment conducted under the regulations (Subpart b, Section 68.25) is less than the distance to any public receptor as defined in Section 68.30, which includes the residential population, schools, hospitals, prisons, parks, and recreational areas, as well as major commercial office and industrial buildings.

❑ Emergency Response Procedures have been coordinated between the stationary source and local emergency planning and response organizations. What this means is that even though no accidental releases with offsite consequences have occurred within the last five (5) years that the facility must, nonetheless, be in dialog with its local emergency response agencies and committees and coordinate potential responses with them.

Program 1 represents the minimum level of compliance for sources subject to the RMP regulations by virtue of having threshold quantities of regulated substances on site.

Program 2 Eligibility

A new subpart C has been added to 40 CFR Part 68 to include the requirements of the Prevention Program for Program 2 processes. Program 2 facilities are those that are neither Program 1 (small sources) or Program 3 facilities. It is easier to identify Program 2 eligibility by looking at smaller facilities eligible for Program 1 on the one hand and large facilities for which Program 3 is mandatory. Those not covered in either of these subgroups qualify for Program 2 RMPs.

Program 3 Eligibility

The Program 3 prevention Program is codified in the new Subpart D of 40 CFR Part 68. As explained above, the subpart adopts the OSHA PSM standard with only minor editorial changes necessitated by the different statutory authorities of the two agencies. Throughout the subpart, "employer" has been changed to "owner or operator," "facility" to "stationary source," and "highly hazardous chemical" to "regulated substance." EPA has reordered the elements somewhat so that the order reflects the progression in which sources will generally implement the program. For example, process

safety information, which is needed for the PHA, now precedes that section. Pre-start-up review, which is the last step of management of change procedures, now follows management of change. The reordering does not reflect any change in the content.

Program 3 applicability is defined by the following three criteria:

❑ The facility does not qualify under Program Level 1
❑ The facility is covered by OSHA process safety management regulations (PSM)
❑ It falls into one of the following SIC Codes:

SIC Code	Description
2611	pulp mills
2812	chlor-alkali
2819	industrial organics, unclassified
2821	plastics and resins
2865	cyclic crudes and intermediates
2869	industrial organics(unclassified)
2873	nitrogen fertilizers
2879	agricultural chemicals (unclassified)
2911	petroleum refineries

If at any time a covered process at a facility no longer meets the eligibility criteria of its program level, the owner/operator must comply with the requirements of the new program level. The RMP must be updated within six months of a change that requires a revised process hazard analysis or hazard review, within six months of a change that requires revised offsite consequence analysis, and within six months of a change that alters the program level. Note that changes in program levels typically will require changes to the level of analysis.

Worst-Case Scenarios

Worse-Case Scenario Reporting

Section 68.25 of the regulation defines worse-case release scenario analysis and reporting.

For Program 1 facilities and processes, one worst-case scenario is required for each process.

For Programs 2 and 3, the regulations require one worst-case release scenario that is estimated to create the greatest distance in any direction to an endpoint provided in Appendix C resulting from an accidental release of regulated substances from covered processes under worst-case conditions, which will be defined in a later section.

Additional worst-case release scenarios for Programs 2 and 3 are required if the worst-case release from another covered process at the facility can potentially affect public receptors differently from those potentially affected by the worst-case scenario previously developed that produces the greatest distance to an endpoint. For example, a accidental release resulting in the greatest distance to an endpoint might occur from one portion of the facility and affect a certain offsite population. Another accident scenario could result in a release that could have a lesser distance to an endpoint and could affect a different offsite area. For example, see Figure 13.1. This figure shows a hypothetical facility with a production area and a shipping depot.

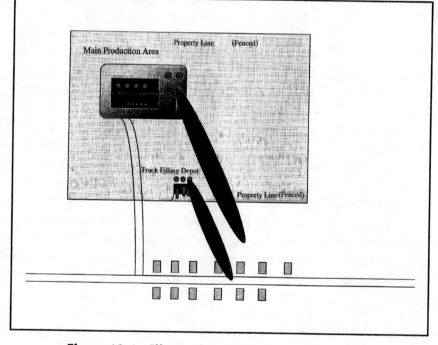

Figure 13.1: Illustration of Distance to Endpoints

This figure shows that a release from a production area in the main process area of the facility could result in a greatest distance to an endpoint; however, a secondary release from the truck filling area could also result in an endpoint off site, which would affect a different area entirely. Therefore, both of these scenarios would have to be analyzed and reported in the RMP.

Determination of Worst-Case Release Quantity

The RMP regulations specifically require that the maximum potential accidental release quantity be calculated as follows:

❑ For substances in a vessel, the greatest amount held in a single vessel, taking into account administrative controls that limit the maximum quantity

❑ For substances in pipes, the greatest amount in a pipe, taking into account administrative controls that limit the maximum quantity

These requirements specifically do not require the inclusion of combined quantities in multiple vessels. A facility is not precluded from looking at such scenarios should they, in its opinion, constitute possible realistic accidental release scenarios. For example, should a vessel be hypothesized to explode and if other nearby vessels contain the same chemical and could potentially be expected to be damaged as a result of vessel A exploding, it would not be inappropriate from a hypothetical point of view to include the multiple additional vessels in the release scenario. Even though the regulations do not require this to be done, in the real world, an explosion of vessel A could possibly result in a loss of the contents of additional vessels, and it would therefore be appropriate for a facility to look at the potential consequences of such multiple failures.

Worst-Case Release Scenario Analysis

The regulations specifically cover what assumptions must be made in worst-case scenario analyses. For toxic gases, the regulations require that regulated toxic substances that are normally gases at ambient temperature, and that are handled as a gas or as a liquid under pressure, be treated in a way that the owner/operator assume that the quantity in the vessel or pipe is released as a gas over a ten-minute interval. The release rate is to be assumed to be the total quantity divided by ten (per minute), unless passive mitigation systems are in place and may be expected to survive the accident itself. Therefore, the source term in pounds per minute will be the pounds of gas or liquid converted to gas divided by ten minutes.

For gases handled as refrigerated liquids at ambient pressure, if the potential release of the substance is not contained by a passive mitigation system or if the contained pool has a depth of one (1) centimeter or less, the owner/operator must assume that the substance is released as a gas in ten minutes.

Mitigation systems can be assumed to contain a refrigerated liquid as a pool, thereby slowing down evaporation. The owner/operator may assume that the quantity in the vessel or pipe is spilled instantaneously to form a liquid pool. The evaporation rate can be calculated at the boiling point of the substance and at the conditions specified in the regulations.

Calculating Evaporation of Pooled Liquids

For liquids that are spilled without passive containment systems, the regulations require that the assumption be made that the liquid spreads to a 1 centimeter deep pool, the area of which is defined as the surface area covered by the spill. Where dikes or other passive mitigation systems are in place, the surface area that contains liquid may be used to calculate the surface area of the pool. The evaporation rate of the spilled liquid can then be calculated, taking into account, for uncontained spills, the surface roughness and surface texture of the area covered by the spill. The volatilization rate must be calculated using the highest daily maximum temperature occurring in the past three years, the temperature of the substance in the vessel, and the concentration of the substance in the mixture or solution.

The release rate to the air is determined from the volatilization rate of the liquid pool. EPA has developed a methodology for this in the RMP Offsite Consequence Analysis Guidance. The guidance document warns that "(it) provides simple methods and reference tables for determining consequence distances for worst-case and alternative release scenarios. Results obtained using (the) methods are expected to be conservative. Conservative assumptions have been introduced to compensate for high levels of uncertainty."(Ref: RMP Offsite Consequence Analysis Guidance, May 24, 1996.)

Considering the conservative approach of the Consequence Analysis Guidance, many facilities may opt for the use of other air dispersion models. By using dispersion models, which are more specific to the characteristics of a release, a facility will likely be able to reduce distances to endpoints and fenceline concentrations. Proprietary and other models are allowable under the RMP regulations, provided the owner/operator gives EPA documentation on the assumptions and mathematical calculations performed in the model and describes the differences between the publicly available model and the proprietary model.

Flammables

Worst-case release scenarios for flammables must assume that the full quantity of a substance results in a vapor cloud explosion. A yield factor of 10% of the available energy released in an explosion must be used to determine the distance to the explosion endpoint if the model used is bases on a TNT-equivalent method.[52] The RMP offsite consequence analysis guidance is recommended for use in determining the distance to the overpressure endpoint. Consideration of passive mitigation systems is allowed for explosives, provided that the mitigation system is capable of withstanding the release event—assuming in this scenario that it would still function as intended.

Owners/operators are required to select the worst-case scenarios for flammables and for explosive regulated substances based on determining which scenario would result in a greater distance to an endpoint made beyond the stationary source boundary. Additionally, if other scenarios could result in a greater distance to an endpoint—including, for example, smaller quantities handled at a higher temperature and pressure or proximity to the boundary of the facility—these alternatives must be examined to determine the worst-case scenario.

Alternative Release Analysis

The owner/operator is required, under the final regulations, to identify and analyze at least one alternative release scenario in which a regulated toxic substance is

held in each covered process and at least one alternative release scenario to represent all flammable substances held in all covered processes. In determining alternative scenarios to consider, facilities are required to examine these areas:

- ❑ Areas where incidents are more likely to occur than a worst-case release scenario
- ❑ Scenarios that will produce an endpoint off site unless no such scenario exists

The regulations require the facilities to include the following release scenarios:

- ❑ Transfer hose releases due to splits or sudden hose uncoupling
- ❑ Process piping releases from failures at flanges, joints, welds, valves and valve seats, and drains or bleeds
- ❑ Process vessel or pump releases due to cracks, seal failure or drain, bleed, or plug failure
- ❑ Vessel overflowing and spill, overpressurization, and venting to relief valves or rupture discs and
- ❑ Shipping container mishandling and breakage or puncture leading to a spill

Assumptions to Apply

The regulations require that the impact assessment of the alternative release be examined in a manner consistent with those used for the worst-case scenario. Fixed meteorological conditions may be assumed, which include the standard lookup techniques provided by EPA as well as proprietary models and detailed air quality models that can reflect site conditions and varying meteorological parameters. If proprietary models are used, the RMP must allow the implementing agency to review the model, and the applicant must describe model features, the model itself, and how it differs from publicly available models.

In selecting the alternative scenarios for analysis, the owner or operator should take into account the five-year accident history of the facility and failure scenarios identified under its hazard assessment.

Chapter 14 will review the specific analytical methods for estimating emissions and for air quality modeling.

---

[5]40 CFR Part 68, 6/20/96.

Choosing Analytical Methods

HAZOP Options

Chapter 2 summarizes the shopping list of hazard analysis options. Which of these is chosen will have an impact on the type of information and the accuracy of information available with respect to calculating potential releases. For example, the safety review, checklist analysis and relative ranking techniques discussed in Chapter 2, Section 2.4 do not allow the computation of release quantities from various portions of a process. Process hazard assessment, HAZOP, fault tree, and event tree analysis allow the calculations of release quantities, assuming that you had process and instrumentation diagrams as well as schematics showing the components in the process and the sizes of each process vessel. Note that if the accident occurs as the release of material contained in piping, the dimensions of the piping are needed. Both the internal diameter of the piping and the length of each pipe run is necessary to calculate the volume contained in a pipe.

Consequence Analysis

EPA did not provide specific guidance in its proposed rule for RMP with respect to calculating worst-case alternative release scenarios, nor with respect to methodology or models for translating the worst-case release into an impact. EPA did not specify a method or technique because it felt that sources would contract with consultants or have available in house appropriate tools to calculate the impacts. EPA received a significant number of comments on the proposed rule and, based on these comments, decided that it would not be appropriate to require site-specific modeling for all facilities. Even though not conducting site-specific modeling would require that applicants ignore site-specific conditions and could potentially generate overly conservative and less realistic estimates of offsite impacts, EPA determined that generic modeling tools are adequate for many facilities and that they would generate "a greater understanding of the hazards posed by substances in emergency planning."[53] Other commenters indicated to EPA that this approach would be acceptable as long as sources were given the flexibility to use any appropriate modeling technique for offsite consequence analysis to take advantage of available expertise and to incorporate site-specific considerations to the hazard assessment.

EPA, taking commenters' suggestions into account, determined that it would develop a generic methodology and reference tables to be part of the offsite assessment guidance to assist sources with the analysis required under the rule. EPA believed "the technical guidance could be revised, expanded, and updated to address the rule requirements." The Methodologies for Offsite Consequence Analysis and look-up tables would be subject to public review prior to publication in the final rule. Once finalized, the tables would be published in technical guidance. EPA added that those who wished to conduct more sophisticated modeling could do so provided that the techniques used accounted for the modeling parameters described in the rule.

Cautionary Note

In recognition of this issue, EPA has prepared draft methodology and reference tables, which were published in January 1996.[54] The publication referenced in this citation, "RMP Offsite Consequence Analysis Guidance," provides guidance for sources wishing to use the look-up table approach. Keeping in mind that this approach is likely to produce worst-case concentrations that exceed any reasonably likely concentration to be produced by an accidental release. Therefore, using this technique, while saving effort and money for a facility, is likely to result in high predicted impacts and an off-site area exceeding the endpoints. In other words, if use of the look-up table does not produce an impact off site, then a source need not resort to more refined and labor and budget intensive techniques. If use of the look-up tables produces a offsite concentration exceeding the endpoint—that is, the distance to the endpoint is greater than the distance to the property line—then a facility should consider using a more refined technique. Finally,

should use of the look-up table produce a predicted concentration that is significantly off site, a source may wish to consider a more refined approach to define the concentrations within the distance to the endpoint.

For example: if the distance to an endpoint is two miles and the distance to the property line is one hundred feet, then there is a substantial area of unknown concentrations between the property line and the distance to the endpoint. Typically, the profile of centerline concentrations will look like Figure 14.1. This figure shows that the distance to maximum ground-level concentration is approximately one-half mile. Note that the figure also shows a property line at one hundred feet and the distance to an endpoint of two miles. If this distance to an endpoint is taken from the look-up table, we know only that we have a concern out to two miles from the facility. We do not know what happened between the facility and that two mile distance. In this example, concentrations are lower near the facility and reach a maximum at about one mile, and then begin

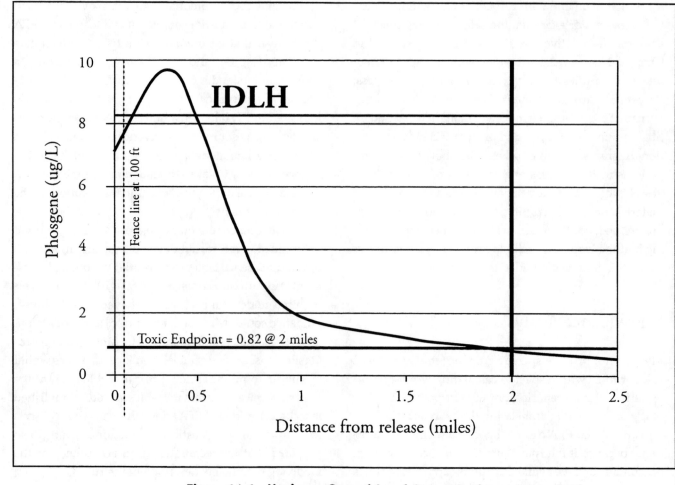

Figure 14.1: Maximum Ground-Level Concentrations

declining until they drop below the endpoint at two miles concentrations. In some instances, it is absolutely critical to know how concentrations behave out to the two-mile endpoint.

Look-up tables will not show the spatial distribution of concentrations surrounding a facility. Assuming a steady-state wind direction, the distance to a uniform concentration profile line (or isoline) will vary with the distance from the centerline. The distance to which a concentration drops below an endpoint value off-axis to a plume will be a function of wind speed and atmospheric stability. Atmospheric dispersion models are needed to calculate this concentration distribution. Additionally, in the real world, wind directions are not constant and, depending on the time frame over which predictions are needed, wind direction will vary. A more refined model is necessary to calculate the concentration distribution over time. All of these factors can be absolutely critical in making informed decisions on possible evacuation or sheltering.

Meteorological Data Relevant to Release Rate Estimation

Meteorological data specified in the final regulations include guidance that the ambient temperature/humidity for the worst-case release analysis of a regulated toxic substance represent the highest daily maximum temperature in the previous three years and average humidity for the site based on temperature/humidity data gathered at the facility or the local meteorological station. The regulations also indicate that the analysis may also be based on twenty-five degrees centigrade and 50% humidity as default parameter values.

The height of the release for the worst-case release must be analyzed assuming a ground level release. For alternative scenario analyses of regulated substance releases, the release height may be determined by the release scenario.

Surface roughness is another indicator of atmospheric stability. Surface roughness may be determined by the owner/operator as either urban or rural, based on the topography accident at the facility. The regulations define "urban" as a topography that includes many obstacles in the immediate area. These could include buildings or trees. "Rural" is applies to an area where there are no buildings and where the terrain is generally flat and unobstructed. This would require, for most facilities, use of urban coefficients. Since urban dispersion coefficients produce greater rates of plume spreading. This is not necessarily a conservative assumption, however it would be accurate for many facilities.

Other U.S. EPA air quality dispersion modeling guidance indicates that urban or rural dispersion coefficients should be selected based on the percentage of land use in the impact area.[55] Typically this is taken at 50%—meaning that if more than 50% of the area would represent rural topography, rural dispersion coefficients should be used.

Modeling dense or neutrally buoyant gas plumes can be based on look-up tables or models that are appropriate for that type of release, as in other types of releases.

For liquid spills that lead to evaporation and transport off site, the temperature of the released substance of refrigerated liquids should be considered to be released at the highest daily maximum temperature based on data from the previous three years appropriate for the operation, or at process temperature, whichever is higher. For alternative scenarios, the temperature may be considered to be that released at a process or ambient temperature that is appropriate for this scenario.

Models

The EPA has recommended the use of several dispersion models; however, facilities may use any model that meets the following criteria:

❏ The model is publicly or commercially available or is a proprietary model that the facility is willing to share with the agency.

❏ The model is appropriate for the chemicals and conditions being modeled.

❏ The facility uses the applicable definitions of worst-case scenarios.

❏ The facility uses the applicable parameters specified in the rule.

Several models are reviewed here; however, the author cannot recommend a specific model that will cover all release scenarios. Therefore, no preference to any specific model should be inferred from the model summaries below.

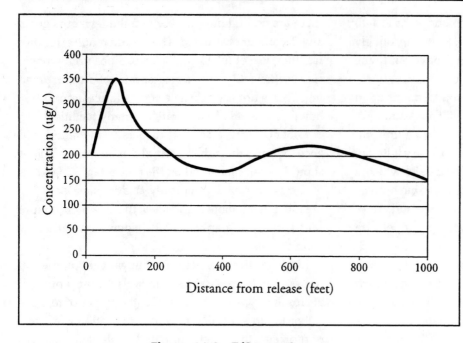

Figure 14.2: T/Screen Output

T/Screen

U.S. EPA has prepared a publicly available modeling tool called T/Screen. It is available at no cost from U.S. EPA at the Technology Transfer Web Site. This model can be used by owners or operators to assist in emergency response planning. It will calculate only centerline concentration profiles, as shown in Figure 14.2.

CAMEO/ALOHA

Additionally, more refined models are also available. A principal one endorsed by EPA is the CAMEO/ALOHA model package. CAMEO stands for Computer Aided Management of Emergency Operations, and ALOHA stands for Aerial Locations of Hazardous Atmospheres. This combination of models and plotting routines allows the calculation of the release of hazardous or toxic substances, including flammable and explosives from spills and process releases. It allows the use of actual meteorological data and will assist owners in calculating the offsite concentrations of regulated substances. Both are available from the National Safety Council. CAMEO was originally developed by NOAA, the National Oceanic and Atmospheric Administration. However, it is now administered and further developed by the National Safety Council. ALOHA allows the calculations of the spatial distribution of concentrations

and plotting of offsite impacts to be undertaken. Information on CAMEO/ALOHA can be obtained at www.nsc.org. Versions for Windows and Macintosh systems are available, for a fee.

CAMEO was originally developed by U.S. EPA and NOAA to help emergency managers in government and industry plan for and mitigate chemical accidents and to comply with requirements under the Emergency Planning and Community Right-to-Know Act of 1986 (SARA Title III). CAMEO is used in emergency response, emergency planning, and for regulatory compliance. It is designed to be used by local emergency planning committees (LEPCs), fire departments, state emergency response commissions (SERC), emergency planners, chemical facilities, health care facilities, universities, and anyone else who needs a computer model to assist in emergency response planning. CAMEO is unique in that it includes a library of safety and emergency response information on more than 4,700 hazardous chemicals. It can also be used to track chemical inventories, both in the community and in transit. It includes a sophisticated emergency air dispersion model, which can be used in hazard assessments and offsite consequence analysis.

Two of the components of CAMEO include the chemical database ALOHA, the air dispersion model, and Marplot, the mapping application. An example of Marplot output is shown as Figure 14.3. This figure taken from the National Safety Council homepage shows a chemical facility, a local highway, and a map of a plume centerline and off-centerline concentrations downwind. Note that, in this example, the plume travels southwesterly towards a hospital. The Marplot portion of the CAMEO suite allows the user to zoom in or zoom out, to do object or layer searching, to do road and base map editing, and to link the image to maps, plans, and other mapping programs, including geographic information system (GIS). CAMEO is available for purchase from the National Safety Council at a government agency price of $375.00 per single user and at a commercial price of $1,050.00 per single user, as of this writing.

Additionally, there are a number of other models that are recommended by EPA for use. These are described in the following sections.

DEGADIS

DEGADIS is a mathematical dispersion model that was developed by the United States Coast Guard. DEGADIS can be used as a refined modeling approach to estimate short-term ambient concentrations and the expected area of exposure to concentrations above specified threshold values for toxic chemical releases. The model is designed for use with dense gases such as LNG, LPG, ammonia, chlorine, and hydrogen fluoride. The model is chemical-specific and predicts dispersion of ground-level, area-source dense gas (or aerosol) clouds released with zero (initial) momentum. The model uses an atmospheric boundary layer approach over flat, level terrain. The model can be used for instantaneous, steady-state, and transient releases of dense gases.

If the plume returns to ground level, as in a negatively buoyant jet, DEGADIS predicts the ensuing ground-level plume dispersion.

SLAB

SLAB is a dispersion model for denser-than-air releases. SLAB was developed by the Lawrence Livermore National Laboratory, with support from the U.S. DOE, USAF Engineering and Services Center, and the American Petroleum Institute. The model allows for a variety of input parameters, including spill type, source properties, spill parameters, field parameters, and meteorological conditions.

The Spill Type parameters include a ground level evaporating pool, an elevated horizontal jet, a stack or elevated vertical jet, and a ground-based instantaneous release. Source properties, including molecular weight, vapor heat capacity, boiling point temperature, heat of vaporization, and liquid heat capacity can be defined for the material being released into the atmosphere. The

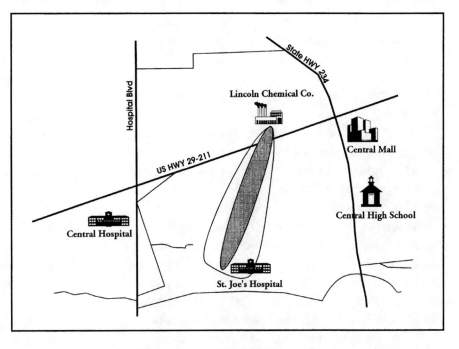

Figure 14.3: Marplot Output[56]

models also incorporates spill characteristics such as temperature of the source material, mass source rate, source area, instantaneous or continuous source duration, and source height.

SCREEN3

EPA's model SCREEN3 estimates maximum ground-level concentrations and the distance to the maximum concentration. The model incorporates the effects of building downwash for both the near wake and far wake regions. The model also successfully estimates concentrations due to inversion break-up and shoreline fumigation. SCREEN3 calculates the maximum concentration at any number of specified distances in flat or elevated simple terrain. The model determines the worst-case concentrations as it examines a full range of meteorological conditions, including all stability classes and wind speeds to find maximum impacts during each model run. SCREEN3 may not be applicable to some sources as it was devised to model these particular sources

- ❑ **Point sources:** stacks, soil vapor extraction vents
- ❑ **Area sources:** landfills, lagoons, VOCs emanating from a SuperFund site
- ❑ **Flares:** burning gas from a landfill gas collection
- ❑ **Volume sources:** leaking gases from a plant, conveyor belts.

SCREEN3 can only model one source at a time and requires source parameters such as emission rate, physical stack height, and stack gas exit velocity.

ISCST3: Industrial Source Complex Short Term Model

The ISCST3 model is used to model primary pollutants and continuous releases of toxic and hazardous waste pollutants. Although the model is not identified as a suggested model by RMP guidance, it is reviewed here for completeness. The model does allow for precipitation scavenging and dry deposition of gases and particulates, and includes both the thermal and mechanical turbulence associated with dispersion in the urban environment. Other models in this section do not treat these effects as well as ISCST3. The Industrial Source Complex model can handle multiple sources, including point, volume, area, and open pit source types. The model can account for the effects of aerodynamic downwash due to nearby buildings on point source emissions. Receptor locations can be specified as gridded and/or discrete receptors in Cartesian or polar coordinates. The ISCST3 model uses real-time meteorological data to account for the atmospheric conditions that affect the distribution of air pollution on the modeling area.

Other Recommended Models

A few dispersion models have been developed by industry for trade-specific operations. For example, British Petroleum developed BP CIRRUS, DuPont developed SAFER, and the Industry Cooperative HF Program developed HGSYSTEM. A number of other models have been listed in EPA's Risk Management Planning, including ARCHIE which was developed by the United States Department of Transportation.

Model Selection

The key as to which of these models to use will depend on the specifics of the facility and the degree to which information is available for applying the model. For example, it makes no sense to use a refined prediction model if real time or statistical meteorological data are not available. If all one has is hypothetical meteorologi-

cal data as specified in the final regulation, a model like TScreen may be sufficient. However, some models have sophisticated algorithms that deal with specific releases.

Although this publication will not recommend specific dispersion models, certain criteria need to be considered in selecting a model and determining modeling techniques.

- ❏ **Suitability:** Is the model applicable to the process? Does the model accurately handle both the physical and thermodynamic parameters of the scenario?
- ❏ **Precedence:** Has the model been used for similar substances and similar parameters by other organizations and agencies?
- ❏ **Evaluation:** Has the model been tested in fluid modeling experiments or in the field? Has the model been well documented and based on sound scientific and technical principles?

In conducting modeling, EPA requires that sources model the downwind dispersion of the worst-case release scenario using atmospheric stability class F. This is a reliable atmospheric stability class and will result in the highest centerline concentrations for certain types of sources. Other types of scenarios—such as unstable conditions producing looping plumes,etc.—may result in higher ground level concentrations. Finally, under high wind speed conditions, neutral or unstable conditions may result in higher downwind concentrations due to building down wash effects. An advantage of refined models is that they can take into account both the actual variation of meteorological conditions and their effects on dispersion and distance to endpoints. Additionally, they can provide a much better depiction of the distribution of concentrations likely to occur from various accidental releases.

Worst-Case Meteorological Conditions

EPA has proposed that sources model with downwind dispersion of the worst-case release scenario using F atmospheric stability and 1.5 meter per second wind speed and model the alternative release scenarios using both the worst-case conditions and the meteorological conditions prevailing at the source. Note that it is unclear as to what EPA means by "meteorological conditions prevailing at the source." Prevailing meteorological conditions could be interpreted to mean average, generally occurring, or frequently occurring conditions.

Since it is possible that worst-case meteorological conditions may occur at the time of an accident, this would not be a conservative assumption to take. Rather, we recommend that operators look at the range of *possible* meteorological conditions and identify the worst-case that would occur for that facility, EPA recommendations of F stability and 1.5 meters per second notwithstanding. This may not represent the worst-case atmospheric conditions for a particular facility and combination off-site receptor locations because such factors as building geometry, distance to property line, and onsite and off-site terrain conditions can effect what constitutes worst-case meteorological conditions. Using actual meteorological data and refined air quality dispersion models represents the best approach to accurately define onsite and offsite impact from accidental releases. EPA, in its guidance, recognizes that a higher wind speed or less stable atmospheric stability class may be used if the owner or operator has local meteorological data applicable to the source that show the lowest recorded wind speed was always greater, or the atmospheric stability class was always less stable during the previous three years.[57] Note that this is not really the issue. The issue is whether alternative meteorological conditions produce higher offsite concentrations or a greater distance to an endpoint.

When considering the use of onsite meteorological data, it is critical that the meteorological instruments be properly sited and be calibrated and maintained in accordance with the manufacturers' recommendations.

Onsite Monitoring

What constitutes appropriate siting for meteorological instruments? First, meteorological data should be taken at a height of ten meters (33 feet) above ground level and in an area free of local obstructions. This means that meteorological towers should be at least ten tower heights away from nearby structures (5 is the absolute minimum) and a similar distance away from tree lines or other significant obstructions. This is to ensure that the wind direction is representative of the prevailing wind directions likely to transport releases off site.

The height of recording of meteorological data should be 10 meters, at a minimum. If releases are likely to occur from higher elevations—for example from flare towers or catalytic crackers—meteorological instruments at a level comparable to the potential height of release should also be considered.

Meteorological instruments must be constantly maintained in accordance with manufacturers' recommendations. Additionally, data should be reviewed and subject to quality control and validation to ensure that the data available at any given time are accurate. Historical data when used for modeling, must be subject to a quality control and validation process to ensure that the data are accurate.

It is easy to introduce bias into data—for instance, if instruments are not properly maintained, wind vanes can stick and anemometers can be subject to bearing drag, which can adversely affect the accuracy of the readings.

A final note on meteorological data is that atmospheric stability cannot be directly measured. Atmospheric stability is normally calculated through one of several means. One is to use the temperature change between 10 meters and 60 meters, for example on a meteorological tower. Relationships between the temperature lapse rate (ΔT) and atmospheric stability have been accepted for many years. These relationships are a useful means of translating the temperature lapse rate into atmospheric stability classifications, ranging from A and B as most unstable to C and D as neutral and to F or G being stable.

Another approach to estimating atmospheric stability is to calculate the standard deviation of wind direction fluctuation. This method ($\sigma\theta$) can be used when meteorological data are only available at one level on a tower. Relationships between sigma theta and atmospheric stability have been developed and accepted by both EPA and state agencies to allow translation of wind direction fluctuation into atmospheric stability. Although either the ΔT or $\sigma\theta$ method can be used when using onsite meteorological data, it is important that meteorological instruments, data recorders, and computers involved in logging and archiving data be accurately installed and routinely calibrated.

Receptor Selection

Whatever refined model is used, it is important to develop an approach to modeling that includes a rational approach to identifying predictions locations (receptors). Typically, screening models like TScreen are used to identify the maximum centerline concentration downwind from a release. Having identified this (Figure 14.2), we can identify the maximum distance to ground level concentration; in this example 150 feet. This occurs under F stability, with 4 meters per second windspeed and downwash conditions. Looking at this centerline concentration profile, it is obvious that similar but different profiles would result under different atmospheric stability classifications and wind speeds. Typically, the screening model is applied for the full range of atmospheric stability and wind speed combinations. As a result, a series of seven atmospheric stability plots for at least three different wind speed ranges is generated. It is possible to identify the distance to maximum concentration under each of these combinations. This information is then used to identify downwind distances for receptor rings around the facility. For example, under A stability, the maximum concentration may occur at 250 meters. A ring of receptors would be placed downwind at this distance. Under B stability, the maximum concentration may occur at half a kilometer and a ring of receptors would be placed at this distance. The result is that a series of 10 downwind distances are identified for purposes of placing receptor rings around the potential accidental release site. These receptor rings result in placing receptors at 10 degree radial distances corresponding to the 10 degree variations in wind directions reported in the meteorological data, or 36 receptors at each downwind distance. The model is then run using offsite or onsite meteorological data to predict the maximum short-term or long-term concentration at each receptor. Plotting programs are then applied to predict the maximum concentration distribution at these receptors under each accidental release scenario.

This results in the most accurate predictions of offsite concentrations.

Environmental Impacts

In the final rule, EPA requires RMPs identify environmental receptors within downwind distance circles and to find distances to endpoints. The EPA defines environmental receptors as natural areas such as national or state parks, forests or monuments or officially designated wildlife sanctuaries, preserves, refuges or areas and federal wilderness areas that can be exposed to accidental releases. All such receptors can typically be found on U.S. geological survey topographic maps based on USGS information. EPA does not require an extensive environmental impact analysis. Rather, EPA requires the RMP identify these areas and relies on environmental agencies who would have access to RMPs to determine whether and what type of impact analysis they would require. Part of the reason EPA did not require detailed environmental analyses is that there is a lack of information regarding the impacts on environmental areas from accidental release of chemicals and other hazardous substances. EPA believes that identification of potentially effected environmental receptors is sufficient for purposes of accidental prevention preparedness and response by the source and at the local level.

[53] 40 CFR Part 68, 6/20/96.

[54] 61 FR 3031, 1/30/96.

[55] United States Environmental Protection Agency, Office of Air Quality Planning and Standards. *Guideline on Air Quality Models (Revised)*. Research Triangle Park, NC, 1995.

[56] Marplot Company.

[57] 40 CFR Part 68, 6/20/96.

Chapter 15

Selecting Inherently Safer Approaches

Some state programs, for example New Jersey's Toxic Catastrophe Prevention Act, require a technology options analysis (TOA). This analysis requires a facility to examine alternative processes that could serve the same purpose as the subject process and be inherently safer.

Case Study: Reducing Risk

An example of the benefits of an inherently safer approach can be seen in examining the case of a electronic manufacturing facility in the midwest. This facility operated a small wastewater treatment operation to treat wastewater for its operations. Although this was a very small wastewater treatment plant, the facility, before an offsite consequence analysis was undertaken, frequently had as much as 10 one-ton cylinders of chlorine on site. Dispersion modeling of the unlikely consequence of 10 tons of chlorine being released into the atmosphere indicated that the plume would exceed IDLH levels for up to five miles off site. Since the plant is located in a densely populated suburban region, this risk was clearly unacceptable. Upon further investigation, it was determined that no more than two cylinders needed to be on site at any one time—one cylinder metering chlorine into the treatment system and another to be used when the cylinder in use was empty. Since it took almost two weeks to empty one cylinder, a maximum of two was all that was required to provide smooth functioning of the wastewater treatment plant and to allow for delays in deliveries of chlorine. Recommendations were made and accepted to reduce the inventory of chlorine from a maximum of 10 one-ton cylinders to a maximum of two. An additional recommendation was made to further restrict the delivery of chlorine cylinders so that delivery vehicles coming onto the site would bring no more than two cylinders to this facility and would not be carrying additional chlorine or other toxic or hazardous substances.

Keep in mind that under the RMP regulations, only one of the one-ton cylinders would need to be assumed to release its contents under the analysis just described above. Nonetheless, it is conceivable (although very unlikely) that all cylinders could release their contents at the same time, resulting in a lethal plume for five miles off site. Under what circumstances could this occur? Probably only if deliberate sabotage were to open the valves or break the valves off all one ton cylinders. It is for this reason, perhaps, that the RMP regulations require only that the release of one container, the largest (in this case they are all the same size), need be considered. Nonetheless, the owner/operator may wish to hypothesize more significant releases than just the maximum container being released.

Note that the RMP regulations require multiple containers to be considered if an explosion or other catastrophe can be hypothesized—which would result in the breaching of more than one storage container. This could occur through the over-pressure of an explosion, or through flying shrapnel created in an explosion. Reducing the quantity of chlorine in storage—or even better, substituting a less hazardous chemical—would clearly be safer from a RMP perspective. However, be sure that the inherently safer RMP scenario does not create other unintended consequences in other areas, such as a more-toxic wastewater.

Management of Change

Inherently safer approaches can also be identified through ongoing attention to hazard identification and through the management of change process under the RMP regulations. The management of change provisions require that owners/operators establish and implement written procedures to manage changes (except for "replacements in kind"). This includes written procedures to manage changes and process chemicals, technology, equipment, procedures, and changes to stationary sources that affect covered processes.

The procedures covering management of change plans must ensure the following considerations are addressed prior to any change:

❑ Technical basis for the proposed change
❑ Impact of change on safety and health
❑ Modifications to operating procedures
❑ Necessary time period for the change
❑ Authorization requirements for the proposed change

Employees who are involved in operating a process, and maintenance and contract employees whose job tasks are affected by a change in the process, must both be informed of and trained in the change prior to the start-up of the affected process. If a change covered by the management of change requirements results in a change in the process safety information required under the RMP regulations, that information must be updated immediately. Likewise, if a change requires a change in the standard operating procedures, the SOPs must also be updated accordingly.

Pre-Start Up Review

Another area in which inherently safer approaches may be identified is through the pre-startup review process. Under Section 68.77, the owner or operator subject to a Program 3 prevention program is required to perform a pre-startup safety review for new stationary sources and for modified sources when the modification is sig-

nificant enough to require a change in the process safety information.

The pre-startup safety review must confirm that, prior to the introduction of the regulated substance in the process, the following precautionary measures are taken:

❑ Construction and equipment is in accordance with design specifications.
❑ Safety, operating, maintenance, and emergency procedures are in place and are adequate.
❑ For new sources, a process hazard analysis has been performed and recommendations have been resolved and implemented before start-up; for modified stationary sources, they meet the requirements contained in the management of change described above, which is Section 68.75.
❑ Finally, training of each employee involved in operating the process must have been completed prior to its initial operation.

EPA encourages, during pre-startup review, an analysis of inherently safer approaches.

Public Outreach

It is important to keep in mind that the RMP documents are filed electronically and the intent is to make them available to the world through Internet access. Because of this, the information contained in the RMPs will be available immediately to the public and to environmental action groups. Therefore, it is highly recommended that facilities covered by the RMP regulations establish an effective community outreach program. An example of the effectiveness of community outreach can be seen by an example of a chemical facility in the mid-Atlantic states. The facility had been subject to some enforcement action and there had been several small releases at the facility. Local residents surrounding the facility became concerned that the plant was not being operated in a safe and efficient manner. The facility undertook a community involvement program to inform the community of operations within the facility and invited the community to participate on a local community involvement committee along with plant environmental and plant production personnel. Over several years and many meetings, a relationship of trust developed between the facility and the community so that when the inevitable small accidents occurred, the community came to the facility's defense rather than being immediately critical of it. This illustrates the point that fear of the unknown is typically worse than knowledge of the facts. The public generally does not know what goes on inside the fenceline of a complex petrochemical or batch chemical operation. Knowing what does go on, what measures are taken to ensure safety, what training is undertaken, what procedures are in place to minimize the potential of an accident occurring, and what procedures are in place to respond to a potential accident, usually helps reassure the community that the facility is doing all that it can to maintain a safe operation.

At the same time, since the process RMP information is made public, and the quantities of materials on site have also been made public in other public submissions, (e.g., the Form R submissions), it is important that the RMP be undertaken diligently and accurately. With today's public access to data, it is very easy for anyone who has the time to determine and look for inconsis- tencies between filings, such as RMP information that indicates different quantities on site than Form R quantities.

Additionally, it must be expected that environmental groups will take the information in RMPs, analyze it, and come to their own conclusions as to whether the facility is operating safely or whether there is an undue risk that may be posed by the quantities of material on site. The same may be said about the adequacy of training, management of change, and other provisions of the RMP regulations. Therefore, it is prudent to examine your RMP carefully, in light of how it may be viewed by the public and environmental groups, before filing it.

A key advantage of conducting the RMP and in looking at it in this way is that changes can be made in the facility, (e.g., at the midwest electronics manufacturing facility where the quantity of material on site was reduced because offsite consequences are not unacceptable).

Chapter 16

The RMP Standard:
A Section-by-Section Analysis

This chapter is a section-by-section analysis of the specific changes that were made during the promulgation of the RMP Standard based on EPA documentation. These are changes that are not otherwise previously described in this book. This chapter is included as a reference tool for the reader because it provides narrative explanations that are otherwise not available by simply referencing the attached 40 CFR Part 68 regulations. The final rule was renumbered to include new sections and subparts. The hazard assessment requirements have been divided into separate sections in Subpart B. The Program 2 prevention program requirements are in Subpart C; Program 3 prevention program elements are in Subpart D. Emergency response requirements are in Subpart E; RMP requirements are in Subpart G. The registration requirement, proposed Sec. 68.12, has been moved to the RMP subpart.

Subpart A: General

Section 68.3: Definitions

Section 68.3, Definitions, has been revised to add or delete a number of definitions.

❑ A definition of *administrative controls* has been added that is derived from the definition used by the Center for Chemical Process Safety (CCPS).

❑ The definition of *analysis of offsite consequences* has been deleted.

❑ A definition of *catastrophic release* has been added that is adapted from OSHA's definition of cata-

strophic release (29 CFR 1910.119); OSHA's language on danger to employees in the workplace has been changed to imminent and substantial endangerment to public health and the environment.

❑ A definition of *classified information* has been added. The definition is adopted from the Classified Information Procedures Act.

❑ As discussed above, a definition of *environmental receptor* has been added to list the receptors of concern.

❑ The definition of *full-time employee* has been deleted.

❑ A definition of *hot work* has been adopted verbatim from the OSHA PSM standard.

❑ The definition of *implementing agency* is adopted as proposed in the SNPRM.

❑ A definition of *injury* has been added.

❑ A definition of *major change* has been added to clarify the types of changes that necessitate actions to manage change. The definition will help sources understand when they are required to take steps to review their activities for new hazards.

❑ A definition of *mechanical integrity* has been added to clarify the requirements of maintenance sections.

❑ A definition of *medical treatment* has been added to clarify what constitutes an injury. The definition is adapted from an OSHA definition used by sources in logging occupational injuries and illnesses.

❏ A definition of *off site* has been changed to clarify that areas within the source would be considered off site if the public has routine and unrestricted access during or outside of business hours. Areas within a source's boundaries that may be considered off site are public roads that pass through sections of the site and natural areas owned by the source to which the public has unrestricted access. For some sites, parking lots within the boundary may be off site if the source cannot restrict access.

❏ A definition of *population* has been added. Population is defined as the public.

❏ A definition of *public* has been added to state that all persons except employees and contractors at the stationary source are members of the public. A number of commenters stated that employees at other facilities should not be considered part of the public. EPA disagrees because these employees may not be trained in protective actions or have protective equipment appropriate for releases from covered processes.

❏ A definition of *public receptor* has been added. Some commenters stated that EPA should include public roads within this definition. EPA decided that inclusion of public roads was unwarranted. EPA recognizes that people on public roads may be exposed during a release. In most cases, however, vehicles on public roads will be able to leave the area quickly and further access can be blocked, especially in isolated areas. If public roads were included, almost no sources would be eligible for Program 1 because there will be public roads leading to the source. In those cases where public roads are heavily traveled, there will be other public receptors near the source and, therefore, the source's processes will not qualify for Program 1.

❏ OSHA's definition of *replacement in kind* has been adopted.

❏ A definition of *typical meteorological conditions* has been added which means the temperature, wind speed, cloud cover, and atmospheric stability class prevailing at the source. Data on the first three of these are available from local meteorological stations (e.g., airports). Atmospheric stability class can be derived from cloud cover data.

❏ The definition of *worst-case release* has been revised to clarify that the release is the one that leads to the greatest distance to the applicable endpoint.

Section 68.10: Applicability

Section 68.10, Applicability, has been revised to change the term "tier" to "program." The section now details the eligibility criteria for all three programs. Paragraph (a) has been revised to be consistent with statutory language on compliance dates. Sources must comply with the requirements by June 21, 1999, three years after EPA first lists a substance, or the date on which a source first becomes subject to this part, whichever is latest. After June 21, 1999, sources that begin using a regulated substance that has been listed for at least three years must be in compliance with the requirements of part 68 on the day they bring the substance on site above a threshold quantity.

❏ The Program 1 eligibility requirements have been revised to clarify that the criteria are applied to a process, not the source as a whole, as discussed above. EPA has amended the List Rule to delete the category of high explosives from the list of regulated substances. The types of accidents that will disqualify a process from Program 1 are now specified in the rule as those accidental releases of a regulated substance that lead to offsite exposure to the substance, its reaction products, over-pressure generated by an explosion involving the substance, or radiant heat generated by a fire involving the substance, which resulted in offsite death or injury (as defined by the rule), or response or restoration activities at an environmental receptor. These accidental release criteria eliminate the need for a definition of significant accidental release, which has been deleted. Offsite environmental response or restoration includes such activities as collection, treatment and disposal of soil, shutoff of drinking water, replacement of damaged vegetation, or isolation of a natural areas due to contamination associated with an accidental release. The distance calculation equation for flammables has been dropped, and the worst-case release endpoint for flammables is specified, which allows the source to use the reference tables or their own methodology to determine the distance to the endpoint. The requirement that the community have an EPCRA emergency response plan has been replaced by a requirement that the source coordinate emergency response procedures with local community responders.

❑ As discussed above, the eligibility criteria for Program 2 and 3 have been changed. Both apply to processes, not sources.

❑ Paragraph (e) states that if a process no longer meets the eligibility criteria of its Program level, the source must comply with the requirements of the new Program level and the update the RMP according to Sec. 68.190. This paragraph clarifies the responsibility of the source when a process becomes ineligible for a Program level (e.g., public receptors move within the distance to an endpoint for a Program 1 process or OSHA changes the applicability of its PSM standard).

Section 68.12: General Requirements

New Section 68.12, General Requirements, has been added to provide a roadmap for sources to identify the requirements that apply to processes in each of the three tiers. The Program 1 requirements, in proposed Sec. 68.13, have been included in this section. Owners or operators of Program 1 processes are required to analyze and document in the RMP the worst-case release to ensure that they meet the eligibility criteria of no public receptors within the distance to the endpoint. As discussed above, the requirement to post signs has been dropped. The certification statement has been revised to be consistent with the eligibility requirements. If a source has more than one Program 1 process, a single certification may be submitted to cover all such processes.

❑ The Program 2 requirements specify the sections of the rule that apply to these processes.

❑ The Program 3 requirements specify the sections of the rule that apply to these processes.

Subpart B: Hazard Assessment

A new Subpart B has been created to cover the hazard assessment requirements. The proposed Sec. 68.15 has been divided into separate sections to cover the param-

eters, the different types of analyses, the identification of offsite populations and environments, documentation and updates, and the five-year accident history. EPA believes that limiting each section to a single topic will make the rule easier to understand.

Section 68.20: Applicable Requirements

Section 68.20 has been added to specify which hazard assessment requirements apply to Program 1, 2, and 3 processes. All sources are required to complete a worst-case release analysis for regulated substances in covered processes, based on the requirements of Sec. 68.25. Program 2 and 3 processes must also perform alternative release analyses required by Sec. 68.28. All sources must complete the five-year accident history for all covered processes.

Section 68.22: Offsite Consequence Analysis

A new Section 68.22, Offsite Consequence Analysis, has been added. Owners or operators who choose to use their own air dispersion modeling tools must use the parameters specified in paragraphs (a), (e), (f), and (g) of this section; they must also use the meteorological parameters specified in paragraph (b) of this section unless they can demonstrate that the conditions do not exist at their site. Paragraph (c) specifies the ambient temperature and humidity for worst case (highest daily maximum over the previous three years and average humidity); if a source uses the guidance, it may use average temperature and humidity (25° C and 50%) as default values. EPA recognizes that these values are less conservative than the worst-case meteorological conditions, but has determined that they represent a reasonable average to be used for developing tables. Providing tables for a variety of temperatures and humidity would have made the guidance much more voluminous and difficult to use. EPA is requiring sources that use dispersion models instead of the guidance to use actual temperature and humidity data applicable to the site. EPA believes this approach represents a reasonable tradeoff. The guidance generates conservative results even with the less conservative assumptions about temperature and humidity; air dispersion modeling will generally produce less conservative results and, therefore, should be based on actual data for these variables. Average data applicable to the source may be used for alternative scenarios. Paragraph (d) requires that the release height for worst-case be at ground level (zero feet). Paragraph (e) specifies that urban or rural topography be used as appropriate in modeling. Paragraph (f) requires sources to use models or tables appropriate for the density of the substance being released (e.g., dense gases must be modeled using tables or models that account for the behavior of dense gases). Dense gases are typically those that are heavier than air, as well as those that form aerosols and behave as if they are heavier than air upon release. For worst-case releases, liquids (other than gases liquefied by refrigeration only) shall be considered to be released at the highest daily maximum temperature or at process temperature, whichever is higher. For alternative scenarios, substances may be considered to be released at ambient or process temperatures, as appropriate. Owners or operators may choose to use EPA's RMP Offsite Consequence Analysis Guidance for their offsite consequence analyses. All of the parameters specified here are reflected in this guidance.

Section 68.25: Worst-Case Release Analysis

A new Section 68.25, Worst-Case Release Analysis, has been added. As discussed above, this section requires one worst-case release for toxics and one for flammables. If additional scenarios, for either class of substances, would potentially expose receptors not exposed by the worst-case release, the additional scenario shall be analyzed and reported. This provision is to take into account the possibility that at large sources, vessels at opposite ends of the source may expose different populations.

The section specifies how the maximum quantity in a vessel or pipe is to be determined, the scenarios to be considered for toxic gases, toxic gases liquefied by refrigeration only, toxic liquids, and flammables, the parameters to be used, consideration of passive mitigation, and factors to be considered in selecting the worst-case scenario. The section also specifies that sources may use proprietary models if the source provides the implementing agency access to the model and explains differences between the model and publicly available models, if requested. This approach will allow sources to use the most appropriate models available, while preserving the transparency of the results.

Section 68.28: Alternative Release Scenario Analysis

A new Section 68.28, Alternative Release Scenario Analysis, has been added. As discussed above, this section requires one alternative release analysis for all flammables held above the threshold in processes at the source and one alternative release analysis for each toxic held above the threshold in processes. For each scenario, the owner or operator must select a scenario that is more likely to occur than the worst case and that will reach an endpoint off site, unless no such scenario exists. The section includes a list of scenarios that owners/operators may want to consider, but does not dictate a particular scenario. EPA has provided additional direction and suggestions for defining these scenarios in the RMP Offsite Consequence Analysis Guidance. As noted above, the section references the parameters to be used and allows consideration of both passive and active mitigation systems. The section specifies factors to be considered in selecting alternative scenarios; specifically, sources shall consider releases that have been documented in the five-year accident history or failure scenarios identified through the PHA or hazard review.

Section 68.30: Offsite Impacts—Population

A new Section 68.30, Offsite Impacts—Population, has been added. This section specifies that populations are to be defined for a circle with a radius that is the distance to the endpoint. Owners or operators are required only to estimate the residential population within the circle to two significant digits and may use Census data to make these estimates. Owners or operators are also required to note, in the RMP, the presence of any major institutions, such as schools, hospitals, prisons, public recreational areas, arenas, and major commercial and industrial developments, but they are not required to estimate the number of people present at such sites. These additional locations are those that would normally be shown on area street maps.

Section 68.33: Offsite Impacts—The Environment

A new Section 68.33, Offsite Impacts—The Environment, has been added. As discussed above, the owners or operators are required only to identify any environmental receptors within the circle with a radius determined by the distance to the endpoint. The owners or operators are not required to assess the potential types or degree of damage that might occur from a release of the substance. The environmental receptors are those that can be identified on U.S. Geological Survey local topographical maps or maps based on U.S.G.S. data.

Section 68.36: Reviewing and Updating the Offsite Consequence Analysis

A new Section 68.36, Reviewing and Updating the Offsite Consequence Analysis, has been added. As proposed, if no changes occur at the site, the analyses must be reviewed and updated at least once every five years. If changes at the site occur that would reasonably be expected either to increase or decrease the distance to the endpoint by a factor of two or more, owners/operators are required to update the offsite consequence analysis within six months. The time for the reanalysis has been changed to six months to make it consistent with the update requirements for the RMP. The proposed requirement for reviewing the analyses based on offsite changes has been deleted. A number of commenters objected to the requirement because it would compel them to track changes over very large areas. Because the distance to the endpoints, especially for toxics, may be as much as 40 km, the area affected could easily exceed 1,000 square miles. EPA agreed with commenters that there was little benefit from requiring sources to track offsite changes and redo analyses because the public is aware of the changes.

Section 68.39: Documentation Related to the Offsite Consequence Analysis

A new Section 68.39, Documentation Related to the Offsite Consequence Analysis, has been added to list the documentation that must be retained on site. For both types of scenarios, the documentation shall include a description of the scenarios identified, assumptions and parameters used, and the rationale for the selection of specific scenarios. Assumptions shall include use of mitigation and any administrative controls that were assumed to limit the quantity that could be released. Documentation must include the effect of the mitigation and controls on the release quantity. The documentation must also include the estimated quantities released, release rates, and duration of release. The owners or operators must also identify the methodology used to determine distance to endpoints (i.e., EPA's guidance or an air dispersion model) and the data used

to estimate population and environmental receptors potentially affected. EPA has deleted the proposed requirement for documentation of endpoints because these are now dictated by the rule. EPA has also dropped the requirement for documentation of distance calculations; distances will either be determined from EPA's reference tables or by an air dispersion model.

Section 68.42: Five-Year Accident History

A new Section 68.42, Five-Year Accident History, has been added. As discussed above, the accident history is limited to accidental releases of listed substances from covered processes only. The only accidental releases that must be included in the history are those that resulted in deaths, injuries, or significant property damage on site, or known offsite deaths, injuries, evacuations, sheltering in place, property damage, or environmental damage. Although language related to the types of environmental damage listed in the proposed rule has been dropped, EPA intends that environmental damage not be limited to environmental receptors; events where any known environmental impact of any kind (e.g., fish or animal kills, lawn, shrub, or crop damage) should be included in the history.

The data required on each accident include date, time, and approximate duration of the release; chemical(s) released; estimated release quantity in pounds; the type of release event and its source; weather conditions (if known); onsite impacts and known offsite impacts; the initiating event and contributing factors (if known); whether offsite responders were notified (if known); and operational or process changes that resulted from the release. Estimates may be provided to two significant digits. EPA expects that for accidents that occur after the publication of this rule, sources will be able to document weather conditions, initiating events and contributing factors, and notification of offsite responders as these items would be part of the incident investigation. The EPA recognizes, however, that for incidents that occur before the rule is final, sources may not have this information unless OSHA PSM already would require the source to gather such information (e.g., initiating event and contributing factors). EPA has dropped the requirement that the concentration of the released substance be reported. Concentration at the point of release is assumed to be 100% except for substances in solution, where the concentration at the point of release is assumed to be the percentage of the solution as held or processed. The data provided will allow the source or the public to estimate the concentration off site.

Because the five-year accident history will initially cover releases that occurred before this rule is promulgated, EPA is requiring reports on weather conditions only if the source has a record. For future releases, EPA encourages the owners or operators keep a record of wind speed and temperature, if possible, as these conditions have a significant impact on the migration of a release off site. The rule specifies that the source must document known offsite impacts. The source is not required to conduct research on this subject, but must report impacts of which it is aware through direct reporting to the source or claims filed, or reasonably should have been aware of from publicly available information. The source is not required to verify the accuracy of public or media reports.

Subpart C: Program 2 Prevention Program

A new Subpart C has been created to include the requirements of the Prevention Program for Program 2 processes.

Section 68.48: Safety Information

New Section 68.48 details the safety information that sources will be required to develop. The information is a subset of the information required under the OSHA rule and is limited to those items that are likely to apply to Program 2 processes: MSDSs, maximum intended inventory, safe upper and lower process parameters, equipment specifications, and the codes and standards used to design, build, and operate the process. Because Program 2 processes are generally simple, EPA determined that items such as process chemistry, process flow diagrams, detailed drawings on equipment, and material and energy balances are not necessary for these processes. Evaluation of consequences of deviations will be handled under the process review and the offsite consequence analysis.

Section 68.48(b): Good Engineering Practices

Section 68.48(b) requires owners or operators to ensure that the process is designed in compliance with good engineering practices. This paragraph states that

compliance with federal or state regulations that address industry-specific safe design or with industry-specific design codes may be used to demonstrate compliance. NFPA-58 for propane handlers and OSHA's rule for ammonia handling (29 CFR 1910.111) are examples of such design codes.

The final paragraph of Sec. 68.48 requires owners or operators to update the safety information if a major change makes it inaccurate.

Section 68.50: Hazard Review

New Section 68.50, Hazard Review, lists the hazards and safeguards that the owners or operators must identify and review. This section states that owners or operators may use checklists, such as those provided in model risk management programs, to conduct the review. For processes that are designed to industry standards (e.g., NFPA-58) or federal/state design rules, owners or operators need only check their equipment closely to ensure that it has been fabricated and installed according to the standards or rules and is being operated appropriately. In this case, the standard or rule-setting body has, in essence, conducted the hazard review and designed the equipment to reduce hazards. Like the PHA required under PSM, the hazard review must be documented and the findings resolved. The review must be updated at least once every five years or when a major change occurs. A streamlined version of the PHA requirement, the review recognizes that for simple processes some of the OSHA requirements—such as the requirement for a team and a person trained in the technique—may not be necessary. Most Program 2 processes will have model risk management programs that will assist owners or operators in conducting the review.

Section 68.52: Operating Procedures

New Section 68.52, Operating Procedures, allows owners or operators to use standardized procedures developed by industry groups or provided in model risk management programs as a basis for the SOPs. Owners or operators will need to review standardized SOPs to ensure that they are appropriate for their operations; some may need to be tailored. The steps covered in the SOP are adapted from the OSHA PSM standard. Certain elements of the PSM requirement (e.g., safety and health consideration) were dropped because they are generally covered in training provided under the OSHA hazard communication standard. Other elements were not included because they are covered by other OSHA rules or may not apply to the kinds of sources in Program 2. The section requires that the SOPs be updated whenever necessary.

Section 68.54: Training

New Section 68.54, Training, is a streamlined version of the OSHA PSM requirement. The primary difference with the OSHA PSM training element is that the documentation requirements have been dropped. EPA believes that for Program 2 sources, which generally will have simple processes and few employees involved in the process, the level of documentation required by OSHA PSM is not needed. This section specifically states that training conducted to comply with other federal or state rules or industry codes may be used to demonstrate compliance with the section if the training covers the SOPs for the process. Workers must be retrained when SOPs change as a result of a major change.

Section 68.56: Maintenance

New Section 68.56, Maintenance, requires owners or operators to prepare and implement procedures for maintenance and train workers in these procedures. The owners or operators are also required to inspect and test process equipment consistent with good engineering practices. The OSHA list of equipment has been dropped because it seemed too detailed for the simpler Program 2 processes. Similarly, the OSHA PSM requirements for documentation, equipment deficiencies, and quality assurance seem too burdensome given the type of processes in Program 2. EPA emphasizes that sources should address equipment deficiencies when they arise.

Sections 68.58 and 68.60: Compliance Audits and Accident Investigation

New Sections 68.58 and 68.60, Compliance Audits and Accident Investigation, are adopted directly from the OSHA PSM standard. EPA believes that these two elements are critical to good prevention practices and that no changes are needed from the OSHA requirements. EPA has added a provision to clearly indicate that audit reports more than five-years old need not be retained.

Subpart D: Program 3 Prevention Program

The Program 3 Prevention Program is codified in new **Subpart D**. As explained above, the subpart adopts the OSHA PSM standard with only minor editorial changes necessitated by the different statutory authorities of the two agencies. Throughout the subpart, "employer" has been changed to "owner or operator," "facility" to "stationary source," and "highly hazardous chemical" to "regulated substance." EPA has additionally reordered the elements somewhat so that the order reflects the progression in which sources will generally implement the program. For example, process safety information, which is needed for the PHA, now precedes that section. Pre-startup review, which is the last step of management of change procedures, now follows management of change. The reordering does not reflect any change in the content.

Section 68.65: Process Safety Information

Section 68.65, Process Safety Information, is adopted directly from OSHA. The only changes are the following: references to other requirements have been changed to reflect the appropriate EPA section numbers; the phrase "highly hazardous chemical" has been changed to "regulated substance"; the word "standard" has been changed to "rule" in paragraph (a); and the date when material and energy balances are needed for new processes has been changed to June 21, 1999. The words "including those affecting the safety and health of employees" has been deleted from the requirement for the evaluation of the consequences of deviations (paragraph (c)(1)(v)) because EPA has no authority to regulate the workplace. Further, EPA believes this change reflects EPA's desire that sources implement one prevention program that protects the safety and health of workers, the public, and the environment and should have no effect on sources already complying with the OSHA PSM rule.

Section 68.67: Process Hazard Analysis

Section 68.67, Process Hazard Analysis, has been adopted from the OSHA rule with a few changes. The OSHA schedule for completion of PHAs has been replaced with the compliance date of this rule; a new sentence has been added to state that PHAs conducted to comply with OSHA PSM are acceptable as the initial

PHA under this rule. These PHAs shall be updated and revalidated based on their OSHA completion date. This provision will ensure that sources do not need to duplicate PHAs already completed or change their update schedule.

Section 68.67(c)(2): Catastrophic Consequences

In paragraph (c)(2), the phrase "in the workplace" was deleted from the requirement to identify previous incidents with the potential for catastrophic consequences because EPA does not have the authority to regulate the workplace. EPA believes that this change will have no effect on the rule; any incident with the potential for catastrophic consequences in the workplace will also have had the potential for catastrophic consequences off site. Similarly, the phrase "on employees in the workplace" was deleted from paragraph (c)(7), which requires a qualitative evaluation of a range of the possible safety and health effects of failure of controls. By deleting the language, rather than changing it, EPA is consistent with its authority without imposing any new requirements on sources. A new sentence was added to paragraph (f) to state that PHAs updated and revalidated under the OSHA rule are acceptable for EPA's purposes. Throughout this section, internal references have been changed.

To maintain consistency with OSHA PSM, proposed paragraph (j), which would have required the evaluation of mitigation and detection systems, has been dropped, as have proposed references to offsite consequences and public health and the environment. Evaluation of mitigation and detection systems is normally part of the PHA process and of management's decisions on implementing recommendations and, therefore, EPA decided that a separate requirement was not needed. EPA will collect information on monitoring, detection, and mitigation systems used in each Program 2 and 3 process as part of the RMP. Proposed paragraph (a), which was advisory, has been dropped.

Section 68.69: Operating Procedures

Section 68.69, Operating Procedures, has been adopted verbatim from OSHA except for changing "employer" to "owner or operator." Proposed paragraph (a) has been deleted to ensure consistency with OSHA.

Section 68.71: Training

Section 68.71, Training, has been adopted verbatim from OSHA except for changing "employer" to "owner or operator" and changes in referenced sections.

Section 68.73: Mechanical Integrity

Section 68.73, Mechanical Integrity, proposed as Maintenance, has been adopted verbatim from OSHA except for changing "employer" to "owner or operator." Proposed paragraph (a) has been deleted to ensure consistency with OSHA. The proposed requirements to develop a critical equipment list, document training, and "maintain" as well as inspect and test under paragraph (d) have been dropped to ensure consistency with OSHA.

Section 68.75: Management of Change

Section 68.75, Management of Change, has been adopted verbatim from OSHA except for changing "employer" to "owner or operator" and changes to referenced sections. Proposed paragraph (a) has been deleted to ensure consistency with OSHA. EPA's proposed paragraph (b), which defined changes not covered by the section, has also been dropped in favor of OSHA's definition of "replacement in kind."

Section 68.77: Pre-Startup Review

Section 68.77, Pre-Startup Review, has been adopted verbatim from OSHA except for changing "employer" to "owner or operator" and changes to referenced sections. Proposed paragraph (a) and the reference to emergency response training in proposed paragraph (c)(4) have been deleted to ensure consistency with OSHA.

Section 68.79: Compliance Audits

Section 68.79, Compliance Audits, has been adopted verbatim from OSHA except for changing "employer" to "owner or operator" and changes to referenced sections. Proposed paragraph (a) has been deleted to ensure consistency with OSHA.

Section 68.81: Accident Investigation

Section 68.81, Accident Investigation, has been adopted verbatim from OSHA except for changing "employer" to "owner or operator"' and "highly hazardous chemical" to "regulated substance" and changes to referenced sections. Proposed paragraphs (a) and (b), the latter of which would have required written procedures, have been deleted to ensure consistency with OSHA. References to significant accidental release have been dropped because the phrase is no longer used. Although EPA has adopted OSHA's language, EPA has changed the definition of "catastrophic release." Consequently, this section requires owners or operators to investigate accidents that resulted in or could reasonably have resulted in a release that presented serious danger to public health or the environment. EPA does not believe that, except in isolated cases, the modification to this provision will require sources to investigate accidents that they would not investigate under the OSHA rule.

Section 68.83: Employee Participation

Section 68.83, Employee Participation, has been adopted verbatim from OSHA except for changing "employer" to "owner or operator." Although EPA did not propose adopting this section, it solicited comments on this issue, and commenters convinced EPA that employee participation is an important component of a complete prevention program.

Section 68.85: Hot Work Permit

Section 68.85, Hot Work Permit, has been adopted verbatim from OSHA except for changing "employer" to "owner or operator." Although EPA did not propose adopting this section, the Agency solicited comments on this provision and decided that it was valuable to maintain consistency with the OSHA PSM elements and that the hot work permit was important to good prevention practices.

Section 68.87: Contractors

Section 68.87, Contractors, has been adopted verbatim from OSHA except for changing "employer" to "owner or operator," changes to referenced sections, and deleting OSHA's paragraph 29 CFR 1910.119(h)(2)(vi). Although EPA did not propose adopting this section, it solicited comments on this issue. Commenters argued that contractor practices are an important component of a complete prevention program. A number of major accidents have resulted from contractor mistakes. EPA agrees with the commenters and has included the provision in the final rule. EPA has, however, deleted the requirement that employers maintain an occupational

injury and illness log for contract employees because it does not have the authority to impose this requirement.

Subpart E: Emergency Response

EPA has placed the emergency response requirements in a new Subpart E and divided the proposed emergency response section into two separate sections, an applicability section and a section to cover the emergency response program.

Section 68.90: Applicability

A new Section 68.90, Applicability, has been added. Because many sources covered by this rule may be too small to handle emergency response themselves, EPA has provided, in this new section, the actions they must take if they will not respond to releases. Specifically, for sources with regulated toxic substances, the source must be addressed in the community emergency response plan developed under EPCRA Section 303. Sources with regulated flammable substances must coordinate response actions with the local fire department. These sources must also establish a mechanism to contact local emergency responders. Sources that do not meet these requirements must comply with EPA's emergency response program requirements.

Section 68.95: Emergency Response Program

Section 68.95, Emergency Response Program, is adopted from Section 68.45 of the proposed rule. The program has four components: an emergency response plan, procedures for use of response equipment and its maintenance, training for employees, and procedures to update the plan after changes to the source. The required elements of the plan are those specified in CAA section 112(r)(7)(B)(ii): procedures for informing the public and local response agencies; documentation of emergency medical treatment; and procedures and measures for emergency response. As explained above, EPA decided that, to avoid inconsistency with other emergency response planning regulations, the rule would be limited to the statutory requirements. Consequently, EPA has deleted the following proposed requirements: documentation of evacuation routes (which should be covered under the emergency action plans required by OSHA under 29 CFR 1910.38); descriptions of all response and mitigation technologies available at the source; documentation of the maintenance and training programs; emergency response drills and exercises; revision of the plan based on the findings of the drills and exercises; and documentation of management's response to findings and a schedule for completion. EPA believes that these requirements are addressed in other federal regulations and, therefore, sources are already completing them. By not including them, EPA, however, avoids the possibility that slightly different wording could lead to unnecessary additional effort on the part of sources.

EPA has added a paragraph (b) to this section to state that compliance with other federal contingency plan regulations or use of the National Response Team's Integrated Contingency Plan Guidance ("One Plan") resulting in a written plan that addresses the elements in paragraph (a) shall satisfy the requirements of the rule, provided that the owner or operator also complies with paragraph (c) of this section.

Paragraph (c) is adopted from proposed paragraph Sec. 68.45(g) and requires coordination of the plan with the local community emergency response plan. References to the local emergency planning committee (LEPC) have been changed to "local emergency response officials" to recognize and include other local groups that may be in charge of coordinating emergency planning. LEPCs would be included in this category.

Subpart G: Risk Management Plan

A new Subpart G, Risk Management Plan, includes three main sections: an executive summary, the registration, and data elements that provide information on the off-site consequence analyses, the five-year accident history, the prevention program, and the emergency response program. The subpart includes separate sections to address each of these, plus sections on submission, certifications, and updates.

Section 68.150: Submission

New Section 68.150, Submission, has been added. As discussed above, an owner or operator shall submit a single RMP for the source, regardless of the number of covered processes or the tiers for which they are eligible. All RMPs will be submitted in a manner and method EPA will specify by the compliance date to a

point designated by EPA; no other submission will be required because other agencies and the public will have access to the submissions online. As required by the CAA, the first RMP must be submitted by June 21, 1999, three years after EPA first lists a substance, or the date on which a source first becomes subject to this part, whichever is latest. As discussed above under applicability, after June 21, 1999, sources that begin using a substance that has been listed for at least three years will be required to submit their RMPs on the date the substance is first on site above the threshold quantity. Sources that begin using such a regulated substance prior to June 21, 1999, will need to be in compliance with the rule on June 21, 1999. The final paragraph states that, except for a classified annex that would not be publicly available, the RMP shall exclude classified information.

Section 68.155: Executive Summary

New Section 68.155, Executive Summary, includes brief descriptions of the following items: the source's prevention and emergency response approach; the stationary source and regulated substances; worst-case release scenario(s) and alternative release scenario(s), including any administrative controls applied to limit the release quantity; the general prevention program and chemical-specific prevention steps; the five-year accident history; the emergency response program; and planned changes to improve safety. EPA anticipates that none of these items should require more than a half page of text. Because this information may be filed electronically, EPA is not asking sources to submit maps of the worst-case or alternative release scenario circles. The data submitted under each of these sections will allow state or local agencies and the public to map the circles.

Section 68.160: Registration

Section 68.160, Registration, replaces proposed Section 68.12. The registration needs to include the following data: stationary source name, street, city, county, state, zip code, latitude, and longitude; the stationary source and corporate Dun and Bradstreet numbers; the name, telephone number, and mailing address of the owner/operator; the name and title of the person responsible for implementation of the risk management program; the name, title, telephone number, and 24-hour telephone number of the emergency contact; the stationary source EPA identifier; the number of full-time employees at the stationary source; whether the stationary source is subject to 29 CFR 1910.119; whether the stationary source is subject to 40 CFR Part 355; and the date on which the stationary source last had a safety inspection by a federal, state, or local government agency.

For each covered process, the source must list the regulated substances present above a threshold quantity (name and CAS number), the maximum quantity of each substance in the process, the SIC code of the process, and the program level that applies to the process. This process information provides a simple method for describing covered processes and identifying program levels.

The reporting of the quantity has been changed; rather than have sources report in ranges, the rule requires that the quantity be reported to two significant digits. EPA has found that the reporting ranges are so broad (generally an order of magnitude) that data analysis is extremely difficult. By limiting the reporting to two significant digits, EPA will allow sources to estimate quantities, but still provide more precise data than are currently available. EPA has added a requirement for reporting full-time employees. These data are easy for sources to provide and will enhance its ability to assess the impact of its rule on businesses of various sizes. The EPA identifier will be the unique number assigned to each source and will allow EPA to cross-reference other reporting done to the Agency. Use of the identifier also means that EPA may not need to collect certain data on this form because they will be available from the identifier database; EPA may revise the requirements when the identifier rule is promulgated.

EPA has deleted the certification statement proposed for the registration because the RMP as a whole will have a certification statement that will cover all elements, including registration. Corrections to the registration will be treated as corrections to the RMP and must be filed within six months of the change, rather than the 60 days proposed for registration changes.

The registration now requires the owners or operators to check off the agency that last conducted a safety inspection at the source and provide the date. The inspection does not need to have been related to prevention practices as defined in this rule, but may instead cover fire safety, workplace safety, etc.

Section 68.165: Reporting Offsite Consequence Analysis

New Section 68.165, Reporting Offsite Consequence Analysis, requires the RMP to include data on one worst-case release scenario for each Program 1 process; and for Program 2 and 3 processes, one worst-case release scenario for toxics and one for flammables (for sources with substances in both hazard classes). If additional worst-case release scenarios are required under Sec. 68.25 for either class, data on that scenario must also be reported. Sources with Program 2 and 3 processes will also provide data on one alternative release scenario to cover all flammables in covered processes and an alternative release scenario for each toxic substance held in covered processes.

For each reported scenario, the owners or operators shall provide the following data: chemical name; physical state (toxics only); basis of results and model (if used); scenario; quantity released in pounds; release rate; duration; wind speed and stability (toxics only); topography (toxics only); distance to endpoint; public and environmental receptors within the distance; passive mitigation considered; and active mitigation (alternative releases only) considered. A number of the data elements are not relevant to all flammable releases; for example, in the worst-case release, flammables are assumed to be released and explode almost instantly so that release rate, duration, wind speed and stability, and topography are not factors in determining distances.

The purpose of requiring these data elements, rather than the proposed summary of the assessment, is to provide the public with the essential estimates of distance to the endpoints and to provide enough data on the release scenario to allow agencies or the public to confirm the distance estimate. With the data provided, a public agency will be able to use EPA's guidance to determine the distance for a particular chemical release and compare that distance with the one reported by the source. This ability will be particularly important when a source has chosen to use an air dispersion model rather than the reference table. The proposed rule approach, which required a summary of the assessment, would have resulted in considerable variation in the information submitted, as happened in the Kanawha Valley exercise. In that case, each source decided on the level of information to provide; although each provided maps, it was not possible, in many cases, to determine how the distances were estimated because much of the underlying data was not reported. EPA believes that these requirements will impose a minimal burden on sources, because they will already have the data from completing the analyses, will ensure that the same data are reported by all sources, and will provide enough data to evaluate the results using publicly available documents and models.

Section 68.168: Five-Year Accident History

New Section 68.168, Five-Year Accident History, simply references the data elements listed in Sec. 68.42(a). The data elements will be reported for each accidental release covered by the accident history requirement.

Section 68.170: Prevention Program/Program 2

New Section 68.170, Prevention Program/Program 2, requires owners or operators with Program 2 processes to list the name of chemical(s) and the SIC code for each item in the Program 2 process; to provide the dates of the most recent revisions or reviews of the prevention program elements; to provide, based on the hazard review, information on the major hazards, process controls, mitigation systems, monitoring or detection systems, and changes since the last hazard review; to list any state or federal regulations of industry-specific design codes or standards being used to demonstrate compliance with prevention program elements; to list the type of training and competency testing used; to provide the date of the most recent change that triggered a review or revision of prevention elements; and to provide the date of the completion of any changes resulting from hazard reviews, audits, or incident investigations. EPA recognizes that not all recommendations resulting from hazard reviews, audits, or incident investigations result in changes; some or all may be resolved without changes. However, if any changes are made, the owners or operators shall report in the RMP the date when such changes are complete or expected to be complete.

Section 68.175: Prevention Program/Program 3

New Section 68.175, Prevention Program/Program 3, requires owners or operators with Program 3 processes to list the name of chemical(s) and the SIC code for each item in the Program 3 process; to provide the dates of the most recent revisions or reviews of the prevention program elements; to provide, based on the

PHA, information on the major hazards, process controls, mitigation systems, monitoring or detection systems, and changes since the last PHA; to list the type of training and competency testing used; to provide the date of the most recent change that triggered a review or revision of prevention elements; and to provide the date of the completion of any changes resulting from PHAs, audits, or incident investigations. As above, EPA recognizes that not all recommendations resulting from PHAs, audits, or incident investigations result in changes; some or all may be resolved without changes. However, if any changes are made, the owners or operators shall report in the RMP the date when such changes are complete or expected to be complete.

Section 68.180: Emergency Response Program

New Section 68.180, Emergency Response Program, requires owners or operators to answer questions about the required content of the emergency response plan, providing the date of the most recent training of employees in the update of the plan, indicate whether the source emergency response plan has been coordinated with the LEPC plan, provide the name and telephone number of the local agency with which the plan has been coordinated, and list other Federal or state emergency planning requirements to which the source is subject.

Section 68.185: Certification

New Section 68.185, Certification, specifies the certification requirements that owners or operators must complete when the RMP is submitted.

Section 68.190: Updating the RMP

New Section 68.190, Updating the RMP, requires the plan to be updated at least once every five years. If a new substance is added to an already covered process or a new covered process is added, the RMP must be updated on the date on which the regulated substance is first present above a threshold quantity. If EPA lists a new substance that the source has above a threshold quantity, the RMP must be updated within three years of the date of listing. If a change at the source leads to a revised offsite consequence analysis, process hazard analysis or review, or a process changes the program level, the RMP must be revised and resubmitted within six months of the change. Subsequent updates will be required within five years of the update.

Subpart H: Other Requirements

A new Subpart H, Other Requirements, has been added.

Section 68.200: Recordkeeping

New Section 68.200, Recordkeeping, simply states that records will be maintained for five years unless otherwise specified in the Program 3 Prevention Program.

Section 68.210: Availability of Information to the Public

New Section 68.210, Availability of Information to the Public, has been added and a paragraph included to provide that classified information is protected under applicable laws, regulations, and executive orders.

Section 68.215: Permit Content and Air Permitting Authority or Designated Agency Requirements

New Section 68.215, Permit Content and Air Permitting Authority or Designated Agency Requirements, has been added to define the requirements for including Part 68 in Parts 70 and 71 permits, as discussed above.

Section 68.220: Audits

Section 68.220, Audits, has been revised to change references in paragraph (a). A new paragraph (c) has been added to specify the sources that have achieved a star or merit rating under OSHA's VPP program will be exempt from audits if the audit program is based on industry accident history or on neutral random oversight and if the source has not had an accidental release that requires investigation under the rule. Paragraph (h) has been revised to clarify that the source must revise the RMP 30 days after completion of the actions detailed in the implementation plan, not 30 days after the issuance of the final determination.

Appendix A

Appendix A has been added to provide the toxic endpoints.

Chapter 17

Conclusions

The RMP regulations represent a significant regulatory program. EPA has been working for years developing regulations and guidance to implement the program that was originally put in place by the Clean Air Act Amendments of 1990. As we have seen, the program parallels several state programs that have been in existence for more than a decade in four states. As a result, there is significant regulatory experience in the state programs that have been running for years. Nonetheless, this new federal program is one of the first to require electronic filing and, from the beginning, the posting of the submissions from a regulated community on the Internet for public view.

Since the program is still evolving and it is likely that additional changes in requirements will be enacted over the next year or so, until the RMPs are due in June of 1999, companies are encouraged to track the regulatory process through reviewing the *Federal Register* and other government publications.

The regulated community is also encouraged to track development and to participate in the development of guidance for the RMP program through involvement in the various work groups established by EPA and through frequent examination of EPA Internet World Wide Web Pages on which updates and new regulations, as well as guidance, are posted before they reach print form in the *Federal Register* or EPA guidance. Some EPA web sites which are worthy of view include the following:

- ❑ epa.gov
- ❑ osha-slc.gov
- ❑ www.epa.gov/swercepp
- ❑ www.nfpa.org (National Fire Protection Association)
- ❑ www.epa.gov/swercepp/acc-pre.html (Chemical Emergency Preparedness and Prevention Office)
- ❑ epa.gov (EPA's home page which provides links to all of the other sites)

Finally, the OSHA site is also important in that it provides background information on the OSHA PSM requirements. The OSHA site is an excellent site with technical links on process safety management at www.osha-slc.gov/SLTC/ProcesSafetyManagement/index.html.

The RMP program represents a challenge to industry. Examine your processes, look for ways to operate with less risk of accidental releases, plan to handle accidents better, and open your information doors to the world.

EPCRA 302: List of Extremely Hazardous Substances

EPCRA 302: List of Extremely Hazardous Substances

CAS No	Chemical name	Note	Reportable quantity (pounds)	Threshold planning quantity (pounds)
75-86-5	Acetone Cyanohydrin		10	1,000
1752-30-3	Acetone Thiosemicarbazide		1,000	1,000/10,000
107-02-8	Acrolein		1	500
79-06-1	Acrylamide	l	5,000	1,000/10,000
107-13-1	Acrylonitrile	l	100	10,000
814-68-6	Acrylyl Chloride	h	100	100
111-69-3	Adiponitrile	l	1,000	1,000
116-06-3	Aldicarb	c	1	100/10,000
309-00-2	Aldrin		1	500/10,000
107-18-6	Allyl Alcohol		100	1,000
107-11-9	Allylamine		500	500
20859-73-8	Aluminum Phosphide	b	100	500
54-62-6	Aminopterin		500	500/10,000
78-53-5	Amiton		500	500
3734-97-2	Amiton Oxalate		100	100/10,000
7664-41-7	Ammonia	l	100	500
300-62-9	Amphetamine		1,000	1,000
62-53-3	Aniline	l	5,000	1,000
88-05-1	Aniline, 2,4,6-Trimethyl-		500	500
7783-70-2	Antimony Pentafluoride		500	500
1397-94-0	Antimycin A	c	1,000	1,000/10,000
86-88-4	ANTU		100	500/10,000
1303-28-2	Arsenic Pentoxide		1	100/10,000
1327-53-3	Arsenous Oxide	h	1	100/10,000
7784-34-1	Arsenous Trichloride		1	500
7784-42-1	Arsine		100	100
2642-71-9	Azinphos-Ethyl		100	100/10,000
86-50-0	Azinphos-Methyl		1	10/10,000
98-87-3	Benzal Chloride		5,000	500
98-16-8	Benzenamine, 3-(Trifluoromethyl)-		500	500
100-14-1	Benzene, 1-(Chloromethyl)-4- Nitro-		500	500/10,000

98-05-5	Benzenearsonic Acid			10	10/10,000
3615-21-2	Benzimidazole, 4,5-Dichloro-2-(Trifluoromethyl)-	g		500	500/10,000
98-07-7	Benzotrichloride			10	100
100-44-7	Benzyl Chloride			100	500
140-29-4	Benzyl Cyanide	h		500	500
15271-41-7	Bicyclo[221]Heptane-2- Carbonitrile, 5-Chloro-6-(((((Methylamino)Carbonyl)O xy)Imino)-, (1s-(1-alpha,2- beta,4-alpha,5-alpha,6E))-			500	500/10,000
534-07-6	Bis(Chloromethyl) Ketone			10	10/10,000
4044-65-9	Bitoscanate			500	500/10,000
10294-34-5	Boron Trichloride			500	500
7637-07-2	Boron Trifluoride			500	500
353-42-4	Boron Trifluoride Compound With Methyl Ether (1:1)			1,000	1,000
28772-56-7	Bromadiolone			100	100/10,000
7726-95-6	Bromine	l		500	500
1306-19-0	Cadmium Oxide			100	100/10,000
2223-93-0	Cadmium Stearate	c		1,000	1,000/10,000
7778-44-1	Calcium Arsenate			1	500/10,000
8001-35-2	Camphechlor			1	500/10,000
56-25-7	Cantharidin			100	100/10,000
51-83-2	Carbachol Chloride			500	500/10,000
26419-73-8	Carbamic Acid, Methyl-, O-(((2,4-Dimethyl-1, 3 Dithiolan-2-- yl)Methylene)Amino)-	d		1	100/10,000
1563-66-2	Carbofuran			10	10/10,000
75-15-0	Carbon Disulfide	l		100	10,000
786-19-6	Carbophenothion			500	500
57-74-9	Chlordane			1	1,000
470-90-6	Chlorfenvinfos			500	500
7782-50-5	Chlorine			10	100
24934-91-6	Chlormephos			500	500
999-81-5	Chlormequat Chloride	h		100	100/10,000
79-11-8	Chloroacetic Acid			100	100/10,000
107-07-3	Chloroethanol			500	500
627-11-2	Chloroethyl Chloroformate			1,000	1,000
67-66-3	Chloroform	l		10	10,000
542-88-1	Chloromethyl Ether	h		10	100
107-30-2	Chloromethyl Methyl Ether	c		10	100
3691-35-8	Chlorophacinone			100	100/10,000

1982-47-4	Chloroxuron			500	500/10,000
21923-23-9	Chlorthiophos	h		500	500
10025-73-7	Chromic Chloride			1	1/10,000
62207-76-5	Cobalt, ((2,2'-(1,2-Ethanediylbis(Nitrilomethylidyne)) Bis(6-Fluorophenolato))(2-)-N,N',O,O')-			100	100/10,000
10210-68-1	Cobalt Carbonyl	h		10	10/10,000
64-86-8	Colchicine	h		10	10/10,000
56-72-4	Coumaphos			10	100/10,000
5836-29-3	Coumatetralyl			500	500/10,000
95-48-7	Cresol, o-			100	1,000/10,000
535-89-7	Crimidine			100	100/10,000
4170-30-3	Crotonaldehyde			100	1,000
123-73-9	Crotonaldehyde, (E)-			100	1,000
506-68-3	Cyanogen Bromide			1,000	500/10,000
506-78-5	Cyanogen Iodide			1,000	1,000/10,000
2636-26-2	Cyanophos			1,000	1,000
675-14-9	Cyanuric Fluoride			100	100
66-81-9	Cycloheximide			100	100/10,000
108-91-8	Cyclohexylamine	l		10,000	10,000
17702-41-9	Decaborane(14)			500	500/10,000
8065-48-3	Demeton			500	500
919-86-8	Demeton-S-Methyl			500	500
10311-84-9	Dialifor			100	100/10,000
19287-45-7	Diborane			100	100
111-44-4	Dichloroethyl ether			10	10,000
149-74-6	Dichloromethylphenylsilane			1,000	1,000
62-73-7	Dichlorvos			10	1,000
141-66-2	Dicrotophos			100	100
1464-53-5	Diepoxybutane			10	500
814-49-3	Diethyl Chlorophosphate	h		500	500
71-63-6	Digitoxin	c		100	100/10,000
2238-07-5	Diglycidyl Ether			1,000	1,000
20830-75-5	Digoxin	h		10	10/10,000
115-26-4	Dimefox			500	500
60-51-5	Dimethoate			10	500/10,000
2524-03-0	Dimethyl Phosphorochloridothioate			500	500
77-78-1	Dimethyl sulfate			100	500
75-78-5	Dimethyldichlorosilane	h		500	500
57-14-7	Dimethylhydrazine			10	1,000

99-98-9	Dimethyl-p-Phenylenediamine			10	10/10,000
644-64-4	Dimetilan	d		1	500/10,000
534-52-1	Dinitrocresol			10	10/10,000
88-85-7	Dinoseb			1,000	100/10,000
1420-07-1	Dinoterb			500	500/10,000
78-34-2	Dioxathion			500	500
82-66-6	Diphacinone			10	10/10,000
152-16-9	Diphosphoramide, Octamethyl-			100	100
298-04-4	Disulfoton			1	500
514-73-8	Dithiazanine Iodide			500	500/10,000
541-53-7	Dithiobiuret			100	100/10,000
316-42-7	Emetine, Dihydrochloride	h		1	1/10,000
115-29-7	Endosulfan			1	10/10,000
2778-04-3	Endothion			500	500/10,000
72-20-8	Endrin			1	500/10,000
106-89-8	Epichlorohydrin	l		100	1,000
2104-64-5	EPN			100	100/10,000
50-14-6	Ergocalciferol	c		1,000	1,000/10,000
379-79-3	Ergotamine Tartrate			500	500/10,000
1622-32-8	Ethanesulfonyl Chloride, 2-Chloro-			500	500
10140-87-1	Ethanol, 1,2-Dichloro-, Acetate			1,000	1,000
563-12-2	Ethion			10	1,000
13194-48-4	Ethoprophos			1,000	1,000
538-07-8	Ethylbis(2-Chloroethyl)Amine	h		500	500
371-62-0	Ethylene Fluorohydrin	c, h		10	10
75-21-8	Ethylene Oxide	l		10	1,000
107-15-3	Ethylenediamine			5,000	10,000
151-56-4	Ethyleneimine			1	500
542-90-5	Ethylthiocyanate			10,000	10,000
22224-92-6	Fenamiphos			10	10/10,000
115-90-2	Fensulfothion	h		500	500
4301-50-2	Fluenetil			100	100/10,000
7782-41-4	Fluorine	k		10	500
640-19-7	Fluoroacetamide	j		100	100/10,000
144-49-0	Fluoroacetic Acid			10	10/10,000
359-06-8	Fluoroacetyl Chloride	c		10	10
51-21-8	Fluorouracil			500	500/10,000
944-22-9	Fonofos			500	500
50-00-0	Formaldehyde	l		100	500
107-16-4	Formaldehyde Cyanohydrin	h		1,000	1,000

23422-53-9	Formetanate Hydrochloride	d, h	1	500/10,000
2540-82-1	Formothion		100	100
17702-57-7	Formparanate	d	1	100/10,000
21548-32-3	Fosthietan		500	500
3878-19-1	Fuberidazole		100	100/10,000
110-00-9	Furan		100	500
13450-90-3	Gallium Trichloride		500	500/10,000
77-47-4	Hexachlorocyclopentadiene	h	10	100
4835-11-4	Hexamethylenediamine, N,N'- Dibutyl-		500	500
302-01-2	Hydrazine		1	1,000
74-90-8	Hydrocyanic Acid		10	100
7647-01-0	Hydrogen Chloride (gas only)	l	5,000	500
7664-39-3	Hydrogen Fluoride		100	100
7722-84-1	Hydrogen Peroxide (Conc >52%)	l	1,000	1,000
7783-07-5	Hydrogen Selenide		10	10
7783-06-4	Hydrogen Sulfide	l	100	500
123-31-9	Hydroquinone	l	100	500/10,000
13463-40-6	Iron, Pentacarbonyl-		100	100
297-78-9	Isobenzan		100	100/10,000
78-82-0	Isobutyronitrile	h	1,000	1,000
102-36-3	Isocyanic Acid, 3,4- Dichlorophenyl Ester		500	500/10,000
465-73-6	Isodrin		1	100/10,000
55-91-4	Isofluorphate	c	100	100
4098-71-9	Isophorone Diisocyanate		100	100
108-23-6	Isopropyl Chloroformate		1,000	1,000
119-38-0	Isopropylmethylpyrazolyl Dimethylcarbamate	d	1	500
78-97-7	Lactonitrile		1,000	1,000
21609-90-5	Leptophos		500	500/10,000
541-25-3	Lewisite	c, h	10	10
58-89-9	Lindane		1	1,000/10,000
7580-67-8	Lithium Hydride	b	100	100
109-77-3	Malononitrile		1,000	500/10,000
12108-13-3	Manganese, Tricarbonyl Methylcyclopentadienyl Methylcyclopentadienyl	h	100	100
51-75-2	Mechlorethamine	c	10	10
950-10-7	Mephosfolan		500	500
1600-27-7	Mercuric Acetate		500	500/10,000
7487-94-7	Mercuric Chloride		500	500/10,000
21908-53-2	Mercuric Oxide		500	500/10,000
10476-95-6	Methacrolein Diacetate		1,000	1,000

760-93-0	Methacrylic Anhydride			500	500
126-98-7	Methacrylonitrile	h		1,000	500
920-46-7	Methacryloyl Chloride			100	100
30674-80-7	Methacryloyloxyethyl Isocyanate	h		100	100
10265-92-6	Methamidophos			100	100/10,000
558-25-8	Methanesulfonyl Fluoride			1,000	1,000
950-37-8	Methidathion			500	500/10,000
2032-65-7	Methiocarb			10	500/10,000
16752-77-5	Methomyl	h		100	500/10,000
151-38-2	Methoxyethylmercuric Acetate			500	500/10,000
80-63-7	Methyl 2-Chloroacrylate			500	500
74-83-9	Methyl Bromide	l		1,000	1,000
79-22-1	Methyl Chloroformate	h		1,000	500
60-34-4	Methyl Hydrazine			10	500
624-83-9	Methyl Isocyanate			10	500
556-61-6	Methyl Isothiocyanate	b		500	500
74-93-1	Methyl Mercaptan	l		100	500
3735-23-7	Methyl Phenkapton			500	500
676-97-1	Methyl Phosphonic Dichloride	b		100	100
556-64-9	Methyl Thiocyanate			10,000	10,000
78-94-4	Methyl Vinyl Ketone			10	10
502-39-6	Methylmercuric Dicyanamide			500	500/10,000
75-79-6	Methyltrichlorosilane	h		500	500
1129-41-5	Metolcarb	d		1	100/10,000
7786-34-7	Mevinphos			10	500
315-18-4	Mexacarbate			1,000	500/10,000
50-07-7	Mitomycin C			10	500/10,000
6923-22-4	Monocrotophos			10	10/10,000
2763-96-4	Muscimol			1,000	500/10,000
505-60-2	Mustard Gas	h		500	500
13463-39-3	Nickel Carbonyl			10	1
54-11-5	Nicotine	c		100	100
65-30-5	Nicotine Sulfate			100	100/10,000
7697-37-2	Nitric Acid			1,000	1,000
10102-43-9	Nitric Oxide	c		10	100
98-95-3	Nitrobenzene	l		1,000	10,000
1122-60-7	Nitrocyclohexane			500	500
10102-44-0	Nitrogen Dioxide			10	100
62-75-9	Nitrosodimethylamine	h		10	1,000
991-42-4	Norbormide			100	100/10,000

0	Organorhodium Complex (PMN-82-147)		10	10/10,000
630-60-4	Ouabain	c	100	100/10,000
23135-22-0	Oxamyl	d	1	100/10,000
78-71-7	Oxetane, 3,3- Bis(Chloromethyl)-		500	500
2497-07-6	Oxydisulfoton	h	500	500
10028-15-6	Ozone		100	100
1910-42-5	Paraquat Dichloride		10	10/10,000
2074-50-2	Paraquat Methosulfate		10	10/10,000
56-38-2	Parathion	c	10	100
298-00-0	Parathion-Methyl	c	100	100/10,000
12002-03-8	Paris Green		1	500/10,000
19624-22-7	Pentaborane		500	500
2570-26-5	Pentadecylamine		100	100/10,000
79-21-0	Peracetic Acid		500	500
594-42-3	Perchloromethylmercaptan		100	500
108-95-2	Phenol		1,000	500/10,000
4418-66-0	Phenol, 2,2'-Thiobis(4- Chloro-6-Methyl)-		100	100/10,000
64-00-6	Phenol, 3-(1-Methylethyl)-, Methylcarbamate	d	1	500/10,000
58-36-6	Phenoxarsine, 10,10'-Oxydi-		500	500/10,000
696-28-6	Phenyl Dichloroarsine	h	1	500
59-88-1	Phenylhydrazine Hydrochloride		1,000	1,000/10,000
62-38-4	Phenylmercury Acetate		100	500/10,000
2097-19-0	Phenylsilatrane	h	100	100/10,000
103-85-5	Phenylthiourea		100	100/10,000
298-02-2	Phorate		10	10
4104-14-7	Phosacetim		100	100/10,000
947-02-4	Phosfolan		100	100/10,000
75-44-5	Phosgene	l	10	10
732-11-6	Phosmet		10	10/10,000
13171-21-6	Phosphamidon		100	100
7803-51-2	Phosphine		100	500
2703-13-1	Phosphonothioic Acid, Methyl-, O-Ethyl O-(4-(Methylthio) Phenyl) Ester		500	500
50782-69-9	Phosphonothioic Acid, Methyl-, S-(2-(Bis(1-Methylethyl)Amino)Ethyl) O- Ethyl Ester		100	100
2665-30-7	Phosphonothioic Acid, Methyl-, O-(4-Nitrophenyl) O-Phenyl Ester		500	500
3254-63-5	Phosphoric Acid, Dimethyl 4-(Methylthio)Phenyl Ester		500	500
2587-90-8	Phosphorothioic Acid, O,O- Dimethyl-S-(2-	c, g	500	500

	Methylthio) Ethyl Ester			
7723-14-0	Phosphorus	b, h	1	100
10025-87-3	Phosphorus Oxychloride		1,000	500
10026-13-8	Phosphorus Pentachloride	b	500	500
7719-12-2	Phosphorus Trichloride		1,000	1,000
57-47-6	Physostigmine	d	1	100/10,000
57-64-7	Physostigmine, Salicylate(1:1)	d	1	100/10,000
124-87-8	Picrotoxin		500	500/10,000
110-89-4	Piperidine		1,000	1,000
23505-41-1	Pirimifos-Ethyl		1,000	1,000
10124-50-2	Potassium Arsenite		1	500/10,000
151-50-8	Potassium Cyanide	b	10	100
506-61-6	Potassium Silver Cyanide	b	1	500
2631-37-0	Promecarb	d, h	1	500/10,000
106-96-7	Propargyl Bromide		10	10
57-57-8	Propiolactone, Beta-		10	500
107-12-0	Propionitrile		10	500
542-76-7	Propionitrile, 3-Chloro-		1,000	1,000
70-69-9	Propiophenone, 4-Amino-	g	100	100/10,000
109-61-5	Propyl Chloroformate		500	500
75-56-9	Propylene Oxide	l	100	10,000
75-55-8	Propyleneimine		1	10,000
2275-18-5	Prothoate		100	100/10,000
129-00-0	Pyrene	c	5,000	1,000/10,000
140-76-1	Pyridine, 2-Methyl-5-Vinyl-		500	500
504-24-5	Pyridine, 4-Amino-	h	1,000	500/10,000
1124-33-0	Pyridine, 4-Nitro-,l-Oxide		500	500/10,000
53558-25-1	Pyriminil	h	100	100/10,000
14167-18-1	Salcomine		500	500/10,000
107-44-8	Sarin	h	10	10
7783-00-8	Selenious Acid		10	1,000/10,000
7791-23-3	Selenium Oxychloride		500	500
563-41-7	Semicarbazide Hydrochloride		1,000	1,000/10,000
3037-72-7	Silane, (4- Aminobutyl)Diethoxymethyl-		1,000	1,000
7631-89-2	Sodium Arsenate		1	1,000/10,000
7784-46-5	Sodium Arsenite		1	500/10,000
26628-22-8	Sodium Azide (Na(N<INF>3))	b	1,000	500
124-65-2	Sodium Cacodylate		100	100/10,000
143-33-9	Sodium Cyanide (Na(CN))	b	10	100
62-74-8	Sodium Fluoroacetate		10	10/10,000

13410-01-0	Sodium Selenate		100	100/10,000
10102-18-8	Sodium Selenite	h	100	100/10,000
10102-20-2	Sodium Tellurite		500	500/10,000
900-95-8	Stannane, Acetoxytriphenyl-	g	500	500/10,000
57-24-9	Strychnine	c	10	100/10,000
60-41-3	Strychnine Sulfate		10	100/10,000
3689-24-5	Sulfotep		100	500
3569-57-1	Sulfoxide, 3-Chloropropyl Octyl		500	500
7446-09-5	Sulfur Dioxide	l	500	500
7783-60-0	Sulfur Tetrafluoride		100	100
7446-11-9	Sulfur Trioxide	b	100	100
7664-93-9	Sulfuric Acid		1,000	1,000
77-81-6	Tabun	c, h	10	10
7783-80-4	Tellurium Hexafluoride	k	100	100
107-49-3	TEPP		10	100
13071-79-9	Terbufos	h	100	100
78-00-2	Tetraethyllead	c	10	100
597-64-8	Tetraethyltin	c	100	100
75-74-1	Tetramethyllead	c, l	100	100
509-14-8	Tetranitromethane		10	500
10031-59-1	Thallium Sulfate	h	100	100/10,000
6533-73-9	Thallous Carbonate	c, h	100	100/10,000
7791-12-0	Thallous Chloride	c, h	100	100/10,000
2757-18-8	Thallous Malonate	c, h	100	100/10,000
7446-18-6	Thallous Sulfate		100	100/10,000
2231-57-4	Thiocarbazide		1,000	1,000/10,000
39196-18-4	Thiofanox		100	100/10,000
297-97-2	Thionazin		100	500
108-98-5	Thiophenol		100	500
79-19-6	Thiosemicarbazide		100	100/10,000
5344-82-1	Thiourea, (2-Chlorophenyl)-		100	100/10,000
614-78-8	Thiourea, (2-Methylphenyl)-		500	500/10,000
7550-45-0	Titanium Tetrachloride		1,000	100
584-84-9	Toluene 2,4-Diisocyanate		100	500
91-08-7	Toluene 2,6-Diisocyanate		100	100
110-57-6	Trans-1,4-Dichlorobutene		500	500
1031-47-6	Triamiphos		500	500/10,000
24017-47-8	Triazofos		500	500
76-02-8	Trichloroacetyl Chloride		500	500
115-21-9	Trichloroethylsilane	h	500	500

327-98-0	Trichloronate	k	500	500
98-13-5	Trichlorophenylsilane	h	500	500
1558-25-4	Trichloro(Chloromethyl)Silane		100	100
27137-85-5	Trichloro(Dichlorophenyl) Silane		500	500
998-30-1	Triethoxysilane		500	500
75-77-4	Trimethylchlorosilane		1,000	1,000
824-11-3	Trimethylolpropane Phosphite	h	100	100/10,000
1066-45-1	Trimethyltin Chloride		500	500/10,000
639-58-7	Triphenyltin Chloride		500	500/10,000
555-77-1	Tris(2-Chloroethyl)Amine	h	100	100
2001-95-8	Valinomycin	c	1,000	1,000/10,000
1314-62-1	Vanadium Pentoxide		1,000	100/10,000
108-05-4	Vinyl Acetate Monomer	1	5,000	1,000
81-81-2	Warfarin		100	500/10,000
129-06-6	Warfarin Sodium	h	100	100/10,000
28347-13-9	Xylylene Dichloride		100	100/10,000
58270-08-9	Zinc, Dichloro(4,4- Dimethyl-5((((Methylamino)Carbonyl) Oxy)Imino)Pentanenitrile)- , (T-4)-		100	100/10,000
1314-84-7	Zinc Phosphide	b	100	500

Title III List of Lists

Consolidated List of Chemicals Subject to the Emergency Planning and Community Right-to-Know Act (EPCRA) and Section 112(r) of the Clean Air Act As Amended April 7, 1997

CAS Number	Chemical Name	Sec 302 (EHS) RQ	Section 304 EHS RQ	Section 304 CERCLA RQ	CAA 112 (r) TQ	Sec 313	RCRA Code
50-00-0	Formaldehyde	500	100	100	15,000	313	U122
50-00-0	Formaldehyde (solution)	500	100	100	15,000	X	U122
50-07-7	Mitomycin C	500/10,000	10	10			U010
50-14-6	Ergocalciferol	1,000/10,000	1,000				
50-18-0	Cyclophosphamide			10			U058
50-29-3	DDT			1			U061
50-32-8	Benzo[a]pyrene			1		313+	U022
50-55-5	Reserpine			5,000			U200
51-03-6	Piperonyl butoxide					313	
51-21-8	Fluorouracil	500/10,000	500			313	
51-21-8	5-Fluorouracil	500/10,000	500			X	
51-28-5	2,4-Dinitrophenol			10		313	P048
51-43-4	Epinephrine			1,000			P042
51-75-2	Nitrogen mustard	10	10			313	
51-75-2	2-Chloro-N-(2-chloroethyl)-N-methylethanamine	10	10			X	
51-75-2	Mechlorethamine	10	10			X	
51-79-6	Urethane			100		313	U238
51-79-6	Carbamic acid, ethyl ester			100		X	U238
51-79-6	Ethyl carbamate			100		X	U238
51-83-2	Carbachol chloride	500/10,000	500				
52-51-7	2-Bromo-2-nitropropane-1,3-diol					313	
52-51-7	Bronopol					X	
52-68-6	Trichlorfon			100		313	
52-68-6	Phosphonic acid, (2,2,2-trichloro-1-hydroxyethyl)-,			100		X	
52-85-7	Famphur			1,000		313	P097
53-70-3	Dibenz[a,h]anthracene			1		313+	U063
53-96-3	2-Acetylaminofluorene			1		313	U005
54-11-5	Nicotine	100	100	100			P075
54-11-5	Nicotine and salts			100			P075
54-11-5	Pyridine, 3-(1-methyl-2-pyrrolidinyl)-,(S)-	100	100	100			P075
54-62-6	Aminopterin	500/10,000	500				
55-18-5	N-Nitrosodiethylamine			1		313	U174
55-21-0	Benzamide					313	
55-38-9	Fenthion					313	
55-38-9	O,O-Dimethyl O-(3-methyl-4-(methylthio) phenyl) est					X	
55-63-0	Nitroglycerin			10		313	P081
55-91-4	Diisopropylfluorophosphate	100	100	100			P043
55-91-4	Isofluorphate	100	100	100			P043
56-04-2	Methylthiouracil			10			U164
56-23-5	Carbon tetrachloride			10		313	U211
56-25-7	Cantharidin	100/10,000	100				

CAS Number	Chemical Name	Sec 302 (EHS) RQ	Section 304 EHS RQ	Section 304 CERCLA RQ	CAA 112 (r) TQ	Sec 313	RCRA Code
56-35-9	Bis(tributyltin) oxide					313	
56-38-2	Parathion	100	10	10		313	P089
56-38-2	Phosphorothioic acid, O,O-diethyl-O-(4-nitrophenyl)	100	10	10		X	P089
56-49-5	3-Methylcholanthrene			10			U157
56-53-1	Diethylstilbestrol			1			U089
56-55-3	Benz[a]anthracene			10		313+	U018
56-72-4	Coumaphos	100/10,000	10	10			
57-12-5	Cyanides (soluble salts and complexes)			10			P030
57-14-7	1,1-Dimethyl hydrazine	1,000	10	10	15,000	313	U098
57-14-7	Dimethylhydrazine	1,000	10	10	15,000	X	U098
57-14-7	Hydrazine, 1,1-dimethyl-	1,000	10	10	15,000	X	U098
57-24-9	Strychnine	100/10,000	10	10			P108
57-24-9	Strychnine, and salts			10			P108
57-33-0	Pentobarbital sodium					313	
57-41-0	Phenytoin					313	
57-47-6	Physostigmine	100/10,000	1*	1*			P204
57-57-8	beta-Propiolactone	500	10	10		313	
57-64-7	Physostigmine, salicylate (1:1)	100/10,000	1*	1*			P188
57-74-9	Chlordane	1,000	1	1		313	U036
57-74-9	4,7-Methanoindan, 1,2,3,4,5,6,7,8,8-octachloro-2,3,	1,000	1	1		X	U036
57-97-6	7,12-Dimethylbenz[a]anthracene			1		313+	U094
58-36-6	Phenoxarsine, 10,10'-oxydi-	500/10,000	500				
58-89-9	Lindane	1,000/10,000	1	1		313	U129
58-89-9	Cyclohexane, 1,2,3,4,5,6-hexachloro-,(1.alpha.,2.al	1,000/10,000	1	1		X	U129
58-89-9	Hexachlorocyclohexane (gamma isomer)	1,000/10,000	1	1		X	U129
58-90-2	2,3,4,6-Tetrachlorophenol			10			
59-50-7	p-Chloro-m-cresol			5,000			U039
59-88-1	Phenylhydrazine hydrochloride	1,000/10,000	1,000				
59-89-2	N-Nitrosomorpholine			1		313	
60-00-4	Ethylenediamine-tetraacetic acid (EDTA)			5,000			
60-09-3	4-Aminoazobenzene					313	
60-11-7	4-Dimethylaminoazobenzene			10		313	U093
60-11-7	Dimethylaminoazobenzene			10		X	U093
60-29-7	Ethane, 1,1'-oxybis-			100	10,000		U117
60-29-7	Ethyl ether			100	10,000		U117
60-34-4	Methyl hydrazine	500	10	10	15,000	313	P068
60-34-4	Hydrazine, methyl-	500	10	10	15,000	X	P068
60-35-5	Acetamide			100		313	
60-41-3	Strychnine, sulfate	100/10,000	10	10			
60-51-5	Dimethoate	500/10,000	10	10		313	P044
60-57-1	Dieldrin			1			P037
61-82-5	Amitrole			10		313	U011
62-38-4	Phenylmercuric acetate	500/10,000	100	100			P092

CAS Number	Chemical Name	Sec 302 (EHS) RQ	Section 304 EHS RQ	Section 304 CERCLA RQ	CAA 112 (r) TQ	Sec 313	RCRA Code
62-38-4	Phenylmercury acetate	500/10,000	100	100			P092
62-44-2	Phenacetin			100			U187
62-50-0	Ethyl methanesulfonate			1			U119
62-53-3	Aniline	1,000	5,000	5,000		313	U012
62-55-5	Thioacetamide			10		313	U218
62-56-6	Thiourea			10		313	U219
62-73-7	Dichlorvos	1,000	10	10		313	
62-73-7	Phosphoric acid, 2-dichloroethenyl dimethyl ester	1,000	10	10		X	
62-74-8	Sodium fluoroacetate	10/10,000	10	10		313	P058
62-74-8	Fluoroacetic acid, sodium salt	10/10,000	10	10		X	P058
62-75-9	N-Nitrosodimethylamine	1,000	10	10		313	P082
62-75-9	Methanamine, N-methyl-N-nitroso-	1,000	10	10		X	P082
62-75-9	Nitrosodimethylamine	1,000	10	10		X	P082
63-25-2	Carbaryl			100		313	U279
63-25-2	1-Naphthalenol, methylcarbamate			100		X	U279
64-00-6	Phenol, 3-(1-methylethyl)-, methylcarbamate	500/10,000	1*	1*			P202
64-18-6	Formic acid			5,000		313	U123
64-19-7	Acetic acid			5,000			
64-67-5	Diethyl sulfate			10		313	
64-75-5	Tetracycline hydrochloride					313	
64-86-8	Colchicine	10/10,000	10				
65-30-5	Nicotine sulfate	100/10,000	100	100			
65-85-0	Benzoic acid			5,000			
66-75-1	Uracil mustard			10			U237
66-81-9	Cycloheximide	100/10,000	100				
67-56-1	Methanol			5,000		313	U154
67-63-0	Isopropyl alcohol (mfg-strong acid process)					313	
67-64-1	Acetone			5,000			U002
67-66-3	Chloroform	10,000	10	10	20,000	313	U044
67-66-3	Methane, trichloro-	10,000	10	10	20,000	X	U044
67-72-1	Hexachloroethane			100		313	U131
68-12-2	N,N-Dimethylformamide			100		313	
68-12-2	Dimethylformamide			100		X	
68-76-8	Triaziquone					313	
68-76-8	2,5-Cyclohexadiene-1,4-dione, 2,3,5-tris(1-aziridin					X	
70-25-7	Guanidine, N-methyl-N'-nitro-N-nitroso-			10			U163
70-30-4	Hexachlorophene			100		313	U132
70-69-9	Propiophenone, 4'-amino	100/10,000	100				
71-36-3	n-Butyl alcohol			5,000		313	U031
71-43-2	Benzene			10		313	U019
71-55-6	1,1,1-Trichloroethane			1,000		313	U226
71-55-6	Methyl chloroform			1,000		X	U226
71-63-6	Digitoxin	100/10,000	100				
72-20-8	Endrin	500/10,000	1	1			P051

CAS Number	Chemical Name	Sec 302 (EHS) RQ	Section 304 EHS RQ	CERCLA RQ	CAA 112 (r) TQ	Sec 313	RCRA Code
72-43-5	Methoxychlor			1		313	U247
72-43-5	Benzene, 1,1'-(2,2,2-trichloroethylidene)bis [4-met			1		X	U247
72-54-8	DDD			1			U060
72-55-9	DDE			1			
72-57-1	Trypan blue			10		313	U236
74-82-8	Methane				10,000		
74-83-9	Bromomethane	1,000	1,000	1,000		313	U029
74-83-9	Methyl bromide	1,000	1,000	1,000		X	U029
74-84-0	Ethane				10,000		
74-85-1	Ethylene				10,000	313	
74-85-1	Ethene				10,000	X	
74-86-2	Acetylene				10,000		
74-86-2	Ethyne				10,000		
74-87-3	Chloromethane			100	10,000	313	U045
74-87-3	Methane, chloro-			100	10,000	X	U045
74-87-3	Methyl chloride			100	10,000	X	U045
74-88-4	Methyl iodide			100		313	U138
74-89-5	Methanamine			100	10,000		
74-89-5	Monomethylamine			100	10,000		
74-90-8	Hydrogen cyanide	100	10	10	2,500	313	P063
74-90-8	Hydrocyanic acid	100	10	10	2,500	X	P063
74-93-1	Methyl mercaptan	500	100	100	10,000	313	U153
74-93-1	Methanethiol	500	100	100	10,000	X	U153
74-93-1	Thiomethanol	500	100	100	10,000	X	U153
74-95-3	Methylene bromide			1,000		313	U068
74-98-6	Propane				10,000		
74-99-7	1-Propyne				10,000		
74-99-7	Propyne				10,000		
75-00-3	Chloroethane			100	10,000	313	
75-00-3	Ethane, chloro-			100	10,000	X	
75-00-3	Ethyl chloride			100	10,000	X	
75-01-4	Vinyl chloride			1	10,000	313	U043
75-01-4	Ethene, chloro-			1	10,000	X	U043
75-02-5	Ethene, fluoro-				10,000		
75-02-5	Vinyl fluoride				10,000		
75-04-7	Ethanamine			100	10,000		
75-04-7	Monoethylamine			100	10,000		
75-05-8	Acetonitrile			5,000		313	U003
75-07-0	Acetaldehyde			1,000	10,000	313	U001
75-08-1	Ethanethiol				10,000		
75-08-1	Ethyl mercaptan				10,000		
75-09-2	Dichloromethane			1,000		313	U080
75-09-2	Methylene chloride			1,000		X	U080
75-15-0	Carbon disulfide	10,000	100	100	20,000	313	P022
75-19-4	Cyclopropane				10,000		
75-20-7	Calcium carbide			10			
75-21-8	Ethylene oxide	1,000	10	10	10,000	313	U115
75-21-8	Oxirane	1,000	10	10	10,000	X	U115

CAS Number	Chemical Name	Sec 302 (EHS) RQ	Section 304 EHS RQ	Section 304 CERCLA RQ	CAA 112 (r) TQ	Sec 313	RCRA Code
75-25-2	Bromoform			100		313	U225
75-25-2	Tribromomethane			100		X	U225
75-27-4	Dichlorobromomethane			5,000		313	
75-28-5	Isobutane				10,000		
75-28-5	Propane, 2-methyl				10,000		
75-29-6	Isopropyl chloride				10,000		
75-29-6	Propane, 2-chloro-				10,000		
75-31-0	Isopropylamine				10,000		
75-31-0	2-Propanamine				10,000		
75-34-3	Ethylidene Dichloride			1,000		313	U076
75-34-3	1,1-Dichloroethane			1,000		X	U076
75-35-4	Vinylidene chloride			100	10,000	313	U078
75-35-4	1,1-Dichloroethylene			100	10,000	X	U078
75-35-4	Ethene, 1,1-dichloro-			100	10,000	X	U078
75-36-5	Acetyl chloride			5,000			U006
75-37-6	Difluoroethane				10,000		
75-37-6	Ethane, 1,1-difluoro-				10,000		
75-38-7	Ethene, 1,1-difluoro-				10,000		
75-38-7	Vinylidene fluoride				10,000		
75-43-4	Dichlorofluoromethane					313	
75-43-4	HCFC-21					X	
75-44-5	Phosgene	10	10	10	500	313	P095
75-44-5	Carbonic dichloride	10	10	10	500	X	P095
75-45-6	Chlorodifluoromethane					313	
75-45-6	HCFC-22					X	
75-50-3	Methanamine, N,N-dimethyl-			100	10,000		
75-50-3	Trimethylamine			100	10,000		
75-55-8	Propyleneimine	10,000	1	1	10,000	313	P067
75-55-8	Aziridine, 2-methyl	10,000	1	1	10,000	X	P067
75-56-9	Propylene oxide	10,000	100	100	10,000	313	
75-56-9	Oxirane, methyl-	10,000	100	100	10,000	X	
75-60-5	Cacodylic acid			1			U136
75-63-8	Bromotrifluoromethane					313	
75-63-8	Halon 1301					X	
75-64-9	tert-Butylamine			1,000			
75-65-0	tert-Butyl alcohol					313	
75-68-3	1-Chloro-1,1-difluoroethane					313	
75-68-3	HCFC-142b					X	
75-69-4	Trichlorofluoromethane			5,000		313	U121
75-69-4	CFC-11			5,000		X	U121
75-69-4	Trichloromonofluoromethane			5,000		X	U121
75-71-8	Dichlorodifluoromethane			5,000		313	U075
75-71-8	CFC-12			5,000		X	U075
75-72-9	Chlorotrifluoromethane					313	
75-72-9	CFC-13					X	
75-74-1	Plumbane, tetramethyl-	100	100		10,000		
75-74-1	Tetramethyllead	100	100		10,000		
75-76-3	Silane, tetramethyl-				10,000		
75-76-3	Tetramethylsilane				10,000		

CAS Number	Chemical Name	Sec 302 (EHS) RQ	Section 304 EHS RQ	Section 304 CERCLA RQ	CAA 112 (r) TQ	Sec 313	RCRA Code
75-77-4	Trimethylchlorosilane	1,000	1,000		10,000	313	
75-77-4	Silane, chlorotrimethyl-	1,000	1,000		10,000	X	
75-78-5	Dimethyldichlorosilane	500	500		5,000	313	
75-78-5	Silane, dichlorodimethyl-	500	500		5,000	X	
75-79-6	Methyltrichlorosilane	500	500		5,000	313	
75-79-6	Silane, trichloromethyl-	500	500		5,000	X	
75-86-5	2-Methyllactonitrile	1,000	10	10		313	P069
75-86-5	Acetone cyanohydrin	1,000	10	10		X	P069
75-87-6	Acetaldehyde, trichloro-			5,000			U034
75-88-7	2-Chloro-1,1,1-trifluoroethane					313	
75-88-7	HCFC-133a					X	
75-99-0	2,2-Dichloropropionic acid			5,000			
76-01-7	Pentachloroethane			10		313	U184
76-02-8	Trichloroacetyl chloride	500	500			313	
76-06-2	Chloropicrin					313	
76-13-1	Freon 113					313	
76-13-1	Ethane, 1,1,2-trichloro-1,2,2,-trifluoro-					X	
76-14-2	Dichlorotetrafluoroethane					313	
76-14-2	CFC-114					X	
76-15-3	Monochloropentafluoroethane					313	
76-15-3	CFC-115					X	
76-44-8	Heptachlor			1		313	P059
76-44-8	1,4,5,6,7,8,8-Heptachloro-3a,4,7,7a-tetrahydro-4,7-			1		X	P059
76-87-9	Triphenyltin hydroxide					313	
77-47-4	Hexachlorocyclopentadiene	100	10	10		313	U130
77-73-6	Dicyclopentadiene					313	
77-78-1	Dimethyl sulfate	500	100	100		313	U103
77-81-6	Tabun	10	10				
78-00-2	Tetraethyl lead	100	10	10			P110
78-34-2	Dioxathion	500	500				
78-48-8	S,S,S-Tributyltrithiophosphate					313	
78-48-8	DEF					X	
78-53-5	Amiton	500	500				
78-59-1	Isophorone			5,000			
78-71-7	Oxetane, 3,3-bis(chloromethyl)-	500	500				
78-78-4	Butane, 2-methyl-				10,000		
78-78-4	Isopentane				10,000		
78-79-5	1,3-Butadiene, 2-methyl-			100	10,000		
78-79-5	Isoprene			100	10,000		
78-81-9	iso-Butylamine			1,000			
78-82-0	Isobutyronitrile	1,000	1,000		20,000		
78-82-0	Propanenitrile, 2-methyl-	1,000	1,000		20,000		
78-83-1	Isobutyl alcohol			5,000			U140
78-84-2	Isobutyraldehyde					313	
78-87-5	1,2-Dichloropropane			1,000		313	U083
78-87-5	Propane 1,2-dichloro-			1,000		X	U083
78-88-6	2,3-Dichloropropene			100		313	

CAS Number	Chemical Name	Sec 302 (EHS) RQ	Section 304 EHS RQ	Section 304 CERCLA RQ	CAA 112 (r) TQ	Sec 313	RCRA Code
78-92-2	sec-Butyl alcohol					313	
78-93-3	Methyl ethyl ketone			5,000		313	U159
78-93-3	Methyl ethyl ketone (MEK)			5,000		X	U159
78-94-4	Methyl vinyl ketone	10	10				
78-97-7	Lactonitrile	1,000	1,000				
78-99-9	1,1-Dichloropropane			1,000			
79-00-5	1,1,2-Trichloroethane			100		313	U227
79-01-6	Trichloroethylene			100		313	U228
79-06-1	Acrylamide	1,000/10,000	5,000	5,000		313	U007
79-09-4	Propionic acid			5,000			
79-10-7	Acrylic acid			5,000		313	U008
79-11-8	Chloroacetic acid	100/10,000	100	100		313	
79-19-6	Thiosemicarbazide	100/10,000	100	100		313	P116
79-21-0	Peracetic acid	500	500		10,000	313	
79-21-0	Ethaneperoxoic acid	500	500		10,000	X	
79-22-1	Methyl chlorocarbonate	500	1,000	1,000	5,000	313	U156
79-22-1	Carbonochloridic acid, methylester	500	1,000	1,000	5,000	X	U156
79-22-1	Methyl chloroformate	500	1,000	1,000	5,000	X	U156
79-31-2	iso-Butyric acid			5,000			
79-34-5	1,1,2,2-Tetrachloroethane			100		313	U209
79-38-9	Ethene, chlorotrifluoro-				10,000		
79-38-9	Trifluorochloroethylene				10,000		
79-44-7	Dimethylcarbamyl chloride			1		313	U097
79-46-9	2-Nitropropane			10		313	U171
80-05-7	4,4'-Isopropylidenediphenol					313	
80-15-9	Cumene hydroperoxide			10		313	U096
80-15-9	Hydroperoxide, 1-methyl-1-phenylethyl-			10		X	U096
80-62-6	Methyl methacrylate			1,000		313	U162
80-63-7	Methyl 2-chloroacrylate	500	500				
81-07-2	Saccharin and salts			100			U202
81-07-2	Saccharin (manufacturing)			100		313	U202
81-81-2	Warfarin	500/10,000	100	100		X	P001
81-81-2	Warfarin, & salts, conc.>0.3%			100		X	P001
81-88-9	C.I. Food Red 15					313	
82-28-0	1-Amino-2-methylanthraquinone					313	
82-66-6	Diphacinone	10/10,000	10				
82-68-8	Quintozene			100		313	U185
82-68-8	PCNB			100		X	U185
82-68-8	Pentachloronitrobenzene			100		X	U185
83-32-9	Acenaphthene			100			
84-66-2	Diethyl phthalate			1,000			U088
84-74-2	Dibutyl phthalate			10		313	U069
84-74-2	n-Butyl phthalate			10		X	U069
85-00-7	Diquat			1,000			
85-01-8	Phenanthrene			5,000		313	
85-44-9	Phthalic anhydride			5,000		313	U190
85-68-7	Butyl benzyl phthalate			100			
86-30-6	N-Nitrosodiphenylamine			100		313	

CAS Number	Chemical Name	Sec 302 (EHS) RQ	Section 304 EHS RQ	Section 304 CERCLA RQ	CAA 112 (r) TQ	Sec 313	RCRA Code
86-50-0	Azinphos-methyl	10/10,000	1	1			
86-50-0	Guthion	10/10,000	1	1			
86-73-7	Fluorene			5,000			
86-88-4	Antu	500/10,000	100	100			P072
86-88-4	Thiourea, 1-naphthalenyl-	500/10,000	100	100			P072
87-62-7	2,6-Xylidine					313	
87-65-0	2,6-Dichlorophenol			100			U082
87-68-3	Hexachloro-1,3-butadiene			1		313	U128
87-68-3	Hexachlorobutadiene			1		X	U128
87-86-5	Pentachlorophenol			10		313	
87-86-5	PCP			10		X	
88-05-1	Aniline, 2,4,6-trimethyl-	500	500				
88-06-2	2,4,6-Trichlorophenol			10		313	
88-72-2	o-Nitrotoluene			1,000			
88-75-5	2-Nitrophenol			100		313	
88-85-7	Dinitrobutyl phenol	100/10,000	1,000	1,000		313	P020
88-85-7	Dinoseb	100/10,000	1,000	1,000		X	P020
88-89-1	Picric acid					313	
90-04-0	o-Anisidine			100		313	
90-43-7	2-Phenylphenol					313	
90-94-8	Michler's ketone					313	
91-08-7	Toluene-2,6-diisocyanate	100	100	100	10,000	313	
91-08-7	Benzene, 1,3-diisocyanato-2-methyl-	100	100	100	10,000	X	
91-20-3	Naphthalene			100		313	U165
91-22-5	Quinoline			5,000		313	
91-58-7	2-Chloronaphthalene			5,000			U047
91-59-8	beta-Naphthylamine			10		313	U168
91-66-7	N,N-Diethylaniline			1,000			
91-80-5	Methapyrilene			5,000			U155
91-93-0	3,3'-Dimethoxybenzidine-4,4'-diisocyanate					313#	
91-94-1	3,3'-Dichlorobenzidine			1		313	U073
91-97-4	3,3'-Dimethyl-4,4'-diphenylene diisocyanate					313#	
92-52-4	Biphenyl			100		313	
92-67-1	4-Aminobiphenyl			1		313	
92-87-5	Benzidine			1		313	U021
92-93-3	4-Nitrobiphenyl			10		313	
93-65-2	Mecoprop					313	
93-72-1	Silvex (2,4,5-TP)			100			
93-76-5	2,4,5-T acid			1,000			U232
93-79-8	2,4,5-T esters			1,000			
94-11-1	2,4-D isopropyl ester			100		313	
94-11-1	2,4-D Esters			100		X	
94-36-0	Benzoyl peroxide					313	
94-58-6	Dihydrosafrole			10		313	U090
94-59-7	Safrole			100		313	U203
94-74-6	Methoxone					313	

CAS Number	Chemical Name	Sec 302 (EHS) RQ	Section 304 EHS RQ	Section 304 CERCLA RQ	CAA 112 (r) TQ	Sec 313	RCRA Code
94-74-6	(4-Chloro-2-methylphenoxy) acetic acid					X	
94-74-6	MCPA					X	
94-75-7	2,4-D, salts and esters			100			U240
94-75-7	2,4-D			100		313	U240
94-75-7	Acetic acid, (2,4-dichlorophenoxy)-			100		X	U240
94-75-7	2,4-D Acid			100		X	U240
94-79-1	2,4-D Esters			100			
94-80-4	2,4-D butyl ester			100		313	
94-80-4	2,4-D Esters			100		X	
94-82-6	2,4-DB					313	
95-06-7	Sulfallate			1*			U277
95-47-6	o-Xylene			1,000		313	U239
95-47-6	Benzene, o-dimethyl-			1,000		X	U239
95-48-7	o-Cresol	1,000/10,000	100	100		313	U052
95-50-1	1,2-Dichlorobenzene			100		313	U070
95-50-1	o-Dichlorobenzene			100		X	U070
95-53-4	o-Toluidine			100		313	U328
95-54-5	1,2-Phenylenediamine					313	
95-57-8	2-Chlorophenol			100			U048
95-63-6	1,2,4-Trimethylbenzene					313	
95-69-2	p-Chloro-o-toluidine					313	
95-80-7	2,4-Diaminotoluene			10		313	
95-94-3	1,2,4,5-Tetrachlorobenzene			5,000			U207
95-95-4	2,4,5-Trichlorophenol			10		313	
96-09-3	Styrene oxide			100		313	
96-12-8	1,2-Dibromo-3-chloropropane			1		313	U066
96-12-8	DBCP			1		X	U066
96-18-4	1,2,3-Trichloropropane					313	
96-33-3	Methyl acrylate					313	
96-45-7	Ethylene thiourea			10		313	U116
97-23-4	Dichlorophene					313	
97-23-4	2,2'-Methylenebis(4-chlorophenol					X	
97-56-3	C.I. Solvent Yellow 3					313	
97-63-2	Ethyl methacrylate			1,000			U118
97-74-5	Bis(dimethylthiocarbamoyl) sulfide			1*			U401
97-77-8	Disulfiram			1*			U403
98-01-1	Furfural			5,000			U125
98-05-5	Benzenearsonic acid	10/10,000	10				
98-07-7	Benzoic trichloride	100	10	10		313	U023
98-07-7	Benzotrichloride	100	10	10		X	U023
98-09-9	Benzenesulfonyl chloride			100			U020
98-13-5	Trichlorophenylsilane	500	500				
98-16-8	Benzenamine, 3-(trifluoromethyl)-	500	500				
98-82-8	Cumene			5,000		313	U055
98-86-2	Acetophenone			5,000		313	U004
98-87-3	Benzal chloride	500	5,000	5,000		313	U017
98-88-4	Benzoyl chloride			1,000		313	
98-95-3	Nitrobenzene	10,000	1,000	1,000		313	U169

CAS Number	Chemical Name	Sec 302 (EHS) RQ	Section 304		CAA 112 (r) TQ	Sec 313	RCRA Code
			EHS RQ	CERCLA RQ			
99-08-1	m-Nitrotoluene			1,000			
99-30-9	Dichloran					313	
99-30-9	2,6-Dichloro-4-nitroaniline					X	
99-35-4	1,3,5-Trinitrobenzene			10			U234
99-55-8	5-Nitro-o-toluidine			100		313	U181
99-59-2	5-Nitro-o-anisidine					313	
99-65-0	m-Dinitrobenzene			100		313	
99-98-9	Dimethyl-p-phenylenediamine	10/10,000	10				
99-99-0	p-Nitrotoluene			1,000			
100-01-6	p-Nitroaniline			5,000		313	P077
100-02-7	4-Nitrophenol			100		313	U170
100-02-7	p-Nitrophenol			100		X	U170
100-14-1	Benzene, 1-(chloromethyl)-4-nitro-	500/10,000	500				
100-25-4	p-Dinitrobenzene			100		313	
100-41-4	Ethylbenzene			1,000		313	
100-42-5	Styrene			1,000		313	
100-44-7	Benzyl chloride	500	100	100		313	P028
100-47-0	Benzonitrile			5,000			
100-75-4	N-Nitrosopiperidine			10		313	U179
101-05-3	Anilazine					313	
101-05-3	4,6-Dichloro-N-(2-chlorophenyl)-1,3,5-triazin-2-ami					X	
101-14-4	4,4'-Methylenebis(2-chloroaniline)			10		313	U158
101-14-4	MBOCA			10		X	U158
101-27-9	Barban			1*			U280
101-55-3	4-Bromophenyl phenyl ether			100			U030
101-61-1	4,4'-Methylenebis(N,N-dimethyl)benzenamine					313	
101-68-8	Methylenebis(phenylisocyanate)			5,000		313#	
101-68-8	MDI			5,000		X	
101-77-9	4,4'-Methylenedianiline			10		313	
101-80-4	4,4'-Diaminodiphenyl ether					313	
101-90-6	Diglycidyl resorcinol ether					313	
102-36-3	Isocyanic acid, 3,4-dichlorophenyl ester	500/10,000	500				
103-85-5	Phenylthiourea	100/10,000	100	100			P093
104-12-1	p-Chlorophenyl isocyanate					313	
104-49-4	1,4-Phenylene diisocyanate					313#	
104-94-9	p-Anisidine					313	
105-46-4	sec-Butyl acetate			5,000			
105-60-2	Caprolactam			5,000			
105-67-9	2,4-Dimethylphenol			100		313	U101
106-42-3	p-Xylene			100		313	U239
106-42-3	Benzene, p-dimethyl-			100		X	U239
106-44-5	p-Cresol			100		313	U052
106-46-7	1,4-Dichlorobenzene			100		313	U072
106-47-8	p-Chloroaniline			1,000		313	P024
106-49-0	p-Toluidine			100			U353
106-50-3	p-Phenylenediamine			5,000		313	

CAS Number	Chemical Name	Sec 302 (EHS) RQ	Section 304 EHS RQ	Section 304 CERCLA RQ	CAA 112 (r) TQ	Sec 313	RCRA Code
106-51-4	Quinone			10		313	U197
106-51-4	p-Benzoquinone			10		X	U197
106-88-7	1,2-Butylene oxide			100		313	
106-89-8	Epichlorohydrin	1,000	100	100	20,000	313	U041
106-89-8	Oxirane, (chloromethyl)-	1,000	100	100	20,000	X	U041
106-93-4	1,2-Dibromoethane			1		313	U067
106-93-4	Ethylene dibromide			1		X	U067
106-96-7	Propargyl bromide	10	10				
106-97-8	Butane				10,000		
106-98-9	1-Butene				10,000		
106-99-0	1,3-Butadiene			10	10,000	313	
107-00-6	1-Butyne				10,000		
107-00-6	Ethyl acetylene				10,000		
107-01-7	2-Butene				10,000		
107-02-8	Acrolein	500	1	1	5,000	313	P003
107-05-1	Allyl chloride			1,000		313	
107-06-2	1,2-Dichloroethane			100		313	U077
107-06-2	Ethylene dichloride			100		X	U077
107-07-3	Chloroethanol	500	500				
107-10-8	n-Propylamine			5,000			U194
107-11-9	Allylamine	500	500		10,000	313	
107-11-9	2-Propen-1-amine	500	500		10,000	X	
107-12-0	Ethyl cyanide	500	10	10	10,000		P101
107-12-0	Propanenitrile	500	10	10	10,000		P101
107-12-0	Propionitrile	500	10	10	10,000		P101
107-13-1	Acrylonitrile	10,000	100	100	20,000	313	U009
107-13-1	2-Propenenitrile	10,000	100	100	20,000	X	U009
107-15-3	1,2-Ethanediamine	10,000	5,000	5,000	20,000		
107-15-3	Ethylenediamine	10,000	5,000	5,000	20,000		
107-16-4	Formaldehyde cyanohydrin	1,000	1,000				
107-18-6	Allyl alcohol	1,000	100	100	15,000	313	P005
107-18-6	2-Propen-1-ol	1,000	100	100	15,000	X	P005
107-19-7	Propargyl alcohol			1,000		313	P102
107-20-0	Chloroacetaldehyde			1,000			P023
107-21-1	Ethylene glycol			5,000		313	
107-25-5	Ethene, methoxy-				10,000		
107-25-5	Vinyl methyl ether				10,000		
107-30-2	Chloromethyl methyl ether	100	10	10	5,000	313	U046
107-30-2	Methane, chloromethoxy-	100	10	10	5,000	X	U046
107-31-3	Formic acid, methyl ester				10,000		
107-31-3	Methyl formate				10,000		
107-44-8	Sarin	10	10				
107-49-3	Tepp	100	10	10			P111
107-49-3	Tetraethyl pyrophosphate	100	10	10			P111
107-92-6	Butyric acid			5,000			
108-05-4	Vinyl acetate	1,000	5,000	5,000	15,000	313	
108-05-4	Acetic acid ethenyl ester	1,000	5,000	5,000	15,000	X	
108-05-4	Vinyl acetate monomer	1,000	5,000	5,000	15,000	X	
108-10-1	Methyl isobutyl ketone			5,000		313	U161

CAS Number	Chemical Name	Sec 302 (EHS) RQ	Section 304 EHS RQ	Section 304 CERCLA RQ	CAA 112 (r) TQ	Sec 313	RCRA Code
108-23-6	Carbonochloridic acid, 1-methylethyl ester	1,000	1,000		15,000		
108-23-6	Isopropyl chloroformate	1,000	1,000		15,000		
108-24-7	Acetic anhydride			5,000			
108-31-6	Maleic anhydride			5,000		313	U147
108-38-3	m-Xylene			1,000		313	U239
108-38-3	Benzene, m-dimethyl-			1,000		X	U239
108-39-4	m-Cresol			100		313	U052
108-45-2	1,3-Phenylenediamine					313	
108-46-3	Resorcinol			5,000			U201
108-60-1	Bis(2-chloro-1-methylethyl)ether			1,000		313	U027
108-60-1	Dichloroisopropyl ether			1,000		X	U027
108-88-3	Toluene			1,000		313	U220
108-90-7	Chlorobenzene			100		313	U037
108-91-8	Cyclohexanamine	10,000	10,000		15,000		
108-91-8	Cyclohexylamine	10,000	10,000		15,000		
108-93-0	Cyclohexanol					313	
108-94-1	Cyclohexanone			5,000			U057
108-95-2	Phenol	500/10,000	1,000	1,000		313	U188
108-98-5	Benzenethiol	500	100	100			P014
108-98-5	Thiophenol	500	100	100			P014
109-06-8	2-Methylpyridine			5,000		313	U191
109-06-8	2-Picoline			5,000		X	U191
109-61-5	Carbonochloridic acid, propylester	500	500		15,000		
109-61-5	Propyl chloroformate	500	500		15,000		
109-66-0	Pentane				10,000		
109-67-1	1-Pentene				10,000		
109-73-9	Butylamine			1,000			
109-77-3	Malononitrile	500/10,000	1,000	1,000		313	U149
109-86-4	2-Methoxyethanol					313	
109-89-7	Diethylamine			100			
109-92-2	Ethene, ethoxy-				10,000		
109-92-2	Vinyl ethyl ether				10,000		
109-95-5	Ethyl nitrite				10,000		
109-95-5	Nitrous acid, ethyl ester				10,000		
109-99-9	Furan, tetrahydro-			1,000			U213
110-00-9	Furan	500	100	100	5,000		U124
110-16-7	Maleic acid			5,000			
110-17-8	Fumaric acid			5,000			
110-19-0	iso-Butyl acetate			5,000			
110-54-3	n-Hexane			5,000		313	
110-54-3	Hexane			5,000		X	
110-57-6	trans-1,4-Dichloro-2-butene	500	500			313	
110-57-6	trans-1,4-Dichlorobutene	500	500			X	
110-75-8	2-Chloroethyl vinyl ether			1,000			U042
110-80-5	2-Ethoxyethanol			1,000		313	U359
110-80-5	Ethanol, 2-ethoxy-			1,000		X	U359
110-82-7	Cyclohexane			1,000		313	U056
110-86-1	Pyridine			1,000		313	U196

CAS Number	Chemical Name	Sec 302 (EHS) RQ	Section 304 EHS RQ	Section 304 CERCLA RQ	CAA 112 (r) TQ	Sec 313	RCRA Code
110-89-4	Piperidine	1,000	1,000		15,000		
111-42-2	Diethanolamine			100		313	
111-44-4	Bis(2-chloroethyl) ether	10,000	10	10		313	U025
111-44-4	Dichloroethyl ether	10,000	10	10		X	U025
111-54-6	Ethylenebisdithiocarbamic acid, salts & esters			5,000		X	U114
111-69-3	Adiponitrile	1,000	1,000				
111-91-1	Bis(2-chloroethoxy) methane			1,000		313	U024
114-26-1	Propoxur			100		313	U411
114-26-1	Phenol, 2-(1-methylethoxy)-, methylcarbamate			100		X	U411
115-02-6	Azaserine			1			U015
115-07-1	Propylene				10,000	313	
115-07-1	Propene				10,000	X	
115-07-1	1-Propene				10,000	X	
115-10-6	Methane, oxybis-				10,000		
115-10-6	Methyl ether				10,000		
115-11-7	2-Methylpropene				10,000		
115-11-7	1-Propene, 2-methyl-				10,000		
115-21-9	Trichloroethylsilane	500	500				
115-26-4	Dimefox	500	500				
115-28-6	Chlorendic acid					313	
115-29-7	Endosulfan	10/10,000	1	1			P050
115-32-2	Dicofol			10		313	
115-32-2	Benzenemethanol, 4-chloro-.alpha.-4-chlorophenyl)-.			10		X	
115-90-2	Fensulfothion	500	500				
116-06-3	Aldicarb	100/10,000	1	1		313	P070
116-14-3	Ethene, tetrafluoro-				10,000		
116-14-3	Tetrafluoroethylene				10,000		
117-79-3	2-Aminoanthraquinone					313	
117-80-6	Dichlone			1			
117-81-7	Di(2-ethylhexyl) phthalate			100		313	U028
117-81-7	Bis(2-ethylhexyl)phthalate			100		X	U028
117-81-7	DEHP			100		X	U028
117-84-0	n-Dioctylphthalate			5,000			U107
117-84-0	Di-n-octyl phthalate			5,000			U107
118-74-1	Hexachlorobenzene			10		313	U127
119-38-0	Isopropylmethylpyrazolyl dimethylcarbamate	500	1*	1*			P192
119-90-4	3,3'-Dimethoxybenzidine			100		313	U091
119-93-7	3,3'-Dimethylbenzidine			10		313	U095
119-93-7	o-Tolidine			10		X	U095
120-12-7	Anthracene			5,000		313	
120-36-5	2,4-DP					313	
120-54-7	Piperidine, 1,1'-(tetrathiodicarbonothioyl)-bis-			1*			U400
120-58-1	Isosafrole			100		313	U141
120-71-8	p-Cresidine					313	

CAS Number	Chemical Name	Sec 302 (EHS) RQ	Section 304 EHS RQ	Section 304 CERCLA RQ	CAA 112 (r) TQ	Sec 313	RCRA Code
120-80-9	Catechol			100		313	
120-82-1	1,2,4-Trichlorobenzene			100		313	
120-83-2	2,4-Dichlorophenol			100		313	U081
121-14-2	2,4-Dinitrotoluene			10		313	U105
121-21-1	Pyrethrins			1			
121-29-9	Pyrethrins			1			
121-44-8	Triethylamine			5,000		313	U404
121-69-7	N,N-Dimethylaniline			100		313	
121-75-5	Malathion			100		313	
122-09-8	Benzeneethanamine, alpha,alpha-dimethyl-			5,000			P046
122-34-9	Simazine					313	
122-39-4	Diphenylamine					313	
122-42-9	Propham			1*			U373
122-66-7	1,2-Diphenylhydrazine			10		313	U109
122-66-7	Hydrazine, 1,2-diphenyl-			10		X	U109
122-66-7	Hydrazobenzene			10		X	U109
123-31-9	Hydroquinone	500/10,000	100	100		313	
123-33-1	Maleic hydrazide			5,000			U148
123-38-6	Propionaldehyde			1,000		313	
123-61-5	1,3-Phenylene diisocyanate					313#	
123-62-6	Propionic anhydride			5,000			
123-63-7	Paraldehyde			1,000		313	U182
123-72-8	Butyraldehyde					313	
123-73-9	2-Butenal, (e)-	1,000	100	100	20,000		U053
123-73-9	Crotonaldehyde, (E)-	1,000	100	100	20,000		U053
123-86-4	Butyl acetate			5,000			
123-91-1	1,4-Dioxane			100		313	U108
123-92-2	iso-Amyl acetate			5,000			
124-04-9	Adipic acid			5,000			
124-40-3	Dimethylamine			1,000	10,000	313	U092
124-40-3	Methanamine, N-methyl-			1,000	10,000	X	U092
124-41-4	Sodium methylate			1,000			
124-48-1	Chlorodibromomethane			100			
124-65-2	Sodium cacodylate	100/10,000	100				
124-73-2	Dibromotetrafluoroethane					313	
124-73-2	Halon 2402					X	
124-87-8	Picrotoxin	500/10,000	500				
126-72-7	Tris(2,3-dibromopropyl) phosphate			10		313	U235
126-98-7	Methacrylonitrile	500	1,000	1,000	10,000	313	U152
126-98-7	2-Propenenitrile, 2-methyl-	500	1,000	1,000	10,000	X	U152
126-99-8	Chloroprene			100		313	
127-18-4	Tetrachloroethylene			100		313	U210
127-18-4	Perchloroethylene			100		X	U210
127-82-2	Zinc phenolsulfonate			5,000			
128-03-0	Potassium dimethyldithiocarbamate			1*		313	U383
128-04-1	Sodium dimethyldithiocarbamate			1*		313	U382
128-66-5	C.I. Vat Yellow 4					313	

CAS Number	Chemical Name	Sec 302 (EHS) RQ	Section 304 EHS RQ	Section 304 CERCLA RQ	CAA 112 (r) TQ	Sec 313	RCRA Code
129-00-0	Pyrene	1,000/10,000	5,000	5,000			
129-06-6	Warfarin sodium	100/10,000	100	100			
130-15-4	1,4-Naphthoquinone			5,000			U166
131-11-3	Dimethyl phthalate			5,000		313	U102
131-52-2	Sodium pentachlorophenate					313	
131-74-8	Ammonium picrate			10			P009
131-89-5	2-Cyclohexyl-4,6-dinitrophenol			100			P034
132-27-4	Sodium o-phenylphenoxide					313	
132-64-9	Dibenzofuran			100		313	
133-06-2	Captan			10		313	
133-06-2	1H-Isoindole-1,3(2H)-dione, 3a,4,7,7a-tetrahydro-2-			10		X	
133-07-3	Folpet					313	
133-90-4	Chloramben			100		313	
133-90-4	Benzoic acid, 3-amino-2,5-dichloro-			100		X	
134-29-2	o-Anisidine hydrochloride					313	
134-32-7	alpha-Naphthylamine			100		313	U167
135-20-6	Cupferron					313	
135-20-6	Benzeneamine, N-hydroxy-N-nitroso, ammonium salt					X	
136-30-1	Carbamodithioic acid, dibutyl-, sodium salt			1*			U379
136-45-8	Dipropyl isocinchomeronate					313	
137-26-8	Thiram			10		313	U244
137-29-1	Copper, bis(dimethylcarbamodithioato-S,S')-			1*			U393
137-30-4	Ziram			1*			P205
137-41-7	Potassium N-methyldithiocarbamate			1*		313	U377
137-42-8	Metham sodium			1*		313	U384
137-42-8	Sodium methyldithiocarbamate			1*		X	U384
138-93-2	Disodium cyanodithioimidocarbonate					313	
139-13-9	Nitrilotriacetic acid					313	
139-25-3	3,3'-Dimethyldiphenylmethane-4,4'-diisocyanate					313#	
139-65-1	4,4'-Thiodianiline					313	
140-29-4	Benzyl cyanide	500	500				
140-76-1	Pyridine, 2-methyl-5-vinyl-	500	500				
140-88-5	Ethyl acrylate			1,000		313	U113
141-32-2	Butyl acrylate					313	
141-66-2	Dicrotophos	100	100				
141-78-6	Ethyl acetate			5,000			U112
142-28-9	1,3-Dichloropropane			5,000			
142-59-6	Nabam					313	
142-71-2	Cupric acetate			100			
142-84-7	Dipropylamine			5,000			U110
143-33-9	Sodium cyanide (Na(CN))	100	10	10			P106
143-50-0	Kepone			1			U142

CAS Number	Chemical Name	Sec 302 (EHS) RQ	Section 304 EHS RQ	Section 304 CERCLA RQ	CAA 112 (r) TQ	Sec 313	RCRA Code
144-34-3	Selenium, tetrakis(dimethyldithiocarbamate)			1*			U376
144-49-0	Fluoroacetic acid	10/10,000	10				
145-73-3	Endothall			1,000			P088
148-18-5	Carbamodithioic acid, diethyl-, sodium salt			1*			U381
148-79-8	Thiabendazole					313	
148-79-8	2-(4-Thiazolyl)-1H-benzimidazole					X	
148-82-3	Melphalan			1			U150
149-30-4	2-Mercaptobenzothiazole					313	
149-30-4	MBT					X	
149-74-6	Dichloromethylphenylsilane	1,000	1,000				
150-50-5	Merphos					313	
150-68-5	Monuron					313	
151-38-2	Methoxyethylmercuric acetate	500/10,000	500				
151-50-8	Potassium cyanide	100	10	10			P098
151-56-4	Ethyleneimine	500	1	1	10,000	313	P054
151-56-4	Aziridine	500	1	1	10,000	X	P054
152-16-9	Diphosphoramide, octamethyl-	100	100	100			P085
156-10-5	p-Nitrosodiphenylamine					313	
156-60-5	1,2-Dichloroethylene			1,000			U079
156-62-7	Calcium cyanamide			1,000		313	
189-55-9	Benzo(rst)pentaphene			10		313+	U064
189-55-9	Dibenz[a,i]pyrene			10		X	U064
189-64-0	Dibenzo(a,h)pyrene					313+	
191-24-2	Benzo[ghi]perylene			5,000			
191-30-0	Dibenzo(a,l)pyrene					313+	
192-65-4	Dibenzo(a,e)pyrene					313+	
193-39-5	Indeno(1,2,3-cd)pyrene			100		313+	U137
194-59-2	7H-Dibenzo(c,g)carbazole					313+	
205-82-3	Benzo(j)fluoranthene					313+	
205-99-2	Benzo[b]fluoranthene			1		313+	
206-44-0	Fluoranthene			100			U120
207-08-9	Benzo(k)fluoranthene			5,000		313+	
208-96-8	Acenaphthylene			5,000			
218-01-9	Benzo(a)phenanthrene			100		313+	U050
218-01-9	Chrysene			100		X	U050
224-42-0	Dibenz(a,j)acridine					313+	
225-51-4	Benz[c]acridine			100			U016
226-36-8	Dibenz(a,h)acridine					313+	
297-78-9	Isobenzan	100/10,000	100				
297-97-2	O,O-Diethyl O-pyrazinyl phosphorothioate	500	100	100			P040
297-97-2	Thionazin	500	100	100			P040
298-00-0	Methyl parathion	100/10,000	100	100		313	P071
298-00-0	Parathion-methyl	100/10,000	100	100		X	P071
298-02-2	Phorate	10	10	10			P094
298-04-4	Disulfoton	500	1	1			P039
300-62-9	Amphetamine	1,000	1,000				

CAS Number	Chemical Name	Sec 302 (EHS) RQ	Section 304		CAA 112 (r) TQ	Sec 313	RCRA Code
			EHS RQ	CERCLA RQ			
300-76-5	Naled			10		313	
301-04-2	Lead acetate			10			U144
301-12-2	Oxydemeton methyl					313	
301-12-2	S-(2-(Ethylsulfinyl)ethyl) O,O-dimethyl ester phosp					X	
302-01-2	Hydrazine	1,000	1	1	15,000	313	U133
303-34-4	Lasiocarpine			10			U143
305-03-3	Chlorambucil			10			U035
306-83-2	2,2-Dichloro-1,1,1-trifluoroethane					313	
306-83-2	HCFC-123					X	
309-00-2	Aldrin	500/10,000	1	1		313	P004
309-00-2	1,4:5,8-Dimethanonaphthalene, 1,2,3,4,10,10-hexachl	500/10,000	1	1		X	P004
311-45-5	Diethyl-p-nitrophenyl phosphate			100			P041
314-40-9	Bromacil					313	
314-40-9	5-Bromo-6-methyl-3-(1-methylpropyl)-2,4-(1H,3H)-pyr					X	
315-18-4	Mexacarbate	500/10,000	1,000	1,000			P199
316-42-7	Emetine, dihydrochloride	1/10,000	1				
319-84-6	alpha-Hexachlorocyclohexane			10		313	
319-84-6	alpha-BHC			10		X	
319-85-7	beta-BHC			1			
319-86-8	delta-BHC			1			
327-98-0	Trichloronate	500	500				
329-71-5	2,5-Dinitrophenol			10			
330-54-1	Diuron			100		313	
330-55-2	Linuron					313	
333-41-5	Diazinon			1		313	
334-88-3	Diazomethane			100		313	
353-42-4	Boron trifluoride compound with methyl ether (1:1)	1,000	1,000		15,000		
353-42-4	Boron, trifluoro[oxybis[methane]]-, (T-4)-	1,000	1,000		15,000		
353-50-4	Carbonic difluoride			1,000			U033
353-59-3	Bromochlorodifluoromethane					313	
353-59-3	Halon 1211					X	
354-11-0	1,1,1,2-Tetrachloro-2-fluoroethane					313	
354-11-0	HCFC-121a					X	
354-14-3	1,1,2,2-Tetrachloro-1-fluoroethane					313	
354-14-3	HCFC-121					X	
354-23-4	1,2-Dichloro-1,1,2-trifluoroethane					313	
354-23-4	HCFC-123a					X	
354-25-6	1-Chloro-1,1,2,2-tetrafluoroethane					313	
354-25-6	HCFC-124a					X	
357-57-3	Brucine			100		313	P018
359-06-8	Fluoroacetyl chloride	10	10				
371-62-0	Ethylene fluorohydrin	10	10				
379-79-3	Ergotamine tartrate	500/10,000	500				

CAS Number	Chemical Name	Sec 302 (EHS) RQ	Section 304 EHS RQ	Section 304 CERCLA RQ	CAA 112 (r) TQ	Sec 313	RCRA Code
422-44-6	1,2-Dichloro-1,1,2,3,3-pentafluoropropane					313	
422-44-6	HCFC-225bb					X	
422-48-0	2,3-Dichloro-1,1,1,2,3-pentafluoropropane					313	
422-48-0	HCFC-225ba					X	
422-56-0	3,3-Dichloro-1,1,1,2,2-pentafluoropropane					313	
422-56-0	HCFC-225ca					X	
431-86-7	1,2-Dichloro-1,1,3,3,3-pentafluoropropane					313	
431-86-7	HCFC-225da					X	
460-19-5	Cyanogen			100	10,000		P031
460-19-5	Ethanedinitrile			100	10,000		P031
460-35-5	3-Chloro-1,1,1-trifluoropropane					313	
460-35-5	HCFC-253fb					X	
463-49-0	1,2-Propadiene				10,000		
463-49-0	Propadiene				10,000		
463-58-1	Carbonyl sulfide			100	10,000	313	
463-58-1	Carbon oxide sulfide (COS)			100	10,000	X	
463-82-1	2,2-Dimethylpropane				10,000		
463-82-1	Propane, 2,2-dimethyl-				10,000		
465-73-6	Isodrin	100/10,000	1	1		313	P060
470-90-6	Chlorfenvinfos	500	500				
492-80-8	C.I. Solvent Yellow 34			100		313	U014
492-80-8	Auramine			100		X	U014
494-03-1	Chlornaphazine			100			U026
496-72-0	Diaminotoluene			10			U221
502-39-6	Methylmercuric dicyanamide	500/10,000	500				
504-24-5	4-Aminopyridine	500/10,000	1,000	1,000			P008
504-24-5	Pyridine, 4-amino-	500/10,000	1,000	1,000			P008
504-60-9	1,3-Pentadiene			100	10,000		U186
505-60-2	Mustard gas	500	500			313	
505-60-2	Ethane, 1,1'-thiobis[2-chloro-	500	500			X	
506-61-6	Potassium silver cyanide	500	1	1			P099
506-64-9	Silver cyanide			1			P104
506-68-3	Cyanogen bromide	500/10,000	1,000	1,000			U246
506-77-4	Cyanogen chloride			10	10,000		P033
506-77-4	Cyanogen chloride ((CN)Cl)			10	10,000		P033
506-78-5	Cyanogen iodide	1,000/10,000	1,000				
506-87-6	Ammonium carbonate			5,000			
506-96-7	Acetyl bromide			5,000			
507-55-1	1,3-Dichloro-1,1,2,2,3-pentafluoropropane					313	
507-55-1	HCFC-225cb					X	
509-14-8	Methane, tetranitro-	500	10	10	10,000		P112
509-14-8	Tetranitromethane	500	10	10	10,000		P112
510-15-6	Chlorobenzilate			10		313	U038

CAS Number	Chemical Name	Sec 302 (EHS) RQ	Section 304 EHS RQ	Section 304 CERCLA RQ	CAA 112 (r) TQ	Sec 313	RCRA Code
510-15-6	Benzeneacetic acid, 4-chloro-.alpha.-(4-chlropheny			10		X	U038
513-49-5	sec-Butylamine			1,000			
514-73-8	Dithiazanine iodide	500/10,000	500				
528-29-0	o-Dinitrobenzene			100		313	
532-27-4	2-Chloroacetophenone			100		313	
533-74-4	Dazomet			1*		313	U366
533-74-4	Tetrahydro-3,5-dimethyl-2H-1,3,5-thiadiazine-2-thio			1*		X	U366
534-07-6	Bis(chloromethyl) ketone	10/10,000	10				
534-52-1	4,6-Dinitro-o-cresol and salts			10			P047
534-52-1	4,6-Dinitro-o-cresol	10/10,000	10	10		313	P047
534-52-1	Dinitrocresol	10/10,000	10	10		X	P047
535-89-7	Crimidine	100/10,000	100				
538-07-8	Ethylbis(2-chloroethyl)amine	500	500				
540-59-0	1,2-Dichloroethylene					313	
540-73-8	Hydrazine, 1,2-dimethyl-			1			U099
540-84-1	2,2,4-Trimethylpentane			1,000			
540-88-5	tert-Butyl acetate			5,000			
541-09-3	Uranyl acetate			100			
541-25-3	Lewisite	10	10				
541-41-3	Ethyl chloroformate					313	
541-53-7	2,4-Dithiobiuret	100/10,000	100	100		313	P049
541-53-7	Dithiobiuret	100/10,000	100	100		X	P049
541-73-1	1,3-Dichlorobenzene			100		313	U071
542-62-1	Barium cyanide			10			P013
542-75-6	1,3-Dichloropropylene			100		313	U084
542-75-6	1,3-Dichloropropene			100		X	U084
542-76-7	3-Chloropropionitrile	1,000	1,000	1,000		313	P027
542-76-7	Propionitrile, 3-chloro-	1,000	1,000	1,000		X	P027
542-88-1	Bis(chloromethyl) ether	100	10	10	1,000	313	P016
542-88-1	Chloromethyl ether	100	10	10	1,000	X	P016
542-88-1	Dichloromethyl ether	100	10	10	1,000	X	P016
542-88-1	Methane, oxybis[chloro-	100	10	10	1,000	X	P016
542-90-5	Ethylthiocyanate	10,000	10,000				
543-90-8	Cadmium acetate			10			
544-18-3	Cobaltous formate			1,000			
544-92-3	Copper cyanide			10			P029
554-13-2	Lithium carbonate					313	
554-84-7	m-Nitrophenol			100			
555-77-1	Tris(2-chloroethyl)amine	100	100				
556-61-6	Methyl isothiocyanate	500	500			313	
556-61-6	Isothiocyanatomethane	500	500			X	
556-64-9	Methyl thiocyanate	10,000	10,000		20,000		
556-64-9	Thiocyanic acid, methyl ester	10,000	10,000		20,000		
557-19-7	Nickel cyanide			10			P074
557-21-1	Zinc cyanide			10			P121
557-34-6	Zinc acetate			1,000			
557-41-5	Zinc formate			1,000			

CAS Number	Chemical Name	Sec 302 (EHS) RQ	Section 304 EHS RQ	Section 304 CERCLA RQ	CAA 112 (r) TQ	Sec 313	RCRA Code
557-98-2	2-Chloropropylene				10,000		
557-98-2	1-Propene, 2-chloro-				10,000		
558-25-8	Methanesulfonyl fluoride	1,000	1,000				
563-12-2	Ethion	1,000	10	10			
563-41-7	Semicarbazide hydrochloride	1,000/10,000	1,000				
563-45-1	3-Methyl-1-butene				10,000		
563-46-2	2-Methyl-1-butene				10,000		
563-47-3	3-Chloro-2-methyl-1-propene					313	
563-68-8	Thallium(I) acetate			100			U214
569-64-2	C.I. Basic Green 4					313	
573-56-8	2,6-Dinitrophenol			10			
576-26-1	2,6-Dimethylphenol					313	
584-84-9	Toluene-2,4-diisocyanate	500	100	100	10,000	313	
584-84-9	Benzene, 2,4-diisocyanato-1-methyl-	500	100	100	10,000	X	
590-18-1	2-Butene-cis				10,000		
590-21-6	1-Chloropropylene				10,000		
590-21-6	1-Propene, 1-chloro-				10,000		
591-08-2	1-Acetyl-2-thiourea			1,000			P002
592-01-8	Calcium cyanide			10			P021
592-04-1	Mercuric cyanide			1			
592-85-8	Mercuric thiocyanate			10			
592-87-0	Lead thiocyanate			10			
593-60-2	Vinyl bromide			100		313	
594-42-3	Perchloromethyl mercaptan	500	100	100	10,000	313	
594-42-3	Methanesulfenyl chloride, trichloro-	500	100	100	10,000	X	
594-42-3	Trichloromethanesulfenyl chloride	500	100	100	10,000	X	
597-64-8	Tetraethyltin	100	100				
598-31-2	Bromoacetone			1,000			P017
598-73-2	Bromotrifluoroethylene				10,000		
598-73-2	Ethene, bromotrifluoro-				10,000		
606-20-2	2,6-Dinitrotoluene			100		313	U106
608-93-5	Pentachlorobenzene			10			U183
609-19-8	3,4,5-Trichlorophenol			10			
610-39-9	3,4-Dinitrotoluene			10			
612-82-8	3,3'-Dimethylbenzidine dihydrochloride					313	
612-82-8	o-Tolidine dihydrochloride					X	
612-83-9	3,3'-Dichlorobenzidine dihydrochloride					313	
614-78-8	Thiourea, (2-methylphenyl)-	500/10,000	500				
615-05-4	2,4-Diaminoanisole					313	
615-28-1	1,2-Phenylenediamine dihydrochloride					313	
615-53-2	N-Nitroso-N-methylurethane			1			U178
621-64-7	N-Nitrosodi-n-propylamine			10		313	U111
621-64-7	Di-n-propylnitrosamine			10		X	U111
624-18-0	1,4-Phenylenediamine dihydrochloride					313	

CAS Number	Chemical Name	Sec 302 (EHS) RQ	Section 304 EHS RQ	Section 304 CERCLA RQ	CAA 112 (r) TQ	Sec 313	RCRA Code
624-64-6	2-Butene, (E)				10,000		
624-64-6	2-Butene-trans				10,000		
624-83-9	Methyl isocyanate	500	10	10	10,000	313	P064
624-83-9	Methane, isocyanato-	500	10	10	10,000	X	P064
625-16-1	tert-Amyl acetate			5,000			
626-38-0	sec-Amyl acetate			5,000			
627-11-2	Chloroethyl chloroformate	1,000	1,000				
627-20-3	2-Pentene, (Z)-				10,000		
628-63-7	Amyl acetate			5,000			
628-86-4	Mercury fulminate			10			P065
630-10-4	Selenourea			1,000			P103
630-20-6	1,1,1,2-Tetrachloroethane			100		313	U208
630-20-6	Ethane, 1,1,1,2-tetrachloro-			100		X	U208
630-60-4	Ouabain	100/10,000	100				
631-61-8	Ammonium acetate			5,000			
636-21-5	o-Toluidine hydrochloride			100		313	U222
639-58-7	Triphenyltin chloride	500/10,000	500			313	
640-19-7	Fluoroacetamide	100/10,000	100	100			P057
644-64-4	Dimetilan	500/10,000	1*	1*			P191
646-04-8	2-Pentene, (E)-				10,000		
675-14-9	Cyanuric fluoride	100	100				
676-97-1	Methyl phosphonic dichloride	100	100				
680-31-9	Hexamethylphosphoramide			1		313	
684-93-5	N-Nitroso-N-methylurea			1		313	U177
689-97-4	1-Buten-3-yne				10,000		
689-97-4	Vinyl acetylene				10,000		
692-42-2	Diethylarsine			1			P038
696-28-6	Dichlorophenylarsine	500	1	1			P036
696-28-6	Phenyl dichloroarsine	500	1	1			P036
709-98-8	Propanil					313	
709-98-8	N-(3,4-Dichlorophenyl)propanamide					X	
732-11-6	Phosmet	10/10,000	10				
757-58-4	Hexaethyl tetraphosphate			100			P062
759-73-9	N-Nitroso-N-ethylurea			1		313	U176
759-94-4	Ethyl dipropylthiocarbamate			1*		313	U390
759-94-4	EPTC			1*		X	U390
760-93-0	Methacrylic anhydride	500	500				
764-41-0	1,4-Dichloro-2-butene			1		313	U074
764-41-0	2-Butene, 1,4-dichloro-			1		X	U074
765-34-4	Glycidylaldehyde			10			U126
786-19-6	Carbophenothion	500	500				
812-04-4	1,1-Dichloro-1,2,2-trifluoroethane					313	
812-04-4	HCFC-123b					X	
814-49-3	Diethyl chlorophosphate	500	500				
814-68-6	Acrylyl chloride	100	100		5,000		
814-68-6	2-Propenoyl chloride	100	100		5,000		
815-82-7	Cupric tartrate			100			
822-06-0	Hexamethylene-1,6-diisocyanate			100		313#	
823-40-5	Diaminotoluene			10			U221

CAS Number	Chemical Name	Sec 302 (EHS) RQ	Section 304 EHS RQ	Section 304 CERCLA RQ	CAA 112 (r) TQ	Sec 313	RCRA Code
824-11-3	Trimethylolpropane phosphite	100/10,000	100				
834-12-8	Ametryn					313	
834-12-8	N-Ethyl-N'-(1-methylethyl)-6-(methylthio)-1,3,5,-tr					X	
842-07-9	C.I. Solvent Yellow 14					313	
872-50-4	N-Methyl-2-pyrrolidone					313	
900-95-8	Stannane, acetoxytriphenyl-	500/10,000	500				
919-86-8	Demeton-S-methyl	500	500				
920-46-7	Methacryloyl chloride	100	100				
924-16-3	N-Nitrosodi-n-butylamine			10		313	U172
924-42-5	N-Methylolacrylamide					313	
930-55-2	N-Nitrosopyrrolidine			1			U180
933-75-5	2,3,6-Trichlorophenol			10			
933-78-8	2,3,5-Trichlorophenol			10			
944-22-9	Fonofos	500	500				
947-02-4	Phosfolan	100/10,000	100				
950-10-7	Mephosfolan	500	500				
950-37-8	Methidathion	500/10,000	500				
957-51-7	Diphenamid					313	
959-98-8	alpha - Endosulfan			1			
961-11-5	Tetrachlorvinphos					313	
961-11-5	Phosphoric acid, 2-chloro-1-(2,3,5-trichlorophenyl)					X	
989-38-8	C.I. Basic Red 1					313	
991-42-4	Norbormide	100/10,000	100				
998-30-1	Triethoxysilane	500	500				
999-81-5	Chlormequat chloride	100/10,000	100				
1024-57-3	Heptachlor epoxide			1			
1031-07-8	Endosulfan sulfate			1			
1031-47-6	Triamiphos	500/10,000	500				
1066-30-4	Chromic acetate			1,000			
1066-33-7	Ammonium bicarbonate			5,000			
1066-45-1	Trimethyltin chloride	500/10,000	500				
1072-35-1	Lead stearate			10			
1111-78-0	Ammonium carbamate			5,000			
1114-71-2	Pebulate			1*		313	U391
1114-71-2	Butylethylcarbamothioic acid S-propyl ester			1*		X	U391
1116-54-7	N-Nitrosodiethanolamine			1			U173
1120-71-4	Propane sultone			10		313	U193
1120-71-4	1,3-Propane sultone			10		X	U193
1122-60-7	Nitrocyclohexane	500	500				
1124-33-0	Pyridine, 4-nitro-, 1-oxide	500/10,000	500				
1129-41-5	Metolcarb	100/10,000	1*	1*			P190
1134-23-2	Cycloate			1*		313	U386
1163-19-5	Decabromodiphenyl oxide					313	
1185-57-5	Ferric ammonium citrate			1,000			
1194-65-6	Dichlobenil			100			
1300-71-6	Xylenol			1,000			

CAS Number	Chemical Name	Sec 302 (EHS) RQ	Section 304		CAA 112 (r) TQ	Sec 313	RCRA Code
			EHS RQ	CERCLA RQ			
1303-28-2	Arsenic pentoxide	100/10,000	1	1			P011
1303-32-8	Arsenic disulfide			1			
1303-33-9	Arsenic trisulfide			1			
1306-19-0	Cadmium oxide	100/10,000	100				
1309-64-4	Antimony trioxide			1,000			
1310-58-3	Potassium hydroxide			1,000			
1310-73-2	Sodium hydroxide			1,000			
1313-27-5	Molybdenum trioxide					313	
1314-20-1	Thorium dioxide					313	
1314-32-5	Thallic oxide			100			P113
1314-62-1	Vanadium pentoxide	100/10,000	1,000	1,000			P120
1314-80-3	Sulfur phosphide			100			U189
1314-84-7	Zinc phosphide	500	100	100			P122
1314-84-7	Zinc phosphide (conc. <= 10%)	500	100	100			U249
1314-84-7	Zinc phosphide (conc. > 10%)	500	100	100			P122
1314-87-0	Lead sulfide			10			
1319-72-8	2,4,5-T amines			5,000			
1319-77-3	Cresol (mixed isomers)			100		313	U052
1320-18-9	2,4-D propylene glycol butyl ether ester			100		313	
1320-18-9	2,4-D Esters			100		X	
1321-12-6	Nitrotoluene			1,000			
1327-52-2	Arsenic acid			1			
1327-53-3	Arsenic trioxide	100/10,000	1	1			P012
1327-53-3	Arsenous oxide	100/10,000	1	1			P012
1330-20-7	Xylene (mixed isomers)			100		313	U239
1332-07-6	Zinc borate			1,000			
1332-21-4	Asbestos (friable)			1		313	
1333-74-0	Hydrogen				10,000		
1333-83-1	Sodium bifluoride			100			
1335-32-6	Lead subacetate			10			U146
1335-87-1	Hexachloronaphthalene					313	
1336-21-6	Ammonium hydroxide			1,000			
1336-36-3	Polychlorinated biphenyls			1		313	
1336-36-3	PCBs			1		X	
1338-23-4	Methyl ethyl ketone peroxide			10			U160
1338-24-5	Naphthenic acid			100			
1341-49-7	Ammonium bifluoride			100			
1344-28-1	Aluminum oxide (fibrous forms)					313	
1397-94-0	Antimycin A	1,000/10,000	1,000				
1420-07-1	Dinoterb	500/10,000	500				
1464-53-5	Diepoxybutane	500	10	10		313	U085
1464-53-5	2,2'-Bioxirane	500	10	10		X	U085
1558-25-4	Trichloro(chloromethyl)silane	100	100				
1563-38-8	Carbofuran phenol			1*			U367
1563-66-2	Carbofuran	10/10,000	10	10		313	P127
1582-09-8	Trifluralin			10		313	
1582-09-8	Benezeneamine, 2,6-dinitro-N,N-dipropyl-4-(trifluor			10		X	

CAS Number	Chemical Name	Sec 302 (EHS) RQ	Section 304 EHS RQ	Section 304 CERCLA RQ	CAA 112 (r) TQ	Sec 313	RCRA Code
1600-27-7	Mercuric acetate	500/10,000	500				
1615-80-1	Hydrazine, 1,2-diethyl-			10			U086
1622-32-8	Ethanesulfonyl chloride, 2-chloro-	500	500				
1634-02-2	Tetrabutylthiuram disulfide			1*			U402
1634-04-4	Methyl tert-butyl ether			1,000		313	
1646-88-4	Aldicarb sulfone			1*			P203
1649-08-7	1,2-Dichloro-1,1-difluoroethane					313	
1649-08-7	HCFC-132b					X	
1689-84-5	Bromoxynil					313	
1689-84-5	3,5-Dibromo-4-hydroxybenzonitrile					X	
1689-99-2	Bromoxynil octanoate					313	
1689-99-2	Octanoic acid, 2,6-dibromo-4-cyanophenyl ester					X	
1717-00-6	1,1-Dichloro-1-fluoroethane					313	
1717-00-6	HCFC-141b					X	
1746-01-6	2,3,7,8-Tetrachlorodibenzo-p-dioxin (TCDD)			1			
1752-30-3	Acetone thiosemicarbazide	1,000/10,000	1,000				
1762-95-4	Ammonium thiocyanate			5,000			
1836-75-5	Nitrofen					313	
1836-75-5	Benzene, 2,4-dichloro-1-(4-nitrophenoxy)-					X	
1861-40-1	Benfluralin					313	
1861-40-1	N-Butyl-N-ethyl-2,6-dinitro-4-(trifluoromethyl) ben					X	
1863-63-4	Ammonium benzoate			5,000			
1888-71-7	Hexachloropropene			1,000			U243
1897-45-6	Chlorothalonil					313	
1897-45-6	1,3-Benzenedicarbonitrile, 2,4,5,6-tetrachloro-					X	
1910-42-5	Paraquat dichloride	10/10,000	10			313	
1912-24-9	Atrazine					313	
1912-24-9	6-Chloro-N-ethyl-N'-(1-methylethyl)-1,3,5-triazine-					X	
1918-00-9	Dicamba			1,000		313	
1918-00-9	3,6-Dichloro-2-methoxybenzoic acid			1,000		X	
1918-02-1	Picloram					313	
1918-16-7	Propachlor					313	
1918-16-7	2-Chloro-N-(1-methylethyl)-N-phenylacetamide					X	
1928-38-7	2,4-D Esters			100			
1928-43-4	2,4-D 2-ethylhexyl ester					313	
1928-47-8	2,4,5-T esters			1,000			
1928-61-6	2,4-D Esters			100			
1929-73-3	2,4-D butoxyethyl ester			100		313	
1929-73-3	2,4-D Esters			100		X	
1929-77-7	Carbamothioic acid, dipropyl-, S-propyl ester			1*			U385

CAS Number	Chemical Name	Sec 302 (EHS) RQ	Section 304 EHS RQ	Section 304 CERCLA RQ	CAA 112 (r) TQ	Sec 313	RCRA Code
1929-82-4	Nitrapyrin					313	
1929-82-4	2-Chloro-6-(trichloromethyl)pyridine					X	
1937-37-7	C.I. Direct Black 38					313	
1982-47-4	Chloroxuron	500/10,000	500				
1982-69-0	Sodium dicamba					313	
1982-69-0	3,6-Dichloro-2-methoxybenzoic acid, sodium salt					X	
1983-10-4	Tributyltin fluoride					313	
2001-95-8	Valinomycin	1,000/10,000	1,000				
2008-41-5	Butylate			1*			U392
2008-46-0	2,4,5-T amines			5,000			
2032-65-7	Methiocarb	500/10,000	10	10		313	P199
2032-65-7	Mercaptodimethur	500/10,000	10	10		X	P199
2074-50-2	Paraquat methosulfate	10/10,000	10				
2097-19-0	Phenylsilatrane	100/10,000	100				
2104-64-5	EPN	100/10,000	100				
2155-70-6	Tributyltin methacrylate					313	
2164-07-0	Dipotassium endothall					313	
2164-07-0	7-Oxabicyclo(2.2.1)heptane-2,3-dicarboxylic acid, d					X	
2164-17-2	Fluometuron					313	
2164-17-2	Urea, N,N-dimethyl-N'-[3-(trifluoromethyl)phenyl]-					X	
2212-67-1	Molinate			1*		313	U365
2212-67-1	1H-Azepine-1 carbothioic acid, hexahydro-S-ethyl es			1*		X	U365
2223-93-0	Cadmium stearate	1,000/10,000	1,000				
2231-57-4	Thiocarbazide	1,000/10,000	1,000				
2234-13-1	Octachloronaphthalene					313	
2238-07-5	Diglycidyl ether	1,000	1,000				
2275-18-5	Prothoate	100/10,000	100				
2300-66-5	Dimethylamine dicamba					313	
2303-16-4	Diallate			100		313	U062
2303-16-4	Carbamothioic acid, bis(1-methylethyl)-S-(2,3-dichl			100		X	U062
2303-17-5	Triallate			1*		313	U389
2312-35-8	Propargite			10		313	
2439-01-2	Chinomethionat					313	
2439-01-2	6-Methyl-1,3-dithiolo[4,5-b]quinoxalin-2-one					X	
2439-10-3	Dodine					313	
2439-10-3	Dodecylguanidine monoacetate					X	
2497-07-6	Oxydisulfoton	500	500				
2524-03-0	Dimethyl chlorothiophosphate	500	500			313	
2524-03-0	Dimethyl phosphorochloridothioate	500	500			X	
2540-82-1	Formothion	100	100				
2545-59-7	2,4,5-T esters			1,000			
2556-36-7	1,4-Cyclohexane diisocyanate					313#	
2570-26-5	Pentadecylamine	100/10,000	100				

CAS Number	Chemical Name	Sec 302 (EHS) RQ	Section 304 EHS RQ	Section 304 CERCLA RQ	CAA 112 (r) TQ	Sec 313	RCRA Code
2587-90-8	Phosphorothioic acid, O,O-dimethyl-5-(2-(methylthio	500	500				
2602-46-2	C.I. Direct Blue 6					313	
2631-37-0	Promecarb	500/10,000	1*	1*			P201
2636-26-2	Cyanophos	1,000	1,000				
2642-71-9	Azinphos-ethyl	100/10,000	100				
2655-15-4	2,3,5-Trimethylphenyl methylcarbamate					313	
2665-30-7	Phosphonothioic acid, methyl-, O-(4-nitrophenyl) O-	500	500				
2699-79-8	Sulfuryl fluoride					313	
2699-79-8	Vikane					X	
2702-72-9	2,4-D sodium salt					313	
2703-13-1	Phosphonothioic acid, methyl-, O-ethyl O-(4-(methyl	500	500				
2757-18-8	Thallous malonate	100/10,000	100				
2763-96-4	5-(Aminomethyl)-3-isoxazolol	500/10,000	1,000	1,000			P007
2763-96-4	Muscimol	500/10,000	1,000	1,000			P007
2764-72-9	Diquat			1,000			
2778-04-3	Endothion	500/10,000	500				
2832-40-8	C.I. Disperse Yellow 3					313	
2837-89-0	2-Chloro-1,1,1,2-tetrafluoroethane					313	
2837-89-0	HCFC-124					X	
2921-88-2	Chlorpyrifos			1			
2944-67-4	Ferric ammonium oxalate			1,000			
2971-38-2	2,4-D chlorocrotyl ester			100		313	
2971-38-2	2,4-D Esters			100		X	
3012-65-5	Ammonium citrate, dibasic			5,000			
3037-72-7	Silane, (4-aminobutyl)diethoxymethyl-	1,000	1,000				
3118-97-6	C.I. Solvent Orange 7					313	
3164-29-2	Ammonium tartrate			5,000			
3165-93-3	4-Chloro-o-toluidine, hydrochloride			100			U049
3173-72-6	1,5-Naphthalene diisocyanate					313#	
3251-23-8	Cupric nitrate			100			
3254-63-5	Phosphoric acid, dimethyl 4-(methylthio) phenyl est	500	500				
3288-58-2	O,O-Diethyl S-methyl dithiophosphate			5,000			U087
3383-96-8	Temephos					313	
3486-35-9	Zinc carbonate			1,000			
3547-04-4	DDE			5,000			
3569-57-1	Sulfoxide, 3-chloropropyl octyl	500	500				
3615-21-2	Benzimidazole, 4,5-dichloro-2-(trifluoromethyl)-	500/10,000	500				
3653-48-3	Methoxone sodium salt					313	
3653-48-3	(4-Chloro-2-methylphenoxy) acetate sodium salt					X	
3689-24-5	Sulfotep	500	100	100			P109

CAS Number	Chemical Name	Sec 302 (EHS) RQ	Section 304 EHS RQ	Section 304 CERCLA RQ	CAA 112 (r) TQ	Sec 313	RCRA Code
3689-24-5	Tetraethyldithiopyrophosphate	500	100	100			P109
3691-35-8	Chlorophacinone	100/10,000	100				
3697-24-3	5-Methylchrysene					313+	
3734-97-2	Amiton oxalate	100/10,000	100				
3735-23-7	Methyl phenkapton	500	500				
3761-53-3	C.I. Food Red 5					313	
3813-14-7	2,4,5-T amines			5,000			
3878-19-1	Fuberidazole	100/10,000	100				
4044-65-9	Bitoscanate	500/10,000	500				
4080-31-3	1-(3-Chloroallyl)-3,5,7-triaza-1-azoniaadamantane c					313	
4098-71-9	Isophorone diisocyanate	100	100			313#	
4104-14-7	Phosacetim	100/10,000	100				
4109-96-0	Dichlorosilane				10,000		
4109-96-0	Silane, dichloro-				10,000		
4128-73-8	4,4'-Diisocyanatodiphenyl ether					313#	
4170-30-3	Crotonaldehyde	1,000	100	100	20,000	313	U053
4170-30-3	2-Butenal	1,000	100	100	20,000	X	U053
4301-50-2	Fluenetil	100/10,000	100				
4418-66-0	Phenol, 2,2'-thiobis[4-chloro-6-methyl-	100/10,000	100				
4549-40-0	N-Nitrosomethylvinylamine			10		313	P084
4680-78-8	C.I. Acid Green 3					313	
4835-11-4	Hexamethylenediamine, N,N'-dibutyl-	500	500				
5124-30-1	1,1'-Methylene bis(4-isocyanatocyclohexane)					313#	
5234-68-4	Carboxin					313	
5234-68-4	5,6-Dihydro-2-methyl-N-phenyl-1,4-oxathiin-3-carbox					X	
5344-82-1	Thiourea, (2-chlorophenyl)-	100/10,000	100	100			P026
5385-75-1	Dibenzo(a,e)fluoranthene					313+	
5522-43-0	1-Nitropyrene					313+	
5598-13-0	Chlorpyrifos methyl					313	
5598-13-0	O,O-Dimethyl-O-(3,5,6-trichloro-2-pyridyl)phosphoro					X	
5836-29-3	Coumatetralyl	500/10,000	500				
5893-66-3	Cupric oxalate			100			
5902-51-2	Terbacil					313	
5902-51-2	5-Chloro-3-(1,1-dimethylethyl)-6-methyl-2,4(1H,3H)-					X	
5952-26-1	Ethanol, 2,2'-oxybis-, dicarbamate			1*			U395
5972-73-6	Ammonium oxalate			5,000			
6009-70-7	Ammonium oxalate			5,000			
6369-96-6	2,4,5-T amines			5,000			
6369-97-7	2,4,5-T amines			5,000			
6459-94-5	C.I. Acid Red 114					313	
6533-73-9	Thallium(I) carbonate	100/10,000	100	100			U215
6533-73-9	Thallous carbonate	100/10,000	100	100			U215

CAS Number	Chemical Name	Sec 302 (EHS) RQ	Section 304		CAA 112 (r) TQ	Sec 313	RCRA Code
			EHS RQ	CERCLA RQ			
6923-22-4	Monocrotophos	10/10,000	10				
7005-72-3	4-Chlorophenyl phenyl ether			5,000			
7287-19-6	Prometryn					313	
7287-19-6	N,N'-Bis(1-methylethyl)-6-methylthio-1,3,5-triazine					X	
7421-93-4	Endrin aldehyde			1			
7428-48-0	Lead stearate			10			
7429-90-5	Aluminum (fume or dust)					313	
7439-92-1	Lead			10		313	
7439-96-5	Manganese					313	
7439-97-6	Mercury			1		313	U151
7440-02-0	Nickel			100		313	
7440-22-4	Silver			1,000		313	
7440-23-5	Sodium			10			
7440-28-0	Thallium			1,000		313	
7440-36-0	Antimony			5,000		313	
7440-38-2	Arsenic			1		313	
7440-39-3	Barium					313	
7440-41-7	Beryllium			10		313	P015
7440-43-9	Cadmium			10		313	
7440-47-3	Chromium			5,000		313	
7440-48-4	Cobalt					313	
7440-50-8	Copper			5,000		313	
7440-62-2	Vanadium (fume or dust)					313	
7440-66-6	Zinc			1,000			
7440-66-6	Zinc (fume or dust)			1,000		313	
7446-08-4	Selenium dioxide			10			
7446-09-5	Sulfur dioxide	500	500				
7446-09-5	Sulfur dioxide (anhydrous)	500	500		5,000		
7446-11-9	Sulfur trioxide	100	100		10,000		
7446-14-2	Lead sulfate			10			
7446-18-6	Thallium(I) sulfate	100/10,000	100	100			P115
7446-18-6	Thallous sulfate	100/10,000	100	100			P115
7446-27-7	Lead phosphate			10			U145
7447-39-4	Cupric chloride			10			
7487-94-7	Mercuric chloride	500/10,000	500				
7488-56-4	Selenium sulfide			10			U205
7550-45-0	Titanium tetrachloride	100	1,000	1,000	2,500	313	
7550-45-0	Titanium chloride (TiCl4) (T-4)-	100	1,000	1,000	2,500	X	
7558-79-4	Sodium phosphate, dibasic			5,000			
7580-67-8	Lithium hydride	100	100				
7601-54-9	Sodium phosphate, tribasic			5,000			
7631-89-2	Sodium arsenate	1,000/10,000	1	1			
7631-90-5	Sodium bisulfite			5,000			
7632-00-0	Sodium nitrite			100		313	
7637-07-2	Boron trifluoride	500	500		5,000	313	
7637-07-2	Borane, trifluoro-	500	500		5,000	X	
7645-25-2	Lead arsenate			1			
7646-85-7	Zinc chloride			1,000			

CAS Number	Chemical Name	Sec 302 (EHS) RQ	Section 304		CAA 112 (r) TQ	Sec 313	RCRA Code
			EHS RQ	CERCLA RQ			
7647-01-0	Hydrochloric acid			5,000			
7647-01-0	Hydrochloric acid (conc 30% or greater)			5,000	15,000		
7647-01-0	Hydrochloric acid (aerosol forms only)			5,000		313	
7647-01-0	Hydrogen chloride (anhydrous)	500	5,000	5,000	5,000	X	
7647-01-0	Hydrogen chloride (gas only)	500	5,000	5,000	5,000	X	
7647-18-9	Antimony pentachloride			1,000			
7664-38-2	Phosphoric acid			5,000		313	
7664-39-3	Hydrogen fluoride	100	100	100		313	U134
7664-39-3	Hydrofluoric acid	100	100	100		X	U134
7664-39-3	Hydrofluoric acid (conc. 50% or greater)	100	100	100	1,000	X	U134
7664-39-3	Hydrogen fluoride (anhydrous)	100	100	100	1,000	X	U134
7664-41-7	Ammonia	500	100	100		313	
7664-41-7	Ammonia (anhydrous)	500	100	100	10,000	X	
7664-41-7	Ammonia (conc 20% or greater)	500	100	100	20,000	X	
7664-93-9	Sulfuric acid (aerosol forms only)	1,000	1,000	1,000		313	
7664-93-9	Sulfuric acid	1,000	1,000	1,000			
7681-49-4	Sodium fluoride			1,000			
7681-52-9	Sodium hypochlorite			100			
7696-12-0	Tetramethrin					313	
7696-12-0	2,2-Dimethyl-3-(2-methyl-1-propenyl)cyclopropanecar					X	
7697-37-2	Nitric acid	1,000	1,000	1,000		313	
7697-37-2	Nitric acid (conc 80% or greater)	1,000	1,000	1,000	15,000	X	
7699-45-8	Zinc bromide			1,000			
7705-08-0	Ferric chloride			1,000			
7718-54-9	Nickel chloride			100			
7719-12-2	Phosphorous trichloride	1,000	1,000	1,000	15,000		
7719-12-2	Phosphorus trichloride	1,000	1,000	1,000	15,000		
7720-78-7	Ferrous sulfate			1,000			
7722-64-7	Potassium permanganate			100			
7722-84-1	Hydrogen peroxide (Conc.> 52%)	1,000	1,000				
7723-14-0	Phosphorus	100	1	1			
7723-14-0	Phosphorus (yellow or white)	100	1	1		313	
7726-95-6	Bromine	500	500		10,000	313	
7733-02-0	Zinc sulfate			1,000			
7738-94-5	Chromic acid			10			
7758-01-2	Potassium bromate					313	
7758-29-4	Sodium phosphate, tribasic			5,000			
7758-94-3	Ferrous chloride			100			
7758-95-4	Lead chloride			10			
7758-98-7	Cupric sulfate			10			
7761-88-8	Silver nitrate			1			
7773-06-0	Ammonium sulfamate			5,000			
7775-11-3	Sodium chromate			10			
7778-39-4	Arsenic acid			1			P010
7778-44-1	Calcium arsenate	500/10,000	1	1			

CAS Number	Chemical Name	Sec 302 (EHS) RQ	Section 304 EHS RQ	Section 304 CERCLA RQ	CAA 112 (r) TQ	Sec 313	RCRA Code
7778-50-9	Potassium bichromate			10			
7778-54-3	Calcium hypochlorite			10			
7779-86-4	Zinc hydrosulfite			1,000			
7779-88-6	Zinc nitrate			1,000			
7782-41-4	Fluorine	500	10	10	1,000	313	P056
7782-49-2	Selenium			100		313	
7782-50-5	Chlorine	100	10	10	2,500	313	
7782-63-0	Ferrous sulfate			1,000			
7782-82-3	Sodium selenite			100			
7782-86-7	Mercurous nitrate			10			
7783-00-8	Selenious acid	1,000/10,000	10	10			U204
7783-06-4	Hydrogen sulfide	500	100	100	10,000	313	U135
7783-07-5	Hydrogen selenide	10	10		500		
7783-35-9	Mercuric sulfate			10			
7783-46-2	Lead fluoride			10			
7783-49-5	Zinc fluoride			1,000			
7783-50-8	Ferric fluoride			100			
7783-56-4	Antimony trifluoride			1,000			
7783-60-0	Sulfur fluoride (SF4), (T-4)-	100	100		2,500		
7783-60-0	Sulfur tetrafluoride	100	100		2,500		
7783-70-2	Antimony pentafluoride	500	500				
7783-80-4	Tellurium hexafluoride	100	100				
7784-34-1	Arsenous trichloride	500	1	1	15,000		
7784-40-9	Lead arsenate			1			
7784-41-0	Potassium arsenate			1			
7784-42-1	Arsine	100	100		1,000		
7784-46-5	Sodium arsenite	500/10,000	1	1			
7785-84-4	Sodium phosphate, tribasic			5,000			
7786-34-7	Mevinphos	500	10	10		313	
7786-81-4	Nickel sulfate			100			
7787-47-5	Beryllium chloride			1			
7787-49-7	Beryllium fluoride			1			
7787-55-5	Beryllium nitrate			1			
7788-98-9	Ammonium chromate			10			
7789-00-6	Potassium chromate			10			
7789-06-2	Strontium chromate			10			
7789-09-5	Ammonium bichromate			10			
7789-42-6	Cadmium bromide			10			
7789-43-7	Cobaltous bromide			1,000			
7789-61-9	Antimony tribromide			1,000			
7790-94-5	Chlorosulfonic acid			1,000			
7791-12-0	Thallium chloride TICl	100/10,000	100	100			U216
7791-12-0	Thallous chloride	100/10,000	100	100			U216
7791-21-1	Chlorine monoxide				10,000		
7791-21-1	Chlorine oxide				10,000		
7791-23-3	Selenium oxychloride	500	500				
7803-51-2	Phosphine	500	100	100	5,000	313	P096
7803-55-6	Ammonium vanadate			1,000			P119
7803-62-5	Silane				10,000		

CAS Number	Chemical Name	Sec 302 (EHS) RQ	Section 304 EHS RQ	Section 304 CERCLA RQ	CAA 112 (r) TQ	Sec 313	RCRA Code
8001-35-2	Toxaphene	500/10,000	1	1		313	P123
8001-35-2	Camphechlor	500/10,000	1	1		X	P123
8001-35-2	Camphene, octachloro-	500/10,000	1	1		X	P123
8001-58-9	Creosote			1		313	U051
8003-19-8	Dichloropropane - Dichloropropene (mixture)			100			
8003-34-7	Pyrethrins			1			
8014-95-7	Oleum (fuming sulfuric acid)			1,000	10,000		
8014-95-7	Sulfuric acid (fuming)			1,000	10,000		
8014-95-7	Sulfuric acid, mixture with sulfur trioxide			1,000	10,000		
8065-48-3	Demeton	500	500				
9006-42-2	Metiram					313	
9016-87-9	Polymeric diphenylmethane diisocyanate					313#	
10022-70-5	Sodium hypochlorite			100			
10025-73-7	Chromic chloride	1/10,000	1				
10025-78-2	Silane, trichloro-				10,000		
10025-78-2	Trichlorosilane				10,000		
10025-87-3	Phosphorus oxychloride	500	1,000	1,000	5,000		
10025-87-3	Phosphoryl chloride	500	1,000	1,000	5,000		
10025-91-9	Antimony trichloride			1,000			
10026-11-6	Zirconium tetrachloride			5,000			
10026-13-8	Phosphorus pentachloride	500	500				
10028-15-6	Ozone	100	100			313	
10028-22-5	Ferric sulfate			1,000			
10031-59-1	Thallium sulfate	100/10,000	100	100			
10034-93-2	Hydrazine sulfate					313	
10039-32-4	Sodium phosphate, dibasic			5,000			
10043-01-3	Aluminum sulfate			5,000			
10045-89-3	Ferrous ammonium sulfate			1,000			
10045-94-0	Mercuric nitrate			10			
10049-04-4	Chlorine dioxide				1,000	313	
10049-04-4	Chlorine oxide (ClO2)				1,000	X	
10049-05-5	Chromous chloride			1,000			
10061-02-6	trans-1,3-Dichloropropene					313	
10099-74-8	Lead nitrate			10			
10101-53-8	Chromic sulfate			1,000			
10101-63-0	Lead iodide			10			
10101-89-0	Sodium phosphate, tribasic			5,000			
10102-06-4	Uranyl nitrate			100			
10102-18-8	Sodium selenite	100/10,000	100	100			
10102-20-2	Sodium tellurite	500/10,000	500				
10102-43-9	Nitric oxide	100	10	10	10,000		P076
10102-43-9	Nitrogen oxide (NO)	100	10	10	10,000		P076
10102-44-0	Nitrogen dioxide	100	10	10			P078
10102-45-1	Thallium(I) nitrate			100			U217
10102-48-4	Lead arsenate			1			
10108-64-2	Cadmium chloride			10			

CAS Number	Chemical Name	Sec 302 (EHS) RQ	Section 304 EHS RQ	Section 304 CERCLA RQ	CAA 112 (r) TQ	Sec 313	RCRA Code
10124-50-2	Potassium arsenite	500/10,000	1	1			
10124-56-8	Sodium phosphate, tribasic			5,000			
10140-65-5	Sodium phosphate, dibasic			5,000			
10140-87-1	Ethanol, 1,2-dichloro-, acetate	1,000	1,000				
10192-30-0	Ammonium bisulfite			5,000			
10196-04-0	Ammonium sulfite			5,000			
10210-68-1	Cobalt carbonyl	10/10,000	10				
10222-01-2	2,2-Dibromo-3-nitrilopropionamide					313	
10265-92-6	Methamidophos	100/10,000	100				
10294-34-5	Boron trichloride	500	500		5,000	313	
10294-34-5	Borane, trichloro-	500	500		5,000	X	
10311-84-9	Dialifor	100/10,000	100				
10347-54-3	1,4-Bis(methylisocyanate)cyclohexane					313#	
10361-89-4	Sodium phosphate, tribasic			5,000			
10380-29-7	Cupric sulfate, ammoniated			100			
10415-75-5	Mercurous nitrate			10			
10421-48-4	Ferric nitrate			1,000			
10453-86-8	Resmethrin					313	
10453-86-8	5-(Phenylmethyl)-3-furanyl)methyl 2,2-dimethyl-3-(2					X	
10476-95-6	Methacrolein diacetate	1,000	1,000				
10544-72-6	Nitrogen dioxide			10			
10588-01-9	Sodium bichromate			10			
10605-21-7	Carbendazim			1*			U372
11096-82-5	Aroclor 1260			1			
11097-69-1	Aroclor 1254			1			
11104-28-2	Aroclor 1221			1			
11115-74-5	Chromic acid			10			
11141-16-5	Aroclor 1232			1			
12002-03-8	Cupric acetoarsenite	500/10,000	1	1			
12002-03-8	Paris green	500/10,000	1	1			
12039-52-0	Selenious acid, dithallium(1+) salt			1,000			P114
12054-48-7	Nickel hydroxide			10			
12108-13-3	Manganese, tricarbonyl methylcyclopentadienyl	100	100				
12122-67-7	Zineb					313	
12122-67-7	Carbamodithioic acid, 1,2-ethanediylbis-, zinc comp					X	
12125-01-8	Ammonium fluoride			100			
12125-02-9	Ammonium chloride			5,000			
12135-76-1	Ammonium sulfide			100			
12427-38-2	Maneb					313	
12427-38-2	Carbamodithioic acid, 1,2-ethanediylbis-, manganese					X	
12672-29-6	Aroclor 1248			1			
12674-11-2	Aroclor 1016			1			
12771-08-3	Sulfur monochloride			1,000			
13071-79-9	Terbufos	100	100				

CAS Number	Chemical Name	Sec 302 (EHS) RQ	Section 304 EHS RQ	Section 304 CERCLA RQ	CAA 112 (r) TQ	Sec 313	RCRA Code
13171-21-6	Phosphamidon	100	100				
13194-48-4	Ethoprop	1,000	1,000			313	
13194-48-4	Ethoprophos	1,000	1,000			X	
13194-48-4	Phosphorodithioic acid O-ethyl S,S-dipropyl ester	1,000	1,000			X	
13356-08-6	Fenbutatin oxide					313	
13356-08-6	Hexakis(2-methyl-2-phenylpropyl)distannoxane					X	
13410-01-0	Sodium selenate	100/10,000	100				
13450-90-3	Gallium trichloride	500/10,000	500				
13463-39-3	Nickel carbonyl	1	10	10	1,000		P073
13463-40-6	Iron, pentacarbonyl-	100	100		2,500	313	
13463-40-6	Iron carbonyl (Fe(CO)5), (TB-5-11)-	100	100		2,500	X	
13474-88-9	1,1-Dichloro-1,2,2,3,3-pentafluoropropane					313	
13474-88-9	HCFC-225cc					X	
13560-99-1	2,4,5-T salts			1,000			
13597-99-4	Beryllium nitrate			1			
13684-56-5	Desmedipham					313	
13746-89-9	Zirconium nitrate			5,000			
13765-19-0	Calcium chromate			10			U032
13814-96-5	Lead fluoborate			10			
13826-83-0	Ammonium fluoborate			5,000			
13952-84-6	sec-Butylamine			1,000			
14017-41-5	Cobaltous sulfamate			1,000			
14167-18-1	Salcomine	500/10,000	500				
14216-75-2	Nickel nitrate			100			
14258-49-2	Ammonium oxalate			5,000			
14307-35-8	Lithium chromate			10			
14307-43-8	Ammonium tartrate			5,000			
14324-55-1	Ethyl Ziram			1*			U407
14484-64-1	Ferbam			1*		313	U396
14484-64-1	Tris(dimethylcarbamodithioato-S,S')iron			1*		X	U396
14639-97-5	Zinc ammonium chloride			1,000			
14639-98-6	Zinc ammonium chloride			1,000			
14644-61-2	Zirconium sulfate			5,000			
15271-41-7	Bicyclo[2.2.1]heptane-2-carbonitrile, 5-chloro-6-((	500/10,000	500				
15339-36-3	Manganese, bis(dimethylcarbamodithioato-S,S')-			1*			P196
15646-96-5	2,4,4-Trimethylhexamethylene diisocyanate					313#	
15699-18-0	Nickel ammonium sulfate			100			
15739-80-7	Lead sulfate			10			
15950-66-0	2,3,4-Trichlorophenol			10			
15972-60-8	Alachlor					313	
16071-86-6	C.I. Direct Brown 95					313	
16543-55-8	N-Nitrosonornicotine					313	

CAS Number	Chemical Name	Sec 302 (EHS) RQ	Section 304 EHS RQ	Section 304 CERCLA RQ	CAA 112 (r) TQ	Sec 313	RCRA Code
16721-80-5	Sodium hydrosulfide			5,000			
16752-77-5	Ethanimidothioic acid, N-[[methylamino)carbonyl]	500/10,000	100	100			P066
16752-77-5	Methomyl	500/10,000	100	100			P066
16871-71-9	Zinc silicofluoride			5,000			
16919-19-0	Ammonium silicofluoride			1,000			
16923-95-8	Zirconium potassium fluoride			1,000			
16938-22-0	2,2,4-Trimethylhexamethylene diisocyanate					313#	
17702-41-9	Decaborane(14)	500/10,000	500				
17702-57-7	Formparanate	100/10,000	1*	1*			P197
17804-35-2	Benomyl			1*		313	U271
18883-66-4	Streptozotocin			1			U206
19044-88-3	Oryzalin					313	
19044-88-3	4-(Dipropylamino)-3,5-dinitrobenzenesulfonamide					X	
19287-45-7	Diborane	100	100		2,500		
19287-45-7	Diborane(6)	100	100		2,500		
19624-22-7	Pentaborane	500	500				
19666-30-9	Oxydiazon					313	
19666-30-9	3-(2,4-Dichloro-5-(1-methylethoxy)phenyl)-5-(1,1-di					X	
20325-40-0	3,3'-Dimethoxybenzidine dihydrochloride					313	
20325-40-0	o-Dianisidine dihydrochloride					X	
20354-26-1	Methazole					313	
20354-26-1	2-(3,4-Dichlorophenyl)-4-methyl-1,2,4-oxadiazolidin					X	
20816-12-0	Osmium tetroxide			1,000		313	P087
20816-12-0	Osmium oxide OsO4 (T-4)-			1,000		X	P087
20830-75-5	Digoxin	10/10,000	10				
20830-81-3	Daunomycin			10			U059
20859-73-8	Aluminum phosphide	500	100	100		313	P006
21087-64-9	Metribuzin					313	
21548-32-3	Fosthietan	500	500				
21609-90-5	Leptophos	500/10,000	500				
21725-46-2	Cyanazine					313	
21908-53-2	Mercuric oxide	500/10,000	500				
21923-23-9	Chlorthiophos	500	500				
22224-92-6	Fenamiphos	10/10,000	10				
22781-23-3	Bendiocarb			1*		313	U278
22781-23-3	2,2-Dimethyl-1,3-benzodioxol-4-ol methylcarbamate			1*		X	U278
22961-82-6	Bendiocarb phenol			1*			U364
23135-22-0	Oxamyl	100/10,000	1*	1*			P194
23422-53-9	Formetanate hydrochloride	500/10,000	1*	1*			P198
23505-41-1	Pirimifos-ethyl	1,000	1,000				
23564-05-8	Thiophanate-methyl			1*		313	U409
23564-06-9	Thiophanate ethyl					313	

CAS Number	Chemical Name	Sec 302 (EHS) RQ	Section 304 EHS RQ	Section 304 CERCLA RQ	CAA 112 (r) TQ	Sec 313	RCRA Code
23564-06-9	(1,2-Phenylenebis(iminocarbonothioyl)) biscarbamic					X	
23950-58-5	Pronamide			5,000		313	U192
23950-58-5	Benzamide, 3,5-dichloro-N-(1,1-dimethyl-2-propynyl			5,000		X	U192
24017-47-8	Triazofos	500	500				
24934-91-6	Chlormephos	500	500				
25154-54-5	Dinitrobenzene (mixed isomers)			100			
25154-55-6	Nitrophenol (mixed isomers)			100			
25155-30-0	Sodium dodecylbenzenesulfonate			1,000			
25167-67-3	Butene				10,000		
25167-82-2	Trichlorophenol			10			
25168-15-4	2,4,5-T esters			1,000			
25168-26-7	2,4-D Esters			100			
25311-71-1	Isofenphos					313	
25311-71-1	2-((Ethoxyl((1-methylethyl)amino]phosphinothioyl]ox					X	
25321-14-6	Dinitrotoluene (mixed isomers)			10		313	
25321-22-6	Dichlorobenzene (mixed isomers)			100		313	
25321-22-6	Dichlorobenzene			100		X	
25376-45-8	Diaminotoluene (mixed isomers)			10		313	U221
25376-45-8	Toluenediamine			10		X	U221
25550-58-7	Dinitrophenol			10			
26002-80-2	Phenothrin					313	
26002-80-2	2,2-Dimethyl-3-(2-methyl-1-propenyl)cyclopropanecar					X	
26264-06-2	Calcium dodecylbenzenesulfonate			1,000			
26419-73-8	Carbamic acid, methyl-, O-(((2,4-dimethyl-1,3-dithi	100/10,000	1*	1*			P185
26471-62-5	Toluenediisocyanate (mixed isomers)			100	10,000	313	U223
26471-62-5	Benzene, 1,3-diisocyanatomethyl-			100	10,000	X	U223
26471-62-5	Toluene diisocyanate (unspecified isomer)			100	10,000	X	U223
26628-22-8	Sodium azide (Na(N3))	500	1,000	1,000		313	P105
26638-19-7	Dichloropropane			1,000			
26644-46-2	Triforine					313	
26644-46-2	N,N'-(1,4-Piperazinediylbis(2,2,2-trichloroethylide					X	
26952-23-8	Dichloropropene			100			
27137-85-5	Trichloro(dichlorophenyl)silane	500	500				
27176-87-0	Dodecylbenzenesulfonic acid			1,000			
27314-13-2	Norflurazon					313	
27314-13-2	4-Chloro-5-(methylamino)-2-[3-(trifluoromethyl)phen					X	
27323-41-7	Triethanolamine dodecylbenzene sulfonate			1,000			

CAS Number	Chemical Name	Sec 302 (EHS) RQ	Section 304 EHS RQ	Section 304 CERCLA RQ	CAA 112 (r) TQ	Sec 313	RCRA Code
27774-13-6	Vanadyl sulfate			1,000			
28057-48-9	d-trans-Allethrin					313	
28057-48-9	d-trans-Chrysanthemic acid of d-allethrone					X	
28249-77-6	Thiobencarb					313	
28249-77-6	Carbamic acid, diethylthio-, S-(p-chlorobenzyl)					X	
28300-74-5	Antimony potassium tartrate			100			
28347-13-9	Xylylene dichloride	100/10,000	100				
28407-37-6	C.I. Direct Blue 218					313	
28772-56-7	Bromadiolone	100/10,000	100				
29232-93-7	Pirimiphos methyl					313	
29232-93-7	O-(2-(Diethylamino)-6-methyl-4-pyrimidinyl)-O,O-dim					X	
30525-89-4	Paraformaldehyde			1,000			
30558-43-1	Ethanimidothioic acid, 2-(dimethylamino)-N-hydroxy-			1*			U394
30560-19-1	Acephate					313	
30560-19-1	Acetylphosphoramidothioic acid O,S-dimethyl ester					X	
30674-80-7	Methacryloyloxyethyl isocyanate	100	100				
31218-83-4	Propetamphos					313	
31218-83-4	3-((Ethylamino)methoxyphosphinothioyl)oxy)-2-buteno					X	
32534-95-5	2,4,5-TP esters			100			
33089-61-1	Amitraz					313	
33213-65-9	beta - Endosulfan			1			
34014-18-1	Tebuthiuron					313	
34014-18-1	N-(5-(1,1-Dimethylethyl)-1,3,4-thiadiazol-2-yl)-N,N					X	
34077-87-7	Dichlorotrifluoroethane					313	
35367-38-5	Diflubenzuron					313	
35400-43-2	Sulprofos					313	
35400-43-2	O-Ethyl O-(4-(methylthio)phenyl)phosphorodithioic a					X	
35554-44-0	Imazalil					313	
35554-44-0	1-(2-(2,4-Dichlorophenyl)-2-(2-propenyloxy)ethyl)-1					X	
35691-65-7	1-Bromo-1-(bromomethyl)-1,3-propanedicarbonitrile					313	
36478-76-9	Uranyl nitrate			100			
37211-05-5	Nickel chloride			100			
38661-72-2	1,3-Bis(methylisocyanate)cyclohexane					313#	
38727-55-8	Diethatyl ethyl					313	
39156-41-7	2,4-Diaminoanisole sulfate					313	
39196-18-4	Thiofanox	100/10,000	100	100			P045

CAS Number	Chemical Name	Sec 302 (EHS) RQ	Section 304 EHS RQ	Section 304 CERCLA RQ	CAA 112 (r) TQ	Sec 313	RCRA Code
39300-45-3	Dinocap					313	
39515-41-8	Fenpropathrin					313	
39515-41-8	2,2,3,3-Tetramethylcyclopropane carboxylic acid cya					X	
40487-42-1	Pendimethalin					313	
40487-42-1	N-(1-Ethylpropyl)-3,4-dimethyl-2,6-dinitrobenzenami					X	
41198-08-7	Profenofos					313	
41198-08-7	O-(4-Bromo-2-chlorophenyl)-O-ethyl-S-propylphosphor					X	
41766-75-0	3,3'-Dimethylbenzidine dihydrofluoride					313	
41766-75-0	o-Tolidine dihydrofluoride					X	
42504-46-1	Isopropanolamine dodecylbenzene sulfonate			1,000			
42874-03-3	Oxyfluorfen					313	
43121-43-3	Triadimefon					313	
43121-43-3	1-(4-Chlorophenoxy)-3,3-dimethyl-1-(1H-1,2,4-triazo					X	
50471-44-8	Vinclozolin					313	
50471-44-8	3-(3,5-Dichlorophenyl)-5-ethenyl-5-methyl-2,4-oxazo					X	
50782-69-9	Phosphonothioic acid, methyl-, S-(2-(bis(1-methylet	100	100				
51026-28-9	Potassium N-hydroxymethyl-N-methyldithiocarbamate			1*			U378
51235-04-2	Hexazinone					313	
51338-27-3	Diclofop methyl					313	
51338-27-3	2-(4-(2,4-Dichlorophenoxy)phenoxy)propanoic acid, m					X	
51630-58-1	Fenvalerate					313	
51630-58-1	4-Chloro-alpha-(1-methylethyl)benzeneacetic acid cy					X	
52628-25-8	Zinc ammonium chloride			1,000			
52645-53-1	Permethrin					313	
52645-53-1	3-(2,2-Dichloroethenyl)-2,2-dimethylcyclopropane c					X	
52652-59-2	Lead stearate			10			
52740-16-6	Calcium arsenite			1			
52888-80-9	Carbamothioic acid, dipropyl-, S-(phenylmethyl) est			1*			U387
53404-19-6	Bromacil, lithium salt					313	
53404-19-6	2,4-(1H,3H)-Pyrimidinedione, 5-bromo-6-methyl-3-(1-					X	
53404-37-8	2,4-D 2-ethyl-4-methylpentyl ester					313	
53404-60-7	Dazomet, sodium salt					313	
53404-60-7	Tetrahydro-3,5-dimethyl-2H-1,3,5-thiadiazine-2-thio					X	

CAS Number	Chemical Name	Sec 302 (EHS) RQ	Section 304		CAA 112 (r) TQ	Sec 313	RCRA Code
			EHS RQ	CERCLA RQ			
53467-11-1	2,4-D Esters			100			
53469-21-9	Aroclor 1242			1			
53558-25-1	Pyriminil	100/10,000	100				
55285-14-8	Carbosulfan			1*			P189
55290-64-7	Dimethipin					313	
55290-64-7	2,3,-Dihydro-5,6-dimethyl-1,4-dithiin 1,1,4,4-tetra					X	
55406-53-6	3-Iodo-2-propynyl butylcarbamate			1*		313	U375
55488-87-4	Ferric ammonium oxalate			1,000			
56189-09-4	Lead stearate			10			
57213-69-1	Triclopyr triethylammonium salt					313	
58270-08-9	Zinc, dichloro(4,4-dimethyl-5((((methylamino)carbon	100/10,000	100				
59669-26-0	Thiodicarb			1*		313	U410
60168-88-9	Fenarimol					313	
60168-88-9	.alpha.-(2-Chlorophenyl)-.alpha.-4-chlorophenyl)-5-					X	
60207-90-1	Propiconazole					313	
60207-90-1	1-(2-(2,4-Dichlorophenyl)-4-propyl-1,3-dioxolan-2-y					X	
61792-07-2	2,4,5-T esters			1,000			
62207-76-5	Cobalt, ((2,2'-(1,2-ethanediylbis(nitrilomethylidyn	100/10,000	100				
62476-59-9	Acifluorfen, sodium salt					313	
62476-59-9	5-(2-Chloro-4-(trifluoromethyl)phenoxy)-2-nitrobenz					X	
63938-10-3	Chlorotetrafluoroethane					313	
64902-72-3	Chlorsulfuron					313	
64902-72-3	2-Chloro-N-(((4-methoxy-6-methyl-1,3,5-triazin-2-yl					X	
64969-34-2	3,3'-Dichlorobenzidine sulfate					313	
66441-23-4	Fenoxaprop ethyl					313	
66441-23-4	2-(4-((6-Chloro-2-benzoxazolylen)oxy)phenoxy)propan					X	
67485-29-4	Hydramethylnon					313	
67485-29-4	Tetrahydro-5,5-dimethyl-2(1H)-pyrimidinone(3-(4-(tr					X	
68085-85-8	Cyhalothrin					313	
68085-85-8	3-(2-Chloro-3,3,3-trifluoro-1-propenyl)-2,2-Dimethy					X	
68359-37-5	Cyfluthrin					313	
68359-37-5	3-(2,2-Dichloroethenyl)-2,2-dimethylcyclopropanecar					X	
69409-94-5	Fluvalinate					313	
69409-94-5	N-(2-Chloro-4-(trifluoromethyl)phenyl)-DL-valine(+)					X	
69806-50-4	Fluazifop butyl					313	

CAS Number	Chemical Name	Sec 302 (EHS) RQ	Section 304 EHS RQ	Section 304 CERCLA RQ	CAA 112 (r) TQ	Sec 313	RCRA Code
69806-50-4	2-(4-(5-(Trifluoromethyl)-2-pyridinyl]oxy]-phenoxy)					X	
71751-41-2	Abamectin					313	
71751-41-2	Avermectin B1					X	
72178-02-0	Fomesafen					313	
72178-02-0	5-(2-Chloro-4-(trifluoromethyl)phenoxy)-N-methylsul					X	
72490-01-8	Fenoxycarb					313	
72490-01-8	(2-(4-Phenoxy-phenoxy)-ethyl)carbamic acid ethyl es					X	
74051-80-2	Sethoxydim					313	
74051-80-2	2-(1-(Ethoxyimino) butyl)-5-(2-(ethylthio)propyl)-3					X	
75790-84-0	4-Methyldiphenylmethane-3,4-diisocyanate					313#	
75790-87-3	2,4'-Diisocyanatodiphenyl sulfide					313#	
76578-14-8	Quizalofop-ethyl					313	
76578-14-8	2-(4-((6-Chloro-2-quinoxalinyl)oxy]phenoxy) propano					X	
77501-63-4	Lactofen					313	
77501-63-4	5-(2-Chloro-4-(trifluoromethyl)phenoxy)-2-nitro-2-e					X	
82657-04-3	Bifenthrin					313	
88671-89-0	Myclobutanil					313	
88671-89-0	.alpha.-Butyl-.alpha.-(4-chlorophenyl) 1H-1,2,4-tri					X	
90454-18-5	Dichloro-1,1,2-trifluoroethane					313	
90982-32-4	Chlorimuron ethyl					313	
90982-32-4	Ethyl-2-((((4-chloro-6-methoxyprimidin-2-yl)-carbon					X	
101200-48-0	Tribenuron methyl					313	
101200-48-0	2-(4-Methoxy-6-methyl-1,3,5-triazin-2-yl)-methylami					X	
111512-56-2	1,1-Dichloro-1,2,3,3,3-pentafluoropropane					313	
111512-56-2	HCFC-225eb					X	
111984-09-9	3,3'-Dimethoxybenzidine hydrochloride					313	
111984-09-9	o-Dianisidine hydrochloride					X	
127564-92-5	Dichloropentafluoropropane					313	
128903-21-9	2,2-Dichloro-1,1,1,3,3-pentafluoropropane					313	
128903-21-9	HCFC-225aa					X	
134190-37-7	Diethyldiisocyanatobenzene					313#	
136013-79-1	1,3-Dichloro-1,1,2,3,3-pentafluoropropane					313	
136013-79-1	HCFC-225ea					X	

CAS Number	Chemical Name	Sec 302 (EHS) RQ	Section 304		CAA 112 (r) TQ	Sec 313	RCRA Code
			EHS RQ	CERCLA RQ			
	** Organorhodium Complex (PMN-82-147)	10/10,000	10				
	Antimony Compounds			***		N010	
	Arsenic Compounds			***		N020	
	Barium Compounds					N040	
	--Except Barium Sulfate (under 313)						
	Beryllium Compounds			***		N050	
	Cadmium Compounds			***		N078	
	Chlordane (Technical Mixture and Metabolites)			***			
	Chlorinated Benzenes			***			
	Chlorinated Ethanes			***			
	Chlorinated Naphthalene			***			
	Chlorinated Phenols			***		N084	
	Chloroalkyl Ethers			***			
	Chlorophenols			***		N084	
	Chromium Compounds			***		N090	
	Cobalt Compounds			***		N096	
	Coke Oven Emissions			1			
	Copper Compounds			***		N100	
	--Except copper phthalocyanine compounds (under 313)##						
	--Except C.I. Pigment Blue 15 (under 313)						
	--Except C.I. Pigment Green 7 (under 313)						
	--Except C.I. Pigment Green 36 (under 313)						
	Cyanide Compounds			***		N106	
	DDT and Metabolites			***			
	Dichlorobenzidine			***			
	Diisocyanates (includes only 20 chemicals)					N120	
	Diphenylhydrazine			***			
	Endosulfan and Metabolites			***			
	Endrin and Metabolites			***			
	Ethylenebisdithiocarbamic acid, salts and esters					N171	
	Fine mineral fibers			***			
	Glycol Ethers			***		N230	
	Haloethers			***			
	Halomethanes			***			
	Heptachlor and Metabolites			***			
	Hexachlorocyclohexane (all isomers) CAS 608-73-1			***			
	Lead Compounds			***		N420	
	Manganese Compounds			***		N450	
	Mercury Compounds			***		N458	

CAS Number	Chemical Name	Sec 302 (EHS) RQ	Section 304		CAA 112 (r) TQ	Sec 313	RCRA Code
			EHS RQ	CERCLA RQ			
	Nickel Compounds			***		N495	
	Nicotine and salts					N503	
	Nitrate compounds (water dissociable)					N511	
	Nitrophenols			***			
	Nitrosamines			***			
	Phthalate Esters			***			
	Polybrominated Biphenyls (PBBs)					N575	
	Polychlorinated alkanes (C10 to C13)					N583	
	Polycyclic aromatic compounds (includes only 19 chemicals)					N590	
	Polycyclic organic matter			***			
	Polynuclear Aromatic Hydrocarbons			***			
	Selenium Compounds			***		N725	
	Silver Compounds			***		N740	
	Strychnine and salts					N746	
	Thallium Compounds			***		N760	
	Warfarin and salts					N874	
	Zinc Compounds			***		N982	

\# Member of diisocyanate category.

\#\# All copper phthalocyanine compounds substituted with only hydrogen and/or bromine or chlorine.

* RCRA carbamate waste; statutory one-pound RQ applies until RQs are adjusted.

** This chemical was identified from a Premanufacture Review Notice (PMN) submitted to EPA. The submitter has claimed certain information on the submission to be confidential, including specific chemical identity.

*** Indicates that no RQ is assigned to this generic or broad class, although the class is a CERCLA hazardous substance. See 50 Federal Register 13456 (April 4, 1985).

! Category codes for reporting under section 313.

40 CFR Part: Chemical Accident Prevention Provisions

Thursday
June 20, 1996

Part III

Environmental Protection Agency

40 CFR Part 68
Accidental Release Prevention
Requirements: Risk Management
Programs Under the Clean Air Act,
Section 112(r)(7); List of Regulated
Substances and Thresholds for
Accidental Release Prevention, Stay of
Effectiveness; and Accidental Release
Prevention Requirements: Risk
Management Programs Under Section
112(r)(7) of the Clean Air Act as
Amended, Guidelines; Final Rules and
Notice

ENVIRONMENTAL PROTECTION AGENCY

40 CFR Part 68

[FRL–5516–5]

RIN 2050–AD26

Accidental Release Prevention Requirements: Risk Management Programs Under Clean Air Act Section 112(r)(7)

AGENCY: Environmental Protection Agency.

ACTION: Final rule.

SUMMARY: The Clean Air Act requires EPA to promulgate regulations to prevent accidental releases of regulated substances and reduce the severity of those releases that do occur. EPA is promulgating rules that apply to all stationary sources with processes that contain more than a threshold quantity of a regulated substance. Processes will be divided into three categories based on: the potential for offsite consequences associated with a worst-case accidental release; accident history; or compliance with the prevention requirements under OSHA's Process Safety Management Standard. Processes that have no potential impact on the public in the case of an accidental release will have minimal requirements. For other processes, sources will implement a risk management program that includes more detailed requirements for hazard assessment, prevention, and emergency response.

Processes in industry categories with a history of accidental releases and processes already complying with OSHA's Process Safety Management Standard will be subject to a prevention program that is identical to parallel elements of the OSHA Standard. All other processes will be subject to streamlined prevention requirements. All sources must prepare a risk management plan based on the risk management programs established at the source. The source must submit the plan to a central point specified by EPA; the plan will be available to state and local governments and the public. These regulations will encourage sources to reduce the probability of accidental releases of substances that have the potential to cause immediate harm to public health and the environment and will stimulate the dialogue between industry and the public to improve accident prevention and emergency response practices.

DATES: The rule is effective August 19, 1996.

ADDRESSES: Supporting material used in developing the proposed rule, supplemental notice, and final rule is contained in Docket No. A–91–73. The docket is available for public inspection and copying between 8:00 a.m. and 5:30 p.m., Monday through Friday (except government holidays) at Room 1500, 401 M St. SW, Washington, DC 20460. A reasonable fee may charged for copying.

FOR FURTHER INFORMATION CONTACT: Craig Matthiessen at (202) 260–8600,

Chemical Emergency Preparedness and Prevention Office, U.S. Environmental Protection Agency, 401 M St. SW, Washington, DC 20460, or the Emergency Planning and Community Right-to-Know Hotline at 1–800–424–9346 (in the Washington, DC, metropolitan area, (703) 412–9810).

SUPPLEMENTARY INFORMATION: *Judicial Review.* Accidental Release Prevention Requirements: Risk Management Programs Under Clean Air Act Section 112(r)(7) were proposed in the Federal Register on October 20, 1993 (58 FR 54190). A supplemental notice was issued on March 13, 1995 (60 FR 13526). This Federal Register action announces the EPA's final decisions on the rule. Under section 307(b)(1) of the Act, judicial review of the Accidental Release Prevention Requirements: Risk Management Programs is available only by the petition for review in the U.S. Court of Appeals for the District of Columbia Circuit within 60 days of today's publication of this final rule. Under section 307(b)(2) of the Act, the requirements that are the subject of today's notice may not be challenged later in civil or criminal proceedings brought by the EPA to enforce these requirements.

Regulated Entities

Entities potentially regulated by this action are those stationary sources that have more than a threshold quantity of a regulated substance in a process. Regulated categories and entities include:

Category	Examples of regulated entities
Chemical Manufacturers	Industrial organics & inorganics, paints, pharmaceuticals, adhesives, sealants, fibers
Petrochemical	Refineries, industrial gases, plastics & resins, synthetic rubber
Other Manufacturing	Electronics, semiconductors, paper, fabricated metals, industrial machinery, furniture, textiles
Agriculture	Fertilzers, pesticides
Public Sources	Drinking and waste water treatment works
Utilities	Electric and Gas Utilities
Others	Food and cold storage, propane retail, warehousing and wholesalers
Federal Sources	Military and energy installations

This table is not intended to be exhaustive, but rather provides a guide for readers regarding entities likely to be regulated by this action. This table lists the types of entities that EPA is now aware could potentially be regulated by this action. Other types of entities not listed in the table could also be regulated. To determine whether a stationary source is regulated by this action, carefully examine the provisions associated with the list of substances and thresholds under § 68.130 (59 FR 4478), the proposed modifications (61

FR 16598, April 15, 1996) and the stay of implementation of the affected provisions until the proposed modifications are final published elsewhere in today's Federal Register, and the applicability criteria in § 68.10 of today's rule. If you have questions regarding the applicability of this action to a particular entity, consult the person listed in the preceding **FOR FURTHER INFORMATION CONTACT** section.

The following outline is provided to aid in reading this preamble:

I. Introduction and Background

A. Statutory Authority
B. Background
II. Discussion of Final Rule
  A. Applicability
  B. Program Criteria and Requirements
  C. Hazard Assessment
  D. Prevention Programs
  E. Emergency Response
  F. Risk Management Plan (RMP)
  G. Air Permitting
  H. Other Issues
III. Discussion of Comments
  A. Tiering
    1. Rationale
    2. Program 1 vs. Program 2 and Program 3 Criteria

I. Introduction and Background

A. Statutory Authority

This rule is promulgated under sections 112(r), 301(a)(1), Title V of the Clean Air Act (CAA) as amended (42 U.S.C. 7412(r), 7601(a)(1), 7661–7661f).

B. Background

The CAA Amendments of 1990 amend section 112 and add paragraph (r). The intent of section 112(r) is to prevent accidental releases to the air and mitigate the consequences of such releases by focusing prevention measures on chemicals that pose the greatest risk to the public and the environment. Section 112(r)(3) mandates that EPA promulgate a list of regulated substances, with threshold quantities; this list defines the stationary sources that will be subject to accident prevention regulations mandated by section 112(r)(7). EPA promulgated its list of substances on January 31, 1994 (59 FR 4478) ("List Rule").

As noted elsewhere in today's Federal Register, EPA has stayed certain provisions of part 68 that were promulgated as part of the List Rule. The stayed provisions are being addressed in amendments to the List Rule, which were proposed in 61 FR 16598 (April 15, 1996). Therefore, EPA has not taken final action on provisions of the Risk Management Program rule that apply to regulated substances, mixtures, and stationary sources addressed by the stayed provisions. Final action will be deferred until EPA takes final action on the proposed amendments to the List Rule.

Section 112(r)(7) mandates that EPA promulgate regulations and develop guidance to prevent, detect, and respond to accidental releases. Stationary sources covered by these regulations must develop and implement a risk management program that includes a hazard assessment, a prevention program, and an emergency response program. The risk management program must be described in a risk management plan (RMP) that must be registered with EPA, submitted to state and local authorities, and made available to the public. On October 20, 1993, EPA published a Notice of Proposed Rulemaking (NPRM) for the section 112(r)(7) regulations (58 FR 54190). (For a summary of the statutory requirements of section 112(r) and related statutory provisions, see the October 20, 1993, NPRM).

Following publication of the proposed rule, EPA held four public hearings and received approximately 770 written comments. Because of these comments, EPA issued a supplemental notice of proposed rulemaking (SNPRM) on March 13, 1995 (60 FR 13526) for comment on: approaches for setting different requirements for sources that pose different levels of hazard (tiering); worst-case releases and other hazard assessment issues; accident information reporting; public participation; inherently safer approaches; and implementation and integration of section 112(r) with state programs, particularly state air permitting programs. EPA held a public hearing on March 31, 1995, in Washington, DC, and received more than 280 written comments. Today's rule reflects EPA's consideration of all comments; major issues raised by commenters and EPA's response are briefly discussed in Section III of this preamble. A summary of all comments submitted and EPA's response to them is available in the Docket (see **ADDRESSES**).

EPA has proposed to delist explosives from § 68.130. Consequently, explosives are not addressed in this rule. EPA had also requested at the time of the final List Rule comments on whether flammable substances, when used as fuel, posed a lesser intrinsic hazard than the same substance handled otherwise (59 FR 4500, January 31, 1994). The comments submitted lacked data that would justify a lesser level of hazard consideration for flammable fuels; hence, the Agency will not adopt a fuel use exemption for purposes of threshold quantity determination.

With today's rule, EPA continues the philosophy that the Agency embraced in implementing the Emergency Planning and Community Right-to-Know Act of

1986 (EPCRA). Specifically, EPA recognizes that regulatory requirements, by themselves, will not guarantee safety. Instead, EPA believes that information about hazards in a community can and should lead public officials and the general public to work with industry to prevent accidents. For example, today's rule requires covered sources to provide information about possible worst-case scenarios. EPA intends that officials and the public use this information to understand the chemical hazards in the community and then engage in a dialogue with industry to reduce risk. In this way, accident prevention is focused primarily at the local level where the risk is found. Further, today's rule builds on existing programs and standards. For example, EPA has coordinated with Occupational Safety and Health Administration (OSHA) and the Department of Transportation (DOT) in developing this regulation. To the extent possible, covered sources will not face inconsistent requirements under these agencies' rules. EPA is encouraging sources to use existing emergency response programs, rather than develop a separate and duplicative program under this rule. In addition, today's rule scales requirements based on the potential risk posed by a source and the steps needed to address the risk, rather than imposing identical requirements on all sources.

To accommodate the concerns of small businesses, EPA is providing guidance with reference tables that covered sources can use to model the offsite consequences of a release. EPA is providing a model RMP guidance for the ammonia refrigeration industry, and will develop similar guidance for propane handlers and drinking water systems. As today's rule is implemented, EPA hopes that other industry sectors will work with EPA to develop model RMPs for other processes, thereby reducing costs for individual sources. Finally, today's rule requires industry to submit RMPs centrally in a format and method to be determined by EPA. Working with stakeholders, EPA will develop mechanisms to allow industry to use appropriate electronic technology to register with EPA and submit RMPs. In turn, all interested parties will be able to access electronically the data in RMPs. This method of submission and access avoids a potentially significant amount of paperwork for all involved parties and promotes uniformity. Users will be able to develop databases for specific purposes and compare RMPs for various sites across the country. In turn, industries' use of the data will promote continuous improvement, for example, through new safety technologies. As the method for submitting RMPs is developed, EPA invites the participation of all stakeholders, including industry, state and local governments, local emergency planning committees, environmental groups, and the general public.

II. Discussion of Final Rule

A. Applicability

The owner or operator of a stationary source that has more than a threshold quantity of a regulated substance in a process must comply with these requirements no later than June 21, 1999; three years after the date on which a regulated substance is first listed under § 68.130; or the date on which a regulated substance is first present in more than a threshold quantity in a process, whichever is later.

B. Program Criteria and Requirements

Under today's rule, processes subject to these requirements are divided into three tiers, labeled Programs 1, 2, and 3.

EPA has adopted the term "Program" to replace the term "Tier" found in the SNPRM to avoid confusion with Tier I and Tier II forms submitted under EPCRA, also known as Title III of the Superfund Amendments and Reauthorization Act of 1986 (SARA Title III). Eligibility for any given Program is based on process criteria so that classification of one process in a Program does not influence the classification of other processes at the source. For example, if a process meets Program 1 criteria, the source need only satisfy Program 1 requirements for that process, even if other processes at the source are subject to Program 2 or Program 3. A source, therefore, could have processes in one or more of the three Programs.

Program 1 is available to any process that has not had an accidental release with offsite consequences in the five years prior to the submission date of the RMP and has no public receptors within the distance to a specified toxic or flammable endpoint associated with a worst-case release scenario. Program 3 applies to processes in Standard Industrial Classification (SIC) codes 2611 (pulp mills), 2812 (chlor-alkali), 2819 (industrial inorganics), 2821 (plastics and resins), 2865 (cyclic crudes), 2869 (industrial organics), 2873 (nitrogen fertilizers), 2879 (agricultural chemicals), and 2911 (petroleum refineries). Program 3 also applies to all processes subject to the OSHA Process Safety Management (PSM) standard (29 CFR 1910.119), unless the process is eligible for Program 1. Owners or operators will need to determine individual SIC codes for each covered process to determine whether Program 3 applies. All other covered processes must satisfy Program 2 requirements. Program requirements and differences are illustrated on Tables 1 and 2:

TABLE 1—PROGRAM ELIGIBILITY CRITERIA

Program 1	Program 2	Program 3
No offsite accident history .... No public receptors in worst-case circle	.... The process is not eligible for Program 1 or 3	Process is subject to OSHA PSM. Process is in SIC code 2611, 2812, 2819, 2821, 2865, 2869, 2873, 2879, or 2911.
Emergency response coordinated with local re-sponders.	....	

TABLE 2—COMPARISON OF PROGRAM REQUIREMENTS

Program 1	Program 2	Program 3
Hazard Assessment: Worst-case analysis	Worst-case analysis .... Alternative releases	Worst-case analysis. Alternative releases.
5-year accident history .... Management Program:	5-year accident history	5-year accident history.
	Document management system	Document management system.

TABLE 2—COMPARISON OF PROGRAM REQUIREMENTS—Continued

Program 1	Program 2	Program 3
Prevention Program: Certify no additional steps needed	Safety Information .... Hazard Review .... Operating Procedures .... Training .... Maintenance .... Incident Investigation .... Compliance Audit	Process Safety Information. Process Hazard Analysis. Operating Procedures. Training. Mechanical Integrity. Incident Investigation. Compliance Audit. Management of Change. Pre-startup Review. Contractors. Employee Participation. Hot Work Permits.
Emergency Response Program: Coordinate with local responders	Develop plan and program	Develop plan and program.
Risk Management Plan Contents: Executive Summary .... Registration .... Worst-case data .... 5-year accident history .... Certification	Executive Summary. Registration .... Worst-case data .... Alternative release data .... 5-year accident history .... Prevention program data .... Emergency response data .... Certification	Executive Summary Registration. Worst-case data. Alternative release data. 5-year accident history. Prevention program data. Emergency response data. Certification.

The owner or operator of a covered process must: (1) prepare and submit a single risk management plan (RMP), including registration that covers all affected processes and chemicals; (2) conduct a worst-case release scenario analysis, review accident history, ensure emergency response procedures are coordinated with community response organizations to determine eligibility for Program 1 and, if eligible, document the worst case and complete a Program 1 certification for the RMP; (3) conduct a hazard assessment, document a management system, implement a more extensive, but still streamlined prevention program, and implement an emergency response program for Program 2 processes; and (4) conduct a hazard assessment, document a management system, implement a prevention program that is fundamentally identical to the OSHA PSM Standard, and implement an emergency response program for Program 3 processes.

Measures taken by sources to comply with OSHA PSM for any process that meets OSHA's PSM standard are sufficient to comply with the prevention program requirements of all three Programs. EPA will retain its authority to enforce the prevention program requirements and the general duty requirements of CAA Section 112(r)(1). EPA and OSHA are working closely to coordinate interpretation and enforcement of PSM and accident prevention programs. EPA will also work with state and local agencies to coordinate oversight of worker and public safety and environmental protection programs.

C. Hazard Assessment

EPA has adopted the worst-case definition proposed in the SNPRM. For all substances, the worst-case release scenario will be defined as the release of the largest quantity of a regulated substance from a vessel or process line failure, including administrative controls and passive mitigation that limit the total quantity involved or the release rate. For most gases, the worst-case release scenario assumes that the quantity is released in 10 minutes. For liquids, the scenario assumes an instantaneous spill; the release rate to the air is the volatilization rate from a pool 1 cm deep unless passive mitigation systems contain the substance in a smaller area. For flammables, the worst case assumes an instantaneous release and a vapor cloud explosion.

For the final rule, EPA has adopted the term "alternative release scenarios" to replace the term "other more likely scenarios" found in the NPRM and SNPRM. The non-worst-case accidental releases for the hazard assessment portion of the risk management plan were presumed "more likely to occur" and "more realistic" than the worst case. EPA believes sources should have flexibility to select non-worst-case scenarios that are the most useful for communication with the public and first responders and for emergency response preparedness and planning.

Catastrophic accidental releases are typically rare events; the words "more likely" suggests certainty of occurrence. Consequently, the scenarios other than worst case provided in the hazard assessment are called alternative release scenarios. For alternative scenarios, sources may consider the effects of both passive and active mitigation systems.

One worst-case release scenario will be defined to represent all toxics, and one worst-case release scenario will be defined to represent all flammables held above the threshold at the source. Additional worst-case release scenario(s) must be analyzed and reported if such a release from another covered process at the source potentially affects public receptors that would not be potentially affected by the first scenario. EPA recognizes that this approach may be problematic for some sources such as batch processors and warehouses where use of listed substances or inventory may vary considerably within an RMP reporting period. EPA suggests that owners or operators of such processes develop a worst-case scenario for future chemical use and inventory based on past practices to minimize the need for frequent revision of their worst-case scenario. For alternative release scenarios, one scenario is required for each toxic substance and one to represent all flammable substances held in covered processes at the source.

An endpoint is needed for the offsite consequence analysis. Appendix A of today's rule lists the endpoints for toxic substances that must be used in worst-case and alternative scenario assessment. The endpoint for a toxic substance is its Emergency Response Planning Guideline level 2 (ERPG–2) developed by the American Industrial Hygiene Association (AIHA). If a substance has no ERPG–2, then the endpoint is the level of concern (LOC) from the Technical Guidance for Hazards Analysis, updated where necessary to reflect new toxicity data. EPA recognizes the limitations associated with ERPG–2 and LOC values and is working with other agencies to develop Acute Exposure Guideline Limits (AEGLs). When these values have been developed and peer-reviewed, EPA intends to adopt them through rulemaking as the toxic endpoints for this rule. For flammables, vapor cloud explosion distances will be based on an overpressure of 1 psi; for alternative flammable releases, radiant heat distances will be based on an exposure of 5 kW/m² for 40 seconds. For vapor cloud fires and jet fires, the lower flammability limit provided by the National Fire Protection Association (NFPA) or other sources shall be used.

EPA selected 1.5 meter per second (m/s) wind speed and F atmospheric stability class as the default worst-case scenario meteorological conditions. If the owner or operator has meteorological data that show that higher minimum wind speeds or less stable atmospheric class conditions existed at the source at all times in the previous three years, then the higher wind speed and different stability class may be used. Alternative release analyses may use site-specific, typical meteorological conditions. If the owner or operator has no data on typical meteorological conditions, then conditions used in the RMP Offsite Consequence Analysis Guidance (3 m/s and D stability), may be used. Although EPA is providing technical guidance and reference tables for worst-case and alternative release scenario assessments, owners or operators may use any generally recognized, commercially or publicly available air dispersion modeling techniques, provided the modeling parameters specified in the rule are used.

For the hazard assessment and the RMP, populations potentially affected are defined as those within a circle that has as its center the point of release and its radius the distance to the toxic or flammable endpoint. Owners or operators may use Census data to define this population, and may update those data if they are inaccurate. EPA suggests that owners or operators use LandView, an electronic publication of environmental, geographic and

demographic information published by EPA and the Bureau of Census. The presence of schools, hospitals, other institutions, public arenas, recreational areas, and large commercial and industrial developments that can be identified on street maps within this circle must be noted in the RMP, but the number of people occupying them need not be enumerated. The presence of environmental receptors within this circle must also be listed. EPA has defined environmental receptors as natural areas such as national or state parks, forests, or monuments; officially designated wildlife sanctuaries, preserves, refuges, or areas; and Federal wilderness areas, that can be exposed to an accidental release. All of these can be identified on local U.S. Geological Survey maps or maps based on USGS data.

The five-year accident history will cover all accidents involving regulated substances, but only from covered processes at the source that resulted in serious on site or certain known offsite impacts in the five years prior to the submission of each RMP. EPA has replaced the definition of significant accidental release with specific definitions of the types of releases to be covered under each of the specific requirements previously associated with this definition.

D. Prevention Programs

EPA has retained the management system requirement proposed in the NPRM, but only for Program 2 and 3 processes. EPA has moved the management system requirement from the prevention program section to the general requirements section because it should be designed to oversee the implementation of all elements of the risk management program. The owner or operator must designate a qualified person or position with overall responsibility for the program and specify the lines of authority if responsibility for implementing individual requirements is assigned to other persons or positions.

In the SNPRM, EPA proposed a Program 2 prevention program that covered training, maintenance, safety precautions, and monitoring, but did not specify any particular actions. EPA solicited comment on whether specific prevention activities should be required for Program 2 sources, such as any of the specific activities initially proposed in the NPRM. For today's rule, EPA has developed seven specific elements for the Program 2 prevention program: safety information (§ 68.48), hazard review (§ 68.50), operating procedures (§ 68.52), training (§ 68.54), maintenance

(§ 68.56), compliance audits (§ 68.58), and incident investigation (§ 68.60). Most Program 2 processes are likely to be relatively simple and located at smaller businesses. EPA believes owners or operators of Program 2 processes can successfully prevent accidents without a program as detailed as the OSHA PSM, which was primarily designed for the chemical industry. EPA combined and tailored elements common to OSHA's PSM and EPA's NPRM to generate Program 2 requirements and applied them to non-petrochemical industry processes. EPA is also developing model risk management programs (and RMPs) for several industry sectors that will have Program 2 processes. These model guidances will help sources comply by providing standard elements that can be adopted to a specific source. EPA expects that many Program 2 processes will already be in compliance with most of the requirements through compliance with other Federal regulations, state laws, industry standards and codes, and good engineering practices.

The Program 3 prevention program includes the requirements of the OSHA PSM standard, 29 CFR 1910.119 (c) through (m) and (o), with minor wording changes to address statutory differences. This makes it clear that one accident prevention program to protect workers, the general public, and the environment will satisfy both OSHA and EPA. For elements that are in both the EPA and OSHA rules, EPA has used OSHA's language verbatim, with the following changes: the replacement of the terms "highly hazardous substance," "employer," "standard" and "facility" with "regulated substance," "owner or operator," "part or rule," and "stationary source"; the deletion of specific references to workplace impacts or to "safety and health;" changes to specific schedule dates; and changes to references within the standard. The "safety and health" and "workplace impacts" references occur in OSHA's PSM standard in process safety information (29 CFR 1910.119 (d)(2)(E)), process hazards analysis (29 CFR 1910.119(e)(3)(vii)), and incident investigation (29 CFR 1910.119(m)(1)). These changes are designed to ensure that OSHA retains its oversight of actions designed to protect workers while EPA retains its oversight of actions to protect public health and the environment and to remove possible interpretations that certain elements of process safety management fail to account for offsite impacts. Commenters were particularly concerned about the phase-in of process hazard analyses

PHAs). Under the final rule, PHAs conducted for OSHA are considered adequate to meet EPA's requirements. They will be updated on the OSHA schedule (i.e., by the fifth anniversary of their initial completion). This approach will eliminate any need for duplicative analyses. Documentation for the PHA developed for OSHA will be sufficient to meet EPA's purposes.

EPA anticipates that sources whose processes are already in compliance with OSHA PSM will not need to take any additional steps or create any new documentation to comply with EPA's program 3 prevention program. Any PSM modifications necessary to account for protection of public health and the environment along with protection of workers can be made when PSM elements are updated under the OSHA requirements. EPA has modified the OSHA definition of catastrophic release, which serves as the trigger for an accident investigation, to include events that present imminent and substantial endangerment to public health and the environment.'' As a result, this rule requires investigation of accidental releases that pose a risk to the public or the environment, whereas the OSHA rule does not. EPA recognizes that catastrophic accidental releases primarily affect the workplace and that this change will have little effect on accident investigation programs already established. However, EPA needs to ensure that deviations that could have had only an offsite impact are also addressed.

. Emergency Response

EPA has adopted the emergency response requirements found in the statute, without additional specific planning requirements beyond those necessary to implement the statute. This action is consistent with the Agency's effort to develop a single Federal approach for emergency response planning. The Presidential Review of federal release prevention, mitigation, and response authorities (required under section 112(r)(10) of the Clean Air Act) found that there is seldom harmony in the required formats or elements of response plans prepared to meet various federal regulations. Accordingly, EPA has committed not to specify new plan elements and/or a specific plan format in today's rule beyond those that are statutorily required. EPA believes that plans developed to comply with other EPA contingency planning requirements and the OSHA Hazardous Waste and Emergency Operations (HAZWOPER) rule (29 CFR 1910.120) will meet most of the requirements for the emergency response program. In addition, EPA and

other National Response Team agencies have prepared Integrated Contingency Plan Guidance ("one plan") (NRT, May 1996). The NRT and the agencies responsible for reviewing and approving federal response plans to which the one plan option applies agree that integrated response plans prepared in the format provided in this guidance will be acceptable and be the federally preferred method of response planning. An emergency response plan that includes the elements specified in this guidance can be used to meet the requirements in today's rule. The final rule also provides relief for sources that are too small to respond to releases with their own employees; these sources will not be required to develop emergency response plans provided that procedures for notifying non-employee emergency responders have been adopted and that appropriate responses to their hazards have been addressed in the community emergency response plan developed under EPCRA (42 U.S.C. 11003) for toxics or coordinated with the local fire department for flammables.

F. Risk Management Plan (RMP)

Owners or operators must submit their first RMP by the date specified in § 68.10. After the RMP is submitted, changes at the source may require updates to the RMP other than the standard update every five years. If a new substance or new process is added, the RMP will need to be revised and submitted by the date the substance is first in the process above the threshold quantity. If changes to processes require revised hazard assessments or PHAs, or if a process changes Program level, the source must submit a revised RMP within six months.

EPA intends that the RMP will be submitted in a method and format to a central point as specified by EPA. States, local entities including local emergency planning committees (LEPCs), and the public will be able to access all RMPs electronically. This process will relieve states and local entities of the burden of filing documents and providing public access to them without limiting these agencies' or the public's access to the information.

The RMP is a multi-purpose document. The CAA requires that the RMP indicate compliance with the regulations and also include the hazard assessment, prevention program, and emergency response program. EPA is mandated to develop a program for auditing RMPs and requiring revisions, where appropriate. The RMP, therefore, must include enough data to allow the implementing agency to determine,

through review of the RMP, whether the source is in compliance with the rule. EPA, however, believes that the RMP must serve another function; to provide information to the public in a form that will be understandable and will encourage the public to use the information to improve the dialogue with sources on issues related to prevention and preparedness.

To meet both of these purposes, the RMP will consist of the source's registration; an executive summary that will provide a brief description of the source's activities as they relate to covered processes and program elements; and data elements that address compliance with each of the rule elements. While the public and implementing agencies could make use of all sections of the RMP, the executive summary will provide text descriptions and give the source a chance to explain its programs in a format that will be easy for communities to read and understand. The data elements will provide the implementing agency with the basic data it needs to assess compliance without asking for detailed documentation. The Agency is considering development of an RMP form where the data elements of the form would provide the implementing agency with the basic data it needs to assess compliance without asking for detailed documentation. All data elements would be checkoff boxes, yes/no answers, or numerical entries.

This approach will provide data that anyone can download or search. States, communities, trade associations, or public interest groups may want to use the data or a subset of the data to create databases that allow them to compare sources in the same industry or same area. For example, a local entity will be able to download data from all reporting sources that are similar to ones in its community to determine whether the quantities stored and process controls used are typical. The information will provide the public with data that will enhance their dialogue with sources. It will also help sources and trade associations to understand practices in their industries and identify practices that could be used to reduce risks. The risk management program documentation will remain at the source and will be available for review by EPA and the implementing agency.

G. Air Permitting

The SNPRM discussed the relationship between section 112(r) and CAA air permitting requirements for sources subject to both provisions. Under the CAA, air permitting authorities must ensure that sources are in compliance with applicable requirements to issue a permit. Because section 112(r) is an applicable requirement, EPA has identified in the final rule the permit conditions and the actions owners or operators and air permitting authorities must take to ensure compliance. The permit must identify part 68 as an applicable requirement and establish conditions that require the owner or operator of the source to submit either a compliance schedule for meeting the requirements of part 68 by the date specified in § 68.10(a) or, as part of the compliance certification submitted under 40 CFR 70.6(c)(5), a certification statement that, to the best of the owner or operator's knowledge, the source is in compliance with all requirements of this part, including the registration and submission of the RMP. The owner or operator must also submit any additional relevant information requested by the air permitting authority or designated agency to ensure compliance with the requirements of this section. If a permit is already issued that does not contain the provisions described above, then, the owner or operator or air permitting authority shall initiate permit revision or reopening according to the procedures in 40 CFR 70.7 or 71.7 to incorporate the terms and conditions as described above. EPA also allows the state to assign the authority to implement and enforce these requirements to another agency or agencies (the "designated agency") to take advantage of resources or accident prevention expertise that might be available in these other agencies. Finally, the air permitting authority or designated agency must: (1) Verify that the source owner or operator has registered and submitted an RMP or a revised plan when required; (2) verify that the source owner or operator has submitted the proper certification or compliance schedule; (3) for some or all sources, use one or more mechanisms such as, but not limited to, a completeness check, source audits, record reviews or facility inspections to ensure that permitted sources are in compliance; and (4) initiate enforcement action, based on the requirements of this section, as appropriate.

H. Other Issues

In the SNPRM, EPA discussed three other issues raised by commenters: accident information reporting, public participation, and inherently safer technologies. EPA has decided not to develop any requirements related to these issues at this time. Although EPA continues to believe that accident reports that provide more detail on the

causes and impacts of accidents could be useful, the Agency has decided to limit such reporting required under this rule to the five-year accident history mandated by the CAA. When necessary, EPA will use its authority to investigate individual accidents and to seek additional information to the extent authorized by CAA section 114 (i.e., to determine compliance with this rule and CAA section 112(r)(1), to support further rule development, and to assist research on hazard assessment).

Secondly, the Agency encourages sources, the public, and local entities to work together on accident prevention issues, but believes that the wide variety and large number of sources subject to this rule make any single mandatory approach to public participation inappropriate. RMP information should be used as the basis for dialogue between the community and sources on accidental release prevention, risk reduction and preparedness for emergency response. Industry and the public should continue to use the LEPC as a mechanism for this dialogue.

Finally, EPA does not believe that a requirement that owners or operators conduct searches or analyses of alternative process technologies for new or existing processes will produce significant additional benefits. Many commenters, including those who support these analyses, indicated that an assessment of inherently safer design alternatives has the most benefit in the development of new processes. Industry generally examines new process alternatives to avoid the addition of more costly administrative or engineering controls associated with a design that may be more hazardous in nature. Although some existing processes may be judged to be inherently less safe than others, EPA believes most of these processes can be safely operated through management and control of the hazards without spending resources searching for unavailable or unaffordable new process technologies. Application of good PHA techniques often reveals opportunities for continuous improvement of existing processes and operations without a separate analysis of alternatives. EPA encourages owners or operators to continue to examine and adopt viable alternative processing technologies, system safeguards, or process modifications to make new and existing processes and operations inherently safer. Through the process and prevention program information in the RMP, sources can demonstrate, and users of the RMP information can observe and promote, progress toward safer processes and operations.

EPA is considering the development of incentives and awards to stimulate inherently safer alternative research and development, public outreach and education, and risk communication efforts. The Agency welcomes ideas and participation in this effort.

III. Discussion of Comments

EPA received 1220 comments, including 180 relevant comments submitted for the List Rule, 757 comments on the NPRM, and 283 comments on the SNPRM. The commenters represented 92 chemical manufacturers, 81 other chemical users, 111 petroleum industry companies, 174 industry trade associations, 40 other trade associations, 58 agricultural supply retailers, 102 propane retailers, 132 explosives users, 29 water treatment facilities, 26 utilities, 66 state agencies, 63 local governments, 8 other Federal agencies, 52 academics and consultants, 61 environmental groups, 6 labor unions, and 31 private citizens. The remaining 88 letters were requests for extensions of the comment period, interim or duplicate sets of comments, or had been sent to the incorrect docket. The major issues raised by the commenters are briefly addressed below; a complete presentation of the Agency's response to the comments received on this rulemaking is available in the Risk Management Program Rule: Summary and Response to Comments in the docket (see ADDRESSES).

Many commenters requested that EPA's list be identical to OSHA's list of highly hazardous substances and no thresholds should be less than OSHA's. These comments were addressed in the final list rule (59 FR 4478; January 21, 1994) and background material related to these issues is available in docket number A–91–74 (see ADDRESSES).

A. Tiering

Commenters on the NPRM suggested that EPA create different levels of requirements for sources that pose different risks. In the SNPRM, EPA proposed three tiers: a low hazard tier for sources whose worst-case release would not affect any public or environmental receptors of concern; a medium hazard tier for sources that were not eligible or covered by the low or high hazard tiers; and a high hazard tier based on either industry sector accident history and number of employees or simply based on the number of employees. Generally, commenters were concerned that all processes at a source would need to be eligible for Program 1 before any process could be. EPA has revised the rule to clarify that eligibility for any tier rogram) is based on process criteria, ot source. If a process meets Program criteria, the owners or operators need ly meet Program 1 requirements for at process even if other processes at e source are subject to Program 2 or rogram 3.

1. Rationale. Only 2 of the 57 mmenters opposed tiering arguing at the CAA mandates that all covered urces be required to complete a full revention program and that Congress ad considered and rejected emptions. One commenter argued that PA had already accounted for differences in size, operations, rocesses, class and categories of urces" in developing the list and resholds. Most commenters supported ering as an appropriate way to cognize different levels of risks and to llow sources and emergency sponders to focus on the highest risk rocesses.

EPA disagrees that the CAA requires ll covered processes to comply with e same detailed risk management rogram. EPA listed regulated bstances because of their inherent azards, such as toxicity and volatility. PA did not consider, nor does the CAA dicate that it may consider, differences in size, operations, rocesses, class and categories of urces" in selecting chemicals or etting thresholds. In establishing ection 112(r)(7) requirements, however, ongress clearly recognized that a "one- ze-fits-all" approach may not be ppropriate for these regulations and irected EPA to consider these factors in e development of the accident revention regulations. Furthermore, PA strongly disputes the assertion that has exempted any source from gulation by creating different rograms for different sources. As noted elow, all covered processes will be ddressed in RMPs that contain hazard ssessment, prevention, and response nformation, as required by statute.

2. Program 1 vs. Program 2 and rogram 3 Criteria. Commenters enerally supported Program 1 for low- isk sources, but argued that few, if any, urces would qualify because the equirements were too stringent.

a. Potential for Offsite Impact. ommenters generally agreed that urces that can demonstrate no offsite mpact should be eligible for Program 1, ut only public health should be onsidered, not environmental impacts. thers stated that only sources posing a hreat of "considerable" impacts should ot be eligible for Program 1. One ommenter stated that EPA's worst-case cenario is unrealistic and its use as a rogram 1 trigger is unreasonable. Other

commenters want EPA to allow site- specific modeling for the offsite consequence analysis, rather than look- up tables.

In today's rule, EPA specifically allows owners or operators to use site- specific air dispersion modeling for their offsite consequence analyses. EPA disagrees that offsite impacts should be limited to "considerable" impacts. When offsite impacts are possible, it may be reasonable to implement some additional measures to reduce accidental releases, especially when the burden of measures such as additional training or safety precautions is low. Programs 2 and 3 provide flexibility to allow source-specific consideration of the appropriate level of effort. Program 1 requires no additional prevention measures, which is only categorically justifiable if such measures would not reduce offsite impact. It is reasonable to couple a no impact criterion with a conservative worst-case scenario to conclude categorically the public would not benefit from additional prevention measures. If no impact can be demonstrated for a conservative worst- case release, then no impact is likely to occur for any other release event, and the process could be judged to pose a low threat to the surrounding area.

EPA has decided that potential impact on environmental receptors resulting from a worst-case scenario will not be a criterion to determine eligibility for Program 1. EPA agrees that very little, if any, data exist on the potential acute environmental impacts or environmental endpoints associated with listed chemicals upon accidental release. In addition, the offsite consequence distances estimated using human acute toxicity or overpressure effects may not be directly relevant to environmental effects. However, owners or operators will be required to document in the RMP the presence of such receptors within the distance determined for the worst case. EPA believes that natural resource agencies and the public will be able to benefit from the environmental receptors information in the RMP in discussions with the source.

b. Accident History for Program 1. Many commenters objected to accident history as a Program 1 criterion, arguing that a process that had a significant accidental release in the previous five years may have been changed to reduce or eliminate future events and public impact. Several commenters suggested that such processes that otherwise meet Program 1 criteria should remain eligible, but be required to justify and document the changes. Some commenters also objected to EPA's

proposed definition of significant accidental release, arguing that many companies and emergency responders conservatively evacuate or shelter-in- place during minor incidents. Under the proposed definition, these actions disqualify a process from Program 1 even if there were no offsite impacts. Some commenters stated that the accident history provision was unnecessary because, by definition, a Program 1 process is not capable of an accidental release that could affect public receptors.

EPA has decided to retain the accident history criterion for Program 1 processes, excluding events with evacuations and shelterings in place, and to drop the definition of significant accidental release. Program 1 eligibility is not a one-time exercise; owners or operators must certify in each RMP that no qualifying releases have occurred since the previous RMP submission and provide current worst-case release data indicating no offsite impacts are anticipated in the future. Program 1 criteria and accident history provide owners or operators an opportunity to demonstrate to the community ongoing excellence in accident prevention and an incentive to search for and implement ways, such as inventory reduction, to reduce the potential for offsite impacts associated with large scale accidental releases. Further, the unique circumstances surrounding past accidents can provide a reality check on the theoretical modeling and worst-case scenario claims used for the offsite consequence assessment and serve to verify that administrative controls and passive mitigation measures work as intended. EPA decided to delete public evacuations or shelterings-in-place as criteria for Program 1 eligibility. EPA is that inclusion of these criteria in Program 1 eligibility may create a perverse incentive not to report releases and it may encourage sources and local emergency officials to take more chances during an event when there may be potential exposures that do not rise to the endpoint specified in this rule but would otherwise be worthy of precautionary actions by the source or by local officials. If the evacuation or sheltering takes place because of a concern for public exposure to an endpoint as specified in this rule, then public receptors necessarily would be under the worst case distance and the process would not be eligible for Program 1 under the criteria of the rule. Owners or operators of processes that meet Program 1 eligibility requirements are required to report a 5 year accident history for that process. If local emergency planners, first responders or the public have concerns about processes in Program 1 because of a past evacuation or sheltering-in-place event, then mechanisms under EPCRA could be used to gather more information from the source about its prevention program (such as EPCRA sections 302(b)(2) [designation of a facility if it does not already handle extremely hazardous substances listed under section 302] and 303(d)(3) [provision of information to the emergency planning committee]) and involve the source in emergency planning. Sources and local first responders should be discussing evacuation and sheltering-in-place criteria and decisions as part of emergency response planning.

c. Other. Many commenters asked that specific industries such as ammonia refrigeration, retail fertilizer outlets, all flammables, and all non-PSM sources be assigned to Program 1. EPA disagrees because each source has unique surroundings that must be considered in the worst-case assessment and each source must demonstrate favorable accident history. All ammonia refrigeration units covered by this rule are already subject to OSHA PSM; many of these have had accidents that affected the community and should be required to complete the requirements of the hazard assessment and emergency response program and provide the community with full RMP information. According to the industry, a typical ammonia fertilizer retailer handles 200 tons of ammonia. Some retailers may be very geographically isolated and can qualify for Program 1, but EPA expects that most will be subject to Program 2. Given the large quantity of ammonia involved, EPA considers it important that the community have information on offsite consequences from these sources and that the owner or operator takes the necessary steps to address accidental release prevention and emergency response.

EPA expects that some sources handling flammables will qualify for Program 1 because the distance to a 1 psi overpressure is generally less than distances to toxic endpoints. Nonetheless, those sources handling flammables in sufficient quantity to generate a potential offsite impact should provide the community with information on hazards and address prevention and response steps. Many sources handling flammables are already subject to PSM; the only additional steps required under this rule are completion of the hazard assessment and emergency response programs and submission of an RMP.

EPA does not agree that non-PSM sources should be assigned to Program 1. Many of these sources could have an accidental release that can affect the community. OSHA exempted retailers because they are covered by other OSHA or state regulations that address workplace safety, not because they are incapable of having offsite impacts. All retailers are in Program 2 unless they can meet Program 1 criteria; thus, they should be taking prevention steps and will be providing the community with information. Compliance with other existing Federal and state programs may satisfy many Program 2 prevention requirements, thereby limiting the burden. In addition, EPA expects to develop model risk management programs for these sectors. Public sources in states without delegated OSHA programs are not covered by OSHA PSM because OSHA is barred by law from regulating them. Nonetheless, these sources may pose a threat to the community. Today's rule places these sources in Program 2.

3. Program 2 vs. Program 3 Criteria. In the SNPRM, EPA's preferred approach assigned sources to Program 3 based on SIC code and number of employees; sources in specified SIC codes with 100 or more full-time employees (FTE) would have been subject to the full program in 3 years; sources in a subset of these SIC codes with 20 to 99 FTEs would have been subject to the full program in 8 years. The alternative was to impose the full program on all sources with more than 100 FTEs. Most SNPRM commenters submitted suggestions and arguments about this approach.

a. Number of Employees. Only two commenters supported using the number of employees as the sole criterion, arguing it would be the easiest approach to implement with the greatest amount of industry participation. Commenters opposed it because the number of employees proposed does not reliably correlate with risk, hazard, or quantity on site, and because it could act as an incentive to reduce employment. In addition, some commenters stated that smaller sources may have fewer resources to manage hazards and, therefore, may pose a greater risk to the public.

EPA agrees and has deleted the number of employees as a Program 3 criterion. Although size of a source in the manufacturing sectors may be related to the quantities on site and complexity of the processes, many other sources may have similar characteristics with fewer employees. Complexity is more directly associated with the type of industry (i.e., SIC code) than with

number of employees; a highly automated process may involve fewer employees and be more complex than a more labor intensive process. Quantity, if relevant, can be directly measured rather than indirectly by number of employees. In addition, EPA was concerned that the data on which the Agency based its proposed approach may not be representative of all accidental releases. These data, drawn from reports to the National Response Center and EPA regions, appear to indicate that larger sources have more and larger accidental releases than do smaller sources. This finding, however, may in part reflect different levels of reporting, rather than different levels of accidents. Both Federal and state officials report that the number of releases has risen in recent years as more sources learn about their reporting obligations. EPA has decided that, because the processes within the SIC codes basically handle the same chemicals in the same way, smaller sources should not be moved to a different Program based on the number of employees.

b. SIC Code. Fifty-seven commenters, particularly those in the oil industry, utilities, and public systems, supported the use of SIC codes based on accident history; 28 commenters opposed it. Supporters argued that industry accident records represented a reasonable criterion for identifying high-risk sources. If an entire industry has a long history without accidental release, it may indicate that the materials handled and handling conditions generate a smaller potential for serious releases or that the industry is effectively controlled by government or industry standards. Some commenters argued that industry accident histories reflect underlying risk better than individual source accident histories because accidents are rare events; a source with no accidental releases over the previous five years is not necessarily safe.

Commenters opposing the use of SIC codes stated that the approach is arbitrary, that accidents with only onsite effects should not be used, that sources in other industry sectors handle similar quantities and pose similar risks, and that sources within an industry that have successful risk management practices are penalized by a few isolated sources within the industry.

EPA has decided to retain the use of SIC codes, adding SIC 2865 based on further review of accident histories, and to add coverage by the OSHA PSM standard as a separate criterion for Program 3. EPA selected the SIC codes by analyzing accident data filed by urces in response to EPA's request for formation in the Accidental Release formation Program (ARIP). ARIP llects data from certain sources that port releases under CERCLA section 13. EPA selected the SIC codes that owed a high frequency of the most rious accidents across a significant rcentage of all sources within the SIC de to avoid mischaracterizing an dustry based on isolated, problematic urces. Data on the selection criteria ere summarized in the SNPRM and e docket at the time of the SNPRM. ne accident history of the cyclic crudes dustry (SIC code 2865) is similar to at of the categories selected. EPA sagrees that only offsite impacts ould be considered; accidental leases that caused death, spitalizations, or injuries on site are so of concern because they indicate gnificant safety problems that could ad to releases that cause impacts fsite. The SIC codes selected by EPA e basically the same ones OSHA lected for its PSM program inspection cus. EPA disagrees that sources are enalized" by this approach because vners or operators of processes in ese SIC codes have an opportunity to esent their safety record, demonstrate e success of their accident prevention ograms, and communicate with the cal community the basis for their risk anagement practices. Sources that ceive Merit or Star status in the OSHA oluntary Protection Program will be vorably distinguished from others in e same industry when implementing encies are selecting sources for audits ee section III.T.1 below).

EPA agrees that serious accidents cur infrequently even at sources with or safety practices and that industry-ide accident records provide a better echanism than the accident history at single source for identifying those ctors whose chemicals and processes ay lead to serious releases. A high roportion of the sources in some SIC des reported releases; EPA's analysis ecifically took into account the umber of reports from individual urces to avoid selecting an SIC code cause of a small number of sources ith serious safety problems.

The OSHA PSM already applies to ost covered processes in the selected C codes. EPA expects that there will e fewer than 400 additional processes signed to Program 3 that are not ready subject to the OSHA PSM andard at the approximately 1,400 urces in these SIC codes and that all these sources will already have other rocesses covered by OSHA PSM. onsequently, fulfilling the RMP

requirements imposes little additional burden.

EPA decided to include all covered processes currently subject to the OSHA PSM standard in Program 3 to eliminate any confusion and inconsistency between the prevention requirements that the owners or operators of such processes must meet. EPA's Program 3 prevention program is identical to the OSHA PSM standard. Including OSHA PSM processes in Program 3, therefore, imposes no additional burden on these processes; the only new requirements for such processes are the hazard assessment, emergency response program, and the RMP, which are the same under Programs 2 and 3.

c. Site-Specific, Risk-based Criteria. Many commenters stated that Program assignment should be based on site-specific risk-based criteria. Accident history is one such criterion and is discussed separately in Section III.A.3.d. Other criteria suggested include population density or proximity, quantity on site, number of substances held above the threshold, process conditions, toxicity, volatility, alternative release scenario results, or combinations of these factors as a risk index.

EPA agrees with commenters that Program assignments should be risk-based to the extent possible; however, as the variety of suggestions indicates, a considerable number of variables would need to be considered. EPA knows of no standard approach or equation that is used and generally accepted. The variety of suggestions indicate the likelihood that any proposed formula would meet opposition. No commenter provided a method to comprehensively address these factors on a nation-wide basis.

An important consideration for EPA in developing the rule provisions for Program assignment was to avoid undue complexity, confusion, and resource expenditure by sources and implementing agencies implementing the rule's criteria. To some extent, EPA has incorporated risk factors, including site-specific factors, in determining which sources are eligible for which Program. For example, Program 1 eligibility already considers the potential for offsite impacts; any process for which there are no public receptors within the distance to an endpoint from a worst-case release may be eligible for Program 1, provided there have been no releases with certain offsite consequences within the previous five years. Today's rule allows sources to consider passive mitigation and administrative controls in conducting the worst-case release analysis. Such

site-specific considerations affect the extent of potential exposure to a worst-case release, and thus are reflected in the Program 1 eligibility criteria. Elements of risk such as process complexity and accident history are also reflected the design of Program 2 and Program 3 requirements and the assignment of processes to these Programs. Program 2 sources generally handle and store regulated substances, but do not react or manufacture them. EPA believes Program 2 sources can take prevention steps that are less detailed than those in the OSHA PSM standard and still accomplish accident prevention that is protective of any population nearby. Program 3 is reserved for processes already subject to the OSHA PSM standard and processes with high accidental release histories. The SIC codes with an accident history selected by EPA for Program 3 are typically complex processes. The PSM standard was designed for, and is particularly appropriate for, these processes.

EPA takes issue with the appropriateness of some of the suggested factors. Meteorological conditions vary too much to be considered in determining a risk level. Chemical quantity alone does not accurately relate to risk because the location and handling conditions can dramatically change the potential for exposures.

In addition, EPA has implementation concerns about a detailed, national, multi-factor, risk-based approach, were it to be feasible. States such as Delaware have used a simple version of a risk-based approach and found that it created serious problems for the state and the sources. Smaller sources and those without technical staff have had great difficulty in implementing the approach and have had to rely on state officials to determine applicability for them. Delaware specifically recommended that EPA not attempt implementing a similar approach on a national basis because of the burden it imposes on the state and the confusion and uncertainty it creates for sources. Delaware has fewer than 100 sources; nationally, EPA estimates that 66,000 sources will be subject to the rule, approximately 62,000 of which are outside of the chemical and refining sectors. If implementing agencies had to help most of these sources determine the index score and Program for each process, not only would the burden on the agencies be extreme, but implementation would also be delayed. Furthermore, were EPA to simply identify risk factors without an index and leave the determination of Program level to sources or implementing agencies, the process for such site-specific determinations would be even more complex and resource intensive for sources and implementing agencies; it would create disincentives for a state to become involved and to take on the role of an implementing agency. EPA believes it is better to have sources and agencies focus their resources on prevention activities.

EPA considered, but decided against, a less comprehensive risk-based approach using proximity or population density as criteria for distinguishing between Program 2 and 3. EPA recognizes that accidental releases from sources near or in densely populated areas may harm more individuals and be perceived to pose a greater risk than other sources. However, as stated above, EPA believes that the type of process, its complexity and accident history should be considered for Program 2 or 3 assignment, regardless of the number of people potentially exposed. In other words, EPA does not believe the streamlined Program 2 prevention elements should apply to a complex Program 3 process just because fewer persons could be potentially exposed or that the Program 3 prevention elements should apply to a Program 2 process because more people could be potentially exposed. EPA believes that populations offsite should be protected from harm based on the type of process; the Program 2 prevention elements, properly applied to the expected types of Program 2 processes, serves to protect off-site populations, just as the Program 3 prevention elements for complex processes serves to protect offsite populations.

If Program assignments were based on the alternative release scenario results, sources would not have the flexibility and latitude in today's rule for these scenarios because more definite criteria would need to be considered to ensure the proper scenarios and results are assessed. This places more emphasis and burden for sources on the offsite consequence assessment rather than on accident prevention and communication with the public and first responders. Furthermore, because active mitigation includes process and control equipment that may fail, considering such equipment in evaluating risk would not be appropriate without detailed review by the source and oversight by the implementing agency.

Some commenters suggested yet another variation of a less comprehensive, "risk"-based approach that would have EPA use a site-specific analysis of likelihood of release to assign Program levels. Many of the same

difficulties in developing a "risk index" for determining Program assignments would apply to an attempt to incorporate likelihood in a more sophisticated manner than EPA was able to do in its analysis of accident history by SIC code. In addition to the substance-specific properties considered as part of the chemical listing criteria, the site-specific likelihood of a release depends on a number of factors, including the appropriateness of the equipment in use, the maintenance of that equipment, operator performance, and safety systems and their performance. Evaluating site-specific likelihood of release requires data on each of these items; such data rarely exist especially for complex processes where a variety of equipment must be evaluated along with the performance of multiple operators and maintenance workers. Using surrogate data (e.g., manufacturer's failure rate data) introduces error of an unknown magnitude to the analysis. Such analyses are very costly and produce results that are, at best, questionable.

EPA also believes that assessing the likelihood of a release at most sites for site-specific individualized Program-level determinations is neither technically feasible nor cost-effective. In most cases, the data do not exist to conduct a meaningful analysis; where they do exist, the cost of developing a defensible analysis and overseeing it could well exceed the cost of compliance with the rule. Such an approach would resemble a permit program, which would be resource-intensive for sources and implementing agencies. EPA determined that the simpler approach for assigning sources to Program 1 would provide regulatory relief for those sources that could not affect the public while allowing other sources to devote their resources to prevention activities rather than to analyses that would be subject to legal challenges.

EPA notes that sources have the flexibility to implement appropriate accident prevention measures based on the hazards and risks discovered in the hazard review or process hazard analysis. The structure of Programs 2 and 3, therefore, reflect site-specific risk criteria. Further, the purpose of the risk management program and RMP effort is to prevent accidents and facilitate local level dialogue about the risks, prevention measures, and emergency response effort in place at the source. The local community and first responders may have far different concerns that should, and can be addressed better through today's

approach than those reflected by a risk index approach.

d. Accident History. Some commenters argued that EPA should assign sources to Program 3 based on the accident history of the source. One commenter suggested that any source with no accidental release that exceeded a reportable quantity (as defined in CERCLA) for the previous five years should be in Program 2. Others argued that a source should be in Program 2 if it had no significant accidental release in the previous five years. Some commenters said that a one-release standard was too stringent and that two or more significant accidental releases should be allowed before a source was assigned to Program 3. Another commenter suggested that a source with no significant accidental releases in the past five years and with few potentially impacted neighbors should be placed in Program 2.

Other commenters opposed this approach, arguing that, in many cases, sources take steps to prevent recurrences following a serious release. In some cases, the offsite impacts from releases are minor and would not justify assigning a source to a particular Program. Other commenters stated that the absence of an accidental release can be indicative of lower risk, but it can also simply mean that a release has not yet occurred. Several commenters noted that a five-year time period is statistically insignificant because accidental releases are infrequent events.

EPA agrees that source-specific accident history is not a reasonable basis for assigning processes to Programs 2 and 3. Given the relative infrequency of serious accidents, a five- or even ten-year period without an accident may not be indicative of safe operations. In addition, the criteria necessary to define the types of past accidental release for the purposes of program classification would need to be based on a wide variety of variables and site-specific factors, which would lead to confusion and unnecessary complexity. Factors such as weather conditions at the time of the release, rather than the size of a source or its management practices, often determine whether a release has offsite consequences. EPA believes that accident history is appropriately used on an industry-wide basis as described above for selection of Program 3 sources. If accidental releases with consequences appear to occur at a large proportion of sources within an SIC code, where similar processes, equipment and chemicals are used, then it is reasonable to conclude that rocesses in that SIC code pose a greater likelihood of a high hazard release than others. This approach removes the need or at least one accident to occur at very source that EPA believes ought to e assigned to a particular Program, specially when such accidents are rare vents. EPA is also concerned that using ource-specific accident history as a iterion would create an incentive for ources to fail to report releases. Finally, EPA has stated, assignments to rogram 2 and 3 also consider the propriateness of the prevention steps r the types of sources. EPA believes at both Programs move sources to eater accident prevention.

e. Other. Some commenters asked that e implementing agency be given iscretion to move a source into a ifferent Program based on local oncerns and knowledge. EPA notes at states have the authority, under the AA, to impose more, but not less, ringent standards than EPA (see CAA ection 112(r)(11)).

A few commenters suggested that rogram 2 be limited to sources for hich a model risk management rogram had been developed. The odels would be designed to reflect sks associated with categories of ources that all use the same type of quipment and handle the substances in e same way (e.g., propane retailers nd users, ammonia retailers). EPA onsidered this approach and decided at the Program 2 prevention program rovides a better, generic prevention pproach for processes for which the ore detailed PSM program would be appropriate. Limiting Program 2 to ose industrial sectors where industry-pecific models are feasible would place ome manufacturing sources at a isadvantage simply because their hemical uses, processes, and quipment were too varied to allow evelopment of a model or because ere are too few sources to justify use f EPA or industry resources to develop model. In addition, if EPA were to mit Program 2 to sources with model rograms, Program 2 regulations would eed sufficient specificity to enforce the se of these models; otherwise, sources ould be able to ignore both PSM and e models. EPA is also concerned that odifying the model plans could stifle nnovation in safety practices. If ndustry codes or other Federal egulations on which parts of the odels may be based were updated, PA would have to revise its models; iven the time needed to propose and dopt regulations, sources might have to elay implementation of new systems nd, in some cases, might be caught etween complying with a revised EPA

or OSHA regulation or state law or complying with the model. Consequently, EPA decided it was better to have models available as guidance, but not require compliance with them. Further, EPA believes that the key elements of good accident prevention practices are captured within the requirements of the Program 2 prevention program. Model programs and plans are likely to build on these approaches, making it easier for sources in Program 2 to use models that are later developed by others.

EPA is working with industry to develop model risk management programs and RMPs for ammonia refrigeration systems, propane distributors and users, and water treatment systems. EPA also expects to develop models for ammonia retailers and wastewater treatment systems. EPA encourages other industrial sectors to work together on additional model development.

4. Program 1 Requirements. Commenters were generally opposed to posting signs, and certification of no environmental impact.

a. Certification of No Environmental Impact. Many commenters stated that it would be "virtually impossible" to certify "no potential for environmental impacts," as required by the SNPRM. Commenters said that the definition of environmental impact was too vague, that the list of environments suggested in the SNPRM was too broad, and that the language seemed to require a full environmental consequence assessment, making the requirement impossible. One commenter noted that companies would find it difficult to assert that there could be "no environmental impacts" even after an environmental consequence assessment reveals insignificant impacts. Two commenters suggested that EPA substitute "low potential for environmental impact" or "no potential for long-term, adverse environmental impact." Other commenters requested that environmental impact be dropped or that the requirement be changed to mirror the Program 1 eligibility criteria with an indication in the RMP that no environmental receptors of concern were within the worst-case distance to an endpoint.

As described above in section III.A.2.a. Potential for Offsite Impact, EPA has decided not to make the presence of environmental receptors a part of the eligibility criteria for Program 1 and has deleted the certification requirement. Instead, owners or operators of all covered processes will have to identify in the RMP any environmental receptors that are within

the distance potentially affected by the worst case.

b. Signs. Commenters generally opposed the SNPRM requirement that sources with Program 1 processes post signs warning of the hazards on site if the only regulated substances present at the site above the threshold quantity were listed for flammability. Commenters stated that local and state fire and safety codes often already require such signs. In addition, sources are already required under EPCRA section 312 to file annual inventories with the LEPC and fire department that identify hazards on site. Signs would have fulfilled the emergency response program requirements for a source. Because Program 1 eligibility will now be determined on a by-process basis rather than by source-wide criteria and because EPA has revised the emergency response program provisions as noted below, EPA has dropped the requirement for signs.

c. Emergency Response Program. In the SNPRM, EPA asked whether additional emergency response planning and coordination should be required for Program 1 processes. Some commenters supported this requirement, while others stated that most sources are already covered by EPCRA and participate in community response planning. Commenters stated that because the worst-case release could not reach public receptors, such efforts were not necessary.

In the final rule, EPA is requiring the owner or operator of a Program 1 process to ensure that any necessary response actions have been coordinated with local response agencies. EPA believes that local responders may become involved in an incident, even if the public is not threatened. No additional CAA-related planning activities are required, however.

d. Other. Many commenters stated that, since Program 1 processes generate no offsite impact, they should be exempt from this rule. One commenter objected to Program 1 because members of the public, particularly first responders and business visitors, could still be hurt by a release. Other commenters suggested that the annual EPCRA section 312 form could be amended to indicate that a source was covered by the rule, replacing the RMP registration form.

The CAA requires that all sources with more than a threshold quantity of a listed substance register an RMP, perform a hazard assessment, and develop accidental release prevention and emergency response programs. Therefore, total exemption of processes that meet Program 1 criteria is not possible. See S. Rep. No. 228, 101st Cong., 1st session, at 208 ("Senate Report") (precursor of RMP provision mandating hazard assessments for sources that exceed threshold for listed substance); 136 Congressional Record S16927 (daily ed. October 27, 1990) (remarks of Sen. Durenburger, sources with more than a threshold quantity are subject to regulations); 136 Cong. Rec. H12879 (daily ed. Oct. 26, 1990)(remarks of Rep. Barton)(all users of hazardous chemicals are required to plan for accidents). Moreover, even if an exemption for processes that exceed a threshold were permissible, the owner or operator would need to take steps that are equivalent to the hazard assessment to establish eligibility for the exemption. The offsite consequence analysis is the most significant burden for a Program 1 process under this rule. The minimal additional actions required in today's rule for Program 1 simply establish a record of eligibility and a response coordination mechanism.

EPA recognizes that emergency responders and site visitors could be hurt by an accidental release from any process, but notes that responder safety is covered by OSHA and EPA under the HAZWOPER regulations. It is the owners' or operators' responsibility to inform visitors about the hazards and the appropriate steps to take in the event of an accidental release from any process subject to today's rule.

Finally, EPA has based the registration information requirements in today's rule on the EPCRA section 312 Tier II form. The CAA requires that the RMP be registered with EPA. Because the EPCRA form is not submitted to EPA, it would not substitute for registration with EPA either in its present or amended form. Completion of the registration portion of the RMP should impose little additional burden on owners or operators. However, EPA recognizes the information overlap between the Tier II form and the RMP registration and is considering use of the RMP registration for the Tier II reporting requirement.

5. Program 2 Requirements. Commenters were generally concerned about the lack of specific requirements for the Program 2 streamlined prevention program and emergency response requirements, and how compliance with other regulations would be incorporated.

a. Streamlined Program. Commenters stated that the Program 2 prevention program does not provide much, if any, regulatory relief because sources would need to address most of the ten elements of the Program 3 prevention program. Others said that the majority of the

sources affected by the rule are already covered by OSHA PSM and chemical industry standards, the Program 2 requirements do not satisfy the CAA mandate, and that only a full process hazard analysis would meet the hazard assessment requirements under section 112(r). Another commenter argued that EPA's statement that sources must comply with the CAA's general duty clause was inadequate because EPA has not used, and has no policy about, the clause.

EPA agrees that the preferred approach in the SNPRM did not provide sufficient detail on Program 2 prevention requirements to distinguish it from Program 3. EPA solicited comments on whether Program 2 should require additional, specific prevention steps. Today's rule provides specific requirements as discussed in section I.D above and in Section IV below. In the RMP, the owner or operator will be required to report on other Federal or state regulations, industry codes, and standards used to comply with prevention elements as well as any major hazards, process controls, mitigation systems, monitoring and detection systems examined in the hazard review. This streamlined prevention program addresses many of the PSM elements as the basis for sound prevention practices, but is tailored to processes with less complex chemical uses; this program provides considerable regulatory relief by substantially reducing the documentation and recordkeeping burden of PSM. In addition, EPA will provide guidance and model risk management programs to further assist Program 2 processes in developing and maintaining good prevention program practices.

EPA disagrees that only a full PHA would meet the requirements of the Act. Section 112(r) does not contain detailed requirements for the hazard assessment, beyond the key components of accidental release scenarios and a five-year accident history. EPA believes that a PHA is more appropriately considered an element of a prevention program, such as PSM. The statute does not mandate detailed PHA engineering analyses for all sources, whether as part of the hazard assessment or the prevention program. EPA believes PHAs involve a more detailed engineering analysis than is necessary to prevent accidents at Program 2 sources. The "hazard review" provisions of Program 2 should be sufficient to detect process hazards at these simpler processes. EPA recognizes that although hazard assessments and PHAs or process hazard reviews are discreet elements

that can be performed independently, hazard assessment results can enhance PHA or process hazards reviews and in turn, the results of the PHA or review can enhance the hazard assessment. EPA encourages owners or operators to make maximum use of the PHA or review and hazard assessment information to manage risks and prevent accidents.

Finally, sources with Program 2 requirements, as well as sources with Program 1 or 3 requirements, must comply with the general duty clause of CAA Section 112(r)(1). The general duty clause provides that owners and operators have a general duty to identify hazards that may result from accidental releases, design and maintain a safe facility, and minimize the consequences of any releases that occur. The general duty clause is a self-executing statutory requirement: it requires no regulations or other EPA action to take effect. The clause provides a separate statutory mechanism that EPA will use in appropriate circumstances to ensure the protection of public health and the environment. To date, EPA has undertaken several inspections designed in part to determine compliance with Section 112(r)(1). As appropriate at a future date, EPA may issue policies or guidance on application of the general duty clause.

b. Other Regulations. Commenters generally agree that OSHA PSM, HAZWOPER, the OSHA hazard communication standard (29 CFR 1910.1200), and NFPA–58 are examples of other regulations or voluntary industry standards that could be cited to meet the requirements of a Program 2 prevention program. Commenters requested that EPA provide a matrix or crosswalk that indicates which other regulations, standards, and codes met specific requirements. One commenter opposed the use of other regulations or referencing of voluntary industry standards, stating that, other than OSHA PSM, no other OSHA standard addresses safety precautions or maintenance. Another commenter objected that this approach creates another documentation burden without any commensurate benefit.

EPA agrees that the SNPRM preferred approach for Program 2 was not specific enough and has provided more detailed requirements in this rule as noted above. EPA continues to believe that many of the Program 2 prevention requirements are already met through industry compliance with existing regulations and voluntary standards. For example, ammonia retailers whose processes are designed to meet the OSHA ammonia handling rule (29 CFR

910.111) should be able to meet the Program 2 requirement that the process design meets good engineering practices. This effectively allows sources to cite compliance with these other regulations and standards instead of developing specific, duplicative elements solely to comply with Program 2. EPA will also use these existing regulations and standards as it develops model programs.

c. Emergency Response Program. Commenters supported considering HAZWOPER programs as adequate to meet the Program 2 emergency response program. A few commenters said that HAZWOPER is inadequate because it does not consider offsite impacts or the environment. Some commenters also said that coverage of a source by an EPCRA community emergency response plan should be sufficient. Others said that any contingency plan developed under Federal or state law should be considered sufficient because the requirements under these programs are generally consistent with EPA's proposed emergency response program; one commenter noted that, for flammable processes, compliance with 29 CFR 1910.38 should be adequate because the response is usually evacuation of employees. Five commenters opposed any requirement that sources with Program 2 processes conduct drills or exercises because they represent lower hazards.

Consistent with its efforts to consolidate Federal emergency planning requirements, EPA has included language in the final rule that will allow any source in compliance with another Federal emergency response program that includes the elements specified in this rule to use that program to meet these requirements. In particular, this applies to response plans prepared in accordance with the National Response Team's Integrated Contingency Plan Guidance ("one plan") (NRT, May 1996). EPA believes that sources should have a single response plan; creation of multiple response plans to meet slightly different Federal or state standards is counterproductive, diverting resources that could be used to develop better response capabilities.

EPA recognizes that some sources will only evacuate their employees in the event of a release. For these sources, EPA will not require the development of emergency response plans, provided that appropriate responses to their hazards have been discussed in the community emergency response plan developed under 42 U.S.C. 11003 for toxics or coordinated with the local fire department for flammables.

B. Offsite Consequence Analysis

1. Worst-Case Release Scenario. EPA proposed in the NPRM to define the worst-case release as the "loss of all of the regulated substance from the process * * * that leads to the worst offsite consequences" and that the scenario should assume "instantaneous release." Hundreds of commenters stated that instantaneous loss of the total process contents is not technically feasible for complex systems and, therefore, represents a non-credible worst case that would provide no useful information to the public or the source for risk communication, accident prevention, and emergency preparedness. Many commenters also argued that this approach differed from the release modeling assumptions contained in EPA's Technical Guidance for Hazards Analysis, which has been the basis for community emergency planning activities under EPCRA. Although some commenters were generally opposed to the concept of worst case, most of the commenters were supportive of an approach similar to that taken in the Technical Guidance.

In response to these comments, EPA proposed in the SNPRM to redefine a worst-case scenario as the release, over a 10-minute period, of the largest quantity of a regulated substance resulting from a vessel or process piping failure. The 10-minute release time is drawn from the Technical Guidance for Hazards Analysis. EPA believes this duration is reasonable and accounts for comments arguing that an "instantaneous" release is unrealistic for large-scale releases.

EPA has decided to adopt the SNPRM approach for worst-case toxic vapor releases in the final rule because most of the SNPRM comments agreed that the redefinition is generally more credible and that the 10-minute time frame particularly applies to vapor releases. Although some commenters argued that this approach still does not account for all process-specific conditions, EPA believes it is reasonable and representative of accident history. EPA notes that owners or operators may use air dispersion modeling techniques that better account for site-specific conditions, provided modeling parameters as specified in the rule are applied. This release scenario will apply to substances that are gases at ambient conditions, including those liquefied under pressure. Gases liquefied by refrigeration only may be analyzed as liquids if the spill would be contained by passive mitigation systems to a depth greater than 1 cm.

Under the SNPRM, worst-case liquid spills were assumed to form a pool in 10 minutes, with the release rate to the air determined by volatilization rate. EPA recognized that this approach differs from the use of an instantaneous release in the Technical Guidance, which EPA cited as an alternative to its favored approach. The few comments received were divided between support of this approach and arguments that the 10-minute time frame was unrealistic for liquid releases (particularly for pipelines and connected equipment) and thus did not properly account for process-specific conditions.

EPA's approach for the liquid worst-case scenario in the final rule is similar to the Technical Guidance methodology, in which the total quantity of liquid in a vessel or pipeline is instantaneously spilled upon failure, considering administrative controls or passive mitigation discussed below. The rate of release to the air is not instantaneous; it is determined by the volatilization rate of the spilled liquid, which depends on the surface area of the pool formed after the spill. The pool surface area is determined by assuming the spilled liquid rapidly spreads out and forms a one-centimeter deep pool, unless passive mitigation systems contain the pool to a smaller area. EPA believes this approach is reasonable because total vessel or pipeline failure will generally lead to immediate and rapid spillage followed by pool volatilization. Further, if the liquid were assumed to spill over a particular time frame rather than instantaneously, owners or operators would need to calculate the amount of vapor emitted to the air as the liquid is spilled, in addition to the volatilization rate as the pool spreads out and reaches its maximum size. Computer-based models are available for such calculations, but they are complex and require considerable data input to use. EPA believes that liquid spillage from a worst-case scenario is likely to be extremely rapid such that the most significant portion of the release rate is given by pool volatilization; consequently, liquid release time is not necessary. Liquid spill rates and times could be reflected in alternative scenarios discussed below.

As proposed, the worst-case for flammables assumes that the total quantity of the substance in the vessel or pipeline vaporizes, resulting in a vapor cloud explosion. If the vapor cloud explosion is modeled using a TNT-equivalent methodology, then a 10 percent yield factor must be used.

EPA requested comment in the SNPRM on whether the worst-case scenario should include an additional amount of substance that could potentially drain or flow from process equipment interconnected with the failed vessel or pipeline. Many commenters opposed this option, suggesting that it is technically uncertain and would have little value in terms of what they saw as EPA's intended purpose for the worst-case assessment. Other commenters requested that "interconnected equipment" be defined and clarified. Given the assumption of rapid release associated with initial equipment failure, EPA agrees that determination of the spill rate from connected piping and equipment is likely to be technically complex, very different from that of the quantity in the vessel or failed pipeline, and likely to extend the duration of volatilization rather than affecting the rate overall. Therefore, EPA has not included this requirement in the final rule.

EPA also sought comment in the SNPRM on options for the determination of the relevant quantity of regulated substance in a vessel or process piping for a worst-case release scenario: the maximum possible vessel inventory (design capacity) at any time without regard for operational practices and administrative controls; the maximum possible vessel inventory unless there are internal administrative controls (written procedural restrictions) that limit inventories to less than the maximum; or historic or projected maximum operating inventories without regard to administrative controls. EPA preferred that the maximum vessel inventory including administrative controls that might limit or raise the vessel quantity to be used in the worst-case assessment and reported in the worst-case release analysis section of the RMP. If the quantity used in the assessment were exceeded (e.g., an administrative control were ignored), then the source would be in violation of the rule (i.e., failure to perform a worst-case analysis) and RMP reporting unless the administrative control was revised, the worst-case analysis updated to reflect any changes in the analysis, and a revised RMP submitted. This approach acknowledges the efforts by sources to increase process safety by intentionally reducing the inventory of regulated substances (e.g., vessels kept at half capacity to allow for process upsets, emergency shutdowns, and deinventorying or maintenance turnarounds). EPA notes that at some sources, as a result of inventory reduction measures, the largest quantity may be held in a transportation

container that is loaded or unloaded at the source (See section P.2).

A few commenters supported the other options, noting that administrative controls may fail, potentially generating a larger scenario. However, the majority of commenters supported EPA's preferred approach based on the historical reliability of such controls at many sources and the role that such a provision could play in encouraging their use at additional locations. Other commenters asked whether mechanical controls, alone or in combination with administrative controls, should be incorporated into the proposal. Although mechanical controls may also serve to limit the quantity, EPA has decided not to include them in the quantity determination for the worst-case release scenario because the definition for administrative control as "written procedural mechanisms used for hazard control" provides a backup for possible failure of mechanical controls. For more discussion of mechanical controls, see section III(B)(2), mitigation systems, below.

In the SNPRM, EPA considered providing the implementing agency with the discretion to determine the appropriate quantity for the worst-case release scenario on a site-specific or industry-specific basis. EPA noted in the SNPRM, and most of the few comments received on this issue agreed, that implementing agency discretion would result in increased administrative burden on the implementing agency and cross-jurisdictional differences in the methodology used for the worst-case analyses. EPA has decided not to incorporate this approach in the final rule. States, however, may impose more stringent requirements, such as additional modeling, under state authority.

In the NPRM worst-case definition, EPA did not specify what constitutes or how to determine the worst offsite consequences. Some commenters indicated that without clear direction, EPA's proposed worst case might not actually capture the scenario that leads to the most severe offsite impact. In the SNPRM, EPA indicated that the worst-case scenario should be the scenario that generates the greatest distance to a specified endpoint (i.e., the toxic vapor cloud or blast wave from a vapor cloud explosion that travels the farthest).

EPA recognizes that there may be other release scenarios that could generate a greater distance than the release from the largest vessel or pipeline. Consequently, EPA has added paragraph (h) to § 68.25 to require owners or operators to consider other scenarios if those scenarios generate

greater distances to the endpoint than the distance generated by the largest vessel or pipeline scenario. Owners or operators need to consider releases from smaller vessels if those vessels contain the substance at higher temperature or pressures or if they are closer to public receptors. In some cases, the largest vessel will be a storage vessel where the substance is held at ambient conditions. A reactor vessel may hold a smaller quantity, but at high pressures and temperatures, generating a release that could travel farther offsite to an endpoint. Vessel location is important, especially at large sources. A smaller vessel located nearer to the stationary source boundary may generate a greater impact distance than a larger vessel farther away. This difference may be particularly important for flammables, because impact distances for flammables are generally shorter than those for toxic releases.

2. Mitigation Systems

a. Worst-case scenario. In the NPRM worst-case scenario, EPA indicated that sources must assume that both active and passive systems fail to mitigate the release. Commenters were generally split between those who wanted passive (as well as certain redundant active) mitigation systems to be included and those who argued that historical evidence from catastrophic releases suggests that the worst case should assume the failure of all such systems. Those who supported mitigation argued that inclusion provides a more credible scenario for improved risk communication, accident prevention, and emergency planning.

EPA proposed in the SNPRM to include passive mitigation systems in the worst-case release scenario as long as the system is capable of withstanding, and continuing to function as intended during and after a destructive event, such as an earthquake, storm, or explosion, which causes a vessel or pipeline to fail. Passive systems such as dikes, catch basins, and drains for liquids, and enclosures for both liquids and gases, could be assumed to mitigate the release. Some commenters opposed this approach, arguing again that the worst case should account for the possibility of passive mitigation failure. The majority supported this approach because the assumption that passive systems specifically designed and installed as protection against a potential catastrophe fail is unrealistic. Furthermore, the approach recognizes and encourages prevention through additional passive mitigation and supports more realistic emergency planning. A few commenters also suggested that active mitigation measures that were unlikely to fail (e.g., redundant or backup systems) should be considered, for similar reasons. Historical data, however, indicate that certain events compromise active mitigation systems (e.g., explosions have destroyed fire water piping systems).

For the final rule, EPA has decided to adopt the SNPRM approach. Passive mitigation systems would be defined as those systems that operate without human, mechanical, or other energy input and would include building enclosures, dikes, and containment walls. EPA also agrees that reservoirs or vessels sufficiently buried underground are passively mitigated or prevented from failing catastrophically. In this case, sources should evaluate the failure of piping connected to underground storage for the worst case or alternative case scenarios. In addition to the requirements outlined in § 68.25, EPA provides guidance on how passive mitigation would affect release rate and distance to endpoints in its RMP Offsite Consequence Analysis Guidance.

b. Alternative scenarios. EPA initially proposed that sources could include passive mitigation systems in their alternative scenario assessments, but that active mitigation systems (e.g., excess flow valves, fail-safe and automatic shutdown valves, scrubbers, flares, deluge systems, and water curtains) would be assumed to fail. Some commenters generally opposed inclusion of any mitigation systems in the hazard assessment, while other commenters noted that the alternative release scenario should recognize and encourage industry accident prevention efforts, specifically the installation of additional mitigation systems, and support more realistic emergency planning.

EPA proposed in the SNPRM to allow sources to consider passive and active mitigation measures in the alternative release scenario assessment. Commenters supported this approach and EPA has decided to retain it in the final rule. EPA agrees that the assumption that both passive and active mitigation measures fail when such measures are specifically designed and installed to mitigate catastrophic releases is unrealistic for the alternative scenarios. Although not required, EPA notes that sources may choose to apply passive and active mitigation measures to a worst-case type scenario to illustrate the capabilities of such systems to reduce the potential impact of a worst-case accidental release. In addition to the requirements outlined in

§ 68.28, EPA provides guidance in its RMP Offsite Consequence Analysis Guidance on how passive and active mitigation would affect release rate and distance to endpoints.

3. Populations Affected. EPA described in the NPRM preamble certain locations (e.g., schools and hospitals) where sensitive populations might be present and proposed in the rule that owners or operators identify potentially exposed populations as part of the offsite consequence assessment. Commenters generally opposed requirements for population surveys; several commenters suggested that Census data or other readily available population information should be sufficient, while other commenters indicated that the LEPC or other local planning entities were the appropriate entity to prepare these data.

EPA believes owners or operators need to be aware of the magnitude of impact on populations associated with the worst-case and alternative scenarios. However, EPA learned that, although much of this information is readily available, identification of some sensitive populations could require considerable effort, especially if the distance to an endpoint generated in the offsite consequence assessment is large or crosses several jurisdictions. Consequently, EPA proposed in the SNPRM that offsite populations be defined using available Census data; information on the number of children and people over 65 could be considered a proxy for sensitive populations, thereby accomplishing the same objective as the proposed rule. EPA also indicated that it has developed a geographic information system, LandView, that will facilitate analysis of resident populations. (LandView can be ordered from the U.S. Bureau of the Census customer service at (301) 457–4100.) In general, commenters agreed with the SNPRM approach. However, some commenters questioned the accuracy of potentially ten-year-old Census data and requested additional flexibility, or a greater role for local government, in this analysis.

EPA has decided to adopt the approach outlined in the SNPRM for the final rule. Sources will be allowed to use available Census data to estimate populations potentially affected. Sources may update these data if they believe the data are inaccurate, but are not required to do so. Populations shall be reported to two significant digits. Because Census data are limited to residential populations, sources will also have to note in the RMP whether other, non-residential populations, such as schools, hospitals, prisons, public

recreational areas or arenas, and major commercial or industrial areas, are within the distance to an endpoint. These institutions and areas are those that can generally be found on local street maps. Sources will not be required to estimate the number of people who might be present at these locations. EPA provides further guidance on the identification of affected populations in its RMP Offsite Consequence Analysis Guidance.

4. Number of Scenarios In the NPRM. EPA required a worst-case release scenario for each regulated substance. Commenters requested clarification, because one substance could be present in more than one process at the source and sources would need to select the "worst" worst case for substances in multiple processes. In addition, one process may have several, similar listed substances and multiple worst-case analyses of similar substances (e.g., flammables) would not provide additional useful information to the public.

EPA proposed in the SNPRM that sources report in the RMP one worst-case release scenario representative of all toxic substances present at the source and one worst-case release scenario representative of all flammable substances present at the source. Even though additional screening analyses to determine the appropriate worst-case scenario might be necessary, this approach reduces to a maximum of two the number of worst-case analyses reported in the RMP by a source. In general, commenters favored this approach, particularly for flammables, which do not produce markedly different adverse effects. A few commenters argued that a single toxic substance should not be considered representative of all toxic substances at a source, since there are considerable differences in toxic endpoint and adverse affect.

EPA has decided to adopt the approach outlined in the SNPRM for the final rule: report one worst-case release scenario for all flammables and one worst-case release scenario for all toxics at the source. EPA notes that the worst-case scenario is designed principally to support a dialogue between the source and the community on release prevention, and not to serve as the sole or primary basis for local emergency planning. The "worst" worst-case release scenario will inform the broadest range of individuals that they may be impacted by the source so that they may participate in dialogue with the source about prevention, preparedness, and emergency response actions. Lesser worst-case release scenarios would not inform any person not already within the range of the "worst" worst case even though the health effects may be different; consequently, EPA believes that only a single toxic worst case is necessary. However, sources must also analyze and report another worst-case release scenario (for flammables or toxics) if such a release from another location at the source potentially affects public receptors different from those potentially affected by the first scenario (e.g., if a large-sized source is located between two communities and has a covered process adjacent to each community).

In the NPRM, EPA did not specify the number of alternative scenarios to be reported for each regulated substance. EPA noted in the preamble that this approach, while providing flexibility, may also create uncertainty about what EPA will consider to be an adequate number of scenarios. While a few commenters argued against scenarios beyond the worst case, many commenters supported a requirement for a maximum of two: the worst case plus one additional scenario; others supported a maximum of three. Many of the commenters noted that local entities could request further information under EPCRA section 303(d)(3) authority if they desired. At the same time, a number of commenters suggested that this determination should be made by the source based on their scenario analysis, perhaps in coordination with a local agency.

In the SNPRM, EPA proposed to require one alternative release scenario for all flammable substances at the source and one alternative scenario for each toxic substance at the source. As discussed above, the listed flammable substances behave similarly upon release and have the same endpoint, while each toxic substance has a different endpoint and different atmospheric behavior. EPA sought comment on whether one toxic substance alternative scenario could represent all toxic substances at a source or in a process. Although commenters generally agreed with the approach for flammables, only a few argued that a single alternative scenario for all toxics was also appropriate; most others supported EPA's proposal.

Upon review of the comments, EPA has decided to adopt the approach outlined in the SNPRM: an alternative release scenario must be reported in the RMP for each toxic held above the threshold at the source, and one alternative scenario must be reported that represents all flammables held above the threshold. As EPA noted in the SNPRM preamble and commenters

echoed, the differences in the hazards posed by individual toxic regulated substances are significant and should be reflected in the alternative scenarios. This information has significant value for emergency planning purposes and could increase public interest in prevention at the source.

5. Technical Guidance The proposed rule required sources to evaluate the consequences (vapor cloud dispersion, blast wave, or radiant heat modeling calculations) associated with the worst-case and alternative release scenarios. EPA did not specify a methodology or models, expecting that sources would have, contract for, or find the expertise and modeling tools needed to perform potentially complex modeling calculations. Because of the potential burden associated with this approach, EPA began working on the development of a set of simple, generic tools that could provide useful results and become part of the technical guidance for the rule. Based on its experience in developing the Technical Guidance for Hazards Analysis and on advice from commenters, EPA understands that a generic methodology depends on approximations to capture a wide variety of situations, will likely ignore site-specific conditions, and potentially may generate overly conservative or less realistic estimates of offsite impacts. In spite of these limitations, EPA believes that generic modeling tools are capable of supporting greater understanding of the hazards posed by substances and emergency planning. Commenters agreed this approach would reduce the burden on smaller sources unfamiliar with such activities as long as use of the guidance was not mandatory, and the guidance addressed specific industry sectors or was used as part of a screening process to focus resources on significant problem areas. Many commenters recommended that sources be given the flexibility to use any appropriate modeling techniques for the offsite consequence analysis to take advantage of expertise and to apply site-specific considerations to the hazard assessment. Other commenters argued that EPA should establish mandatory guidelines or specify certain dispersion modeling tools to make release scenario results more comparable across sources. Some commenters were concerned about the development of modeling tools by EPA outside of the rulemaking process and requested the opportunity to participate in their development.

In the SNPRM, EPA stated it would develop a generic methodology and reference tables in an offsite consequence assessment guidance to assist sources with the analyses required

by the rule. EPA believed that the Technical Guidance could be revised, expanded, and updated to address the rule requirements. The methodologies and tables would be subject to public review prior to publication of the final rule; once finalized, the tables would replace the Technical Guidance. EPA added that sources that wish to conduct more sophisticated modeling could do so, provided the techniques used account for the modeling parameters described in the rule. Alternatively, EPA proposed that only Program 2 sources use the guidance; Program 3 sources would be required to conduct their own dispersion modeling.

Most commenters supported the SNPRM approach, especially if sources were given the option to use their own site-specific modeling. Some commenters argued that the generic methodology and reference tables and the option for site-specific modeling should be applied to processes in all three Programs, while others suggested that they be applied only to a specific Program. In recognition of these comments, EPA prepared draft modeling methodologies and reference tables, provided an opportunity for their review (see 61 FR 3031, January 30, 1996), and has published them as the RMP Offsite Consequence Analysis Guidance. EPA intends to conduct peer review of the RMP Offsite Consequence Analysis Guidance and will revise it as appropriate. For the final rule, EPA will allow sources in all Programs to use the guidance or conduct their own site-specific modeling, provided the modeling techniques used account for the parameters described in the rule. For example, EPA's Office of Air Quality Planning and Standards has prepared a publicly available modeling tool called TScreen that can assist owners and operators with consequence assessments. EPA also encourages local emergency planners, fire departments, and others who use tools such as CAMEO/ALOHA or other modeling techniques to assist businesses in their community who may need help in their modeling efforts. EPA believes the final rule approach takes advantage of the broad range of expertise and modeling tools already available and will provide more useful results at the local level for chemical emergency prevention, preparedness, and response. This approach will also stimulate accidental release modeling research, new and existing model development, and model validation to generate new tools for better understanding of hazards and the behavior of substances in accidental release situations.

6. Modeling Parameters. a. Endpoints. In the NPRM, EPA did not specify toxic or flammable substance endpoints that must be used in the offsite consequence assessment modeling. Most commenters recommended that EPA specify endpoints to provide a consistent basis for modeling; many favored the use of existing standards or guidelines, primarily the emergency response planning guidelines (ERPGs) developed by the American Industrial Hygiene Association for toxic substances. For flammables, commenters suggested overpressure, heat radiation, and explosion or flammability limits. In addition to other specific standards, a few commenters recommended a hierarchy of values if certain levels for some chemicals were not available.

In the SNPRM, EPA indicated that it would select one endpoint for each toxic substance for use in the offsite consequence assessment methodology and sought comment on whether it should use a single endpoint to the extent possible (e.g., the Immediately Dangerous to Life and Health (IDLH) value developed by the National Institute for Occupational Safety and Health (NIOSH), unless one does not exist for a substance), or a hierarchy of endpoints (e.g., ERPGs; if one does not exist, then the IDLH; and finally toxicity data if no other value is available). EPA also asked whether overpressure or both overpressure and radiant heat effects should be used for flammable substance endpoints. Some commenters supported the use of ERPG values for the toxic substance endpoint, or a hierarchy of values beginning with the ERPG. Others opposed IDLH or the IDLH divided by 10 for technical reasons.

EPA agrees with commenters that one toxic endpoint should be set for each substance. The endpoint for each listed toxic substance is provided in Appendix A to the final rule. The endpoint, applicable whether the source uses the EPA guidance or conducts site-specific modeling described below, is the AIHA ERPG-2 or, if no ERPG-2 is available, the level of concern (LOC) developed for the Technical Guidance, corrected where necessary to account for new toxicity data. The LOCs that were based on IDLHs have been updated only if the IDLHs were revised between the original LOC listing in 1987 and the 1995 IDLH revisions. The most recent IDLH revisions were not used because they were based on a methodology that EPA has not reviewed; the previous IDLH methodology was reviewed by EPA's Science Advisory Board for use as LOCs. EPA chose the ERPG-2 first because ERPGs are subject to peer review and are specifically developed

by a scientific committee for emergency planning to protect the general public in emergency situations. The ERPG-2 represents the maximum airborne concentration below which the committee judges that nearly all individuals could be exposed for up to an hour without experiencing or developing irreversible or other serious human health effects or symptoms that could impair their ability to take protective action. EPA rejected the ERPG-3, which is a lethal exposure level, because it is not protective enough of the public in emergency situations. About 30 listed toxic substances have ERPGs. EPA chose to use LOC levels for substances with no ERPG because LOCs have been peer reviewed by EPA's Science Advisory Board, they are intended to be protective of the general public for exposure periods of up to an hour, they are widely used by the emergency response planning community, and, for a majority of the listed toxic substances, there are no acceptable alternatives. EPA notes that, for substances with both values, the LOC is comparable to, and in some cases is identical to, the ERPG-2.

EPA recognizes potential limitations associated with the ERPG and LOC and is working with other agencies to develop Acute Exposure Guideline Limits (AEGLs). See Establishment of a National Advisory Committee for Acute Exposure Guideline Levels (AEGLs) for Hazardous Substances, (60 FR 55376; October 31, 1995). When these values have been developed and peer-reviewed, EPA intends to adopt them, through rulemaking, as the toxic endpoint for substances under this rule.

As proposed, vapor cloud explosion distances will be based on an overpressure of 1 psi, and for analysis of worst-case releases, a yield factor of 10 percent. Yield factors (the percentage of the available energy released in the explosion process) can vary considerably. EPA selected 10 percent to generate conservative worst-case consequences. For flammables, EPA selected a radiant heat exposure level of 5 kW/m² for 40 seconds as recommended by the commenters, and, for vapor cloud fire and jet fire dispersion analysis, the lower flammability limit (LFL) as specified by NFPA or other recognized sources.

b. Meteorology. In the NPRM, EPA proposed that sources model the downwind dispersion of the worst-case release scenario using an F atmospheric stability class and 1.5 m/s wind speed and model the alternative release scenarios using both the worst-case conditions and the meteorological

conditions prevailing at the source. EPA did not revise the meteorological assumptions in the SNPRM.

Several commenters argued that the worst-case meteorological conditions were too conservative or not applicable on a national basis and that site-specific conditions should be used, while others agreed that for worst case, minimum wind speeds and the most stable atmospheric conditions should be used. In the final rule, EPA has decided that sources must conduct worst-case dispersion modeling using an F atmospheric stability class and a 1.5 m/s wind speed. A higher wind speed or less stable atmospheric stability class may be used if the owner or operator has local meteorological data applicable to the source that show that the lowest recorded wind speed was always greater or the atmospheric stability class was always less stable during the previous three years.

In the final rule, EPA also requires sources to conduct alternative release scenario dispersion modeling using the typical meteorological conditions applicable to the source. If meteorological data are not available, typical conditions in the RMP Offsite Consequence Analysis Guidance may be used. EPA believes typical meteorological conditions should be used to generate realistic hazard assessments for communication with the public and first responders and for emergency planning.

C. Consideration of Environmental Impact

The issue of whether and how environmental impacts should be addressed in the hazard assessment and the rule in general drew considerable comment. The comments divide into three questions: Should EPA consider environmental impacts from accidental releases? If so, which environments should be identified? What constitutes an environmental impact?

1. Inclusion of Environmental Impacts. Environmental groups argued that the CAA requires assessment of potential impacts to the environment and that the environmental receptors listed in the SNPRM should be broadened. One commenter stated that since the CAA Amendments of 1990 strengthened limits of continuous air toxic emissions, wildlife is now threatened more by accidental releases. However, the majority of commenters on this issue, principally industry groups, opposed consideration of the environment because it is adequately protected by other environmental statutes, environmental protection in section 112(r) relates only to emergency

response, and Congress intended in section 112(r) for the environment to be addressed only to the extent that human health is protected. Several commenters argued that flammable substances were unlikely to generate environmental impacts. Commenters also stated that many industries have voluntarily developed nature reserves around their sources, often at the urging of government agencies. Additional regulations based on "environmental" impact consideration would "penalize" these sources for their efforts. Finally, two commenters noted that EPA's endpoints are based on acute human effects; applying these to the environment may not be valid.

EPA disagrees that section 112(r) was not intended to protect the environment as well as human health. Although section 112(r)(5) links the threshold quantity to human health, section 112(r)(3) requires EPA to select substances that could impact human health and the environment. EPA agrees that the only time sections 112(r)(7)(B)(I) and (ii) mention protection of the environment is in conjunction with emergency response; however, this is also true for protection of human health. Congress did not intend to limit concern about either impact strictly to emergency response procedures; Congress may not have mentioned either impact relative to prevention because the act of preventing an accident eliminates the impact on both. When accidents occur, human health and the environment need protection. By mentioning both impacts in the response or post accident phase, Congress was stressing its concern for the environment as well as human health. Given the integrated nature of the RMP, it would be an inappropriately narrow reading of CAA section 112(r)(7)(B) to say environmental impacts must be ignored in hazard assessments and in the design of the prevention program, but must be accounted for in emergency response. In addition, section 112(r)(9) provides authority for EPA to take emergency action when an actual or threatened accidental release of a regulated substance may cause imminent and substantial endangerment to human health, welfare, or the environment. Clearly, section 112(r)(9) allows EPA to take action to prevent, as opposed to simply respond to, accidental releases to protect the environment. Because section 112(r)(7) is intended to prevent situations that could lead to emergency orders under section 112(r)(9), it is logical to conclude that Congress meant EPA to develop regulations that would

prevent accidental releases that could cause environmental damage. Although the consequences may not be precisely known, EPA believes that impacts could occur at environmental receptors located within the distance to a human acute exposure endpoint associated with a worst-case or alternative scenario because wildlife may be more sensitive or require less exposure to cause an adverse effect than humans.

2. Environmental Receptors to Be Considered. In the SNPRM, EPA proposed that sources report in their RMP which sensitive environments listed by the National Oceanographic and Atmospheric Administration (NOAA) for the Clean Water Act are within the distance determined by the worst-case or alternative case scenario. A few commenters argued that the list should include state and local level analogues to Federal entities (e.g., state parks), all surface waters that are fishable or swimmable or supply drinking water, and ground water recharge areas. Many commenters opposed the NOAA list, arguing that the list is extremely broad, covers millions of acres in primarily rural areas, and contains areas that are difficult for both the regulated community and the government to clearly identify (e.g., habitat used by proposed threatened or endangered species, cultural resources, and wetlands). They stated that the NOAA list is not appropriate for this rule because it represents guidance applicable to offshore sources, and to a limited number of very large onshore sources, that could have catastrophic oil spills. A few commenters suggested limiting the list to Federal Class I areas designated under the CAA prevention of significant deterioration program, or reducing the list of sensitive areas to national parks and the designated critical habitat for listed endangered species, and limiting environmental concern to those accidents that generate a significant and long-term impact, such as an actual "taking" of an endangered species.

For the final rule, EPA has not used the NOAA list. Instead EPA requires owners or operators to indicate in the RMP the environmental receptors located within circles whose radii are the distances to an endpoint for the worst-case and alternative release scenarios. EPA agrees with commenters that the locations of certain natural resources are difficult to identify. Consequently, EPA has defined environmental receptors as natural areas such as national or state parks, forests, or monuments; officially designated wildlife sanctuaries, preserves, refuges, or areas; and Federal wilderness areas,

that can be exposed to an accidental release. All such receptors typically can be found on local U.S. Geological Survey (USGS) maps or maps based on USGS data. Habitats of endangered or threatened species are not included because the locations of these habitats are frequently not made public to protect the species. Natural resource agencies will have access to the RMP information and can raise concerns with local officials about potential harm to these habitats, as necessary. Local emergency planners and responders may want to consult with environmental management agencies as part of emergency preparedness.

3. Level of Analysis Required. In the SNPRM, EPA proposed that sources only identify sensitive environments within the area of the worst-case release rather than analyzing potential impacts. A few commenters opposed this approach, stating that the CAA requires that sources analyze impacts. Most commenters supported EPA's position because extensive expertise at considerable cost is required to adequately assess all environmental impacts associated with the environments list EPA provided. Commenters stated that this cost would make fewer resources available for prevention activities and providing no benefit. Other commenters noted that much of the data needed for such analyses is not available.

EPA agrees that extensive environmental analysis is not justified. Irreversible adverse effect exposure level data for the wide variety of environmental species potentially exposed in an accidental release event are not available for most of the listed substances. EPA believes that identification of potentially affected environmental receptors in the RMP is sufficient for purposes of accident prevention, preparedness, and response by the source and at the local level.

D. Program 3 Consistency with OSHA PSM Standard

1. Prevention Program. In EPA's original proposal, the prevention program requirements were based on the elements of OSHA's PSM standard (29 CFR 1910.119), and some commenters supported this approach. But EPA added a paragraph to each OSHA prevention program element to explain the purpose of the provision and, in some instances, added additional recordkeeping, reporting, or substantive provisions to ensure that statutory requirements were met. Several commenters argued that these additions cause confusion and appear to require sources to create two separate

evention programs, which could use conflicting inspection and inforcement actions and greater cost for urces that must comply with both the SHA and EPA requirements. Many immenters suggested that EPA simply reference the OSHA requirements.

EPA agrees that the Program 3 evention program requirements iould be identical to OSHA's PSM andard to avoid confusion and dundant requirements and to ensure at sources develop one accidental lease prevention program that protects orkers, the general public, and the ivironment. Therefore, EPA has moved e Management System requirement ee section I.D) supported by most immenters to a section separate from e Prevention Program and deleted the itroductory paragraphs and odifications to the PSM language. The gency recognizes that many workplace izards also threaten public receptors

and that the majority of accident prevention steps taken to protect workers also protect the general public and the environment; thus, a source owner or operator responsible for a process in compliance with the OSHA PSM standard should already be in compliance with the Program 3 prevention program requirements.

EPA did not cross-reference sections of the PSM standard in today's rule because, under Office of Federal Register requirements at 1 CFR 21.21(c)(2), EPA cannot adopt OSHA's requirements. EPA and OSHA have separate legal authority to regulate chemical process safety to prevent accidental releases. Furthermore, cross-referencing the OSHA standard would be tantamount to a delegation of authority to set standards in this area from the Administrator of EPA to the Secretary of Labor, because OSHA would be able to modify the PSM

requirements without an EPA rulemaking under CAA § 307(d). The Senate explicitly considered and rejected the possibility of the Administrator delegating to OSHA responsibility for hazard assessment. Senate Report at 226. As that term was used in the Senate bill, hazard assessment included many of the elements of PSM.

With the exception of some key terms and phrases, the Program 3 prevention program language in the final rule is identical to the OSHA standard language (the rulemaking docket contains a side-by-side analysis of the OSHA standard and EPA rule text with word differences highlighted). Most of the differences are terms based on specific legislative authorities given to OSHA or EPA that have essentially the same meaning:

OSHA term	EPA term
ghly hazardous substance	Regulated substance.
nployer	Owner or operator.
icility	Stationary source.
andard	Rule or part.

EPA also agrees with commenters that sound process safety management systems ideally address chemical accident revention in a way that protects workers, the public, and the environment. Since OSHA's responsibility is to protect orkers, there are phrases in the OSHA standard that are designed to focus employer attention on accidents that fect the workplace. It could be argued that these phrases inadvertently exclude consideration of offsite impacts. EPA as deleted the phrases noted below to ensure that all sources implement process safety management in a way that rotects not only workers, but also the public and the environment:

OSHA PSM requirement	EPA program 3 requirement
910.119(d)(2)(E) An evaluation of the consequences of deviations, including those affecting the safety and health of employees.	68.65(c)(1)(v) An evaluation of the consequences of deviations.
910.119(e)(3)(ii) The identification of any previous incident which had a likely potential for catastrophic consequences in the workplace.	68.67(c)(2) The identification of any previous incident which had a likely potential for catastrophic consequences.
910.119(e)(3)(vii) A qualitative evaluation of a range of the possible safety and health effects of failure of controls on employees in the workplace.	68.67(c)(7) A qualitative evaluation of a range of the possible safety and health effects of failure of controls.
910.119(m)(1) The employer shall investigate each incident which resulted in, or could reasonably have resulted in a catastrophic release of a highly hazardous chemical in the workplace.	68.81(a) The owner or operator shall investigate each incident which resulted in, or could reasonably have resulted in a catastrophic release of a regulated substance.

EPA also made changes to specific chedule dates to coordinate with the SHA PSM requirements, made internal ferences consistent, and added a rovision to the PHA section pecifically grandfathering all OSHA HAs and allowing sources to update nd revalidate these PHAs on their SHA schedule. EPA believes these iodifications do not cause source wners or operators to make major djustments to their PSM systems tablished under OSHA. These minor iodifications ultimately lead to the evelopment of one comprehensive rocess safety management system itisfying both OSHA and EPA that

works to prevent accidents affecting workers, the public, and the environment.

EPA also modified the OSHA definition of catastrophic release, which serves as a trigger for an accident investigation, to include events "that present imminent and substantial endangerment to public health and the environment." This modification, in combination with the changes noted above, ensure that sources covered by both OSHA and EPA requirements must investigate not only accidents that threaten workers, but also those that threaten the public or the environment. EPA agrees with commenters and

recognizes that most catastrophic accidental releases affect workers first. However, the Agency also believes that there are accidental release situations where workers are protected but the public and the environment are threatened, e.g. vessel overpressurizations that cause emergency relief devices to work as designed and vent hazardous atmospheres away from the workplace and into the air where they are carried downwind. Although many sources through the PHA process will have recognized and addressed the potential impact offsite associated with safety measures that protect workers (e.g. an emergency vent scrubber system), EPA believes that the requirements in today's rule ensure that all sources routinely consider such possibilities and integrate the protection of workers, the public, and the environment into one program.

2. Enforcement. Many commenters expressed concern for conflicting audit procedures, interpretations, and enforcement actions when EPA and OSHA auditors inspect the same processes. EPA has no authority to exempt a source covered under the PSM standard and today's rule from any prospect of an EPA enforcement action for violations of section 112(r) and EPA regulations issued under it. EPA and OSHA are working closely to ensure that enforcement actions are based on consistent interpretations and coordinated to avoid overlapping audits. Such coordination in enforcement was recognized as an appropriate method for exercising the Administrator's duty to coordinate the EPA program with OSHA (Senate Report at 244).

3. Exemptions. Many commenters suggested that the Agency exempt small businesses or certain industry sectors because the rule is too costly, some industries are already subject to substantial regulation by other Federal or state agencies, OSHA exempts certain industries from the PSM standard, and some sources have effective self-policing regimes in place.

Regardless of whether the source is covered under some other Federal, state, or local program, EPA has no authority to exempt a source that has more than a threshold quantity of a regulated substance from complying with the risk management program rule (CAA section 112(r)(7)(B)(ii)). EPA established the tiered approach to acknowledge that different industries pose different potential risks to human health and the environment and that elements of other regulatory programs may serve to prevent accidents. EPA believes that owners or operators can indicate in their Program and RMP how compliance with other particular regulations and standards satisfies Program or RMP elements, thereby, avoid duplication. Only those processes in certain SIC codes or covered by OSHA's PSM standard must implement the full PSM program under Program 3. A source owner or operator can demonstrate compliance with the Program 2 or 3 prevention program under today's rule for a covered process by showing that it complies with the PSM standard. This approach is consistent with the authority to set different standards for different types of sources under CAA section 112(r)(7)(B)(I).

E. Relationship to Air Permitting

Several commenters on the NPRM requested that EPA clarify the relationship between the risk management program and the air permit program under Title V of the CAA for sources subject to both requirements. In the SNPRM, EPA indicated that in Title V, section 502(b)(5)(A), Congress clearly requires that permitting authorities must have the authority to "assure compliance by all sources required to have a permit under this title with each applicable standard, regulation or requirement under this Act." EPA further states in part 70.2 that "Applicable Requirement means * * * (4) Any standard or other requirement under section 112 of the Act, including any requirement concerning accident prevention under section 112(r)(7) of the Act; * * *" Consequently, EPA must require that air permitting authorities implementing Title V permit programs be able to assure compliance with section 112(r). In the SNPRM, EPA attempted to identify the section 112(r) "applicable requirements," clarify the minimum content of part 70 permits with respect to these requirements, and to specify the role and responsibilities of the part 70 permitting authority in assuring compliance with these requirements.

The sections below address the major issue areas raised by commenters on the SNPRM. More detail can be found in the Risk Management Program Rule: Summary and Response to Comments in the Docket. The SNPRM also addressed the role and responsibilities of the implementing agency with respect to section 112(r). This issue is addressed separately in Section R below.

1. General relationship between the part 68 and air permitting programs. Some commenters agreed with EPA's proposed role for the air permitting authority with respect to section 112(r), but encouraged EPA to avoid new, confusing, and duplicative state and source permitting requirements. A few commenters suggested that all part 68 requirements should become permit conditions, that it be fully enforced through the part 70 permitting program, and that anything less violates the CAA. Most commenters (state air permitting authorities and industry), opposed EPA's proposal stating that Congress did not intend, and legislative history does not support, section 112(r) to be implemented or enforced through the Title V permit program.

EPA agrees that Congress did not intend for section 112(r) to be implemented and enforced primarily through Title V and recognizes the potential for confusion and burden on sources and air permitting authorities associated with section 112(r). EPA believes that the requirements in today' rule are flexible, impose minimal burden, address the concerns raised by commenters and satisfy the CAA requirement for assurance of compliance with section 112(r) as an applicable requirement for permitting. The requirements apply only to sources subject to both part 68 and parts 70 or 71; there are no permitting requirement on sources subject solely to part 68. EPA agrees that ideally, one authority should implement part 68 oversight; however, air permitting authorities should not be responsible for implementation just as implementing agencies should not be responsible for permitting (see implementing agency discussion in Section R, below). The air permitting authority has the flexibility under today's rule to obtain assistance, expertise or resources from other agencies in fulfilling its responsibilities with respect to section 112(r). This will foster interaction and coordination of ai pollution, pollution prevention, public and worker safety and health and environmental programs at the state and local levels leading to more effective oversight.

2. Impact of EPA's proposal on air permitting programs. Several commenters stated that EPA's proposal places an unreasonable burden on air permitting programs because states would need to amend or develop new legislative authority and implementing regulations which diverts limited state resources away from the development and operation of more important routine emissions permit programs.

EPA disagrees that today's rule places an unreasonable burden on air permitting programs. Part of the approval process for a state air permitting program is confirmation that states have the authority to ensure that sources are in compliance with air toxics requirements under section 112 including section 112(r). The provisions of section 68.215 are sufficient to meet the obligations under part 70. Thus, for state and local agencies that have approved part 70 programs, states would need to develop new legislative authorities only if they seek delegation to implement part 68 beyond the narrow responsibilities provided in § 68.215 (see Section R, below). State obligations under § 68.215, which should be covered by permit fees (see section E.11, below), should not impose a substantial burden on state resources because the rule streamlines the RMP requirements and establishes centralized recordkeeping for RMPs.

3. Part 68 as an "applicable requirement" under part 70. As described above, the CAA requires that air permitting authorities ensure that sources are in compliance with applicable requirements as a condition of permitting. In the preamble of previous rulemakings for part 70 (57 FR 32301), EPA indicated that the definition of "applicable requirement" under Title V includes "any requirement under section 112(r) to prepare and register a risk management plan (RMP)." This explanatory statement preceded development of part 68, which implements section 112(r)(7). In the SNPRM, EPA proposed more specific provisions to assure compliance with applicable requirements for section 112(r) than the part 70 preamble so that air permitting authority responsibility is clear. EPA believed that all elements of part 68 are applicable requirements; however, compliance with applicable requirements could be assured by including generic terms in permits and certain minimal oversight activities. Together, these steps ensure that permitted sources fulfill their accident prevention and information sharing responsibilities.

EPA proposed standard permit conditions that would allow air permitting authorities to verify compliance with part 68. Commenters stated that alteration of the part 70 rule definition of the term 'applicable requirement' under the part 68 rulemaking is inappropriate and that the role of the air permitting authority with respect to section 112(r) should be defined in part 70 rulemakings rather than in part 68.

EPA's action today does not alter the definition of "applicable requirements" under 40 CFR 70.2, which already includes "any requirement concerning accident prevention under section 112(r)(7)." Rather, EPA is establishing very simple permit terms and flexible, minimal oversight responsibilities that will assure compliance with part 68. EPA disagrees that part 68 cannot establish more specific terms for permits than those given in part 70 or 71 with respect to section 112(r). As mentioned in the SNPRM preamble, part 70 does not preclude EPA from clarifying or even expanding air permitting responsibilities. Specific permit requirements are useful to clearly establish the minimum permit conditions and state responsibilities essential to ensuring compliance with part 68 and to reduce uncertainties that may lead to overly broad interpretations of the requirements. However, air permitting authorities still have the

flexibility to establish additional terms for the permit if it so chooses.

4. Role of the air permitting authority. In the SNPRM, EPA proposed certain air permitting authority responsibilities necessary to ensure that sources are in compliance with part 68 for purposes of permitting. Commenters stated that the role of the Title V permitting authority should be defined in part 70, not in part 68 and opposed EPA's proposal arguing that it causes unnecessary confusion for sources. Commenters also argued that air permitting authorities do not have the relevant expertise needed and that states should have the flexibility to implement risk management programs in whichever agency they see fit. Other commenters argued that air permitting authorities, without section 112(l) delegation, could not accept the responsibilities assigned by the SNPRM and that EPA was unlawfully attempting to delegate the responsibility for implementing section 112(r) to the state permitting authorities. Several commenters believed the permitting authority should have no responsibilities beyond those set forth in EPA's April 13, 1993, policy memorandum from John Seitz, Director of the Office of Air and Quality Planning and Standards (OAQPS), to EPA Regional Air Division Directors, available in the docket because states invested significant resources and effort into the development of their programs, guided by this EPA memorandum. However, a state permitting authority stated that the EPA memorandum did not account for many of the key program elements, including the necessary incorporation of standard permit conditions. Many commenters also opposed requiring extensive details or all aspects of part 68 compliance in the permit, finding this approach excessive and overly burdensome on both state air permitting authorities and sources and contrary to the law and Congressional intent in that it would have required section 112(r)(7) to be fully implemented by state permit programs.

Several commenters were concerned that a single violation of part 68 could potentially be enforced by both the permitting authority and the implementing agency. One commenter suggested that the only case where a violation of a part 68 requirement should also be considered a violation of part 70 would be the failure to register an RMP on time under the requirements of § 68.12. Another commenter requested that, at § 68.58(b)(3), EPA should allow the state the discretion to determine whether a penalty should be assessed. Several commenters, uncertain how the Programs proposed by EPA in

the SNPRM would affect the role of the permitting authority, suggested that EPA develop a process to inform states of the tiering approach and to exclude Program 1 and 2 sources from additional permitting requirements.

EPA believes that part 68 should more clearly define the role of the air permitting authority with respect to section 112(r). Part 70 requirements were established well before part 68 and are therefore vague. Consequently, EPA is using part 68 to clarify the applicable requirements, to specify permit terms and to establish the minimum permit conditions and activities to avoid misinterpretations and to ensure compliance with part 68. EPA agrees that air permitting authorities may not have the expertise necessary with respect to part 68; consequently, the requirements in today's rule only specify the actions the state must take to assure that sources have met their part 68 responsibilities while giving the state flexibility to assign or designate by agreement entities other than the permitting authority to carry out these activities. The elements in today's rule are the minimal components of a successful compliance program; anything less falls short of the statutory requirements of assuring compliance with all applicable requirements. EPA also disagrees that it is forcing delegation on air permitting authorities to implement section 112(r). As described in the SNPRM and above, air permitting authorities must ensure that sources are in compliance with applicable requirements for purposes of permitting. This is not section 112(r) implementation (see section R below). EPA is merely specifying more clearly the requirements already upon air permitting authorities; without the specification given in today's rule, it could be argued that air permitting authorities are obligated to review and evaluate the adequacy of RMP submissions. EPA agrees that oversight of the adequacy of part 68 compliance, including RMPs, is not an appropriate activity for the air permitting authority and is more appropriately an implementing agency duty. Delegation of these implementing agency activities can only be accomplished through a delegation consistent with part 63, subpart E.

EPA also maintains that the air permitting authority role should be more specifically defined than that offered by the April 13, 1993, memorandum. The April 1993 policy was prepared prior to the NPRM and SNPRM, it does not account for implementation of the risk management program by the source (as opposed to implementation of the plan), and there is no mechanism, such as a review of the RMP by the permitting authority, to ensure that the plan contains the elements required by part 68. These deficiencies were previously indicated by EPA in a June 24, 1994, memorandum from John Seitz and Jim Makris, Director of the Chemical Emergency Preparedness and Prevention Office (CEPPO) to EPA Regional Division Directors, which stated that "approval criteria in the April 13 memorandum may not be sufficient to ensure compliance with all 'applicable requirements' established" in the risk management program rule. EPA acknowledges that states may have invested considerable resources and effort in development of air permitting programs based on the April 13, 1993 policy. However, EPA also believes that the minimum requirements and flexibility offered by today's rule allow air permitting authorities to fold these activities into their programs with minimal burden. EPA recognizes that there may be multiple agency oversight related to permitting and part 68. As mentioned above, today's rule allows the air permitting authority the flexibility to use other agencies, such as the implementing agency or a designated agency (upon agreement), to better coordinate at the state and local level. In addition, EPA must note that there is no 'approval' of either initial or revised RMP submissions.

EPA agrees that requiring the permit to contain extensive details of part 68 compliance goes well beyond the need for part 70 permits to assure compliance with applicable section 112(r) requirements and it would impose considerable resource and expertise burdens on the permitting authority. EPA has maintained that it is not appropriate to include risk management program elements as permit conditions since these elements will be highly source-specific and subject to change as the source develops and implements its programs.

While enforcement would primarily occur using part 68 authority, EPA agrees that the permitting authority also has the authority to pursue violations under part 70 and sources could be subject to multiple violations. This is no different from any other standard promulgated by EPA that becomes an applicable requirement for permitting. EPA agrees that the air permitting authority has the discretion to coordinate with the implementing agency with respect to penalty assessment associated with § 68.58(b)(3) in the SNPRM (§ 68.215(e)(4) under today's rule).

Finally, the tiering (Program) approach benefits sources as well as air permitting authorities. EPA has simplified the tiering provisions so sources and air permitting authorities should be able to readily determine the Program requirements each process must satisfy, leading to more effective oversight. EPA has also streamlined the RMP reporting requirements and is working on electronic submission of RMP information which serve to reduce the burden on air permitting authorities and implementing agencies.

5. Title V permit application contents. Many commenters stated that sources regulated under parts 70 or 71 and part 68 should only be required to certify whether they are subject to section 112(r) in their initial permit application to allow timely processing. Although EPA indicated that it did not want the RMP included in permit applications or in the permit, many commenters stated their opposition because the additional time required for RMP review could delay permit grants and, in some states, the RMP could be included in the source's permit. Several commenters suggested that the air permitting authority should decide whether it wants the RMP; one commenter stated that sources would have a significant incentive to comply with such a request, given the permitting authority's ability to withdraw an application shield. Others stated that the permitting authority should be prohibited from asking for the RMP as part of the permit application.

As EPA has indicated, the RMP should not be submitted with the permit application or made part of the permit. EPA is working to streamline permit application requirements and has indicated that the minimum with respect to section 112(r) is a "check box" for the source to note whether it is subject to section 112(r), and either certification that the source is in compliance with part 68 or has a plan for achieving compliance. Any other requirements are up to the air permitting authority. All sources will be required to submit their RMP to a central point to be specified by EPA and will be immediately available to local responders and the state which may elect to make it available to air permitting authorities.

6. Air permit contents. EPA proposed in the SNPRM that each permit contain standard conditions that address key compliance elements in part 68 and mechanisms for compliance plans, certifications and revisions. Although EPA indicated it did not believe the RMP should be part of the permit, two commenters suggested that it should be

included while most others indicated that it should not or that the air permitting authority should decide. Several commenters supported no more than the four conditions proposed in the SNPRM while others suggested requirements including: prompt development and updating of a complete RMP; no conditions other than an indication that a source is subject to part 68; provisions stating the need to register according to § 68.12; a condition stating that the source will comply with all part 68 requirements; and a standard provision recognizing that the implementing agency has the section 112(r) enforcement authority.

Except for the provisions of § 68.215(a), EPA does not believe that the RMP or all or any portion of the remainder of part 68 should become permit conditions because the RMP and part 68 elements will be highly source-specific and subject to frequent change introducing unnecessary complexity and delaying permit implementation. The provisions of § 68.215 should allow the air permitting authority to implement the conditions in a standardized way across many sources with minimal burden. EPA has revised § 68.215 to require that all permits contain a statement listing part 68 as an applicable requirement and that conditions shall be added that require the source to submit a compliance schedule for meeting the requirements of part 68 or, as part of the compliance certification all permitted sources must submit under 40 CFR 70.6(c)(5), a certification statement that, to the best of the owner or operator's knowledge, the source is in compliance with all requirements of this part, including the registration and submission of the RMP. EPA had amended the authority citation for part 68 to include CAA Title V because EPA is promulgating permit terms and oversight duties. Consistent with parts 70 and 71, the permit shield provisions of parts 70 and 71 would not apply to the substantive requirements of part 68 because the detailed substantive requirements of part 68 are not addressed in the Title V permit or permit application. If a permit without these conditions has already been issued, then when the permit comes up for renewal under part 70 or 71 requirements (40 CFR Part 70.7), the owner or operator shall submit an application for a revision to its permit to incorporate these conditions. The suggested alternative conditions, not adopted, generally help assure compliance only with portions of part 68, such as registration or the preparation of the RMP, or omit critical information, such as whether the source is subject to part 68 or what its compliance status is. The implementing agency's enforcement authority is apparent on the face of the CAA.

7. Completeness review. As part of ensuring compliance, EPA proposed in the SNPRM that within a certain time-frame the air permitting authority must verify that an RMP containing the required elements had been submitted and indicated in the preamble that it would assist air permitting authorities by developing a checklist. EPA stated that this review is independent of completeness reviews required for permit applications to avoid interfering with the permit process. Further, air permitting authorities could arrange for other agencies, including the implementing agency, to perform the completeness review. EPA also requested comment on whether the permitting authority should be able to require sources to make revisions to an RMP.

Most commenters disagreed with this proposal arguing that if a completeness check is necessary, it should be performed by the implementing agency since most air permitting authorities will not have the technical expertise (e.g., chemical process safety) required to adequately review RMPs for technical completeness. Commenters also argued that a completeness review would be merely procedural, it duplicates effort without creating any real benefit, it consumes scarce resources, and it leads to inconsistent RMP review without ensuring the source is in compliance with risk management program requirements. Some commenters suggested that the completeness review could be better defined only as a review of source self-certification that a complete RMP was submitted rather than a substantive review. Some commenters generally agreed that completeness checks should be completed within sixty days. Finally, most commenters argued that only the implementing agency should be able to require revisions to the RMP. Otherwise, another revision review, appeal and verification process would be necessary, duplicating the process already established for the implementing agency.

Based on these comments, EPA has decided not to require that air permitting authorities perform a completeness check as part of the verification of compliance with part 68. EPA has modified the rule requirements so that the air permitting authority may elect for itself one or more appropriate mechanisms (such as source audits, record reviews, source inspections or

completeness checks) and time-frame in conjunction with source certifications, to ensure that permitted sources are in compliance with the part 68 requirements. Without some kind of oversight, source self-certification is not a sufficient means of compliance assurance, given that an RMP contains information essential at the local level for emergency prevention, preparedness, and response and is not subject to routine, case-by-case review for quality. These oversight mechanisms do not need to be used on each source in order to be effective. EPA agrees that the review for quality or adequacy of the RMP is best accomplished by the implementing agency on a frequency and scope that may vary. EPA is willing to work with air permitting authorities on guidance, checklists or other tools to assist in the development of compliance mechanisms related to the RMP. In addition, EPA is willing to assist air permitting authorities in electronic checks once the electronic system for RMP submittal is developed. EPA emphasizes that if an RMP completeness check is used by the air permitting authority, it should remain independent of the completeness determination for the permit application. The RMP will most likely be submitted at a different time than a permit application, since almost all permit applications will have been submitted well in advance of the risk management program rule deadline. If the completeness check determines that an incomplete RMP has been submitted, the permitting authority can request additional information under § 68.215(b) and should coordinate with the implementing agency on necessary RMP revisions. The completeness checks are facial reviews of RMPs to verify that there are no omissions. Such checks could be performed on a select basis and occasionally integrated with a multi-purpose source inspection conducted to ensure that the air source is in compliance with its permit.

8. Interaction of the implementing agency and the permitting authority. In the SNPRM, EPA attempted to delineate the specific requirements unique to the air permitting authority and the implementing agency. The role of the state is described in more detail in E.4 while the implementing agency is discussed in R. Commenters on the SNPRM suggested that EPA should require the implementing agency to certify to permitting authorities whether part 68 sources regulated under part 70 are in compliance with part 68 requirements. Such certification should be deemed sufficient to "assure

compliance" with the applicable requirement under part 70. Other commenters suggested that the permitting authority could simply consult with the implementing agency when it believes there is a problem requiring attention or that the implementing agency should notify the permitting authority of any problems in part 68 compliance, so that the permitting authority may then expand the permit conditions accordingly.

EPA does not believe it is necessary to define the interaction between the permitting authority and the implementing agency. Ideally, this coordination and interaction should occur at the state or local level. Coordination of other CAA programs (Title V, SBAP, and other 112 programs) with the 112(r) program will ensure that the programs are more consistently implemented and enforced, while easing regulatory burden and providing the public greater access to information. However, when EPA is the implementing agency, it stands ready to work with air permitting authorities on oversight associated with permitting and enforcement of the part 68 requirements. Today's rule also provides the state the flexibility to assign some or all of its responsibilities by prior cooperative agreements or memoranda of understanding to the implementing agency or another state, local, or Federal "designated agency." EPA recognizes that each state is structured differently and will have different impediments and opportunities; therefore each state has the flexibility to place the program in an appropriate agency or department, including the air permitting agency.

9. The "designated agency." In the SNPRM, EPA proposed to define the designated agency as the state or local agency designated by the air permitting authority as the agency responsible for the review of an RMP for completeness. This provision was designed to give the air permitting authority the flexibility to obtain expertise from other agencies to fulfill its responsibilities. Several commenters believed the SNPRM does not clearly allow the permitting authority to delegate tasks to a designated agency and the permitting authority should be able to delegate more than the completeness review, e.g., enforcement. Some commenters requested that EPA redefine the term to allow permitting authorities to delegate tasks to EPA or other Federal agencies; while one commenter argued that EPA should not allow the permitting authority to designate EPA as the designated agency.

EPA agrees that the definition should be revised to give the air permitting authority more flexibility. EPA has dropped the mandatory completeness review, added broader implementation and enforcement activities, and included Federal agencies in the designated agency definition. Thus, a "designated agency" may be any state, local, or Federal agency designated by the state as the agency to carry out the provisions of § 68.215, provided that such designation is in writing and, in the case of a Federal agency, consented to by the agency. The parties to any such designation should negotiate the terms and details of any agreements.

10. Reopening part 70 permits to incorporate section 112(r) requirements. In the preamble to the SNPRM, EPA indicated that part 68 requirements should be incorporated into part 70 or 71 permits using the part 70 administrative amendment process because of the timing difference between part 68 and air permitting. Most commenters agreed with this approach or indicated that permits should not be reopened at all; instead, sources that submitted permit applications prior to promulgation of the final section 112(r) regulations should not be subject to enforcement action under Title V until after the first renewal of the permit (i.e., after 5 years).

As discussed under section E.6, if a permit without the necessary part 68 conditions has already been issued, then the owner or operator or air permitting authority shall initiate a permit revision or reopening according to the procedures detailed in 40 CFR 70.7 or 71.7 to incorporate the terms and conditions under paragraph (a) of § 68.215. Although EPA has not completed part 70 permit streamlining efforts, the requirements for permit revisions or reopenings should be complete by the time sources will be required to be in compliance with the part 68 requirements. Under the most recent part 70 proposal, the part 68 requirements would be classified as "less environmentally significant" and the associated procedures would be followed. Sources with such permits shall be subject to enforcement under authorities other than Title V.

11. Use of Title V funds. In the SNPRM, EPA indicated that activities conducted by air permitting authorities should be covered by fees collected under part 70 since part 68 is an "applicable requirement." EPA also acknowledged that air permitting authorities may not have planned for section 112(r) activities and requested input on alternative funding mechanisms or whether resources

would need to be reduced in other programs to allow completion of part 68 responsibilities.

Several commenters raised concerns about the impact of the section 112(r) requirements on state and local air permitting authorities because funding will be needed and it may not be possible in the current political climate for the permitting authorities to raise the necessary fees through Title V. Some commenters argued that funding decisions should be left up to the air permitting authorities.

EPA agrees that funding decisions regarding the part 68 program should be made at the discretion of the state and local agencies. However, air permitting authorities need to be aware that the CAA requires states to impose permit fees that are sufficient to cover the direct and indirect costs of implementing the permit program, including part 68 activities and activities conducted by state designated agencies. EPA believes the straight-forward and flexible requirements established in today's rule impose minimal additional burden on air permitting authorities. Funding associated with section 112(r) implementation is addressed in section R, below.

12. Other issues. In the SNPRM preamble, EPA stated that it worked closely with and directly involved several state and local air program officials and state emergency response and prevention representatives in the development of the preamble and regulatory language to prepare the approaches described. EPA stated that the proposed approaches "best reflect the concerns of the states about air permit program implementation and the needs for comprehensive participation in chemical accident prevention, preparedness, and response at the state and local level." Two commenters disagreed, arguing that in January 1995, the National Governors Association (NGA) and ECOS (organization of state environmental officials) presented numerous recommendations to EPA Assistant Administrator Mary Nichols for changes in several clean air programs; regarding section 112(r), NGA/ECOS recommended that Title V permitting authorities be required only to certify that an RMP has been submitted. These commenters believe that the SNPRM fails to adequately address states' central concern; requiring permitting authorities to review RMPs will encumber an already overtaxed system.

Although EPA disagrees that the proposal fails to adequately address states' concerns, EPA agreed that the air

permitting authority requirements could be more sharply focused to minimize the burden. EPA believes that today's rule is the product of many hours of hard work with state and local air permitting authorities to recognize their concerns and to develop a rule that is effective, flexible and imposes the least economic burden possible.

F. General Definitions

1. Significant Accidental Release. In the NPRM, EPA proposed to define significant accidental release as "any release of a regulated substance that has caused or has the potential to cause offsite consequences such as death, injury, or adverse effects to human health or the environment or to cause the public to shelter in place or be evacuated to avoid such consequences." This definition was key to the applicability of a number of rule requirements, including hazard assessment, accident history, and accident investigation. Only four of more than 115 commenters supported this proposal arguing that the definition should be protective of the public and should consider inconvenience to the public and precautionary measures taken. Other commenters argued that Congress intended for the section 112(r) rules to address catastrophic releases, not those with minor impacts, and that this definition overly broadens the scope of the rule diverting resources and increasing cost for little additional benefit. Many commenters stated that "injury" and "adverse effects" are undefined and could mean any health impact from irreversible effects to minor irritation requiring no medical treatment. "Potential to cause" was also considered too vague. As discussed in Section III.C, many commenters objected to consideration of environmental impacts. Commenters also opposed sheltering-in-place and evacuation as criteria because these actions are often precautionary and, in many cases, are later viewed as unnecessary and may discourage owners or operators from making recommendations to evacuate or shelter-in-place. Several commenters submitted alternative definitions where injuries were limited to those that require hospitalization, adverse effects were limited to serious effects, and environmental effects were limited to those that generate human deaths or hospitalizations. Some suggested that all environmental effects be dropped.

EPA agrees that the definition as proposed was too vague and subject to a wide variety of interpretations. In addition, EPA decided that a single definition does not adequately address e criteria needed for all affected ections of the rule. For example, the ve-year accident history requirement epends on the offsite impacts enerated by the accident while ndpoint criteria are used for the worst-ase and alternate scenario offsite onsequence assessments. onsequently, EPA has decided to drop e definition and instead identify the riteria for the types of releases or npacts that should be addressed by the ppropriate requirement. EPA has onsidered the suggestions offered by ommenters and added definitions of e terms "environmental receptor," injury," "medical treatment," and public receptor" and adopted (with odifications as described above) the SHA definition of catastrophic release. PA notes that sources should be aware at within the definition of Injury, irect consequences include effects aused by shrapnel and debris set in notion by a vapor cloud explosion. EPA dopted its Medical Treatment efinition from one OSHA uses for ogging occupational injuries and lness. Finally, under the nvironmental and public receptor efinitions, sources should note that ertain parks and recreational areas may e both if the public could be exposed s a result of an accidental release.

2. Stationary Source. Commenters equested that EPA state whether the erm stationary source covers the entire facility" or simply a single process and rovide guidance on which equirements apply source-wide and rhich are process-specific. EPA also eceived comments regarding the elationship or overlap between the tationary source definition and DOT egulations. These are discussed in ection III.P.2 below.

In the List and Thresholds rule, EPA efined stationary source to include an ntire "facility." Sources will be equired to submit one RMP and one egistration as part of that RMP for all rocesses at the source with more than threshold quantity of a regulated ubstance. Although the management ystem applies to all Program 2 and 3 rocesses, the prevention program lements are process-specific. The azard assessment requirements apply o the regulated substances, but only in overed processes. As a practical matter, he emergency response program will robably apply to the entire source lthough technically it applies only to overed processes.

3. Process. Several commenters rgued that the definition of process was usceptible to overly expansive nterpretations and asked that certain ctivities such as storage at sources or

distribution terminals be excluded. Many commenters sought clarification of "close proximity" and "interconnected vessel." Commenters also wanted the definition to be consistent with OSHA.

EPA adopted OSHA's definition of process in the original proposal and for the final rule. This definition specifically covers storage (as well as handling and processing) of regulated substances. EPA disagrees that storage-only sources are adequately covered by SPCC regulations since the regulations under SPCC and OPA–90 cover oil terminals and releases to water. This rule is directed at accidental releases of regulated substances (not including oil) to the ambient air. Generally, OSHA PSM also covers these chemical terminals; consequently, the only additional steps these sources will need to take will be to conduct the hazard assessment and submit the RMP, as existing emergency response plans may meet the emergency response program requirements.

Since EPA's definition is identical to OSHA's, EPA will coordinate interpretations of the definition of process with OSHA to ensure that the rule is applied consistently. OSHA has stated that processes are in "close proximity" if a release from one could lead to a release from the other. Owners or operators must be able to demonstrate that an "effective barrier" exists to prevent a release from one process from affecting another. OSHA has interpreted "interconnected vessel" to mean vessels connected by any means, such as piping, valves or hoses, even if these are occasionally disconnected. EPA will also adhere to these interpretations.

4. Offsite. One commenter stated that EPA's proposed definition of offsite should be expanded to include the air above and below the point of release to cover exposure to the upper atmosphere and groundwater. Another asked EPA to limit the definition to areas frequented by the public. Two commenters opposed including areas on site where the public has access because OSHA already covers these areas.

In the final rule, EPA has retained a definition of offsite as "areas beyond the property boundary of the stationary source or areas within the property boundary to which the public has routine and unrestricted access during or outside business hours." OSHA's jurisdiction includes visitors that may be on the property of a facility who are conducting business as employees of other companies but does not necessarily extend to casual visitors or to areas within a facility boundary to

which the public has routine and unrestricted access at any time.

5. Other Definitions. Commenters raised questions about several other definitions. Three commenters suggested changes or clarifications to the definition of accidental release. EPA's definition is the statutory definition. Commenters also proposed modifications to the definition of "analysis of offsite consequence." As noted above, EPA has determined that this definition is not needed and has deleted it from the final rule.

Commenters sought clarification of the definition of mitigation systems and whether personnel should be considered an active mitigation system. Others asked for a list of passive mitigation systems and provided proposals. These commenters also objected to limiting passive systems to those that capture or control released substances; they suggested that systems that are designed to prevent releases or control the volume or rate of a release, such as vent/catch tanks, quench tanks, blowdown tanks, elevated stacks and high velocity stacks, adsorbents including carbon beds, neutralization tanks, double-walled vessels or pipelines, chemical sewers, closed drain header systems for flammables, vapor-liquid separators, fire barriers, explosion-resistant walls, isolation distances, barriers to prevent free access of air flow after a release, containment buildings, pre-charged water spray systems, closed vent systems, and filters should also be considered passive mitigation. One commenter suggested that active mitigation systems should be defined as those that require manual activation or an energy source (other than gravitational attraction) to perform their intended function.

For the final rule, EPA has decided to define passive mitigation systems as those systems that operate without human, mechanical, or other energy input and would include building enclosures, dikes, and containment walls but excludes active mitigation systems such as excess flow valves, fail-safe systems, scrubbers, flares, deluge systems, and water curtains. In addition to the requirements outlined in §§ 68.25 and 68.28, EPA provides further guidance on the consideration of the effect of passive mitigation in its RMP Offsite Consequence Analysis Guidance. EPA does not believe that all systems designed to prevent releases or control the volume or rate of a release should be considered passive mitigation, consistent with its intent to reflect the potential for failure of any system that requires human, mechanical, or other energy inputs.

G. Risk Management Plan (RMP)

In the NPRM, EPA proposed that owners or operators of stationary sources covered by the requirements submit an RMP summarizing the key elements of its risk management program. In the NPRM preamble, EPA indicated that summaries of the information requested (e.g., hazard assessment and emergency response program) would provide the most useful information to the public and local agencies without overburdening them with unneeded detailed information. EPA further stated that the RMP should serve to provide local and state agencies and the public with sufficient information to determine if additional details are needed. These details would be available, if needed, to implementing agency officials conducting audits or compliance inspections.

1. Level of Detail. Most commenters agreed with EPA's proposal noting that the public should be able to identify key hazard and risk management information from the RMP without being overwhelmed by extraneous documentation that is more appropriately maintained on site. A detailed submission would not be cost-effective and could threaten plant security; these commenters expressed fears of terrorism, thieves, and saboteurs.

Other commenters disagreed and argued that summaries would not provide enough information while "full disclosure" would support an informed public. Some commenters argued that the public could be misled by a summary derived from a "full" RMP withheld from the public by the source. Further, several commenters made the general argument that right-to-know provisions should be strengthened and that the public should be given full access to all risk management program information including PHAs and actual operating procedures. Individual commenters also requested public access to specific information regarding such details as worst-case scenarios and descriptions of chemical accidents. Some commenters argued that an informed public and public scrutiny, in general, can act as a powerful force in reducing risk and preventing accidents at stationary sources.

EPA agrees that an informed public is a key element of sound chemical emergency prevention, preparedness, and response. However, EPA also believes that it is essential for the public to focus on the information essential at the local level for prevention, preparedness, and response and has decided to maintain its proposed requirement that the RMP provide certain information about the risk management programs at a source. EPA notes that its previous use of the word summary was not intended to imply that the source prepares a "full" RMP document from which a source extracts summary information that is shared with the public. Rather, the source is obligated to develop certain information about the hazards, prevention, and emergency response programs from the array of documentation at the source to prepare an RMP. EPA believes it would be impractical to require sources to share all documentation used for the safe operation of the processes at a source. Not only is much of this information likely to be confidential, but significant technical expertise and time are necessary to extract, understand, and to make meaningful judgments about the adequacy of the information. The RMP will consist of an executive summary and required data elements addressing all elements of the risk management program as described below. Detailed supporting documentation will be maintained on site available to the implementing agency for review.

2. RMP Contents. Most commenters requested that EPA generally limit the level of detail required, the number of scenarios, or the number of pages in the RMP. Other commenters recommended EPA require submission of only information specified in the CAA and incorporate other detailed information by reference. Commenters also noted that documenting each action taken to address a hazard, the date on which the action started (or is scheduled to start), and the actual or scheduled completion date would prove impractical. EPA received many comments stating that the requirement that exact dates on which training, emergency exercises, or rescue drills, are conducted would be impractical and unnecessary.

Commenters seeking more comprehensive RMPs argued in favor of requiring an index or bibliography of detailed information or a catalog of all available documents, an investigation and analysis of all other credible release scenarios, and submission of assumptions, methodology, and modeling methods used to determine worst-case accidents.

As described above, EPA is considering development of a reporting mechanism and form to collect key data elements. As discussed below, this approach will foster electronic submission and immediate availability to Federal, state and local entities, and the public. To make such submission possible, EPA wants to collect data that generally can be reported by numerical information, yes/no answers, and check boxes. For the offsite consequence analyses, owners or operators will be asked to provide distance to the endpoint, populations and environments affected, and enough of the data used to determine these distances so that local entities and the public can check the distance against the distance derived from EPA's reference tables or a model identified in the RMP. If EPA's guidance was not used, sources will need to indicate which models were used. Many of the parameters for modeling are set in the rule and do not need to be respecified in the RMP. The rule requires only one alternative release scenario per toxic substance and one for all flammables; owners or operators may submit additional scenarios.

For prevention programs, owners or operators must provide information (primarily dates) that will allow the implementing agency to assess whether the source is in compliance with the rule elements. For the PHA, owners or operators must state which technique was used for each covered process, the general hazards associated with the chemicals and process, the process controls in use, mitigation and monitoring or detection systems in use, and changes instituted since the last PHA (Program 3) or hazard review (Program 2) update. Through lists and checkoff boxes, EPA can collect a significant amount of information on current safety practices without requiring sources to develop lengthy documentation that would have proved a burden to both the source and any government or public data user and reduced the potential for electronic submission. EPA believes this approach provides the Agency and others with a mechanism for identifying industry practices and controls from almost 70,000 sources that would not be feasible otherwise. EPA notes that some of the largest chemical sources and refineries may be providing data on 30 or more processes. In the format proposed in the NPRM, these sources might have submitted several thousand pages each; analyzing such submissions would have been a daunting task for the implementing agencies and probably would have made it impossible for public interest groups to review an industry as a whole. With electronic submission, such reviews will be easier. The implementing agency or EPA can seek additional details from individual sources, as needed. EPA has eliminated the requirement to provide dates of training and emergency exercises or rills because the Agency agrees that his amount of detail is unnecessary and impractical.

3. Submission. In the NPRM preamble, EPA proposed that computer software be developed that would provide sources with a standard format for completing the information required in the RMP; that local authorities be allowed to designate the state as the receiving entity; or that RMPs be submitted only on request from the state, or local entity.

Many commenters, particularly those in the potentially regulated community, supported submission of the RMP upon request or mandatory submission to the implementing agency with submission by request to other organizations. Others recommended submission to the LEPC and public with submission by request to the implementing agency, and SERC. Most commenters favored reducing the paperwork burden and electronic submission because it would reduce time and errors, provide more consistency, and make information more useful for the LEPC and regulatory agencies. Only two commenters opposed electronic filing because all sources may not have the computer capability.

Commenters also supported the development of a standard RMP format regardless of whether the RMP is submitted electronically because standardization would ensure submissions were manageable and useful and would ease burdens on both regulated and reviewing entities.

EPA has decided to work toward electronic submission of RMPs. The Agency believes this will meet numerous objectives of the program and will address several issues. First, electronic submission would reduce the burden on regulated and receiving entities. The Agency has noted that information management of regulatory documents is not a cost-free requirement, and that duplication of effort, including system development, personnel resources, and storage and maintenance efforts could be significant. Electronic submissions would reduce the paperwork burden on sources and state and local governments and would further serve to comply with the Paperwork Reduction Act of 1995, which supports the maximum feasible use of electronic submission. Second, EPA wishes to limit the information management burden on local entities so they can focus on the chemical safety issues raised by this rule.

Third, electronic submissions would benefit affected communities and the general public. Besides having the RMP provide the statutorily required

information on compliance with the regulations to the implementing agency, EPA believes the specific value of RMP information is for the local community to understand its community's risk from chemical accidents and to help them work with sources using these chemicals to reduce such risks. The Agency believes this objective would not be served well with a centralized paper information source and that using an electronic medium would support better access to information. With electronic submission of RMPs to a central point, states, local entities, and the public will have access to all RMPs electronically. RMP information may also be made available on-line via libraries and other institutions. Electronic submissions further address the issue of standardized RMPs. The RMP data elements included in the submission will be checkoff boxes, yes/ no answers, or numerical entries to ease the burden of submission and reception and will promote consistency and uniformity. The Agency intends to develop technical guidance for the submission of the RMPs, which will provide for submission and receipt of an electronic formatted document containing the data elements outlined in §§ 68.160 through 68.180.

4. Other Issues. In the NPRM, EPA proposed that RMPs be resubmitted within six months of an information change. Several commenters argued it would generate a continual flow of paperwork and recommended an update frequency requirement of once a year.

EPA has retained the requirement that the RMP be resubmitted within six months of the elimination of a substance in a process or at the source, a change in Program status for a process, or if a process change at the source requires a revised hazard assessment or hazard review/PHA. To be consistent with the statutory requirements for compliance, the RMP would also have to be updated on the date an already regulated substance becomes present in a process above the threshold or within three years of the date when EPA lists a new substance. EPA believes that with a standardized format and electronic filing, updates can be rapidly and easily made, and this information should be promptly shared. EPA changed the update schedule for hazard assessments to make them consistent with the RMP update. EPA also specified when offsite consequence analyses require update; the rule states that these analyses need to be reviewed and changed if on-site changes may be reasonably expected to change the distance to an endpoint by a factor of two or more. EPA notes that this change is likely to reduce the

number of updates required. For PHAs, only major changes to a process or installation of new processes is likely to trigger a revised PHA. EPA expects that relatively few sources will need to update either their offsite consequence analyses or PHAs/hazard reviews more frequently than once every five years because the majority of sources have simple processes that do not change frequently. Chemical industry sources may need to submit more updates if processes are changing significantly. The RMP should reflect such significant changes.

EPA proposed that RMPs be submitted to implementing agencies, SERCs, and LEPCs, and be made available to the public. Several commenters recommended that additional parties, local fire officials in particular, also receive RMPs. One commenter stated that EPCRA requires various reports go to local fire departments, and another commenter noted that RMP information may be better used by emergency management agencies, fire departments, and hazardous materials teams. Because EPA plans to have RMPs submitted to and available from a central point in electronic format, any agency that wants the information will be able to access it directly on-line. The RMP will be immediately available to local responders and the state. Thus, this manner of submission fulfills the requirements of CAA section 112(r)(7)(B)(iii). Additional submission requirements are, therefore, unnecessary.

The Department of Defense (DOD) commented concerning the lack of a rule provision explicitly declaring that information that is classified under applicable laws and Executive Orders (E.O.s) is not to be included in the RMP. EPA is clarifying that such classified information is protected from disclosure by including a specific regulatory exemption for such information. Furthermore, EPA is clarifying that no provision of part 68 requires the disclosure of classified information in violation of Federal law, regulations, or E.O.s. Finally, EPA is also promulgating a definition of "classified information" that adopts the definition under the Classified Information Procedures Act.

EPA has found no relevant statutory language superseding or impliedly repealing the Classified Information Procedures Act or applicable E.O.s regarding disclosure of classified information, nor has EPA found any legislative history indicating that Congress intended to supersede or repeal these provisions when it established the requirement to prepare publicly-available RMPs. The provision for exemptions from standards and limitations established under CAA section 112 narrowly addresses the procedures for an exemption when "the President determines that the technology to implement such standard is not available and * * * it is in the national security interests of the United States to do so." CAA § 112(i)(4). The focus of section 112(i)(4) is on the technical capability to meet a limitation; for example, the provision would apply when an emission standard requires a control device that precludes national security-related equipment from functioning. Section 112(i)(4) does not consider or address the availability or distribution of classified information to the public, nor does the legislative history demonstrate that such disclosure was contemplated.

The requirement of section 112(r)(7)(B)(iii) to make RMPs publicly available must read in congruence with the provisions prohibiting disclosure of classified information. "Classified information," as defined by the Classified Information Procedures Act, 18 U.S.C. App. 3, section 1(a), is "any information or material that has been determined by the United States Government pursuant to an Executive order, statute, or regulation, to require protection against unauthorized disclosure for reasons of national security. * * *" "National security * * * means the national defense and foreign relations of the United States" 18 U.S.C. App. 3, section 1(b). Criminal penalties exist for unauthorized disclosure of classified information that has been designated by the Department of Defense or defense agencies for limited or restricted dissemination or distribution. 18 U.S.C. 793. It is not reasonable to interpret the CAA to require the disclosure of classified information in violation of criminal law. It has been EPA's long-standing policy to interpret information disclosure provisions in its statutes as being consistent with national security law to the maximum extent possible and to require such information to be maintained in accordance with the originating agency's requirements. *Federal Facilities Compliance Strategy* (November 1988), at page V–6. Therefore, EPA is promulgating language in § 68.150(d) to clarify its intent with respect to the disclosure of classified information in RMPs by specifically exempting classified information from the RMP except by means of a classified annex submitted to appropriately cleared Federal or state representatives with proper security

clearances. Furthermore, EPA is promulgating § 68.210(b) to clarify that disclosure of classified information is controlled by the Classified Information Procedures Act, E.O.s 12958 and 12968, and other laws, regulations, and E.O.s applicable to classified information. Finally, in § 68.3, EPA is defining classified information by promulgating the definition under the Classified Information Procedures Act.

H. Prevention Program

In the NPRM preamble, EPA noted that the CAA requires the risk management program to include a prevention program that covers safety precautions and maintenance, monitoring, and employee training measures. Because OSHA PSM covers this same set of elements, EPA proposed a prevention program that adopted and built on OSHA PSM. The proposed requirements for EPA's prevention program included a management system requirement and sections covering nine elements: process hazard analysis, process safety information, operating procedures (SOPs), training, maintenance, pre-startup review, management of change, safety audits, and accident investigation.

To assist in describing its prevention program, EPA included a section in its preamble comparing its prevention program to OSHA PSM standard. EPA noted that with the exception of the management system requirement, the proposed prevention program covered the same elements as OSHA's PSM and generally used identical language except where the statutory mandates of the two agencies dictated differences. EPA added introductory paragraphs to most sections to provide additional information. Further, in some of the sections, EPA proposed additional requirements and established different deadlines. The majority of comments EPA received concerned conflicts and differences between EPA's proposed requirements and OSHA PSM standard.

In the final rule, the Program 3 prevention program is the OSHA PSM standard for parallel elements, with minor wording changes to address statutory differences. For elements that are in both the EPA and OSHA rules, EPA has used OSHA's language verbatim, changing only certain regulatory terms (e.g., highly hazardous chemical to regulated substance and employer to owner/operator) and dates. The sections of the OSHA PSM standard were not cross-referenced for the reasons discussed in section III.D of this preamble. Key issues under PSM are discussed below; the remainder are

addressed in the Response to Comments Document.

Management. In the NPRM preamble, EPA stated the purpose of its proposed management system is to ensure integration of all prevention program elements. EPA proposed that owners or operators identify a single person or position that has the overall responsibility for the development, implementation, and integration of the risk management program requirements. When responsibility for implementing individual requirements of the risk management program is assigned to persons other than the person designated, the names or positions of these people shall be documented and the lines of authority defined through an organization chart or similar document.

Several commenters agreed with this approach because it serves a useful purpose and many PSM sources already implement management systems. Many commenters opposed the requirement for submission of an organization chart of their source because it would be of no value to EPA and that continual updating would waste company resources.

EPA has decided to maintain its management system requirements in the final rule for sources with processes in Program 2 and 3, but has moved it to general requirements (§ 68.15) because it is the entire risk management program that should be managed, not just the prevention program. EPA has also revised the requirement to provide flexibility in indicating lines of authority; an organization chart is not absolutely required and is not included in the RMP.

Management of Change. Some commenters objected to EPA's definition of replacement in kind, asking that EPA adopt the OSHA PSM definition. Other commenters stated that management of change procedures should only be implemented when the changes had the potential to increase the risk (e.g., an increase in inventory, an introduction of a new substance).

As part of its efforts to strengthen coordination between the two programs, EPA will use the OSHA definition for "replacements in kind": "a replacement which satisfies the design specification." OSHA defined this term to address a concern expressed by commenters on its standard that failing to define "replacements in kind" could result in misunderstandings such as employers believing that only a replacement with the same brand and model number could be characterized as a "replacement in kind." OSHA promulgated a definition in recognition of these comments, and EPA understands it to reflect a concept understood in industry.

Further, EPA does not agree that management of change requirements should exclude changes that reduce the risk of an accidental release. The Agency does not believe that only changes to "critical systems" should be subject to management of change procedures. As EPA stated in the NPRM preamble, most process changes improve process safety or efficiency. However, even these changes may result in unintended effects when source owners and operators fail to evaluate the consequences of the change. Therefore, the Agency continues to believe that a change that reduces the risk of an accidental chemical release may, nonetheless, be an appropriate subject for a management of change procedure. Failure to subject such changes to a management of change process could inadvertently result in a change that was believed to lower risk when such a change, in fact, increases risk. Regarding the comment about critical systems, EPA notes that chemical processes are integrated systems, and that a change in one part of the process can have unintended effects in other parts of the system—irrespective of whether the system is "critical." Consequently, EPA agrees with OSHA that source owners and operators must establish and implement written management of change procedures for any change to a regulated substance, process technology, or equipment and any change to a source that affects the covered process.

Other Provisions. Several commenters stated that EPA should include in its risk management program the OSHA PSM provisions on contractors, employee participation, and hot work permits that EPA had not proposed in its prevention program. The NPRM solicited comment on whether to include these provisions (58 FR 54205; October 20, 1993). Commenters argued that contractors have been responsible for a number of accidents that have affected the public and the environment. Commenters presented the same argument to support inclusion of the hot work permit requirements. A substantial number of commenters also argued that employee participation is a key factor in successful implementation of PSM. A few commenters supported EPA's initial position that these requirements were more properly OSHA concerns.

In response to the former commenters' arguments and to ensure consistency between the elements of the two rules, EPA has decided to add these sections to its Program 3 prevention program. EPA believes that each of these elements

is important to the implementation of an effective prevention program. Worker participation in PHAs and other elements is critical to the success of process safety because workers are intimately familiar with the process and equipment operation, possible failure modes and consequences of deviations. It also serves as a mechanism for greater communication and understanding of specific process hazards (as opposed to the general chemical hazards) and the importance of developing and following proper procedures. Similarly, contract employees have been involved in a number of major accidents in recent years; for example, the explosion in Pasadena, Texas, in 1989, which killed 23 workers, has been attributed to improper maintenance practices by contractor employees. Oversight of contractors, therefore, can be critical for accident prevention. Finally, hot work permits ensure that use of flame or spark-producing equipment is carefully controlled. Not only are many of the listed substances highly flammable, but fires in the vicinity of vessels or pipes containing the toxic substances can lead to releases of these substances.

I. Accident History

In the NPRM, EPA required sources to document a five-year history of releases that caused or had the potential to cause offsite consequences for each regulated substance handled at the source. EPA specified that the accident history should include the nature of any offsite consequences, such as deaths, injuries, hospitalizations, medical treatments, evacuations, sheltering-in-place, and major offsite environmental impacts such as soil, groundwater, or drinking water contamination, fish kills, and vegetation damage.

A few commenters argued that releases with only the potential for offsite consequences should not be included, while other commenters were evenly divided on whether near-miss events should be included in the accident history. A number of commenters indicated that releases with on-site consequences should be added to the accident history. Several commenters requested that EPA clarify that the accident history applies only to covered processes.

In recognition of these comments, in the final rule, only those accidents from covered processes that resulted in deaths, injuries, or significant property damage on-site, or known offsite deaths, injuries, evacuations, sheltering in place, property damage, or environmental damage need to be included in the five-year accident history. Near-miss accidents or

accidents with only the potential for offsite consequences (that did not meet any of the previous criteria) would not need to be included. Because the accident history is, by statute, an aspect of the hazard assessment, and the hazard assessment provisions apply only to covered processes, EPA believes that requiring the accident history to address accidental releases from processes not covered by this rule would be inconsistent with the structure of part 68. EPA notes that such releases may be subject to reporting under other statutes; the Agency may investigate such releases to determine the need for a response action under CERCLA and to determine whether CAA section 112(r)(1) has been violated.

J. Emergency Response Program

In the proposed rule, EPA required sources to develop an emergency response plan that defines the steps the source and each employee should take during an accidental release of a regulated substance. EPA noted that most sources are already required to have at least part of the emergency response plan in place as a result of other EPA (Spill Prevention, Control, and Countermeasures and Resource Conservation and Recovery Act) and OSHA (emergency action plans and HAZWOPER) regulations and requested comment on how the proposed requirements could best be integrated with these existing programs to minimize duplication. Many of the commenters were particularly concerned with the potential for increased duplication of emergency planning requirements at the state and Federal levels that would require expenditure of additional resources without improving source emergency response capabilities. Most of these commenters suggested that EPA allow compliance with other Federal regulatory programs to meet the mandate of the Clean Air Act for an emergency response program, while other commenters recommended that EPA work with other agencies to develop a format for a single, comprehensive response plan for the source. Some commenters addressed related concerns with respect to state program or voluntary initiatives.

EPA has decided to adopt the emergency response requirements found in the statute, without additional specific planning requirements. This action is consistent with the Agency's effort to develop a single Federal approach for emergency response planning. The Review of Federal Authorities for Hazardous Materials Accident Safety, (required under section

112(r)(10) of the Clean Air Act) reported little harmony in the required formats or elements of response plans prepared to meet various Federal regulations. Accordingly, EPA has committed not to specify new plan elements or a specific plan format in today's rule. EPA believes that plans developed to comply with other EPA contingency planning requirements and the OSHA Hazardous Waste and Emergency Operations (HAZWOPER) rule (29 CFR 1910.120) will meet the requirements for the emergency response program provided that they address the elements in section 68.95(a). EPA believes that coordination of the emergency response plan with the community emergency response plan will help ensure that offsite response issues are addressed. In addition, EPA and other National Response Team agencies have prepared Integrated Contingency Plan Guidance ("one plan") (NRT, May 1996). An emergency response plan that includes the elements specified in this guidance can be used to meet the requirements in today's rule. The final rule also provides relief for sources that are too small to respond to releases with their own employees; these sources will not be required to develop emergency response plans provided that appropriate responses to their hazards have been discussed in the community emergency response plan developed under EPCRA (42 U.S.C. 11003) for toxics or coordinated with the local fire department for flammables.

K. Registration

In the NPRM, EPA proposed that sources register with the EPA Administrator by three years after the publication date of the final rule, or within three years of the date on which a source becomes subject to the risk management program requirements as mandated by the CAA. While a number of commenters agreed with this proposal, a greater number requested that EPA accelerate the registration to between six months and two years of promulgation of the rule so that implementing agencies could better determine resource allocation and conduct more extensive outreach and technical assistance to sources developing risk management programs and preparing RMPs.

EPA agrees that earlier registration could aid outreach efforts and help implementing agencies focus resources. However, since the first RMP need not be submitted until June 21, 1999, an earlier, pre-registration would impose an additional burden on sources. Some sources may reduce inventories, make process modifications or switch

chemicals prior to the first RMP due date and, consequently, will not be subject to the rule. If EPA required a pre-registration, these sources would have to deregister at that time. Further, states and local agencies already have information gathered under EPCRA section 312 that could be used for early identification and outreach to sources covered by this rule. EPA is also working with trade associations and other representatives of affected industries to ensure that sources are aware of the rule. Instead, in today's rule, the registration is included as part of the RMP to limit the number of filings made by sources.

EPA also proposed that sources submit written registration information. A number of commenters advocated either the modification of existing forms (e.g., the EPCRA Tier II form) or an electronic filing system for the submission of this information. Since the RMP and the registration are consolidated into one submission, this issue is addressed generally in Section III.G.

Under the proposed rule sources would need to submit an amended notice to the Administrator and the implementing agency within 60 days if information in the registration is no longer accurate. Many commenters argued that six months or a year is needed to ensure compliance with the certification requirements. EPA agrees with commenters and in the final rule has lengthened the time for submission of an amended registration to six months which should be enough time to modify the information and to electronically resubmit the registration and RMP.

L. Model Risk Management Programs

Commenters supported the development of model risk management programs and RMPs, stating that the models were needed by smaller businesses and public systems that lack the expertise to implement process safety management. Commenters specifically supported development of models for industries with well-understood processes and practices, such as chlorination systems, propane and ammonia retailers, and refrigeration systems. A few commenters asked that the models be made available for public review. Others said the models should be published as guidance, not regulations.

EPA is working with industry groups to develop model programs for ammonia refrigeration, propane handling, and water treatment. After having provided the public with an opportunity to review a draft of the ammonia model

program, EPA today is issuing a guidance on a model program for this industry (see Model Risk Management Program for Ammonia Refrigeration). EPA encourages other industry groups to work with the Agency to develop models for their sectors. EPA notes that the models are particularly relevant to sources with Program 2 processes. Because EPA has adopted the OSHA PSM standard, EPA has not provided an EPA guidance on PSM compliance. EPA will also publish general technical guidance to help sources understand and comply with the rule which will include Program 2 prevention program guidance. The RMP Offsite Consequence Analysis Guidance contains reference tables for the offsite consequence analysis, which can be used instead of site-specific modeling. EPA emphasizes that the models are guidance, not regulations; sources are not required to use them.

M. Implementing Agency Audits

EPA originally proposed in § 68.60 seven criteria an implementing agency could use to determine whether to audit a source's RMP. EPA also proposed that the implementing agency have the authority to determine whether an RMP should be revised and to direct the owner or operator to make revisions. Many commenters suggested that the Agency lacked statutory authority to specify measures to correct risk management program elements through the RMP, and that RMP changes based on implementing agency directives will be costly.

EPA or other implementing agencies have general inspection and enforcement authority under CAA sections 112(r)(7)(E), 113, and 114 to compel source owners and operators to correct deficiencies in the risk management program. EPA intends to use the audit process as a way to verify the quality of the program summarized in the RMP. When it is reasonable, EPA will require modifications to the RMP that may lead to quality improvements in the underlying program.

EPA notes that many commenters were uncertain of the distinction among audits conducted under § 68.220, reviews by the permitting authority under § 68.215, and inspections. CAA section 112(r)(7)(B)(iii) requires EPA to develop, by regulation, a system for auditing RMPs. These audits will review the information submitted by sources to determine whether the source is in compliance with the rule elements. For example, the implementing agency will consider whether the dates for reviews and revisions of various elements are consistent with the steps sources are equired to take. If a source reported a major change on a date later than the last date on which safety information and operating procedures were reviewed, the implementing agency would seek further information about why such reviews had not been conducted and require updates if the agency determined that the source should have reviewed the documents. Audits may be detailed paper reviews or may be done at a source to confirm that on-site documentation is consistent with reported information.

In contrast, the air permitting authority or its designated agency may be reviewing the RMP for completeness, rather that the quality of the RMP contents. Inspections are generally more extensive in scope than audits although they may include a review of the accuracy of the RMP information. Inspections will consider whether the source is in compliance with part 68 as a whole, not just with the RMP requirements, and may review both the documentation kept at the source and operating practices.

Regarding comments that making changes to the RMP would be too costly, EPA has endeavored to ameliorate the cost burden of this rule by using a tiering approach to make the risk management program elements on which the RMP rests appropriate for sources of various sizes and complexity. In addition, EPA is considering development of a standard RMP reporting format and data elements, which should significantly reduce the time and effort necessary to revise the RMP. Any source owner or operator can further limit the costs associated with revising its RMP by submitting a timely, complete, and valid plan in the first instance.

N. Public Participation

In the SNPRM, EPA requested comments on how public participation in the risk management program process might be encouraged. EPA's preferred approach was to encourage the public and sources to use existing groups, primarily the LEPC, as a conduit for communications between the source and the public throughout the RMP development process. A substantial number of commenters supported this approach, stating that the LEPC was well placed to interpret the RMP information for the public. Commenters said that LEPCs and their member organizations have considerable experience and have established rapport in dealing with the community. Others stated that this role is a logical extension of current LEPC

responsibilities under EPCRA, although funding for LEPCs was a concern.

A number of commenters opposed this approach because some LEPCs are not functional and that LEPCs are not a substitute for public participation. A few LEPCs also objected to assuming any additional role. Commenters suggested that EPA should require public participation in the development of the RMP and require all major sources to have a public participation strategy. Industry commenters generally opposed any mandated public participation requirements because direct involvement in risk management program development would delay the process and would represent an unwarranted and inappropriate interference in management and site control responsibilities. A few commenters supported the SNPRM suggestion that public participation be limited to sources with Program 3 processes because these sources represent the greatest risk. Other commenters opposed this idea, preferring the decision to be left to local authorities.

EPA has not adopted any specific public participation requirements. EPA plans to make the RMP immediately available to any member of the public. LEPCs and others will be able to compare their sources with similar sources in other areas to determine whether quantities on sites, process controls, mitigation systems, and monitoring systems are significantly different. This information will give the public an opportunity to gain a better understanding of local industries and carry on a more informed dialogue with sources on their prevention practices. EPA continues to encourage sources to work with the LEPCs and other community groups to provide information to the public and ensure an on-going dialogue during and after RMP development and submission. The public is a valuable resource and a key stakeholder in chemical accident prevention, preparedness, and response at the local level.

A number of commenters said that EPA should prohibit the public from triggering an audit through petitions because this approach would open the process to litigation; a petition process would be expensive, time-consuming, and increase the time needed to complete the RMP. Some commenters said it would impose an excessive burden on the implementing agency. Two commenters favored public petitions to trigger audits. One said that the audits should be conducted by qualified third parties, subject to community selection and supervision.

EPA has not included public petitions as a mechanism for periodic audits of sources under § 68.220. States, however, are able to adopt more stringent requirements.

O. Inherently Safer Technologies

In response to the NPRM, a number of commenters stated that EPA should require sources to conduct "technology options analyses" to identify inherently safer technologies. In the SNPRM, EPA solicited comments on this issue, but did not propose a requirement for such analyses.

A number of commenters stated that EPA should require analyses of inherently safer technologies, at least for sources with Program 3 processes or new processes. Some commenters argued that inherent safety is primary prevention (directed at the source of the hazard), while EPA's proposed requirements are secondary prevention (control of the hazard). One commenter asked that sources be required to provide full economic and technical analyses of options. Commenters argued that without a technology options analysis requirement, industry will not conduct these analyses because, unlike its pollution prevention efforts, EPA has provided no incentive for safer plants.

Other commenters strongly opposed any requirement for these analyses because PHA teams regularly suggest viable, effective (and inherently safer) alternatives for risk reduction, which may include features such as inventory reduction, material substitution, and process control changes. These changes are made as opportunities arise, without regulation or adopting of completely new and unproven process technologies. Commenters said that similar analyses are frequently conducted during the design phase of a process or source where there are sufficient economic incentives to design a process with as few costly additional safety features as possible without new EPA requirements. Commenters also said that a requirement would prove costly, without providing commensurate benefits.

EPA has decided not to mandate inherently safer technology analyses. EPA does not believe that a requirement that sources conduct searches or analyses of alternative processing technologies for new or existing processes will produce additional benefits beyond those accruing to the rule already. As many commenters, including those that support such analyses, pointed out, an assessment of inherently safer design alternatives has the most benefit in the development of new processes. Industry generally examines new process alternatives to avoid the addition of more costly administrative or engineering controls to mitigate a design that may be more hazardous in nature. Although some existing processes may be superficially judged to be inherently less safe than other processes, EPA believes these processes can be safely operated through management and control of the hazards without spending resources searching for unavailable or unaffordable new process technologies. Good PHA techniques often reveal opportunities for continuous improvement of existing processes and operations. EPA encourages sources to continue to examine and adopt viable alternative processing technologies, system safeguards, or process modifications to make new and existing processes and operations inherently safer. EPA included questions related to process modifications in the RMP so that sources can demonstrate, and users of the RMP information can observe, progress toward safer processes and operations.

P. Coverage by Other Regulations

A large number of commenters expressed concerns about duplication between the risk management program rule and other Federal and state regulations. Issues related to overlap between this rule and OSHA PSM are discussed in Section III.D of this preamble; issues related to overlap between this rule and other emergency response planning regulations are discussed in Section III.J of this preamble.

1. General Issues. A substantial number of commenters stated that EPA had failed to consider other regulations to which sources are subject that cover some of the same requirements as this rule. They noted that many sources are covered by DOT rules, other EPA rules, OSHA rules, and, in some cases, other agency or state rules. Some commenters argued that these other regulations essentially prevent accidents and, therefore, this rule is not needed. Commenters stated that EPA should define jurisdictional and enforcement boundaries so that sources subject to multiple regulations are not subjected to multiple enforcement actions for the same violation. Other commenters said that EPA should clearly identify which similar requirements imposed by other programs satisfy this rule and what additional steps are needed. Some commenters said that any source covered by another, similar rule should be excluded from this rule. Others suggested that EPA explicitly cross-reference other applicable rules. A few

commenters stated that EPCRA reporting requirements provide ample information to local entities and no further reporting is needed.

EPA disagrees with some of these comments. Except for the OSHA PSM rule, no other rule cited by the commenters addresses accidental releases of regulated substances to the extent that today's rule does. Some Federal and state rules for certain industries provide design standards; compliance with these rules will satisfy parts of today's rule. For example, sources in compliance with 29 CFR 1910.111 for handling of anhydrous ammonia may not need to take additional steps to ensure the safe design of the process. These other standards generally do not cover training, maintenance, hazards analysis, and accident investigation, which are all key elements in process safety management. In addition, none of the Federal rules require offsite consequence analyses or reporting to the public on the results of these analyses and on prevention steps. Information submitted under EPCRA, which consists primarily of annual inventories, is not equivalent to the RMP information.

Nevertheless, EPA agrees with commenters that duplication should be minimized, which is why the emergency response and Program 2 prevention program steps recognize that meeting other requirements will satisfy elements of this rule. The model risk management programs that EPA is developing with industry will explicitly cite other regulations, as well as codes and standards, that satisfy specific elements of this rule.

2. DOT Transportation Regulations. Commenters concerned with overlap with DOT regulations focused on two issues: pipeline regulations, and loading/unloading and storage regulations. Commenters asked EPA to exclude pipelines and transportation containers connected for loading or unloading since these are adequately covered by DOT regulations. Some commenters disagreed and wanted loading and unloading of transportation containers to be included because many accidents occur during these procedures.

In the final List Rule, EPA defined stationary source to include "transportation containers that are no longer under active shipping orders and transportation containers that are connected to equipment at the stationary source for the purposes of temporary storage, loading, or unloading." One commenter stated that the 1993 oleum release in Richmond, California, demonstrated that DOT

regulations do not adequately address risk management of loading and unloading. The other commenters, however, said that loading and unloading were covered by DOT regulations and should not be subject to this rule. They noted that DOT has adopted regulations requiring training for anyone who loads or unloads hazardous materials. They further said that at distribution centers, regulated substances are not used or processed, and, if in packages, the containers are not opened.

Several commenters were concerned that EPA regulation in this area could create problems with DOT's preemption of state rules. Under U.S. law, states may not adopt regulations in certain specified areas that are not substantively the same as DOT rules or in other areas that pose an obstacle to DOT goals under Federal Hazardous Materials Transportation Law. If state laws are authorized by Federal law, however, states could develop different requirements than DOT imposes. In this case, the commenter said, if EPA were to regulate loading and unloading under the CAA, the states would have the authority under the CAA to impose more stringent requirements on this activity.

EPA disagrees with the commenters concerning the scope of the Hazardous Materials Transportation Act preemption authority in this area. EPA's definition of stationary source clearly covers transportation containers only when they are no longer in transportation in commerce and was addressed in the List Rule. EPA believes commenters have overstated the extent of any preemption problem. EPA's interpretation today is consistent with DOT's, as explained in "California and Los Angeles County Requirements Applicable to the On-Site Handling and Transportation of Hazardous Materials—Preemption Determination" (60 FR 8774, 8776–78, February 15, 1995). EPA notes that in many cases warehouses and wholesalers take delivery of materials and resell them; EPA considers this storage to be covered by today's rule. EPA believes that DOT standards for container integrity satisfy process safety information requirements. The same applies to DOT standards for training requirements for loading and unloading; that training satisfies the training requirements of this rule for loading and unloading. Requirements for the PHA only apply to connections to transportation containers and for storage of containers.

3. Other EPA Regulations. Many commenters stated that other EPA regulations cover the same activities and

hould be deferred to or referenced to prevent duplicative requirements and enforcement. A number of commenters said that regulations under the Clean Water Act, specifically the Spill Prevention, Control, and Countermeasure (SPCC) and Oil Pollution Act of 1990 (OPA–90) rules, duplicate many of the provisions of this rule. Other commenters argued the Underground Storage Tank (UST) rules require sources to comply with requirements equivalent to many of the notification, prevention, and emergency response provisions. A few commenters stated that EPCRA already covers the right-to-know provisions; others stated that the risk management program regulations should support existing EPCRA rules. Three commenters said that EPA should exempt any source covered by the Resource Conservation and Recovery Act (RCRA) because the rules under that act already impose comprehensive risk management requirements.

As discussed in Section III.J, emergency response plans developed under SPCC, OPA–90, or RCRA can be used to meet the emergency response requirements of this rule. EPA notes, however, that SPCC, OPA–90, and UST rules do not address storage, handling, and release prevention for regulated substances. SPCC and OPA–90 rules apply to oil; UST rules apply to oil and gasoline. The processes addressed by these rules, therefore, do not overlap with the processes covered by today's rule.

RCRA requirements apply only to certain activities undertaken at sources that may be subject to the requirements of today's final rule. As noted above, EPA anticipates that emergency response plans developed under RCRA can be used to meet the emergency response requirements of this rule. In addition, certain training and other release prevention activities required under RCRA may satisfy certain of the prevention program requirements for Program 2 processes.

4. Other Federal Regulations. A number of commenters stated that EPA should not cover outer continental shelf (OCS) sources because they are adequately regulated under the Marine Mineral Service, Pipeline Safety Act, and OPA–90. The mining industry said that they should not be covered because their handling of explosives is regulated in great detail by the Mine Safety and Health Administration and the Bureau of Alcohol, Tobacco, and Firearms. In its proposed rule (61 FR 16598, April 15, 1996), EPA has proposed to delist explosives and proposed a stay of the affected list provisions; elsewhere in

today's Federal Register, EPA has stayed implementation of the affected provisions until these changes are finalized. OCS sources are not subject to part 68 because the connection between this part and protection of ambient air quality is too remote; therefore, CAA section 328 proscribes EPA's jurisdiction.

5. State and Local Regulations. Commenters sought clarification of how risk management programs implemented under state laws in Delaware, New Jersey, California, and Nevada would be treated. Some commenters said sources complying with these state rules should be grandfathered into EPA's rule for at least five years. California commenters asked that risk management prevention programs (RMPPs) developed and submitted under California's rule be considered in lieu of the required RMP. Some commenters asked that documentation created to meet the state requirements be considered adequate to meet EPA's program so that additional documentation need not be created just to meet slightly different rules. A few commenters suggested that EPA should explicitly preempt any state risk management program regulations that are not submitted to and approved by EPA. Other states said that EPA should defer to state rules on hydrogen sulfide and propane.

None of the four state risk management program rules is identical to EPA's or each other. The Delaware, New Jersey, and Nevada programs closely parallel the OSHA PSM rule; the California program is less specific. EPA expects that sources in compliance with these state programs will have completed most of the steps required under EPA's rule. EPA notes that these sources are generally also covered by OSHA PSM and, therefore, should be in compliance with a significant portion of EPA's rule.

In relation to the request for grandfathering, EPA does not have the authority to grandfather compliance with programs that the Agency has not reviewed and approved. EPA expects that these four states will seek delegation of the 112(r) program under CAA section 112(l). At that time, EPA will review the state programs and approve them if they are as stringent as EPA's rule and meet other section 112(l) requirements. If states are granted delegation, they will have the authority to grandfather previous compliance. Because the CAA specifically grants states the right to impose more stringent regulations, EPA cannot preempt state programs as one commenter requested.

EPA believes that substitution of the RMPP for the RMP for California sources is not feasible. The California RMPPs are voluminous documents, submitted per process, not per source. These documents could not be submitted electronically. Because EPA is concentrating on submission of data elements, EPA believes that its RMP requirements can be met quickly by any source that has completed an RMPP. Completion of the RMP will not impose a large burden on sources. If the RMPP has summary sections, these may be directly transferable for use as the executive summary.

In regard to other state laws, states may include them as part of their CAA section 112(l) submission for EPA's review and approval. These laws, however, must be as stringent as EPA's; that is, they must cover all elements of the rule with requirements that at least match EPA's. EPA notes that state propane laws are generally based on NFPA–58, which EPA is using to help develop its model risk management program for propane distributors and users. Therefore, sources in compliance with NFPA–58 requirements may meet many of the requirements of Program 2, as defined in the model.

Q. Industry-Specific Issues

A number of industries submitted comments on issues that were particular to them, in many cases seeking exemption from the rule.

1. Oil and Gas Facilities. Industry commenters argued that components of the oil and gas industries should be excluded from EPA's risk management program; in particular, that EPA should exempt the following operations and facilities from RMP requirements:

• Atmospheric storage and transfer of flammable liquids;
• Retail facilities;
• Marketing terminals and bulk plants;
• Remote, low-risk petroleum operations;
• Oil and gas exploration, production and processing facilities;
• Crude oil separation, handling, and storage operations;
• Subsurface hydrocarbon reservoirs;
• All transportation and facilities incident to transportation; and
• Outer continental shelf facilities.

Commenters noted that these industries and facilities pose a low risk to the public for a number of reasons. Significant accidental releases are highly unlikely because these facilities handle materials which, given site conditions, have limited potential for release to the air or offsite impacts. Existing regulations reduce the potential for significant accidental releases. Additionally, commenters argued that the RMP provisions extend beyond EPA's statutory authority and run counter to the Domestic Natural Gas and Oil Initiative established by President Clinton.

Commenters stated that most of the exploration and production facilities are remotely located and argued that even the tiering approach that EPA proposed in the SNPRM did not provide adequate relief for these sources, which pose minimal risks. They noted that OSHA specifically excludes remotely located sources, retail facilities, DOT-regulated sources, and atmospheric storage tanks. A number of commenters said that EPA had never included most of these sources in its economic analysis, implying that EPA did not intend to cover them in these regulations; they requested an explicit statement to that effect. One commenter opposed an exemption for oil and gas sources and pipeline and other transportation companies, arguing that these sources have some of the most common or worst accidents.

EPA does not agree that marketing terminals or bulk plants should be excluded if there are regulated substances present above their threshold quantities. Although EPA did not specifically exempt gasoline and naturally occurring hydrocarbons (e.g., crude oil), it did not intend to cover regulated flammables in these mixtures. In its proposed rule (61 FR 16598, April 15, 1996), EPA has proposed to revise the criteria for flammable mixtures and to exclude naturally occurring hydrocarbons prior to processing at a gas processing plant or refinery. Flammable mixtures would be covered only if they met all of the NFPA–4 criteria. Gasoline and crude oil are listed with NFPA 3 flammability ratings in NFPA 325 M, Fire Hazard Properties of Flammable Liquids, Gases, and Volatile Solids, 1991. Elsewhere in today's Federal Register, EPA has stayed implementation of the risk management program rule for substances and processes that would be affected by the proposed changes. As EPA explained in the preamble to the final list rule, the Agency has not adopted OSHA's exemption for atmospheric storage of flammables because, unlike OSHA, EPA has listed only flammable gases and highly volatile flammable liquids. EPA considers these substances to be intrinsically hazardous, regardless of storage conditions and, therefore, does not believe it is appropriate to provide an exemption for such tanks.

2. Retail Facilities. The rule is expected to cover a substantial number of retail facilities, specifically those handling propane and ammonia as a fertilizer. Approximately 100 commenters requested that EPA exempt propane retailers from coverage under the risk management program, primarily due to the effectiveness of the existing regulatory structure for the industry (in particular, NFPA Standard 58). At the same time, more than 50 commenters requested that EPA exempt agricultural chemical retailers (with inventories of ammonia fertilizer) from coverage under the risk management program because of the existing state and Federal regulation of these operations.

a. Propane Retailers. Commenters argued that the primary thrust of the proposed regulations is to preclude unwarranted risk to the surrounding community from an accidental failure of a storage tank. They stated that the basic purpose of NFPA 58, the Storage and Handling of Liquefied Petroleum Gases, is to prevent such releases through design and engineering. This standard requires fire safety analyses, distance separation between the storage tank and surrounding exposures, and approval of plans for new or existing facilities by local authorities. They noted that NFPA 58 has been adopted as state law in 48 of the 50 states and that the two remaining states (California and Texas) have similar rules. They said that propane storage containers are manufactured strictly to the specifications of the American Society of Mechanical Engineers. According to commenters, emergency response planning is already covered by NFPA–58, OSHA, and DOT. Because of compliance with this standard and state law, commenters argued that the rule would not provide any improvement in safety. A number of commenters argued that propane was a heating fuel, not a chemical, and did not pose the same level of risk as larger quantities of propane held and used as a chemical feedstock. One commenter noted that OSHA had exempted retailers and propane when used as a fuel.

In contrast, one state, which also regulates propane under its state risk management program law, argued that propane is not sufficiently regulated. It stated:

Fire authorities inspect each new facility before propane is introduced. They concentrate on adequate fire water supply, electrical code compliance, and distance separation requirements. Some fire authorities are not technically capable of determining if the facility piping system complies with NFPA 58. There are no follow-up inspections to

assure continuing compliance and no requirements under NFPA 58 for training distribution plant operators or mechanics, written maintenance programs, or procedures to control change. During our inspections, we have identified some facilities that were not in conformance with NFPA 58.

EPA does not agree with commenters who are seeking exemption of propane retailers and users. In a supplemental notice, EPA sought comment on whether flammable substances, when used as a fuel, posed a lesser intrinsic hazard than the same substances handled otherwise; no data were submitted to EPA to justify this position. Further, EPA has considerable accident data for propane that illustrate its potential to affect the public located nearby. As a result, EPA continues to believe that the hazard posed by propane is inherent and does not vary with its use. Because of a lack of data justifying a different level of hazard for flammables used as fuel, the Agency will not adopt a fuel use exemption similar to that provided by OSHA.

Furthermore, EPA notes that many propane retailers are relatively close to other commercial buildings and the community. Should a fire or explosion occur, the community could be substantially impacted. EPA believes the community and sources need to be aware of the potential risk and understand the steps the source is taking to limit the potential for a release. Because EPA recognizes that the full PSM standard is not appropriate for propane retailers, EPA has assigned propane retailers and users to Program 2. Compliance with most aspects of Program 2 should be simple. For example, use of tanks that meet relevant ASME standards and retention of the material safety data sheets required by OSHA will satisfy the safety information requirements of § 68.48. Furthermore, EPA is developing a model risk management program to help sources comply. This model is being based on NFPA–58 standards, where they apply, so that sources already in compliance with NFPA–58 will be in substantial compliance with Program 2. The model will help sources comply with other elements in a cost-effective manner.

b. Ammonia Retailers. Ammonia is sold as a fertilizer from agricultural retailers, primarily in the Middle West, Great Plains, and West. Commenters stated that the retail fertilizer industry is already governed by OSHA's Health and Safety Standards, which are specifically applicable to the storage and handling of anhydrous ammonia. They noted that this standard (29 CFR 1910.111) is based on ANSI K61.1 and sets forth extensive quirements applicable to the design, nstruction, location, installation, and peration of anhydrous ammonia cilities. Measures designed to dequately provide for the prevention of d response to accidental releases are integral part of this standard. Some mmenters said that if EPA did not empt retail sources, ammonia retailers ould be deemed to be in compliance ith the prevention program. In dition, commenters said they are gulated under state laws and are bject to EPCRA reporting quirements. Many commenters argued at retail fertilizer sources have an cellent safety record. They stated that tail fertilizer facilities are limited in ze, do not involve complex processing d manufacturing operations, and are cated in rural areas; consequently, ey present a low risk to the rrounding communities. Commenters jected to the regulations because they ould impose a substantial burden on hat are small operations. Some mmenters argued that, because ngress had granted EPA the authority exempt ammonia when held by a rmer for use as a fertilizer, EPA could ant retail ammonia sources the same emption.

Although EPA recognizes that other gulatory programs address safety for ricultural retailers and that such perations do not involve complex rocessing or manufacturing, EPA sagrees with the conclusions of these mmenters. According to the industry, e typical ammonia retailer has 200 ns of ammonia on site at times. Even rural areas, release of even a fraction this quantity could affect the mmunity. Sources constructed and perated consistent with the relevant NSI standard will meet the EPA rule r subjects addressed by both. EPA cognizes the OSHA standard for hydrous ammonia handling and opes to work with the ammonia dustry to develop a model risk anagement program for ammonia tailers. This model would be based on e OSHA standard, where applicable. he standard, however, does not clude some elements mandated by the AA as part of the prevention program, ecifically training and maintenance rograms. In addition, EPA believes that ere is a further need to convey formation on hazards and risk anagement practices of these perations to the public and local ntities. The model will provide uidance to help sources comply with ese elements in a cost-effective anner. Finally, EPA does not agree at the Congressionally allowed

exemption of farmers can be extended to non-farmers. See 136 Cong. Rec. S2284 (March 7, 1990) (colloquy between Sens. Kerrey and Chafee).

3. Refrigeration Systems. A number of commenters stated that ammonia used in a refrigeration system should be exempted from this rule because these systems pose little risk to the public. One commenter said that EPA should exempt roof-mounted air handlers, pipes, and components. Some commenters said that the industry was already overregulated and the imposition of this rule would be a burden.

The CAA requires EPA to impose this rule on any source with more than a threshold quantity of a regulated substance. Therefore, EPA cannot exempt ammonia refrigeration systems that contain more than 10,000 pounds of ammonia. In addition, ammonia refrigeration plants have had a substantial number of accidents where the ammonia has migrated offsite, indicating that these systems do pose a risk to the public. At the same time, it should be noted that all of these refrigeration systems are already covered by the OSHA PSM standard. Consequently, the only additional steps sources will have to take are to conduct the hazard assessment, comply with the emergency response requirements, and file the RMP. EPA worked with the International Institute of Ammonia Refrigeration to develop a model risk management program that will facilitate compliance and reduce the burden on sources (Model Risk Management Program for Ammonia Refrigeration). For most of these sources, which have only one chemical, the RMP will be a very brief document.

4. Other Operations. Comments were submitted on a range of other industries.

The warehouse industry said that it should be exempted where material is received and shipped in packages that are not opened; commenters noted that they are covered by DOT packaging regulations. EPA believes that warehouses must be covered if they have more than a threshold quantity of a regulated substance. Under the OSHA definition of process, which EPA has adopted, packages of a substance stored in the same room may be counted toward the threshold quantity if the packages could release their contents in the same event. EPA notes that warehouse fires have created major incidents in the past 10 years, and the Agency believes that warehouses should take the steps necessary to prevent and mitigate such incidents. EPA is interested in working with the industry to create a model risk management

program that would help sources develop a hazard assessment process that can account for potentially changing contents of a warehouse.

Batch processors face related problems with changing chemicals on site. EPA is willing to work with industry to develop a generic approach to risk management programs. EPA believes, however, that most batch processors will already be covered by OSHA PSM. The RMP Offsite Consequence Analyses Guidance will reduce the burden of developing multiple release scenario analyses. To minimize the need for continual revision of their worst-case scenario to accommodate periodic inventory changes, sources such as warehouses and batch processors may want to analyze their expected chemical inventory in developing a scenario that represents the worst case for the foreseeable future, even if the substance is not currently in use at the source.

A number of commenters raised questions about coverage of POTWs. A specific concern was EPA's statement in the NPRM that substances in waste streams would not be covered by the rule. This statement is based on the belief that the regulated toxic substances will not constitute more than one percent of any waste stream received by a POTW. Consequently, they will not be considered in calculations of threshold quantities. No waste stream is likely to meet EPA's flammability criteria. POTWs are likely, however, to be covered because of regulated substances they use to treat wastes.

R. Implementing Agency Delegation

EPA received a number of comments to the NPRM regarding the role and potential burden on LEPCs, SERCs, and other local agencies that may result from implementation of the risk management program. In the SNPRM preamble, EPA indicated that EPA and the states share the responsibility for protecting public health and the environment and encouraged state and local agencies to seek delegation for this program because their participation is essential to successful chemical accident prevention, preparedness and response and recognized by the legislative history and the CAA section 112(r) requirements by requiring that RMPs be submitted to states and local planning entities. States are already involved in chemical emergency preparedness and planning through the requirements of EPCRA.

Commenters on the SNPRM requested that the final rule clearly state that EPA is the implementing agency unless a state or local agency is granted a delegation of authority under section 112(l). Several commenters indicated that EPA should allow states the flexibility to designate the most appropriate implementing agency, such as OSHA or the state agency that administers and enforces the OSHA PSM standard, rather than mandating the air permitting authority or a SERC agency in the final rule. A number of commenters on the SNPRM and NPRM suggested that existing local emergency planning agencies (e.g., LEPCs, fire departments) would be best suited to serve as implementing agencies, in part because they are closest to the communities at risk. However, many commenters (including LEPCs that commented) argued that LEPCs would be unprepared to take on such a burden and that even a minimal role in implementing section 112(r), including mere storage of RMPs, would overwhelm their limited resources and technical expertise. In addition, commenters indicated that LEPCs, as mostly volunteer agencies, would not and could not have the authority necessary to implement and enforce the RMP rule.

The implementing agency is the state or local agency that obtains delegation of the section 112(r) program under section 112(l). As stated in the definition of Implementing Agency in today's rule, until a state or local agency is granted delegation of the risk management program under CAA section 112(l), EPA will serve as the implementing agency. States may select any state or local agency to implement this program, including an air permitting authority or a state OSHA program, provided the agency has the expertise, legal authority and resources to implement the program; the state must also have the authority to enforce the program. EPA realizes that, in most cases, LEPCs will not have the authority to be implementing agencies, but they should be involved as much as possible in the program.

Commenters on the SNPRM suggested that EPA should avoid adding specific implementation details to the final rule so that states would have the flexibility to develop or continue programs that meet local needs. Other commenters, however, suggested that EPA should issue delegation guidance and to define the elements of an adequate state program to avoid inconsistent interpretations and implementation of the rule. Commenters representing companies that operate in several states were particularly concerned about maintaining uniform implementation.

EPA has not added specific state or local implementation requirements to today's rule because the Agency already promulgated sufficient provisions for delegation of accident prevention programs under section 112(r) to states and local authorities under 40 CFR part 63, subpart E, which implements CAA § 112(l). As EPA discussed in the SNPRM, implementing agencies will be responsible for such tasks as reviewing RMP information, auditing and inspecting a percentage of sources annually, requiring revisions to the RMP as necessary, and assisting the permitting authority in ensuring compliance. States have the flexibility to implement their own programs, however the CAA requires that state or local program requirements must be as stringent as EPA's and must include EPA regulated substances and processes. This means that California, Delaware, Nevada, and New Jersey will need to revise their existing program requirements, substance lists, and in some cases, thresholds, to meet EPA's requirements and to obtain section 112(r) delegation. EPA intends to issue additional guidance that will help state and local agencies obtain program delegation. EPA must review delegation requests submitted under 40 CFR part 63, subpart E to ensure that state and local programs requirements are as stringent as EPA's. With respect to nationwide uniform implementation, EPA notes that the CAA specifically grants states the right to develop more stringent requirements; consequently, there may be state-to-state variations. Many states, however, are prohibited under their state laws from adopting regulations that are more stringent than Federal rules.

One commenter on the NPRM indicated that EPA's estimation of the costs of implementing the section 112(r) program is extremely low, representing demands that are 65 to 75 percent lower than those experienced by states implementing similar programs. LEPCs and state governments were concerned about the imposition of section 112(r) requirements on state and local governments as an unfunded mandate. Several state agencies indicated that the considerable financial burden imposed by section 112(r) implementation would prohibit them from seeking section 112(l) delegation. Commenters encouraged EPA to develop guidance on potential funding mechanisms, including descriptions of the fee systems used by existing state programs for accidental release prevention. Several commenters indicated that the political climate at the state and local level would make it impossible to levy new, or raise existing, fees.

Since states are not required to seek delegation of this program, it does not constitute an unfunded mandate (see also section V.C). Before EPA grants delegation, state or local agencies must show that they have the resources to implement and enforce the risk management program rules. EPA recognizes that there is no Federal funding associated with implementation of section 112(r) but believes that the tiered program levels and centralized electronic submission of RMPs in today's rule substantially reduces the cost and resource demand for state and local entities seeking delegation. State and local agencies that fully implement section 112(r) will be able to develop and operate a program that best fits their individual needs, resources, and structures. As part of consideration of the costs to implement section 112(r), state and local agencies should also weigh the benefits of integrating accident prevention with pollution prevention, environmental protection, and worker and public health and safety at the state level, and the benefits to local industry associated with state, rather than Federal, implementation of this program. Many states and local agencies have established a close working relationship with the sources in their jurisdiction. In addition, a number of state and local publicly owned sources are covered by this rule; state implementation can serve to enhance compliance that may otherwise require increased coordination with EPA. Although other states have successfully "self-funded" their accident prevention programs with various state authorized fees, EPA recognizes that it may be difficult for state or local agencies to generate the resources necessary to fund full section 112(r) implementation.

Several commenters on the SNPRM requested guidance and training for sources, local entities, and implementing agencies on understanding hazard assessments, and conducting program inspections, reviews, and audits. EPA recognizes the need for guidance and training for implementing agencies and sources. EPA plans to modify and to continue offering its four-day Chemical Safety Audit workshop to other federal agency representatives, state and local government officials, and industry representatives as an introduction to chemical process safety, current industry chemical accident prevention practices and understanding the elements of the risk management program. EPA is ready to assist state and local agencies through its regional offices to coordinate state and local rograms and to help in obtaining program delegation and development of resources to fund state or local programs. Region 4 in Atlanta, Georgia, for example, has developed an integrated section 112(r) work group of state and local air pollution control, ERC, and LEPC representatives who participate in workshops, seminars, and pilot studies designed to foster local program implementation and to build a support network. EPA also continues to work with NOAA to enhance modeling and information management tools contained in the Computer Aided Management of Emergency Operations (CAMEO) and Areal Locations of Hazardous Atmospheres (ALOHA) software for local emergency planners and responders.

Two commenters on the NPRM requested that EPA address the issue of tort liability in the event that an accidental release occurs after an RMP has been submitted to the implementing agency. One other commenter believed that the implementing agency must be held accountable for RMP content while another believed that EPA must ensure that adequate limits to implementing agency liability exist.

The primary responsibility for accident prevention rests with the owners or operators of sources. Section 112(r) does not create a basis for implementing agency tort liability under federal law. CAA § 112(r)(1). When EPA is the implementing agency, it is immune from tort liability under state law. States that are implementing agencies generally will have protection from liability under their state laws. If a state has waived its sovereign immunity, EPA cannot take steps to alter that situation. EPA encourages states concerned about this issue to discuss the matter with their attorneys general to determine whether state law protects them from liability.

. Accident Information Reporting

In the SNPRM, EPA discussed the possibility of additional accident reporting to support a variety of future accident prevention activities. EPA proposed that sources either submit an OSHA PSM or Program 3 investigation report for certain accidental releases or a survey form that collects certain accident data. Otherwise EPA could use existing authorities to collect additional accident data from existing information, as needed.

Most commenters opposed EPA's proposal for additional accident reporting requirements, especially the collection of accident investigations prepared under Program 3 or OSHA PSM, because it increases costs, it

would have no benefit, it generates significant liability issues, and it would divert limited resources away from activities with greater public health benefit. Commenters supported the use of existing reports since this approach should not generate an additional burden, such reports are available through EPA and OSHA under other regulations and they should be adequate for the objectives outlined by EPA.

EPA agrees with commenters and has decided not to adopt any additional accident reporting requirements. EPA will rely on the five-year accident history for the immediate future and, based on that information, determine whether additional information and requirements are needed. EPA has the authority under CAA section 114 to investigate releases and seek additional information as needed.

T. Other Issues

1. OSHA VPP. In the SNPRM, EPA asked whether the OSHA Voluntary Protection Program (VPP) protects public health and the environment and suggested that one approach to third party review (discussed below) would be to assign sources that participate in VPP to Program 2. Many commenters supported VPP participation as a criterion for assigning a source to Program 2. Several of these commenters noted, however, that because VPP sources are probably already covered by OSHA PSM, assigning them to Program 2 would provide no reduction in burden or regulatory relief. One commenter suggested that EPA could allow VPP sources the flexibility to determine, with the LEPC, what the offsite consequence analysis would cover. Seven commenters opposed VPP participation as a Program 2 criterion because VPP does not address offsite consequences, no evidence was presented that PSM is being carried out adequately at VPP sources, and this approach would discriminate against other voluntary programs.

After consideration of the comments, EPA has decided not to use VPP participation as a Program 2 criterion, but has adopted language in the final rule to exempt sources with a Star or Merit ranking under OSHA's VPP from selection for audits based on the criteria in § 68.220 (b)(2) and (b)(7); such a source may be audited if it has an accidental release that requires an accident investigation under these regulations. This decision recognizes that such sources have active accident prevention programs and should not be regarded in the same way as other sources within the same industry or as other sources in general. In addition, it

thus provides a similar degree of benefit with respect to EPA auditing as it does with respect to OSHA auditing. EPA agrees that VPP sources would gain no benefit by assignment to Program 2. EPA does not believe it is appropriate to adjust the hazard assessment requirements for VPP sources; this information is essential to local emergency preparedness and response and for public dialogue.

2. Qualified Third Party. In the SNPRM, EPA sought comments on whether sources should be allowed to have qualified third parties assist them in achieving and maintaining compliance. Eight commenters supported third party reviews as a way to reduce implementing agency efforts. One commenter stated that sources should be required to hire a qualified third party to assess their activities. Most commenters, however, expressed some reservations including greater cost if sources were required to hire third parties, when many sources already have staff qualified to implement the risk management program. Commenters said that a third party review would be particularly costly for retailers who will have model programs and stated that use of third parties would add another layer of bureaucracy to the process. A number of commenters said that EPA should fund third parties. Commenters also stated that use of third parties might confuse the issue of who was responsible for safety and for enforcement; they said that EPA must make it clear that the owner or operator of the source remains responsible for accidents and that the implementing agency retains enforcement authority. Finally, several commenters asked who would determine the qualifications of a qualified third party.

EPA is not requiring use of qualified third parties in this rule. EPA, however, endorses the concept of offering sources the option of using third parties to assist owner/operators in meeting their obligations under the rule. Based on the comments, EPA recognizes that any third party proposal must:

• Not weaken the compliance responsibilities of source owner/operators;

• Offer cost savings and benefits to the industry, community, and implementing agencies that significantly exceed the cost of implementing the qualified third party approach;

• Lead to a net increase in process safety, particularly for smaller, less technically sophisticated sources; and

• Promote cost-effective agency prioritization of implementing agency oversight resources.

Several key issues need further discussion before the use of a qualified third party may be offered as an option. These include qualification criteria, certification procedures, liability, and other critical issues associated with the use of a qualified third party. Therefore, following promulgation of this rule, EPA proposes to call a meeting to solicit input from trade associations, professional and technical societies, states, and other interested parties to address these issues and investigate the need for developing a process and a national exam to qualify third parties.

3. Documentation. Commenters expressed a number of concerns about the level of recordkeeping and the availability of information. Some commenters stated that records need to be maintained for longer than five years; commenters suggested 10 years, 20 years, and the life of the source. One commenter suggested that records should be kept for the life of the process and then seven years thereafter to ensure that records would be available if a lawsuit was initiated. Industry commenters said that only current documents and data should be maintained to prevent confusion from having multiple versions of the same document. One commenter stated that policies and procedures should be kept until they are superseded, then they should be destroyed; retaining old, superseded information is unsafe and unacceptable and can result in accidents.

One commenter said that sources should be required to develop and maintain a master index or catalogue of documents relevant to the proposed rule to support public access. Another commenter stated that, in addition to

maintaining records supporting the implementation of the risk management program, the owner or operator should submit the records to the implementing agency. A third commenter said that the rule should require that all records supporting compliance with the rule be organized and readily available through the designated contact person at the source to the implementing agency for inspection.

Other commenters said the proposed recordkeeping was excessive. One stated that EPA is forcing industries towards "defensive universal recordkeeping," retaining mountains of documents because EPA has not specified what records need to be kept. Another commenter said that an examination of the proposal indicated that no fewer than about 22 separate written documents are required to be maintained on site or submitted to the responsible regulatory agency and other parties. One commenter noted that more resources will be spent on filling out paperwork than on actual spill prevention.

In the final rule, EPA has adopted the OSHA PSM language for Program 3 processes; therefore, documentation for PSM elements is dictated by that rule. For other elements of the risk management program and for processes in other tiers, EPA has set a period of five years for the maintenance of supporting documentation. EPA agrees with commenters that only current versions of documents and procedures should be retained. On the issue of records submitted to the implementing agency, EPA believes that the provisions outlined in the final rule (as described in Subpart G to part 68) will limit the volume of such documentation. The

implementing agency and EPA will have access to all on-site documentation when needed. Much of the on-site documentation will be confidential and protected under Section 114(c) of the CAA. The burden on the implementing agency will be substantially reduced because it will not have to establish protected trade secret files and procedures.

Finally, EPA agrees with commenters that level of recordkeeping should be kept as low as possible consistent with EPA's statutory mandate. EPA has reduced the documentation requirements for Program 2 processes (particularly with respect to the prevention program) because it believes that for these sources, the benefit of the records does not offset the cost of creating and maintaining files.

IV. Section-by-Section Analysis of the Rule

This section discusses specific changes to the rule that are not otherwise described in this preamble. The rule has been renumbered to include new sections and subparts. The hazard assessment requirements have been divided into separate sections in subpart B. The Program 2 prevention program requirements are in subpart C; Program 3 prevention program elements are in Subpart D. Emergency response requirements are in subpart E, RMP requirements in subpart G. The registration requirement, proposed § 68.12, has been moved to the RMP subpart. Tables 3 and 4 present the distribution of NPRM and SNPRM sections and derivation of final rule sections.

TABLE 3.—DISTRIBUTION TABLE

NPRM and SNPRM citations	Final rule citations
68.3 Definitions	68.3 Definitions.
68.10 Applicability	68.10 Applicability.
68.12 Registration	68.160 Registration.
68.13 No Impact Sources (Tier 1)	68.10(b) Applicability.
	68.12(b) General Requirements.
68.14 Streamlined Risk Management Program (Tier 2)	Subpart C Program 2 Prevention Program (68.48–68.60).
68.15 Hazard Assessment	Subpart B Hazard Assessment (68.20–68.42).
68.20 Prevention Program—Purpose	Deleted.
68.22 Prevention Program—Management System	68.15 Management.
68.24 Prevention Program—Process Hazard Analysis	68.67 Process Hazard Analysis.
68.26 Prevention Program—Process Safety	68.65 Process Safety Information.
68.28 Prevention Program—Standard Operating Procedures	68.69 Operating Procedures.
68.30 Prevention Program—Training	68.71 Training.
68.32 Prevention Program—Maintenance (mechanical integrity)	68.73 Mechanical Integrity.
68.34 Prevention Program—Pre-Startup Review	68.77 Pre-Startup Review.
68.36 Prevention Program—Management of Change	68.75 Management of Change.
68.38 Prevention Program—Safety Audits	68.58 Compliance Audits.
	68.79 Compliance Audits.
68.40 Prevention Program—Accident Investigation	68.60 Incident Investigation.
	68.81 Incident Investigation.
68.45 Emergency Response Program	68.95 Emergency Response Program.

TABLE 3.—DISTRIBUTION TABLE—Continued

NPRM and SNPRM citations	Final rule citations
3.50 Risk Management Plan	Subpart G Risk Management Plan (68.150–68.190).
3.55 Recordkeeping Requirements	68.200 Recordkeeping.
3.58 Permit Content and Air Permitting Authority Requirements	68.215 Permit Content and Air Permitting Authority or Designated Agency Requirements.
3.60 Audits	68.220 Audits.

TABLE 4.—DERIVATION TABLE

Final rule citations	NPRM and SNPRM citations
3.3 Definitions	68.3 Definitions.
3.10 Applicability	68.10 Applicability, SNPRM 68.13.
3.12 General Requirements	SNPRM 68.13, 68.14.
3.15 Management	68.22 Prevention Program—Management.
3.20 Applicability (Hazard Assessment)	68.10 Applicability.
3.22 Offsite Consequence Analysis Parameters (Hazard Assessment).	68.15(e) Hazard Assessment.
3.25 Worst-Case Release Analysis (Hazard Assessment)	68.15(c) Hazard Assessment.
3.28 Alternative Release Analysis (Hazard Assessment)	68.15(d) Hazard Assessment.
3.30 Defining Offsite Impacts—Population (Hazard Assessment)	68.15(e)(3) Hazard Assessment.
3.33 Defining Offsite Impacts—Environment (Hazard Assessment)	68.15(e)(4) Hazard Assessment.
3.36 Review and Update (Hazard Assessment)	68.15(g) Hazard Assessment.
3.39 Documentation (Hazard Assessment)	68.15(h) Hazard Assessment.
3.42 Five-year Accident History (Hazard Assessment)	68.15(f) Hazard Assessment.
3.48 Safety Information (Program 2)	68.14(b) Streamlined Risk Management Program (Tier 2); 68.26 Process Safety Information.
3.50 Hazard Review (Program 2)	68.14(b) Streamlined Risk Management Program (Tier 2); 68.24 PHA.
3.52 Operating Procedures (Program 2)	68.14(b) Streamlined Risk Management Program (Tier 2); 68.28 SOPs.
3.54 Training (Program 2)	68.14(b) Streamlined Risk Management Program (Tier 2); 68.30 Training.
3.56 Maintenance (Program 2)	68.14(b) Streamlined Risk Management Program (Tier 2); 68.32 Maintenance.
3.58 Compliance Audits (Program 2)	68.38 Prevention Program—Safety Audits.
3.60 Incident Investigation (Program 2)	68.40 Prevention Program—Incident Investigation.
3.65 Process Safety Information (Program 3)	68.26 Prevention Program—Process Safety.
3.67 Process Hazard Analysis (Program 3)	68.24 Prevention Program—Process Hazard Analysis.
3.69 Operating Procedures (Program 3)	68.28 Prevention Program—Standard Operating Procedures.
3.71 Training (Program 3)	68.30 Prevention Program—Training.
3.73 Mechanical Integrity (Program 3)	68.32 Prevention Program—Maintenance (mechanical integrity).
3.75 Management of Change (Program 3)	68.36 Prevention Program—Management of Change.
3.77 Pre-Startup Review (Program 3)	68.34 Prevention Program—Pre-Startup Review.
3.79 Compliance Audits (Program 3)	68.38 Prevention Program—Safety Audits.
3.81 Accident Investigation (Program 3)	68.40 Prevention Program—Accident Investigation.
3.83 Employee Participation (Program 3)	68.24(f) Process Hazard Analysis.
3.85 Hot Work Permit (Program 3)	NPRM Preamble (58 FR 54205).
3.87 Contractors (Program 3)	NPRM Preamble (58 FR 54205).
3.90 Applicability (Emergency Response)	68.45(a) Emergency Response Program.
3.95 Emergency Response Program	68.45(b)–(f) Emergency Response Program.
3.150 Submission (Risk Management Plan)	68.50(a) Risk Management Plan.
3.155 Executive Summary (Risk Management Plan)	68.50(a) Risk Management Plan.
3.160 Registration (Risk Management Plan)	68.12 Registration.
3.165 Offsite Consequence Analysis (Risk Management Plan)	68.50(c) Risk Management Plan.
3.168 Five-Year Accident History (Risk Management Plan)	68.15(f) Hazard Assessment.
3.170 Prevention Program/Program 2 (Risk Management Plan)	68.14(b) Streamlined Risk Management Program (Tier 2); 68.50(g).
3.175 Prevention Program/Program 3 (Risk Management Plan)	68.50(g) Risk Management Plan.
3.180 Emergency Response Program (Risk Management Plan)	68.50(e) Risk Management Plan.
3.185 Certification (Risk Management Plan)	68.50(g) Risk Management Plan. 68.13(a) No Impact Sources.
3.190 Updates (Risk Management Plan)	68.50(h) Risk Management Plan.
3.200 Recordkeeping	68.55 Recordkeeping Requirements.
3.210 Availability of Information to the Public	42 U.S.C. 7412.
3.215 Permit Content and Air Permitting Authority or Designated Agency Requirements.	68.58 Permit Content and Air Permitting Authority Requirements.
3.220 Audits	68.60 Audits.
Appendix A—Table of Toxic Endpoints	68.15(h)(3)(iii) Hazard Assessment.

Section 68.3, Definitions, has been revised to add or delete a number of definitions. A definition of administrative controls has been added that is derived from the definition used

by the Center for Chemical Process Safety (CCPS).

The definition of analysis of offsite consequences has been deleted.

A definition of catastrophic release has been added that is adapted from OSHA's definition of catastrophic release (29 CFR 1910.119); OSHA's language on danger to employees in the workplace has been changed to imminent and substantial endangerment to public health and the environment.

A definition of classified information has been added. The definition is adopted from the Classified Information Procedures Act.

The proposed definition of covered process is unchanged.

The proposed definition of designated agency has been revised to indicate that the state, not the state air permitting authority, shall select an agency to conduct activities required by § 68.215.

As discussed above, a definition of environmental receptor has been added to list the receptors of concern.

The definition of full-time employee has been deleted.

A definition of hot work has been adopted verbatim from the OSHA PSM standard.

The definition of implementing agency is adopted as proposed in the SNPRM.

A definition of injury has been added.

A definition of major change has been added to clarify the types of changes that necessitate actions to manage change. The definition will help sources understand when they are required to take steps to review their activities for new hazards.

A definition of mechanical integrity has been added to clarify the requirements of maintenance sections.

A definition of medical treatment has been added to clarify what constitutes an injury. The definition is adapted from an OSHA definition used by sources in logging occupational injuries and illnesses.

The proposed definition of mitigation has been changed by adding a definition of active mitigation.

A definition of offsite has been changed to clarify that areas within the source would be considered offsite if the public has routine and unrestricted access during or outside of business hours. Areas within a source's boundaries that may be considered offsite are public roads that pass through sections of the site and natural areas owned by the source to which the public has unrestricted access. For some sites, parking lots within the boundary may be offsite if the source cannot restrict access.

A definition of population has been added. Population is defined as the public.

A definition of public has been added to state that all persons except employees and contractors at the stationary source are members of the public. A number of commenters stated that employees at other facilities should not be considered part of the public. EPA disagrees because these employees may not be trained in protective actions or have protective equipment appropriate for releases from covered processes.

A definition of public receptor has been added. Some commenters stated that EPA should include public roads within this definition. EPA decided that inclusion of public roads was unwarranted. EPA recognizes that people on public roads may be exposed during a release. In most cases, however, vehicles on public roads will be able to leave the area quickly and further access can be blocked, especially in isolated areas. If public roads were included, almost no sources would be eligible for Program 1 because there will be public roads leading to the source. In those cases where public roads are heavily traveled, there will be other public receptors near the source and, therefore, the source's processes will not qualify for Program 1.

OSHA's definition of replacement in kind has been adopted.

The definition of significant accidental release has been deleted.

A definition of typical meteorological conditions has been added which means the temperature, wind speed, cloud cover, and atmospheric stability class prevailing at the source. Data on the first three of these are available from local meteorological stations (e.g., airports). Atmospheric stability class can be derived from cloud cover data.

The definition of worst-case release has been revised to clarify that the release is the one that leads to the greatest distance to the applicable endpoint.

Section 68.10, Applicability, has been revised to change the term "tier" to "Program." The section now details the eligibility criteria for all three programs. Paragraph (a) has been revised to be consistent with statutory language on compliance dates. Sources must comply with the requirements by June 21, 1999, three years after EPA first lists a substance, or the date on which a source first becomes subject to this part, whichever is latest. After June 21, 1999, sources that begin using a regulated substance that has been listed for at least three years must be in compliance with the requirements of part 68 on the

day they bring the substance on site above a threshold quantity.

The Program 1 eligibility requirements have been revised to clarify that the criteria are applied to a process, not the source as a whole, as discussed above. EPA has deleted requirements for explosives because the Agency is proposing to delist explosives. The types of accidents that will disqualify a process from Program 1 are now specified in the rule as those accidental releases of a regulated substance that led to offsite exposure to the substance, its reaction products, overpressure generated by an explosion involving the substance, or radiant heat generated by a fire involving the substance which resulted in offsite death or injury (as defined by the rule), or response or restoration activities at an environmental receptor. These accidental release criteria eliminate the need for a definition of significant accidental release, which has been deleted. Offsite environmental response or restoration would include such activities as collection, treatment and disposal of soil, shutoff of drinking water, replacement of damaged vegetation, or isolation of a natural areas due to contamination associated with an accidental release. The distance calculation equation for flammables has been dropped, and the worst-case release endpoint for flammables is specified which allows the source to use the reference tables or their own methodology to determine the distance to the endpoint. The requirement that the community have an EPCRA emergency response plan has been replaced by a requirement that the source coordinate emergency response procedures with local community responders.

As discussed above, the eligibility criteria for Program 2 and 3 have been changed. Both apply to processes, not sources.

Paragraph (e) states that if a process no longer meets the eligibility criteria of its Program level, the source must comply with the requirements of the new Program level and the update the RMP according to § 68.190. This paragraph clarifies the responsibility of the source when a process becomes ineligible for a Program level (e.g., public receptors move within the distance to an endpoint for a Program 1 process or OSHA changes the applicability of its PSM standard).

Proposed § 68.12, Registration, has been dropped. Registration requirements are now part of the RMP requirements in subpart G, § 68.160.

New § 68.12, General Requirements, has been added to provide a roadmap r sources to use to identify the requirements that apply to processes in ch of the three tiers. The Program 1 requirements, in proposed § 68.13, have en included in this section. Owners or erators of Program 1 processes are quired to analyze and document in the MP the worst-case release to ensure at they meet the eligibility criteria of public receptors within the distance the endpoint. As discussed above, the quirement to post signs has been opped. The certification statement has en revised to be consistent with the igibility requirements. If a source has ore than one Program 1 process, a ngle certification may be submitted to ver all such processes.

The Program 2 requirements specify e sections of the rule that apply to ese processes.

The Program 3 requirements specify e sections of the rule that apply to ese processes.

Proposed § 68.22, Management, has en moved from the prevention ogram to § 68.15 in subpart A-General. he section has been adopted as oposed except that the purpose ntence in paragraph (a) has been opped and a phrase at the beginning paragraph (b) has been deleted as necessary.

A new subpart B has been created to ver the hazard assessment quirements. The proposed § 68.15 has en divided into separate sections to ver the parameters, the different types analyses, the identification of offsite opulations and environments, ocumentation and updates, and the ve-year accident history. EPA believes at limiting each section to a single pic will make the rule easier to nderstand.

Section 68.20 has been added to ecify which hazard assessment quirements apply to Program 1, 2, and processes. All sources are required to omplete a worst-case release analysis r regulated substances in covered ocesses, based on the requirements of 8.25. Program 2 and 3 processes must so perform alternative release analyses quired by § 68.28. All sources must omplete the five-year accident history r all covered processes.

A new § 68.22 has been added to list e parameters to be used in the offsite onsequence analyses. Owners or erators who choose to use their own r dispersion modeling tools must use e parameters specified in paragraphs), (e), (f), and (g) of this section; they ust use the meteorological parameters ecified in paragraph (b) of this section nless they can demonstrate that the onditions do not exist at their site. aragraph (c) specifies the ambient

temperature and humidity for worst case (highest daily maximum over the previous three years and average humidity); if a source uses the guidance, it may use average temperature and humidity (25° C and 50 percent) as default values. EPA recognizes that these values are less conservative than the worst-case meteorological conditions, but determined that they represent a reasonable average to be used for developing tables. Providing tables for a variety of temperatures and humidity would have made the guidance much more voluminous and difficult to use. EPA is requiring sources that use dispersion models instead of the guidance to use actual temperature and humidity data applicable to the site. EPA believes this approach represents a reasonable tradeoff. The guidance generates conservative results even with the less conservative assumptions about temperature and humidity; air dispersion modeling will generally produce less conservative results and, therefore, should be based on actual data for these variables. Average data applicable to the source may be used for alternative scenarios. Paragraph (d) requires that the release height for worst-case be at ground level (zero feet). Paragraph (e) specifies that urban or rural topography be used as appropriate in modeling. Paragraph (f) requires sources to use models or tables appropriate for the density of the substance being released (e.g., dense gases must be modeled using tables or models that account for the behavior of dense gases). Dense gases are typically those that are heavier than air as well as those that form aerosols and behave as if they are heavier than air upon release. For worst-case releases, liquids (other than gases liquefied by refrigeration only) shall be considered to be released at the highest daily maximum temperature or at process temperature, whichever is higher. For alternative scenarios, substances may be considered to be released at ambient or process temperatures as appropriate. Owners or operators may choose to use EPA's RMP Offsite Consequence Analysis Guidance for their offsite consequence analyses. All of the parameters specified here are reflected in this guidance.

A new § 68.25 has been added on the worst-case release analysis. As discussed above, the section requires one worst-case release for toxics and one for flammables. If additional scenarios, for either class of substances, would potentially expose receptors not exposed by the worst-case release, the additional scenario shall be analyzed and reported. This provision is to take

into account the possibility that at large sources, vessels at opposite ends of the source may expose different populations.

The section specifies how maximum quantity in a vessel or pipe is to be determined, the scenarios to be considered for toxic gases, toxic gases liquefied by refrigeration only, toxic liquids, and flammables, the parameters to be used, consideration of passive mitigation, and factors to be considered in selecting the worst-case scenario. The section also specifies that sources may use proprietary models if the source provides the implementing agency access to the model and explains differences between the model and publicly available models, if requested. This approach will allow sources to use the most appropriate models available, while preserving the transparency of the results.

A new § 68.28 has been added on alternative release scenario analysis. As discussed above, the section requires one alternative release analysis for all flammables held above the threshold in processes at the source and one alternative release analysis for each toxic held above the threshold in processes. For each scenario, the owner or operator shall select a scenario that is more likely to occur than the worst case; and that will reach an endpoint offsite, unless no such scenario exists. The section includes a list of scenarios that owners/operators may want to consider, but does not dictate a particular scenario. EPA has provided additional direction and suggestions for defining these scenarios in the RMP Offsite Consequence Analysis Guidance. As noted above, the section references the parameters to be used and allows consideration of both passive and active mitigation systems. The section specifies factors to be considered in selecting alternative scenarios; specifically, sources shall consider releases that have been documented in the five-year accident history; or failure scenarios identified through the PHA or hazard review.

A new § 68.30 has been added on defining offsite impacts—population. The section specifies that populations are to be defined for a circle with a radius that is the distance to the endpoint. Owners or operators are required only to estimate the residential population within the circle to two significant digits and may use Census data to make these estimates. Owners or operators are also required to note, in the RMP, the presence of any major institutions, such as schools, hospitals, prisons, public recreational areas, arenas, and major commercial and industrial developments, but they are not required to estimate the number of people present at such sites. These additional locations are those that would normally be shown on area street maps.

A new § 68.33 has been added on defining offsite impacts to the environment. As discussed above, the owners or operators are required only to identify any environmental receptors within the circle with a radius determined by the distance to the endpoint. The owners or operators are not required to assess the potential types or degree of damage that might occur from a release of the substance. The environmental receptors are those that can be identified on U.S. Geological Survey local topographical maps or maps based on U.S.G.S. data.

A new § 68.36 has been added to list the requirements for reviewing and updating the offsite consequence analysis. As proposed, if no changes occur at the site, the analyses must be reviewed and updated at least once every five years. If changes at the site occur that would reasonably be expected either to increase or decrease the distance to the endpoint by a factor of two or more, owners/operators are required to update the offsite consequence analysis within six months. The time for the reanalysis has been changed to six months to make it consistent with the update requirements for the RMP. The proposed requirement for reviewing the analyses based on offsite changes has been deleted. A number of commenters objected to the requirement because it would have compelled them to track changes over very large areas. Because the distance to the endpoints, especially for toxics, may be as much as 40 km, the area affected could easily exceed 1,000 square miles. EPA agreed with commenters that there was little benefit from requiring sources to track offsite changes and redo analyses because the public is aware of the changes.

A new § 68.39 has been added to list the documentation related to the offsite consequence analyses that must be retained on site. For both types of scenarios, the documentation shall include a description of the scenarios identified, assumptions and parameters used, the rationale for the selection of specific scenarios; assumptions shall include use of mitigation and any administrative controls that were assumed to limit the quantity that could be released. Documentation shall include the effect of the mitigation and controls on the release quantity. The documentation shall also include the estimated quantities released, release

rates, and durations of release. The owners or operators shall also identify the methodology used to determine distance to endpoints (i.e., EPA's guidance or an air dispersion model) and the data used to estimate population and environmental receptors potentially affected. EPA has deleted the proposed requirement for documentation of endpoints because these are now dictated by the rule. EPA has also dropped the requirement for documentation of distance calculations; distances will either be determined from EPA's reference tables or by an air dispersion model.

A new § 68.42 has been added to detail the requirements for the five-year accident history. As discussed above, the accident history is limited to accidental releases of listed substances from covered processes only. The only accidental releases that must be included in the history are those that resulted in deaths, injuries, or significant property damage on site, or known offsite deaths, injuries, evacuations, sheltering in place, property damage, or environmental damage. Although language related to the types of environmental damage listed in the proposed rule has been dropped, EPA intends that environmental damage not be limited to environmental receptors; events where any known environmental impact of any kind (e.g., fish or animal kills, lawn, shrub, or crop damage), should be included in the history.

The data required on each accident include date, time, and approximate duration of the release; chemical(s) released; estimated quantity in pounds; the type of release event and its source; weather conditions (if known); on-site impacts and known offsite impacts; the initiating event and contributing factors (if known); whether offsite responders were notified (if known); and operational or process changes that resulted from the release. Estimates may be provided to two significant digits. EPA expects that for accidents that occur after the publication of this rule, sources will be able to document weather conditions, initiating events and contributing factors, and notification of offsite responders as these items would be part of the incident investigation. The Agency recognizes, however, that for incidents that occur before the rule is final, sources may not have this information unless OSHA PSM already would require the source to gather such information (e.g., initiating event and contributing factors). EPA has dropped the requirement that the concentration of the released substance be reported.

Concentration at the point of release is assumed to be 100 percent except for substances in solution, where the concentration at the point of release is assumed to be the percentage of the solution as held or processed. The data provided will allow the source or the public to estimate the concentration offsite.

Because the five-year accident history will initially cover releases that occurred before this rule is promulgated, EPA is requiring reports on weather conditions only if the source has a record. For future releases, EPA encourages the owners or operators keep a record of wind speed and temperature if possible as these conditions have a significant impact on the migration of a release offsite. The rule specifies that the source must document known offsite impacts. The source is not required to conduct research on this subject, but must report impacts of which it is aware through direct reporting to the source or claims filed, or reasonably should have been aware of from publicly available information. The source is not required to verify the accuracy of public or media reports.

A new subpart C has been created to include the requirements of the prevention program for Program 2 processes.

New § 68.48 details the safety information that sources will be required to develop. The information is a subset of the information required under the OSHA rule and is limited to those items that are likely to apply to Program 2 processes: MSDSs, maximum intended inventory, safe upper and lower process parameters, equipment specifications, and the codes and standards used to design, build, and operate the process. Because Program 2 processes are generally simple, EPA determined that items such as process chemistry, process flow diagrams, detailed drawings on equipment, and material and energy balances are not necessary for these processes. Evaluation of consequences of deviations will be handled under the process review and the offsite consequence analysis.

Paragraph (b) of § 68.48 requires owners or operators to ensure that the process is designed in compliance with good engineering practices. The paragraph states that compliance with Federal or state regulations that address industry-specific safe design or with industry-specific design codes may be used to demonstrate compliance. NFPA–58 for propane handlers and OSHA's rule for ammonia handling (29 CFR 1910.111) are examples of such design codes.

The final paragraph of § 68.48 requires owners or operators to update the safety information if a major change makes it inaccurate.

New § 68.50 sets the requirements for hazard review. The section lists the hazards and safeguards that the owners or operators must identify and review. The section states that owners or operators may use checklists, such as those provided in model risk management programs, to conduct the review. For processes that are designed to industry standards (e.g., NFPA–58) or federal/state design rules, owners or operators need only check their equipment closely to ensure that it has been fabricated and installed according to the standards or rules and is being operated appropriately. In this case, the standard or rule-setting body has, in essence, conducted the hazard review and designed the equipment to reduce hazards. Like the PHA required under PSM, the hazard review must be documented and the findings resolved. The review must be updated at least once every five years or when a major change occurs. A streamlined version of the PHA requirement, the review recognizes that for simple processes some of the OSHA requirements, such as the requirement for a team and a person trained in the technique, may not be necessary. Most Program 2 processes will have model risk management programs that will assist owners or operators in conducting the review.

New § 68.52 covers operating procedures. The section allows owners or operators to use standardized procedures developed by industry groups or provided in model risk management programs as a basis for the SOPs. Owners or operators will need to review standardized SOPs to ensure that they are appropriate for their operations; some may need to be tailored. The steps covered in the SOP are adapted from the OSHA PSM standard. Certain elements of the PSM requirement (e.g., safety and health consideration) were dropped because they are generally covered in training provided under the OSHA hazard communication standard. Other elements were not included because they are covered by other OSHA rules or may not apply to the kinds of sources in Program 2. The section requires that the SOPs be updated whenever necessary.

New § 68.54 covers training and is a streamlined version of the OSHA PSM requirement. The primary difference with the OSHA PSM training element is that the documentation requirements have been dropped. EPA believes that for Program 2 sources, which generally will have simple processes and few employees involved in the process, the level of documentation required by OSHA PSM is not needed. The section specifically states that training conducted to comply with other Federal or state rules or industry codes may be used to demonstrate compliance with the section if the training covers the SOPs for the process. Workers must be retrained when SOPs change as a result of a major change.

New § 68.56 covers maintenance and requires owners or operators to prepare and implement procedures for maintenance and train workers in these procedures. The owners or operators are also required to inspect and test process equipment consistent with good engineering practices. The OSHA list of equipment has been dropped because it seemed too detailed for the simpler Program 2 processes. Similarly, the OSHA PSM requirements for documentation, equipment deficiencies, and quality assurance seem too burdensome given the type of processes in Program 2. EPA emphasizes that sources should address equipment deficiencies when they arise.

New §§ 68.58 and 68.60 on compliance audits and accident investigation are adopted directly from the OSHA PSM standard. EPA believes that these two elements are critical to good prevention practices and that no changes are needed from the OSHA requirements. EPA has added a provision to clearly indicate that audit reports more than five-years old need not be retained.

The Program 3 prevention program is codified in new subpart D. As explained above, the subpart adopts the OSHA PSM standard with only minor editorial changes necessitated by the different statutory authorities of the two agencies. Throughout the subpart, "employer" has been changed to "owner or operator," "facility" to "stationary source," and "highly hazardous chemical" to "regulated substance." EPA has reordered the elements somewhat so that the order reflects the progression in which sources will generally implement the program. For example, process safety information, which is needed for the PHA, now precedes that section. Pre-startup review, which is the last step of management of change procedures, now follows management of change. The reordering does not reflect any change in the content.

Section 68.65, process safety information, is adopted directly from OSHA. The only changes are the following: references to other requirements have been changed to reflect the appropriate EPA section numbers; the phrase "highly hazardous chemical" has been changed to "regulated substance"; the word "standard" has been changed to "rule" in paragraph (a); and the date when material and energy balances are needed for new processes has been changed to June 21, 1999. The words "including those affecting the safety and health of employees" has been deleted from the requirement for the evaluation of the consequences of deviations (paragraph (c)(1)(v)) because EPA has no authority to regulate the workplace. Further, EPA believes this change reflects EPA's desire that sources implement one prevention program that protects the safety and health of workers, the public and the environment and should have no effect on sources already complying with the OSHA PSM rule.

Section 68.67, process hazard analysis, has been adopted from the OSHA rule with a few changes. The OSHA schedule for completion of PHAs has been replaced with the compliance date of this rule; a new sentence has been added to state that PHAs conducted to comply with OSHA PSM are acceptable as the initial PHA under this rule. These PHAs shall be updated and revalidated based on their OSHA completion date. This provision will ensure that sources do not need to duplicate PHAs already completed or change their update schedule.

In paragraph (c)(2), the phrase "in the workplace" has been deleted from the requirement to identify previous incidents with the potential for catastrophic consequences because EPA does not have the authority to regulate the work place. EPA believes that this change will have no effect on the rule; any incident with the potential for catastrophic consequences in the workplace will also have had the potential for catastrophic consequences offsite. Similarly, the phrase "on employees in the workplace" has been deleted from paragraph (c)(7), which requires a qualitative evaluation of a range of the possible safety and health effects of failure of controls. By deleting the language, rather than changing it, EPA is consistent with its authority without imposing any new requirements on sources. A new sentence has been added to paragraph (f) to state that PHAs updated and revalidated under the OSHA rule are acceptable for EPA's purposes. Throughout this section, internal references have been changed.

To maintain consistency with OSHA PSM, proposed paragraph (j), which would have required the evaluation of mitigation and detection systems, has been dropped, as have proposed references to offsite consequences and public health and the environment. Evaluation of mitigation and detection systems is normally part of the PHA process and of management's decisions on implementing recommendations and, therefore, EPA decided that a separate requirement was not needed. EPA will collect information on monitoring, detection, and mitigation systems used in each Program 2 and 3 process as part of the RMP. Proposed paragraph (a), which was advisory, has been dropped.

Section 68.69, Operating Procedures, has been adopted verbatim from OSHA except for changing "employer" to "owner or operator." Proposed paragraph (a) has been deleted to ensure consistency with OSHA.

Section 68.71, Training, has been adopted verbatim from OSHA except for changing "employer" to "owner or operator" and changes in referenced sections. Proposed paragraph (a) has been deleted to ensure consistency with OSHA, as has proposed paragraph (e).

Section 68.73, Mechanical Integrity proposed as Maintenance, has been adopted verbatim from OSHA except for changing "employer" to "owner or operator." Proposed paragraph (a) has been deleted to ensure consistency with OSHA. The proposed requirements to develop a critical equipment list, document training, and "maintain" as well as inspect and test under paragraph (d) have been dropped to ensure consistency with OSHA.

Section 68.75, Management of Change, has been adopted verbatim from OSHA except for changing "employer" to "owner or operator" and changes to referenced sections. Proposed paragraph (a) has been deleted to ensure consistency with OSHA. EPA's proposed paragraph (b), which defined changes not covered by the section, has also been dropped in favor of OSHA's definition of "replacement in kind."

Section 68.77, Pre-Startup Review, has been adopted verbatim from OSHA except for changing "employer" to "owner or operator" and changes to referenced sections. Proposed paragraph (a) and the reference to emergency response training in proposed paragraph (c)(4) have been deleted to ensure consistency with OSHA.

Section 68.79, Compliance Audits, has been adopted verbatim from OSHA except for changing "employer" to "owner or operator" and changes to referenced sections. Proposed paragraph (a) has been deleted to ensure consistency with OSHA.

Section 68.81, Accident Investigation, has been adopted verbatim from OSHA except for changing "employer" to

"owner or operator" and "highly hazardous chemical" to "regulated substance" and changes to referenced sections. Proposed paragraphs (a) and (b), the latter of which would have required written procedures, have been deleted to ensure consistency with OSHA. References to significant accidental release have been dropped because the phrase is no longer used. Although EPA has adopted OSHA's language, EPA has changed the definition of catastrophic release. Consequently, this section requires owners or operators to investigate accidents that resulted in or could reasonably have resulted in a release that presented serious danger to public health or the environment. EPA does not believe that, except in isolated cases, the modification to this provision will require sources to investigate accidents that they would not investigate under the OSHA rule.

Section 68.83, Employee Participation, has been adopted verbatim from OSHA except for changing "employer" to "owner or operator." Although EPA did not propose adopting this section, the Agency solicited comments on this issue, and commenters convinced the Agency that employee participation is an important component of a complete prevention program.

Section 68.85, Hot Work Permit, has been adopted verbatim from OSHA except for changing "employer" to "owner or operator." Although EPA did not propose adopting this section, the Agency solicited comments on this provision and decided that it was valuable to maintain consistency with the OSHA PSM elements and that the hot work permit was important to good prevention practices.

Section 68.87, Contractors, has been adopted verbatim from OSHA except for changing "employer" to "owner or operator," changing to referenced sections, and deleting OSHA's paragraph 29 CFR 1910.119(h)(2)(vi). Although EPA did not propose adopting this section, the Agency solicited comments on this issue. Commenters argued that contractor practices are an important component of a complete prevention program. A number of major accidents have resulted from contractor mistakes. EPA agrees with the commenters and has included the provision in the final rule. EPA has, however, deleted the requirement that employers maintain an occupational injury and illness log for contract employees because the Agency does not have the authority to impose this requirement.

EPA has placed the emergency response requirements in a new Subpart E and divided the proposed emergency response section into two separate sections, an applicability section and a section to cover the emergency response program.

A new § 68.90, Applicability, has been added. Because many sources covered by this rule may be too small to handle emergency response themselves, EPA has provided, in this new section, the actions they must take if they will not respond to releases. Specifically, for sources with regulated toxic substances, the source must be addressed in the community emergency response plan developed under EPCRA section 303. Sources with regulated flammable substances must coordinate response actions with the local fire department. These sources must also establish a mechanism to contact local emergency responders. Sources that do not meet these requirements must comply with EPA's emergency response program requirements.

Section 68.95, Emergency Response Program, is adopted from § 68.45 of the proposed rule. The program has four components: an emergency response plan, procedures for use of response equipment and its maintenance, training for employees, and procedures to update the plan after changes to the source. The required elements of the plan are those specified in CAA section 112(r)(7)(B)(ii): procedures for informing the public and local response agencies; documentation of emergency medical treatment; and procedures and measures for emergency response. As explained above, EPA decided that, to avoid inconsistency with other emergency response planning regulations, the rule would be limited to the statutory requirements. Consequently, EPA has deleted the following proposed requirements: documentation of evacuation routes (which should be covered under the emergency action plans required by OSHA under 29 CFR 1910.38); descriptions of all response and mitigation technologies available at the source; documentation of the maintenance and training programs; emergency response drills and exercises; revision of the plan based on the findings of the drills and exercises; and documentation of management's response to findings and a schedule for completion. EPA believes that these requirements are addressed in other Federal regulations and, therefore, sources are already doing them. By not including them, EPA, however, avoids the possibility that slightly different wording could lead to unnecessary additional effort on the part of sources.

EPA has added a paragraph (b) to this section to state that compliance with other Federal contingency plan regulations or use of the National Response Team's Integrated Contingency Plan Guidance ("One Plan") that results in a written plan that addresses the elements in paragraph (a) shall satisfy the requirements of the rule, provided that the owner or operator also complies with paragraph (c) of this section.

Paragraph (c) is adopted from proposed paragraph § 68.45(g) and requires coordination of the plan with the local community emergency response plan. References to the local emergency planning committee (LEPC) have been changed to 'local emergency response officials' to recognize and include other local groups that may be in charge of coordinating emergency planning. LEPCs would be included in this category.

A new Subpart G has been created to cover the Risk Management Plan. The Risk Management Plan includes three main sections, an executive summary, the registration, and data elements that provide information on the offsite consequence analyses, the five-year accident history, the prevention program, and the emergency response program. The subpart includes separate section to address each of these, plus sections on submission, certifications, and updates.

New § 68.150, Submission, has been added. As discussed above, an owner or operator shall submit a single RMP for the source, regardless of the number of covered processes or the tiers for which they are eligible. All RMPs will be submitted in a manner and method EPA will specify by the compliance date to point designated by EPA; no other submission will be required because other agencies and the public will have access to the submissions on-line. As required by the CAA, the first RMP must be submitted by June 21, 1999, three years after EPA first lists a substance, or the date on which a source first becomes subject to this part, whichever is latest. As discussed above under applicability, after June 21, 1999, sources that begin using a substance that has been listed for at least three years will be required to submit their RMPs on the date the substance is first on site above the threshold quantity. Sources that begin using such a regulated substance prior to June 21, 1999 will need to be in compliance with the rule on June 21, 1999. The final paragraph states that, except for a classified annex that would not be publicly available, the RMP shall exclude classified information.

New § 68.155 details the requirements for the executive summary. The summary shall include brief descriptions of the following items: the source's prevention and emergency response approach; the stationary source and regulated substances; worst-case release scenario(s) and alternative release scenario(s), including any administrative controls applied to limit the release quantity; the general prevention program and chemical-specific prevention steps; the five-year accident history; the emergency response program; and planned changes to improve safety. EPA anticipates that none of these items should require more than a half page of text. Because this information may be filed electronically, EPA is not asking sources to submit maps of the worst-case or alternative release scenario circles. The data submitted under each of these sections will allow state or local agencies and the public to map the circles.

Section 68.160, Registration, replaces proposed § 68.12. The registration shall include the following data: stationary source name, street, city, county, state, zip code, latitude, and longitude; the stationary source and corporate Dun and Bradstreet numbers; the name, telephone number, and mailing address of the owner/operator; the name and title of the person responsible for implementation of the risk management program; the name, title, telephone number, and 24-hour telephone number of the emergency contact; the stationary source EPA identifier; the number of full-time employees at the stationary source; whether the stationary source is subject to 29 CFR 1910.119; whether the stationary source is subject to 40 CFR part 355; and the date on which the stationary source last had a safety inspection by a Federal, state, or local government agency.

For each covered process, the source must list the regulated substances present above a threshold quantity (name and CAS number), the maximum quantity of each substance in the process, the SIC code of the process, and the Program level that applies to the process. This process information provides a simple method for describing covered processes and identifying Program levels.

The reporting of the quantity has been changed; rather than have sources report in ranges, the rule requires that the quantity be reported to two significant digits. EPA has found that the reporting ranges are so broad (generally an order of magnitude) that data analysis is extremely difficult. By limiting the reporting to two significant digits, EPA will allow sources to estimate

quantities, but still provide more precise data than are currently available. EPA has added a requirement for reporting full-time employees. These data are easy for sources to provide and will enhance the Agency's ability to assess the impact of its rule on businesses of various sizes. The EPA identifier will be the unique number EPA will assign to each source and will allow EPA to cross reference other reporting to the Agency. Use of the identifier also means that EPA may not need to collect certain data on this form because they will be available from the identifier database; EPA may revise the requirements when the identifier rule is promulgated.

EPA has deleted the certification statement proposed for the registration because the RMP as a whole will have a certification statement that will cover all elements, including registration. Corrections to the registration will be treated as corrections to the RMP and must be filed within six months of the change, rather than the 60 days proposed for registration changes.

The registration now requires the owners or operators to check off the agency that last conducted a safety inspection at the source and provide the date. The inspection does not need to have been related to prevention practices as defined in this rule, but may instead cover fire safety, workplace safety, etc.

New § 68.165 covers the requirements for reporting on the offsite consequence analysis. As discussed in Section III.B, the RMP shall include data on one worst case release scenario for each Program 1 process; and, for Program 2 and 3 processes, one worst case release scenario for toxics and one for flammables (for sources with substances in both hazard classes). If additional worst-case release scenarios are required under § 68.25 for either class, data on that scenario must also be reported. Sources with Program 2 and 3 processes will also provide data on one alternative release scenario to cover all flammables in covered processes and an alternative release scenario for each toxic substance held in covered processes.

For each reported scenario, the owners or operators shall provide the following data: chemical name; physical state (toxics only); basis of results and model (if used); scenario; quantity released in pounds; release rate; duration; wind speed and stability (toxics only); topography (toxics only); distance to endpoint; public and environmental receptors within the distance; passive mitigation considered; and active mitigation (alternative releases only) considered. A number of the data elements are not relevant to all flammable releases; for example, in the worst-case release flammables are assumed to be released and explode almost instantly so that release rate, duration, wind speed and stability, and topography are not factors in determining distances.

The purpose of requiring these data elements, rather than the proposed summary of the assessment, is to provide the public with the essential estimates of distance to the endpoints and provide enough data on the release scenario to allow agencies or the public to confirm the distance estimate. With the data provided, a public agency will be able to use EPA's guidance to determine the distance for a particular chemical release and compare that distance with the one reported by the source. This ability will be particularly important when a source has chosen to use an air dispersion model rather than the reference table. The proposed rule approach, which required a summary of the assessment, would have resulted in considerable variation in the information submitted, as happened in the Kanawha Valley exercise. In that case, each source decided on the level of information to provide; although each provided maps, it was not possible, in many cases, to determine how the distances were estimated because much of the underlying data was not reported. EPA believes that these requirements will impose a minimal burden on sources, because they will already have the data from completing the analyses, will ensure that the same data are reported by all sources, and will provide enough data to evaluate the results using publicly available documents and models.

New § 68.168 on the five-year accident history simply references the data elements listed in § 68.42(a). The data elements will be reported for each accidental release covered by the accident history requirement.

New § 68.170, Prevention Program/ Program 2, requires owners or operators with Program 2 processes to list the name of chemical(s) in, and SIC code for, the Program 2 process; to provide the dates of the most recent revisions or reviews of the prevention program elements; to provide, based on the hazard review, information on the major hazards, process controls, mitigation systems, monitoring or detection systems, and changes since the last hazard review; to list any state or federal regulations of industry-specific design codes or standards being used to demonstrate compliance with prevention program elements; to list the type of training and competency testing used; to provide the date of the most

recent change that triggered a review or revision of prevention elements; and to provide the date of the completion of any changes resulting from hazard reviews, audits, or incident investigations. EPA recognizes that not all recommendations resulting from hazard reviews, audits, or incident investigations result in changes; some or all may be resolved without changes. However, if any changes are made, the owners or operators shall report in the RMP the date when such changes are complete or expected to be complete.

New § 68.175, Prevention Program/ Program 3, requires owners or operators with Program 3 processes to list the name of chemical(s) in, and SIC code for, the Program 3 process; to provide the dates of the most recent revisions or reviews of the prevention program elements; to provide, based on the PHA, information on the major hazards, process controls, mitigation systems, monitoring or detection systems, and changes since the last PHA; to list the type of training and competency testing used; to provide the date of the most recent change that triggered a review or revision of prevention elements; and to provide the date of the completion of any changes resulting from PHAs, audits, or incident investigations. As above, EPA recognizes that not all recommendations resulting from PHAs, audits, or incident investigations result in changes; some or all may be resolved without changes. However, if any changes are made, the owners or operators shall report in the RMP the date when such changes are complete or expected to be complete.

New § 68.180, Emergency Response Program, requires owners or operators to answer questions about the required content of the emergency response plan, providing the date of the most recent training of employees update of the plan, indicate whether the source emergency response plan has been coordinated with the LEPC plan, provide the name and telephone number of the local agency with which the plan has been coordinated, and list other Federal or state emergency planning requirements to which the source is subject.

New § 68.185, Certification, specifies the certification requirements that owners or operators must complete when the RMP is submitted.

New § 68.190 details the requirements for updating the RMP. The plan must be updated at least once every five years. If a new substance is added to an already covered process or a new covered process is added, the RMP must be updated on the date on which the regulated substance is first present

above a threshold quantity. If EPA lists a new substance that the source has above a threshold quantity, the RMP must be updated within three years of the date of listing. If a change at the source leads to a revised offsite consequence analysis, process hazard analysis or review, or a process changes Program level, the RMP must be revised and resubmitted within six months of the change. Subsequent updates will be required within five years of the update

A new Subpart H, Other Requirements, has been added.

New § 68.200, Recordkeeping, simply states that records will be maintained for five years unless otherwise specified in the Program 3 prevention program.

New § 68.210, Availability of information to the public, has been added and a paragraph included to provide that classified information is protected under applicable laws, regulations, and executive orders.

New § 68.215, Permit content and air permitting authority or designated agency requirements, has been added to define the requirements for including part 68 in Part 70 and 71 permits, as discussed above.

Section 68.220, Audits, has been revised to change references in paragraph (a). A new paragraph (c) has been added to specify the sources that have achieved a star or merit rating under OSHA's VPP program will be exempt from audits if the audit program is based on industry accident history or on neutral random oversight and if the source has not had an accidental release that requires investigation under the rule. Paragraph (h) has been revised to clarify that the source must revise the RMP 30 days after completion of the actions detailed in the implementation plan, not 30 days after the issuance of the final determination.

Appendix A has been added to provide the toxic endpoints.

V. Required Analyses

A. E.O. 12866

Under Executive Order (E.O.) 12866 (58 FR 51735; October 4, 1993), EPA must determine whether a regulatory action is "significant" and, therefore, subject to OMB review and the requirements of the E.O. The Order defines "significant regulatory action" as one that is likely to result in a rule that may:

(1) Have an annual effect on the economy of $100 million or more or adversely affect in a material way the economy, a sector of the economy, productivity, competition, jobs, the environment, public health or safety, or state, local, or tribal government or communities.

(2) Create a serious inconsistency or otherwise interfere with an action taken or planned by another agency;

(3) Materially alter the budgetary impact of entitlements, grants, user fees, or loan programs or the rights and obligations of recipients thereof; or

(4) Raise novel legal or policy issues arising out of legal mandates, the President's priorities, or the principles set forth in the E.O.

Under terms of E.O. 12866, EPA has determined that today's final rulemaking is a "significant regulatory action." EPA, therefore, has developed an economic impact analysis for the final rule, (Economic Analysis in Support of Final Rule on Risk Management Program Regulations for Chemical Accidental Release Prevention), which is available in the docket.

In developing the final rule, EPA notes that it has taken actions to streamline requirements whenever possible and has tailored the requirements through the use of programs. This approach differed from the proposed rule, which imposed what are now Program 3 requirements on all sources and processes. EPA has also changed substantially the requirements for two elements of the rule, the offsite consequence analysis and the RMP. For the offsite consequence analysis, EPA decided to develop methodologies and look-up tables so sources would not need to spend resources obtaining air dispersion models; EPA also reduced the requirements to define offsite populations by allowing sources to use census data and to identify only those institutions and developments that appear on local maps (as opposed to identifying day care centers and nursing homes). For the RMP, EPA has limited the requirements for information to that which can be reported as data elements. In contrast, the rule as proposed would have required sources to document for each process all major hazards, the consequences of each of these hazards, the risk reduction steps taken to address each hazard, and the consequences of each risk reduction step. The result would have been, for large, complex sources, documents of a 1,000 pages or more.

To analyze the cost impacts of the various approaches, EPA considered three possible options in the final EIA: the final rule, an option that imposed final rule Program 3 requirements on all sources, and an option that imposed proposed rule requirements on all sources. The last of these options was considered to evaluate the impact of changing the requirements for the offsite consequence analysis and RMP.

Based on the final list and thresholds, EPA estimates that approximately 66,100 sources will be affected by the rule. EPA expects that about 360 sources and approximately 410 processes will be eligible for Program 1. These sources are primarily gas processors that, because they are remote and unstaffed, are not covered by OSHA PSM. EPA also estimated that approximately 50 processes using toluene di-isocyanate (TDI) may qualify for Program 1 based on the relatively low volatility of TDI. Program 2 is expected to include 40,200 sources and 47,700 processes; these sources include all retailers, propane users, public drinking water and wastewater systems and public electric utilities not subject to OSHA PSM, wholesalers, processes at Federal facility processes, and non-chemical manufacturers. Program 3 is expected to cover 25,500 sources and 43,800 processes. These sources include manufacturers, electric utilities, POTWs and drinking water sites covered by OSHA PSM, wholesalers, ammonia refrigeration systems, gas utilities, gas processors, and Federal facilities. All of these sources are already covered by OSHA PSM for at least one regulated substance; EPA estimates that about 370 non-OSHA Program 3 processes in the specified SIC codes will be covered.

Sources that already have a high quality PSM program would not need to take any additional actions to satisfy EPA's Program 3 prevention program, but the analysis assumed that many sources may still be in the process of improving their PSM programs after achieving initial compliance. The public scrutiny expected to follow submission of the RMP is likely to encourage sources to ensure that their prevention efforts are fully implemented and effective. To account for these efforts, the analysis assumed that sources covered by OSHA would improve training, maintenance, and management oversight and, in some cases, institute additional capital improvements.

The rule provides sources three years to come into compliance with the rule. The rule, however, will impose continuing costs as sources implement their risk management programs. Initial compliance, therefore, covers the cost of meeting the requirements of the rule by the three-year compliance date. These costs are presented as a single figure, but are assumed to be incurred over a three-year period. Total costs to industry were estimated by multiplying the estimated unit costs of compliance with the risk management program elements by the estimated number of affected sources. Because many sources already implement some of the risk

management requirements (e.g., training), cost estimates were adjusted to account for the expected likelihood that a source is already human health (death or injury), responses to these threats (evacuations, sheltering in place) threats to the environment, and economic damages (lost production, property damages, and litigation). Additional benefits may be provided by making information available to the public in the RMP. These benefits, however, cannot be quantified.

B. Regulatory Flexibility Act

In accordance with the Regulatory Flexibility Act of 1980, Federal agencies must evaluate the impacts of rules on small entities and consider less burdensome regulatory alternatives. As originally proposed in 1993, EPA believes that the rule would have created a severe, adverse impact on small manufacturers. In February 1995, EPA published a supplemenatal proposal which introduced a tiering approach for this regulation. By using the tiering approach and streamlining the Program 2 requirements, this final rule significantly reduces the impact on small businesses. The tiering approach also significantly reduces the impact on small communities.

EPA has developed a Regulatory Flexibility Analysis for this final rule evaluating the effects on small entities, which is presented in Chapter 7 of the EIA. The number of small manufacturers was estimated to be 960 sources with fewer than 20 FTEs, and 2,000 sources with between 20 and 99 FTEs. The number of small non-manufacturers is more difficult to determine. Virtually all retailer and wholesalers have fewer than 100 FTEs. Industry estimates, however, indicate that about 80 percent of the affected retailers may be owned by larger companies; the analysis assumed that 3,700 retailers were small businesses. No information was available to estimate the percentage of wholesalers that might be owned by large corporations. The analysis assumed that all wholesalers were small. The total number of small businesses, therefore, was estimated to be 8,160.

Public drinking water and waste water systems affected by the rule generally serve a minimum of 10,000 people. Approximately 980 water systems are estimated to serve between 10,000 and 25,000 people. Approximately 500 water systems are estimated to serve between 25,000 and 50,000 people. Consequently, 1,480 drinking water systems would be considered small governmental entities. The number of small POTWs was estimated to include all systems treating less than 10 mgd and 59 percent of those treating between 10 and 25 mgd (based on the ratio of drinking water systems in this category that serve populations below 50,000). Approximately 2,600 POTWs were estimated to serve between 10,000 and 25,000 people and 180 to serve between 25,000 and 50,000, for a total of 2,800 POTWs. A total of approximately 4,300 small governmental entities would be affected by this rule.

The total number of small entities affected by this rule was estimated to be 12,500 or 19 percent of the affected universe. No detailed analysis of the impact on small entities was performed because of the relatively low cost of the rule for small entities. Initial costs are considerably less than one percent of sales for all small manufacturers. Subsequent year costs will be even lower. Costs for non-manufacturers are very low (less than $1,000 per year for initial compliance). These sums do not impose a serious adverse burden on these sources. Only chemical manufacturers with complex processes and 20 to 99 FTEs have initial costs that exceed $6,000 per year. The costs for these sources, $28,000 to $30,000 per year for the first three years, represent less than 0.5 percent of sales. It should be noted that all of the costs for small manufacturers assume that the sources will take additional efforts, above their actions to comply with the OSHA rule, to improve the quality of the risk management programs. If they do not take additional actions, their costs would be substantially lower.

C. Unfunded Mandates Reform Act

Title II of the Unfunded Mandates Reform Act of 1995 (UMRA), Public Law 104–4, establishes requirements for Federal agencies to assess the effects of their regulatory actions on state, local, and tribal governments and the private sector. Under section 202 of UMRA, EPA must generally prepare a written statement, including a cost-benefit analysis for proposed and final rules with "Federal mandates" that may result in expenditures to state, local, and tribal governments, in the aggregate, or to the private sector, of $100 million or more in any one year. Before promulgating an EPA rule for which a written statement is needed, section 205 of UMRA generally requires EPA to identify and consider a reasonable number of regulatory alternatives and adopt the least costly, most cost-effective, or least burdensome alternatives that achieves the objectives of the rule. The provisions of section 205 do not apply when they are

inconsistent with applicable law. Moreover, section 205 allows EPA to adopt an alternative other than the least costly, most cost-effective, or least burdensome alternative if the Administrator publishes with the final rule an explanation of why the alternative was not adopted. Before EPA establishes any regulatory requirements that significantly or uniquely affect small governments, including tribal governments, it must have developed under section 203 of UMRA, a small government agency plan. The plan must provide for notifying potentially affected small governments, enabling officials of affected small governments to have meaningful and timely input into the development of the regulatory proposals with significant Federal intergovernmental mandates, and informing, educating, and advising small governments on compliance with the regulatory requirements.

EPA has determined that this rule contains a Federal mandate that may result in expenditures of $100 million or more for state, local, and tribal governments, in the aggregate, or to the private sector, in any one year. Accordingly, EPA has prepared, under section 202 of the UMRA, a written statement which is summarized below.

EPA is required to promulgate this rule under CAA section 112(r). In the first and third year of initial compliance, the cost of the rule to the regulated community will exceed $100 million; in all subsequent years the costs will be below $100 million. EPA has developed an economic impact analysis, discussed above, that evaluates several regulatory alternatives. EPA has adopted the least costly of these alternatives. EPA estimates that annualized costs for state and local governments will be $13 million; annualized costs for the private sector are estimated to be $72 million.

Consistent with the intergovernmental consultation provisions of section 204 of the UMRA and Executive Order 12875 "Enhancing the Intergovernmental Partnership," EPA has involved state, local and business representatives in focus groups to develop the rule. EPA included representatives of state government in the rulemaking workgroup process, available to the public under CAA section 114(c) and 40 CFR part 2; EPA does not believe that any of the requested information will be considered confidential.

The public reporting burden will depend on the regulatory program into which the 66,100 sources are placed. The public reporting burden for rule familiarization is estimated to range from 4 to 68 hours per source for all

three program tiers. The public reporting burden to prepare and submit the registration and other RMP element is estimated to be 0.5 hours for sources with only Program 1 processes, between 6.0 and 11.25 hours for Program 2 sources, and between 6.25 and 30.5 hours for Program 3 sources. The RMP is submitted once, at the end of the three year compliance period. The public recordkeeping burden to maintain on-site documentation is estimated to range from 10 to 180 hours for Program 2 sources and from 52 to 1,200 hours for Program 3 sources. On-site documentation must be developed and maintained on an ongoing basis, which varies by rule element; based on the statute of limitation for this rule, documentation must generally be maintained for five years. The total annual public reporting burden for rule familiarization, to complete the RMP, and to maintain on-site documentation is estimated to be about 3.36 million hours over three years, or an annual burden of 1.119 million hours. No capital costs are expected to be incurred to maintain or submit this documentation.

Burden means the total time, effort, or financial resources expended by person to generate, maintain, retain, or disclose or provide information to or for a Federal agency. This includes the time needed to review instructions; develop, acquire, install, and use technology and systems for the purposes of collecting, validating, and verifying information, processing and maintaining information, and disclosing and providing information; adjust the existing ways to comply with any previously applicable instructions and requirements; train personnel to be able to respond to a collection of information; search data sources; complete and review the collection of information; and transmit or otherwise disclose the information.

E. Submission to Congress and the General Accounting Office

Under section 801(a)(1)(A) of the Administrative Procedures Act (APA) as amended by the Small Business Regulatory Enforcement Fairness Act of 1996, EPA submitted a report containing this rule and other required information to the U.S. Senate, the U.S. House of Representatives and the Comptroller General of the General Accounting Office prior to publication of the rule in today's Federal Register. This rule is a "major rule" as defined by section 804(2) of the APA as amended.

st of Subjects in 40 CFR Part 68

Environmental protection, Chemicals, azardous substances, tergovernmental relations.

Dated: May 24, 1996.

arol M. Browner,

dministrator.

For the reasons set out in the reamble, 40 CFR Part 68 is amended as llows:

ART 68—[AMENDED]

1. The authority citation for part 68 is vised to read as follows:

Authority: 42 U.S.C. 7412(r), 7601(a)(1), 61–7661f.

2. Part 68 is amended by designating Subpart C (§§ 68.100—3.130) as Subpart F.

ubpart A—[Amended]

4. Section 68.3 is amended to add the llowing definitions:

8.3 Definitions.

Act means the Clean Air Act as mended (42 U.S.C. 7401 et seq.)

* * * *

Administrative controls mean written rocedural mechanisms used for hazard ontrol.

AIChE/CCPS means the American nstitute of Chemical Engineers/Center r Chemical Process Safety.

* * * *

API means the American Petroleum stitute.

ASME means the American Society of echanical Engineers.

Catastrophic release means a major ncontrolled emission, fire, or xplosion, involving one or more gulated substances that presents nminent and substantial endangerment public health and the environment.

Classified information means lassified information'' as defined in e Classified Information Procedures ct, 18 U.S.C. App. 3, section 1(a) as any information or material that has en determined by the United States overnment pursuant to an executive der, statute, or regulation, to require rotection against unauthorized isclosure for reasons of national curity.''

Covered process means a process that as a regulated substance present in ore than a threshold quantity as etermined under § 68.115.

Designated agency means the state, cal, or Federal agency designated by e state under the provisions of 68.215(d) .

* * * *

Environmental receptor means natural areas such as national or state parks, forests, or monuments; officially designated wildlife sanctuaries, preserves, refuges, or areas; and Federal wilderness areas, that could be exposed at any time to toxic concentrations, radiant heat, or overpressure greater than or equal to the endpoints provided in § 68.22(a) , as a result of an accidental release and that can be identified on local U. S. Geological Survey maps.

Hot work means work involving electric or gas welding, cutting, brazing, or similar flame or spark-producing operations.

Implementing agency means the state or local agency that obtains delegation for an accidental release prevention program under subpart E, 40 CFR part 63. The implementing agency may, but is not required to, be the state or local air permitting agency. If no state or local agency is granted delegation, EPA will be the implementing agency for that state.

Injury means any effect on a human that results either from direct exposure to toxic concentrations; radiant heat; or overpressures from accidental releases or from the direct consequences of a vapor cloud explosion (such as flying glass, debris, and other projectiles) from an accidental release and that requires medical treatment or hospitalization.

Major change means introduction of a new process, process equipment, or regulated substance, an alteration of process chemistry that results in any change to safe operating limits, or other alteration that introduces a new hazard.

Mechanical integrity means the process of ensuring that process equipment is fabricated from the proper materials of construction and is properly installed, maintained, and replaced to prevent failures and accidental releases.

Medical treatment means treatment, other than first aid, administered by a physician or registered professional personnel under standing orders from a physician.

Mitigation or mitigation system means specific activities, technologies, or equipment designed or deployed to capture or control substances upon loss of containment to minimize exposure of the public or the environment. Passive mitigation means equipment, devices, or technologies that function without human, mechanical, or other energy input. Active mitigation means equipment, devices, or technologies that need human, mechanical, or other energy input to function.

NFPA means the National Fire Protection Association.

Offsite means areas beyond the property boundary of the stationary source, and areas within the property boundary to which the public has routine and unrestricted access during or outside business hours.

OSHA means the U.S. Occupational Safety and Health Administration.

Owner or operator means any person who owns, leases, operates, controls, or supervises a stationary source.

Population means the public.

* * * * *

Public means any person except employees or contractors at the stationary source.

Public receptor means offsite residences, institutions (e.g., schools, hospitals), industrial, commercial, and office buildings, parks, or recreational areas inhabited or occupied by the public at any time without restriction by the stationary source where members of the public could be exposed to toxic concentrations, radiant heat, or overpressure, as a result of an accidental release.

* * * * *

Replacement in kind means a replacement that satisfies the design specifications.

RMP means the risk management plan required under subpart G of this part.

SIC means Standard Industrial Classification.

* * * * *

Typical meteorological conditions means the temperature, wind speed, cloud cover, and atmospheric stability class, prevailing at the site based on data gathered at or near the site or from a local meteorological station.

* * * * *

Worst-case release means the release of the largest quantity of a regulated substance from a vessel or process line failure that results in the greatest distance to an endpoint defined in § 68.22(a).

5. Section 68.10 is added to subpart A to read as follows:

§ 68.10 Applicability.

(a) An owner or operator of a stationary source that has more than a threshold quantity of a regulated substance in a process, as determined under § 68.115, shall comply with the requirements of this part no later than the latest of the following dates:

(1) June 21, 1999;

(2) Three years after the date on which a regulated substance is first listed under § 68.130; or

(3) The date on which a regulated substance is first present above a threshold quantity in a process.

(b) Program 1 eligibility requirements. A covered process is eligible for

Program 1 requirements as provided in § 68.12(b) if it meets all of the following requirements:

(1) For the five years prior to the submission of an RMP, the process has not had an accidental release of a regulated substance where exposure to the substance, its reaction products, overpressure generated by an explosion involving the substance, or radiant heat generated by a fire involving the substance led to any of the following offsite:

(i) Death;

(ii) Injury; or

(iii) Response or restoration activities for an exposure of an environmental receptor;

(2) The distance to a toxic or flammable endpoint for a worst-case release assessment conducted under Subpart B and § 68.25 is less than the distance to any public receptor, as defined in § 68.30; and

(3) Emergency response procedures have been coordinated between the stationary source and local emergency planning and response organizations.

(c) Program 2 eligibility requirements. A covered process is subject to Program 2 requirements if it does not meet the eligibility requirements of either paragraph (b) or paragraph (d) of this section.

(d) Program 3 eligibility requirements. A covered process is subject to Program 3 if the process does not meet the requirements of paragraph (b) of this section, and if either of the following conditions is met:

(1) The process is in SIC code 2611, 2812, 2819, 2821, 2865, 2869, 2873, 2879, or 2911; or

(2) The process is subject to the OSHA process safety management standard, 29 CFR 1910.119.

(e) If at any time a covered process no longer meets the eligibility criteria of its Program level, the owner or operator shall comply with the requirements of the new Program level that applies to the process and update the RMP as provided in § 68.190.

6. Section 68.12 is added to subpart A to read as follows:

§ 68.12   General requirements.

(a) General requirements. The owner or operator of a stationary source subject to this part shall submit a single RMP, as provided in §§ 68.150 to 68.185. The RMP shall include a registration that reflects all covered processes.

(b) Program 1 requirements. In addition to meeting the requirements of paragraph (a) of this section, the owner or operator of a stationary source with a process eligible for Program 1, as provided in § 68.10(b), shall:

(1) Analyze the worst-case release scenario for the process(es), as provided in § 68.25; document that the nearest public receptor is beyond the distance to a toxic or flammable endpoint defined in § 68.22(a); and submit in the RMP the worst-case release scenario as provided in § 68.165;

(2) Complete the five-year accident history for the process as provided in § 68.42 of this part and submit it in the RMP as provided in § 68.168;

(3) Ensure that response actions have been coordinated with local emergency planning and response agencies; and

(4) Certify in the RMP the following: "Based on the criteria in 40 CFR 68.10, the distance to the specified endpoint for the worst-case accidental release scenario for the following process(es) is less than the distance to the nearest public receptor: [list process(es)]. Within the past five years, the process(es) has (have) had no accidental release that caused offsite impacts provided in the risk management program rule (40 CFR 68.10(b)(1)). No additional measures are necessary to prevent offsite impacts from accidental releases. In the event of fire, explosion, or a release of a regulated substance from the process(es), entry within the distance to the specified endpoints may pose a danger to public emergency responders. Therefore, public emergency responders should not enter this area except as arranged with the emergency contact indicated in the RMP. The undersigned certifies that, to the best of my knowledge, information, and belief, formed after reasonable inquiry, the information submitted is true, accurate, and complete. [Signature, title, date signed]."

(c) Program 2 requirements. In addition to meeting the requirements of paragraph (a) of this section, the owner or operator of a stationary source with a process subject to Program 2, as provided in § 68.10(c), shall:

(1) Develop and implement a management system as provided in § 68.15;

(2) Conduct a hazard assessment as provided in §§ 68.20 through 68.42;

(3) Implement the Program 2 prevention steps provided in §§ 68.48 through 68.60 or implement the Program 3 prevention steps provided in §§ 68.65 through 68.87;

(4) Develop and implement an emergency response program as provided in §§ 68.90 to 68.95; and

(5) Submit as part of the RMP the data on prevention program elements for Program 2 processes as provided in § 68.170.

(d) Program 3 requirements. In addition to meeting the requirements of

paragraph (a) of this section, the owner or operator of a stationary source with a process subject to Program 3, as provided in § 68.10(d) shall:

(1) Develop and implement a management system as provided in § 68.15;

(2) Conduct a hazard assessment as provided in §§ 68.20 through 68.42;

(3) Implement the prevention requirements of §§ 68.65 through 68.87;

(4) Develop and implement an emergency response program as provided in §§ 68.90 to 68.95 of this part; and

(5) Submit as part of the RMP the data on prevention program elements for Program 3 processes as provided in § 68.175.

7. Section 68.15 is added to subpart A to read as follows:

§ 68.15   Management.

(a) The owner or operator of a stationary source with processes subject to Program 2 or Program 3 shall develop a management system to oversee the implementation of the risk management program elements.

(b) The owner or operator shall assign a qualified person or position that has the overall responsibility for the development, implementation, and integration of the risk management program elements.

(c) When responsibility for implementing individual requirements of this part is assigned to persons other than the person identified under paragraph (b) of this section, the names or positions of these people shall be documented and the lines of authority defined through an organization chart or similar document.

8. Subpart B—is added to read as follows:

Subpart B—Hazard Assessment

Sec.
68.20   Applicability.
68.22   Offsite consequence analysis parameters.
68.25   Worst-case release scenario analysis.
68.28   Alternative release scenario analysis.
68.30   Defining offsite impacts — population.
68.33   Defining offsite impacts — environment.
68.36   Review and update.
68.39   Documentation.
68.42   Five-year accident history.

Subpart B—Hazard Assessment

§ 68.20   Applicability.

The owner or operator of a stationary source subject to this part shall prepare a worst-case release scenario analysis as provided in § 68.25 of this part and complete the five-year accident history as provided in § 68.42. The owner or erator of a Program 2 and 3 process ust comply with all sections in this bpart for these processes.

68.22   Offsite consequence analysis rameters.

(a) Endpoints. For analyses of offsite nsequences, the following endpoints all be used:

(1) Toxics. The toxic endpoints ovided in Appendix A of this part.

(2) Flammables. The endpoints for ammables vary according to the enarios studied:

(i) Explosion. An overpressure of 1 si.

(ii) Radiant heat/exposure time. A diant heat of 5 kw/m² for 40 seconds.

(iii) Lower flammability limit. A wer flammability limit as provided in FPA documents or other generally cognized sources.

(b) Wind speed/atmospheric stability ass. For the worst-case release alysis, the owner or operator shall use wind speed of 1.5 meters per second d F atmospheric stability class. If the wner or operator can demonstrate that cal meteorological data applicable to e stationary source show a higher inimum wind speed or less stable mosphere at all times during the revious three years, these minimums ay be used. For analysis of alternative enarios, the owner or operator may se the typical meteorological nditions for the stationary source.

(c) Ambient temperature/humidity. or worst-case release analysis of a gulated toxic substance, the owner or perator shall use the highest daily aximum temperature in the previous ree years and average humidity for the te, based on temperature/humidity ata gathered at the stationary source or a local meteorological station; an wner or operator using the RMP Offsite onsequence Analysis Guidance may se 25°C and 50 percent humidity as alues for these variables. For analysis f alternative scenarios, the owner or perator may use typical temperature/ umidity data gathered at the stationary urce or at a local meteorological ation.

(d) Height of release. The worst-case lease of a regulated toxic substance all be analyzed assuming a ground vel (0 feet) release. For an alternative enario analysis of a regulated toxic bstance, release height may be etermined by the release scenario.

(e) Surface roughness. The owner or perator shall use either urban or rural pography, as appropriate. Urban eans that there are many obstacles in e immediate area; obstacles include uildings or trees. Rural means there are o buildings in the immediate area and

the terrain is generally flat and unobstructed.

(f) Dense or neutrally buoyant gases. The owner or operator shall ensure that tables or models used for dispersion analysis of regulated toxic substances appropriately account for gas density.

(g) Temperature of released substance. For worst case, liquids other than gases liquified by refrigeration only shall be considered to be released at the highest daily maximum temperature, based on data for the previous three years appropriate for the stationary source, or at process temperature, whichever is higher. For alternative scenarios, substances may be considered to be released at a process or ambient temperature that is appropriate for the scenario.

§ 68.25   Worst-case release scenario analysis.

(a) The owner or operator shall analyze and report in the RMP:

(1) For Program 1 processes, one worst-case release scenario for each Program 1 process;

(2) For Program 2 and 3 processes:

(i) One worst-case release scenario that is estimated to create the greatest distance in any direction to an endpoint provided in Appendix A of this part resulting from an accidental release of regulated toxic substances from covered processes under worst-case conditions defined in § 68.22;

(ii) One worst-case release scenario that is estimated to create the greatest distance in any direction to an endpoint defined in § 68.22(a) resulting from an accidental release of regulated flammable substances from covered processes under worst-case conditions defined in § 68.22; and

(iii) Additional worst-case release scenarios for a hazard class if a worst-case release from another covered process at the stationary source potentially affects public receptors different from those potentially affected by the worst-case release scenario developed under paragraphs (a)(2)(i) or (a)(2)(ii) of this section.

(b) Determination of worst-case release quantity. The worst-case release quantity shall be the greater of the following:

(1) For substances in a vessel, the greatest amount held in a single vessel, taking into account administrative controls that limit the maximum quantity; or

(2) For substances in pipes, the greatest amount in a pipe, taking into account administrative controls that limit the maximum quantity.

(c) Worst-case release scenario—toxic gases.

(1) For regulated toxic substances that are normally gases at ambient temperature and handled as a gas or as a liquid under pressure, the owner or operator shall assume that the quantity in the vessel or pipe, as determined under paragraph (b) of this section, is released as a gas over 10 minutes. The release rate shall be assumed to be the total quantity divided by 10 unless passive mitigation systems are in place.

(2) For gases handled as refrigerated liquids at ambient pressure:

(i) If the released substance is not contained by passive mitigation systems or if the contained pool would have a depth of 1 cm or less, the owner or operator shall assume that the substance is released as a gas in 10 minutes;

(ii) If the released substance is contained by passive mitigation systems in a pool with a depth greater than 1 cm, the owner or operator may assume that the quantity in the vessel or pipe, as determined under paragraph (b) of this section, is spilled instantaneously to form a liquid pool. The volatilization rate (release rate) shall be calculated at the boiling point of the substance and at the conditions specified in paragraph (d) of this section.

(d) Worst-case release scenario—toxic liquids.

(1) For regulated toxic substances that are normally liquids at ambient temperature, the owner or operator shall assume that the quantity in the vessel or pipe, as determined under paragraph (b) of this section, is spilled instantaneously to form a liquid pool.

(i) The surface area of the pool shall be determined by assuming that the liquid spreads to 1 centimeter deep unless passive mitigation systems are in place that serve to contain the spill and limit the surface area. Where passive mitigation is in place, the surface area of the contained liquid shall be used to calculate the volatilization rate.

(ii) If the release would occur onto a surface that is not paved or smooth, the owner or operator may take into account the actual surface characteristics.

(2) The volatilization rate shall account for the highest daily maximum temperature occurring in the past three years, the temperature of the substance in the vessel, and the concentration of the substance if the liquid spilled is a mixture or solution.

(3) The rate of release to air shall be determined from the volatilization rate of the liquid pool. The owner or operator may use the methodology in the RMP Offsite Consequence Analysis Guidance or any other publicly available techniques that account for the modeling conditions and are recognized by industry as applicable as part of

current practices. Proprietary models that account for the modeling conditions may be used provided the owner or operator allows the implementing agency access to the model and describes model features and differences from publicly available models to local emergency planners upon request.

(e) Worst-case release scenario—flammables. The owner or operator shall assume that the quantity of the substance, as determined under paragraph (b) of this section, vaporizes resulting in a vapor cloud explosion. A yield factor of 10 percent of the available energy released in the explosion shall be used to determine the distance to the explosion endpoint if the model used is based on TNT-equivalent methods.

(f) Parameters to be applied. The owner or operator shall use the parameters defined in § 68.22 to determine distance to the endpoints. The owner or operator may use the methodology provided in the RMP Offsite Consequence Analysis Guidance or any commercially or publicly available air dispersion modeling techniques, provided the techniques account for the modeling conditions and are recognized by industry as applicable as part of current practices. Proprietary models that account for the modeling conditions may be used provided the owner or operator allows the implementing agency access to the model and describes model features and differences from publicly available models to local emergency planners upon request.

(g) Consideration of passive mitigation. Passive mitigation systems may be considered for the analysis of worst case provided that the mitigation system is capable of withstanding the release event triggering the scenario and would still function as intended.

(h) Factors in selecting a worst-case scenario. Notwithstanding the provisions of paragraph (b) of this section, the owner or operator shall select as the worst case for flammable regulated substances or the worst case for regulated toxic substances, a scenario based on the following factors if such a scenario would result in a greater distance to an endpoint defined in § 68.22(a) beyond the stationary source boundary than the scenario provided under paragraph (b) of this section:

(1) Smaller quantities handled at higher process temperature or pressure; and

(2) Proximity to the boundary of the stationary source.

§ 68.28 Alternative release scenario analysis.

(a) The number of scenarios. The owner or operator shall identify and analyze at least one alternative release scenario for each regulated toxic substance held in a covered process(es) and at least one alternative release scenario to represent all flammable substances held in covered processes.

(b) Scenarios to consider. (1) For each scenario required under paragraph (a) of this section, the owner or operator shall select a scenario:

(i) That is more likely to occur than the worst-case release scenario under § 68.25; and

(ii) That will reach an endpoint offsite, unless no such scenario exists.

(2) Release scenarios considered should include, but are not limited to, the following, where applicable:

(i) Transfer hose releases due to splits or sudden hose uncoupling;

(ii) Process piping releases from failures at flanges, joints, welds, valves and valve seals, and drains or bleeds;

(iii) Process vessel or pump releases due to cracks, seal failure, or drain, bleed, or plug failure;

(iv) Vessel overfilling and spill, or overpressurization and venting through relief valves or rupture disks; and

(v) Shipping container mishandling and breakage or puncturing leading to a spill.

(c) Parameters to be applied. The owner or operator shall use the appropriate parameters defined in § 68.22 to determine distance to the endpoints. The owner or operator may use either the methodology provided in the RMP Offsite Consequence Analysis Guidance or any commercially or publicly available air dispersion modeling techniques, provided the techniques account for the specified modeling conditions and are recognized by industry as applicable as part of current practices. Proprietary models that account for the modeling conditions may be used provided the owner or operator allows the implementing agency access to the model and describes model features and differences from publicly available models to local emergency planners upon request.

(d) Consideration of mitigation. Active and passive mitigation systems may be considered provided they are capable of withstanding the event that triggered the release and would still be functional.

(e) Factors in selecting scenarios. The owner or operator shall consider the following in selecting alternative release scenarios:

(1) The five-year accident history provided in § 68.42; and

(2) Failure scenarios identified under §§ 68.50 or 68.67.

§ 68.30 Defining offsite impacts—population.

(a) The owner or operator shall estimate in the RMP the population within a circle with its center at the point of the release and a radius determined by the distance to the endpoint defined in § 68.22(a).

(b) Population to be defined. Population shall include residential population. The presence of institution (schools, hospitals, prisons), parks and recreational areas, and major commercial, office, and industrial buildings shall be noted in the RMP.

(c) Data sources acceptable. The owner or operator may use the most recent Census data, or other updated information, to estimate the population potentially affected.

(d) Level of accuracy. Population shall be estimated to two significant digits.

§ 68.33 Defining offsite impacts—environment.

(a) The owner or operator shall list in the RMP environmental receptors within a circle with its center at the point of the release and a radius determined by the distance to the endpoint defined in § 68.22(a) of this part.

(b) Data sources acceptable. The owner or operator may rely on information provided on local U.S. Geological Survey maps or on any data source containing U.S.G.S. data to identify environmental receptors.

68.36 Review and update.

(a) The owner or operator shall review and update the offsite consequence analyses at least once every five years.

(b) If changes in processes, quantities stored or handled, or any other aspect of the stationary source might reasonably be expected to increase or decrease the distance to the endpoint by a factor of two or more, the owner or operator shall complete a revised analysis within six months of the change and submit a revised risk management plan as provided in § 68.190.

§ 68.39 Documentation

The owner or operator shall maintain the following records on the offsite consequence analyses:

(a) For worst-case scenarios, a description of the vessel or pipeline and substance selected as worst case, assumptions and parameters used, and the rationale for selection; assumptions shall include use of any administrative ontrols and any passive mitigation that ere assumed to limit the quantity that ould be released. Documentation shall clude the anticipated effect of the ontrols and mitigation on the release uantity and rate.

(b) For alternative release scenarios, a escription of the scenarios identified, ssumptions and parameters used, and e rationale for the selection of specific cenarios; assumptions shall include se of any administrative controls and ny mitigation that were assumed to mit the quantity that could be released. ocumentation shall include the effect f the controls and mitigation on the lease quantity and rate.

(c) Documentation of estimated uantity released, release rate, and uration of release.

(d) Methodology used to determine istance to endpoints.

(e) Data used to estimate population nd environmental receptors potentially ffected.

68.42   Five-year accident history.

(a) The owner or operator shall clude in the five-year accident history ll accidental releases from covered rocesses that resulted in deaths, njuries, or significant property damage n site, or known offsite deaths, njuries, evacuations, sheltering in lace, property damage, or nvironmental damage.

(b) Data required. For each accidental elease included, the owner or operator hall report the following information:

(1) Date, time, and approximate uration of the release;

(2) Chemical(s) released;

(3) Estimated quantity released in ounds;

(4) The type of release event and its ource;

(5) Weather conditions, if known;

(6) On-site impacts;

(7) Known offsite impacts;

(8) Initiating event and contributing actors if known;

(9) Whether offsite responders were otified if known; and

(10) Operational or process changes hat resulted from investigation of the elease.

(c) Level of accuracy. Numerical stimates may be provided to two ignificant digits.

9. Subpart C is added to read as ollows:

ubpart C—Program 2 Prevention Program

ecs.

8.48 Safety information.
8.50 Hazard review.
8.52 Operating procedures.
8.54 Training.
8.56 Maintenance.
8.58 Compliance audits.
8.60 Incident investigation.

Subpart C—Program 2 Prevention Program

§68.48   Safety information.

(a) The owner or operator shall compile and maintain the following up-to-date safety information related to the regulated substances, processes, and equipment:

(1) Material Safety Data Sheets that meet the requirements of 29 CFR 1910.1200(g);

(2) Maximum intended inventory of equipment in which the regulated substances are stored or processed;

(3) Safe upper and lower temperatures, pressures, flows, and compositions;

(4) Equipment specifications; and

(5) Codes and standards used to design, build, and operate the process.

(b) The owner or operator shall ensure that the process is designed in compliance with recognized and generally accepted good engineering practices. Compliance with Federal or state regulations that address industry-specific safe design or with industry-specific design codes and standards may be used to demonstrate compliance with this paragraph.

(c) The owner or operator shall update the safety information if a major change occurs that makes the information inaccurate.

§68.50   Hazard review.

(a) The owner or operator shall conduct a review of the hazards associated with the regulated substances, process, and procedures. The review shall identify the following:

(1) The hazards associated with the process and regulated substances;

(2) Opportunities for equipment malfunctions or human errors that could cause an accidental release;

(3) The safeguards used or needed to control the hazards or prevent equipment malfunction or human error; and

(4) Any steps used or needed to detect or monitor releases.

(b) The owner or operator may use checklists developed by persons or organizations knowledgeable about the process and equipment as a guide to conducting the review. For processes designed to meet industry standards or Federal or state design rules, the hazard review shall, by inspecting all equipment, determine whether the process is designed, fabricated, and operated in accordance with the applicable standards or rules.

(c) The owner or operator shall document the results of the review and ensure that problems identified are resolved in a timely manner.

(d) The review shall be updated at least once every five years. The owner or operator shall also conduct reviews whenever a major change in the process occurs; all issues identified in the review shall be resolved before startup of the changed process.

§68.52   Operating procedures.

(a) The owner or operator shall prepare written operating procedures that provide clear instructions or steps for safely conducting activities associated with each covered process consistent with the safety information for that process. Operating procedures or instructions provided by equipment manufacturers or developed by persons or organizations knowledgeable about the process and equipment may be used as a basis for a stationary source's operating procedures.

(b) The procedures shall address the following:

(1) Initial startup;

(2) Normal operations;

(3) Temporary operations;

(4) Emergency shutdown and operations;

(5) Normal shutdown;

(6) Startup following a normal or emergency shutdown or a major change that requires a hazard review;

(7) Consequences of deviations and steps required to correct or avoid deviations; and

(8) Equipment inspections.

(c) The owner or operator shall ensure that the operating procedures are updated, if necessary, whenever a major change occurs and prior to startup of the changed process.

§68.54   Training.

(a) The owner or operator shall ensure that each employee presently operating a process, and each employee newly assigned to a covered process have been trained or tested competent in the operating procedures provided in §68.52 that pertain to their duties. For those employees already operating a process on June 21, 1999, the owner or operator may certify in writing that the employee has the required knowledge, skills, and abilities to safely carry out the duties and responsibilities as provided in the operating procedures.

(b) Refresher training. Refresher training shall be provided at least every three years, and more often if necessary, to each employee operating a process to ensure that the employee understands and adheres to the current operating procedures of the process. The owner or operator, in consultation with the employees operating the process, shall determine the appropriate frequency of refresher training.

(c) The owner or operator may use training conducted under Federal or state regulations or under industry-specific standards or codes or training conducted by covered process equipment vendors to demonstrate compliance with this section to the extent that the training meets the requirements of this section.

(d) The owner or operator shall ensure that operators are trained in any updated or new procedures prior to startup of a process after a major change.

§ 68.56   Maintenance.

(a) The owner or operator shall prepare and implement procedures to maintain the on-going mechanical integrity of the process equipment. The owner or operator may use procedures or instructions provided by covered process equipment vendors or procedures in Federal or state regulations or industry codes as the basis for stationary source maintenance procedures.

(b) The owner or operator shall train or cause to be trained each employee involved in maintaining the on-going mechanical integrity of the process. To ensure that the employee can perform the job tasks in a safe manner, each such employee shall be trained in the hazards of the process, in how to avoid or correct unsafe conditions, and in the procedures applicable to the employee's job tasks.

(c) Any maintenance contractor shall ensure that each contract maintenance employee is trained to perform the maintenance procedures developed under paragraph (a) of this section.

(d) The owner or operator shall perform or cause to be performed inspections and tests on process equipment. Inspection and testing procedures shall follow recognized and generally accepted good engineering practices. The frequency of inspections and tests of process equipment shall be consistent with applicable manufacturers' recommendations, industry standards or codes, good engineering practices, and prior operating experience.

§ 68.58   Compliance audits.

(a) The owner or operator shall certify that they have evaluated compliance with the provisions of this subpart at least every three years to verify that the procedures and practices developed under the rule are adequate and are being followed.

(b) The compliance audit shall be conducted by at least one person knowledgeable in the process.

(c) The owner or operator shall develop a report of the audit findings.

(d) The owner or operator shall promptly determine and document an appropriate response to each of the findings of the compliance audit and document that deficiencies have been corrected.

(e) The owner or operator shall retain the two (2) most recent compliance audit reports. This requirement does not apply to any compliance audit report that is more than five years old.

§ 68.60   Incident investigation.

(a) The owner or operator shall investigate each incident which resulted in, or could reasonably have resulted in a catastrophic release.

(b) An incident investigation shall be initiated as promptly as possible, but not later than 48 hours following the incident.

(c) A summary shall be prepared at the conclusion of the investigation which includes at a minimum:

(1) Date of incident;

(2) Date investigation began;

(3) A description of the incident;

(4) The factors that contributed to the incident; and,

(5) Any recommendations resulting from the investigation.

(d) The owner or operator shall promptly address and resolve the investigation findings and recommendations. Resolutions and corrective actions shall be documented.

(e) The findings shall be reviewed with all affected personnel whose job tasks are affected by the findings.

(f) Investigation summaries shall be retained for five years.

10. Subpart D is added to read as follows:

Subpart D—Program 3 Prevention Program

Sec.
68.65   Process safety information.
68.67   Process hazard analysis.
68.69   Operating procedures.
68.71   Training.
68.73   Mechanical integrity.
68.75   Management of change.
68.77   Pre-startup review.
68.79   Compliance audits.
68.81   Incident investigation.
68.83   Employee participation.
68.85   Hot work permit.
68.87   Contractors.

Subpart D—Program 3 Prevention Program

§ 68.65   Process safety information.

(a) In accordance with the schedule set forth in § 68.67, the owner or operator shall complete a compilation of written process safety information before conducting any process hazard analysis required by the rule. The compilation of written process safety information is to enable the owner or operator and the employees involved in operating the process to identify and understand the hazards posed by those processes involving regulated substances. This process safety information shall include information pertaining to the hazards of the regulated substances used or produced by the process, information pertaining to the technology of the process, and information pertaining to the equipment in the process.

(b) Information pertaining to the hazards of the regulated substances in the process. This information shall consist of at least the following:

(1) Toxicity information;

(2) Permissible exposure limits;

(3) Physical data;

(4) Reactivity data;

(5) Corrosivity data;

(6) Thermal and chemical stability data; and

(7) Hazardous effects of inadvertent mixing of different materials that could foreseeably occur.

Note to paragraph (b): Material Safety Data Sheets meeting the requirements of 29 CFR 1910.1200(g) may be used to comply with this requirement to the extent they contain the information required by this subparagraph.

(c) Information pertaining to the technology of the process.

(1) Information concerning the technology of the process shall include at least the following:

(i) A block flow diagram or simplified process flow diagram;

(ii) Process chemistry;

(iii) Maximum intended inventory;

(iv) Safe upper and lower limits for such items as temperatures, pressures, flows or compositions; and,

(v) An evaluation of the consequences of deviations.

(2) Where the original technical information no longer exists, such information may be developed in conjunction with the process hazard analysis in sufficient detail to support the analysis.

(d) Information pertaining to the equipment in the process.

(1) Information pertaining to the equipment in the process shall include:

(i) Materials of construction;

(ii) Piping and instrument diagrams (P&ID's);

(iii) Electrical classification;

(iv) Relief system design and design basis;

(v) Ventilation system design;

(vi) Design codes and standards employed;

(vii) Material and energy balances for processes built after June 21, 1999; and

(viii) Safety systems (e.g. interlocks, detection or suppression systems).

(2) The owner or operator shall document that equipment complies with recognized and generally accepted good engineering practices.

(3) For existing equipment designed and constructed in accordance with codes, standards, or practices that are no longer in general use, the owner or operator shall determine and document that the equipment is designed, maintained, inspected, tested, and operating in a safe manner.

§8.67 Process hazard analysis.

(a) The owner or operator shall perform an initial process hazard analysis (hazard evaluation) on processes covered by this part. The process hazard analysis shall be appropriate to the complexity of the process and shall identify, evaluate, and control the hazards involved in the process. The owner or operator shall determine and document the priority order for conducting process hazard analyses based on a rationale which includes such considerations as extent of the process hazards, number of potentially affected employees, age of the process, and operating history of the process. The process hazard analysis shall be conducted as soon as possible, but not later than June 21, 1999. Process hazards analyses completed to comply with 29 CFR 1910.119(e) are acceptable as initial process hazards analyses. These process hazard analyses shall be updated and revalidated, based on their completion date.

(b) The owner or operator shall use one or more of the following methodologies that are appropriate to determine and evaluate the hazards of the process being analyzed.

(1) What-If;
(2) Checklist;
(3) What-If/Checklist;
(4) Hazard and Operability Study (HAZOP);
(5) Failure Mode and Effects Analysis (FMEA);
(6) Fault Tree Analysis; or
(7) An appropriate equivalent methodology.

(c) The process hazard analysis shall address:

(1) The hazards of the process;
(2) The identification of any previous incident which had a likely potential for catastrophic consequences.
(3) Engineering and administrative controls applicable to the hazards and their interrelationships such as appropriate application of detection methodologies to provide early warning of releases. (Acceptable detection methods might include process monitoring and control instrumentation with alarms, and detection hardware such as hydrocarbon sensors.);

(4) Consequences of failure of engineering and administrative controls;
(5) Stationary source siting;
(6) Human factors; and
(7) A qualitative evaluation of a range of the possible safety and health effects of failure of controls.

(d) The process hazard analysis shall be performed by a team with expertise in engineering and process operations, and the team shall include at least one employee who has experience and knowledge specific to the process being evaluated. Also, one member of the team must be knowledgeable in the specific process hazard analysis methodology being used.

(e) The owner or operator shall establish a system to promptly address the team's findings and recommendations; assure that the recommendations are resolved in a timely manner and that the resolution is documented; document what actions are to be taken; complete actions as soon as possible; develop a written schedule of when these actions are to be completed; communicate the actions to operating, maintenance and other employees whose work assignments are in the process and who may be affected by the recommendations or actions.

(f) At least every five (5) years after the completion of the initial process hazard analysis, the process hazard analysis shall be updated and revalidated by a team meeting the requirements in paragraph (d) of this section, to assure that the process hazard analysis is consistent with the current process. Updated and revalidated process hazard analyses completed to comply with 29 CFR 1910.119(e) are acceptable to meet the requirements of this paragraph.

(g) The owner or operator shall retain process hazards analyses and updates or revalidations for each process covered by this section, as well as the documented resolution of recommendations described in paragraph (e) of this section for the life of the process.

§68.69 Operating procedures.

(a) The owner or operator shall develop and implement written operating procedures that provide clear instructions for safely conducting activities involved in each covered process consistent with the process safety information and shall address at least the following elements.

(1) Steps for each operating phase:
(i) Initial startup;
(ii) Normal operations;
(iii) Temporary operations;
(iv) Emergency shutdown including the conditions under which emergency

shutdown is required, and the assignment of shutdown responsibility to qualified operators to ensure that emergency shutdown is executed in a safe and timely manner.

(v) Emergency operations;
(vi) Normal shutdown; and,
(vii) Startup following a turnaround, or after an emergency shutdown.

(2) Operating limits:
(i) Consequences of deviation; and
(ii) Steps required to correct or avoid deviation.

(3) Safety and health considerations:
(i) Properties of, and hazards presented by, the chemicals used in the process;
(ii) Precautions necessary to prevent exposure, including engineering controls, administrative controls, and personal protective equipment;
(iii) Control measures to be taken if physical contact or airborne exposure occurs;
(iv) Quality control for raw materials and control of hazardous chemical inventory levels; and,
(v) Any special or unique hazards.
(4) Safety systems and their functions.

(b) Operating procedures shall be readily accessible to employees who work in or maintain a process.

(c) The operating procedures shall be reviewed as often as necessary to assure that they reflect current operating practice, including changes that result from changes in process chemicals, technology, and equipment, and changes to stationary sources. The owner or operator shall certify annually that these operating procedures are current and accurate.

(d) The owner or operator shall develop and implement safe work practices to provide for the control of hazards during operations such as lockout/tagout; confined space entry; opening process equipment or piping; and control over entrance into a stationary source by maintenance, contractor, laboratory, or other support personnel. These safe work practices shall apply to employees and contractor employees.

§68.71 Training.

(a) Initial training. (1) Each employee presently involved in operating a process, and each employee before being involved in operating a newly assigned process, shall be trained in an overview of the process and in the operating procedures as specified in §68.69. The training shall include emphasis on the specific safety and health hazards, emergency operations including shutdown, and safe work practices applicable to the employee's job tasks.

(2) In lieu of initial training for those employees already involved in operating a process on June 21, 1999 an owner or operator may certify in writing that the employee has the required knowledge, skills, and abilities to safely carry out the duties and responsibilities as specified in the operating procedures.

(b) Refresher training. Refresher training shall be provided at least every three years, and more often if necessary, to each employee involved in operating a process to assure that the employee understands and adheres to the current operating procedures of the process. The owner or operator, in consultation with the employees involved in operating the process, shall determine the appropriate frequency of refresher training.

(c) Training documentation. The owner or operator shall ascertain that each employee involved in operating a process has received and understood the training required by this paragraph. The owner or operator shall prepare a record which contains the identity of the employee, the date of training, and the means used to verify that the employee understood the training.

§ 68.73 Mechanical integrity.

(a) Application. Paragraphs (b) through (f) of this section apply to the following process equipment:
(1) Pressure vessels and storage tanks;
(2) Piping systems (including piping components such as valves);
(3) Relief and vent systems and devices;
(4) Emergency shutdown systems;
(5) Controls (including monitoring devices and sensors, alarms, and interlocks) and,
(6) Pumps.

(b) Written procedures. The owner or operator shall establish and implement written procedures to maintain the on-going integrity of process equipment.

(c) Training for process maintenance activities. The owner or operator shall train each employee involved in maintaining the on-going integrity of process equipment in an overview of that process and its hazards and in the procedures applicable to the employee's job tasks to assure that the employee can perform the job tasks in a safe manner.

(d) Inspection and testing. (1) Inspections and tests shall be performed on process equipment.
(2) Inspection and testing procedures shall follow recognized and generally accepted good engineering practices.
(3) The frequency of inspections and tests of process equipment shall be consistent with applicable manufacturers' recommendations and good engineering practices, and more frequently if determined to be necessary by prior operating experience.

(4) The owner or operator shall document each inspection and test that has been performed on process equipment. The documentation shall identify the date of the inspection or test, the name of the person who performed the inspection or test, the serial number or other identifier of the equipment on which the inspection or test was performed, a description of the inspection or test performed, and the results of the inspection or test.

(e) Equipment deficiencies. The owner or operator shall correct deficiencies in equipment that are outside acceptable limits (defined by the process safety information in § 68.65) before further use or in a safe and timely manner when necessary means are taken to assure safe operation.

(f) Quality assurance. (1) In the construction of new plants and equipment, the owner or operator shall assure that equipment as it is fabricated is suitable for the process application for which they will be used.
(2) Appropriate checks and inspections shall be performed to assure that equipment is installed properly and consistent with design specifications and the manufacturer's instructions.
(3) The owner or operator shall assure that maintenance materials, spare parts and equipment are suitable for the process application for which they will be used.

§ 68.75 Management of change.

(a) The owner or operator shall establish and implement written procedures to manage changes (except for "replacements in kind") to process chemicals, technology, equipment, and procedures; and, changes to stationary sources that affect a covered process.
(b) The procedures shall assure that the following considerations are addressed prior to any change:
(1) The technical basis for the proposed change;
(2) Impact of change on safety and health;
(3) Modifications to operating procedures;
(4) Necessary time period for the change; and,
(5) Authorization requirements for the proposed change.
(c) Employees involved in operating a process and maintenance and contract employees whose job tasks will be affected by a change in the process shall be informed of, and trained in, the change prior to start-up of the process or affected part of the process.
(d) If a change covered by this paragraph results in a change in the process safety information required by § 68.65 of this part, such information shall be updated accordingly.

(e) If a change covered by this paragraph results in a change in the operating procedures or practices required by § 68.69, such procedures or practices shall be updated accordingly.

§ 68.77 Pre-startup review.

(a) The owner or operator shall perform a pre-startup safety review for new stationary sources and for modified stationary sources when the modification is significant enough to require a change in the process safety information.
(b) The pre-startup safety review shall confirm that prior to the introduction of regulated substances to a process:
(1) Construction and equipment is in accordance with design specifications;
(2) Safety, operating, maintenance, and emergency procedures are in place and are adequate;
(3) For new stationary sources, a process hazard analysis has been performed and recommendations have been resolved or implemented before startup; and modified stationary sources meet the requirements contained in management of change, § 68.75.
(4) Training of each employee involved in operating a process has been completed.

§ 68.79 Compliance audits.

(a) The owner or operator shall certify that they have evaluated compliance with the provisions of this section at least every three years to verify that the procedures and practices developed under the standard are adequate and are being followed.
(b) The compliance audit shall be conducted by at least one person knowledgeable in the process.
(c) A report of the findings of the audit shall be developed.
(d) The owner or operator shall promptly determine and document an appropriate response to each of the findings of the compliance audit, and document that deficiencies have been corrected.
(e) The owner or operator shall retain the two (2) most recent compliance audit reports.

§ 68.81 Incident investigation.

(a) The owner or operator shall investigate each incident which resulted in, or could reasonably have resulted in a catastrophic release of a regulated substance.
(b) An incident investigation shall be initiated as promptly as possible, but not later than 48 hours following the incident.
(c) An incident investigation team shall be established and consist of at least one person knowledgeable in the

rocess involved, including a contract mployee if the incident involved work the contractor, and other persons ith appropriate knowledge and xperience to thoroughly investigate nd analyze the incident.

(d) A report shall be prepared at the onclusion of the investigation which icludes at a minimum:

(1) Date of incident;

(2) Date investigation began;

(3) A description of the incident;

(4) The factors that contributed to the cident; and,

(5) Any recommendations resulting om the investigation.

(e) The owner or operator shall stablish a system to promptly address nd resolve the incident report findings nd recommendations. Resolutions and orrective actions shall be documented.

(f) The report shall be reviewed with l affected personnel whose job tasks e relevant to the incident findings cluding contract employees where pplicable.

(g) Incident investigation reports shall retained for five years.

68.83   Employee participation.

(a) The owner or operator shall evelop a written plan of action garding the implementation of the nployee participation required by this ction.

(b) The owner or operator shall onsult with employees and their presentatives on the conduct and evelopment of process hazards nalyses and on the development of the her elements of process safety anagement in this rule.

(c) The owner or operator shall rovide to employees and their presentatives access to process hazard nalyses and to all other information quired to be developed under this lle.

68.85   Hot work permit.

(a) The owner or operator shall issue hot work permit for hot work perations conducted on or near a overed process.

(b) The permit shall document that e fire prevention and protection quirements in 29 CFR 1910.252(a) ave been implemented prior to eginning the hot work operations; it all indicate the date(s) authorized for ot work; and identify the object on hich hot work is to be performed. The ermit shall be kept on file until ompletion of the hot work operations.

68.87   Contractors.

(a) Application. This section applies contractors performing maintenance repair, turnaround, major renovation,

or specialty work on or adjacent to a covered process. It does not apply to contractors providing incidental services which do not influence process safety, such as janitorial work, food and drink services, laundry, delivery or other supply services.

(b) Owner or operator responsibilities. (1) The owner or operator, when selecting a contractor, shall obtain and evaluate information regarding the contract owner or operator's safety performance and programs.

(2) The owner or operator shall inform contract owner or operator of the known potential fire, explosion, or toxic release hazards related to the contractor's work and the process.

(3) The owner or operator shall explain to the contract owner or operator the applicable provisions of subpart E of this part.

(4) The owner or operator shall develop and implement safe work practices consistent with § 68.69(d), to control the entrance, presence, and exit of the contract owner or operator and contract employees in covered process areas.

(5) The owner or operator shall periodically evaluate the performance of the contract owner or operator in fulfilling their obligations as specified in paragraph (c) of this section.

(c) Contract owner or operator responsibilities. (1) The contract owner or operator shall assure that each contract employee is trained in the work practices necessary to safely perform his/her job.

(2) The contract owner or operator shall assure that each contract employee is instructed in the known potential fire, explosion, or toxic release hazards related to his/her job and the process, and the applicable provisions of the emergency action plan.

(3) The contract owner or operator shall document that each contract employee has received and understood the training required by this section. The contract owner or operator shall prepare a record which contains the identity of the contract employee, the date of training, and the means used to verify that the employee understood the training.

(4) The contract owner or operator shall assure that each contract employee follows the safety rules of the stationary source including the safe work practices required by § 68.69(d).

(5) The contract owner or operator shall advise the owner or operator of any unique hazards presented by the contract owner or operator's work, or of any hazards found by the contract owner or operator's work.

11. Subpart E is added to read as follows:

Subpart E—Emergency Response

Sec.
68.90   Applicability.
68.95   Emergency Response Program.

Subpart E—Emergency Response

§ 68.90   Applicability.

(a) Except as provided in paragraph (b) of this section, the owner or operator of a stationary source with Program 2 and Program 3 processes shall comply with the requirements of § 68.95.

(b) The owner or operator of stationary source whose employees will not respond to accidental releases of regulated substances need not comply with § 68.95 of this part provided that they meet the following:

(1) For stationary sources with any regulated toxic substance held in a process above the threshold quantity, the stationary source is included in the community emergency response plan developed under 42 U.S.C. 11003;

(2) For stationary sources with only regulated flammable substances held in a process above the threshold quantity, the owner or operator has coordinated response actions with the local fire department; and

(3) Appropriate mechanisms are in place to notify emergency responders when there is a need for a response.

§ 68.95   Emergency response program.

(a) The owner or operator shall develop and implement an emergency response program for the purpose of protecting public health and the environment. Such program shall include the following elements:

(1) An emergency response plan, which shall be maintained at the stationary source and contain at least the following elements:

(i) Procedures for informing the public and local emergency response agencies about accidental releases;

(ii) Documentation of proper first-aid and emergency medical treatment necessary to treat accidental human exposures; and

(iii) Procedures and measures for emergency response after an accidental release of a regulated substance;

(2) Procedures for the use of emergency response equipment and for its inspection, testing, and maintenance;

(3) Training for all employees in relevant procedures; and

(4) Procedures to review and update, as appropriate, the emergency response plan to reflect changes at the stationary source and ensure that employees are informed of changes.

(b) A written plan that complies with other Federal contingency plan regulations or is consistent with the approach in the National Response Team's Integrated Contingency Plan Guidance ("One Plan") and that, among other matters, includes the elements provided in paragraph (a) of this section, shall satisfy the requirements of this section if the owner or operator also complies with paragraph (c) of this section.

(c) The emergency response plan developed under paragraph (a)(1) of this section shall be coordinated with the community emergency response plan developed under 42 U.S.C. 11003. Upon request of the local emergency planning committee or emergency response officials, the owner or operator shall promptly provide to the local emergency response officials information necessary for developing and implementing the community emergency response plan.

12. Subpart G is added to read as follows:

Subpart G—Risk Management Plan

Sec.

Subpart G—Risk Management Plan

§ 68.150 Submission.

(a) The owner or operator shall submit a single RMP that includes the information required by §§ 68.155 through 68.185 for all covered processes. The RMP shall be submitted in a method and format to a central point as specified by EPA prior to June 21, 1999.

(b) The owner or operator shall submit the first RMP no later than the latest of the following dates:

(1) June 21, 1999;

(2) Three years after the date on which a regulated substance is first listed under § 68.130; or

(3) The date on which a regulated substance is first present above a threshold quantity in a process.

(c) Subsequent submissions of RMPs shall be in accordance with § 68.190.

(d) Notwithstanding the provisions of §§ 68.155 to 68.190, the RMP shall exclude classified information. Subject to appropriate procedures to protect such information from public disclosure, classified data or information excluded from the RMP may be made available in a classified annex to the RMP for review by Federal and state representatives who have received the appropriate security clearances.

§ 68.155 Executive summary.

The owner or operator shall provide in the RMP an executive summary that includes a brief description of the following elements:

(a) The accidental release prevention and emergency response policies at the stationary source;

(b) The stationary source and regulated substances handled;

(c) The worst-case release scenario(s) and the alternative release scenario(s), including administrative controls and mitigation measures to limit the distances for each reported scenario;

(d) The general accidental release prevention program and chemical-specific prevention steps;

(e) The five-year accident history;

(f) The emergency response program; and

(g) Planned changes to improve safety.

§ 68.160 Registration.

(a) The owner or operator shall complete a single registration form and include it in the RMP. The form shall cover all regulated substances handled in covered processes.

(b) The registration shall include the following data:

(1) Stationary source name, street, city, county, state, zip code, latitude, and longitude;

(2) The stationary source Dun and Bradstreet number;

(3) Name and Dun and Bradstreet number of the corporate parent company;

(4) The name, telephone number, and mailing address of the owner or operator;

(5) The name and title of the person or position with overall responsibility for RMP elements and implementation;

(6) The name, title, telephone number, and 24-hour telephone number of the emergency contact;

(7) For each covered process, the name and CAS number of each regulated substance held above the threshold quantity in the process, the maximum quantity of each regulated substance or mixture in the process (in pounds) to two significant digits, the SIC code, and the Program level of the process;

(8) The stationary source EPA identifier;

(9) The number of full-time employees at the stationary source;

(10) Whether the stationary source is subject to 29 CFR 1910.119;

(11) Whether the stationary source is subject to 40 CFR part 355;

(12) Whether the stationary source has a CAA Title V operating permit; and

(13) The date of the last safety inspection of the stationary source by a Federal, state, or local government agency and the identity of the inspecting entity.

§ 68.165 Offsite consequence analysis.

(a) The owner or operator shall submit in the RMP information:

(1) One worst-case release scenario for each Program 1 process; and

(2) For Program 2 and 3 processes, one worst-case release scenario to represent all regulated toxic substances held above the threshold quantity and one worst-case release scenario to represent all regulated flammable substances held above the threshold quantity. If additional worst-case scenarios for toxics or flammables are required by § 68.25(a)(2)(iii), the owner or operator shall submit the same information on the additional scenario(s). The owner or operator of Program 2 and 3 processes shall also submit information on one alternative release scenario for each regulated toxic substance held above the threshold quantity and one alternative release scenario to represent all regulated flammable substances held above the threshold quantity.

(b) The owner or operator shall submit the following data:

(1) Chemical name;

(2) Physical state (toxics only);

(3) Basis of results (give model name if used);

(4) Scenario (explosion, fire, toxic gas release, or liquid spill and vaporization);

(5) Quantity released in pounds;

(6) Release rate;

(7) Release duration;

(8) Wind speed and atmospheric stability class (toxics only);

(9) Topography (toxics only);

(10) Distance to endpoint;

(11) Public and environmental receptors within the distance;

(12) Passive mitigation considered; and

(13) Active mitigation considered (alternative releases only);

§ 68.168 Five-year accident history.

The owner or operator shall submit in the RMP the information provided in § 68.42(b) on each accident covered by § 68.42(a).

§ 68.170 Prevention program/Program 2.

(a) For each Program 2 process, the owner or operator shall provide in the RMP the information indicated in paragraphs (b) through (k) of this section. If the same information applies more than one covered process, the owner or operator may provide the information only once, but shall indicate to which processes the information applies.

(b) The SIC code for the process.

(c) The name(s) of the chemical(s) covered.

(d) The date of the most recent review or revision of the safety information and a list of Federal or state regulations or industry-specific design codes and standards used to demonstrate compliance with the safety information requirement.

(e) The date of completion of the most recent hazard review or update.

(1) The expected date of completion of any changes resulting from the hazard review;

(2) Major hazards identified;

(3) Process controls in use;

(4) Mitigation systems in use;

(5) Monitoring and detection systems in use; and

(6) Changes since the last hazard review.

(f) The date of the most recent review or revision of operating procedures.

(g) The date of the most recent review or revision of training programs;

(1) The type of training provided—classroom, classroom plus on the job, on the job; and

(2) The type of competency testing used.

(h) The date of the most recent review or revision of maintenance procedures and the date of the most recent equipment inspection or test and the equipment inspected or tested.

(i) The date of the most recent compliance audit and the expected date of completion of any changes resulting from the compliance audit.

(j) The date of the most recent incident investigation and the expected date of completion of any changes resulting from the investigation.

(k) The date of the most recent change that triggered a review or revision of safety information, the hazard review, operating or maintenance procedures, or training.

68.175 Prevention program/Program 3.

(a) For each Program 3 process, the owner or operator shall provide the information indicated in paragraphs (b) through (p) of this section. If the same information applies to more than one covered process, the owner or operator may provide the information only once, but shall indicate to which processes the information applies.

(b) The SIC code for the process.

(c) The name(s) of the substance(s) covered.

(d) The date on which the safety information was last reviewed or revised.

(e) The date of completion of the most recent PHA or update and the technique used.

(1) The expected date of completion of any changes resulting from the PHA;

(2) Major hazards identified;

(3) Process controls in use;

(4) Mitigation systems in use;

(5) Monitoring and detection systems in use; and

(6) Changes since the last PHA.

(f) The date of the most recent review or revision of operating procedures.

(g) The date of the most recent review or revision of training programs;

(1) The type of training provided—classroom, classroom plus on the job, on the job; and

(2) The type of competency testing used.

(h) The date of the most recent review or revision of maintenance procedures and the date of the most recent equipment inspection or test and the equipment inspected or tested.

(i) The date of the most recent change that triggered management of change procedures and the date of the most recent review or revision of management of change procedures.

(j) The date of the most recent pre-startup review.

(k) The date of the most recent compliance audit and the expected date of completion of any changes resulting from the compliance audit;

(l) The date of the most recent incident investigation and the expected date of completion of any changes resulting from the investigation;

(m) The date of the most recent review or revision of employee participation plans;

(n) The date of the most recent review or revision of hot work permit procedures;

(o) The date of the most recent review or revision of contractor safety procedures; and

(p) The date of the most recent evaluation of contractor safety performance.

§ 68.180 Emergency response program.

(a) The owner or operator shall provide in the RMP the following information:

(1) Do you have a written emergency response plan?

(2) Does the plan include specific actions to be taken in response to an accidental releases of a regulated substance?

(3) Does the plan include procedures for informing the public and local agencies responsible for responding to accidental releases?

(4) Does the plan include information on emergency health care?

(5) The date of the most recent review or update of the emergency response plan;

(6) The date of the most recent emergency response training for employees.

(b) The owner or operator shall provide the name and telephone number of the local agency with which the plan is coordinated.

(c) The owner or operator shall list other Federal or state emergency plan requirements to which the stationary source is subject.

§ 68.185 Certification.

(a) For Program 1 processes, the owner or operator shall submit in the RMP the certification statement provided in § 68.12(b)(4).

(b) For all other covered processes, the owner or operator shall submit in the RMP a single certification that, to the best of the signer's knowledge, information, and belief formed after reasonable inquiry, the information submitted is true, accurate, and complete.

§ 68.190 Updates.

(a) The owner or operator shall review and update the RMP as specified in paragraph (b) of this section and submit it in a method and format to a central point specified by EPA prior to June 21, 1999.

(b) The owner or operator of a stationary source shall revise and update the RMP submitted under § 68.150 as follows:

(1) Within five years of its initial submission or most recent update required by paragraphs (b)(2) through (b)(7) of this section, whichever is later.

(2) No later than three years after a newly regulated substance is first listed by EPA;

(3) No later than the date on which a new regulated substance is first present in an already covered process above a threshold quantity;

(4) No later than the date on which a regulated substance is first present above a threshold quantity in a new process;

(5) Within six months of a change that requires a revised PHA or hazard review;

(6) Within six months of a change that requires a revised offsite consequence analysis as provided in § 68.36; and

(7) Within six months of a change that alters the Program level that applied to any covered process.

(c) If a stationary source is no longer subject to this part, the owner or operator shall submit a revised registration to EPA within six months indicating that the stationary source is no longer covered.

13. Subpart H is added to read as follows:

Subpart H—Other Requirements

Sec.
§ 68.200 Recordkeeping.
§ 68.210 Availability of information to the public.
68.215 Permit content and air permitting authority or designated agency requirements.
68.220 Audits.

Subpart H—Other Requirements

§ 68.200 Recordkeeping.

The owner or operator shall maintain records supporting the implementation of this part for five years unless otherwise provided in Subpart D of this part.

§ 68.210 Availability of information to the public.

(a) The RMP required under subpart G of this part shall be available to the public under 42 U.S.C. 7414(c).

(b) The disclosure of classified information by the Department of Defense or other Federal agencies or contractors of such agencies shall be controlled by applicable laws, regulations, or executive orders concerning the release of classified information.

§ 68.215 Permit content and air permitting authority or designated agency requirements.

(a) These requirements apply to any stationary source subject to this part 68 and parts 70 or 71 of this Chapter. The 40 CFR part 70 or part 71 permit for the stationary source shall contain:

(1) A statement listing this part as an applicable requirement;

(2) Conditions that require the source owner or operator to submit:

(i) A compliance schedule for meeting the requirements of this part by the date provided in § 68.10(a) or;

(ii) As part of the compliance certification submitted under 40 CFR 70.6(c)(5), a certification statement that the source is in compliance with all requirements of this part, including the registration and submission of the RMP.

(b) The owner or operator shall submit any additional relevant information requested by the air permitting authority or designated agency.

(c) For 40 CFR part 70 or part 71 permits issued prior to the deadline for registering and submitting the RMP and which do not contain permit conditions described in paragraph (a) of this section, the owner or operator or air

permitting authority shall initiate permit revision or reopening according to the procedures of 40 CFR 70.7 or 71.7 to incorporate the terms and conditions consistent with paragraph (a) of this section.

(d) The state may delegate the authority to implement and enforce the requirements of paragraph (e) of this section to a state or local agency or agencies other than the air permitting authority. An up-to-date copy of any delegation instrument shall be maintained by the air permitting authority. The state may enter a written agreement with the Administrator under which EPA will implement and enforce the requirements of paragraph (e) of this section.

(e) The air permitting authority or the agency designated by delegation or agreement under paragraph (d) of this section shall, at a minimum:

(1) Verify that the source owner or operator has registered and submitted an RMP or a revised plan when required by this part;

(2) Verify that the source owner or operator has submitted a source certification or in its absence has submitted a compliance schedule consistent with paragraph (a)(2) of this section;

(3) For some or all of the sources subject to this section, use one or more mechanisms such as, but not limited to, a completeness check, source audits, record reviews, or facility inspections to ensure that permitted sources are in compliance with the requirements of this part; and

(4) Initiate enforcement action based on paragraphs (e)(1) and (e)(2) of this section as appropriate.

§ 68.220 Audits.

(a) In addition to inspections for the purpose of regulatory development and enforcement of the Act, the implementing agency shall periodically audit RMPs submitted under subpart G of this part to review the adequacy of such RMPs and require revisions of RMPs when necessary to ensure compliance with subpart G of this part.

(b) The implementing agency shall select stationary sources for audits based on any of the following criteria:

(1) Accident history of the stationary source;

(2) Accident history of other stationary sources in the same industry;

(3) Quantity of regulated substances present at the stationary source;

(4) Location of the stationary source and its proximity to the public and environmental receptors;

(5) The presence of specific regulated substances;

(6) The hazards identified in the RMP; and

(7) A plan providing for neutral, random oversight.

(c) Exemption from audits. A stationary source with a Star or Merit ranking under OSHA's voluntary protection program shall be exempt from audits under paragraph (b)(2) and (b)(7) of this section.

(d) The implementing agency shall have access to the stationary source, supporting documentation, and any area where an accidental release could occur.

(e) Based on the audit, the implementing agency may issue the owner or operator of a stationary source a written preliminary determination of necessary revisions to the stationary source's RMP to ensure that the RMP meets the criteria of subpart G of this part. The preliminary determination shall include an explanation for the basis for the revisions, reflecting industry standards and guidelines (such as AIChE/CCPS guidelines and ASME and API standards) to the extent that such standards and guidelines are applicable, and shall include a timetable for their implementation.

(f) Written response to a preliminary determination.

(1) The owner or operator shall respond in writing to a preliminary determination made in accordance with paragraph (e) of this section. The response shall state the owner or operator will implement the revisions contained in the preliminary determination in accordance with the timetable included in the preliminary determination or shall state that the owner or operator rejects the revisions in whole or in part. For each rejected revision, the owner or operator shall explain the basis for rejecting such revision. Such explanation may include substitute revisions.

(2) The written response under paragraph (f)(1) of this section shall be received by the implementing agency within 90 days of the issue of the preliminary determination or a shorter period of time as the implementing agency specifies in the preliminary determination as necessary to protect public health and the environment. Prior to the written response being due and upon written request from the owner or operator, the implementing agency may provide in writing additional time for the response to be received.

(g) After providing the owner or operator an opportunity to respond under paragraph (f) of this section, the implementing agency may issue the owner or operator a written final determination of necessary revisions to e stationary source's RMP. The final etermination may adopt or modify the visions contained in the preliminary etermination under paragraph (e) of is section or may adopt or modify the ubstitute revisions provided in the sponse under paragraph (f) of this ection. A final determination that lopts a revision rejected by the owner r operator shall include an explanation f the basis for the revision. A final etermination that fails to adopt a ubstitute revision provided under aragraph (f) of this section shall

include an explanation of the basis for finding such substitute revision unreasonable.

(h) Thirty days after completion of the actions detailed in the implementation schedule set in the final determination under paragraph (g) of this section, the owner or operator shall be in violation of subpart G of this part and this section unless the owner or operator revises the RMP prepared under subpart G of this part as required by the final determination, and submits the revised RMP as required under § 68.150.

(i) The public shall have access to the preliminary determinations, responses, and final determinations under this section in a manner consistent with § 68.210.

(j) Nothing in this section shall preclude, limit, or interfere in any way with the authority of EPA or the state to exercise its enforcement, investigatory, and information gathering authorities concerning this part under the Act.

14. Part 68 Appendix A is added to read as follows:

APPENDIX A TO PART 68—TABLE OF TOXIC ENDPOINTS

[As defined in § 68.22 of this part]

CAS No.	Chemical name	Toxic endpoint (mg/L)
07–02–8	Acrolein [2-Propenal]	0.0011
07–13–1	Acrylonitrile [2-Propenenitrile]	0.076
14–68–6	Acrylyl chloride [2-Propenoyl chloride]	0.00090
07–18–6	Allyl alcohol [2-Propen-1-ol]	0.036
07–11–9	Allylamine [2-Propen-1-amine]	0.0032
664–41–7	Ammonia (anhydrous)	0.14
664–41–7	Ammonia (conc 20% or greater)	0.14
784–34–1	Arsenous trichloride	0.010
784–42–1	Arsine	0.0019
0294–34–5	Boron trichloride [Borane, trichloro-]	0.010
637–07–2	Boron trifluoride [Borane, trifluoro-]	0.028
53–42–4	Boron trifluoride compound with methyl ether (1:1) [Boron, trifluoro[oxybis[methane]]-, T-4	0.023
726–95–6	Bromine	0.0065
5–15–0	Carbon disulfide	0.16
782–50–5	Chlorine	0.0087
0049–04–4	Chlorine dioxide [Chlorine oxide (ClO2)]	0.0028
7–66–3	Chloroform [Methane, trichloro-]	0.49
42–88–1	Chloromethyl ether [Methane, oxybis[chloro-]	0.00025
07–30–2	Chloromethyl methyl ether [Methane, chloromethoxy-]	0.0018
170–30–3	Crotonaldehyde [2-Butenal]	0.029
23–73–9	Crotonaldehyde, (E)-, [2-Butenal, (E)-]	0.029
06–77–4	Cyanogen chloride	0.030
08–91–8	Cyclohexylamine [Cyclohexanamine]	0.16
9287–45–7	Diborane	0.0011
5–78–5	Dimethyldichlorosilane [Silane, dichlorodimethyl-]	0.026
7–14–7	1,1-Dimethylhydrazine [Hydrazine, 1,1-dimethyl-]	0.012
06–89–8	Epichlorohydrin [Oxirane, (chloromethyl)-]	0.076
07–15–3	Ethylenediamine [1,2-Ethanediamine]	0.49
51–56–4	Ethyleneimine [Aziridine]	0.018
5–21–8	Ethylene oxide [Oxirane]	0.090
782–41–4	Fluorine	0.0039
0–00–0	Formaldehyde (solution)	0.012
10–00–9	Furan	0.0012
02–01–2	Hydrazine	0.011
647–01–0	Hydrochloric acid (conc 30% or greater)	0.030
4–90–8	Hydrocyanic acid	0.011
647–01–0	Hydrogen chloride (anhydrous) [Hydrochloric acid]	0.030
664–39–3	Hydrogen fluoride/Hydrofluoric acid (conc 50% or greater) [Hydrofluoric acid]	0.016
783–07–5	Hydrogen selenide	0.00066
783–06–4	Hydrogen sulfide	0.042
3463–40–6	Iron, pentacarbonyl- [Iron carbonyl (Fe(CO)5), (TB–5–11)-]	0.00044
8–82–0	Isobutyronitrile [Propanenitrile, 2-methyl-]	0.14
08–23–6	Isopropyl chloroformate [Carbonochloride acid, 1-methylethyl ester]	0.10
26–98–7	Methacrylonitrile [2-Propenenitrile, 2-methyl-]	0.0027
4–87–3	Methyl chloride [Methane, chloro-]	0.82
9–22–1	Methyl chloroformate [Carbonochloridic acid, methylester]	0.0019
0–34–4	Methyl hydrazine [Hydrazine, methyl-]	0.0094
24–83–9	Methyl isocyanate [Methane, isocyanato-]	0.0012
4–93–1	Methyl mercaptan [Methanethiol]	0.049
56–64–4	Methyl thiocyanate [Thiocyanic acid, methyl ester]	0.085
5–79–6	Methyltrichlorosilane [Silane, trichloromethyl-]	0.018
3463–39–3	Nickel carbonyl	0.00067
697–37–2	Nitric acid (conc 80% or greater)	0.026

APPENDIX A TO PART 68—TABLE OF TOXIC ENDPOINTS—Continued

[As defined in § 68.22 of this part]

CAS No.	Chemical name	Toxic endpoint (mg/L)
10102–43–9	Nitric oxide [Nitrogen oxide (NO)]	0.031
8014–95–7	Oleum (Fuming Sulfuric acid) [Sulfuric acid, mixture with sulfur trioxide]	0.010
79–21–0	Peracetic acid [Ethaneperoxoic acid]	0.0045
594–42–3	Perchloromethylmercaptan [Methanesulfenyl chloride, trichloro-]	0.0076
75–44–5	Phosgene [Carbonic dichloride]	0.0008
7803–51–2	Phosphine	0.0035
10025–87–3	Phosphorus oxychloride [Phosphoryl chloride]	0.0030
7719–12–2	Phosphorus trichloride [Phosphorous trichloride]	0.028
110–89–4	Piperidine	0.022
107–12–0	Propionitrile [Propanenitrile]	0.0037
109–61–5	Propyl chloroformate [Carbonochloridic acid, propylester]	0.010
75–55–8	Propyleneimine [Aziridine, 2-methyl-]	0.12
75–56–9	Propylene oxide [Oxirane, methyl-]	0.59
7446–09–5	Sulfur dioxide (anhydrous)	0.0078
7783–60–0	Sulfur tetrafluoride [Sulfur fluoride (SF4), (T-4)-]	0.0092
7446–11–9	Sulfur trioxide	0.010
75–74–1	Tetramethyllead [Plumbane, tetramethyl-]	0.0040
509–14–8	Tetranitromethane [Methane, tetranitro-]	0.0040
7750–45–0	Titanium tetrachloride [Titanium chloride (TiCl4) (T-4)-]	0.020
584–84–9	Toluene 2,4-diisocyanate [Benzene, 2,4-diisocyanato-1-methyl-]	0.0070
91–08–7	Toluene 2,6-diisocyanate [Benzene, 1,3-diisocyanato-2-methyl-]	0.0070
26471–62–5	Toluene diisocyanate (unspecified isomer) [Benzene, 1,3-diisocyanatomethyl-]	0.0070
75–77–4	Trimethylchlorosilane [Silane, chlorotrimethyl-]	0.050
108–05–4	Vinyl acetate monomer [Acetic acid ethenyl ester]	0.26

[FR Doc. 96–14597 Filed 6–19–96; 8:45 am]

BILLING CODE 6560–50–M

---

40 CFR Part 68

[FRL–5516–6]

List of Regulated Substances and Thresholds for Accidental Release Prevention; Final Rule—Stay of Effectiveness

AGENCY: Environmental Protection Agency (EPA).

ACTION: Final rule.

SUMMARY: On April 15, 1996, the Environmental Protection Agency (EPA) proposed several modifications to provisions of the rule listing regulated substances and establishing threshold quantities under section 112(r) of the Clean Air Act as amended (List Rule Amendments). The proposed List Rule Amendments, if promulgated in a final rule, would clarify or establish that part 68 does not apply to several types of processes and sources. In addition, EPA proposed, pursuant to Clean Air Act section 301(a)(1), 42 U.S.C. 7601(a)(1), to stay the effectiveness of provisions that would be affected by the proposed List Rule Amendments, for so long as necessary to take final action on the proposed List Rule Amendments. EPA received no adverse public comment on the short-term stay. Today EPA is amending part 68 to promulgate the

stay, under which owners and operators of processes and sources that EPA has proposed not be subject to part 68 would not become subject to part 68 until EPA has determined whether to proceed with the List Rule Amendments. The effect of today's action will be to give owners and operators of sources affected by the proposed List Rule Amendments the same amount of time to achieve compliance with the requirements of part 68 as owners and operators of other sources in the event that EPA does not proceed with the List Rule Amendments as proposed.

EFFECTIVE DATE: June 20, 1996.

FOR FURTHER INFORMATION CONTACT: Vanessa Rodriguez, Chemical Engineer, Chemical Emergency Preparedness and Prevention Office, Environmental Protection Agency (5101), 401 M St. SW., Washington, DC 20460, (202) 260–7913.

SUPPLEMENTARY INFORMATION:

I. Background and Discussion

On April 15, 1996, EPA proposed amendments to regulations in 40 CFR part 68 that, inter alia, list regulated substances and establish threshold quantities for the accident prevention provisions under Clean Air Act section 112(r). 61 FR 16598. Readers should refer to that document for a complete discussion of the background of the rule affected. The amendments proposed in

that document ("List Rule Amendments") would, if promulgated, delete explosives from the list of regulated substances, modify threshold provisions to exclude flammable substances in gasoline and in naturally occurring hydrocarbon mixtures prior to entry into a processing unit or plant, modify the threshold provisions for other flammable mixtures, and clarify the definition of stationary source with respect to transportation, storage incident to transportation, and naturally occurring hydrocarbon reservoirs.

On the same date, EPA proposed to stay provisions of part 68 that were affected by the proposed List Rule Amendments until such time as EPA takes final action on the proposed List Rule Amendments. 61 FR 16606. EPA proposed a stay of 18 months because it believed such a period would be sufficient to take final action on the List Rule Amendments and believed that owners and operators affected by the List Rule Amendments should have the same certainty about whether they are subject to part 68 as owners and operators of other sources have when they begin their regulatory compliance planning. In general, owners and operators of sources subject to the "Risk Management Program" final rule promulgated elsewhere in today's Federal Register, have three years from today to achieve compliance with part 68.

248

NASA's Lewis Safety Management and Safety Permit System

NASA Lewis Safety Manual

Chapter 1

LEWIS SAFETY MANAGEMENT AND THE SAFETY PERMIT SYSTEM

Revision Date: 7/97

Figures must be viewed by hard copy (NASA/LeRC Safety Manual) located at the LeRC Library

1.1 PROGRAM

1.1.1 Scope

The Lewis Safety Management Program includes a Centerwide Lewis Safety Organization that provides the technical expertise and the safety orientation necessary to execute the Program functions and responsibilities; a safety control and accident reporting system that handles all the potential hazards known to exist at Lewis; a safety education and training system; and a Lewis safety publication.

1.1.2 Applicability

The instructions of the Lewis Safety Management Program apply to the Cleveland Center and the Plum Brook Station.

1.1.3 Authority

The authority for the Program is derived from the "NASA Basic Safety Manual" (NHB 1700.1, Vol. 1 B).

1.1.4 Policy

It is Lewis policy to administer its operations so as to reduce or eliminate all potential hazards, thereby avoiding undue risk and accidents that can result in loss of life, injury to personnel, damage to property, or loss of research operating time and effectiveness. To this end, a definite, comprehensive Safety Management Program encompassing every applicable phase of Center activity shall be established and implemented. Using the dictates of sound engineering judgment, Lewis will follow recognized safety codes and standards in all operations, including the modification or construction of facilities.

1.1.5 General Considerations

The Lewis Safety Management Program must consider both the Lewis safety environment and basic safety management.

The Lewis safety environment. Safety considerations at the Center are many and complex as a result of the following:

(a) The diversity of R&D operations in propulsion, power, and energy-related research

(b) The potentially hazardous character of the materials, fluids, test equipment, and processes involved

(c) The continual turnover of experiments and the constantly changing nature of research test operations

(d) The range and depth of the technical competence that is required to manage a safety program in such an environment

Basic safety management. For effective operation, Center safety management must provide

(a) The means of identifying, locating, and eliminating or controlling all potential hazards known to exist at Lewis

(b) The means of establishing and maintaining such employee safety data as specific hazard exposure, training, medical examinations, accident reports, and so on

(c) General compliance with "Occupational Safety and Health Administration (OSHA) Standards" (29 CFR).

(d) The means of integrating all of these into a coordinated Centerwide safety operations plan

1.1.6 Basic Responsibilities

Lewis Director. The Center Director is responsible for the establishment of a Lewis Safety and Accident Prevention Program in accordance with federal regulations, the "NASA Basic Safety Manual," NHB 1700.1, Vol. 1 B, and other related guidelines set up by NASA Headquarters.

Lewis Safety Organization. The Lewis Safety Organization includes the Executive Safety Board; the Institutional Safety Office; Area Safety Committees; the Aviation Safety Officer; the Electrical Applications and the Process Systems Safety Committees; Plum Brook Reactor Facility Safety Committee; the Office of Health Services; the Environmental Management Office (EMO), including the Radiation Safety Committee and the Environmental Pollution Control Board. It is broadly responsible for

(a) Promulgating Lewis safety policies and developing an effective Safety Management Program, including definition and implementation of the Center safety and accident prevention plan

(b) Evaluating Program effectiveness

(c) Developing appropriate recommendations and corrective actions to improve Program effectiveness

(d) Establishing and/or approving in-house safety standards, regulations, and criteria, and reviewing and monitoring operational compliance therewith

(e) Reviewing installations and equipment and issuing Safety Permits to operate facilities

Chief of the Institutional Safety Office. The Chief of the Institutional Safety Office (ISO) is responsible for the overall management, coordination, and documentation of the Lewis Safety Management Program and, in conjunction with the ESB, for the implementation of Center safety policies and directives. The ISO Chief also serves as the Center focal point of communications on all life safety matters and on functional safety relationships between the Center and NASA Headquarters.

Supervisors. All organization supervisors have a prime responsibility for compliance with pertinent safety requirements (including those related to housekeeping and shop safety) and for ensuring the effectiveness of the Lewis Safety Management Program as it affects their specific activities. This responsibility includes, but is not limited to, the following:

(a) Knowing pertinent Lewis safety requirements; communicating these requirements to subordinate personnel; mandating compliance with these requirements; and monitoring this compliance

(b) Knowing about and ensuring adherence to Lewis safety approval procedures

(c) Reviewing the work proposals of subordinates to ensure that all potential hazards are properly identified and evaluated, that procedures for safe operation and effective emergency rescue have been developed, and that the cognizant Area Safety Committee evaluation is obtained

(d) Personally surveying their work areas and recognizing potential hazards therein; analyzing statistics on accidents and near accidents in these areas; and initiating or recommending corrective action where required

(e) Supplying the Institutional Safety Office with the necessary technical input for the development of safe operating procedures, emergency rescue procedures, or any other safety documentation deemed necessary by the Institutional Safety Office

(f) Providing direction for continuing safety education and training for subordinate personnel in accordance with the standards and criteria established by the Institutional Safety Office

Employees. Each Lewis employee is responsible for

(a) Exercising reasonable care and caution in the safe performance of his or her work assignments and in the conduct of any activity at the Center

(b) Possessing knowledge of Lewis safety regulations, safe operating procedures, and emergency rescue procedures affecting his or her individual work area and work assignments and complying therewith

(c) Reporting the development or appearance of any potentially hazardous condition to his or her supervisor, to the Division Safety Representative, to the Institutional Safety Office, or to the Area Safety Committee chairman

1.1.7 Operating Responsibilities and Procedures

The specific operating responsibilities, procedures, and related requirements for the implementation of the Safety Management Program are reflected in the chapters of this Manual.

1.2 LEWIS SAFETY ORGANIZATION

1.2.1 Scope

The Lewis Safety Organization includes the Executive Safety Board; the Institutional Safety Office; Area Safety Committees; the Aviation Safety Officer; the Electrical Applications and the Process Systems Safety Committees; Plum Brook Reactor Facility Safety Committee; the Occupational Medical Services; the Environmental Management Office, including the Radiation Safety Committee and the Environmental Pollution Control Board.

The responsibilities and authorities of the Lewis Safety Organization are described in subsequent paragraphs.

1.2.2 Applicability

The Lewis Safety Organization directives apply to the Cleveland Center and the Plum Brook Station.

1.2.3 Authority

The authority for this organization comes from the "NASA Basic Safety Manual," NHB 1700.1, Vol. 1 B, and the "NASA Safety and Health Handbook," NHB 2710.1.

1.2.4 Objectives

The Lewis Safety Organization is structured to

(a) Ensure a safe work environment for conducting Lewis operations

(b) Avoid loss of life, injury of personnel, damage to or loss of property, and disruption of operations

(c) Ensure that an organized and systematic approach is used to identify and control potential safety hazards

(d) Obtain thorough and timely safety reviews and approvals for all technical operations at Lewis

(e) Instill safety awareness in all Lewis employees

(f) Provide specialized technical knowledge essential to continuing safety maintenance on a Centerwide basis

1.2.5 Executive Safety Board

The Executive Safety Board (ESB) serves as the Center's safety policy- and decision-making board and is responsible for the overall direction of the Lewis Safety Program. The ESB reports to the Center Director and is responsible for ensuring that all aspects of safety at Lewis are properly addressed and that the objectives of the program are met. The Center Deputy Director or his appointee serves as chairman of the ESB.

Responsibilities. The responsibilities of the ESB are to

(a) Establish a system of safety committees, advisory panels, and investigating committees to conduct detailed third-party reviews of specified Lewis operations and take necessary action to ensure safe operations within the limits of prescribed authority

(b) Oversee and monitor the activities of the committees and panels comprising the Lewis Safety Organization to ensure that they are appropriately staffed and operating

(c) Establish (or abolish) committees and panels and use consultants and experts as deemed necessary

(d) Report to the Center Director at least annually, providing a summary of the principal activities of the Lewis Safety Organization that includes an evaluation of its accomplishments and progress and an identification of problems or other matters requiring the attention of Lewis management

(e) Review, evaluate, and resolve any disputes on safety matters referred to it by any of the subdivisions of the Lewis Safety Organization

(f) Refer to the Director any Center safety disputes felt to warrant his attention and decision; acquaint the Director with significant major risks, for his concurrence about acceptability; ensure that such referrals include at least the following information: background, principal issues involved, pros and cons from a safety standpoint, hazard or risk analysis, and the Board's final evaluation and recommendation

(g) Provide policy and technical direction to the Lewis Safety Director to ensure uniformity and consistency of safety operations throughout Lewis

(h) Meet at the call of the chairman

Authority. In addition to the authority implicit in performing the functions and responsibilities described in Section 1.2.5, the ESB or any member thereof has the authority to stop and forbid any operation about which there is a safety concern, until an appropriate review and determination can be made. Exercise of this authority requires immediate notification to the chairman of the ESB and the chairman of the Area Safety Committee involved. The ESB has the authority to overrule any subordinate Lewis Safety Organization element except where Nuclear Regulatory Commission requirements are involved.

1.2.6 Lewis Institutional Safety Office

Chief of the Institutional Safety Office. The primary function of the Chief of the ISO is to implement, manage, and coordinate the Lewis Safety Program through his/her staff, which includes the Lewis Safety Officer, and the various committees. The Chief of the ISO reports on the overall Lewis Safety Program to the Executive Safety Board. The staff supporting the ISO Chief shall provide competent engineering judgment and analysis in executing safety policy and responsibility.

Responsibilities: The responsibilities of the Chief of the ISO are to

(a) Implement safety policies formulated by the Executive Safety Board (ESB) and perform those safety functions required by this Manual and other applicable regulations and directives

(b) Manage, implement, coordinate, and review the Lewis Safety Permit program

(c) Serve as consultant on safety matters to Lewis senior staff and management

(d) Assist the Lewis Procurement Officer in determining the adequacy of contractor safety programs and approve the content and the scope of the programs

(e) Maintain the Lewis Safety Manual and ensure that drafts of all proposed chapters for the Manual are distributed to the members of the ESB and the Environmental Pollution Control Board, and to the chairmen of cognizant safety committees and advisory panels, for review before publication

(f) Ensure that all material to be included in the Lewis Safety Manual has received prior written approval of the ESB and of the chairman of the Environmental Pollution Control Board, as appropriate

(g) Serve as the executive secretary to the ESB and as an ex-officio member of all safety committees and those investigating committees and advisory panels associated with the ESB

(h) Maintain the Lewis Emergency Preparedness Plan

Authority: The Chief of the ISO has the authority to terminate any operation of questionable safety until an appropriate review and determination can be made. Exercise of this authority requires immediate notification to both the chairman of the ESB and the chairman of the Area Safety Committee involved

Lewis Safety Officer. The Lewis Safety Officer ensures proper implementation of safety operations throughout the Center. The Lewis Safety Officer reports to and receives technical direction from the Chief of the ISO.

Responsibilities: The responsibilities of the Lewis Safety Officer are to

(a) Implement safety policies and perform those safety functions required by this Manual and other applicable regulations and directives

(b) Administer the expiration notification process for the Lewis Safety Permit program

(c) Maintain a safety information library containing codes, manuals, handbooks, the hazards inventory, information files, records, and references

(d) Monitor, through safety staff, contractor activities onsite to ensure compliance with all applicable safety standards and regulations

(e) Keep illness and injury records in accordance with OSHA regulations and prepare quarterly and annual reports to the Department of Labor and other relevant government agencies

(f) Manage, and coordinate emergency responses to Center accidents and mishaps

Authority: The Lewis Safety Officer has the authority to shut down any operation of questionable safety, until an appropriate review and determination can be made. Exercise of this authority requires immediate notification to the Chief of the ISO, the chairman of the ESB and the chairman of the Area Safety Committee involved.

1.2.7 Aviation Safety Officer

The Lewis general safety program concerned with airworthiness and flight safety is implemented by the Aviation Safety Officer (ASO). This officer participates with the Area 1 Safety Committee in the review of Safety Permit Requests for proposed operations involving flight research and program support aircraft assigned to Lewis. The ASO also serves as an ex-officio member of the Area 1 Safety Committee.

Responsibilities. The responsibilities of the ASO are to

(a) Review and evaluate proposed modifications to Lewis aircraft and the aircraft assigned to support Lewis programs, and review and evaluate operating procedures, performance requirements, and restrictions for missions on these aircraft

NOTE: The term "modification" refers to any alteration, addition, or removal of aircraft structure, components, equipment, or instrumentation, including equipment or instrumentation used for research purposes. The term "mission" refers to any flight of Lewis aircraft or aircraft assigned to support Lewis programs.

(b) Provide technical guidance on safety aspects of flight programs

(c) Maintain surveillance of aviation activities for conformance with prescribed directives, standards, procedures, and Safety Permit (NASA Form C-919) restrictions, and initiate corrective action when required

(d) Review aviation training and assess personnel qualifications to ensure safety of operations

(e) Review and approve Flight Work Order forms (NASA Form C-500) as required

(f) Report to the ESB at designated meetings

Authority. In addition to the authority necessary to implement assigned responsibilities, the ASO has the authority to shut down any operation or activity on which there is a question of aircraft flight safety, until an appropriate technical review can be conducted. Exercise of this authority requires immediate notification to the chairman of the ESB, the chairman of the Area 1 Safety Committee, and the Chief of the ISO.

1.2.8 Process Systems Safety Committee

The Process Systems Safety Committee (PSSC) ensures that the central service systems of the Center are designed to, and in fact do, operate in a safe manner. Central service systems include the systems and equipment for conveying, supplying, generating, removing, distributing, or processing liquids and gases and the prime machinery for each process system leading to and terminating at the test cell or an area of a research setup.

NOTE: The following systems are specifically included: central air and exhaust systems, fire and domestic water systems, carbon dioxide systems, steam systems, natural gas systems, heating plants, cooling tower water systems, cooling towers, wet and dry coolers, industrial waste basins and the lines leading to them, general purpose and mobile cryogenic equipment, pressure vessels and related systems, and the Engine Component Research Laboratory underground fuel storage and distribution system.

Responsibilities. In order to ensure the safe operation of the central service systems of the Center, the Process Systems Safety Committee has been charged with the following specific responsibilities:

(a) Establish acceptable safety standards and review specific proposals for modifications or additions to facilities, equipment, or operations involving process systems

(b) Oversee application of NHB 1700.6, "Guide for Inservice Inspection of Ground-Based Pressure Vessels and Systems"

(c) Approve and issue the Safety Permit for those proposals that meet Lewis safety requirements

(d) Supply the cognizant Area Safety Committee chairman with copies of the Safety Permits issued by the PSSC, calling attention to approved modes or levels of operation of the central systems so that Area Safety Committees do not approve research operations exceeding authorized bounds (Conversely, Area Safety Committees and Safety Permit requestors are expected to notify the PSSC of activities that are likely to affect the process systems.)

(e) Recommend, subject to the review and approval of the Executive Safety Board (ESB), minimum acceptable safety standards within the scope of the functions set forth in Section 1.2.8

(f) Advise Area Safety Committees and other organizational elements, upon request, about the safety aspects of specific proposals involving process systems

(g) Maintain technical surveillance of and keep informed of current activities in assigned area of responsibility, to anticipate problems and minimize safety-related conflicts between organizational elements

(h) Submit to the ESB significant concerns or unresolved questions regarding the granting of permits and the assessment of major risks

(i) Report, through the Committee chairman, to the ESB at its designated meetings

Authority. In addition to the authority necessary to implement the Committee's assigned responsibilities, the chairman of the Process Systems Safety Committee has the authority to shut down any operation or activity on which there is a question of process systems safety, until an appropriate technical review can be conducted. Exercise of this authority requires immediate notification to the chairman of the ESB, the chairman of the Area Safety Committee concerned, and the Chief of the ISO.

1.2.9 Electrical Applications Safety Committee

The Electrical Applications Safety Committee reviews all major electrical power systems leading to facility test cells or research setups and issues the Safety Permit to cover activities that cross safety area boundaries. The prime safety responsibility of the Committee is the power distribution system, including all substations, power transformers, and switchgear rated at 2400 volts or higher. For systems of 480 volts or less that lead to facility test cells or research setups, the power system interface is at the main distribution panels. The Committee is charged also with reviewing novel electrical applications. It provides copies of its Safety Permit forms to cognizant Area Safety Committees and ensures that Area Safety Committees do not approve research operations exceeding authorized bounds. As with the Process Systems Safety Committee (see Sec. 1.2.8), Area Safety Committees and originators of a Safety Permit Request are expected to notify the Electrical Applications Safety Committee when proposals are likely to impact the safety of electrical power systems.

Responsibilities. Specific responsibilities of the Electrical Applications Safety Committee are to

(a) Review specific proposals for the design, construction, alteration, or removal of electrical power systems or special electrical applications, and approve and issue a Safety Permit for those proposals that meet Lewis safety requirements

(b) Recommend, subject to review and approval of the ESB, minimum acceptable safety standards within the scope of the functions set forth in Section 1.2.9

(c) Advise Area Safety Committees, the Process Systems Safety Committee, and other organizational elements, upon request, about the safety aspects of specific proposals involving electrical applications

(d) Maintain technical surveillance of and keep informed of activities in assigned area of responsibility, to anticipate problems and minimize safety-related conflicts between organizational elements

(e) Submit to the ESB significant concerns or unresolved questions regarding the granting of permits and the assessment of major risk

(f) Report, through the Committee chairman, to the ESB at its designated meetings

Authority. In addition to the authority necessary to implement the Committee's assigned responsibilities, the chairman of the Electrical Applications Safety Committee has the authority to shut down any operation or activity on which there is a question of electrical power systems safety, until an appropriate technical review can be conducted. Exercise of this authority requires immediate notification to the chairman of the ESB, the chairman of the Area Safety Committee concerned, and the Chief of the ISO.

1.2.10 Plum Brook Reactor Facility Safety Committee

The Plumb Brook Reactor Facility Safety Committee ensures compliance with the Nuclear Regulatory Commission (NRC) licenses for the Plum Brook Reactor Facility (PBRF) and the Mockup Reactor contained within the PBRF. The current licenses, which expire in 1997, define a condition to possess-but-not-operate. The PBRF Safety Committee reviews all matters with safety implications, to ensure that plans, technical specifications, safety analyses, the radiator safety program, and written procedures provide protection to the worker, the facility, and the environment. In addition, it ensures that activities authorized under the license are conducted without endangering the health and safety of the public. The Committee concerns itself with radiation safety, industrial hygiene, and industrial safety; minimizing public and employee radiation exposure is a prime consideration. The Committee consists of four or more members, at least one of which shall have a nuclear background and one a familiarity with the conditions of the facility. The Radiation Safety Officer shall also be a member.

Responsibilities. The Plum Brook Reactor Facility Safety Committee responsibilities are to

(a) Approve new and revised PBRF procedures and facility changes that have safety implications, thereby ensuring that such procedures and changes are safe and consistent with NRC licenses and regulations

(b) Review any license change request prior to submitting it to the NRC

(c) Conduct periodic reviews and inspections of activities and records, to determine if the radiation controls and other safety controls required at the PBRF are being met

(d) Review and approve corrective actions that are proposed to preclude repetition of incidents, malfunctions, and personnel errors affecting facility safety

(e) Maintain technical surveillance of and keep informed of current activities at the PBRF, to anticipate safety-related problems

(f) Approve the method to control and maintain inventories of radioactive materials procured and disposed of

(g) Provide review, surveillance, and guidance as directed by the charter of the Committee

(h) Submit to the ESB significant concerns or unresolved questions regarding the granting of permits and the assessment of major risks

(i) Report, through the Committee chairman, to the ESB at its designated meetings

Authority. In addition to the authority necessary to implement the Committee's assigned responsibilities, the chairman of the Plum Brook Reactor Facility Safety Committee has the authority to shut down any operation or activity on which there is a question of safety, until an appropriate technical review can be made. Exercise of this authority requires immediate notification to the chairman of the ESB and the Chief of the ISO.

1.2.11 Area Safety Committees

The Area Safety Committees conduct third-party reviews of all proposed installations and operations in their assigned areas to ensure that the proposed design and/or operation is consistent with the dictates of sound engineering judgment and acceptable health and safety standards. (Safety areas of the Cleveland Center and the Plum Brook Station are shown in the Lewis Telephone Directory.)

Responsibilities. Area Safety Committee responsibilities are to

(a) Review specific proposals for all research operations, for modifications or additions to facilities and equipment, or for any project that may affect safety within the assigned safety areas

(b) Approve and issue permits for those proposals that meet Lewis safety requirements as prescribed in Section 1.5.5, Forms and Rules

(c) Maintain technical surveillance of and keep informed of current activities in assigned area of responsibility to anticipate problems and minimize safety-related conflicts between organizational elements

(d) Recommend, subject to the review and approval of the ESB, minimum acceptable safety standards within the scope of the functions set forth in Section 1.2.11

(e) Obtain comments and advice from advisory panels, the Institutional Safety Office, and the Environmental Management Office concerning matters that fall within their areas of specialization

(f) Make periodic surveys (at least annually) of plant and research operations within assigned areas and report results thereof to the Chief of the ISO

(g) Ensure that activities presenting significant risk to persons or property have a formal readiness review by the requester's line management prior to issuing a Safety Permit

(h) Submit to the ESB significant concerns or unresolved questions regarding the granting of permits and the assessment of major risks

(i) Report, through the Committee chairman, to the ESB at designated meetings

Specific committees' responsibilities. Besides the responsibilities set forth in Section 1.2.11, the following responsibilities apply to specific committees:

Area 1 Safety Committee: This Committee issues the required Safety Permit to cover all operations, maintenance, and R&D modifications of Lewis aircraft or other aircraft operated in support of Lewis programs and requiring the presence of Lewis personnel. Before issuing a Safety Permit, the Committee routes it to the Aviation Safety Officer for review and concurrence.

Area 6 Safety Committee: In implementing its responsibilities, this Committee coordinates with the Radiation Safety Committee, which has specific responsibilities to the Nuclear Regulatory Commission (NRC) in meeting established NRC requirements.

Area 9 Safety Committee: This Committee is responsible for all of the Plum Brook Station except the Plum Brook Reactor Facility, which is under cognizance of the PBRF Safety Committee.

Authority. In addition to the authority necessary to implement the Committee's assigned responsibilities, the chairman of each Area Safety Committee has the authority to shut down any operation or activity in the assigned area on which there is a question of safety, until an appropriate technical review can be made. Exercise of this authority requires immediate notification to the chairman of the ESB and the Chief of the ISO.

1.2.12 Occupational Medical Services

For the protection of employees Lewis maintains a comprehensive occupational medicine program under the direction of the Lewis Medical Director. Services provided under the program include investigation of the medical aspects of personal injury cases, medical diagnosis and treatment of occupational injuries, first aid, a physical fitness program, and the Health Screening Clinic. The responsibilities of the Occupational Medical Services are described in Section 1.4, Lewis Occupational Medicine Program.

1.2.13 Environmental Management Office (EMO)

EMO is responsible for the recognition, measurement, and recommended control of hazardous factors in the work environment that can cause illness, disease, or impaired well-being. EMO serves as consultant to the Lewis staff on matters of environmental quality, industrial hygiene, and health physics (including radiation safety). The responsibilities of EMO are described in Section 1.3.8.

1.3 LEWIS ENVIRONMENTAL QUALITY ORGANIZATION

1.3.1 Scope

The Lewis Environmental Quality Organization includes the Environmental Pollution Control Board (EPCB), the Occupational Medical Services, EMO, and the Radiation Safety Committee (RSC).

The responsibilities and authority of the Environmental Quality Organization are described in the following paragraphs.

1.3.2 Applicability

The provisions listed herein are applicable to the Cleveland Center and the Plum Brook Station.

1.3.3 Authority

The authority of the Lewis Environmental Quality Organization comes from NHB 8800.11, "Implementing the Provisions of the National Environmental Policy Act"; "The Occupational Safety and Health Act (1970)," Section 19; Executive Order 11514, "Protection and Enhancement of Environmental Quality"; Executive Order 12196, "Occupational Safety and Health Programs for Federal Employees"; Executive Order 12088, "Federal Compliance with Pollution Control Standards"; Executive Order 11752, "Prevention, Control, and Abatement of Environmental Pollution at Federal Facilities"; and the "NASA Basic Safety Manual," NHB 1700.1 (Vol. 1 B).

1.3.4 Objectives

The Lewis Environmental Quality Organization is structured to

(a) Instill environmental awareness in all Lewis employees

(b) Provide specialized technical knowledge essential to continuing protection and enhancement of environmental quality on a Centerwide basis

(c) Maintain control over potential environmental hazards, consistent with pertinent environmental standards and guidelines and sound engineering and operating practices

(d) Provide Lewis management with a centralized source of information on matters of environmental quality and control

1.3.5. Policy

It is Lewis policy to operate in a manner that provides a safe and healthful workplace for employees; that complies with all laws and regulations pertaining to health and the environment; and that protects and enhances the surrounding community and the environment, consistent with the mission of the Center.

Responsibility for implementing this policy lies with line management and all employees. The Environmental Quality Organization is responsible for providing guidance and oversight of implementation and for making periodic reports to regulatory agencies and others. Line management must ensure that operations under its control are operated consistent with these instructions and guidance from the Environmental Quality Organization.

1.3.6 Environmental Pollution Control Board

The Lewis Environmental Pollution Control Board serves as the Center environmental policy- and decision-making board. It is responsible for the overall direction of the Lewis Environmental Quality Organization. The Board is responsible for assuring the Center Director that all aspects of environmental quality are properly addressed and that program objectives are met.

Responsibilities. Specific responsibilities of the Board are to

(a) Recommend, to the Center Director, policies and practices for improvement in environmental health

(b) Provide environmental policy and direction to the Chief of the Environmental Management Office

(c) Coordinate with the Lewis Safety Organization to ensure third-party functional review of all Lewis R&D activities

(d) Serve as an appeal channel on unresolved questions pertaining to the environmental sensitivity of Lewis operations, and review, evaluate, and resolve any disputes

(e) Review existing or potential environmental problems and submit to the Center Director, along with the Board's evaluation and recommendations, any disputes that warrant the Director's attention and decision

(f) Develop systematic procedures to ensure a timely transfer of information and an understanding of programs affecting the environment, taking alternative courses of action into consideration

(g) Ensure that information about existing or potential environmental problems is made available to all appropriate levels of Lewis management

(h) Review NASA regulations, policies, and procedures relating to environmental pollution control and inform the Center Director of any Lewis operational deficiencies or inconsistencies therewith

(i) Review environmental impact assessments and statements related to Lewis operations; transmit assessments or statements with applicable recommendations to the cognizant NASA Headquarters organization

(j) Exchange pollution control data and research results with other Governmental agencies

(k) Meet quarterly, or as otherwise necessary, and submit to the Director a written report of the results of the meetings

Authority. In addition to the authority necessary to ensure performance of its stated responsibilities, the Environmental Pollution Control Board, or any member thereof, has the authority to close down any operation having a serious negative impact on the environment, until an appropriate review and assessment can be made. Exercise of this authority requires immediate notification to the chairman of the Environmental Pollution Control Board, the Chief of the Office of Environmental Programs, the chairman of the Area Safety Committee having jurisdiction in the area involved, and the chairman of the Executive Safety Board.

1.3.7 Occupational Medical Services

For the protection of employees, Lewis maintains a comprehensive occupational health program under the direction of the Lewis Medical Officer. This program provides investigation of the medical aspects of personal injury cases, medical diagnosis and treatment of occupational injuries, a physical fitness program, health screening clinic, and first aid. The Lewis Medical Officer serves as a member of the Environmental Pollution Control Board. The responsibilities of the Occupational Medical Services are described in LMI 1800.1, as revised, "Lewis Occupational Medicine Program," and Section 1.4.5 herein.

1.3.8 The Environmental Management Office

EMO is responsible for recognizing, measuring, and recommending control of hazards in the work environment that can cause illness, disease, or impaired well-being. The EMO serves as a consultant to the Lewis staff on matters of environmental quality, industrial hygiene, and health physics, and ensures compliance in these areas.

The responsibilities of the EMO are to

(a) Implement policies formulated by the Environmental Pollution Control Board

(b) Maintain appropriate handbooks, information files, and references, and serve as consultant on environmental quality, industrial hygiene, and radiation safety matters to the Lewis staff

(c) Assist the Lewis Procurement Officer in reviewing the environmental quality programs of contractors

(d) Make surveys of work areas on a periodic basis, collect samples associated with potentially toxic or other environmental hazards, and coordinate these efforts with cognizant personnel in the required technical specialties

(e) Advise Area Safety Committees (1) on the pollution control aspects of specific proposals to install, remove, or alter waterborne waste disposal facilities or air pollution control equipment in their areas; and (2) on the industrial hygiene aspects of specific proposals to install, remove, or alter systems, equipment, or operations

(f) Review requests for a Safety Permit to determine whether such requests concern matters under the cognizance of the Office, and when necessary, coordinate with Area Safety Committees in third-party reviews of proposed activities

(g) Review the precautions taken by operating officials with respect to controlling the acquisition of unusually toxic or radioactive materials; supervising the distribution, use, accountability, and disposal of toxic or radioactive materials; disposing of waterborne wastes through the various Lewis sewer systems; discharging exhaust, vent, or waste gases into the atmosphere; and monitoring systems designed to safeguard the health of persons associated with sources of pollution or exposed to toxic materials

(h) Evaluate these precautions, report to the Environmental Pollution Control Board on their effectiveness, and recommend changes if necessary

(i) Recommend, subject to review and approval by the Environmental Pollution Control Board, minimum acceptable environmental quality standards for operations involving toxic and noxious materials and pollution sources

(j) Request special experiments and investigations to delineate potential environmental hazards and evaluate the proposed methods of their control

(k) Verify compliance throughout Lewis with all pertinent regulations applicable to the prevention, control, and abatement of air and water pollution

(l) Keep abreast of developments and requirements in the fields of industrial hygiene, air and water pollution control, and health physics

(m) Review each Purchase Request for chemicals and hazardous materials, evaluate the hazard potential for each commodity, obtain copies of the Material Safety Data Sheet for hazardous materials, and distribute copies to interested persons

(n) Fulfill additional responsibilities pertaining to the Lewis Occupational Medicine Program described in LMI 1800.1

(o) Report to the Environmental Pollution Control Board at its regularly scheduled meetings

The Chief of the Environmental Management Office serves as the executive secretary to the Environmental Pollution Control Board and as the chairman of the Radiation Safety Committee.

Authority. The Chief of the Environmental Management Office is authorized to shut down any operation on which there is a question of health hazard or on which there is a source of contamination that exceeds established air and water pollution control limits, pending an appropriate review. Exercise of this authority requires immediate notification to the chairman of the Environmental Pollution Control Board, the chairman of the Area Safety Committee involved, and the chairman of the Executive Safety Board.

1.3.9 Radiation Safety Committee

The Radiation Safety Committee provides advice, technical expertise, and guidance to minimize and/or eliminate health hazards associated with using, transporting, storing, and handling radioactive materials and sources of ionizing radiation. The Committee was established under the broad nuclear byproduct material license for the Cleveland Center to review the associated radiation program and to verify compliance with Nuclear Regulatory Commission regulations.

Responsibilities. The Radiation Safety Committee responsibilities are to

(a) Review quarterly, or at more frequent intervals as directed by the Environmental Pollution Control Board, the precautions taken by operating officials with respect to regulating the acquisition of radioactive sources, materials, and equipment; and controlling the distribution, use, accountability, and disposal of radioactive materials and equipment

(b) Evaluate these precautions and their effectiveness, and report to the Environmental Pollution Control Board, recommending changes or improvements considered appropriate

(c) Recommend, subject to review and approval by the Environmental Pollution Control Board, minimum acceptable environmental quality standards for operations involving radioactivity

(d) Advise Area Safety Committees about ionizing radiation safety aspects of specific proposals to install, remove, or alter radioactive sources, materials, equipment, or operations

(e) Review each Safety Permit request referred by the Environmental Management Office

(f) Keep abreast of developments in and requirements for radiation safety

(g) Request special experiments and investigations when such activities are consistent with Lewis environmental quality objectives and policies

(h) Report to the Environmental Pollution Control Board at its regularly scheduled meetings

Authority. The chairman of the Radiation Safety Committee is authorized to shut down any operation on which there is a question of radiation safety, until an appropriate review can be made. Exercise of this authority requires immediate notification to the chairman of the Environmental Pollution Control Board, the chairman of the Area Safety Committee involved, and the chairman of the Executive Safety Board.

NOTE: Because of Nuclear Regulatory Commission requirements, the Radiation Safety Committee will not be overruled on decisions that reject experiments, facility modifications, or operating procedures on the basis of NRC safety requirements.

1.4 LEWIS OCCUPATIONAL MEDICINE PROGRAM

1.4.1 Scope

The Lewis Occupational Medicine Program, administered by the Occupational Medical Services, is a comprehensive health and safety management program that includes all aspects of health protection for Lewis employees. In order to provide continuity within these health and safety functions, the Lewis Medical

Director is a consultant/advisor to the Executive Safety Board and the Environmental Pollution Control Board. The Lewis Occupational Medicine Program practices such preventive medicine techniques as appropriate physical examinations and appraisal of health hazards in the work environment, along with emergency care, and diagnosis and treatment of occupational diseases and injuries.

1.4.2 Authority

The authority for the Lewis Occupational Medicine Program comes from Public Law 89 554, "Government Organization and Employees," Public Law 90 83, "Federal Employees Pay and Allowances, Etc.," and Public Law 91 596, "Occupational Safety and Health Act, 1970"; Executive Order 12196, "Occupational Safety and Health Programs for Federal Employees"; NHB 2710.1, "NASA Safety and Health Handbook, Occupational Safety and Health Programs"; and NMI 3792.1, "NASA Employee Assistance Program."

1.4.3 Applicability

These instructions apply to all Lewis organizational elements.

1.4.4 Policy

The Lewis Occupational Medicine Program is to be used to maintain, conserve, and improve the health of Lewis employees and to evaluate any physical, chemical, or bacteriological hazards that may be present in the employee's work environment.

Nothing in this section is to be construed as running counter to or establishing standards less comprehensive than those set forth in local, state, and Federal health regulations.

1.4.5 Responsibilities

Lewis Executive Safety Board and Environmental Pollution Control Board. These Boards are responsible for monitoring the Lewis Occupational Medicine Program, which is coordinated and implemented by them and the following Lewis health and safety groups: the Occupational Medical Services; the Environmental Management Office; the Institutional Safety Office; the Radiation Safety Committee; and the cognizant Area Safety Committee.

Lewis Medical Director. Through the Director of the Office of Health Services, the Medical Director

(a) Provides professional services for examining, diagnosing, and treating employee illness or injury and maintains records needed in the operation of the program

(b) Furnishes medical information to and assists the Lewis Human Resources Management Division, as required, in resolving questions about the placement and utilization of employees

(c) Consults with appropriate supervisors regarding employees who, in the judgment of a physician, may be allowed to work only if limitations on their physical activity are observed. (This applies also to new employees with physical handicaps and to employees returning to work after an illness or injury. The judgment of the employee's physician is given full consideration in such situations.)

(d) Keeps the Center Director informed, through the Chief of the Institutional Safety Office, of all cases of significant accidental injury to personnel, especially about the diagnosis, nature, and extent of injuries. This is done by direct and timely oral communication and includes subsequent followup medical reports. The severity of injuries (first aid, reportable, or lost time) is classified in accordance with Occupational Safety and Health Administration (OSHA) recordkeeping requirements.

(e) Ensures that kitchens and cafeterias are periodically inspected for conformance with local, state, and Federal health regulations

(f) Approves, prior to installation or introduction into the work area, such items as footpaths, first aid kits, salt tablets, air fresheners, and so forth

(g) Establishes procedures in conjunction with local medical facilities for emergency referral and treatment of injuries and illnesses

(h) Serves as Medical Review Official for the Lewis Drug-Free Workplace Program

(i) Serves as consultant to the Environmental Pollution Control Board

(j) Administers the Health Screening Program

(k) Administers the Physical Fitness Program

The Chief of the Environmental Management Office

(a) Coordinates with the Lewis Medical Director to provide professional services, and maintains the records necessary for operating the environmental health programs

(b) Provides advice on and criteria for environmental systems, shielding and absorption materials, sanitation provisions, illumination standards, noise, dust, ionizing and nonionizing radiation, vibration, temperature-humidity standards, air- and water-pollution controls, and exposure to toxic substances and biological agents

(c) Maintains a work area surveillance program that includes collecting and analyzing samples associated with potentially toxic hazards; performs periodic and special surveys of the physical environment for noise, dust, vibration, radiation, and such

(d) Develops or obtains environmental health and safety facilities and monitoring equipment commensurate with program needs

(e) Provides technical support as required by the Occupational Medical Services

(f) Recommends medical monitoring of certain Lewis personnel after reviewing Safety Permit Requests, Purchase Requests, and in-field monitoring and inspection activities. (Medical monitoring may include periodic physical examinations and/or laboratory analyses as appropriate to the potential hazard exposure of each employee.)·

Chief of the Institutional Safety Office. The Chief of the Institutional Safety Office

(a) Coordinates with the Lewis Medical Director to provide professional services and maintains records necessary for the operation of the safety programs

(b) Monitors illness and injury records in accordance with OSHA regulations

(c) Provides quarterly and annual reports to the Department of Labor

First-line supervisor. It is the responsibility of the first-line supervisor to discuss with employees under his or her jurisdiction the potential exposures and health hazards in their work assignments and to make arrangements to monitor those who are exposed to potential environmental hazards. The supervisor also semiannually reviews the changes in work assignments and facilities that influence the health monitoring program. The names of employees with potential hazard exposure are forwarded to the cognizant division office along with the identity of the material or condition of concern. The division chief collects and forwards these names to the Environmental Management Office for forwarding to the Medical Director

Employees. It the responsibility of all employees to maintain high standards of personal hygiene, health, and physical fitness and to notify their first-line supervisor of potential exposures to environmental health hazards in their work assignments.

1.4.6 Program Elements

Procedures for service-connected medical conditions and emergencies. There are procedures in place for the following conditions:

Illness or injury: When any illness, service-connected injury, or health emergency occurs during work hours, the employee notifies his or her supervisor, if possible, and immediately reports to Medicine Services. If a service-connected illness becomes apparent during off-duty hours, the employee notifies his or her supervisor and Medical Services within 24 hours unless the incident occurs during a weekend or similar off-duty period, in which case notification is made at the start of the next work day. If the employee is treated by his or her personal physician for a work-related condition during off-duty hours, this fact must be reported. First-line supervisors are to inform all personnel under their jurisdiction of these requirements.

Accidental spill or exposure: If an accidental spill of hazardous substance or exposure to a hazardous material or condition occurs, the employee concerned immediately notifies Medical Services of the incident and then notifies his or her supervisor of the incident, even if no injury is apparent.

First aid: Selected personnel are trained and properly equipped to render first-aid treatment on all shifts in critical areas of operation at the Center.

Health examinations. Health examinations are offered as follows:

(a) Special health examinations are conducted for some replacement employees, and periodic reexaminations are required for certain jobs. Such periodic examinations are required for special vehicle operators, crane operators, pilots, and employees in critical occupations where job performance could affect the health or safety of other Lewis employees.

(b) A medical monitoring program has been established for the protection of the health and safety of employees exposed to a potentially hazardous environment in a regular work assignment. First-line supervisors must notify Medical Services whenever there is a change in the potential exposure of any of their employees to hazardous substances or conditions.

(c) Each employee may take advantage of a complete physical examination once every 3 years and partial examinations in the intervening years.

Emergency services. Ill or seriously injured personnel at the Center are transported to Medical Services by emergency vehicle unless otherwise instructed by that office. Emergency transportation at the Plum Brook Station is to the appropriate local medical facilities or hospital.

Emergency vehicle service: Emergency vehicle service may be obtained by dialing 911 at the Cleveland Center or Plum Brook Station and stating the location of the patient and the nature of the injury or illness, if known. The individual making the call should ensure that someone is at an appropriate place to direct emergency vehicle attendants to the patient. Details of the Lewis Emergency Call System are given in the Lewis Safety Manual, Chapter 21, Mishap Reporting and Accident Investigation.

Emergency treatment: Medical Services provides emergency treatment to employees to the extent feasible within the capability of available staff and facilities. If the treatment required is outside the scope of available staff or facilities, the employee is provided transportation to suitable external medical facilities. Upon return from treatment at such external medical facilities, the employee is to report to Medical Services.

Contractor emergency care: Contractor employees may receive medical care from Medical Services for such emergency services as control of bleeding, application of dressings or splints, treatment and evaluation of potentially life-threatening injuries or illness, or alleviation of pain and suffering prior to being transported to a medical facility off the Center. The ambulance service responds to contractor injuries and illnesses when necessary, and it may transport con- tractor employees to the hospital if the Lewis Medical Officer, a Lewis nurse, or the ambulance squad leader judges it appropriate.

Therapeutic service: Therapeutic service is a normal dispensary function available from Medical Services for the treatment of nonemergency occupational and nonoccupational injuries and illnesses. Many of these services, including followup on emergency treatment, are rendered by nurses under the supervision of a physician.

The scope of the program does not permit extensive treatment of nonoccupational injury or illness; this is the province of the employee's private physician. However, in the interest of keeping the employee on the job, reducing lost time, or relieving suffering, employees may be afforded care for minor medical-office-type illnesses or injuries.

At the written request of an employee's private physician and under his or her prescription and with the concurrence of the Lewis Medical Director, Medical Services administers medicines, changes dressings, and provides available therapy in the interest of keeping the employee on the job and saving the time he or she might spend in seeking treatment at his or her personal physician's office.

Medical release. Following any illness or injury that results in an absence from work of 10 or more consecutive work days, the employee must obtain a medical release from his or her physician or hospital, as applicable, and report to Medical Services prior to returning to his or her duty station. This requirement is established to safeguard employees and to determine their fitness to return to duty. This requirement applies to Exchange employees as well as to other NASA employees. If there is any question about the advisability of returning to work, the lack of a physician's written medical release precludes the employee from returning to work until such permission is obtained.

Preventive services. Annually, Lewis civil service employees are offered an extensive physical examination. Employees are contacted automatically around the time of their birthdays to set up appointments; no independent action on the part of the employee is required. Employees are also encouraged to take advantage of other preventive services offered, such as health education programs on topics important to employee health, and the immunization service for overseas travelers.

Review and modification of facilities. Periodic reviews are conducted to investigate the existence of potential environmental health hazards in the work areas of the Center. When, in the professional opinion(s) of the Medical Director, the Environmental Health Officer, the Radiation Safety Committee, the cognizant Area Safety Committee, or the Safety Officer, environmental conditions are deemed to constitute a hazard to the health of an employee, studies are to be conducted to determine a means of modifying or eliminating such hazardous conditions. The Safety Officer is responsible for implementing the recommendations of such studies.

Records. The Medical Director establishes and maintains a medical file for each employee who is examined by Medical Services, including those whose work requires exposure to potential health hazards. This file is maintained in accordance with the Privacy Act and is considered to be privileged information; information therefrom is conveyed to persons outside Medical Services only as follows:

(a) To an employee's private physician or to the employee's representative upon the request and written permission of the employee

(b) To the chairman of the Executive Safety Board, the chairman of the Environmental Pollution Control Board, cognizant members of the Human Resources Management Division staff, and appropriate management officials, in the form of findings of fact, conclusions, and recommendations, when such information is necessary to evaluate the employee's ability to do his or her job, the employee's eligibility for disability retirement, or the employee's conformance with prescribed health standards

Radiation exposure records of individual employees are maintained by the Environmental Management Office.

1.5 SAFETY PERMIT SYSTEM

1.5.1 Scope

The objectives of the Safety Permit System are to avoid undue risks, injury to personnel, damage to property, or disruption of operations by:

- Assuring that a systematic approach is used to identify and control potential hazards
- Obtaining an independent, thorough, and timely safety review of all technical designs, tests, and operations
- Permitting the operation of facilities, systems/subsystems and experiments within safe constraints
- Control changes to permitted facilities system/subsystems and experiments
- Instilling safety awareness in all employees

The Safety Permit constitutes a license to operate a facility or piece of equipment within the constraints listed on the Permit. All proposed activities, operations, and tests shall be reviewed by the Safety Committee Chairperson to determine if a Safety Permit is required. The Safety Permit System described in this Chapter typically does not cover construction and maintenance activities (see Chapter 17).

The need for a Safety Permit is determined by the Safety Committee Chairperson by reviewing the nature and extent of the hazards associated with the proposed activity. The following hazard categories may be useful in identifying and evaluating hazards associated with an activity (these hazard categories are defined in Appendix A):

- Collision
- Chemical
- Corrosion
- Electrical Shock
- Explosion
- Fire
- High Noise
- Implosion
- Loss of Habitable Atmosphere
- Biological
- Radiation
- Temperature Extremes

Examples of activities/operations which may involve hazards and may require a Safety Permit include (Note: This is not an all-inclusive list):

- Use of Fuels or Oxidizers
- Use of Chemicals or Other Hazardous Materials
- Use of Compressed Gases
- High Temperature Operations (Over 140 degF)
- Use of High Voltage Electrical Power
- Use of Ionizing Radiation Sources
- Use of Lasers
- Use of Pressurized Vessels or Systems
- High Speed Rotating Equipment

- Use of Vacuum Systems
- Use of Cryogens
- Aircraft Operations
- Suspended Load Operations
- Modifications to permitted operations

1.5.2 Applicability

These instructions on the Safety Permit System apply to all Cleveland and Plum Brook Station facilities and technical operations and to organizational elements and personnel involved in offsite operations.

1.5.3 Authority

The authority for the Safety Permit System comes from the Lewis Safety Manual, Section 1.2, Lewis Safety Organization, and Section 1.3, Lewis Environmental Quality Organization.

1.5.4 Policy

It is the responsibility of cognizant personnel assigned to a system or operation to ensure that its design and operations are safe. All systems should be designed to fulfill fail-safe requirements and to avoid an unsafe situation in an interfacing system. A Safety Permit Request must be submitted to the cognizant Safety Committee Chairperson for all proposed Lewis test operations.

Expired Safety Permits. Operation of any facility, rig, system, or experiment is forbidden if the governing Safety Permit has expired. All personnel are under instructions not to operate or perform work unless the activity is covered by a valid permit. The Institutional Safety Office maintains a file of all Safety Permits, maintains the SafePerm program, and provides notification of expiring permits 60 days prior to expiration.

Stop Work Authority. Safety Committee Chairpersons have the authority to shut down any operation or activity in their assigned areas on which there is a question of safety, until an appropriate review can be made. Exercise of this authority requires immediate notification to the Chairperson of the Executive Safety Board and the Chief of the Institutional Safety Office.

Modifications to rigs or operational limits. A Safety Permit is invalidated by any change in the apparatus, operating conditions, or mode of operation from those described in the Permit and supporting documentation, unless the change has been approved by the cognizant Safety Committee.

1.5.5 The Lewis Safety Organization

The Lewis Safety Organization is described in Section 1.2 of this Manual. Specifically, the roles and responsibilities of the Aviation Safety Officer, the Process Systems Safety Committee, the Electrical Applications Safety Committee, the Area Safety Committees, and the Radiation Safety Committee are defined in Sections 1.2.7, 1.2.8, 1.2.9, 1.2.11, and 1.3.9 respectively. Refer to these sections for further information.

Safety areas of the Cleveland Center and the Plum Brook Station are shown in the Lewis Telephone Directory.

1.5.6 The Lewis Safety Program

The Lewis Safety Program is described in Section 1.1 of this Manual, with additional elements of the Safety Program described in the various chapters of this Manual and the Lewis Environmental Programs Manual. Refer to Appendix C for chapter references for specific systems and operations.

1.5.7 Process

A "Safety Permit Requester's Guide" is available from the Safety Committee Chairperson or the Institutional Safety Office.

A flowchart showing the safety permit process is shown in Appendix B. (This flowchart can be used as a check sheet throughout this process.)

The degree of detail, rigor, and formality required for the Safety Permit review is dependent on the complexity, hazards, and uniqueness of the test. Communication with the Safety Committee early and often will assure a smooth and thorough safety review process.

Initiating the Safety Permit Request. The following steps are required to initiate a Safety Permit Request:

(a) When a decision has been made to undertake a new activity, the conceptual design has been agreed on, and the general location has been selected, the responsible person (the Safety Permit requester) contacts the Safety Committee Chairperson and describes the design, siting considerations, operating conditions, the need for a Qualified Operators List (NASA Form C-580), and so forth. Note: Some Safety Permits are issued for facilities, and the requester needs to be aware of permitted facilities to ensure compliance within the specified parameters.

(b) If the Committee, after reviewing the information provided by the requester, decides there is no attendant potential hazard, it notifies the requester and the Institutional Safety Office via memo that no Safety Permit is required.

(c) If a hazard is judged to exist, then the Committee shall conduct an appropriate safety review before issuing a Safety Permit. The Chairperson advises the requester on the nature and detail of documentation and analyses (see Section 1.5.9) that should accompany the formal Safety Permit Request. Also, the number and nature of additional meetings are established. The Committee may counsel the requester to consult with advisory bodies and may furnish examples of the documentation it requires. The key element is early notification of and continuing involvement by the Safety Committee through incremental progress meetings.

(d) When the design is complete, and typically 60 days prior to the planned initiation of operations (depending on the scope and complexity of the planned activity), the requester prepares and submits the Safety Permit Request (NASA Form C-923), the Qualified Operators List (C-580), and supporting documentation (see Section 1.5.8) to the Chief of the initiating branch for review and signature.

(e) The Safety Permit Request package is then submitted to the Safety Committee Chairperson.

(f) The Safety Committee Chairperson forwards a copy of the Safety Permit Request package to the Institutional Safety Office (ISO). The ISO conducts a parallel review to ensure compliance with OSHA regulations and NASA safety standards. In addition, the ISO determines if EMO should review the permit request for environmental, industrial hygiene, hazardous chemical, or health physics requirements. If the ISO determines that a review by EMO is required, the ISO forwards a copy of the Safety Permit Request package to EMO for parallel review.

(g) The ISO determines the appropriate Hazard Level Identification sticker, indicating appropriate emergency response measures. After the ISO (and EMO, if necessary) have reviewed the package, the copy of the Safety Permit Request package with their comments is returned to the Safety Committee Chairperson.

Approval of the Request and Issuance of the Safety Permit

(a) The Safety Committee conducts a review of the proposed operation. Reviews are normally conducted by at least 2 Committee members. In no case should the review be made by a single member. The Safety

Committee may call on advisory personnel (contact the ISO for. In no case should the review be made by a single member. The Safety Committee may call on advisory personnel (contact the ISO for a list of advisory personnel) to assist it. Opinions, concurrences, or clarifications are to be documented and preserved as part of the review record. If changes are required on the Safety Permit Request, the package is returned to the requester. After making the required changes, the requester resubmits the request to the Safety Committee Chairperson.

(b) After the Safety Committee, approves the issuance of a Safety Permit, the Chairperson prepares the Safety Permit with appropriate operating conditions included. The Chairperson signs the original Safety Permit and the Qualified Operators List.

(c) The Safety Committee Chairperson retains the original of the Safety Permit, the Safety Permit Request, Qualified Operators List, and all supporting documentation for the Committee files. Copies of the Safety Permit (with the colored hazard identification sticker attached), the Qualified Operator List, and the Safety Permit Request are sent to the requester. Copies of the Permit (without supporting documentation) are also sent to the Lewis Institutional Safety Office (and other organizations as required) by the Safety Committee Chairperson.

(d) The requester posts the copy of the approved Safety Permit (together with an attached copy of the Safety Permit Request and the Qualified Operator List) in a conspicuous place at the specified site, or if more practical, in the applicable control center of the site. It is also recommended that applicable Material Safety Data Sheets (MSDS's) be posted with this package.

Operations under a Safety Permit

The Safety Permit allows the requester to begin the operation or experiment. The permit outlines the operations which are covered and includes any operating conditions which must be met in order to maintain safe operations.

Any deviations from the procedures stated on the Safety Permit must be reviewed by the Safety Committee Chairperson. Failure to comply with the procedures and operating conditions found on the Safety Permit any accompanying documentation will result in termination of the operation by the Safety Committee Chairperson.

Safety-related questions on a permitted operation by the building manager or other parties working in the area should be brought to the attention of the Safety Committee Chairperson or the Institutional Safety Office.

Modification of a Safety Permit

If there is a change required in the purpose, procedures, operational limits, constraints, or design of the activity while the existing permit is in force, a modification of the Safety Permit must be requested. To accomplish this the requester informs the Safety Committee Chairperson (via memo) of the proposed modification(s). Modifications include changes in operations or conditions beyond the operational limits/envelope specified on the Safety Permit. The accom- panying documentation should consist primarily of amendments to the documents originally submitted, together with the appropriate explanatory narrative. The cognizant Safety Committee then conducts the necessary review. For minor changes (with no new or different hazards), the Safety Committee Chairperson responds to the requester with an approval memo, which the requester shall post with the Safety Permit package. For major changes, the Safety Committee Chairperson requests that a formal amendment process (a Safety Permit Renewal/Modification Form or new permit request) be initiated.

Safety Permits are typically issued for a one-year period. There may be permitted activities which the Safety Committee determine to be relatively benign and unchanging (generally not testing-related activities) where the Committee is willing to issue a two-year or three-year Permit. The decision to issue a multi-year Permit is at the discretion and control of the Safety Committee Chairperson.

Renewal of a Safety Permit

A notification of expiration will be sent to the permit holder by the Institutional Safety Office sixty (60) days prior to expiration. Expiration notices are also sent to the Safety Committee Chairperson, the Building Manager, and the assigned Safety Engineer.

If there are no changes to the operation and the activity will not be completed before the Safety Permit expires, then at least 30 days prior to the Safety Permit expiration, the requester shall

- Ensure that all documentation submitted with the original Safety Permit Request is accurate and up-to-date. Ensure that all limit switches, warning lights, detection systems, interlocks, and other safety features are functional.
- Complete a Safety Permit Renewal/Modification Request Form (NASA-C-590) and obtain the branch chief's approval. Send this form to the Safety Committee Chairperson at least 30 days before expiration.

The Safety Committee will then conduct a review. The depth of this review will depend on the number of changes and any other factors brought to light by recent operating history. After the Safety Committee reviews the renewal request and approves renewal, the Safety Committee Chairperson makes the necessary revisions to the expiration date on the original Permit and initials the change. A copy of the renewed Safety Permit (with the hazards identification sticker attached) and a copy of the Safety Permit Renewal Request are sent to the requester. Copies are also sent to the Lewis Institutional Safety Office. The originals are retained in the Safety Committee files. The requester then posts the renewed permit, the renewal request, the original Safety Permit Request, and the updated Qualified Operators List.

Completion of an activity

Upon completion of the operation or activity covered by a Safety Permit, the responsible individual

(a) Removes, dates, and signs the copy of the Safety Permit in the space provided and returns the Safety Permit to the Safety Committee Chairperson.

(b) Coordinates phase out of the operation, disposition of equipment, and removal and proper disposal of all hazardous material in accordance with the applicable safety standards. Contact the Health, Safety, and Environmental (HS&E) Help Line (3-8848) for assistance with chemical disposal.

The Chairperson removes the original Safety Permit from the files, marks the original and copy canceled, forwards the copy to the Lewis Institutional Safety Office, and retains the files for three years. The Lewis Institutional Safety Office files the canceled permit.

1.5.8 Forms

Safety Permit Request (NASA Form C-923). Form C-923 (Attachment 1 in Appendix D) constitutes formal application for permission to operate a facility, rig, system, experiment, or such. The formal request shall be submitted to the cognizant Safety Committee approximately 60 days prior to the contemplated initiation of operation. As described previously, notification of and discussions with the cognizant Safety Committee is required at the time the conceptual design is completed so that the specific requirements for analyses, drawings, and the like may be established.

Safety Permit (NASA Form C-919). Form C-919 (Attachment 2 in Appendix D) indicates that a facility, rig, system, experiment, or operation has been reviewed by a Safety Committee; it constitutes a license to operate the facility within the constraints indicated thereon. A Safety Permit is valid for a 1-, 2-, or 3-year period from the date of issue, as determined by the cognizant Safety Committee.

Safety Permit Renewal/Modification Request (NASA Form C-590). A Safety Permit

Renewal/Modification Request (Attachment 3 in Appendix D) shall be submitted no later than 30 days prior to the expiration date of the Safety Permit or planned modification. The routing of the Renewal/Modification Request is the same as for an initial Safety Permit Request.

Qualified Operators List (NASA Form C-580). Form C-580 (Attachment 4 in Appendix D) lists qualified operators and describes the experience and training requirements for each operator. This document should be used only in conjunction with a valid Safety Permit.

Users Radiological Training and Experience Record (NASA Form C-197). When the use of radioactive materials or radiation-producing equipment is involved, a C 197 for each user must be attached. A user is defined as a person qualified by training and experience to use radioactive material and ionizing radiation-producing devices in a safe manner. The user is responsible for the safekeeping of material and equipment, as specified in the Safety Permit under his or her control.

1.5.9 Supporting Documentation

The Safety Committee Chairperson will advise the requester of the supporting documentation which will be needed with the Safety Permit Request. A list of supporting documentation and requirements for specific systems is provided in Appendix C for guidance. Typically, the supporting documentation required with a Safety Permit Request will include:

Description of the Activity

- Test objectives
- Test description
- Technical description of the test rig, systems, equipment, etc. - A brief technical description of the experiment or activity should include the desired range of environmental test parameters and cite factors such as maximum stored energy and quantity-distance criteria.
- Location of the activity
- Duration and frequency of operations

Drawings and Figures

- Drawings, (dated and with approval signatures) of such equipment as test hardware; control systems; laser systems; electrical systems for the facility, cell, or test rig, and flow systems, showing physical characteristics such as:
    o Line size, cable size
    o Materials of construction
    o Design, operating, and test pressures, flows, and temperatures
    o Important power, control, and instrumentation components (including interlocks and permissives)
    o Important structural components, such as supports and anchors
    o Class of electrical equipment
- Schematics, showing electrical or fluid flow circuits for the test facility and all interfaces with facility support systems
- Parts lists and/or component lists
- Plot Plan - A drawing of the test area showing equipment, type and location of personnel-protective equipment, warning signs, barricades, evacuation routes, and/or warning lights used during testing must be provided.
- Barricade Plan

Design Criteria

To minimize the chance of failure, an analysis of design limits and/or redline operating limits (with analytical methods used and results of supporting calculations) must be provided. Wherever possible, designs are to be fail-safe or fail-passive. Safety factors or safety margins and quantity-distance criteria must be provided, as appropriate. Other design criteria include:

- System or project requirements
- Design approach and assumptions
- Applicable codes and guidelines used
- Supporting calculations
- Design and Operating Limits
- Quality Assurance Plan
- Configuration Control requirements
- Test or Inspection documentation (e.g. pressure tests of pressure vessels)

Hazards Analysis

Early in the program development, hazardous conditions need to be identified and corrective actions determined. The requester should refer to the generic hazard list in Appendix A, and use the Safety Permit Request to generate an initial hazard assessment. The Safety Committee Chairperson will inform the requester of the need for a formal hazards analysis, such as Preliminary Hazards Analysis, Failure Mode and Effects Analysis, Fault Hazards Analysis, Operational Hazard Analysis, and Fault Tree Analysis (refer to the Lewis Product Assurance Manual, PAI 220, Hazard Analysis Preparation). The identification of potential hazards shall be an integral and mandatory part of the development of the Safety Permit Request. The severity of failures are to be identified and categorized as follows:

Hazard class	Severity	Effect of equipment failure or operational error
I	Catastrophic	Death, serious injury, or mission loss
II	Critical	Severe injury or major property damage(>$25,000)
III	Marginal	Minor injury or property damage (<$25,000)
IV	Negligible	No injury or property damage (system function can be restored in short time with repair or maintenance procedures)

The probability that a hazard will occur during the planned operational life of a system is to be described in the hazard analyses through a qualitative hazard probability ranking:

Hazard ranking	Probability of hazard
A	Likely to occur immediately
B	Likely to occur in time
C	May occur in time
D	Unlikely to occur

Where appropriate, supporting rationale for assigning a hazard probability shall be documented in hazard analysis reports.

The combination of the hazard class (severity) and hazard ranking (probability) leads to the Risk Assessment Code, shown in the Table below. A Risk Assessment Code of High is unacceptable and must be reduced to medium or low prior to issuance of a Safety Permit.

PROBABILITY OF HAZARD OCCURRENCE	HAZARD SEVERITY CATEGORY			
	I	II	III	IV
A	High	High	Medium	Medium
B	High	High	Medium	Low
C	High	Medium	Medium	Low
D	Medium	Medium	Low	Low

Operational Information

- Initial checkout plan
- Operating Procedures/Checklists, including normal startup, shutdown, and operations (these shall be approved by a knowledgeable supervisor or project authority prior to Safety Committee review)
- Emergency Plans and Shutdown Procedures - An emergency reaction plan including all procedures for shutdown, sequence of notifications, and so on must be provided.
- Equipment or system limits
- List of alarms, shutdowns, and permissives
- Access control requirements

Maintenance Information

- Maintenance procedures and schedules (for items which have safety implications)
- Logbooks or maintenance data sheets (for items which have safety implications)
- Lockout/tagout procedures
- Recertification requirements

Radiation or Radioactive Material Information. A description of a radioactive material or a radiation emitting device. This description would include the physical form, chemical form, type of radiation activity, radiation safety procedures, and detection instruments. Note: Radiographers only have a notification requirement to EMO.

Training of qualified operators. When the circumstances of the activity warrant special training personnel, a Qualified Operator List shall be submitted. The Qualified Operator List includes the names of the personnel who are assigned to operate or are responsible for the test rig, experiment, or operation, along with a description of the experience and training requirements.

Buddy system. The required level of protection to ensure the safety of personnel is prescribed in the Lewis Safety Manual, Chapter 22, The Lewis Buddy System.

Emergency Evacuation Plan. Operators should be aware of impact operation may have on the building evacuation plan. Evacuation plan information should be coordinated with the Building Managers. Refer to Chapter 27 of the Lewis Safety Manual for information on emergency evacuation plans.

See Appendix C for additional system-specific documentation requirements.

The supporting documentation should be sufficient to allow the reviewers to understand and assess the hazards that are involved in the activity, the safety standards applied, the operational safeguards planned, and the like. In general, the amount or extent of necessary supporting docu- mentation depends on the complexity of the experiment, the risk of failure, and the severity of a failure.

1.5.10 Qualified Operators

Requester. The Safety Permit requester completes NASA Form C-580, Qualified Operators List, and submits it to the cognizant Safety Committee Chairperson together with the NASA Form C-923, Safety Permit Request. The requester also includes supporting documentation, as required, of the applicable training programs provided to personnel listed on the C-580.

The operators training program, as documented by the C-580, should include, but not be limited to, developing safety awareness and making operators fully knowledgeable of and alert to potential hazards that could exist within their work environments.

Requester's Supervisor. The requester's supervisor approves the Qualified Operators List and ensures that training programs have been conducted as required.

Cognizant Safety Committee. The Safety Committee reviews and signs the NASA Form C-580, Qualified Operators List. The Safety Permit shall not be issued until the Qualified Operators List is approved.

1.5.11 Responsibilities

Requester (usually the project engineer). The requester's responsibilities are to

(a) Notify the cognizant Safety Committee Chairperson, after the conceptual design is approved, of the forthcoming new operation, and arrange for an introductory meeting.

(b) Prepare the Safety Permit Request and arrange for all required supporting documentation, allowing for appropriate lead time.

(c) Supplying the Institutional Safety Office with the necessary technical input for the development of safe operating procedures, emergency rescue procedures, or any other safety documentation deemed necessary by the Institutional Safety Office.

(d) Respond to all action items and requests for further information levied by the cognizant Safety Committee.

(e) Take necessary and timely action to obtain renewal of a Safety Permit.

(f) Ensure that the operation is conducted in accordance with the operating conditions specified on the Safety Permit.

(g) Advise the cognizant Safety Committee of contemplated changes to the operation or equipment and take necessary action to obtain a revised Safety Permit.

(h) Take necessary action to close out a Safety Permit on completion of operations.

(i) May appeal rejections through their Division Chief and the Chief of ISO. The appeal shall be ruled on by the ESB.

(j) Ensure that activities presenting significant risk to persons or property have a formal readiness review by the requester's line management.

Supervisors. All organization supervisors have a prime responsibility for compliance with pertinent safety requirements (including those related to housekeeping and shop safety) and for ensuring the effectiveness of the Lewis Safety Management Program as it affects their specific activities. Their responsibility for the Safety Permit process includes the following:

(a) Knowing pertinent Lewis safety requirements; communicating these requirements to subordinate personnel; mandating compliance with these requirements; and monitoring this compliance.

(b) Knowing about and ensuring adherence to the Lewis Safety Permit process, including the review and approval procedures.

(c) Reviewing and approving the Safety Permit Request and supporting documentation submitted by their subordinates to ensure that all potential hazards are properly identified and evaluated, and that procedures for safe operation and effective emergency rescue have been developed.

(d) Reviewing and approving the Qualified Operators List.

(e) Ensuring that the cognizant Safety Committee evaluation is obtained.

(f) Personally surveying their work areas and recognizing potential hazards therein; analyzing statistics on accidents and near accidents in these areas; and initiating or recommending corrective action where required.

(g) Providing direction for continuing safety education and training for subordinate personnel in accordance with the standards and criteria established by the Institutional Safety Office.

Cognizant Safety Committee. Safety Committees conduct third party reviews of all proposed installations and operations in their assigned areas to insure that the proposed design and operations are consistent with the dictates of sound engineering judgment and acceptable safety and health standards. The responsibilities of the cognizant Safety Committee are to:

(a) Conduct reviews of proposals for all research operations, for modifications or additions to facilities and equipment, and for any activities that affect safety within the assigned safety areas; approve and issue Safety Permits for those proposals that meet Lewis safety requirements, contingent on receiving sufficiently complete technical information that satisfies all questions relative to safety and on being satisfied that fail-safe requirements have been fulfilled. (Requesters may appeal rejections through the initiating division chief and the Chief of the Institutional Safety Office, to the Executive Safety Board.)

(b) Notify the requester and the Institutional Safety Office via memo when it has determined that a Safety Permit is not required.

(c) Consult, as required, with the Institutional Safety Office, EMO, and advisory personnel, on safety and environmental matters that fall within their areas of specialization. All reviews and concurrences are to be a part of the safety review documentation and should be available for any required mishap investigation.

(d) Specify, when appropriate, the need for qualified operators or any special conditions on which the approval is based.

(e) Refer major safety issues or questions of significant risk assessment to the Executive Safety Board.

Lewis Institutional Safety Office. Responsibilities of the Institutional Safety Office are to

(a) Administer, coordinate, and implement the Safety Permit Program at the Cleveland Center and the Plum Brook Station.

(b) Participate in all safety permit reviews.

(c) Maintain technical surveillance of and keep informed of current activities in assigned area of responsibility to anticipate problems and minimize safety-related conflicts between organizational elements.

(d) Conduct quarterly surveys of facilities and research operations within assigned areas and report results to the Chief of the Institutional Safety Office and the Safety Committee Chairperson (reference Chapter 24 of this manual).

(e) Manage the SafePerm system, and issue expiration notices to the requester, Safety Committee Chairperson, ISO representative, and Building Manager.

(f) Provide overall surveillance of the Safety Permit system.

Executive Safety Board. Responsibilities of the Executive Safety Board are to

(a) Review and evaluate disputes concerning safety conditions, in the deliberations of a Safety Permit and in all major risk assessments submitted to it by a cognizant Safety Committee.

(b) Submit to the Director a written report reflecting its evaluations and recommendations on major risk assessments.

EXCEPTION: When Nuclear Regulatory Commission (NRC) requirements are involved, decisions of the Radiation Safety Committee for Cleveland cannot be overruled.

Responsibilities of the EMO are to

(a) Review requests for Safety Permits as required, examining them for impact on the environment, for creation of radiological hazards, or for hazards to the worker because of toxic materials or hazardous conditions; consult with advisory panels or Safety Committees concerning matters under their cognizance.

(b) Indicate concurrence by documenting any special requirements to the Safety Committee Chairperson.

1.5.12 Safety Permit Hazard Level Identification

A color-coded sticker affixed to the Safety Permit provides immediate identification of the potential hazard level and the instructions for emergency action to be taken. The color codes used and their meanings are as follows:

Safety Permit Hazard Identification

Color Code	Hazard Level	Take action?	Emergency action
Red	Unique; high explosion potential, high toxicity, nuclear radiation, etc.	ONLY on advice of knowledgeable person (Project manager or alternate)	NOTIFY "Emergency Contact" named on Safety Permit
Yellow	Potential of fire involving liquid metals, high voltage, etc.	Yes	Use DRY chemicals ONLY; then notify "Emergency Contact" named on Safety Permit
Green	No unusual or unique hazard	Yes	Use water, dry chemicals, or CO2; then notify "Emergency Contact" named on Safety Permit

1.5.13 Offsite Operations

Lewis employees at another NASA center or Government agency. If an operation is conducted at a site or in facilities of another NASA center or Government agency, or in their aircraft or vessels, the safety review and approval procedures of the Center or agency govern and are to be complied with; a Lewis Safety Permit is not required. The Lewis employee in charge must take positive action on his or her own initiative to ascertain the host organization's requirements for safety approval and must see that they are fulfilled. No Lewis operation may be conducted without such safety approval. In addition, the Lewis employee in charge must inform the Lewis Institutional Safety Office, by letter, of the nature and character of the offsite operation. The Chief of the ISO is not responsible for reviewing and approving the operation (this is the responsibility of the host organization). However, if the Lewis employee has a significant concern based on his or her experience and expertise, the employee may request that the Chief, Institutional Safety Office or the Chairman of the Lewis Executive Safety Board have the matter appropriately investigated through a formal request to the host organization.

Lewis employees at unhosted site. If Lewis personnel conduct an offsite operation where there is no host organization, and if the whole organization has no properly approved safety procedures in effect or the whole organization places all or part of the safety approval under Lewis' responsibility, the operation is subject to the same rules and regulations set forth in the Lewis Safety Manual for onsite operations. All such offsite operations require preparation of a Safety Permit Request in accordance with this Manual. The offsite request is submitted to the Lewis Institutional Safety Office for appropriate safety review and determination.

Government-retained offsite personnel. Non-Government members of an offsite research team, when retained as Government experts or consultants (i.e., special Government employees), are also required to observe the pertinent regulations of the Lewis Safety Manual. The Lewis employee in charge ensures that a copy of such regulations and related instructions is made available. Safety regulations of other Government agencies involved are recognized as a part of the total safety requirement for the program and are to be adhered to by all Lewis personnel concerned.

Appendix A - Generic Hazard List

The determination of need for a Safety Permit requires that the hazards associated with the activity be identified and evaluated. The following is a list of hazard categories which may be useful in identifying and evaluating the hazards associated with an activity.

COLLISION
>Items breaking loose and impacting others items. You hit it or it hits you. Caused by structural failure, procedural error, or inadequate handling of equipment.

CHEMICAL
>The release of toxic, flammable, corrosive, condensible or particular matter. Caused by leakage, spillage, loose objects, abrasion, growth or component failure.

ELECTRICAL SHOCK
>Personnel injury or fatality due to electrical current passing through any portion of the body. Caused by contact with energized circuits, procedural error, component failures, static discharge or environmental conditions.

TEMPERATURE EXTREMES
>Injury to persons or damage to equipment due to departure of temperature from normal range. Extreme heat or cold caused by fire or cryogenics due to compartment failure or procedural error. Results in burns or structural damage.

FIRE

SAFETY PERMIT REQUEST	DATE RECEIVED (Completed by Committee Chair)	PERMIT NUMBER (To be provided by Committee Chair)

TITLE: _____

(Limited to 70 characters including blank spaces)

TO: _____ **SAFETY COMMITTEE**
(Provide area number or special committee name)

FROM: _____
(Safety Permit Requester, print name)

EMERGENCY CONTACTS (Provide information below for an emergency contact and alternate knowledgeable of activity. The Safety Permit Requester can be an Emergency Contact)	**ORGANIZATION**	**WORK PHONE**	**MAIL STOP**

NAME	**WORK PHONE**	**HOME PHONE**	**LOCATION OF ACTIVITY:** _____ (Indicate facility name, number, cell)
			EXPECTED DURATION (Indicate month and year)

ACTIVITY SCHEDULE (Mark an X below for all that apply)			**Start:**	**Complete:**
Workday	Night	Weekend	**TEST RUN LENGTH** (Hours, days) :	

DESCRIBE ACTIVITY (If a precedence exists for this activity, provide details including related safety permit number(s)).

Mark with an X the Supporting Documentation Attached:

Technical Description	NASA-C-580 Qualified Operators List
Schematics, Drawings	NASA-C-197 Users Radiological Training and Experience Record
Parts List	Pressure System Test Certification
Plot/Barricade Plan	List of Alarms and Shutdowns
Hazards Analysis	Emergency Response Plan/Shutdown Procedures
Operating Procedures/Check Sheets	Laser Documentation
Lockout/Tagout Procedures	Radiation or Radioactive Material Information
Material Safety Data Sheets	Other (Specify)

ENVIRONMENTAL DISCHARGE PRODUCTS (Provide below the name(s) and estimated amounts of the discharge product(s), what it will be discharged to (e.g., air, sewer), plans for abatement/treatment, the method of detection used to measure the amount/type of discharge, and the frequency of discharge sampling. Indicate if none.)

SAFETY PERMIT REQUESTER (Sign and date)	**SUPERVISOR OF REQUESTER** (Print name, sign and date)	**WORK PHONE**

NASA TECHNICAL SUPERVISOR (Required if Safety Permit Requester is a contractor. Print name, sign and date)	**WORK PHONE**	**INSTRUCTIONS:** Send this request and all supporting documentation to the appropriate Safety Committee Chairperson. Refer to the Lewis Safety Manual, Chapter 1, for additional information.

NASA-C-923 Page 1 of 4 (Revision 9-94)

HAZARD CATEGORY

Hazard Category	Controls
COLLISION	Overspeed Control
	Crane Proofloading
	Guards
	Lockout/Tagout Procedures
	Barricade Plan
	Blast Shield
	Critical Speed Analysis
	Triburst Calculations
	Other
CHEMICAL	Ventilation
	Detectors
	Proper Storage
	Personal Protective Equipment
	HazCom Training
	Proper Labeling
	Spill Response Procedures
	Respiratory Protection Program
	Other
ELECTRICAL SHOCK	Grounding
	Guards
	Designed per NEC
	Current limiting devices
	Lockout/Tagout Procedures
	Other
TEMPERATURE EXTREMES	Temperature Controls
	Temperature Alarms
	Personal Protective Equipment
	Other

HAZARD CATEGORY

Hazard Category	Controls
FIRE	Control or Removal of Ignition Sources
	Ventilation of Combustion Gases
	Over-Temperature Protection
	Smoke/Fire Detectors
	Fire Suppression
	Other
EXPLOSION/IMPLOSION	Designed per ASME Boiler & Pressure Vessel Code and LSM Chapter 7
	Temperature Controls
	Relief Devices
	Detectors
	Alarms
	Pressure System Test per LSM Chapter 7
	Quantity-Distance Calculations
	Contamination Control
	Barricade Plan
	Welding Inspection
	Other
HIGH NOISE	Engineering Controls
	Hearing Protection
	Barricade Plan
	Signs
	Hearing Conservation Program
	Other
CORROSION	Corrosion-resistant materials
	Other

HAZARD CATEGORY

LASER RADIATION	Laser Radiation Form
	Compliance with ANSI Z136.1
	Interlocks
	Annual Eye Exams
	Shielding
	Barricade Plan
	Signs
	Other
NUCLEAR RADIATION	NRC License Review
	Radiation Detection Equipment
	Shielding
	Barricade Plan
	Signs
	Other
OTHER RADIATION	Shielding
	Barricade Plan
	Signs
	Other
LOSS OF HABITABLE ATMOSPHERE	Ventilation
	Detectors
	Confined Space Entry Procedures
	Temperature Control
	Other
BIOLOGICAL	Personal Protective Equipment
	Bloodborne Pathogen Program
	Disposal Methods
	Other
OTHER	

SAFETY PERMIT

National Aeronautics and Space Administration
Lewis Research Center
Cleveland, OH

TITLE:

(Limited to 70 characters including blank spaces)

PERMIT NUMBER		LOCATION OF ACTIVITY:
		(Indicate facility name, number, cell)

EMERGENCY CONTACTS			DATE ISSUED (Month and year)	COLOR OF STICKER TO BE ATTACHED HERE (Red, yellow or green)
NAME	**WORK PHONE**	**HOME PHONE**		
(Knowledgeable person)				
(Alternate)			EXPIRATION DATE (Month and year)	

ACTIVITY DESCRIPTION:

SAFETY COMMITTEE CONDITIONS FOR CONDUCTING ACTIVITY:

SAFETY PERMIT REQUESTOR (Print name)	ORGANIZATION	WORK PHONE	MAIL STOP

SAFETY PERMIT REVIEWERS (Print names)

SAFETY COMMITTEE CHAIRPERSON (Signature)	ACTIVITY COMPLETED (Return to Safety Committee Chairperson)	
	SAFETY PERMIT REQUESTOR (Signature)	DATE

NASA-C-919 Page 1 of 2 (Revision 9-94)

SAFETY PERMIT	National Aeronautics and Space Administration Lewis Research Center Cleveland, OH

TITLE:

(Limited to 70 characters including blank spaces)

PERMIT NUMBER		LOCATION OF ACTIVITY:
		(Indicate facility name, number, cell)

CONTINUATION SHEET FROM PAGE 1: (Note the section from page 1 that is being appended)

NASA-C-919 Page 1 of 2 (Revision 9-94)

SAFETY PERMIT RENEWAL-CHANGE REQUEST	DATE RECEIVED (Completed by Committee Chair)	PERMIT NUMBER (To be renewed or changed)

TITLE:

_____

(From Safety Permit to be renewed or changed. Note proposed title changes below. Limited to 70 characters including blank spaces)

TO: _____ SAFETY COMMITTEE	FROM: _____
(Provide area number or special committee name)	(Safety Permit Requester, print name)

PERMIT ISSUE DATE (Month and year)		ORGANIZATION	WORK PHONE	MAIL STOP
PERMIT EXPIRATION DATE (Month and year)				

A REVIEW IS REQUIRED OF THE ACTIVITIES AND SUPPORTING DOCUMENTATION ASSOCIATED WITH THE SAFETY PERMIT TO BE RENEWED OR CHANGED. AFTER CONDUCTING THIS REVIEW, MARK AN X IN THE APPROPRIATE BOX BELOW.

	This review identified no new hazards and no changes to the design, operations, constraints, information or supporting documentation from the original Safety Permit Request.
	This review identified changes which are described in detail below.

DESCRIPTION OF CHANGES (Include details of changes to the information from the original Safety Permit Request (e.g., Emergency Contacts) and changes to the supporting documentation (e.g., Qualified Operators List))

SAFETY PERMIT REQUESTER (Sign and date)	SUPERVISOR OF REQUESTER (Print name, sign and date)	WORK PHONE

NASA TECHNICAL SUPERVISOR (Required if Safety Permit Requester is a contractor. Print name, sign and date)	WORK PHONE	INSTRUCTIONS: Attach a copy of the original Safety Permit to this request along with any modified supporting documentation and send to the appropriate Safety Committee Chairperson. Refer to the Lewis Safety Manual, Chapter 1, for additional information.

NASA-C-590 (Revision 9-94)

Risk Management Plan Data Elements

1. REGISTRATION

Source identification

a. Name _____

b. Street _____

c. City _____

d. County _____

e. State _____

f. Zip _____

g. Latitude _____

h. Longitude _____

Source Dun and Bradstreet Number _____

a. Name of corporate parent company (if applicable) _____

b. Dun and Bradstreet number of corporate parent company (if applicable) _____

Owner/operator

a. Name _____

b. Phone _____

c. Mailing address _____

Name and title of person responsible for Part 68 implementation _____

_____

Emergency contact

a. Name _____

b. Title _____

c. Phone _____

d. 24-hour phone _____

For each covered process:

Chemical name	CAS number	Quantity SIC code	Program level

EPA Identifier _____

Number of full-time employees _____

Covered by

a. OSHA PSM   1. ___ Yes   2. ___ No

b. EPCRA Section 302   1. ___ Yes   2. ___ No

c. CAA Title V Operating Permit   1. ___ Yes   2. ___ No

Last safety inspection

Date _____

By

___ OSHA   ___ EPA   ___ Fire Department   ___ Not Applicable

___ State OSHA   ___ State EPA   ___ Other: _____

2. TOXICS: WORST CASE (Complete at least one.)

Chemical name _____

Physical state

a. ___ Gas

b. ___ Liquid

Results based on

a. ___ Reference table

b. ___ Modeling

c. Model used _____

Scenario

a. ___ Explosion

b. ___ Fire

c. ___ Toxic gas release

d. ___ Liquid spill and vaporization

Quantity released _____ **lbs**

Release rate _____ **lbs/min.**

Release duration (if modeled) _____ **min.**

Wind speed _____ **m/sec**

Stability class _____

Topography (check one)

a. ___ Urban

b. ___ Rural

Distance to endpoint _____ **miles**

Residential population within distance (number) _____

Public receptors (check all that apply)

a. ___ Schools

b. ___ Residences

c. ___ Hospitals

d. ___ Prisons

e. ___ Public recreational areas or arenas

f. ___ Major commercial, office, or industrial areas

Environmental receptors within distance (check all that apply)

a. ___ National or state parks, forests, or monuments

b. ___ Officially designated wildlife sanctuaries, preserves, or refuges

c. ___ Federal wilderness areas

Passive mitigation considered (check all that apply)

a. ___ Dikes

b. ___ Enclosures

c. ___ Berms

d. ___ Drains

e. ___ Sumps

f. ___ Other (specify)

3. TOXICS: ALTERNATIVE RELEASES (complete for each toxic)

Chemical _____

Physical state

a. ___ Gas

b. ___ Liquid

Results based on

a. ___ Reference table

b. ___ Modeling

c. Model used _____

Scenario (check one)

a. ___ Transfer hose failure

b. ___ Pipe leak

c. ___ Vessel lea

d. ___ Overfilling

e. ___ Rupture disk/relief valve

f. ___ Excess flow valve failure

g. ___ Other (specify):

_____

Quantity released _____ **lbs**

Release rate _____ **lbs/min.**

Release duration _____ **min.**

Wind speed _____ **m/sec**

Stability class _____

Topography (check one)

a. __ Urban

b. __ Rural

Distance to endpoint _____ **miles**

Residential population within distance (number) _____

Public receptors (check all that apply)

a. ___ Schools   d. ___ Prisons

b. ___ Residences   e. ___ Public recreational areas or arenas

c. ___ Hospitals   f. ___ Major commercial, office, or industrial areas

Environmental receptors within distance (check all that apply)

a. ___ National or state parks, forests, or monuments

b. ___ Officially designated wildlife sanctuaries, preserves, or refuges

c. ___ Federal wilderness areas

Passive mitigation considered (check all that apply)

a. ___ Dikes   d. ___ Drains

b. ___ Enclosures   e. ___ Sumps

c. ___ Berms   f. ___ Other (specify)_____

Active mitigation considered (check all that apply)

a. ___ Sprinkler systems   d. ___ Neutralization   g. ___ Scrubbers

b. ___ Deluge system   e. ___ Excess flow valve   h. ___ Emergency shutdown systems

c. ___ Water curtain   f. ___ Flares   i. ___ Other (specify)

4. FLAMMABLES WORST CASE (complete one)

Chemical _____

Results based on (check one)

a. ___ Reference table

b. ___ Modeling

c. Model used _____

Scenario (check one)

a. ___ Vapor cloud explosion

b. ___ Fireball

Quantity released _____ **lbs**

Endpoint used _____

Distance to endpoint _____ **miles**

Residential population within distance (number) _____

Public receptors (check all that apply)

a. ___ Schools   d. ___ Prison

b. ___ Residences   e. ___ Public recreational areas or arenas

c. ___ Hospitals   f. ___ Major commercial, office, or industrial areas

Environmental receptors within distance (check all that apply)

a. ___ National or state parks, forests, or monuments

b. ___ Officially designated wildlifesanctuaries, preserves, or refuges

c. ___ Federal wilderness areas

Passive mitigation considered (check all that apply)

a. ___ Dikes

b. ___ Fire walls

c. ___ Blast walls

d. ___ Enclosures

e. ___ Other (specify) _____

5. FLAMMABLES ALTERNATIVE RELEASES (complete one)

Chemical _____

Results based on (check one)

a. ___ Reference table

b. ___ Modeling

c. Model used _____

Scenario (check one)

a. ___ Vapor cloud explosion

b. ___ Fireball

c. ___ BLEVE

d. ___ Pool fire

e. ___ Jet fire

f. ___ Vapor cloud fire

Quantity released _____ lbs

Endpoint used _____

Distance to endpoint _____ miles

Residential population within distance (number) _____

Public receptors (check all that apply)

a. ___ Schools

b. ___ Residences

c. ___ Hospitals

d. ___ Prisons

e. ___ Public recreational areas or arenas

f. ___ Major commercial, office, or industrial areas

Environmental receptors within distance (check all that apply)

a. ___ National or state parks, forests, or monuments

b. ___ Officially designated wildlife sanctuaries, preserves, or refuges

c. ___ Federal wilderness areas

Passive mitigation considered (check all that apply)

a. ___ Dikes   b. ___ Fire walls   c. ___ Blast walls

Active mitigation considered (check all that apply)

a. ___ Sprinkler systems   c. ___ Water curtain

b. ___ Deluge system   d. ___ Excess flow valve

6. FIVE-YEAR ACCIDENT HISTORY (complete the following for each release)

Date _____

Time _____

Release duration _____

Chemical(s) _____

Quantity released (lbs) _____

Release event

a. ___ Gas release   d. ___ Explosion

b. ___ Liquid spill/evaporation   e. ___ Valve

c. ___ Fire   f. ___ Pump

Release source

a. ___ Storage vessel   c. ___ Process vessel

b. ___ Piping   d. ___ Transfer hose

Weather conditions at time of event (if known)

a. Wind speed/direction _____   d. Precipitation present _____

b. Temperature _____   e. Unknown _____

c. Stability class _____

Onsite impacts

a. Deaths _____ (number)

b. Injuries _____ (number)

c. Property damage ($) _____

Known offsite impacts

a. Deaths _____ (number)

b. Hospitalizations _____ (number)

c. Other medical treatment _____ (number)

d. Evacuated _____ (number)

e. Sheltered _____ (number)

f. Property damage ($) _____

g. Environmental damage _____ (specify type)

Initiating event

a. ___ Equipment failure

b. ___ Human error

c. ___ Weather condition

d. ___ Overpressurization

e. ___ Upset condition

f. ___ By-pass condition

g. ___ Maintenance activity/Inactivity

h. ___ Process design

i. ___ Unsuitable equipment

j. ___ Unusual weather condition

k. ___ Management error

Contributing factors (check all that apply)

a. ___ Equipment failure

b. ___ Human error

c. ___ Improper procedures

Offsite responders notified

a. ___Yes   b. ___ No

Changes introduced as a result of the accident

a. ___ Improved/upgrade equipment

b. ___ Revised maintenance

c. ___ Revised training

d. ___ Revised operating procedures

e. ___ New process controls

f. ___ New mitigation systems

g. ___ Revised emergency response plan

h. ___ Changed process

i. ___ Reduced inventory

j. ___ Other: _____

k. ___ None

7. PREVENTION PROGRAM coordinated

a. Name _____

b. Telephone number _____

Subject to (check all that apply)

a. ___ OSHA 1910.38 (Emergency Action Plan)

b. ___ OSHA 1910.120 (HAZWOPER)

c. ___ Clean Water Act/SPCC

d. ___ RCRA

e. ___ OPA-90

f. ___ State EPCRA Rules/Law

g. ___ Other (specify): _____

Sample RMP for the Propane Industry

Chemical Emergency Preparedness and Prevention Office (CEPPO)

Sample Risk Management Plan
under the Clean Air Act Amendments, Section 112(r)

A sample RMP (including both the Executive Summary and Data Elements) for a propane facility follows. This sample is NOT the Model RMP for the propane industry, and does NOT represent the electronic or paper format for RMP's that EPA will accept. The official reporting format is currently being developed.

EXECUTIVE SUMMARY

1. Accidental release prevention and emergency response policies:

In this distribution facility, we handle propane which is considered hazardous by EPA. The same properties that makes propane valuable as a fuel also makes it necessary to observe certain safety precautions in handling propane to prevent unnecessary human exposure, to reduce the threat to our own personal health as well as our co-workers, and to reduce the threat to nearby members of the community. It is our policy to adhere to all applicable Federal and state rules and regulations. Safety depends upon the manner in which we handle propane combined with the safety devices inherent in the design of this facility combined with the safe handling procedures that we use and the training of our personnel.

Our emergency response program is based upon the NPGA's LP-Gas Safety Handbook, "Guidelines for Developing Plant Emergency Procedures" and "How to Control LP-Gas Leaks and Fires". The emergency response plan includes procedures for notification of the local fire authority and notification of any potentially affected neighbors.

2. The stationary source and regulated substances handled.

- The primary purpose of this facility is to repackage and distribute propane to both retail and wholesale customers. Propane is used by our retail customers as a fuel. Propane is received by rail car and by truck (transports) and stored in three storage tanks. Propane is distributed to retail customers by delivery trucks (bobtails) and to wholesale customers by bobtails and transports. We also fill Department of Transportation (DOT) containers for use by retail customers. This facility has equipment for unloading rail cars and transports and equipment to load bobtails, transports and DOT containers. Access to the site is restricted to authorized facility employees, authorized management personnel and authorized contractors.
- The regulated substance handled at this distribution facility is propane.

The maximum amount of propane that can be stored at this plant is <u>400,000</u> pounds.

3. The worst-case release scenario(s) and the alternative release scenario(s), including administrative controls and mitigation measures to limit the distances for each reported scenario.

- Worst-Case Scenario. - Failure of my largest storage tank when filled to the greatest amount allowed would release 222,000 pounds of propane. Company policy limits the maximum filling capacity of this tank to 88% at 60 F. It is assumed that the entire contents are released as vapor which finds an ignition source, 10% of the released quantity is assumed to participate in the resulting explosion.
- The distance to the endpoint of 1 psi for the worst-case scenario is 0.47 miles.
- Alternative Scenario. - A pull-away causing failure of a 25 foot length of 4 inch hose. The excess flow valves function to stop the flow. The contents of the hose is released. The resulting

unconfined vapor travels to the lower flammability limit.
- The distance to the endpoint for the lower flammability limit for the alternative scenario is less than 317 feet. This release has the possibility of extending beyond the facility boundary.

4. The general accidental release prevention program and the specific prevention steps.

This distribution facility complies with EPA's Accidental Release Prevention Rule and with all applicable state codes and regulations. This facility was designed and constructed in accordance with NFPA-58. All of our drivers have been thoroughly trained using the NPGA's Certified Employee Training Program (CEPT).

5. Five-year accident history.

We had an accidental release of propane that ignited on 1/28/95. No one off-site was injured and no off-site damage occurred but the adjacent highway was closed.

6. The emergency response program.

This facility's emergency response program is based upon the NPGA's LP-Gas Handbook, "Guidelines for Developing Plant Emergency Response Procedures" and "How to Control LP-Gas Leaks and Fires". We have discussed this program with the New Castle County Local Emergency Planning Committee and the Newark Fire Department. A representative of the Newark Fire Department visited this plant on June 25, 1994.

7. Planned changes to improve safety.

This facility was constructed in 1968 and is in compliance with the NFPA-58 Standard, 1967 Edition. In 2000 we plan to do extensive maintenance and upgrade the facility to NFPA-58, 1998 Edition.

RISK MANAGEMENT PLAN DATA ELEMENTS

1. REGISTRATION

1.1 Source identification:

a. Name: Super Safe Propane Distributors

b. Street: Propane Court

c. City: Their Fair City **d. County:** Coutyname **e. State:** ST **f. Zip:** 55555

g. Latitude: 7705'00" **h. Longitude:** 3852'30"

1.2 Source Dun and Bradstreet number: 12-3456-7899

1.3 a. Name of corporate parent company (if applicable): N/A

b. Dun and Bradstreet number of corporate parent company (if applicable): N/A

1.4 Owner/operator:

a. Name: Firstname Lastname **b. Phone:** (555) 555-5555

c. Mailing address: P.O. Box 5555, Their Fair City, ST 55555

1.5 Name and title of person responsible for part 68 implementation: Firstname M. Lastname

1.6 Emergency contact:

a. Name: Firstname M. Lastname **b. Title:** Vice President

c. Phone: (555) 555-5555 **d. 24-hour phone:** (555) 555-1212

1.7 For each covered process:

a. 1. Chemical name: 2. CAS number: 3. Quantity: 4. SIC code: 5. Program level:

Propane : 74-98-6 : 400,000 : 5172 : Level 2

b. 1. Chemical name: 2. CAS number: 3. Quantity 4. SIC code: 5. Program level:

c. 1. Chemical name: 2. CAS number: 3. Quantity 4. SIC code: 5. Program level:

1.8 EPA Identifier: To be determined

1.9 Number of full-time employees: 5

1.10 Covered by:

a. OSHA PSM: 1. ____ Yes **2.** X No

b. EPCRA section 302: 1. X Yes **2.** ____ No

c. CAA Title V operating permit: 1. ____ Yes **2.** X No

1.11 Last safety inspection:

Date: By:

a. 3/20/95 **b.** ____ OSHA

c. ____ State OSHA

d. ____ EPA

e. X State EPA

f. ____ Fire department

g. ____ Other (specify)

h. ____ Not applicable

4. WORST CASE (FLAMMABLES)

(Note: This section will be replaced once EPA has finalized the submittal format.)

4.1 Chemical: Propane

4.2 Results based on (check one):

a. X Reference Table

b. _____ Modeling

c. _____ Model used _____

4.3 Scenario (check one):

a. X Vapor cloud explosion

b. _____ Fireball

c. _____ BLEVE

d. _____ Pool Fire

e. _____ Jet Fire

4.4 Quantity released: 222,000 lbs

4.5 Endpoint used: 1 psi

4.6 Distance to endpoint: 0.47 miles

4.7 Population within distance: 25

4.8 Public receptors (check all that apply):

a. _____ Schools

b. X Residences

c. _____ Hospitals

d. _____ Prisons

e. _____ Public recreational areas or arenas

f. _____ Major commercial or industrial areas

4.9 Environmental receptors within distance (check all that apply):

a. _____ National or state parks, forests, or monuments

b. _____ Officially designated wildlife sanctuaries, preserves, or refuges

c. _____ Federal wilderness areas

4.10 Passive mitigation considered (check all that apply):

a. _____ Dikes

b. ____ Fire Walls

c. ____ Blast Walls

d. ____ Enclosures

e. ____ Other (specify)

5. ALTERNATIVE SCENARIOS (FLAMMABLES)

(Note: This section will be replaced once EPA has finalized the submittal format.)

5.1 Chemical: Propane

5.2 Results based on (check one):

a. X Reference Table

b. ____ Modeling

c. ____ Model used _____

5.3 Scenario (check one):

a. ____ Vapor cloud explosion

b. X Fireball

c. ____ BLEVE

d. ____ Pool Fire

e. ____ Jet Fire

5.4 Quantity released: 69 lbs **5.5 Endpoint used:** LFL

5.6 Distance to endpoint: .06 miles **5.7 Population within distance:** 0

5.8 Public receptors (check all that apply):

a. ____ Schools

b. ____ Residences

c. ____ Hospitals

d. ____ Prisons

e. ____ Public recreational areas or arenas

f. ____ Major commercial or industrial areas

5.9 Environmental receptors within distance (check all that apply):

a. ____ National or state parks, forests, or monuments

b. ____ Officially designated wildlife sanctuaries, preserves, or refuges

c. ____ Federal wilderness areas

5.10 Passive mitigation considered (check all that apply):

a. ____ Dikes

b. ____ Fire Walls

c. ____ Blast Walls

5.11 Active mitigation considered (check all that apply):

a. ____ Sprinkler Systems

b. ____ Deluge Systems

c. ____ Water Curtain

d. X Excess Flow Valve

6. FIVE-YEAR ACCIDENT HISTORY

(complete for each release)

(Note: This section will be replaced once EPA has finalized the submittal format.)

6.1 Date: 1/28/95 **6.2 Time:** 8:05 AM

6.3 Release duration: 10 Minutes

6.4 Chemical(s): Propane

6.5 Quantity released (lbs): 50

6.6 Release event:

6.7 Release source:

a. X Gas release **a.** ____ Storage vessel

b. ____ Liquid spill/evaporation **b.** ____ Piping

c. X Fire **c.** ____ Process vessel

d. ____ Explosion **d.** X Transfer hose

e. ____ Valve

f. X Pump

6.8 Weather conditions at time of event (if known):

a. Wind speed/direction _____

b. Temperature _____

c. Stability class _____

d. Precipitation present <u>No </u>

e. Unknown <u>X </u>

6.9 On-site impacts:

a. Deaths _____ (number)

b. Injuries _____ (number)

c. Property damage <u>$325 </u>

6.10 Known offsite impacts:

a. Deaths <u>0 </u>(number)

b. Hospitalizations <u>0 </u>(number)

c. Other medical treatment <u>0 </u>(number)

d. Evacuated <u>0 </u>(number)

e. Sheltered <u>0 </u>(number)

f. Property damage ($) <u>0</u>

g. Environmental damage <u>0 </u>(specify type)

6.11 Initiating event:

6.12 Contributing factors (check all that apply):

a. _____ Equipment failure **a.** ____ Equipment failure

b. <u>X </u>Human error **b.** <u>X </u>Human error

c. _____ Weather condition **c.** ____ Improper procedures

d. ____ Overpressurization

e. ____ Upset condition

f. ____ By-pass condition

g. ____ Maintenance activity/Inactivity

h. ____ Process design

I. ____ Unsuitable equipment

j. ____ Unusual weather condition

k. ____ Management error

6.13 Offsite responders notified **a.** X Yes **b.** ____ No

6.14 Changes introduced as a result of the accident

a. ____ Improved/upgrade equipment

b. X Revised maintenance

c. ____ Revised training

d. ____ Revised operating procedures

e. ____ New process controls

f. ____ New mitigation systems

g. X Revised emergency response plan

h. ____ Changed process

I. ____ Reduced inventory

j. ____ Other

k. ____ None

8. PREVENTION PROGRAM 2

(For Each Program 2 Process)

(Note: This section will be replaced once EPA has finalized the submittal format.)

8.1 SIC code for process: <u>5172</u>

8.2 Chemicals:

a. Propane

8.3 Safety information:

a. The date of the most recent review or revision of the safety information: <u>5/23/96</u>

b. A list of Federal or state regulations or industry-specific design codes and standards used to demonstrate compliance with safety information requirement:

1. X NFPA 58 (or state law based on NFPA 58)

2. ____ OSHA 1910.111

3 . ____ ASTM

4 . X ANSI standards

5 . X ASME standards

6 . ____ other (specify)

7 . ____ None

8.4 Hazard Review:

a. The date of completion of the most recent hazard review or update: 5/24/96

b. The expected date of completion of any changes resulting form the hazard review: 5/24/96

c. Major hazards identified (check all that apply):

1 . ____ Toxic release

2 . X Fire

3 . X Explosion

4 . ____ Runaway reaction

5 . ____ Polymerization

6 . ____ Overpressurization

7 . ____ Corrosion

8 . X Overfilling

9. ____ Contamination

10 . X Equipment failure

11. ____ Loss of cooling, heating, electricity, instrumentation air

12. ____ Earthquake

13. ____ Floods (flood plain)

14. ____ Tornado

15. ____ Hurricanes

16. ____ Other

d. Process controls in use (check all that apply):

1. ____ Vents

2. X Relief valves

3. ____ Check valves

4. ____ Scrubbers

5. ____ Flares

6. X Manual shutoffs

7. X Automatic shutoffs

8. ____ Interlocks

9. ____ Alarms and procedures

10. ____ Keyed bypass

11. ____ Emergency air supply

12. ____ Emergency power

13. ____ Backup pump

14. X Grounding equipment

15. ____ Inhibitor addition

16. ____ Rupture disks

17. X Excess flow device

18. ____ Quench system

19. ____ Purge system

20. ____ Other

e. Mitigation systems in use (check all that apply)

1. ____ Sprinkler system

2. ____ Dikes

3. ____ Fire walls

4. ____ Blast walls

5. ____ Deluge systems

6. ____ Water curtain

7. ____ Enclosure

8. ____ Neutralization

9. ____ Other

f. Monitoring/detection systems in use

1. ____ Process area detectors

2. ____ Perimeter monitors

3. ____ Other

g. Changes since last hazard review update (check all that apply)

1. ____ Reduction in chemical inventory

2. ____ Increase in chemical inventory

3. ____ Change in process parameters

4. ____ Installation of process controls

5. ____ Installation of process detections systems

6. ____ Installation of perimeter monitoring systems

7. ____ Installation of mitigating systems

8. ____ Other

9. X None required recommended

8.5 The date of the most recent review or revision of operating procedures: <u>6/4/96</u>

8.6 Training:

a. The date of the most recent review or revision of training programs: <u>6/5/96</u>

b. The type of training provided:

1. ____ Classroom

2. X Classroom plus on the job

3. ____ On the job

4. ____ Other

c. The type of competency testing used:

1 . X Written tests

2 . ____ Oral tests

3 . X Demonstration

4 . X Observation

5 . ____ Other

8.7 Maintenance:

a. The date of the most recent review or revision of maintenance procedures: 6/15/96

b. The date of the most recent equipment inspection or test: 6/16/96

c. The equipment inspected or tested: Pump

8.8 Compliance audits:

a. The date of the most recent compliance audit: 6/30/96

b. The expected date of completion of any changes resulting from the compliance audit: 6/30/96

8.9 Incident investigation:

a. The date of the most recent incident investigation: 1/28/95

b. The expected date of completion of any changes resulting from the investigation: 3/30/95

8.10 The date of the most recent change that triggered a review or revision of safety information, the hazard review, operating or maintenance procedures, or training: 6/16/96

9. EMERGENCY RESPONSE

(Note: This section will be replaced once EPA has finalized the submittal format.)

9.1 Do you have a written emergency response plan?: a. X Yes **b.** ____ No

9.2 Does the plan include specific actions to be taken in response to an accidental release of a regulated substance?: a. X Yes **b.** ____ No

9.3 Does the plan include procedures for informing the public and local agencies responsible for responding to accidental releases?: a. X Yes **b.** ____ No

9.4 Does the plan include information on emergency health care?: a. X Yes **b.** ____ No

9.5 The date of the most recent review or update of the emergency response plan: 2/28/96

9.6 The date of most recent emergency response training for employees: 3/10/96

9.7 The name and telephone of the local agency with which the plan is coordinated:

a. Name: <u>Newark Fire Department</u> **b. Telephone number:** <u>(302) 888-1212 or 311</u>

9.8 Subject to (check all that apply):

a. ____ OSHA 1910.38 (Emergency Action Plan)

b. ____ OSHA 1910.120 (HAZWOPER)

c. ____ Clean Water Act / SPCC

d. ____ RCRA

e. ____ OPA-90

f. ____ State EPCRA Rules / Law

g. ____ Other (specify)

||EPA Homepage ||OSWER Homepage ||CEPPO Homepage ||Search EPA||

||Comments to EPA||Comments to CEPPO ||EPCRA Hotline ||

Maintained by the Chemical Emergency Preparedness and Prevention Office (CEPPO), Office of Solid Waste and Emergency Response (OSWER), U.S. Environmental Protection Agency (EPA)

URL:http://www.epa.gov/swercepp/pubs/sample.html

Last Updated: May 21, 1997

Index

PC #	ENVIRONMENTAL TITLES	Pub Date	Price
585	Book of Lists for Regulated Hazardous Substances, 8th Edition	1997	$79
4088	CFR Chemical Lists on CD ROM, 1997 Edition	1997	$125
4089	Chemical Data for Workplace Sampling & Analysis, Single User	1997	$125
512	Clean Water Handbook, 2nd Edition	1996	$89
581	EH&S Auditing Made Easy	1997	$79
587	E H & S CFR Training Requirements, 3rd Edition	1997	$89
4082	EMMI-Envl Monitoring Methods Index for Windows-Network	1997	$537
4082	EMMI-Envl Monitoring Methods Index for Windows-Single User	1997	$179
525	Environmental Audits, 7th Edition	1996	$79
548	Environmental Engineering and Science: An Introduction	1997	$79
578	Environmental Guide to the Internet, 3rd Edition	1997	$59
560	Environmental Law Handbook, 14th Edition	1997	$79
353	Environmental Regulatory Glossary, 6th Edition	1993	$79
625	Environmental Statutes, 1998 Edition	1998	$69
4098	Environmental Statutes Book/Disk Package, 1998 Edition	1997	$208
4994	Environmental Statutes on Disk for Windows-Network	1997	$405
4994	Environmental Statutes on Disk for Windows-Single User	1997	$139
570	Environmentalism at the Crossroads	1995	$39
536	ESAs Made Easy	1996	$59
515	Industrial Environmental Management: A Practical Approach	1996	$79
4078	IRIS Database-Network	1997	$1,485
4078	IRIS Database-Single User	1997	$495
510	ISO 14000: Understanding Environmental Standards	1996	$69
551	ISO 14001: An Executive Repoert	1996	$55
518	Lead Regulation Handbook	1996	$79
478	Principles of EH&S Management	1995	$69
554	Property Rights: Understanding Government Takings	1997	$79
582	Recycling & Waste Mgmt Guide to the Internet	1997	$49
603	Superfund Manual, 6th Edition	1997	$115
566	TSCA Handbook, 3rd Edition	1997	$95
534	Wetland Mitigation: Mitigation Banking and Other Strategies	1997	$75

PC #	SAFETY AND HEALTH TITLES	Pub Date	Price
547	Construction Safety Handbook	1996	$79
553	Cumulative Trauma Disorders	1997	$59
559	Forklift Safety	1997	$65
539	Fundamentals of Occupational Safety & Health	1996	$49
535	Making Sense of OSHA Compliance	1997	$59
563	Managing Change for Safety and Health Professionals	1997	$59
589	Managing Fatigue in Transportation, *ATA Conference*	1997	$75
4086	OSHA Technical Manual, Electronic Edition	1997	$99
598	Project Mgmt for E H & S Professionals	1997	$59
552	Safety & Health in Agriculture, Forestry and Fisheries	1997	$125
613	Safety & Health on the Internet, 2nd Edition	1998	$49
597	Safety Is A People Business	1997	$49
463	Safety Made Easy	1995	$49
590	Your Company Safety and Health Manual	1997	$79

Electronic Product available on CD-ROM or Floppy Disk

PLEASE CALL OUR CUSTOMER SERVICE DEPARTMENT AT (301) 921-2323 FOR A FREE PUBLICATIONS CATALOG.

Government Institutes
4 Research Place, Suite 200 • Rockville, MD 20850-3226
Tel. (301) 921-2323 • FAX (301) 921-0264
E mail: giinfo@govinst.com • Internet: http://www.govinst.com

GOVERNMENT INSTITUTES ORDER FORM

GI ... **GI**

4 Research Place, Suite 200 • Rockville, MD 20850-3226 • Tel (301) 921-2323 • Fax (301) 921-0264
Internet: *http://www.govinst.com* • E-mail: *giinfo@govinst.com*

3 EASY WAYS TO ORDER

1. Phone: **(301) 921-2323**
Have your credit card ready when you call.

2. Fax: **(301) 921-0264**
Fax this completed order form with your company purchase order or credit card information.

3. Mail: **Government Institutes**
4 Research Place, Suite 200
Rockville, MD 20850-3226
USA
Mail this completed order form with a check, company purchase order, or credit card information.

PAYMENT OPTIONS

❏ **Check** (*payable to Government Institutes in US dollars*)

❏ **Purchase Order** (this order form must be attached to your company P.O. <u>Note:</u> All International orders must be pre-paid.)

❏ **Credit Card** ❏ *VISA* ❏ MasterCard ❏ AMERICAN EXPRESS

Exp.____/____

Credit Card No. _____

Signature _____
Government Institutes' Federal I.D.# is 52-0994196

CUSTOMER INFORMATION

Ship To: (Please attach your Purchase Order)

Name: _____

GI Account# (*7 digits on mailing label*): _____

Company/Institution: _____

Address: _____
(please supply street address for UPS shipping)
_____

City: _____ State/Province: _____

Zip/Postal Code: _____ Country: _____

Tel: ( ) _____

Fax: ( ) _____

E-mail Address: _____

Bill To: (if different than ship to address)

Name: _____

Title/Position: _____

Company/Institution: _____

Address: _____
(please supply street address for UPS shipping)
_____

City: _____ State/Province: _____

Zip/Postal Code: _____ Country: _____

Tel: ( ) _____

Fax: ( ) _____

E-mail Address: _____

Qty.	Product Code	Title	Price

❏ **New Edition No Obligation Standing Order Program**
Please enroll me in this program for the products I have ordered. Government Institutes will notify me of new editions by sending me an invoice. I understand that there is no obligation to purchase the product. This invoice is simply my reminder that a new edition has been released.

15 DAY MONEY-BACK GUARANTEE
If you're not completely satisfied with any product, return it undamaged within 15 days for a full and immediate refund on the price of the product.

Subtotal_____
MD Residents add 5% Sales Tax_____
Shipping and Handling (see box below)_____
Total Payment Enclosed_____

Within U.S:	**Outside U.S:**
1-4 products: $6/product	Add $15 for each item (Airmail)
5 or more: $3/product	Add $10 for each item (Surface)

SOURCE CODE: BP01